CHILDREN WITH HANDICAPS:
A Review of Behavioral Research

CHILDREN WITH HANDICAPS:
A Review of Behavioral Research

Gershon Berkson

LEA LAWRENCE ERLBAUM ASSOCIATES, PUBLISHERS
1993   Hillsdale, New Jersey   Hove and London

Lawrence Erlbaum Associates, Inc., Publishers
365 Broadway
Hillsdale, New Jersey 07642

Library of Congress Cataloging-in-Publication Data

Berkson, Gershon.
 Children with handicaps : a review of behavioral research /
Gershon Berkson.
  p. cm.
 Includes bibliographical references and indexes.
 ISBN 0-89859-987-3 (alk. paper)
  1. Developmentally disabled children—Psychology—Abstracts.
2. Developmentally disabled children—Abstracts. I. Title.
 [DNLM: 1. Child Development Disorders. 2. Handicapped—
psychology. 3. Social Behavior—in infancy & childhood. WS
350.8.S6 B513c]
RJ506.D47B47 1993
155.45'1—dc20
DNLM/DLC
for Library of Congress   92-49570
                                                               CIP

Books published by Lawrence Erlbaum Associates are printed on acid-free paper, and their
bindings are chosen for strength and durability.

Printed in the United States of America
10 9 8 7 6 5 4 3 2 1

For *Samuel* and *Daniel*
and the rest of their generation

Contents

II INDIVIDUAL PSYCHOLOGY

III SOCIAL PSYCHOLOGY

Preface

Psychological research on children with mental and physical handicaps began 200 years ago. Its major development awaited maturation of psychology as an empirical science and social movements for child welfare and education. This book is a record of research as it was accomplished in the 1980s. At the end of the 19th century, behavioral research on handicapped children could at best be characterized as pioneering. By the 1990s, it had become a vigorous activity, with scientists producing hundreds of articles a year. The consequences has been a level of detail in theory and factual support that simply was not available before then.

This volume is written for people who know something about psychology and education, but who are unfamiliar with research on children and handicaps. This might include parents of children with disabilities, upper level undergraduate students, graduate students who are looking for a research topic, and my colleagues in developmental psychology and education of normal children who might wish to familiarize themselves with the recent developments in the study of deviations in behavioral development.

There are 11 chapters, organized into three sections. The first section of four chapters deals with general issues: History and general concepts; classification and prevalence; causes; and diagnosis. The second section is concerned with individual psychology: sensorimotor processes and brain organization; learning and memory; higher mental processes and language; and motivation, personality, and psychopathology. The final three chapters deal with social psychology and its applications: social processes; treatment; and follow-up studies and adult life in the community.

I have tried to make the literature review extensive and representative of the primary literature of the 1980s. However, the reader should not expect it to be either exhaustive, to cover much work between 1945 and 1980 or after 1990, or to include many book chapters. The approach taken was first to screen all of the abstracts published in *PsychScan-LDMR* and *PsychScan-Developmental Psychology* from the period 1984–1989. I express appreciation to the American Psychological Association because, without this publication, the project would not have been possible in its current form.

Abstracts summarizing research that was obviously flawed or papers that were mainly the expression of a person's opinions were excluded from further consideration. Book chapters were rarely included because *PsychScan* did not include them at that time and because including them would have made the project too large. About 5,000 abstracts remained and were categorized into seveal topic areas.

Lilian Tosic prepared a computerized database of these references organized under the topics, and she obtained copies of each article and kept the copies in order so that I could use them as I wrote the chapters. When the chapters were written, she proofread the references. I thank her for her work and especially for the care with which she accomplished the job.

From the 5,000 articles that emerged from the search through the abstracts, I included for further consideration mainly those that I judged to be the best representatives in any particular research area. Sometimes this was easy to do because there was so little competent research in the area; sometimes it was difficult because there was a great deal of good work and space prevented me from including all of the good references.

After writing drafts of the chapters, I asked certain people to give me feedback on some of them. Especially helpful were Rathe Karrer, Leon Miller, and Arnold Sameroff; my students Grace Baranek, Theresa Schultz, and Marrea Winnega; and two anonymous editorial reviewers.

I wish also to acknowledge the remarkable support that I received from the taxpayers of the State of Illinois through the Institute for the Study of Developmental Disabilities and the Psychology Department of the University of Illinois at Chicago. Especially understanding were Kenneth Swiatek and Rathe Karrer. For the 5 years of the project, I was given the time and financial support that it took to complete the work. I hope that the book will be seen as useful by those who supported it.

My family contributed in ways that they may not be aware of. I tried to emulate Suzanne Raphael Berkson's creativity, of course without success. Adam Berkson, Jennie Berkson Edelstein, and David Edelstein tolerated my talking at them and kept me thinking about pragmatic implications.

Theodore Cohn kept in touch and always asked how the book was going. Carmel Berkson kept alive the idea of where this book came from.

Finally, a word should be said about the role of the U.S. federal government in support of the research reviewed in this book. Beginning in the 1950s, billions of dollars were contributed to the development of services for children with mental and physical handicaps. A much smaller, but significant, amount of support was also given to behavioral research through the National Institute of Child Health and Human Development, the National Institute of Mental Health, and the U.S. Department of Education. When seen together as it is in this book, this research is a major accomplishment. Credit for this accomplishment certainly must be given to parents of children with handicaps, their effective representatives to the Congress, and particular members of the Senate and the House of Representatives who have worked to assure annual support of research programs. Special mention must also be made of the very few men and women in the Executive Branch, working in these institutes, who have espoused behavioral research, fighting for it with all of their substantial sophistication and idealism.

Gershon Berkson

I

General Issues

1

Introduction

Almost everyone has a physical or mental handicap. Most handicaps are minor and do not prevent a person from getting along in the world. Those readers who wear glasses have such minor handicaps. These people are fortunate that their handicap is correctable. But they also are aware that, without their glasses, they can experience significant problems.

Other readers may have more severe disabilities or may have a relative or friend who has one. Perhaps they are sitting in a wheelchair, are wearing a hearing aid, or have had a long course of psychotherapy. Perhaps they have a brother who is mentally retarded or a sister who is said to have a significant learning disability. Maybe they know a child who has been abused by adults or who abuses others. About 15% of school children have a disability severe enough to require special help over an extended period of time. Not all of them need help throughout their childhood, and many—perhaps most— ultimately become reasonably happy adults who contribute significantly to society.

Children with handicaps and their families often experience great unhappiness, much of which is preventable. Modern industrialized nations also spend significant amounts of money providing services for handicapped children. Reducing unhappiness of families of children with handicaps, helping them to be more effective, and providing services in a cost-effective manner are all achievable and obviously desirable goals.

Although this book is about children with handicapping conditions, it is

3

not intended to help the reader to ameliorate the condition of any specific child. The technical training required for helping children properly comes with graduate training in a specialized field such as clinical or counseling psychology, special education, medicine, occupational therapy, physical therapy, speech, nursing, or rehabilitation. Instead, this book provides an introduction to the concepts of developmental psychology that are particularly germane to handicapped children.

Nor is this book intended to be a conventional textbook on the psychology of children with handicaps, organized according to clinical category and reviewing what is known. It is a review of the research done in the 1980s, organized according to psychological process. The book is directed toward educated parents, advanced students, and to those of my colleagues who would like to get a first look at recent work with handicapped children.

There is a strong tendency to break research on handicapping conditions of children into subfields, primarily along traditional classification lines. That is, the research literatures on children with learning disabilities, with mental retardation, with autism, or with oppositional disorders, for example, tend to be published in different journals and read by different groups of people. Although these literatures do often emphasize different things, there is also a remarkable amount of overlap between them. The overlap is seen, not only with respect to the topics studied, and at the conceptual and methodological levels, but also with respect to major results. A deficit in short-term memory, low social acceptance of children with handicaps by normal peers, and the general effectiveness of peer instruction are examples. Therefore, the book is organized, not along conventional classification lines, but according to general psychological processes such as learning or social behavior.

The book assumes that handicapped children are, first and foremost, children. People often see handicapped individuals as embodiments of their handicap. They talk of *the* retarded, *the* hearing impaired, *the* autistic. Whereas it is true that people with handicaps do have special problems, the tendency to focus on their problems and not to treat them as people has historically been detrimental to them. Thus, this book is organized around the ideas of traditional developmental psychology, using concepts about individual differences that have emerged during the last century.

In summary, this book recognizes that the categories of disorders of development are different, but they overlap significantly. The problems common to all handicaps are perhaps as important as the differences between handicapping conditions. Children with chronic physical handicaps certainly are different from children with oppositional disorder, and both groups are characteristically different from children with learning disabilities. However, there may be substantial overlap between these categories, and all of the categories may share some characteristics (e.g., low social acceptance). In dealing with specific individuals on a day-to-day basis, clinicians know that what is done for the children is perhaps less dependent on their diagnostic category than on the severity of their disability, the support of the family, and the availability of specific treatments. Therefore, this book not only views the handicapped child from the perspective of general developmental psychology but also emphasizes the things that children with handicaps have in common.

According to the central emphasis of this book, science and a reformist spirit have combined to increase our understanding of the nature of handicaps and have promoted the integration of handicapped children into general society. Science without reform and the reformist spirit without tough-minded conceptualization have never worked in the interests of handicapped people. Only when the human mind and the human heart work together have the interests of children with handicaps been served.

In this first chapter, the historical development of study and services for children with handicaps is reviewed. I hope to make clear that ideas about handicapped children accelerated rapidly in their scope, precision, and accuracy beginning in the 18th century and have become increasingly sophisticated since then.

Although a casual look at the experience of children with handicaps in modern society is not always encouraging (e.g., when school programs lose their funding), a careful look shows that knowledge and the providing of services has advanced steadily in the last 200 years. Hopefully, this will continue.

SOCIAL LIVING IN PREHISTORIC TIMES

Individuals with physical abnormalities have been part of society since well before the evolution of humankind. There is evidence of this in the existence of handicapped individuals in subhuman primate groups. Monkey and ape groups include individuals who have fallen from trees or who have been injured by predators. The injuries may be minor, but there are reported instances of severe limb or skull fractures (Schultz, 1956). Handicapped individuals may survive in natural animal groups when their injury does not actually interfere with foraging or escape from predators. In other words, the injury may not be handicapping.

Injured animals may survive and live in a group because group living itself can provide aid to adaptation. Mother monkeys provide care that compensates for even severe injuries, and other members of the group may "babysit" injured babies, as they do other young of the group. Such compensatory care tends to decline as the handicapped infant becomes older, and the older infant may then be taken by a predator. However, in certain environments, where predation pressure is low and food is plentiful, handicapped animals may live to be adults (Berkson, 1974).

Neanderthals, a species closely related to our own, also lived in groups. Disabling arthritis and other illnesses were common in Neanderthal individuals (M. S. Goldstein, 1969; Straus & Cave, 1957). There is also a published description of a Neanderthal male who had experienced severe injuries to the head and arm when he was young. This Neanderthal lived to be an adult. The injury probably prevented use of his right arm, and he used his teeth to hold an object when it was necessary to use both "hands" (Solecki, 1971; Stewart, 1958). Thus, even before the evolution of modern Homo sapiens, at least some injured and handicapped individuals survived and were part of society.

THE ANCIENT WORLD

The advent of human culture brought with it complicated reactions to handicapped people. We do not know much about the everyday life of people with mental and physical impairments before 2,000 years ago. However, it is certain that they participated in society. Achondroplastic dwarfs lived in ancient Egypt (figurines displayed at the Oriental Institute of the University of Chicago; Scheerenberger, 1983). Reference to blindness was widespread in the literature and visual arts of the ancient world (Esser, 1961). Cretinism was a condition recognized very early (Boyage et al., 1987). Apparently, chronic impairments as well as disease were a fact of life in the ancient world.

Religious leaders and philosophers had different views about how society should respond to handicapped people. Ancient Judaism cursed people who directed blind people away from their path (Deuteronomy, 27, 18), and traditional Christian (Kanner, 1964) and Islamic (Koran, 4th sura, 4th verse) traditions were likewise protective of handicapped people.

It sometimes was customary in the ancient Greek city states to euthanize obviously disabled newborn infants by exposure. At other times, governments forbade such practices. Aristotle (Politics, *VII*, 16) recognized that exposure for control of population numbers was not customary but thought that no handicapped newborn baby should be reared. In the *Republic*, Plato had an elaborate plan for planned breeding in the education of the philosopher kings. However, such eugenics ideas apparently did not apply beyond the newborn period for the general population.

The ancient world clearly recognized handicapped children and attitudes toward them ranged from kind protection to attempts to eliminate them. Exposure was continued or forbidden in various places throughout history (Edgerton, 1970; Sumner, 1906/1940) and continues in modified form today

(Duff &. A. Campbell, 1973). Everyday life for those children whose handicaps developed or were recognized after the newborn period must have been difficult, although we know that some lived as "fools" in the houses of the aristocracy for at least 1,000 years, beginning during the Roman empire (Kanner, 1964).

Judeo-Christian tradition protected handicapped children. However, when medieval thinkers conceived of the erroneous idea that mental illness is a manifestation of the devil, ferocious physical punishment and even death were espoused for mentally afflicted children as a means of ridding the body of the devil. And this was not the last period in which handicapped people were visited with widespread and systematic persecution based on ignorance.

THE BASIS OF MODERN IDEAS
IN THE 18TH CENTURY

Empiricist Philosophy

By the beginning of the 17th century, several modern developments had begun. The distinction between mental illness and mental retardation had been recognized (Woolfson, 1984). Pedro Ponce de Leon had taught manual communication to a deaf boy (Lane, 1984), and Francesco Lucas had made use of large letters cast in wood for instruction of the blind (Jourdain, 1916, footnote 1, p. 9). However, it was not until 150 years later that formal special education for handicapped people really got its start.

The 17th and 18th centuries were a time filled with armed civil strife as well as a glorious expansion of conceptions about what is possible for human beings. Education was slowly recovering from its near obliteration after the fall of Rome. The development of towns and commerce had brought with it the recognition of the need for an educated populace, and scientific study began to replace scholarship based on reference to authority.

It was in this context that education and study of handicapped people began in the 18th century. The first influence was from a group of English and French philosophers whose central interest was to determine how the human mind is formed. These philosophers agreed that experience is necessary for the development of the mind. Perhaps the most influential of these philosophers was John Locke (1632–1704), who wrote widely on science and government. His ideas about handicapping conditions were contained in *Some Thoughts Concerning Education* and *An Essay Concerning Human Understanding*. His essay on education was a compendium of suggestions about ways of educating an upper-class child. In it he recognized the existence of individual differences between children and indicated that instruction should be fitted to those differences. His more influential publication was the *Essay on Human Understanding*, in which he espoused four ideas that were to have great impact. First, he denied the existence of innate ideas. He based this denial of innate ideas partly on the fact that young children and mentally retarded people did not appear to him to have innate ideas.

Locke also believed that the mind is built on the basis of sense experience and the mind's reflection on those experiences. He predicted that congenitally blind people would have poorly developed ideas of visual experiences such as color. He also thought that blind people who regained their sight would have difficulty recognizing objects by sight because they had not had experience with them.

In addition, Locke indicated that mentally retarded people differ from mentally ill people in their processing of information. He thought that mentally retarded people have dull sensations, that is, that they do not experience events fully. Mentally ill people are normal in the intensity of their perceptions, but they combine ideas abnormally. Thus, Locke made an essential distinction between mentally ill and mentally retarded people, which is based on an analysis of psychological processes.

Finally, Locke pointed out that nonhandicapped people are similar in some ways to handicapped people. Specifically, mentally ill people combine ideas in strange ways, but this is often true, at times, of nonhandicapped individuals as well. Ideas are formed by the coincidence of experiences and by more or less perfect reflections on those experiences. Experience is generally haphazard and reflections on those experiences can be fallible, so the thought processes of normal people can sometimes resemble those of mentally ill people.

Locke's four ideas were embedded in his essay and were not necessarily intended to foster understanding of handicapped people. Instead, they were used to illustrate Locke's points about the growth and functioning of the human mind. A more direct influence on blind, deaf, and mentally retarded people came from France in the first half of the 18th century, during the 50 years before the French Revolution. In this period, a democratic movement was asserting itself against a rigidly authoritarian monarchy and aristocracy. One manifestation of this democratic movement on behalf of the "rights of man" was a belief in universal education. Some form of universal education had been espoused by Martin Luther 200 years before, but support for the right of every child for education was not widespread until the Enlightenment of 18th-century France.

Three French philosophers were deeply interested in education, in individual differences, and in handicapped people. They were Jean-Jacques Rousseau (1712–1778), Etienne Bonnot de Condillac (1715–1780), and Denis

Diderot (1713–1784). These three men were among the leaders of the attack on the "old regime" represented by the monarchy and the aristocracy. They knew each other, and indeed they were frequent dinner companions. Therefore, though there were differences in their writings, it is not surprising that their general approach often was quite similar.

They believed that education of the mind is largely through the senses. In his *Emile*, a treatise on the ideal education, Rousseau expressed the view that young children should receive sense-training. This involves the systematic exposure of children to sensations so that they have practice in measuring, counting, weighing, and comparing. As is pointed out here, this idea had an important influence on later systems of education for handicapped children.

Rousseau emphasized that children differ from each other and that education must be adapted to these differences. Rousseau was quite clear in stating that some of these differences are native, whereas other philosophers (e.g., Diderot's *Second Discourse*) accounted for individual differences on the basis of the person's experiential history. Whatever the source of individual differences, the importance of these differences and their consequence to education was made clear by these philosophers.

A more explicit reference to handicapped people came from the interest of these philosophers in the consequences of loss of one of the senses. They believed that because the mind is developed from experience, a person with a sensory loss might have a specific deficit in conceiving certain ideas. An example would be the concept of visual color for a person who has been blind since birth. The crucial test of this idea would come, not only from asking a blind person about colors, but from observing people who had cataracts removed (to determine whether they could identify objects visually). A Dr. Molyneux proposed this problem to Locke. It was developed in great detail by Condillac in his *Treatise on Sensations* (1754) and his *Essay on the Origin of Human Knowledge* (1756) and by Diderot in his *Letter on the Blind* (1749) and *Addition to the Letter on the Blind* (see Jourdain, 1916).

The problem was of great importance, first of all, because it constituted a test of the sensationist view of the development of the mind. It was also important because it could be exposed to scientific test. That is it depended on actual formal observations rather than casual observations and suppositions about what might be true. This scientific approach was possible not only because it was becoming customary in an increasingly scientific age, but also because medical care was progressing rapidly. For instance, the removal of cataracts to improve vision was becoming a feasible method of surgery (Jourdain, 1916, footnote 1, p. 144).

Condillac and Diderot both referred to actual cases in great detail, using them to evaluate the philosophical ideas they were considering. It turned out that vision was indeed a problem for people who had cataracts removed.

(But, because of technical problems, this result was uncertain until 200 years later, when studies with animals reared in visually deprived conditions confirmed and defined the nature of the deficits.)

Pioneers of Organized Special Education

During the 18th century, handicapped people either were cared for within the family or were neglected. In aristocratic families, they received some education, which helped some to prominent places in society. For instance, Nicholas Saunderson was a visually handicapped man who ultimately became a famous mathematician and university professor. Maria Theresa von Paradis was a blind musician who gave concerts throughout Europe. However, most handicapped people either stayed in their home, begged, wandered the countryside, or lived in institutions. Some deaf people had contact with each other. When they did, they communicated with manual signs that they apparently taught each other. Thus, education for handicapped children was either private and in the home or rudimentary.

Organized education began in France in the 18th century. At that time there was a general movement to universal education, because of the influence of the empiricist philosophers, because educational procedures had been in use, and perhaps most of all, because a small group of pioneers demonstrated that organized education is possible for handicapped people.

The first of these pioneers was Jacob Rodrigues Pereire (1715–1780). Members of Pereire's family were deaf. The young Pereire resolved to teach them how to communicate. He drew on the work of 17th-century teachers of the deaf to teach his sister and others how to speak and read lips. His method used manual signs as well as speech, and he was at least partially successful. His most important contributions included instructing the members of his family as well as other children, and the development of support for education of the deaf among the nobility.

At least as important as Pereire was Charles-Michel de l'Epee (1712–1789). Like the other pioneers, he undertook to teach one or two people at first, using existing methods. In Epee's case, it was two deaf sisters that he encountered on a visit to their home. He found them essentially isolated from the rest of society, and he resolved to teach them to communicate with hearing people. He developed a system of manual signs that stood for French words. He believed that once deaf people had learned French words, they could be taught to read French. Before this time, hearing-handicapped people used a sign language that permitted them to communicate with each other but not with other French people.

Besides developing a sign language and educating individual deaf students, Epee founded the first school for the deaf and trained several disciples who began schools for deaf children in France and other countries. Pereire and Epee were at odds about the possibilities of Pereire's goal of teaching spoken language to congenitally deaf people. This conflict about goals and methods for education of deaf children has continued until this century (Lane, 1984).

Epee's most influential disciple was Roch-Ambrose Sicard (1742–1822). Sicard was a flamboyant personality who made famous the successes in teaching the deaf. He made Epee's system more practical, and he revived Epee's school, which was failing after Epee died. At least as important, he was the teacher of Jean Massieu, the first deaf teacher of deaf children (Lane, 1984). He also influenced the careers and work styles of Valentin Hauy and Jean Itard, pioneers in the education of blind and mentally retarded children.

Valentin Hauy (1745–1822) was also influenced by the movement to educate people with sensory handicaps. He had been encouraged by Sicard's successes with deaf children and by the personal support of Maria Theresa von Paradis. He began by using techniques that blind people had previously developed for reading, writing, and traveling. These techniques included reading by touch with wooden letters, with letters made by pricking paper with a pin, and with mathematical tables and maps. In working with his first student, Hauy discovered that the boy could read raised and embossed letters on paper. His most important contribution, however, was the establishment of the first organized school for the blind in 1784 (Farrell, 1956).

Periere, Epee, Sicard, and Hauy were stimulated by the humanitarian movements of their time and were motivated mainly by a desire to improve the social condition of people with sensory handicaps. Jean Itard (1774–1838), a physician and teacher of deaf children, was motivated by humanitarian concerns. However, he also had philosophical interests. In 1798, a 12-year-old boy who was said to have been captured in the forests of Aveyron, was brought to Paris. This "Wild Boy of Aveyron" was regarded as mentally retarded and incurable by Phillipe Pinel, the most prominent reforming psychiatrist of the day. Indeed, the fact that the child engaged in body-rocking, needed to keep things in their place, had no language, and was unkempt and dirty in his habits (Itard, 1962) would today be consistent with a diagnosis of severe mental retardation with autistic features.

Itard believed it possible that the boy's condition might have resulted from social deprivation during the 5 or more years it was believed he had spent in the warm forests of southern France. Itard thought that if Locke and Condillac were correct about the importance of experience in the development of the mind, it should be possible with intensive education to "develop him physically and morally." Itard undertook the boy's education with five goals: (a) to interest him in social life; (b) to awaken his senses; (c) to extend his range of ideas; (d) to lead him to use speech; and (e) to induce him to employ the simplest mental operations and afterward inducing the application of these mental processes to the objects of instruction.

After only 9 months, there were remarkable changes in the boy's condition. He attended to things, understood instructions, was clean in his body and habits, slept in a bed, could associate some letters with objects, and could say a few words appropriately. In fact, he had been changed from a nonsocial human to one who could participate in society, although in a primitive way. Itard proved that even a severely mentally disabled individual was educable.

On the other hand, 5 years later, despite continuing and intensive educational efforts, it was also clear that the boy was never going to be a normal person. Itard concluded that although education is possible with such a child, doing so becomes more difficult if the education begins after 5 years of age.

Itard's work was another, and spectacular, demonstration with handicapped children that education is possible for all children. His study added to the work of the pioneering educators of deaf and blind children. Together, they showed that handicapping conditions are not a permanent immutable characteristic, inevitably excluding people from participating in society. It showed that whereas education does not necessarily eliminate a condition completely, it can have profound positive effects on a person's life.

THE 19TH CENTURY

Most of the basic ideas that underlie modern special education and research on handicaps in children were developed by the end of the 19th century. In this section we review four intellectual movements that formed the basis for 20th-century thought. The expansion and institutionalization of special education paralleled the growth of education in general. The study of individual differences contributed to description of children's special needs. Child study emerged from this interest in individual differences and from certain theories of evolution. Parallel to these movements was also the study of brain anatomy and how the mind works.

Expansion of Special Education

Epee's disciples founded a dozen schools for hearing-impaired people in his lifetime, and by the time Sicard died, there were five times that number (Lane, 1984). Before Hauy died in 1822, at least 12 schools for the blind had been established throughout Europe (Farrell, 1956). The numbers increased steadily and spread to the New World before the middle of the 19th century.

In addition to numbers, the next 200 years saw a rapid expansion in the refinement of the ideas underlying services for handicapped children. Educational procedures became more detailed, descriptions of the nature of handicapping conditions became more thorough, and an understanding of causes of these conditions became deeper. Hundreds of physicians, teachers, and scientists became involved. Among these were Louis Braille, the inventor of the widely used reading system for visually handicapped people, Thomas Gallaudet, who established the first college for deaf people, and Dorothea Dix, a reformer who improved living conditions for prisoners, mentally ill people, and mentally retarded people.

Two men who worked at the beginning of the 19th century stand out because of the general impact of their work. Both were physicians, reformers, teachers, and skilled administrators. The first was Edouard Seguin (1812–1880). Seguin undertook to educate severely retarded children (at that time called "idiots"). The foremost authorities of the time were sceptical about the possibility of educating retarded people. Seguin understood that severely retarded people can be abnormal physiologically, but he was stimulated by the reformist ideas of Henri Saint-Simon and was encouraged by Itard and the psychiatrist Jean Esquirol to make an attempt to educate "idiots." Beginning in 1837, he worked with a few children at the Bicetre, an institution in Paris.

Seguin succeeded dramatically. Not only was he able to improve the functioning of these mentally handicapped children, but he was also able to conceive of special education in a way that seems familiar even now. Seguin believed that mental deficiency is a brain disorder caused by prenatal factors such as undernutrition and the drinking of alcohol by the mother. He therefore espoused prenatal care to prevent the physiological disorder. He also thought early detection of the condition was important. And for optimum results, he believed that a cooperative relationship between the school and the parents should begin immediately after the condition is detected.

The educational program was wideranging and specific, with instructions that took into account individual differences between children. Sense training was part of the curriculum, but a wide range of physical exercises, practice in imitation, speech training, some reading, social skills training, and discipline were also included. The final chapter of his book on "idiocy" (Seguin, 1907) is a plan for the residential schools in which the training would be done. Seguin was specific about the environments in which training would take place. He distinguished between schools and institutions, which are temporary placements, and asylums, which are more permanent custodial programs for homeless, severely disabled children. Seguin emigrated to the United States in 1848. He spent most of the remainder of his life developing the kinds of institutions described in his book and in writing.

While in the United States, Seguin became one of several reformers who were developing social services for people with mental illness, mental retardation, and sensory disorders. One of the most influential of these reformers was Samuel Gridley Howe (1801–1876). Howe was born and reared in Boston, Massachusetts. He studied medicine and expected to enter a lucrative medical practice in the Boston area. However, his ambition, adventurous spirit, and idealism led him to quite a different career.

Immediately after medical school, he became a physician in the Greek revolution against the Ottoman empire. He used his medical skills there, but often was a soldier and a fundraiser for this cause. He returned from the war at the age of 29 determined not to practice medicine. However, he was not quite sure what to do. By chance, he met members of a committee who were organizing a school for the blind for New England. In this chance encounter, Howe was asked whether he would consider becoming the director of the new school. He agreed. Thus, he became the director of the first school for the blind in the United States, the Perkins School, which is still in existence.

Howe's most famous accomplishment was the demonstration that children who are both deaf and blind can be educated. He taught four of these children, the most famous being Laura Bridgman. Laura was a highly intelligent child. Her education began at 7 years of age, after a number of years in which she had been taught some signs by an older friend. Thus, a lively mind, fostered by supportive early experience, prepared her for the intensive instruction she received from the staff of Howe's school. She grew up to be a teacher in the Perkins School and an international figure (Schwartz, 1956).

In the 1840s, Howe became interested in the plight of severely retarded children. In this crusade he accomplished several noteworthy things. As head of a commission to review the needs for services for retarded people in Massachusetts, he undertook the first scientific survey of the prevalence of mental retardation. He did this first by sending a letter to the clerks of each community in the state, asking them to identify the mentally retarded people in their community. However, this approach did not produce satisfactory results. The informants either did not respond, or they did not have the appropriate information. Howe then sent a person into a large number of communities to find the mentally retarded people. This person looked in the poor houses and asked around the small communities. In this way, Howe found several hundred people who needed schooling. The legislature allowed a small amount of money to start a school for mentally retarded children at the Perkins School. The school for the retarded was soon separated from the school for the blind and became what is now called the Fernald School in Waltham, Massachusetts.

The report of the commission (Howe, 1848), in addition to estimating prevalence of mental retardation and needs for services, also summarized what was then known about mental retardation. The report differentiated mental retardation from other forms of mental disorder. It also pointed out that there are different degrees of mental retardation expressed as three different levels. It guessed at the causes of mental retardation, pointing out (only partially correctly) that it seems to run in families, that it is associated with sexual self-abuse (not correct), and that it can be caused by nutritional deficits and alcohol consumption. The report also described one type of mental retardation, cretinism. Perhaps most important, it emphasized how different mentally retarded people are from one another.

Howe went on to exert his influence to support Dorothea Dix in her crusade to improve the condition of prisons and institutions for mentally ill people, and he became active in the movement to abolish slavery. In all, his vigor, idealism, and intelligence were to have significant impact on the development of social services in the United States.

Between the publication of John Locke's *Essay Concerning Human Understanding* and the establishment of Pereire's school for the deaf, 50 years had passed. It took another 20 years for Epee's school and still another 20 years until Hauy established his school for visually handicapped children. Itard's experiment with the Wild Boy of Aveyron occurred more than 100 years after Locke. Seguin's class for the retarded at the Bicetre began a generation later, and the Massachusetts legislature approved $2,500 for the first school for the retarded in the United States more than 150 years after Locke. Progress was thus slow at first, but special education developed with increasing speed during the 19th century. The progress was fostered by advances in the description of individual differences.

Describing Individual Differences

It is obvious that people differ from one another. Plato and Rousseau, for instance, recognized individual differences and said that it was important to take them into account in education. Medical tradition also held that groups of symptoms (i.e., syndromes) are sometimes associated with particular causes and could be treated with special procedures. In addition, at the beginning of the 18th century, Linneaus classified all animal and plant species known at that time in an effort to put them into some order.

All of these influences affected the psychiatrists of the late 18th and 19th century. Phillipe Pinel, for instance, wrote a brief treatise classifying mental disorders, including various forms of mental illness and mental retardation. In the next generation, Jean Esquirol did the same in a more elaborate way. Both of them distinguished cretinism from other forms of mental retardation and pointed to the fact that mental retardation may be more or less severe. The classifications by Seguin and Howe did not progress much further than that of Esquirol, but their descriptions of individual cases of mental retardation were more detailed.

Although Pinel, Esquirol, Seguin, and Howe did bring some order into the description of mental illness and mental retardation, these classifications were often different from those we use today. At least as important, there was no special classification for children. Special attention to description of children waited until the end of the 19th century.

In 1850, it was thought that the disorders of childhood were probably the same as those of adulthood. Sensory disorders, such as visual and hearing handicap were recognized. Also mental illness and mental retardation were distinguished from sensory handicaps and from each other. It was believed that dementia, a disorder of intelligence, was different from mental retardation in that it occurs only in adulthood, whereas mental retardation begins before birth or in childhood. Otherwise, specific disorders of childhood were not yet recognized.

With the exception of cretinism, which was still incompletely defined, none of the syndromes of childhood disorders such as Down syndrome, fetal alcohol syndrome, dyslexia, cerebral palsy, or childhood depression had been described. In addition, although it was known that causes of childhood disorder occurred prenatally and others postnatally, the guesses about causes were not associated with any syndrome. Moreover, they were sometimes vague or incorrect. For instance, Seguin believed that mental retardation is due to prenatal malnutrition. Although this can sometimes be true, the statement is so vague that it has little use in practice. Howe believed that mental retardation and other disorders were the result of sinful living, which is also so vague that it is generally useless.

Thus, at the middle of the 19th century, although individual differences were recognized, the classification of disorders of children and the search for causes of these disorders had hardly begun. From then until now, our understanding of children's psychological disorders has gradually improved under the influence of three general historical factors: The first is a continuation of the qualitative description of cases in the search for subcategories that can be associated with specific causes. The second has been the development of refined methods for measuring psychological processes. The third is an ever increasing interest in children that is derived from the aforementioned educational movements and from the theory of evolution.

Before proceeding, it is necessary to digress a bit to describe a now discredited belief that was popular and influential in the last century. Howe's idea that mental deficiency could result from sin was only one example of the widely held view that the way people behave and the environmental influences on them become part of the heredity they pass on to their children. When behavior is dissolute or the environment unfavorable, it was thought that there could be an effect on the person's own body and that whatever was in the structure of the body was passed to the children as a hereditary degeneration. This belief declined rapidly after modern gene theory (which separates somatic cells from the cells that carry hereditary information) was promulgated at the turn of this century.

In the 19th century, both heredity and environment were regarded as important in child development. There was general agreement that people could inherit the consequences of their parents' life-style. Upright habits could have beneficial effects to the family's evolutionary status; dissolute ways could bring degeneration, and ultimately extinction, to the hereditary stock. The consequences of this erroneous view were to have harmful effects on handicapped people.

On the other hand, degeneration theory did foster the belief that handicapping conditions could result from environmental causes and might therefore be preventable. The view that excessive alcohol consumption, poor nutrition, and inadequate health care during pregnancy were associated with some cases of handicap ultimately was proven to be true, and the idea that there could be intergenerational effects presaged modern research on environmental effects that last beyond a single generation.

We return now to the search for subcategories and the causes of developmental disorders. Case histories, categorization, and the search for causes had been improving during the early part of the 19th century. The decade of the 1860s produced several notable advances. W. J. Little described several cases of cerebral palsy associated with difficulties at birth, particularly a deprivation of oxygen. Little noted also that some of his cases were mentally retarded (i.e., that cerebral palsy and mental retardation could be associated).

At about the same time H. J. Down classified mentally retarded people according to a fallacious racial category system. He thereby discovered Down syndrome (originally called mongolism). Down's racial categories were never accepted because people with Down syndrome resemble members of the Mongolian race only superficially. However, the incorrect association by name remained until about 1970. Down's racial theory, which was motivated by degeneration theory, also never was accepted widely as an etiological statement. In fact, the etiology of Down syndrome remained controversial until 1959 when it was shown that Down syndrome is associated with a chromosome abnormality.

The great British psychiatrist, Henry Maudsley, included a chapter on childhood psychiatric disorders in his text entitled *The Pathology of Mind* (1890). This is a remarkable book, not only because it includes a classification of childhood psychiatric disorders, but also because it attempts to describe abnormal mental phenomena in terms of normal processes. He began his chapter on children with an analysis of normal infant development and then went on to show how psychopathology may develop as a deviation from normal processes. In the course of his description, he described several forms of insanity (including the recently controversial category of childhood depression).

Thus, by the end of the 19th century, modern classification concepts and certain ideas about etiology had begun. Most important, a scientific approach to qualitative description, classification, and searches for causes had become well established.

At the time that qualitative description of cases was becoming more detailed and scientific, the quantitative analysis of psychological processes also was developing. The credit for initiation of scientific psychological testing is ordinarily given to Francis Galton (1822–1911). However, it should be noted that Howe included a kind of psychological test in his commission report. The survey in Howe's commission report described psychological ratings of 574 people with respect to tactile sensibility, language skill, attention, ability to count, and manifestation of sexual passion, among other things. It also included ratings of health, whether parents were "drunkards," and measures of cranial dimensions. All of these "scores" were taken from detailed case histories and were either yes–no scores or ratings on a 10-point scale. Howe's survey certainly was the first quantitative description of individual differences among mentally retarded people.

Galton receives the credit for pioneering the description of individual differences because he actually tested performance on standard tasks (i.e., tasks given in essentially the same way to everyone). Galton was interested in individual differences because he was deeply concerned with human evolution. He believed that human beings could be made better through "eugenics," a term he invented. Eugenics is a program for improving the human race through selective breeding and improvement of social conditions. Galton wished to describe human abilities as they were in his time. To do that, he constructed scientific measurements of the human faculties.

The notion that the human mind is made up of several, relatively independent faculties or abilities has been with us since people began to think about the human mind (e.g., Aristotle). Included among these faculties are sensation, perception, memory, and language. Groups of abilities can be divided into more specific abilities, and the exact number of faculties is probably not definable exactly. It is also true that, most of the time, the faculties are not independent of one another. For example, one must perceive something in order to remember it.

Galton set out to measure the functioning of at least some human faculties and to see how they vary in different people. He invented tests of relatively simple psychological abilities and asked how individual differences were statistically distributed. He showed his tests did measure something and that they were easy and quick to administer. He also showed that the scores on the tests tend to be distributed according to the "Gaussian" or normal distribution. Finally, he also showed that scores on his tests tend to correlate with each other. That is, people who score high on one test tend to score high on others, and those who score low tend to score low on many tests.

This correlation of scores led Galton and his student, Pearson, to believe that a common factor could explain the correlation among scores. To the extent that scores are correlated, one might talk, not so much about specific faculties, but about a common factor called intelligence. The argument about whether human intelligence is most properly considered as a general factor or as a group of separate processes continues to this day. When considering handicapped children, one may ask whether it is most appropriate to consider specific process deficits such as dyslexia or more general deficits such as mental retardation. Spearman (1927) gave the most appropriate answer: "Really to measure any intelligence-process whatsoever, due account must be taken, not only of the said factor shared with all others, but also of the supplementary factor peculiar to itself" (p. 351).

In other words, the nature of a process, including its association with other processes, should be the focus of analysis.

Galton's ideas are included in his *Inquiries into the Human Faculty and Its Development* (1883). This book also includes the first statement of his eugenics program. The ideas in the program were taken up by others later and turned into a social movement that was to do great harm to ethnic minorities and to handicapped people. The movement continues today in more benign form (Spaulding & Balch, 1983).

Galton's intent was positive. He wished to improve the lives of people. However, he was limited by the ignorance of his time, which unfortunately had a powerful social impact through the actions of people who pay no attention to the implications of later scientific ideas.

In the generation following Galton, several people used mental tests for practical purposes, most notably Alfred Binet (1857–1911). He was an experimental psychologist who had spent most of his career studying topics popular in French psychological laboratories at the time: suggestion, hypnotism, individual differences in head size, and thinking. At the turn of the century, he was caught up by the interest in child psychology that was also common, published articles on individual differences, and participated in the development of special schools for mildly retarded children in France.

Historically, there had been little problem in identifying blind, deaf, or severely retarded children. Their disabilities were so obvious that anyone could tell they needed special help. However, the situation was not as clear with less obvious disabilities. Binet was struck by the lack of precision in the contemporary methods used for identifying children with mental handicaps. Head size, head shape, and answers to survey questions were about all that were available. These were not adequate for identifying the milder disabilities that would affect school performance. Binet set out to develop a test that would identify children who would be appropriate for the education that the public schools were planning.

He had been studying handicapped children for many years, so he knew that single test questions were not enough. More important, he knew that tests of complex thinking would predict school performance better than would simple tests of attention, sensation, and motor abilities. He proceeded to develop groups of questions, and he administered them to normal and handicapped children of different ages. He found that certain of the tests differentiated between the normal and handicapped children. At least as important, he showed that the handicapped children scored like younger normal children. That is, they were retarded in their mental development (T. Wolf, 1973).

The idea that "idiots" are arrested in their development had been recognized by Locke, Howe, and Maudsley. However, Binet was able to describe the degree of retardation and associate it with a particular age level. In doing so, he invented the concept of *mental level* (later called *mental age*). He felt it was possible to place children at a specific mental level by administering his tests. As a result, this permitted a statement of the school grade placement that was appropriate for the child. This association of mental level with grade placement has remained one of the most powerful tools available to us. When an intelligence test is used properly, it provides a valid prediction of the general level of schooling appropriate for the child.

Although his tests showed that some handicapped children perform at a younger level than one would expect from their chronological age, Binet believed that these children were not necessarily simply delayed in their development. He thought, for instance, that they might have deficits in attention that younger normal children did not have. He was never able to prove this position, however, and the issue has remained controversial until this day.

Binet never took the obvious step of converting the mental level to a measure of growth rate. This was accomplished by William Stern a few years later. It involved division of mental age (MA) by the child's chronological age (CA), thereby producing a growth rate measure, the intelligence quotient (MA / CA = IQ). In turn, this produced the concept of a delay in development: People with a low IQ develop more slowly. Delay concepts like this have been applied to a number of handicapping conditions, for instance as one theory of learning disabilities.

The tradition of mental testing to determine needs for service has been one of the most active aspects of modern psychology. Modern attacks on the misuse of intelligence tests have increased in recent years. These attacks appropriately concentrate on inappropriate construction and application of the tests rather than on the need to use them for the planning of services. As is pointed out here, tests that were developed later tended to focus somewhat more on specific processes rather than on general intelligence. Before we proceed to the analysis of such processes, we consider the rapid growth in child study at the turn of the 20th century.

The Beginnings of Scientific Study of Children

Universal education was espoused as part of the Enlightenment, organized special education began in the 18th century, and the study of individual differences began in the 19th century. The scientific study of children did not really begin until the end of the 19th century. In the period between 1880 and 1900, William Preyer, G. Stanley Hall, James Mark Baldwin, and Sigmund Freud separately published monumental works that were to set the stage for much of 20th-century research on children.

These four workers were strongly influenced by two ideas about evolution that had developed during the previous century: adaptation and recapitulation. *Adaptation* is a central process in the evolution of new species of animals (including human beings), and adaptation is also important in the changing relationship between the individual organism and its environment. Thus, the plasticity of species over generations and of individuals within a generation was a central theme in the theories of evolution.

Early concepts of adaptation (e.g., LaMarck's theory) did not clearly distinguish between species and individual adaptation, and even Charles Darwin believed that changes in the individual could be transmitted to its offspring through direct effects on body cells. This general point of view was consistent with the degeneration theory reviewed earlier. It also emphasized the importance of environmental change and of learning in adaptation of both species and individual.

One consequence of the idea of adaptation was an emphasis on learning in the comparative study of higher animals. Animal psychologists like George Romanes, Leonard Hobhouse, and Edward Thorndike all were interested in learning processes because they saw them as important for adaptation as part of evolution. The extended period of infancy in higher animals was also emphasized because it was thought that the period of growth was the time that animals learned most.

Other animal psychologists emphasized the instinctual behaviors that matched the animal to its environment. Instincts might involve some learning, but they were universal in any species, and their form and behavior were determined primarily by hereditary factors. Thus, for instance, emotional expressions were believed by Darwin to be characteristic of a particular species, to serve as social communication, and to evolve.

A second main theme in evolutionary theory that influenced the major child psychologists of the end of the 19th century was *recapitulation* theory (sometimes called the biogenetic law). According to recapitulation theory, during its development, the individual goes through stages that its species had gone through in its evolution. Embryos and young children were thought to pass through states that not only seemed like those of the adult form of lower animals but actually represented those adult forms. For instance, during one phase of its development the human embryo is seen to have gill slits like those of a fish.

Recapitulation theory, in its 19th-century form, ultimately was rejected for two reasons. First, the stages that appear to be like the stages of the adult form of lower animals are not exactly like those adult forms. Second, the biogenetic law held that the embryo's development represented not only the phylogenetic history of the animal but also special adaptations of the species. In other words, the embryonic development in each species is made up of two aspects, its phylogenetic history and special adaptations to the environment in which the species grew. However, it was not always possible to be sure whether a particular trait represents the phylogenetic history or the individual species adaptations. A theory is judged by the success of its predictions. It lost favor because the predictions of the biogenetic law were unclear.

Nevertheless, at the end of the 19th century, many people took the biogenetic law as a satisfactory theory. It had a great influence on the pioneers of child study. Analysis of the relationship between individual and phylogenetic development was a natural outcome of the biogenetic law. The first person to look at child development in these terms was William Preyer (1841–1897). Preyer set out to detail the development of the child from conception through the first 3 years of life in order to describe how the child's development was recapitulating human evolution. He was not the first person to describe his children. Tiedemann had done so in the 18th century, and Charles Darwin had kept a diary of his son's behavioral development.

However, Preyer was the first to study his children so carefully and to do so in the context of a theory—evolutionary theory. His great work, *The Mind of the Child* (1890/1973), was first published in 1881. It is a careful descriptive study of the development of the senses, the will, and the intellect in young children. The emphasis in the book is not so much to catalogue the ages at which behaviors may normally be seen. Preyer acknowledged that children grow at different rates so that the same behaviors mature at different times in different children. He was more interested in the organization of behavioral development and believed that all children go through the same stages.

Preyer's description of the development of children was based not only on an interest in human development. He also compared the development of children with the development of animals. He believed that development itself is one kind of adaptation, and he wished to learn how development evolved. For instance, he believed that the extended developmental period of higher animals is related to their increased capacity for higher thought. Preyer believed that many behaviors of the infant reflect the infant's evolutionary history. Although he acknowledged the influence of experience on development, he also thought that heredity (i.e., the child's evolutionary past) is also reflected in its behavioral growth.

G. Stanley Hall (1844–1924), the first American child psychologist, was also strongly influenced by the biogenetic law. In his two-volume work on *Adolescence,* he presented the view that, at puberty, children leave a state in which their instinctive behaviors have become matched to their environments. Their new situation reduces them to a state of nature, so far as some of the higher faculties are concerned, and they must adapt to the new situation that puberty brings. If they do not adapt successfully, it is possible that they will degenerate into dissolute ways (quotation in Grinder, 1967, p. 218).

Hall followed a strict interpretation of the biogenetic law, seeing a reflection of evolutionary history in many behaviors of growing children. James Mark Baldwin (1861–1934) took quite a different position. He rejected a strict interpretation of recapitulation because it did not make sense to him that a child would have to pass through all of the forms that are characteristic of its animal ancestors. Instead, he believed that a capacity to adapt through spontaneous action, repetition, habit, and the pleasure–pain principle are the products of evolution and that natural selection works on those individuals who have adapted by taking advantage of experience. This functional view therefore emphasized the influence of ontogeny on phylogeny rather than the reverse (Baldwin, 1894).

Hall and Baldwin also were interested in the social adaptation of the child. However, the person who emphasized adaptation in the context of social life in the most influential way was Sigmund Freud (1856–1939). There was much in Freud's developmental theory that was not new. His belief in stages of development, in the unconscious part of the mind, in conscious processes, in the importance of early development, in sex, in instinct, and in adaptation were his expressions of ideas that had been discussed frequently in the previous 200 years. However, his integration of these ideas and his emphasis on socialization in the context of the family were unique, influencing the subsequent study of child development in fundamental ways.

Freud's theory of child development was a "social learning" theory in which the child's instincts are satisfied more or less successfully through interaction with the people in its family. The child learns to adapt to the reality of social life. But because interactions are imperfect, the child may fail to progress completely through the biologically regulated major stages of childhood. The child may even regress to an earlier point of development in moments of crisis. Fixations at one point in a stage or regression to an earlier stage can be pathological, and they may be more likely in people who are constitutionally susceptible because of abnormal sexuality of their parents (S. Freud, 1938, p. 624).

In this brief description of Freud's theory, one can detect elements of the theory of evolution. His emphasis on adaptation is a central aspect of all evolutionary theories. The assumption that there are hereditary instincts and that biology drives progress through hierarchically organized developmental stages are vestiges of recapitulation theory. Finally, his regression theory is a form of constitutional degeneration theory.

The interest in child study at the end of the 19th century was partly due to the expansion of the movement for universal education. At least as important, however, was the influence of theories of evolution that had developed at the beginning of the century. One consequence was an emphasis on adaptation that was the central principle in evolutionary theory. From this principle came a functional approach that emphasized learning in a social context.

A second important influence of evolutionary theories was the hierarchical concept of child development. Children develop through a predictable sequence of universal stages. At first, it was thought that these stages are determined by phylogenetic hierarchies, that is, that "ontogeny recapitulates phylogeny." However, a strict relationship between developmental sequences and evolution was questioned later, leaving the issue of the relationship between individual and species development for future generations (Gould, 1977). However, it was clear that careful observation of children over a significant amount of time was regarded as necessary to understand how development is organized. The longitudinal study had been born.

Research on the Brain and the Mind

The 19th century brought with it an expansion of special education, a refinement of the description of individual differences, and the beginning of scientific study of children. One more movement, the study of brain function and the relation of mind to brain was to have an important influence on 20th-century understanding of handicapped children.

A central issue in this research was whether the brain functions as a whole or whether individual psychological faculties are controlled by different parts of the brain. The modern view is the one presented by one of the pioneers of brain physiology, Pierre Flourens (1794–1867). Flourens did careful experiments that showed that destruction of specific brain areas not only had specific effects on behavior but also more general ones. This is because the different parts of the brain work in concert with one another.

Thus, removal of one part of the brain destroys not only a specific function but also the integrating influence of that part.

Study of the brain was accomplished with animal experiments and also by study of people who had specific brain lesions. A famous case studied by Paul Broca (1824–1880) was of a man admitted to the Bicetre Hospital with only one problem, an inability to speak. When the patient died, Broca examined the man's brain and found a restricted lesion in the left frontal cerebral hemisphere. This correlation of specific symptom with local lesion was to become a standard way of studying brain localization.

John Hughlings Jackson (1835–1911) was a clinical neurologist who made several contributions to the understanding of the brain, using clinical methods. Hughlings Jackson was strongly influenced by the theory of evolution. He conceived of levels of the nervous system, organized according to phylogenetic level. He believed that, as evolution proceeds, levels of the brain are added to organize increasingly complex mental activities. Thus, the cerebral cortex is not only the most advanced part of the nervous system in evolutionary terms, but Hughlings Jackson also thought that it organizes higher thought. When a person deteriorates intellectually the nervous system degenerates through evolutionary levels in reverse as the higher centers of the nervous system give way to lower levels of organization.

Jackson's ideas about deterioration with brain injury was to result in a new view about diagnosis. He believed that if skills are lost, they are replaced by other more primitive skills. It seemed important to him to describe, not only the losses of skills, but also the behaviors that remain or emerge. He felt that this emphasis on the remaining or emerging skills was as informative as counting what has been lost.

Jackson also made contributions to localization of function within the brain by writing about epilepsy. He showed that different types of seizure are associated with abnormalities in different parts of the brain. He also was one of the first to write extensively about agnosias, aphasias, and apraxia, the bizarre disorders of perception and language associated with specific brain lesions.

The issue of localization of function in the nervous system was part of a larger exploration of the relationship between mind and body, or behavior and brain function. Philosophers had discussed this issue in great depth prior to the 19th century, but the issue did not become scientific until that time. Much of this research was carried out by experimental psychologists who had been trained as philosophers, physicians, and physicists.

Foremost among these experimental psychologists were Gustav T. Fechner (1801–1887) and Wilhelm Wundt (1832–1920). Fechner developed the science of psychophysics. He was a physicist who set out to determine how the mind responds to external events. More specifically, he wished to determine whether judgments of changes in the intensity of stimuli are directly proportional to the changes themselves. It happens that they are not directly proportional. This means that the psychology of the individual is not an exact reflection of the physical world. The brain makes a conversion of physical to psychic phenomena. At least as important, it is possible to demonstrate that this is true and to measure the mind–body relationship in a quantitative way.

Fechner's work is important in the history of the psychology of children with handicaps because the methods he developed for psychophysics are exactly those that are used today to assess sensory and other psychological functioning. Procedures for testing vision, hearing, and other senses, for example, are based directly on the elegant experimental methods that Fechner developed and used.

Wundt was interested in a great many things, including anthropology and animal behavior. However, he is best known for studies of how the mind is structured and how it works. Like Preyer, he was interested in the way the general mind works, rather than in individual differences. In his studies of mental processes, he used the laboratory method (i.e., studying responses in highly controlled conditions) and introspection by trained observers, rather than "tests" like those used by Galton or Binet. In other words, he believed in studying the mind intensively.

Perhaps because Wundt and his followers were not very interested in individual differences (including age differences), Wundt's type of experimental psychology did not begin to influence the study of children until the middle of the 20th century. However, the work of the early experimental psychologists did form a new science that flourished in the 20th century and ultimately became a central movement in the study of children with handicaps.

THE 20TH CENTURY

By the beginning of the 20th century, most of the basic ideas that we now hold about handicapped children had been developed. Handicapped people can and should be educated. They have special needs but usually can live reasonably normal lives. There are great differences between them, just as there are between all people. It is appropriate to think about handicapped children in the context of general principles of development. These principles include descriptions of normative developmental processes and sequences. They also include statements about the hereditary and environmental contributions to development.

The turn of the century brought with it an expansion and unprecedented detailing of these ideas (A. D. B. Clarke & A. M. Clarke, 1987; Summers, 1986). Scientific and technical advances, combined with a social reformist spirit, were to bring new services to a much wider range of children and to foster the idea that handicapped people can participate normally in society with the same legal rights as the general population.

However, before the reformist ideologies of the post-World War II period provided a force for integrating handicapped people into everyday life, two generations of handicapped people were to endure the effects of the eugenics movement of the early part of the century.

The Eugenics Movement

Francis Galton had stimulated the idea that, with controlled breeding, it would be possible to improve the mental quality of the human species. This notion was based on two false premises: First, psychological processes are organized into relatively simple separate faculties; second, mental characteristics are determined mainly by hereditary, rather than environmental, influences. Modern genetics and psychological research have shown that psychological characteristics are related in complex ways, that their development is complex, and that both heredity and environment always interact to produce all psychological characteristics. Thus, any simplistic program of mental eugenics probably is not feasible.

At the beginning of this century, however, the complexities of heredity and of psychology were not yet appreciated, and the eugenics movement was a clear possibility for many people. Eugenicists disagreed about how to proceed (Cravens, 1978, p. 47). Some believed in a positive approach, such as the one espoused by Galton. He thought, for instance, that support of early marriage would increase reproduction of those classes of society to be favored. He explicitly avoided speaking of repression of less-favored classes, believing it would "ensue indirectly as a matter of course" (Galton, 1907/1973, p. 219).

In the next generation, others did favor negative methods such as restriction of immigration, segregating people in institutions, and compulsory sterilization laws. The eugenics movement in the United States became an influential political movement characterized by a racist doctrine and a simplistic hereditarian philosophy. It assumed that many handicaps are transmitted mainly by heredity and that preventing reproduction by handicapped people was the best way to go about preventing a "swamping" of the population with handicaps.

Many people supported the general goals of the eugenics movement. Laws restricting immigration from eastern and southern Europe and favoring "Nordic" populations were supported on eugenics grounds, and 30 U.S. state legislatures passed compulsory sterilization law between 1907 and 1931 (Cravens, 1978, p. 53). However, the eugenics movement had already reached its peak by 1930 and declined thereafter though vestiges can still be discerned (Spaulding & Balch, 1983).

Perhaps the most important influence leading to its decline was a revulsion against the racist ideas that had come to be its theme. The idea that some racial groups in society are superior or more advanced than others had received some support in the United States, but the idea was seen to be inimical to the ideals on which the U.S. government was based. In Europe, this idea had become an important part of the program of the National Socialist party in Germany, which led to the genocide of ethnic minorities during the 1930s and 1940s.

Not only had eugenics shown itself to be antidemocratic and destructive, but the assumption that it was based on scientific principles proved to be false. Eugenics was based on a simplistic genetic idea that heredity directly and solely affects behavior and its disabilities. This view of genetics was challenged by discoveries in genetics beginning about 1910. These discoveries showed that environments affect hereditary transmission. Heredity and environment interact to produce all characteristics, mental and physical. The statement that heredity alone produces most changes in an individual's behavior became meaningless.

In addition to advances in experimental genetics, the new science of cultural anthropology was making the case that apparent race differences in behavior are as easily attributable to cultural differences as to hereditary differences. Anthropologists were also denying that race or ethnic differences are hierarchically organized. That is, they showed that one ethnic group could not be shown to be more advanced in evolution than another. Biological and cultural evolution were said to be independent processes interacting with one another.

This new scientific outlook introduced a complexity of analysis that undercut the simplistic thinking of the eugenicists. During the 1920s, many discussions about eugenics issues occurred, and public support for the eugenics movement gradually died. But the consequences for handicapped people would take another generation to work themselves out. The sterilization laws were never widely used, but mentally retarded, mentally ill, epileptic, blind, and deaf people were to be maintained in institutions whose main function was custodial and separatist.

Mainstreaming and Normalization

While the eugenics movement was growing and then declining, special education expanded steadily. First, classes for more severely handicapped children were provided in the educational system. These classes were generally in separate schools or separate classrooms. Then, special services were provided in regular classrooms for children with special needs. Finally, there was a move to educate handicapped children in regular classes, the so-called *mainstreaming movement*.

As we have shown, special education began on the basis of a reformist ideal. Seguin conceived of three types of placement: day schools, short-term residential programs, and long-term custodial placement. By the beginning of the 20th century, special education in day schools had become established and was increasing. Long-term residential placements in institutions were steadily increasing in size. Short-term residential schools were declining in importance, consistent with their reduced importance in general education.

The typical special class or school was smaller than average so that the teacher could respond to the special needs of the individuals in the class. The curriculum in these classes was specialized for the different handicaps. For instance, classes for blind children emphasized travel and braille reading skills in addition to regular subjects. Curricula for hearing-handicapped pupils concentrated on communication skills, whereas mentally retarded students learned general subjects adjusted to their mental age level. In addition, all students learned simple vocational skills that were appropriate for the time.

The long-term residential institutions gradually changed from the benevolent environments that Seguin conceived of in the 1840s into the overcrowded "warehouses" of the 1960s. At the turn of the century, it was not simple to distinguish some hearing-handicapped, epileptic, mentally retarded, criminal, or mentally ill people from each other. As a result, initially all of these groups were placed in the same increasingly crowded institutions. As it became clear that these groups had different needs, special institutions were established. However, most of the institutions became environments having essentially no educational purpose and devoted to keeping people alive (but not necessarily very healthy; hepatitis was endemic in many institutions). People spent their lives in large buildings with scores of other people of the same sex, regularly shifted from a bedroom to a bare and crowded day-room or to an exercise yard. These institutions ultimately became overcrowded, with people minimally supervised by a few poorly educated staff members.

Segregated special education and institutions in rural areas were characteristics of services for handicapped children until after World War II. Beginning in the 1950s, several factors led to a movement to *normalize* the lives of handicapped children. This movement made major changes in the lives of handicapped children and adults, but it cannot yet be counted as completely successful.

Perhaps the most important factor was ideological and legal. Democratic ideals had been fostered by events before and especially during World War II. Social democracy in Europe and traditional democratic ideals in the

United States had been challenged by racist theories and totalitarian governments. The defeat of the antidemocratic forces during World War II prepared the way for several democratic movements that were to find some expression in law. For example, civil rights and feminist political action produced voting rights laws and affirmative action regulations that strengthened the political influence and access to employment of ethnic minorities and women in the United States. It was in the context of this struggle for equal rights that legislation for handicapped people provided some assurance of equal access to the general society.

One specific result of this movement was legislation guaranteeing access to all public buildings for physically handicapped people. Architectural changes such as ramps and transportation services for people who were unable to use public transportation also were consequences of this democratic movement.

As important as these physical changes was a federal law (Public Law 94–142) guaranteeing education for all handicapped children. Although never fully funded, this law stipulates that all handicapped children have a right to education in "the least restrictive environment," that is, in a situation as much like a regular classroom as possible.

This law had been fostered by a second influence on special education. Scientific studies of the efficacy of special classes had shown that a handicapped child could be educated as well, and less expensively, in the regular class. Thus, scientific assessment of efficacy had been added to ideological considerations to foster a movement to mainstream handicapped children.

Ideology, science, and finances also influenced a dismantling of the large institutions. Before the 1960s, children were being placed in institutions to spend the rest of their lives there. By 1990, institutions continued to exist but mainly housed severely handicapped people. The populations of the institutions had decreased significantly, and the programs were reasonably well-staffed.

The normalization movement had been imported from Sweden to the United States (Nirje, 1985). The philosophy of this movement centered on the idea that a handicapped person should live in as normal an environment as possible. This included life in the community, perhaps in homelike residences, and in schools, working places, and recreation programs that are part of the general community.

On the basis of this ideology, many mildly handicapped people were moved from institutions to reasonably normal community environments. This movement was fostered by the development of psychotropic drugs that were shown to reduce symptoms in many mentally ill people. Another contributing factor to deinstitutionalization was studies that had shown that institutional living retards emotional and cognitive growth. Finally, it became apparent to many public administrators that deinstitutionalization would reduce the state's expense to maintain handicapped people. Instead of state funding of institutions, community living meant that support for the handicapped person could be undertaken by parents, philanthropic agencies, and federal government sources.

The dismantling of segregated special classes and of large institutions was thus fostered by ideological, scientific, and fiscal considerations. At this writing, this movement is still underway, but may be losing its force because of problems that have emerged in community placement (see chap. 11).

Child Study

In addition to eugenics, special education, and the movement favoring integration of handicapped people into general society, the 20th century has seen a refinement in the description of child development and of the understanding of the causes of handicapping conditions. Child study has had three major themes, the analysis of hereditary and environmental influences on behavior, the description of motor and cognitive development, and the study of social development.

The analysis of the relative influences of heredity and environment dates back to Greek philosophy and was an enduring philosophical problem until the middle of the 20th century. The philosopher, of the Enlightenment and the social reformers who followed them emphasized the role of experience in psychological development. Francis Galton and the proponents of Eugenics favored a hereditarian emphasis. It was not until the 20th century that scientists understood that both heredity and environment, working together, are necessary for the development of any physical or mental characteristic. Moreover, "environment" could mean not only postnatal experience but also the chemical environments necessary for growth. In sum, the question was not whether heredity or environment are important or even whether one is more important than the other. The main question for the 20th century became "how do hereditary and environmental factors exert their influence on any specific behavior?"

This view of the role of heredity and of experiential and chemical environments in development was to have important implications for handicapped children. It fostered the view that even if children have a hereditary disorder, they can and should be educated. It was also consistent with the idea that experience, by itself, might not be sufficient for mental development. That is, the same education can have different effects on children who have had different developmental histories.

A second theme in the study of child development in the 20th century was the description of normative behavioral development. This tradition, begun by Preyer and Binet, depended on the idea that development is organized into typical universal sequences. Thus, normal children sit at about 6 to 8 months of age, say their first words when about a year old, and so forth. The description of these universal patterns has developed during the 20th century so that much detailed knowledge about developmental sequences is now available. When looked at very closely, it becomes clear that the sequences are not as uniform as they appear when looked at crudely. However, for rough practical diagnostic purposes, the range of times and the sequence of occurrence of various behaviors are reasonably predictable.

Sometimes rough diagnoses are not enough. When more precision and accuracy are needed, the concepts and procedures developed by experimental child psychologists have provided a new level of description and analysis not possible with traditional tests in the Galton and Binet traditions. Intensive study of perception, learning, memory, thinking, and even social behavior has become possible in the last 50 years and holds great promise for the future.

The detailed description of normal development has produced an average standard against which the development of children with handicaps can be assessed. Thus, delays in specific motor or cognitive behaviors or in general behavioral development can be detected as deviations with the precision of a number of months. Recently, longitudinal studies have permitted, not only the description of typical age of appearance of specific behaviors but also organization of the sequences themselves. No doubt this will someday result in a more sophisticated understanding of what was once thought to be universal sequencing and thus in more subtle diagnosis of individual development.

In addition to the general causes of development, the description of behavioral development, and the study of psychological processes, a fourth theme in child study during this century has concerned itself with the development of social relationships. Sigmund Freud initiated this line of investigation. However, Freud never actually observed the social development of children. There was some study of the social relationships of children by his followers in the first half of the 20th century. However, it was not until the 1950s that the intensive scientific study of child social development began.

At that time, scientists and clinicians working in the psychoanalytic, behaviorist, and ethology (animal behavior) traditions developed a social learning approach that emphasized how children learn specific things from the important people they grow up with. For instance, children model on and become like the people around them, especially adults who are both powerful and loving. Other scientists studied ways in which children first become socially attached to their mothers, and they described individual differences in attachment.

These studies showed that social attachments are reciprocal. That is, not only do infants attach socially to their parents, but parents develop relationships with their children. And these responses of parents are different when the children are different from each other. These ideas of reciprocity and responses to individual differences were to be important in the analysis of parent–child interactions in the study of social development of children with handicaps.

Similarly, studies of children who had been reared in institutions or of animals who had been raised without mothers were to be important for our views of handicapped children. These studies showed that maternal deprivation can have devastating effects on the social development of children. The deprivation effects include withdrawal, fearfulness, and abnormal behaviors characteristic of some mentally ill children.

Individual Differences

Besides eugenics, special education, and child study, the description of individual differences produced dramatic changes in the 20th century, both through psychological measurement and syndrome description.

Prior to the turn of the century, there were no techniques available for the objective standardized description of human behavior outside of the laboratory. Now there are hundreds of tests, surveys, and questionaires that can detect and describe delays and deviations in development. The emergence of these assessment methods depended on several principles that became the basis for quantitative description of human behavior and its deviations.

The first principle indicated that behavior can be described quantitatively and it is desirable to do so. Quantification was seen as a complement to qualitative description, making it more precise. For instance, the statement that a child is delayed in reading by 2 years is a more useful statement than one asserting that the child has problems in reading but in no other academic area. According to a second principle, whereas each child is unique, this uniqueness is defined best by looking at the child in standard situations. Observing a child's response to standard test questions or in a standard free-play situation, for example, provides the basis for defining the dimensions that describe that child's unique qualities.

A third principle forming the basis of testing technologies of the 20th century is the idea that describing a particular person involves comparing that person with others, usually of the same age. This principle made formal the idea that saying that a child is handicapped is really a statement of how the child is the same as other children and how different.

Modern behavioral description also involved assessment of the quality of the tasks or questions used to describe people. The most basic criterion of whether an assessment procedure is adequate is a statement of its reliability, that is, the degree to which the task or question produces the same description every time it is administered. The second criterion of the quality of a test is its validity (i.e., the degree to which the procedure actually measures what it was intended to measure).

Not all modern tests embody the principles that are made possible by the field of behavioral measurement. Tests of sensory acuity (mainly of vision or hearing) do have these characteristics of being quantitative, standardized, reliable, and valid. Intelligence tests and school achievement tests may have them but sometimes are used inappropriately. Tests of personality are helpful in describing the child but do not always fulfill the criteria listed previously very well and must therefore be used with caution.

Nevertheless, progress in the technology of behavioral assessment has produced clear advances in the clinical description of the behavior of handicapped children. This progress has provided a much clearer conception of the nature of handicaps than was available at the end of the 19th century and has been an essential aid to the sophisticated and sensitive diagnosis of childhood disorders.

Syndromes and Causes

In addition to the description of children along multiple quantitative dimensions, the 20th century has seen the emergence of categories of handicap that have sometimes been related to the cause of the disorder. One reason that clinical categories are sought is to find the unique causes of the disorder. During the 20th century, several syndromes have been discovered. Childhood autism, fetal alcohol syndrome, dyslexia, phenylketonuria, and Fragile-X syndrome are only a few of the hundreds of conditions that have been defined.

Most of the syndromes are defined by specific physical characteristics. Behavioral characteristics are rarely unique to the syndrome. Thus, fetal alcohol syndrome is defined by certain features of the face and by a history of prenatal exposure to alcohol that is quite specific. However, the mild mental retardation also associated with fetal alcohol syndrome is not specific and is not unique to this syndrome.

Some categories are defined completely by behavior. Learning disabilities, hyperactivity, and dyslexia are examples. However, in these cases, there is still substantial controversy about which behaviors are to be used in the definition of the syndrome. Thus, the nature of the categories, let alone their cause, remains a mystery.

Finding causes for conditions that are well-defined by physical characteristics has advanced significantly during the past 30 years. Down syndrome is a disorder associated with a defect in part of a chromosome pair. Phenylke-tonuria is a severe type of mental deficiency caused by a specific genetic defect in metabolism of one amino acid. The search for causes has been most successful for those well-defined physical syndromes that have generalized behavioral consequences. Less success has come from the search for specific behavioral syndromes.

On the other hand, behavior has been a very sensitive marker that something has gone wrong during development. In the last century, there was a dim understanding that alcohol during pregnancy and inadequate diets could produce general behavioral handicaps. In this century, these ideas were confirmed scientifically and the role of environmental poisons, drugs, viruses, inadequate parenting, and cultural factors all were specified and demonstrated. The effects of all these classes of conditions are often marked by behavioral handicaps as their most significant consequence.

Treatments

Though specific behavioral syndromes are not always possible to define, and though there is no clear scientific relationship between specific causes and specific behavioral patterns, the 20th century has seen remarkable progress in the understanding of how children's behavioral handicaps are deter-mined. This understanding has led to prevention of these disorders. At the same time, three approaches to providing treatment have also been devel-oped essentially independent of the search for causes. These treatments include drug therapies, psychotherapy, and behavior modification.

Modern drug therapies to normalize behavior in handicapped children were first used in the 1930s as a result of the finding that drugs having a stimulating effect in adults tend to depress hyperactivity in children. This effect is not yet understood, but it has had an impressive positive effect in helping hyperactive children maintain their attention on important things. Since the 1930s, several psychotropic medications have been developed for use with children with behavioral disorders.

There are two main difficulties in using drugs with children. First, they sometimes have side-effects such as interfering with normal growth or inducing abnormal movements if used in large quantities over long periods of time. In addition, these drugs are often used more than is warranted by the child's problems. Sometimes the drugs are used for children who do not need them; sometimes more medication is given than is appropriate. In the latter case, the drug given to suppress undesirable behaviors may also suppress desirable ones.

The use of psychotropic drugs therefore can be useful but sometimes inappropriate. Psychotherapy and behavior modification are used either independent of drug therapy or complementary to it. Psychotherapy rose from the moral treatments of the 19th century, but more specifically from the psychoanalytic therapy developed by Freud and his collaborators and followers. The main purpose of psychotherapy is the intensive analysis of a person's ideas in order to help with adaptation. Mental analysis, complemented by suggestion, hypnotism, and other procedures had been developed in France in the 19th century. Freud and the people he influenced emphasized self-understanding through long-term analysis of the person's present ideas in the light of past social experience.

Freud's psychotherapeutic method emphasized analysis of early social history but was carried out primarily with adult patients at first. Children's ideas are quite different from those of adults, and the language of very young children is limited. This required different approaches in psychotherapy. It was not until the 1930s that psychotherapy of children was pioneered by Melanie Klein, Anna Freud, and Virginia Axline, who used play and drawing as well as talking in the psychotherapy of children. Approaches to psychotherapy have multiplied since the 1930s. Most recently, therapy of families of children with handicaps has become part of psychological treatment. Overall, a complex set of treatments has become available for analysis of the emotional problems.

These traditional psychotherapies emphasize analysis of the children's ideas about themselves and the social world. Behavior modification comes from a different tradition that emphasizes the effective change of specific behaviors. The direct roots of behavior modification reside in the behaviorist movement that began with the learning theories of the first half of the 20th century. John B. Watson, Ivan P. Pavlov, and Edward L. Thorndike all espoused the view that behavior, rather than the inner workings of the mind, were the appropriate focus for a scientific study of the traditional problems of human behavior. Their followers—Clark Hull, Edward Tolman, E. R. Guthrie, and B. F. Skinner—developed complex and sophisticated theories of learning as general accounts of human behavior.

Skinner, particularly, was interested in how the study of specific behaviors could be used to advance the welfare of human society. Skinner's students developed a scientific technology, using basic learning procedures (e.g., discrimination, generalization, and reinforcement) to reduce the symptoms of mentally ill and mentally retarded children and adults. These procedures can be very powerful and are in wide use. They can be applied to reduce undesirable behaviors, such as inappropriate aggression and self-injurious behaviors and to increase desirable skills like self-feeding, dressing, and language. In addition, a central feature of the approach involves formal assessment of whether the procedures used actually have worked in the individual case.

In the last 10 years, drug therapy, traditional psychotherapy and behavioral approaches have been used in combination with one another. Many studies have shown that the effects of drugs and behavior modification are more beneficial when used in combination than when either is administered independently. Moreover, cognitive behavioristic psychotherapy is a recent application of behavioral principles to more complex behaviors such as images and ideas. Thus, the three traditionally separate therapeutic approaches have been found, at least in some instances, to be complementary.

GENERAL CONCEPTS

The history of scientific study and social reform on behalf of children with handicaps is well-advanced. Basic concepts, established methods, and traditional issues are defined clearly. Of course, the experienced clinician or teacher often feels inadequate when confronted with specific problems and often cannot do what is needed to help children with handicaps and their families. Scientists feel much confusion about their concepts and their methods when they go beyond general statements, especially in trying to deal with specific children. Yet, as this chapter has attempted to show, we are very far ahead of where we were even 50 years ago. Progress has been steady.

In the chapters that follow, I hope to present to the reader the picture as it was reflected in the research of the 1980s. In doing so, I repeatedly refer to seven general concepts that underlie much thinking about children with handicaps. These concepts were available 100 years ago, and they continue to motivate research and services today. The following questions are often asked in considering individual children: How severe is the disorder? Is there more than one problem? What is the child's developmental status? What is the nature of the disorder? How does the child adapt to its environment, and how does the environment respond? What caused the handicapping condition? What can be done about it?

Severity

Samuel Gridley Howe emphasized that mental retardation is graded according to severity. This most obvious characteristic of a disability was apparent early in the history of thinking about children's handicaps. The difference between a child with a mild transitory learning disorder and one with a profound problem that affects every area of functioning throughout its life is more important for practical purposes than are other differences between children. A child with mild, correctable, astigmatism can live a normal life, whereas another child who has difficulty seeing even with maximum correction may have special problems throughout life.

Multiple Handicap

In addition to a single handicap, the question of the possible existence of multiple handicaps is an important aspect of the clinical picture of many children with disabilities. For instance, whereas it may be convenient to think of children as being either chronically ill, blind, hearing-handicapped, mentally retarded, or emotionally handicapped, in fact, many children with disabilities are handicapped in more than one way. Multiple handicap tends to be related to severity. Children who are severely handicapped also tend to have more than one handicap. Thus, severely retarded children may have cerebral palsy, sensory disorders, and/or one of several chronic illnesses.

There are important consequences from the understanding that children with handicaps may have more than one disability and that multiple handicap tends to be related to severity of the disorder(s). Most important, the competent professional understands that in diagnosing and treating a child, one must consider the possibility that more than one handicap exists. A broad diagnostic approach, and a treatment program that takes into account all of the handicaps involved, is preferable to an approach that responds only to the most obvious disability.

Developmental Level

The effect of any event in the child's life also depends on the child's development level, usually marked by chronological age. Not only does education vary with age, but drug effects, psychotherapy, and behavior modification all have different effects at different age levels. Moreover, causes of developmental disorders, such as lead intoxication, hypoxia, and parenting abnormalities have qualitatively different effects at different developmental levels. Thus, a "developmental" approach is essential in considering handicapping conditions.

Nature of the Handicap

In addition to severity, multiple handicaps, and developmental status, a fourth important general consideration is the nature of the handicapping condition. The differences between categories, syndromes, or types of developmental disorder can be obvious. One would not expect an intelligent child with cerebral palsy to have the same problems in adapting to the social environment as does a mentally retarded child with normal motor functioning.

But the differences between categories should not be overdrawn. There are some problems that most handicapped children share. For instance, irrespective of their diagnosis, many handicapped children are not accepted socially by their peers. Moreover, their families generally suffer financial burdens that are greater than those borne by families of nonhandicapped children. These two sources of stress can produce a higher risk for emotional problems in any handicapped child, not just those who are categorized as having emotional problems. Thus, the nature of the handicap includes not only how handicapped children differ from each other but also the things that they share.

As important as defining how the child with handicaps is different from normal is a statement of how handicapped children are the same as other children. Although people often see handicapped people in terms of the problems the children have, most handicapped children are very much like other children of the same age or developmental status. Handicapped children think of themselves as essentially normal and expect to be accepted as such. In fact, the abilities and motives of most handicapped children are normal for their age.

Handicap as an Ecological Concept

Some environments make disabilities more obvious than do others. School, for instance, taxes the intellectual abilities of children increasingly as they grow older. As a result, some intellectual handicaps become more obvious in the later school years than they are either earlier or in adulthood. This is only one example of the principle that adaptation is determined, not only by the characteristics of the child, but also by the demands of the environment. In other words, "handicap" is an ecological concept.

Causes and Prevention

As a consequence of the understanding that handicap is an ecological concept, one seeks to improve adaptation through several approaches. The first approach is preventing the condition in the first place. Prevention requires, first, basic research into the causes of disorders of development. Then, public health measures can be instituted so that specific conditions can be eliminated altogether. The reduction of poliomyelitis, cretinism, Tay-Sachs disease, and Down syndrome are all instances where this has been accomplished in industrial societies, if not universally.

Treatment

Prevention research and public health programs have yet to eradicate children's handicaps. In those cases in which the child's characteristics and the environment interact to produce a problem in adaptation, education of the child and modification of the environment can reduce the problem. The goal of education is to change the child's behavior so that it is more consistent with society's expectations. On the other hand, society can also change so that people with handicaps can participate more fully. Braille signs in elevators, ramps for buildings, special transportation, interpreters for people with hearing handicaps, and laws guaranteeing social equality are all ways that society has modified itself to enable handicapped children to participate more fully.

SUMMARY

Individuals with handicaps were part of society before the evolution of human culture. Attitudes toward handicapped people have been ambivalent since ancient times and continue to be complex now. Throughout history, people with handicaps have been vilified, overprotected, supported, or regarded as essentially like any other people.

Organized services for children with handicaps began in the 18th century. The services were motivated by revolutionary movements espousing the universal rights of human beings. Empiricist philosophies supported the idea that all people can benefit from education, and the importance of universal education for democracy became an accepted assumption.

Organized education and scientific psychology spread during the 19th century. In particular, the study of individual differences and of developmental processes became established. These movements were fostered by theories of evolution and by studies of brain functioning and experimental psychology. Degeneration theory and recapitulation theory were widely accepted before they lost influence in the 20th century.

The 20th century opened with the eugenics movement, which separated people with handicaps from society. At the same time, however, expansion of special education was continuous. The eugenics movement lost its force in the 1930s, and the normalization movement took its place. Understanding of the nature and causes of disorders of development became more refined, which had important effects on prevention and treatment of handicapping conditions.

The following seven concepts have been important in thought about disorders of development: severity, multiple handicap, developmental level, nature of the handicap, handicap as an ecological concept, causes, and treatment. These concepts appear often in the remaining chapters of this book.

2

Categories and Prevalence

Our review of the history of thinking about children's handicaps has shown that, by the end of the 19th century, the broad categories of handicapping conditions had been defined. In the 20th century, thinking about classification became more formal and refined so that several classification systems have emerged. This chapter describes the main types of handicap in children and provides rough estimates of the prevalence of the various conditions.

At least as important, the chapter reviews ways in which classification systems are constructed and their uses. It concludes that current classification of handicapping conditions are more complex and confusing than one might expect at first. Moreover, current behavioral classification systems seem to be useful mainly for general assignment to treatment programs rather than for detailed planning of treatment or for analysis of causes. Some reasons for the limitations in current classification systems are reviewed in this chapter and also the next one.

Classification begins with the description of individuals. Each child has a unique pattern of physical and behavioral characteristics that can be described, and this description can be used for planning that child's treatment and education. However, this description must be done in terms of categories or dimensions that can be applied to more than one child. For instance, age, height, intelligence quotient, presence or absence of abnormal movements, degree of visual impairment, activity level, aggression, and ability to use community transportation are only a few of the almost infinite number of ways in which a child can be described.

The use of appropriate categories or dimensions to describe the individual child allows parents and professionals to detect patterns in the child's behavior and to learn whether the child is similar to other children in important ways. If it turns out that the child is similar to others, it may be that treatments that have been successful with these other children might also be successful in this case. Thus, the use of appropriate descriptors allows grouping of children so that prevention and treatment of their handicap becomes possible.

Grouping children into categories also allows an estimate of the number of children who have the disorder (prevalence) or who have ever had it (incidence). Estimating the number of children with a disorder allows government administrators to plan services for children with that disorder. If one knows that the prevalence of childhood autism is much lower than the prevalence of speech disorders, then program administrators may establish fewer training programs for teachers of autistic children than for communication specialists.

Prevalence rates also are necessary for the study of prevention of specific disorders. If prevalence rates of a disorder are related to specific environmental factors, then those environmental factors may be a cause of the disorder. One instance of such an epidemiological study involved the demonstration of the relationship between endemic cretinism (a form of mental deficiency) and low levels of iodine in the diet.

As becomes evident, the development of categories of handicap and the estimate of prevalence rates are not necessarily simple and straightforward. Category systems change, and different ones are used for different purposes. Specific categories are not mutually exclusive, and the differences between categories may not be discrete. Even when categories are clear, data sources for developing prevalence rates are not always scientific, and prevalence estimates therefore can vary.

Despite these problems, categories of children's handicaps are useful. There is, in fact, general agreement on the major categories. An autistic child will not be confused with a sociable child having rheumatic heart disease. This agreement allows imprecise, but useful, prevalence rate estimates and general service program planning. The development of category systems has come far since the 19th century. Their further development, using scientific approaches, will improve those that exist.

CLASSIFICATION

Purposes of Classification

When describing any child, we use words that can be applied to other children. A particular individual may be young, happy, spoiled, a brother, poor, and so on. Thus, our picture of a unique person comes from a comparison with others. This use of descriptors that can be applied to others is also central to classifying a child with handicaps.

We often use the same categories or dimensions in talking about handicapped children as we use for describing children with no handicaps. Thus, handicapped children also may be young, happy, spoiled, a brother, poor, and so on. However, there are also special descriptors that apply to handicaps. Retardation, visual impairment, psychosis, and learning disability are terms that are not applied to children who have no special problems.

There are several reasons that we use special classification systems for children with handicaps (Blashfield &. Draguns, 1976b). Perhaps the most widely used function of classification systems is communication. Identifying a child as handicapped in a special way permits professionals to talk with one another about a specific child and about groups of children having similar characteristics. Moreover, some clinicians (Werry, 1985) believe that parents experience significant relief from anxiety when they are told that their child is a member of a particular diagnostic group. The parent perceives that the professional person understands what their child is like, what the cause is of the condition, and what to expect in the future.

But not all classifications permit statements about cause and what to expect in the future. In the ideal, knowing the child's condition may help in detecting the etiology, or cause, of the condition and to predict what is the course, or future, of the condition.

Knowing the condition, its etiology, and its future course might help in understanding the nature of the disorder. That is, classification could lead to an understanding of how the disease process works. Historically, this relationship between, classification, course, etiology, and theory have led to improved prevention or treatment of conditions that are medical.

Unfortunately, the history of the classification of problems of behavior has not been as successful. Although it is true that there are many conditions defined by both physical and behavioral characteristics, the same is not true of conditions in which only behavior forms the basis of classification or in which the physical symptoms are very generalized. Thus, Down syndrome, fetal alcohol syndrome, phenylketonuria, and cretinism (all of which are associated with behavioral disorders that are general and severe) are also characterized by specific physical characteristics and specific causes. On the other hand, conduct disorders, mental retardation, and learning disabilities are all defined by general behavioral characteristics only. Their causes are unknown or multiple, and prevention and treatment programs for them are only very general. Thus, behavioral classification does not yet guarantee increased understanding, prevention, or differential treatment (Ysseldyke, Christenson, Thurlow, &. Bakewell, 1989).

Behavioral classification does, however, provide the basis for communication about the child. It also helps organize the way in which information about children is collected. Diagnostic procedures or research are accomplished with very different questions in mind if the children are visually impaired than if they have a motor impairment. Treatment and its evaluation are different for a child with cerebral palsy than for one with dyslexia, even though the cause or course of either are not very well understood.

The Risk of Labeling

Classification of handicaps in childhood has a number of potential uses, but there are also two major risks from use of a classification system. One of these is the possibility that a child will be misclassified and therefore placed in a treatment setting from which no benefit can be obtained. One notable example is the placement of hearing-impaired children into custodial institutions for mentally retarded children after an inadequate hearing evaluation. There are cases of children living a lifetime in such institutions without the staff being aware that they are not mentally retarded.

A second risk comes from the possibility of problems caused by the label itself. Several people (e.g., Hobbs, 1975) have expressed the view that placing a child in a diagnostic category itself influences people's responses to the child, with the result that the child's self-concept begins to match that of the label and the child begins to behave abnormally. In other words, it is thought that the label causes behavioral pathology. Especially poignant is the fact that simply providing a child with needed special services can act as a negatively valued label (Bak, Cooper, Dobroth, & Siperstein, 1987).

This labeling perspective makes sense if one views the classification process as just another example in which people assign attributes to children, and children respond by living up (or down) to the attributes assigned to them. If one believes that by telling children they are gifted, one can increase their self-confidence, ambition, and performance, one might also believe that if one tells children they are learning disabled, they might lose confidence and ambition and perform poorly in school.

Although the existence of the labeling effect is plausible, the situation is more complicated than it might initially appear. First, in the case of children with severe handicaps, it is unlikely that the labeling effect itself has caused the handicap. The behavior of children with spinal injuries may be influenced by what the people around them say about them, but the spinal injury and its behavioral consequences are certainly at least as potent as the diagnostic label. It is not credible that the label produced the spinal injury.

The labeling issue has therefore been applied mainly in the case of normal children or children with mild handicaps. Here the question is whether the label itself causes or accentuates disabilities. The answer (Guskin, 1978) appears to be that, whereas the label might have deleterious effects, its effects are not very strong. Of course, people do apply negatively valued labels to children with handicaps and to normal children also (R. W. Smith, Osborne, Crim, & Rhu, 1986). However, the results of studies of the effects of the labels on self-concept and on performance do not give a clear negative picture.

The overall conclusion, therefore, espouses that whereas there may be a risk of deleterious effects from labeling children as handicapped, the evidence for this negative effect is not very strong. In any case, it must also be recognized that there are benefits if the classification of the child provides access to special services the child may need. In the individual case, the potential benefits of classification must be balanced with the possible detrimental effects of labeling.

Sources of Variation in Classification Systems

There are a number of systems for classification of children's handicaps and these systems vary significantly. In this section, several issues are summarized that describe this variation. The first issue is the purpose of the classification system. Some systems summarize symptoms, others emphasize etiology, others concentrate on treatment, and still others attempt to deal with all three of these purposes, at least implicitly.

A second source of variation is the type of information about the child. Some systems emphasize the notes and summaries that the clinician makes when interviewing the child and the family (Towle & Schwarz, 1987). Others use standard checklists of symptoms filled out by parents and/or teachers. These different sources of information produce different pictures of the child (Achenbach & Edelbrock, 1978, 1984; Achenbach, McConaughy, & Howell, 1987) in the same classification system and also different classification systems.

Another distinction between classification systems has to do with whether they emphasize symptoms or syndromes. A *symptom* is one abnormal characteristic of the child, whereas a *syndrome* is a group of symptoms regularly occurring together and often associated with a unique etiology. For instance, mental retardation is a very general symptom. Down syndrome includes mental retardation, several associated physical characteristics, and a chromosomal abnormality thought to cause the mental and physical abnormalities.

Physically defined syndromes certainly exist. A central question is whether behavioral syndromes exist or whether the classes of behavioral abnormalities in children are merely groups of symptoms that have no intrinsic connection with one another. The research on this issue is meager, but what has been done suggests that there are at least some broadly defined behavioral syndromes that are regularly found (Achenbach & Edelbrock, 1984; Edelbrock & Costello, 1988).

A fourth issue concerns the basic concepts used in clinical classification. Should discrete categories be used to form the classes, or should the classes be points on continuous dimensions? Is it best to describe mental retardation as a qualitatively different condition from normal intelligence or as the lower end of the normal distributions of intelligence and adaptive behavior? The answer to this difficult question depends on the handicap and on the classifier. It is easier to think of early infantile autism as a discrete category because autistic children are so different from normal children. On the other hand, it is also possible to think of autistic children as very different socially, not as qualitatively different. Some classifiers tend to emphasize discrete categories (e.g., Curry & R. J. Thompson, 1985), whereas others emphasize dimensions (e.g., Quay, 1979).

There probably is no absolute solution to this issue, and it may be that different handicapping conditions require different ways of description. Partly, it is a matter of analysis technique. Cluster analytic procedures require discrete categories, whereas factor analysis allows continuous dimensions. Nevertheless, the distinction between discrete category and continuous dimension does make for differences in classification systems.

The issue of categories versus dimensions is related to the question of whether overlapping categories are permitted in the classification system. That is, may a child be named in more than one category (e.g., learning disability, attention deficit disorder, and chronic illness)? Certain category systems allow use of only one class at a time or at best a "primary" diagnosis and a "secondary" diagnosis. Others permit multiple dimensions or axes to be named if appropriate for a particular child. The use of multiple classes when necessary is appropriate because multiple descriptors are perhaps the norm rather than the exception.

Finally, the different classification systems differ in the degree to which their classes strive for inclusiveness versus reliability. Blashfield and Draguns (1976a) made the point that the coverage of a classification system tends to be inversely related to its reliability. That is, to the extent that a classification system attempts to cover all children, it must include poorly defined categories that tend to have low interrater agreement. Some systems attempt to include a wide range of children, others have a more limited scope.

There are thus several systems for classifying psychological disorders of children. These systems vary according to their purpose, their data source, the units they use, their degree of overlap, and the coverage for which they aim. It is no wonder that there is some confusion in the classification of childhood disorders of behavior.

Criteria for Successful Classification Systems

If classification systems differ from one another, how do we know which one(s) to use? There are four criteria that are generally acknowledged as helpful in making a choice (Blashfield & Draguns, 1976a). The first of these criteria is reliability or the degree to which diagnosticians agree when presented with the same information about a case. Thus, at minimum, clinicians using the same classification system must agree about which classes to use in describing specific children.

Reliability between diagnosticians tends to be higher if the diagnostic classes in a system are defined explicitly; if the diagnosticians are trained to use the system; if there is plentiful information about the case; and if the diagnosticians are consistent in using the system (i.e., if there is good intradiagnostician reliability).

As a matter of fact, reliability tends to vary from moderate to fairly high (90% agreement), depending on the nature of the data source and the complexity of the classification system (Achenbach & Edelbrock, 1984). The sources of information about a child are important to specify because sources differ significantly. Parents differ from children and from each other (Kolko, Kazdin, & Meyer, 1985; Webster-Stratton, 1988). Different groups of educational personnel also have different perspectives in classification (Garvar & Schmelkin, 1989).

Coverage is a second criterion for determining the usefulness of a classification system. In this regard, the systems that cover only mental retardation (Grossman, 1973) or psychological disorders of children with average intelligence (Rutter & Garmezy, 1983) would not be regarded as useful as the various editions of the *Diagnostic and Statistical Manual of the American Psychiatric Association* (American Psychiatric Association, 1980, 1987). On the other hand, as indicated earlier, broader coverage tends to go with lower reliability.

The third and fourth criteria of success of a system have to do with two kinds of validity, that is, the extent to which the system actually classifies what it is intended to classify. Descriptive validity refers to the validity of the classes themselves. Descriptive validity may be thought of in terms of the homogeneity of the classes. That is, are the children in a diagnostic class more like each other, with respect to the appropriate characteristics, than they are like children in the other classes?

Homogeneity within class does not mean that all children in a class are exactly like each other. Variation between children within a classification is expected and often is useful for refined distinctions among them. However, children within a class should be more alike than they are like children in other classes in the system. Children with dyslexia should all have significant reading problems. Children with mental retardation may also have difficulty reading, but the reading problems of mentally retarded children should be different from those of dyslexics.

The fourth criterion is predictive validity. On the basis of classification, one would like to know the course of the children's disorder over time and perhaps even their response to a treatment specified by an understanding of their condition. Evaluating a classification using the predictive validity criterion requires careful follow-up studies, perhaps with evaluation of treatment to determine whether different groups have different life courses or respond to treatment differently. Unfortunately, in the area of behavioral disorders of children, this type of evaluation is rarely carried out.

The substantial variability between classification systems and the absence of their complete evaluation precludes any conclusive statements about which classification systems are the best. In practice, there is general agreement on some broad categories that classify children with a substantial amount of ambiguity. As becomes evident, this ambiguity has implications for treatment of the individual case and for the planning of programs for children with handicaps.

PREVALENCE

In the previous section, we indicated that two purposes of classification are planning of services and research into the causes of handicapping conditions. Both program planning for groups of children and the search for causes require precise estimates of the number of children with each type of condition. This part of the chapter considers the ways in which such estimates of prevalence are derived. This section shows that prevalence figures for handicapping conditions in childhood vary widely, and it points to some reasons why this might be true.

Prevalence and Incidence

The terms *prevalence* and *incidence* mean different things. Prevalence refers to the number of children who have a condition at any moment in time. Incidence is defined as the number of children who have ever had the disorder in question. Thus, the prevalence of the common cold is usually not very high, but its incidence in the general population is virtually 100%.

Prevalence and incidence rates are close to each other when the condition is chronic, severe, and when it is discovered early. Many of the conditions discussed later in this chapter have these three characteristics. Severe cerebral palsy, for instance, is discovered during the first year of life, remains evident throughout the life of the individual, and often significantly affects the person's adaptation.

The prevalence and incidence of severe cerebral palsy tend to be similar. The case with mild disorders is different. To the extent that mild cases go undiscovered until later and affect children's adaptation only during special times (for instance when they engage in competitive sports), prevalence and incidence values may be different.

Prevalence refers to a statement about the existence of a condition at only one point in time, whereas incidence describes rates over the full life span, so it is simpler to study prevalence than it is to describe incidence. Moreover, prevalence may be more useful when one is interested more in what is happening right now than in long-term effects. Prevalence rates are more useful for administrative program planning and for assessing causes that have immediate effects. Therefore, there is more research on prevalence than incidence of childhood behavioral disabilities. Consequently, we emphasize prevalence over incidence in what follows.

In addition to the distinction between prevalence and incidence, it is also important to distinguish between true prevalence and administrative prevalence. Many children with handicaps do not receive special services and are therefore not counted in prevalence surveys conducted by service agencies. True prevalence refers to the actual number of handicapped children in the population. Administrative prevalence is the number of children counted by a service agency. Of course, under these definitions, true prevalence is always higher than administrative prevalence.

General Prevalence of Handicapping Conditions

The U.S. Office of Education has estimated that 4.3 million U.S. school children receive educational services for one or more handicapping conditions. This amounts to about 1 in 10 school children or a prevalence rate of 10% (National Institute of Handicapped Research, 1985; also see Casby, 1989 for more recent but similar figures). This figure is close to the 8% given by Vikan (1985) for the sum of prevalence of problems primarily of a psychological nature (5%), hyperkinesis (0.4%), and mental retardation (2.6%) in a population of Norwegian school-age children. Vikan's figure would be higher if he had included sensory disorders, motor disabilities, chronic health problems, speech disorders, and so forth.

Therefore the overall administrative prevalence of handicapping conditions in school children is at least 10%. However, the variation in prevalence is as significant as the general level. For instance, prevalence estimates for psychiatric disorders in children have ranged from 5% to 29.8% (Vikan, 1985). This means that, if one were to add other disabilities, it might be possible to say that between one-third and one-half of all school children need services for a handicapping condition at any one time. Although this is possible, it seems unlikely that such a high figure is accurate. Therefore, sources of variation in prevalence rates are of interest.

Sources of Variation in Prevalence Rates

Perhaps the main sources of high prevalence rates are loose definitions of categories, unreliable and invalid data, and data from differing sources. Normal children within the general population often show deviant behaviors (Achenbach & Edelbrock, 1981; L. C. Miller, Hampe, Barrett, & Noble, 1971). These behaviors may not be regarded by clinicians as evidence of chronic pathology needing treatment but may be seen by relatives and teachers as serious problems. As indicated in the previous section on classification, very broad definitions of a condition will increase the number of people who are counted as having the condition.

Many conditions are defined by continuous dimensions, thus it is not always clear where to draw the line in defining the category. At what level of vision impairment should a child be defined as legally blind? What is the IQ that defines mental retardation? Is a mild fear to be regarded as an abnormal condition requiring treatment?

There are no perfect answers to these questions. Sometimes the definition is the result of agreement by a committee, and this agreement may or may not become broadly accepted. For instance, the IQ definition of mental retardation is often an IQ below 70 or 75. However, rarely, an IQ of 55 or 85 have been used and have resulted in small or large prevalence rates, respectively. In general, clearly stated definitions of handicaps tend to be restricted to obvious handicapping conditions and therefore result in conservative prevalence estimates.

Definitions of conditions may also be determined by the resources available for providing treatment, rather than the reverse. If society determines, through legislation, that it wishes to serve children with a particular type of handicap, such children may be "found." Finding cases may be done by clinicians who know of a child who needs services but is not receiving them for legal or financial reasons. If the child can honestly be fitted into the category under the definition required by the legislation providing the funds for the new services, the child is then "counted," thereby increasing the prevalence for the condition. Unfortunately, changes in style of definition can bar children from receiving services. Perhaps the recent reduction in the prevalence rate of mild mental retardation is an instance (MacMillan, 1989; Zetlin & Murtaugh, 1990).

Unreliable and invalid data sources is another and related basis of ambiguous and high prevalence rates. Sometimes experienced administrators make informal prevalence estimates as part of an assessment of needs for services in a particular geographical area that is their responsibility. As another example, parents, teachers, and other staff who work with children are sometimes casually asked to describe children with a view to assessing prevalence rates. Such informal methods tend to be unreliable and invalid, thereby resulting in invalid prevalence estimates.

The best approach to evaluating true prevalence appears to be a formal study with two steps. First, people who know the children well estimate whether they have an adaptive problem or demonstrate deviant behavior, perhaps by observing their behavior in relation to a well-defined symptom checklist. Then, children are seen by a person who may not know them very well but who is well-acquainted with the characteristics of children with handicaps. This process is more likely to produce a valid estimate of whether or not the child has a significant problem (Vikan, 1985).

Correlates of Prevalence

The overall result of a conservative definition and a valid information-collecting procedure is a low but stable estimate of prevalence. But once a valid measure of prevalence is obtained, there continue to be real variations in rates. These variations are associated with certain personal and environmental factors such as sex, age, geography, culture, and social class. We allude to them briefly here to show how they can influence prevalence rates.

One of the most pervasive predictors of prevalence rates is the sex of the child. Rates for most behavioral problems tend to be higher for boys than for girls, though there are some significant exceptions, such as Turner's syndrome (McCauley, Kay, Ito, & Treder, 1987; see also Achenbach & Edelbrock, 1981). There have been several attempts to explain the gender effect. Included among the hypotheses are sex-linked heredity, experientially or hormonally based behavioral differences, and differential social acceptability of deviance in the two sexes. However, as yet, there is no general explanation of sex differences in the prevalence of handicapping conditions. Indeed, it is possible that different mechanisms account for sex differences in prevalence of various conditions.

A second correlate of variation in prevalence is age. In the first place, there are changes in the meaning of a condition with development. If there are changes in the organization of behavior as a child grows, one might reasonably suppose that there is also "discontinuity" in the meaning of childhood disorders at different age periods. The manifestation of depression, for instance, is different in infancy, middle childhood, adolescence, adulthood, and among elderly people. One may then ask whether the conditions are comparable at all. That is, comparisons of rates at different times are not meaningful if the disorder is not the same at various times in the life span (Beitchman, Wekerle, & Hood, 1987; Breslau & Marshall, 1985; McDermott, 1984; Minde, 1988; O'Donnell, Leicht, F. L. Phillips, Marnett, & Horn, 1988).

When the definition of the disorder is reasonably constant over age, prevalence rates can be compared and the rates can vary in predictable ways. The typical form of prevalence rate changes over age for mild mental retardation. Not many cases are detected prior to school age, and prevalence grows in the high school years as academic work becomes increasingly difficult. After graduation, the rate drops as the students find jobs and begin to live independently.

These age changes emphasize that a person can be handicapped at one time and not at another. The changes dramatize the principle that handicaps in children are defined, not only by the characteristics of the children, but also by the demands of the environment in which the children live. In other words, handicap is an *ecological concept*. It is defined by the interaction of the characteristics of the children and of their environment.

This ecological principle is further illustrated by studies showing that prevalence rates vary with geography and culture. One careful study of well-matched populations (Rutter, Cox, Tupling, Berger, & Yule, 1975) concluded that rates of emotional disorders and conduct disturbances were twice as high in the inner city of London, England than they were on the Isle of Wight. The basis for the different prevalence rates were not explained definitely, but differential migration rates out of the two areas by families with normal children was cited as a possibility.

There are differing prevalence rates among special education categories across the United States and also some variation between countries at least in some categories (Frankenberger & Harper, 1988; Keller, Ball, & Hallahan, 1987). On the other hand, certain categories associated with behavior disturbance seem to have only minor prevalence variation in different countries (Achenbach, Verhulst, Baron, & Althaus, 1987; Cederblad, 1988).

Often related to geographical differences is social class. Handicaps are definitely more prevalent in families who have lower income (C. J. Phillips, Hon, B. Smith, & Sutton, 1986). Perhaps access to prenatal medical care, adequate education, and psychological services partly explain this difference. Whatever the cause, the variation in prevalence rates as a correlate of social class illustrates that more than the characteristics of individuals must be taken into consideration when thinking about prevalence.

MAJOR CLASSIFICATION SYSTEMS

There are several more or less formal systems of classification of childhood disorders in use. At this time, none of them is universally accepted, and some are continually evolving. However, there are some generally recognized categories of behavior disorders of children. In the remainder of this chapter, we review representative classification systems used by professionals working with handicapped children and then summarize the characteristics and prevalence rates of the major categories.

The most carefully worked out and widely used classification system is that developed under the auspices of the American Psychiatric Association. Known as *Diagnostic and Statistical Manual* (*DSM-III* and *DSMIII-R*), it includes the latest versions of a classification system that is continually being revised in accord with clinical experience and research findings (Robins & Helzer, 1986).

The system consists of several dozen carefully defined categories that can be subsumed under larger headings within five major "axes." Sinclair and Alexson (1985) attempted to simplify the system and presented data on inpatient and outpatient children in a psychiatric service. One of their most significant findings revealed that the majority of their 591 subjects received multiple diagnoses, which the *DSM-III* system allows. This overlap of categories is a main characteristic of all category systems (e.g., Baker & Cantwell, 1987a; Reiss, 1990; Van Hasselt, Kazdin, & Hersen, 1986).

The broad coverage, careful definition of the categories, and wide use are strengths of the *DSM-III* and *DSM-IIIR*. However, the system has been criticized because it has been difficult to demonstrate reliability and validity with the detailed categories and because the categories allow only a statement of whether or not a condition exists, rather than a quantitative statement of the degree of a disorder (Achenbach & Edelbrock, 1984).

The *DSM-III* is used by psychiatrists and many psychologists. Educators use another, less formal, system made up of a few generally defined categories whose definitions and names are not always the same. Forness and Cantwell (1982) listed the special education categories and their relationship to certain *DSM-III* diagnoses. Some of the categories (e.g., mental retardation) are defined clearly and are reliable and valid. Others (e.g., behavior disorder) are controversial because they are less reliable.

The *DSM-III* and educational systems represent efforts at consensus in the psychiatric and educational professional communities about the ways in which children's handicaps should be classified. They represent a good deal of clinical experience. To the extent that they provide reliable and valid labeling of children, they are useful for clinical and research purposes. On the other hand, these systems seem to work better when the cases are severe, when the categories are broad, and when the classes are well-defined, reliable, and valid.

Recently, there have been several attempts to build classification systems by using objective evaluations analyzed with multivariate statistical methods (Achenbach & Edelbrock, 1978, 1984; Quay, 1979). As with the less formal clinical methods, these procedures attempt to integrate various sources of information into a picture of what the child looks like. However, in this more objective approach, there is an attempt to make the source of the information about the child uniform, reliable, and valid. Thus, checklists, formal observations, and tests with known validity are used uniformly for each of the children being classified.

Then the information is integrated using multivariate statistics such as factor analysis or cluster analysis. In factor analysis, correlations between measures are searched to detect any underlying dimensions that most succinctly summarize the information. In cluster analysis, the data are analyzed so that groupings of scores emerge.

As with the less formal clinical methods, the classification depends on the nature of the information that is considered. Different categories emerge from checklists filled out by parents than those presented by teachers (Achenbach & Edelbrock, 1978). Of course, no valid categories can emerge when invalid data sources are used. In addition, there is a certain amount of judgment involved in the application of the statistical procedures, as there is in the clinical methods. Thus, rotation of factors and size of clusters both involve a subjective element. To the extent that both involve a subjective element, the informal and statistical approaches are not completely different. However, it does seem that the objective methods attempt to exclude ideology, use procedures that can be described formally, and encourage a uniformity of approach that allows assessment of reliability.

When these objective procedures have been used with an adequate data base, patterns consistent with at least some of the general classifications have emerged (Curry & R. J. Thompson, 1985; Gajar, Hale, Kuzovich, & Saxe, 1984; Kline, Lachar, & Gdowski, 1988; M. A. Stein & O'Donnell, 1985; R. J. Thompson, 1985). There is general agreement that there is a cluster consisting of fighting, disobedience, and destructiveness; one composed of shyness, hypersensitivity, and withdrawal; and a third cluster involving distractibility, short attention span, and overactivity. In addition, physical disabilities and cognitive disorders such as mental retardation and learning disabilities seem to be yet other dimensions that define handicapped populations.

In short, the classification systems all recognize some general categories defined by either informal or formal methods. These general categories have different names in different systems and their definition and measurement are not always exactly the same. Moreover, any child may have more than one of these symptom clusters so that there can be overlap among them. Thus, even the general categories are not sharply defined or mutually exclusive.

MAIN CATEGORIES
OF HANDICAPPING CONDITIONS

Keeping in mind that the main categories overlap, we can proceed to describe their general characteristics and prevalence. It is important to remember that a child with mental retardation or a learning disability may also be troubled with an emotional disturbance or someone with a physical handicap may also have difficulty in academic subjects. Thus, even the major categories of handicap are useful abstractions, but should not be applied too strictly.

Sensory Impairments

The major sensory impairments include functional losses in vision and in audition. As anyone who wears glasses knows, mild visual problems are very prevalent. There are many forms of visual disability. These include myopia, astigmatism, and strabismus, among many others. Ordinarily, visual problems are detected as a result of routine screening examinations given in school. Children who demonstrate difficulty seeing at home, in the classroom, or as a result of formal screening tests are appropriately seen by an opthalmologist (a physician who specializes in disorders of the visual system) or an optometrist (a professional who specializes in testing visual function). As a result of careful testing, glasses or other visual corrections may be prescribed.

Auditory disorders are likewise complex. They are also detected informally at home or in the school, and routine screening tests are a feature of initial screening programs in most schools. Children who are suspected of having a significant hearing loss may be seen by an otorhinolaryngologist (a physician dealing with disorders of the ear, nose, and throat) or an audiologist (an expert in formal routine testing of hearing).

The fields of visual and hearing disorders each have elaborate classification systems that describe the syndromes associated with loss of sight or hearing. Parents and other people who work with children need not be experts in disorders of vision and hearing. However, they should be sensitive to the possibility of sensory handicaps and have some idea of their possible influence on development. It is obvious that a severe visual disorder can interfere with reading in the school years. However, it is also true that in the preschool period, sensory disorders can have important influences on cognitive and language development (Fraiberg & Freedman, 1964).

Because of the complexity of the classification systems for sensory handicaps, the existence of undetected sensory disorders in the preschool period, the high level of corrected visual disorders, and the association of sensory disabilities with other handicaps, prevalence estimates cannot be exact. However, a very conservative figure is 0.26%, a figure derived from a count of the number of children with sensory handicaps who receive special services in schools (National Institute of Handicapped Research, 1985).

Motor Handicaps

Motor handicaps also constitute a complex group of disorders. They include delay of development, cerebral palsy, motor paralyses, diffuse disorders of coordination, and motor problems associated with bone malformations or injuries. Motor handicaps may be associated with other types of disorders such as sensory handicaps and intellectual problems, but they may also exist by themselves. The overall prevalence of motor disorders is at least 0.14% (National Institute of Handicapped Research, 1985).

Delays of motor development are often discovered in infancy during routine pediatric examinations. If some delay is suspected, it may be confirmed by an infant development schedule administrated by a developmental psychologist. Mild delays of motor development are often temporary and do not signify any chronic disorder. However, severe delays of more than a few months during the first year may predict more extensive pathology, including other motor disorders, intellectual retardation, and/or psychopathology.

Cerebral palsy is a group of motor disorders associated with an injury to the brain. The form that cerebral palsy takes depends on the area of the brain affected. Thus, for instance, spastic paralyses result from lesions in the cerebral cortex, whereas athetoid movements are associated with the basal ganglia. Brain damage in children is rarely localized, so motor handicaps may be mixed and variable (Blair & Stanley, 1985). They may affect all four limbs (quadriplegia), either the arms or legs (diplegia), or one limb. Moreover, involvement of the four limbs may differ in degree.

Motor paralyses result, not only from injury to the brain, but also from spinal cord disorders. Full transection, or even partial cutting of the spinal cord through malformation, disease, or injury, can produce severe paralyses that interfere with adaptation in important ways (Tew & Laurence, 1985). The limbs that are affected depends on the level of the spinal cord involved.

Many children with handicaps experience difficulty with diffuse problems in motor coordination, especially in fine motor skills (Henderson, 1987). Not all children with mild coordination problems have serious handicaps to adaptation, though they might experience difficulties in sports or in penmanship. However, as with sensory handicaps, coordination problems are suggestive of a possibly more significant handicap that should receive attention.

Motor problems may also result from bone malformations that are part of a specific or a more generalized developmental problem. In either case, difficulty in manipulating the environment or getting around in it produces problems in adaptation.

Sensory and motor problems are not always recognized as important in producing psychological problems and in complicating the effects of other handicapping conditions. However, they can be very important, and should not be neglected by parents and professionals. Sophisticated methods for correction of sensory disorders and for some motor conditions are available and can be used even in infancy.

Mental Retardation

Disorders of attention, perception, and thinking constitute a large general overlapping group of disorders that become especially important during the school years. The classification of some of these disorders is confused, partly because they are conceptualized poorly, but also because they are difficult to measure precisely. Mental retardation, pervasive developmental disorders, learning disabilities, dyslexia, attention deficit disorders, perceptual handicap, and hyperactivity are all controversial categories whose definition and procedures of measurement are not yet universally agreed upon.

Mental retardation (sometimes called mental handicap, mental subnormality, or mental deficiency) is a general category defined by low intelligence, failures of adaptation, and age of onset. Low general intelligence is the main characteristic of mental retardation. This means that children with mental retardation have a generalized deficiency in cognitive skills relative to other children of the same age. Another way of saying this is that they are slow in their general mental development and they may have difficulties in attention, perception, memory, and thinking. Although mentally retarded children may be stronger in some skills than in others, and a very few have special memory skills in music and computing (Treffert, 1988), mentally retarded children are generally low in all intellectual attainments.

People with low intelligence are not called mentally retarded unless they also have some problem in adaptation. An adult with a very low IQ who can hold a job, lives independently, and does not inappropriately depend on others as a source of income would not, according to current practice, be defined as mentally retarded (However, see Barnett, 1986 and Zigler, Balla, & Hodapp, 1984).

Thus, to be labeled as mentally retarded, one must have a low IQ and also have troubles that require special care. Finally, mental retardation must have begun during the childhood years. This restriction of the mental retardation diagnosis to conditions beginning in childhood differentiates it from conditions beginning in adulthood that also are associated with low IQ and adaptive difficulty (e.g., conditions associated with brain deterioration during adulthood).

The prevalence of mental retardation is about 1% of the general population, although in the school years it can be substantially higher (Diaz-Fernandez, 1988; McLaren & Bryson, 1987; McQueen, Spence, Garner, Pereira, & Winsor, 1987; Rantakallio & von Wendt, 1986; Kuo-Tai, 1988).

Within the category of mental retardation, three, four, or five levels are traditionally described. The least severely affected are children who have difficulty with academic materials during the school years, but who often can become independent when they reach adulthood. The borderline group constitutes a large population with IQs between 75 and 90, which often is underserved in special education (MacMillan, 1989). Mild or educable mentally retarded people have IQs ranging from roughly 55 to 75. They can learn to read a newspaper and compute simple arithmetic and often are independent in adulthood. These two groups constitute the large majority (85%) of the mentally retarded population.

Moderately or trainable retarded children can learn to dress themselves, have simple speech, and can work at surprisingly complicated tasks in sheltered workshops when they are adults. The least prevalent are the severely/profoundly or custodial group (Berkson & Landesman-Dwyer, 1977). These people rarely develop beyond the level of a normal 2- to 3-year-old child mentally, although their bodies often develop reasonably normally. They sometimes learn simple speech and most can communicate simply with sign language if taught to do so. However, the severely/profoundly retarded group ordinarily require life-long care. They constitute less than 5% of the mentally retarded population or 0.1% of the general population.

The simplicity of the classification of mental retardation is somewhat illusory. There are great individual differences among mentally retarded people, even at the same intellectual level. Some have socioemotional problems (Polloway, M. H. Epstein, & Cullinan, 1985; Reiss, 1990). A few are even criminals, though the number of retarded people who break the law has been overemphasized in the past (Spruill & May, 1988).

Pervasive Developmental Disorders

To illustrate some of the characteristics of individual disorders and the ways that are used to define them, we continue with pervasive developmental disorders, that is, autism, childhood schizophrenia, and related problems. These are very rare conditions that represent profound adaptive problems in thinking, language, and social relationships. Their characteristics have become increasingly clear during the last 50 years and, no doubt, will become more clear in the future.

Autism is defined partly by its onset earlier than 30 months of age, whereas childhood schizophrenia develops later. In addition, autism is characterized by difficulties in formation of social relationships, profound problems in language and communication, and by restricted and stereotyped behavior patterns. Autistic children do not use many symbols, whereas symbol use of schizophrenic children is varied and complex, but also abnormal, and may depend on a reduced information-processing capacity (Atlas & Lapidus, 1987; Rutter & Schopler, 1987; Schneider & Asarnow, 1987; Volkmar, D. J. Cohen, Hoshino, Rende, & Paul, 1988).

Both conditions are very rare, but autism is more common and has received far more study. Therefore it is emphasized in the discussion that follows. Approximately 80% of autistic children score below normal on IQ tests. Thus, most have a significant delay in development. However, even when that delay is taken into account, more severely delayed children seem oblivious to caretaking adults, they express themselves minimally, they show a low level of interest in exploring objects, they avoid sounds, and they engage in ritualistic behavior to a degree not found in comparable normal children (Wenar, Ruttenberg, Kalish-Weiss, & E. G. Wolf, 1986).

The causes of autism are unknown but are thought to be prenatal and not social. A major malformation in the cerebellum has recently been implicated. The recognition that autistic children differ greatly from each other has led to attempts to subclassify the group (Rescorla, 1988; B. Siegel, Anders, Ciaranello, Bienenstock, & Kraemer, 1986; Volkmar, D. J. Cohen, Bregman, Hooks, & Stevenson, 1989). These attempts must be regarded as preliminary at this time.

There have been several recent studies of the prevalence of autism in Asia, Europe, and the United States. All have turned up rates of .03% to .13%, with fluctuations that may point to environmental causes (e.g., Burd, Fisher, & Kerbeshian, 1987; Ciadella & Mamelle, 1989; C. Gillberg, 1988; Tanoue, Oda, Asano, & Kawashima, 1988).

Learning Disabilities

We turn now to the concept of Learning Disabilities and the associated concepts of dyslexia, minimal brain damage (MBD), perceptual handicap, attention deficit disorder, and hyperactivity. All of these categories are controversial, mainly because they have been overextended. That is, although there are cases that fit restricted definitions of these concepts, in practice looser definitions have been applied so that the restricted concept has lost much of its meaning.

A case in point is the concept of learning disabilities. This field has struggled recently to define itself from its conceptual sources: the medical-neurological approach, the information-processing and cognitive strategies approach; the developmental delay concept; applied behavior analysis; and educational approaches (Adelman & L. Taylor, 1986; Coplin & Morgan, 1988; Kavale & Forness, 1986; Poplin, 1988; Torgesen, 1986). It is now generally recognized that each of these perspectives provides a set of concepts that may be useful in the individual case.

Historically, a learning-disabled child was defined as one whose academic performance in one academic area (perhaps reading) is behind the child's ability more than 2 years. Thus, the disability is restricted in its range, and there is a discrepancy between academic performance and tested general

ability. In these two ways, a learning disability differs from mental deficiency, because the latter is characterized by a general delay and academic
performance is usually at the level expected from ability. In practice,
learning disability has been used to characterize any child with a learning
problem who cannot be called mentally deficient, no matter how broad the
range of disabilities and what the discrepancy from tested ability level
(Furlong & Yanagida, 1985; but see also L. Wilson, Cone, Bradley, & Reese,
1986).

The overextension of the more restricted definition has not only increased the apparent prevalence of Learning Disability, but also has made
the field confusing. Ames (1985) described this confusion and estimates that
if the more conservative definition is used the prevalence of learning disabilities would be about 5%. Gregory, Shanahan, and Walberg (1985) reported
an even lower prevalence of 2.7% for specific learning disabilities when a
self-report method was used with high school sophomores. In general, the
prevalence is estimated on average at about 4.5% (McNutt, 1986).

Despite the confusion, some agreement is emerging (C. R. Reynolds, 1985;
Strawser & Weller, 1985; Tittemore, Lawson, & Inglis, 1985; L. R. Wilson,
1985). These authorities provide a scientific basis for the concept that
learning disability is defined by a discrepancy between ability level and
academic performance and this discrepancy must be a significant one indicating adaptive failure.

Moreover, there is agreement that the concept of Learning Disabilities
denotes a heterogenous group of children and it is worthwhile looking for
subgroups (Kavale & Forness, 1987; Lewandowski, 1985; Speece, J. D.
McKinney, & Appelbaum, 1985). A conventional route for subtyping has
been through analysis of subtest patterns on neuropsychological test batter-
ies. Such patterns are found, but they tend to disappear when account is
taken of general intelligence (Morgan & T. L. Brown, 1988). Other subtyping
approaches focus on memory (Swanson, 1988a, 1988b), language (Feagans &
Appelbaum, 1986), academic skills (Share, Moffitt, & Silva, 1988), personality
(J. D. McKinney, 1989), and adaptive behaviors (Weller & Strawser, 1987).

Especially important has been the question of whether the subtypes are
stable over time. This question involves identifying membership in one of
several subgroups with a follow-up of the same children at a significant time
later. There are not many of these longitudinal studies. Those that exist
permit one to say that there is some stability of groupings over long periods
of development. However, there is less assurance that children will remain
in the same subgroup over time (Feagans & Appelbaum, 1986; Spreen &
Haaf, 1986; J. D. McKinney & Speece, 1986). No doubt more studies in this
area would illuminate the subgroup issue.

Before leaving the general topic of learning disabilities, we can allude to
the substantial overlap between learning disabilities and other problems.

Attention has been drawn to the higher levels of behavior problems in the classroom and also to an increased risk for delinquency in children with learning disabilities (Bender, 1987a, 1987b; Eliason & Richman, 1988; Larson, 1988; Spreen, 1989). This relationship is important to note, although it need not be overdrawn. That is, not all children with learning disabilities break the law, and not all delinquent children have learning disabilities. There have been a number of reviews that have attempted to account for any relationship that there might be, but it is unlikely that anything definitive can be concluded until both learning disabilities and behavior problems are better defined.

Dyslexia

Perhaps the most widely discussed form of learning disability is dyslexia, a relatively specific problem in reading. The broadest definition of dyslexia includes those children whose reading skills are delayed for any reason. Thus, poor education, neurological disorder, and developmental delay can all be predictors of poor reading, and these would all be counted in this broadest definition. A more specific concept of dyslexia involves a comparison of reading performance with the child's age and intelligence. Thus, specific reading retardation is counted only if reading performance is well below expectation for the child's age and intelligence.

It is rare for dyslexia to be specific. Many studies have shown that it is associated with a number of cognitive deficits. There may, in fact, be several subtypes of dyslexia (Morris, Blashfield, & Satz, 1986). However, what those subtypes are probably will not be understood until we have a coherent theory of reading. In other words, reading involves many processes. Problems with one or more of these processes can interfere with the development of reading performance (Levi & Piredda, 1986; M. W. Lovett, 1984).

The prevalence of developmental dyslexia varies widely, depending on the definition of the disorder and geographical variables. The broad definition produces a prevalence of about 16%, whereas more restrictive definitions result in prevalence estimates of 3% to 5% (Lindgren, deRenzi, & Richman, 1985; Silva, McGee, & Williams, 1985). Prevalence rates are higher in the United States than they are in Italy, perhaps due to differences in the complexity of the English language as compared with Italian (Lindgren, deRenzi, & Richman, 1985).

Attention Deficit Disorder

Interest in learning disabilities received an impetus in the 1940s from studies by Heinz Werner and applications of his work to education by Alfred Strauss

(Kavale & Forness, 1984; A. A. Strauss & Lehtinen, 1947). According to Strauss' central idea, some children suffer from minor brain damage that is manifested in perceptual problems, attention deficits, and hyperactivity. The result was a complex of overlapping diagnoses variously called minimal brain damage, perceptual handicap, attention deficit disorder, and hyperactivity.

All of these categories are sometimes used inappropriately and thus have lost credibility in some quarters. Minimal brain damage (MBD) may be properly used by a physician to describe a child who has minor neurological signs in the course of a neurological examination. The signs may, for instance, include minor and transitory weakness on one side of the body. Sometimes they are not confirmed by other neurological examinations (Denckla, LeMay, & Chapman, 1985; Matousek, Rasmussen, & C. Gillberg, 1984). MBD can reliably be described and may be associated with behavioral abnormality. However, in many cases, the minor signs are transitory and prediction of future behavioral and educational problems is imperfect (I. C. Gillberg, 1985). Thus, the category of MBD must be treated with caution (Carey & McDevitt, 1981).

Perceptual handicap is a characteristic of some children (A. A. Strauss & Lehtinen, 1947). These children have difficulty, for instance, copying a design that is set before them. However, in cases like this the problem is not clear: Is perception the problem or is it translating the perceived image to the drawing act? Because of ambiguities like this, perceptual handicap is no longer as popular a diagnosis. More common diagnoses, at this time, are attention deficit disorder (ADD) and hyperactivity.

The concepts of attention disorder and hyperactivity are often confused with one another. Children who cannot sit still are thought to be inattentive to their lessons in school. A distinction between attention deficit disorder and hyperactivity was made in one *DSM-III*, and careful observational studies have defined the distinction empirically (Dienske, DeJonge, & Sanders-Woudstra, 1985). More recently the distinction was dropped from the *DSM-III* system, but this action has been challenged (Lahey, Schaughency, Hynd, & Carlson, & Nieves, 1987; see also Barkley, 1987).

A child who does not attend engages in nonfunctional use of material; often fails to finish activities; acts prematurely or redundantly; infrequently reacts to requests and questions; has difficulty with tasks that require fine discrimination, sustained vigilance, or complex organization; and/or improves in achievement markedly when supervised intensively. As may be seen, this is a broad definition of attention deficit. It should be no surprise that children with many disorders will have problems like those listed and children with attention disorders have difficulties in school (Edelbrock, Costello, & Kessler, 1984; Sinclair, Guthrie, & Forness, 1984). A later chapter points out that the concept of attention is complex, and sometimes the expected differences between children with and without ADD are not observed (e.g., Samuels & N. L. Miller, 1985).

A child who is hyperactive engages in excessive standing up, walking, running, and climbing; does not remain seated for long during tasks; frequently makes redundant movements; shifts excessively from one activity to another; and/or often starts talking, asking, or requesting. Children who are judged by teachers to be hyperactive are indeed more active when observed systematically (Luk, 1985; Rutter, 1983). However, this elevated activity level expresses itself differently at different ages (S. B. Campbell, 1985; G. Weiss & Hechtman, 1980).

Inattentive, hyperactive children sometimes are disturbing to their parents, teachers, and peers. In fact, children with aspects of the ADD-hyperactivity complex are often judged to be behaviorally disturbed (Bohline, 1985; Davidson, 1987; Edelbrock et al., 1984). Thus, the definition of this complex concept is not only vague, but it overlaps significantly with other major categories.

It is, therefore, not too surprising that prevalence rates of ADD-MBD-Hyperactivity vary widely (E. Taylor & Sandberg, 1984; G. Weiss & Hechtman, 1980). The variation in definition, age, sex, types of data source, and cultural factors (Shen, Wang, & Yang, 1985; Yao, Solanto, & Wender, 1988) produce estimates up to 35%. However, most estimates are less than 9% for boys and even less for girls (Szatmari, Offord, & Boyle, 1989).

Speech and Language Disorders

Communication disorders are basically disorders of motor and/or cognitive organization. However, in the major classification systems, they are treated as a separate group of disorders of speech and language. Speech disorders involve the motor organization of speech articulation. Common examples are stuttering, reduction of syllables, and delays of maturity of speech articulation. There is evidence that these problems with speech articulation are related to a more general difficulty with motor organization (Cross & Luper, 1983), but subclasses are no doubt important (Rentschler, 1984).

Language disorders comprise difficulties in understanding and/or expressing words or using them in a social context (Beitchman et al., 1989). Most language disorders are correlated with age (Schery, 1985), and there is a clear relationship between language disorders and dyslexia (Morice & Slaghuis, 1985; Seidenberg, Bruck, Fornarolo, & Backman, 1985; Silva, McGee, & S. M. Williams, 1983). Language disorders also include writing problems, but there have not been recent studies of writing in children with handicaps (Borge-Osorio & Salzano, 1987).

Lately, there has been interest in the relation between language disorders and psychiatric disturbance (Baker & Cantwell, 1987). This relationship is not unique. Language problems are common in many handicapping conditions, for example in children with mental retardation (Enderby & Phillipp, 1986). On the whole, the more general or severe the language disorder, the more likely it is to be associated with another problem group like attention deficit disorder or autism (Beitchman, Hood, Rochon, & Peterson, 1989; Beitchman, Nair, Clegg, Ferguson, & Patel, 1986; Cantwell & Baker, 1987).

Perhaps this is one reason that speech and language disorders are second only to learning disabilities in prevalence in the schools. The U.S. Office of Education estimates that almost 3% of children in schools receive services for speech problems. Other estimates include prevalence figures of 1.1% (Gregory, Shanahan, & Walberg, 1985) and 7.6% to 10.4% (Silva et al., 1983).

Emotional, Behavioral, and Conduct Disorders

Most of the categories of disability discussed here have had conduct disorders associated with them, but there are children who are classified as emotionally, behaviorally, or conduct disordered without having other problems. In the past, it was thought that children who are intelligent, but who had adaptive difficulties that included such behaviors as shyness, low self-concept, hyperactivity, bed-wetting, aggression, disrespect, or were antisocial in other ways could all be included in a single category called emotionally disturbed or behaviorally disordered. Empirical studies have shown that the general categorization is not appropriately descriptive, and it may be that the more explicit one gets about the behavior of the individual child, the more useful.

There are many manifestations of emotional disorder (Rutter & Garmezy, 1983; Quay, 1979). Fears; anxiety; shyness; being perceived as overly aggressive; destructive or chronically disobedient; stealing in the company of others; having bad companions; truancy; and staying out late are common problems of any group of children. When parents or teachers believe that these problems interfere with the child's adaptation or happiness, the child may be referred for professional help.

It is possible to describe children by listing specific deviant behaviors that they show. This may be accomplished by having a parent and/or teacher fill out a checklist of behaviors that many children demonstrate. There are many such checklists (Achenbach & Edelbrock, 1984; Boyle & S. C. Jones, 1985). A typical checklist (Achenbach & Edelbrock, 1981) contains 20 social competence items and 118 behavior problem items.

When viewed generally, behavior disorders of children fall into two large dimensions, *undercontrolled* and *overcontrolled*. Undercontrolled behaviors include hyperactivity, aggression, and delinquent behaviors. Overcontrolled behaviors are represented by anxiety, depression, somatic complaints, and obsessive-compulsive behavior (Achenbach & Edelbrock, 1984).

Another empirically derived classification distinguishes undersocialized conduct disorders from socialized conduct disorders. Undersocialized disorders involve consistent physical violence when the child also has poor interpersonal relationships. Socialized conduct disorders are seen in children whose relationship with others is generally good. Delinquent behavior by gang members might be one example of this subcategory (Quay, Routh, & Shapiro, 1987). Sometimes both subcategories are seen as two extremes of a single dimension of antisocial behavior (Loeber & Schmaling, 1985). Whichever way they are conceived, they are troublesome for parents and teachers.

These dimensional approaches are useful because they seek commonalities among the many symptoms that can be described as emotional, behavioral, or conduct disorders. Another approach has been the intensive study of the sources, relationships and treatment of specific behaviors, like fire-setting (e.g., Kolko & Kazdin, 1986). This approach that works with a clearly defined symptom is not being used as much as are less reliable, but broader categories, like aggression. However, it may become more common following the development of the widely used checklists of behavioral abnormalities.

In considering the prevalence of emotional, behavioral, or conduct disorders, one must take into account the rates of the very common seemingly identical behaviors of normal children (McGuire & Richman, 1987; Pfeffer, Zuckerman, Plutchik, & Mizruchi, 1987). Situational factors are also important (Bullock, Zagar, Donahue, & Pelton, 1985; Cullinan, M. H. Epstein, & Kauffman, 1984).

Eating disorders are important in the preschool period and, in different ways, in adolescence (Faust, 1987; Murray, 1986; Muuss, 1986). Enuresis (bed-wetting) is not regarded as a significant problem until school-age, though it occurs in most children before. Lying and stealing are almost universal in children. However, they are not regarded as pathological unless they frequently occur inappropriately and with other problem behaviors (Stouthamer-Loeber & Loeber, 1986). In some gang cultures, they are even regarded as normal and desirable behaviors in certain circumstances. Sex offenses have received consideration recently (G. E. Davis & Leitenberg, 1987).

When both the parent and teacher agree that a child has a particular problem, the prevalence of the problem is generally low, and under those circumstances it tends to be pervasive and chronic. Prevalence estimates of serious mental illness in children vary according to the definition of the disorder, age of the child, the measuring instrument, geography, and other variables. Estimates as low as 4.6% and as high as 29.8% have been set forth (McGee, Silva, & S. M. Williams, 1984).

Of special interest recently has been a group of symptoms that are labeled as depression. Depression was recognized in children 100 years ago (Maudsley, 1890), but it was essentially ignored until quite recently. Psychoanalytic theories of depression in adults seemed to exclude the possibility in children. However, with the continuing interest in depression in adults and the growing recognition of the importance of such phenomena as infantile depression following maternal deprivation, sadness, low affect accompanied by aggression, and self-poisoning and suicide in children and adolescents (e.g., Kerfoot, 1988; Neiger & Hopkins, 1988) research on depression in children began to grow.

The definition of depression in children is especially difficult. Surely its manifestations are not exactly the same in adults and its definition changes with age. For instance, low appetite is one symptom of depression in adults, but poor eating is common in as many as a third of 6 year olds (Digdon & Gotlib, 1985). Thus, one could not use low appetite to define depression in young children. Nevertheless, extreme and chronic sadness, hopelessness, and suicide are main conceptual and behavioral characteristics in childhood as well as adulthood, and many ways of measuring them are emerging (Kerr, Hoier, & Versi, 1987).

Using this kind of criterion, the administrative prevalence is 2% to 3%, but studies using broader definitions and seeking true prevalence rates find very high levels (Quay, Routh, & Shapiro, 1987).

Overall, then, the last decade has seen an increasing clarification of the nature of childhood emotional, behavioral, and conduct disorders. This growth has been a consequence of increasing specification of the behaviors involved and the development of formal ways of describing them, mainly with checklists. There is general recognition that the manifestation and perhaps the basic character of these problems changes with development so that the causes of most of them are sought in developmental processes that are social in nature. There is much overlap between these problems and other kinds of handicapping conditions. Estimates of prevalence vary from 5% to more than 30% as a result of variations in definition, measurement, situation, and who is making the estimate.

Chronic Health Disorders

There is one more significant group of children with handicaps that is not generally included in classifications of children with behavioral disorders. Nevertheless, many of these children live in special circumstances, and they share some of the problems of adaptation experienced by other children with handicaps. Children with asthma (Mrazek, 1986; Rutter, Tizard, & Whitmore, 1970), diabetes (C. S. Holmes & Richman, 1985; Ryan, Longstreet,

& Morrow, 1985), cancer (Bearison & Pacifici, 1984), sickle-cell disease (Hurtig & L. S. White, 1986), obesity (Israel & Shapiro, 1985), cystic fibrosis (Breslau & Marshall, 1985), and many other conditions have special problems that are attended to in medical settings. However, they are not always dealt with adequately in families or schools.

Children with mental retardation, learning disabilities, communication disorders, and emotional and conduct disorders often also have health problems (Rutter et al., 1970). However, children who do not have mental disorders and even gifted children (Hemmings, 1985) can also be afflicted with chronic and serious medically handicapping illnesses.

The prevalence of these illnesses is relatively high. Rutter and colleagues (1970) estimated a prevalence rate of 5.5%. This rate includes all physically handicapping conditions (including sensory and motor handicaps and mild, but chronic, health disorders). The prevalence served in schools (National Institute for Handicapped Research, 1985) is said to be 0.13%. Thus the true prevalence is probably somewhere between these two figures, but has not been assessed recently.

It is likely that the psychological accompaniments of specific chronic medical conditions in children will be studied more intensively in the future because interest in the subject seems to be growing.

SUMMARY

Classification of children with handicaps begins with the understanding that every child is an individual having a unique combination of behavioral characteristics. Although each child is different from every other, it is possible to describe children by reference to concepts that apply to other children. Perhaps some dimensions or categories are unique to children with handicaps.

There are three major purposes for classifying children with handicaps: communication, planning treatment programs, and discovering the causes of the handicapping conditions. For these purposes, it is important to know how prevalence rates of the conditions vary.

Classifying or labeling children carries with it the risk that the label may itself cause pathology through an effect on self-concept and performance. The evidence for a labeling effect exists, but the effect is apparently not powerful.

In classifying children, one must first decide whether to use discrete categories or continuous dimensions. Overlapping categories and multiple dimensions are most appropriate. Four characteristics: Reliability, coverage, descriptive validity, and predictive validity are criteria for evaluating classification systems.

Several classification systems exist and are used to a different extent by different professions. None fulfills the aforementioned criteria completely, but they are being refined continually. There is, however, agreement on the major classifications of handicap and on the fact that categories overlap extensively.

Prevalence estimates of childhood handicap vary widely, but 10% to 15% is a conservative figure. Variation of prevalence is as important as the average. Variation is determined by methodological considerations (definitions and the nature of data sources). It is also predicted by individual and environmental factors (age, sex, social class, and culture).

3

Causes of Developmental Disorders

The first two chapters have emphasized the many factors associated with individual differences between handicapped children. Some general principles have been set out, and the main classes of developmental disorders of behaviors have been discussed. Missing in the discussion has been an emphasis on the causes or etiology of developmental disorders. In this chapter, we add a consideration of etiology because it is centrally important to later chapters on family processes and on treatment.

Interest in the etiology of behavioral orders of development comes from two sources. The first is the strong tendency among families of developmentally handicapped children to wish to attribute some cause to their child's handicap. The second interest in the study of causes of developmental disorders comes from the need to prevent handicapping conditions. Prevention is practical in many instances and perhaps is the ultimate treatment for disorders of development. For instance, recent advances in the understanding of the hereditary causes have lead to active family-planning programs involving genetic counseling. Lack of iodine was a major cause of mental retardation before the importance of a small amount of iodine in the diet was understood. Extreme forms of social deprivation during early postnatal development have been shown to have important effects on later adaptation. Understanding of the importance of social factors has led to social programs such as out-of-home adoption that have corrected abnormal early social environments.

The purpose of this chapter, then, is to review the topic of etiology of behavioral disorders of development. This is done by describing some principles of normal development. Then, representative causes of developmental disorders are reviewed. The theme that individual differences result from varied and complex causes is developed. The discussion emphasizes the idea that simple explanations are not adequate for solving the needs of developmentally disabled children. Finally, the implications of this knowledge for specific prevention programs are outlined (Rutter, 1985a).

NORMAL AND ABNORMAL DEVELOPMENT

Normal Development

Abnormalities of development occur against a background of the constantly emerging and changing structure of behavior. This dynamic movement is determined by both hereditary and environmental factors entwined so that their influence often cannot be differentiated. Variability between individuals is also there from the start. The genetic message is different for each fertilized cell, and the child therefore begins a unique developmental path beginning at conception. Throughout the child's growing period, the general hereditary structure of the species maintains its guiding influence. However, the hereditary message can be modified in significant ways by the chemical and experiential environments the child happens to be in. Thus, both an enduring species-specific form and also modifications in the structure of heredity can occur throughout development.

Development proceeds rapidly. During the 9 months before birth, hereditary–environmental interactions involve mainly chemical environments. Programmed and fortuitous changes in hormone levels and also intrauterine nutrition produce significant changes in the rapidly changing structure of the body.

As particular parts of the body change and emerge, those that are in the process of change are particularly susceptible to environmental influences. This is true, whether the chemical changes arise within the body or from outside of it. Thus, there are times when parts of body organs are particularly sensitive to environmental influences. These times are called critical or sensitive periods (Bornstein, 1989; Colombo, 1982).

Chemical factors continue to influence the structure of the body after birth. Nutrition and hormonal changes continue to influence the path determined by the hereditary messages. However, experience begins increasingly to affect the child's progress. As perceptual and learning processes mature, the experiential environment of the child takes on a major role in influencing the ways in which the child develops. The increasingly important intertwined dimensions of sensory, cognitive, and social experiences are discerned, and they add what is perhaps the most important source of plasticity, learning (R. M. Lerner & Hood, 1986).

Abnormal Development

These general principles of normal development also serve as a guide for concepts of abnormal growth. The complexity and speed of developmental changes mean that patterns of abnormal behavior will be complex and quite different for different individuals. From this idea comes the concept of a continuum of reproductive casualty. Pasamanick and Knobloch (1966) first pointed out that abnormalities in development can be conceived of as a continuum of severity. Some abnormal conditions result in the death of the fetus quite early in development, whereas others manifest themselves in only very mild deviations that do not affect adaptation very much (for instance, correctable mild visual disorders). Between these two extremes is a continuum of casualty.

The continuum of reproductive casualty can be seen in the context of two-factor theories of causes of developmental disorders. These theories (e.g., Zigler, 1967) propose that there are two general causes of developmental disorders. The first type is a cause that is an extreme variant of a normal process. It is an unusually large deviation from a normal distribution. The second type is a definite pathological process, caused by abnormal hereditary or environmental conditions that tend to produce more severe disabilities. The two-factor theory and the continuum of reproductive casualty suggest that there will be more cases of severe disabilities than expected by chance from the normal distribution.

Not only is there a continuum of reproductive casualty resulting in a two-factor picture of the distribution of disabilities, but it is also true that a child can have more than one handicap. This is no surprise when one considers that an abnormal condition can have its effect over time and it can produce its effect on systems that develop simultaneously. Thus, multiple handicap is a common occurrence in developmentally disabled children. The more severe the disability, the more likely that multiple systems will be involved.

Individuality of patterning of disorders is another consequence of the complexity of development. Just as each normal person is different, (Rowe & Plomin, 1981) disabled children also are varied. The last chapter discussed how this variability can confuse some conventional classifications of disorder, and later chapters deal with the implication of this variability for individualized treatment.

Beyond the complexity of development, there are principles that account for the resistance of the growing child to abnormalities in development. Considering that normal development is the result of fine-tuning of thousands of intertwined processes, it is surprising that children grow up as normal as they do. One reason for the surprising stability in growth patterns is the species-specific hereditary patterning that guides growth throughout life. Maturation patterns tend to follow these hereditary guides and to resist changes in them (McCall, 1981).

Another way stability of development is achieved is through plasticity that assures modifications of body and behavior appropriate for adequate adaptation of the children to their environment. This plasticity is conferred by an overproduction of cells during growth periods and by learning. The consequence is a modification of development in the direction of normality.

Development tends to be normal, but abnormalities do occur when these conservative tendencies are inadequate. Hereditary messages may be abnormal from the beginning of development. Or some chemical or experiential environment may affect the developmental course in an abnormal way. Hereditary abnormalities can result from abnormalities in single genes, from more than one gene, or from malformations in one or more chromosomes. The source of these genetic causes may be familial, that is, they may be transmitted through the parental germ cells. Or the genetic material carrying the genetic message may be altered during the course of development by some environmental agent.

Environmental toxins (teratogens) can also exert their effect on growing cells without affecting hereditary material at all. The number of teratogens that the human child is exposed to is immense, and they work by withdrawing nutrition from the system or by interfering with normal biochemical processes. Teratogens produce abnormalities by acting either over extended periods of time or by exerting their influence over brief critical periods. It becomes evident that more than one teratogen can produce abnormalities simultaneously. Alcohol, drugs, undernutrition, and various infections are a common combination of factors characterizing a particular lifestyle, working over an extended period, to produce varied and devastating effects on children.

Method

The main point up to here has been that the interaction of heredity and environment in complex systems results in varied patterns of individual differences, including abnormalities. Given the complexity of causes, it might seem impossible to determine what has been the cause in any individual case. As it is sometimes said, there may be too many variables to come up with definite conclusions. To some extent this pessimistic view has some support. Often, potential etiological agents are confounded or confused with each other because they are always present simultaneously in the same kind of case.

This is apparent in the earlier example of alcohol, drugs, and undernutrition as etiological agents that are present together. To make the situation even more difficult, some variables are, by their nature, poorly defined. For example, socioeconomic status (SES) is a general variable often confounded with other etiological agents.

The search for causes, therefore, is sometimes difficult, and the reader should beware of the problems involved. On the other hand, much specific information about causes of developmental disabilities has been acquired through scientific study. This information is firm and has been used to inform parents and to prevent disorders of development. The information has been collected using a variety of methods that can be classified into three general approaches: simultaneous, retrospective, and prospective methods.

The *simultaneous* approach involves describing characteristics of a developmentally disabled person that exist at the current time. An example would be studies of the brains of autistic children or of the home environment of depressed children (Downey & Coyne, 1990; Murakami, Courchesne, Press, Yeung-Courchesne, & Hesselink, 1989). Such studies can be done with a small number of people and then are called case studies. Or they may be done with formal data collection, using statistical methods with large numbers of cases. Then they are known as epidemiological studies. In either instance, care must be taken in defining the symptoms or syndromes carefully, in selecting the associated variables to be studied, and in using appropriate comparison groups (Levy, Zoltak, & Saelens, 1988). When done properly, the simultaneous method allows the clinician or scientist to state possible causes of disabling conditions. However, the simultaneous approach does not ordinarily permit definitive statements about cause.

In the *retrospective* method, the focus is on the history of the cases. Examples would be a determination of whether a group of mentally retarded children had suffered more birth injuries than a comparable nonhandicapped group or a look at the patterns of occurrence of phenylketonuria (PKU) in the ancestry of a child with PKU. Again, the syndrome and variables must be defined accurately with this method. At least as important with the retrospective method is ascertainment that sampling is unbiased (Widom, 1988). The retrospective method is particularly susceptible to the difficulty that, because of the passage of time, certain data will not be available for a complete picture (Simons, Ritchie, Mullett, & Liechty, 1986). Thus, whereas retrospective studies tend to be relatively inexpensive and provide unique information, results from them must be viewed with great care.

Perhaps the most valid types of investigation are the various forms of *prospective* studies. Prospective investigations involve the follow-up of cases where a suspected specific etiological agent has been identified. Follow-up studies of children who have experienced low levels of oxygen at birth or who have been raised in educationally impoverished environments would be examples. Also included in this type of study are the many experiments with animals that seek to determine the consequences on development of prenatal infections or other potential teratogens. Prospective studies, perhaps more than the other two classes, allow definitive conclusions about causes of developmental disorders. This is particularly true when experimental procedures (i.e., random assignment of experimental and control conditions) are employed. Naturally, this is most feasible with animal models. However, it is also possible in studies with humans when a deficiency condition exists and specific treatment with supplements are undertaken. For instance, the role of protein deficiency in later development can be assessed with controlled protein supplementation procedures.

Prospective investigations do have problems. In the first place, they tend to be very expensive. Imagine how difficult it would be to keep track of a sufficiently large group of children who had experienced brain hemorrhages at birth in order to find out whether they would have difficulties in school. Thus, one of the main problems in prospective studies is to avoid attrition, the loss of the sample. It is particularly important to avoid differential attrition between the potentially disabled group and the comparison group that is expected to have no special problem. Despite these difficulties, when there is a choice, the prospective study is preferred over the simultaneous and retrospective methods.

GENERAL RISK FACTORS

Some of the causes of developmental disorders are relatively specific. However, several etiological categories are quite general. They include chronic illness and accidents; prematurity and other high risk factors; socioeconomic status; and parent intelligence and education. This section reviews these generalized concepts. Then we turn to more specific causes.

Before we proceed, it is important to note that causes of developmental disorders often have unpredictable effects. As we show later, children who have a severe illness early in life can, and often do, develop normally later on. On the other hand, it is also possible that a seemingly minor abnormality can have widespread and devastating effects on behavior.

It is also true that causes of developmental disorders can extend their effects beyond single generations. Although it is easier to demonstrate an etiological effect from one generation to another (i.e., from parents to their children), it is also possible to demonstrate transgenerational effects (Beach, Gershwin, & Hurley, 1982; Wehmer & Porter, 1970). Typically these effects have been demonstrated in animal studies of nutritional deprivation and of stress. A great deal is not understood about how these transgenerational effects are transmitted through the second generation to the third, but the practical significance for the human condition is clear: Once an etiological agent is demonstrated, programs to prevent the condition may have to be continued for a long time.

Chronic Illness and Accidents

The least well-studied predictors of psychological disorders of children are chronic illnesses and accidents. However, there is adequate evidence now to point to the association between these factors and both behavioral and cognitive disorders. Chronic illnesses such as early onset diabetes mellitus predict problems in visual-spatial abilities. Surveys point to an association between chronic illnesses and various psychiatric diagnoses such as neuroses, conduct disorders, and hyperactivity (Cadman, Boyle, Szatmari, &. Offord, 1987; Rovet, Ehrlich, &. Hoppe, 1988).

Accidents are very common in early childhood, but they ordinarily result in minor injuries that apparently have no long-term effect. In one study of a well-supervised day-care center, there were 1,324 accidents during a 42-month observation period. However only 4 of them required referral to a physician, and none of them was regarded as serious (Elardo, Solomons, &. Snider, 1987). On the other hand, children do occasionally suffer head injuries that, when severe, can result in adaptive difficulties (J. M. Fletcher, Ewing-Cobbs, Miner, Levin, &. Eisenberg, 1990).

High Risk Status and Prematurity

The concept of high risk refers to any condition that has been shown to have deleterious effects later. This category may include general conditions like prematurity, severe illness such as hyaline membrane disease, specific genetic conditions like Down syndrome, and impoverished educational and/or social environments. The concept of high risk is so inclusive that it is not very useful for specific predictions about the presence or character of behavioral disorders. Moreover, its meaning has changed rapidly over recent decades (Kopp &. Krakow, 1983). The concept of high risk, therefore, may be regarded as a term, still in common use, which has only general meaning.

A more useful term is prematurity. This term does have its expected meaning, that is, a child who is born much earlier than the norm (average of 40 weeks of gestation age). However, it is sometimes difficult to determine exactly when a child was conceived because the mother's estimate of her last menstrual period is not always valid (she may not remember the date of the period accurately, or spotting may have occurred after conception). The child's maturity can be estimated from an examination of its physical and neurological status (Volpe, 1981). However, this examination is not regarded as completely accurate by itself. In practice, gestation age is estimated by a combination of the mother's estimate of last menstrual period and the examination of the maturity of the child.

Prematurity is also defined in terms of birth weight. Although this may not seem as generally valid as gestation age (because families and ethnic groups in various countries tend to vary in size), in practice, birth weight is used often. Prematurity is defined as a weight of 2,500 grams or less. This weight was chosen because children below that birth weight tended to have health problems. However, nursery care has improved so dramatically in the last 10 years, at least in industrialized societies, that 1,500 grams is beginning to replace 2,500 grams as the weight below which neonatologists begin to express concern.

Although health status is not used as a definer of prematurity, small children who are born early may also have health problems involving difficulties in breathing, maintenance of a steady heart beat, and feeding. More mature infants may also have these problems, but premature babies are particularly subject to them. On the other hand, many premature babies require no special medical care.

Follow-up studies of premature birth have shown a mixed picture (Kopp, 1983). In the first place, because care of premature babies has improved, more small babies are surviving. Thus, infants below 1,500 grams routinely live, and it is even possible to save infants lighter than 500 grams. The consequences of this change in caregiving are both positive and negative. On the positive side, many more children who previously would have died now survive, and many who would have had behavioral problems later no longer manifest these problems. On the negative side, many very low birth weight babies are found, at follow-up, to have some significant disability.

In addition, whereas it is sometimes possible to show that premature children subsequently suffer from disorders of behavior such as mental retardation, learning disabilities, and emotional handicaps of various kinds (H. G. Taylor & J. M. Fletcher, 1983; Zubrick, Macartney, & Stanley, 1988), it is also true that many premature children seem to be essentially normal when they grow up. Statements that the premature groups may have some problem do not necessarily refer to all or even most of the children in the premature groups (Largo, Molinari, Pinto, Weber, & Duc, 1986; Ruff, Mc-Carton, Kurtzberg, & Vaughan, 1984). Also, the differences between premature and full-term babies, although statistically significant, tend to be small.

Consistent with the concept of multiple handicaps, it is the smallest babies with severe health problems who generally are at greatest risk for developmental delay, cerebral palsy, and other disorders. Thus, it is not so much high risk status or premature birth that predicts behavioral problems, but very low birth weight, intraventricular hemorrhages, and associated health problems that seem to be important. Still more complicating is that follow-up studies have shown that children who appear quite normal at birth may begin to manifest disorders of development later. This delayed effect may occur because a body organ that was affected prenatally may not normally begin to function until later on. For instance, brain structures that subserve motor development begin to form quite early, but a child does not normally walk until about 1 year of age, and the effect of an injury to those brain structures will not be evident until the child is 1 or more years old (A. M. Elliman, Bryan, & A. D. Elliman, 1986). Another explanation for delayed effects are the social influences mentioned later (Bradley, Caldwell, Rock, Casey, & Nelson, 1987).

Whatever the explanation, the implications are clear: The effects of risk status and prematurity may be considered cumulative, and life events at all periods of development are significant.

A most important predictor of the degree of disability in later childhood appears to be the social environment in which the child is reared. More is said later about the influence of the home and of social class in the determination of developmental disorders. However, it is now becoming increasingly clear (Sameroff & Chandler, 1975) that the outcome of high risk birth is importantly affected by the nature of the social environment in which the child is reared. Children with a severe disability at birth may have their disability reduced by rearing in an environment having full opportunities for medical care, early intervention, and later educational opportunities, whereas a mild disability may be exacerbated by rearing in an impoverished environment. The importance of the social environment for the ultimate outcome of high risk births is one of the surprises that have been turned up by follow-up studies of high risk children. It once again emphasizes importance of events throughout the growth period (G. Gottlieb, 1983).

Social Class

Several extensive and careful studies have shown that whereas the biological factors mentioned earlier predict later disabilities, the social class, home environment, and intelligence or education level of parents are perhaps the strongest independent predictors of later problems (Broman, P. L. Nichols, & Kennedy, 1975; Dutton, 1985; L. S. Siegel et al., 1982; K. R. White, 1982). Exactly how these general variables moderate later development is not yet understood, but the fact that there is a correlation between them and later development seems to be clear. In this section, we discuss the definitions of each variable and also factors that may mediate the relationship between social class, home environment, and education on the one hand and development on the other.

The general concepts underlying social class are occupational status and income. The precise measurement of social class varies, and there is no generally accepted method (C. W. Mueller & Parcel, 1981; Gottfried, 1985). However, occupational status and education are common ways of defining social class. The measures of development with which social class are correlated ordinarily are various measures of development, such as scores on the Bayley Scales of Infant Development, intelligence, or school performance.

Social class predicts developmental level significantly, but only to a moderate degree, that is, the independent correlation coefficient is about .22 (K. R. White, 1982). This means that although poor families tend to have more children with developmental problems, there are also many exceptions. Brilliant, talented individuals do grow up in impoverished homes. Thus, simplistic statements about the relationship between poverty and developmental disabilities are not valid. On the other hand, the relationship between SES and school achievement stands as one of the clearly validated results in modern social science (R. C. Nichols, 1981).

There is a central problem in interpreting the relationship between social class and later behavior because we do not yet know what mediates the relationship. We might believe that lower social class causes developmental problems. However, low income could not directly cause behavioral difficulties. It is not lack of resources itself that produces difficulties. Rather, lack of adequate prenatal medical care, the potential poor intellectual support of cognitive growth, or the unfavorable physical environments (Proshansky & Kaminoff, 1981) that go along with poverty are at least conceivably more direct causes of developmental problems.

It may not be so much that the variables associated with poverty cause later developmental disorders but that the disorders of development, running in a family, are the causes of poverty. That is, it is possible that the causal relationship intrinsic to the correlation between development and poverty is ambiguous. We return to this possibility when we consider polygenic inheritance. For now, remember that although there is a clear moderate relationship between social class and later behavioral problems, the causal factors mediating this correlation are not clear.

Home Environment

As we indicated earlier, the strength of most predictors of later development is modest. Social class, for instance, with its correlation of .22 predicts only about 4% of the variability in academic achievement. Home environment variables seem to be more successful predictors. On average, they correlate $r = .57$ with academic achievement and therefore predict the square of .57, or somewhat more than 25% of the variability in academic achievement. Thus, home environment seems to be the best statistical predictor of academic success. Yet, the correlation is modest.

There are many ways of defining the home environment. These include family stability, reading materials in the home, parent aspirations for the child, and amount of cultural activities. As is shown later, some of these factors do influence later development and some are not as effective. However, the home environment has been an important global idea because of its predictive success and its appeal to common sense.

It should surprise no one that children who come from home environments that support intellectual development should perform better in school. However, the causal direction of this relationship is not as clear. Perhaps children are academically successful because they have books in the home or because their parents have educational aspirations for their children. It is equally plausible, however, that the causal direction is the reverse. That is, parents may buy books and think of advanced education for children who have clear ability and show interest in such things. Of course, both possibilities may be true.

Parent Intelligence and Education

Some of the same points can be made for the well-established correlation between parent IQ or maternal education (Broman et al., 1975) and children's intellectual development. Again, the correlations are well-established and moderate. In fact, parent intelligence predicts a child's later behavioral development more strongly than does the child's own rate of development when it is an infant (Ulvund, 1984).

The exact nature of the causal direction or of the mediating variables are unclear. For instance, although it is conceivable that a relationship between parent IQ and developmental level might be hereditary, the characteristics of the home alluded to earlier might be determined to some extent by parent intelligence, especially when one or more parents are mentally retarded.

In summary, the general characteristics of social class, home environment, and parent intellectual level show some relationship with later developmental problems. However, the direction or the nature of the relationships is not clear. In fact, it is possible that the correlation between social class, home environment, and parent intellectual level on the one hand and child's development on the other may represent many causes.

HEREDITARY CAUSES

Hereditary factors are important in the etiology of developmental disorders. Later we discuss specific hereditary syndromes. First, however, more general considerations are reviewed. There are several sources for the belief that heredity is important in causing developmental disorders. First, as already stated, heredity is involved in the development of all behaviors, normal or abnormal. One cannot conceive of behavior emerging without the guidance of DNA templates in the context of biochemical and experiential environments. Second, many kinds of developmental disorders can be found in several members of a family. We show that familial disorders do not necessarily prove hereditary causation. However, specific familial patterns sometimes do indicate that hereditary factors are involved. Third, sometimes behavior disorders are associated with physical disorders that we know to be caused by hereditary factors. In such cases, it is a pretty good guess that the behavioral disorder is also caused by a hereditary process.

On the other hand, hereditary etiology is often inappropriately invoked when there is no evidence of another etiological mechanism. Thus, in the absence of definitive evidence that a biochemical factor or experience is the sole factor involved, people sometimes guess that a hereditary factor might be the cause. This fairly common tendency is an action based on ignorance of what is happening and therefore is not appropriate.

Before continuing, it may be helpful to distinguish between *hereditary*, *genetic*, and *congenital*, because these terms are sometimes confused. The term *hereditary* is the one we use when referring to those (usually) familial factors transmitted to the embryo, in the form of DNA, which guide development throughout life. Genetics is sometimes used synonymously with heredity because it also refers to the actions of genes. However, the term *genetic* is also used as a synonym for "development" so that it can be confusing. The term *congenital* is something quite different. It refers to behaviors or other characteristics that are present at birth. We have already seen that things present at birth are the result of interaction of hereditary and prenatal environmental factors. Thus, congenital means a characteristic that is the result of prenatal factors that may or may not be exclusively hereditary.

Method

There are several ways that one can confirm a hereditary diagnosis of a developmental disorder. Perhaps the most direct is to show that the behavioral disorder is associated with a specific abnormality of genes or chromosomes. A typical example would be Down syndrome, a form of mental retardation associated with certain physical characteristics and an abnormality of the 21st chromosome that can be detected by visual examination of a photograph of the chromosomes of typical cells. Note that by viewing chromosomes, one is not examining the biochemical, anatomical, or behavioral results of the chromosomal abnormality. It is the photo of the chromosomes (called a karyotype) that is the evidence of the hereditary etiology.

The remaining methods for detecting hereditary influences are even less direct. They all depend on a look at the relationship between disabled people and members of their family, using either retrospective or simultaneous methods. One asks, first, whether the disabling condition occurs in other members of the family more than one would expect from the general population. If the condition occurs in at least some other family members, one can then test whether hereditary transmission is via one, two, or more genes; whether the transmission is sex-linked; whether the genes are dominant or recessive; and the degree of expression of the genes. These pedigree analyses are done one case at a time and are useful mainly for conditions where one or two genes are involved.

When many genes are involved (that is polygenic inheritance), procedures that statistically analyze the correlations from many people is the preferred approach. If a condition is heritable, not only may there be other people in the family who have the disorder, but the likelihood of two people having the disorder is related to the closeness of their relationship. For instance, the occurrence of schizophrenia among family members can be predicted from their degree of relationship (Faraone & Tsuang, 1985).

There is some difficulty in accepting a hereditary explanation from higher correlations among closer relatives because closer relatives not only share hereditary histories but also tend to live in similar environments. Therefore, it is possible that the greater association of disabling conditions among closer relatives is a result of environmental factors, not heredity. In other words, disabilities may be familial without being hereditary.

Two general methods have been used to try to separate environmental from hereditary factors in family studies. Twin studies involve the comparison of twins from single-celled pregnancies (monozygotic twins) with twins who are born at the same time, but from different fertilized eggs (dyzygotic twins). To the extent that a condition is heritable, monozygotic twins should be more similar to each other than would be dizygotic twins. The comparison of these two types of twins is used because, although their hereditary relationships are different, the differences in the environments of the twin pairs of the two classes are assumed to be equivalent.

Adoption studies attempt to separate the influences of heredity and environment by evaluating the relationships between adopted children and their biological parents and the adoptive parents. In other words, the correlations of the children's behavior with their adoptive or biological parents are contrasted (Bergeman & Plomin, 1988; Plomin, Loehlin, & DeFries, 1985). This would seem to be an ideal way to separate heredity from environment. However, adoption studies are very difficult to accomplish without biasing factors (such as selective adoption procedures). In any case there are few adoption studies of developmentally handicapped children (Daniels & Plomin, 1985).

Polygenic Inheritance

Most of the studies on heritability of general categories of developmental disorders have been studies of twins demonstrating a heritable component in the etiology of the disorder. For instance, twin studies of childhood autism (Folstein & Rutter, 1977) and of learning disabilities and speech and language disorders (Pennington & S. D. Smith, 1983) point to heredity as important in causing these disorders. However, heritability is not always possible to demonstrate. For instance, one study of familial mental retardation showed no greater similarity between monozygotic than dizygotic twins (P. L. Nichols, 1984).

Even when a heritable influence is demonstrable, sometimes it is more apparent with some aspects of the disability than others. Howie (1981) showed, with a twin study, that certain forms of speech disorder are heritable whereas others are not. This means that generalized statements about the heritability of any of the major clinical categories may be questionable. Put more positively, it seems as though it is at the level of specific behaviors such as hyperactivity, spelling problems, and reading disorders that heritability analyses are most productive (Folstein & Rutter, 1988; J. Stevenson, Graham, Fredman, & McLoughlin, 1987; J. Stevenson & Graham, 1988; Decker & Bender, 1988).

Whereas it therefore seems possible to make some statements about heritability from twin studies, more specific statements about how much a trait is determined by heredity, which genes are involved and how the genes work in producing a disability may not be as clear. Heritability quotients that attempt to describe the proportion of individual variability in behavior accounted for by hereditary variability are common aspects of these general heritability studies. The difficulty with these heritability quotients is rooted in the fact that they depend on random sampling procedures not possible in most studies of human behavior. These heritability quotients tend to be tied to the particular sample studied, they tend to be unstable from study to study, and they change with age in prospective studies (R. S. Wilson, 1985). Thus, a statement that heredity is involved can be made from these twin studies, but it is unclear how much heredity is involved.

Although heredity seems to be demonstrable, studies of the role of heredity in the etiology of developmental disorders do not ordinarily specify which genes are involved. Usually, all that can be said is that the inheritance involves more than one, two, or three genes among the tens of thousands of genes that take part in human development (Pennington & Bruce, 1988). However, the studies of specific inheritance deal only with a small proportion of cases of children with developmental disabilities. When inheritance is demonstrable, most cases are concerned with polygenic inheritance that is nonspecific.

The results of these general heritability studies cannot be very specific about the particular genes involved, but they are also not explicit about the ways that the genes interact or express themselves. Dominance, additivity, and degrees of expressivity are often hypothesized characteristics of the action of the multiple genes involved. However, these characteristics are more successfully described in the case of single gene models than they are in the case of polygenic inheritance models.

In summary, the confounding of hereditary and environmental variables is a problem in testing the role of heredity in the etiology of most developmental disorders of behavior. Although there are problems with twin studies that compare monozygotic with dizygotic twins, comparisons of twin types have been the main way of reducing this confounding. Studies of twins have shown that many general classes of developmental disorders are at least partly influenced by hereditary mechanisms, although some specific disorders are not. Even when the role of heredity is suggested, the specific way it acts is undetermined.

Specific Hereditary Causes

In the majority of cases, the etiology of developmental disorders of behavior is undefined. Either the suspected etiology is very general, as in the case of the general etiologies already discussed, or the cause of the disability is unknown. However, in perhaps 25% of cases the etiology is known and well defined. Hundreds of these specific causes of disability have been described, and their mechanisms of action are fairly well understood. Unfortunately, however, these specific causes are rare recessive genetic disorders or extreme environmental conditions that also occur infrequently. In addition, there is little reason to believe that specific causes produce specific behavioral patterns. Thus, whereas there has been dramatic progress in defining some causes of developmental disorders of behavior, this progress has applied to a minority of cases and has not resulted in the definition of many discrete syndromes of behavioral disorders.

Hereditary messages in humans are carried on 23 pairs of chromosomes in humans. Each chromosome is made up of thousands of genes, each of which is a complex DNA strand. The structure of the chromosomes and genes are established at conception. However, they and the manner in which the hereditary message is expressed can be modified in radical ways as development proceeds, especially during early stages of cell division. These modifications in the hereditary material and the way it works depend on the chemical milieu of the cells as they grow to form body structures. Alterations in this milieu during prenatal life can cause major changes in anatomical structures that mediate behavior and can modify the physiology of these structures.

Chromosome Disorders

Disorders of chromosomes can be devastating because so much genetic material is involved. The nature of the abnormality is determined by the specific pair of chromosomes affected, although to a certain extent, this principle can be overstated if one is describing behavioral effects.

The most common chromosomal disorder is Down syndrome. This syndrome is characterized by up to 50 physical abnormalities and almost always is associated with mental retardation. The syndrome was once thought to be caused by hormone deficiencies, because many people with Down syndrome do have abnormal hormone levels. However, the discovery that this syndrome is associated with an extra chromosome on the 21st chromosome pair convinced scientists that the basic etiological problem in Down syndrome is the abnormality in the hereditary material. This abnormality causes the whole syndrome, including the hormonal defects. This is another example that correlated factors do not necessarily demonstrate a causal relationship.

There is variability within Down syndrome. This is partly due to variability in the chromosomal defect. That is, different parts of the chromosome may be affected in different cases, and this is related to the character of the physical symptoms. Moreover, in a minority of cases, the chromosomes of only some of the person's cells are affected (mosaic cases). In these people, it is possible that the intellectual deficit is less marked (Gibson, 1978).

Variability among people with Down syndrome depends not only on the specific chromosomal defect, but also on the social history of the child. Those children reared from infancy in the depriving environments of the state-operated institutions of 30 to 80 years ago became severely retarded, whereas those raised at home with early educational intervention are now best described as mildly to moderately retarded (Hanson, 1981).

Perhaps the most surprising thing about Down syndrome is that there are few characteristic psychological patterns. Stereotypes about the syndrome have abounded (Gibson, 1978). For instance, people with Down syndrome have been said to be characteristically pleasant and musical. However, neither of these stereotypes has been validated. When groups of people with Down syndrome have been compared with groups of retarded people of equal intelligence, about the only difference that repeatedly has emerged has been a specific auditory processing deficit in the Down syndrome group. Thus, whereas there clearly is a syndrome of physical defects associated with the extra chromosome on the 21st pair, there is little clear evidence for a syndrome of behavioral characteristics.

Two other chromosome disorders that affect behavior are abnormalities of the pair of chromosomes that determine the sex of the individual. In normal women, the 23rd pair of chromosomes is made up of two chromosomes that are quite similar, but not identical. This pair is known as the X-X pair. Normal men also have one X chromosome, but it is paired with a Y chromosome. The Y chromosome has genes that activate certain hormones early in development, resulting in the individual being a male. Abnormalities in the sex chromosomes can occur in several ways that have different manifestations.

These sex-linked abnormalities are first detected through pedigree analyses when an abnormality is found more in one sex than in another. Sometimes only males or only females are affected. One example of a common sex-linked abnormality is the Fragile-X syndrome (De La Cruz, 1985; Madison, Mosher, & George, 1986). The behavioral aspects of this syndrome include mental retardation and sometimes autistic characteristics. When these general symptoms are found with a physical break at a certain point of the X chromosome, the diagnosis of Fragile-X syndrome may be made.

Females may also have the Fragile-X chromosomal abnormality. However, when they do, they do not show the behavioral disorders as severely as males, probably because their normal X chromosome provides the genetic message for normal growth. However, these females sometimes pass on the Fragile-X defect to their male children who then may be mentally retarded (Hagerman & Sobesky, 1989).

The Fragile-X syndrome produces generalized behavioral disorders, as do most chromosomal defects. This is because many developmental processes are affected with a pervasive genetic problem. However, an exception to this principle of a pervasive behavioral effect is Turner's syndrome. This syndrome involves the existence of only one X chromosome. There is neither an X nor a Y chromosome paired with this X. As a result, all cases of Turner's syndrome are female. The single X chromosome guides development reasonably normally, although girls with Turner's syndrome are short in stature. Their IQ is normal, but they tend to have a specific and severe deficit in spatial reasoning. The deficits in individuals with a single X chromosome demonstrate that the paired X chromosomes in nonhandicapped females are not identical and each chromosome, by itself, is not adequate to direct growth. The deficits also suggest that normal spatial reasoning is controlled at least partly by genes on the 23rd chromosome pair.

Gene Disorders

There are several thousand genes on each chromosome. Influenced by chemical or experiential environments, each gene guides one or more processes that may culminate in specific behavior. Sometimes the gene controls a process that is important to many other processes and so has a general effect. In that case, the gene's effect is said to be pleiotropic. We have already shown that chromosomes have pleiotropic effects on behavior. In this section, a pleiotropic effect of single genes is also emphasized.

The best known example of a genetic cause of developmental disorders is phenylketonuria (PKU). This condition was first discovered with pedigree analysis and involves a single recessive gene. Subsequent biochemical analyses demonstrated that the gene, when present, controls one of the steps in the conversion of phenylalanine into tyrosine, a protein essential in many physiological processes. In the absence of the gene, an excess of phenylalanine develops. The practical result is severe mental retardation. In other words, the absence of only one gene, controlling only one step in an essential metabolic process, produces a pleiotropic effect.

Genes that produce defects are often recessive. That is, they do not produce the defect unless they are present on each chromosome of a pair. In the case of single gene defects, this occurs in about 25% of the offspring when both parents are carriers of the gene. Thus, the defective gene may be present in a population without expressing itself completely in all affected individuals. It is important to note that recessive genes may be present and transmitted without being evident in all affected individuals.

Gene defects also result from the action of dominant genes, that is, genes that produce an abnormal condition whenever they are present on only one chromosome. In contrast with recessive genes, severe defects produced by dominant genes tend to die out of the population because they are always expressed and interfere with life or reproduction (except when the gene has its effect late in the reproductive period).

In the case of either deleterious recessive or dominant genes, the incidence of the conditions is very low. For instance, the incidence of PKU is about 1/15,000 births. Thus, although there are several disorders that have been clearly associated with single gene abnormalities (Omenn, 1976), the overall prevalence of single-gene disorders is minor relative to chromosomal disorders and to the general, nonspecific disorders reviewed earlier. Nevertheless, the importance of gene disorders is great because the relative simplicity of the gene-biochemistry relationship has led to an understanding of the nature of these relationships and because this understanding has led to successful procedures for preventing these devastating disorders.

Although not quite as advanced, pedigree analyses have also pointed to single gene causes in some cases of learning disabilities and speech disorders. Just as the discovery of Fragile-X syndrome provided understanding of the cause of some cases of mild and moderate mental retardation, pedigree analyses have begun to discover that some cases of learning disabilities and speech disorders are possibly associated with single or two-gene defects (Pennington & Bruce, 1988; Pennington & S. D. Smith, 1983). However, in these cases, the biochemical analyses have not yet been accomplished.

Chromosome and gene analyses have shown that severe and generalized behavioral consequences can be the result of pervasive defects in hereditary material or in relatively simple defects having pleiotropic effects. There are few instances yet of specific genetic influences having highly specific behavioral effects. This is not surprising because the translation of the genetic message must go through a myriad of developmental processes at the cell and organ level before it is expressed as a behavioral pattern. The next section, reviews what some of these intermediate stages are like, especially showing the way in which abnormal chemical environments can interfere with the guides given by heredity.

CHEMICAL ENVIRONMENTS

Heredity produces the intricate chemical milieu in which the development of anatomical structures and physiological and behavioral functions develop. As shown earlier, the chemical milieu itself affects the hereditary messages and also subsequent development. Thus, as soon as a child is conceived, the complex interplay of hereditary and environmental factors begins. This section reviews representative instances of chemical factors working on development. Those presented have been shown to produce abnormal development of behavior. These factors ordinarily are studied in the prenatal period because the fetus is often vulnerable to them. However, chemical factors can produce abnormalities at any time during the life span, and some chemical conditions (e.g., lack of oxygen from the air) can be more important after than before birth.

Malformations produced by biochemical factors can sometimes be predicted if one knows four factors: the nature of the chemical agent; its intensity or dose level; the time during development when it acts; and when its effects are observed.

The biochemical effect depends partly on the specific nature of the chemical abnormality. Specific types of nutritional deficits or toxic agents, including infections, can have relatively specific effects, as in the case of the fetal alcohol syndrome (discussed later). However, as with the pleiotropic hereditary effects, effects of a specific agent can be general. Thus, behavioral effects of protein, vitamin, and trace metal deficiencies, and toxic effects of drugs, heavy metals, and viral and parasite infections tend to be variable.

This variation is at least partly due to the intensity of the agent. Chemical effects ordinarily increase with the amount of the agent. However, these increasing effects do not always occur. In the first place, some agents (such as vitamin A) can be beneficial at low dose levels but become harmful when too much is ingested. That is, a simple linear function does not necessarily describe the nature of the dose–effect relationship. With other agents (such as lead), it is clear that high levels produce severe developmental disorders and very low levels produce none. However, the very important situation with intermediate levels is still not clear, even after many years of painstaking epidemiological research.

Variable effects of chemical agents also result because the time in development at which the agents exert their effect can be as important as the nature of the agent. The same dose level of X-radiation has very different effects at different times in development. This is because X-radiation interferes with the growth of those anatomical structures developing at the time the agent is having its effects. These timing or critical period effects can be so accurate that they have been used, with great precision, to map structural development in animals.

The effect of an agent depends, not only on the nature of the agent, the amount of the agent, and the time that the agent affects the organism, but also when the effect is observed. Thus, as indicated at the beginning of this chapter, a behavioral defect may emerge later in the development of a child even though the structure subserving that behavior may have been destroyed by a chemical agent much earlier in development. This occurs because, in development, behavior emerges as a result of the interaction of many anatomical structures working together.

Variability of behavioral effects of chemical agents therefore depends on the nature of the agent, on its dose, and on temporal factors. There is one other general source of variability that we have met before, the relation of the chemical agent with other causes of developmental disorders. In humans, chemical teratogens are often confounded with other causes. For instance, pregnant women who habitually use drugs such as heroin or cocaine also tend to drink large amounts of alcohol, be undernourished, receive inadequate medical care, and come from low SES environments. It is not surprising that these women tend to have children with developmental disorders. However, it is not always clear to which variable or variables the disorders are attributable.

The relation of chemicals with other factors may also be interactive. That is, the effect of a specific chemical agent may depend on hereditary or experiential factors. For instance, thyroid deficiencies seem to be more devastating in individuals reared in environments characterized by impoverished experiences, and enriching the experiential environment appears to be an important way to moderate the effects of teratogens (Sameroff & Chandler, 1975).

Nutrition

In the following paragraphs, we review those chemical factors that have been studied extensively. Nutritional deficits, specifically low calorie and/or protein levels in the diet, have received much attention because children throughout the world suffer severe undernutrition. The study of the effects of food deficiency have been carried out in some third-world countries. Undernutrition is often confounded with experiential (for instance, social) deprivation (Salt, Galler, & Ramsey, 1988), so experimental studies employing food supplementation has been an important method of study. This approach involves providing supplemental protein or calories to children without altering their environment in other ways. As may be imagined, accomplishing this kind of project in a rural, third-world environment is not easy, and results sometimes are difficult to interpret (Z. Stein & Susser, 1985). So, studies of animals reared in controlled environments with different levels of specific food substances are also an important feature of the literature.

The literature in this area is controversial. Sometimes, no behavioral effects of undernutrition are found even when there are physical growth deficiencies (Z. Stein, Susser, Saenger, & Marolla, 1972). However, there are a number of important instances in which a behavioral effect of protein or calorie deficiency is evident. The most interesting of these studies show little effect of protein deprivation on learning but significant effects on temperamental and motivational variables (D. E. Barrett, Radke-Yarrow, & Klein, 1982). These studies are noteworthy because they are among the most meticulous in the literature. In monkeys and in children (Ricciuti, 1981; Z. Stein & Susser, 1985) studies of nutritional deficiencies and supplementation have shown fewer effects on conventional tests of learning and cognitive development than on attention, motivation, activity level, and temperament. It is likely, of course, that unmotivated individuals may learn less in practical situations. However, these studies of undernutrition show that it is as much motivational as learning processes that is affected.

Other forms of undernutrition are placental insufficiency of the prenatal period and asphyxia associated with birth. Both of these conditions are complex in that several factors seem to be involved. Also, they represent a situation in which a severe disorder in the period of early development can turn out to have negligible effects later. Placental insufficiency refers to an abnormality that results in inadequate nutrition of the fetus, including perhaps an inadequate supply of oxygen. The result is a significantly lower growth rate. Neonatal asphyxia involves a limitation in the supply of oxygen to the child as it is being born. The consequences may be subsequent severe intellectual and motor disorders such as cerebral palsy. In the cases of both placental insufficiency and neonatal asphyxia, several factors may be occurring simultaneously, and it is not always clear what is the etiological agent. In the case of placental insufficiency, oxygen deprivation may be part of the picture. However, other nutritional factors such as carbohydrates and proteins may also be deficient. In the case of neonatal asphyxia, not only is there reduced oxygen, but there is also elevated carbon dioxide, which produces an acidic condition thought to be more important than the reduced oxygen in producing brain damage. Thus, a confused picture emerges from what was once thought to be a relatively simple etiologic picture.

Placental insufficiency and neonatal asphyxia can produce severe defects during and immediately after birth. Indeed these severe defects may endure throughout life in the form of severe general behavioral disorders. However, follow-up studies generally show that most children who seemed to be severely disabled at birth ultimately recover. Children who initially appear as though they will never recover from their initial deficits turn out in school to perform up to their age peers. It is unclear yet to what this remarkable plasticity is due. However, overproduction of cells, emergence of new neurological structures, and compensation by experiential environments are all possible explanations.

Hormones

Complex and interactive patterns are also apparent in the case of abnormalities produced by hormonal imbalance. Sex, thyroid, and growth hormones are all chemical factors secreted by the body at special times during the growth period. Their action may affect many organ systems (as in the case of growth and thyroid hormone), or they may be more specific. Ordinarily, these factors are finely balanced with each other, and behavioral growth proceeds normally. However, sometimes there is a deficiency or an excess of one or more hormones, and then behavioral development can be altered.

Behavioral abnormalities resulting from hormone imbalance can be somewhat specific. For instance, variations in growth hormone produce differences in body stature but have not been shown to affect general cognitive development (M. O. Smith et al., 1985). Deficiencies in thyroid hormone secretion produce mental retardation, as well as certain physical abnormalities (J. W. Davenport & Dorcey, 1972), whereas excesses of thyroid hormone sometimes result in psychopathology. Variations in sex hormones seem to affect temperament and sex-related behaviors but do not influence one's conception of oneself as male or female (Ehrhardt & Meyer-Bahlburg, 1981). Thus, the behavioral effects of different hormonal abnormalities may be quite different from one another.

As with hereditary factors, hormonal factors interact with experience. The effects of hormone abnormalities are not necessarily overcome completely by favorable environments, but they can be ameliorated. On the other hand, hormone deficiencies may be exacerbated by environments that do not support cognitive growth. This principle is best illustrated by a study by J. W. Davenport, Gonzalez, Carey, Bishop, and Hagquist (1976), who reared thyroid-deficient rats in environments that were either empty or had many objects in them. They showed that subsequent performance in maze learning was superior in the "enriched" group, and their performance was almost comparable to that of controls. If we may generalize to humans from this study, we should treat thyroid-deficient infants not only with thyroid hormone but also assure that they are reared in educationally enriched environments.

Environmental Toxins

Hereditary and hormonal factors are therefore important in causing developmental disorders of behaviors. Understanding their various actions provides some opportunity for preventing developmental disorders, but perhaps such prevention will be difficult. However, there is a larger class of causes that potentially can more easily be controlled. This is the group of environmental toxins including heavy metals (lead, mercury); addictive substances (alcohol, heroin); therapeutic drugs (dilantin, thalidomide); food additives; and infections (viruses and parasites). With the exception perhaps of alcohol, none of these agents has very specific effects. That is, the way in which they are manifested depends more on dose level and time of action. However, these causes of developmental disorders are very important because of their devastating effects and because the effects are at least theoretically preventable.

Ingesting lead or mercury in large amounts produces severe illness and death or profound brain damage resulting in mental deficiency. There is general agreement on this clinical finding, and it has produced legislation limiting heavy metal in the air and in paint (that very young children may put in their mouths). There is less agreement about the possible harmful effects of small amounts of lead in the environment. Some investigators (e.g., Needleman, Schell, Bellinger, Leviton, & Allred, 1990) believe that even low levels of lead in the environment produce defects and these defects can be subtle disorders of perception and learning, as well as of classroom learning. Other research workers (Silva, P. Hughes, S. Williams, & Faed, 1988), acknowledge that high concentrations of lead produce severe problems, but find only small effects of lower concentrations when confounded factors such as parent intelligence and SES are controlled. This disagreement exists because evaluating levels of heavy metals in body organs is sometimes tricky. For instance, blood levels of lead are affected by degree of exposure to the sun. Also, disorders of behavior that are subtle sometimes are difficult to assess reliably. The weight of the evidence, however, seems to point to the heavy metals as a teratogen whose effect on behavior is proportional to the amount ingested over time.

There seems to be little question now that if a pregnant woman drinks a substantial amount of alcohol, her baby is at risk for developmental defects (West & Prinz, 1987). The defects may be manifested as a syndrome called the fetal alcohol syndrome. This group of symptoms includes specific facial features and also mild mental retardation or learning disability. There also may be a more generalized cognitive disorder (Abel, 1980; Streissguth, Landesman-Dwyer, Martin, & Smith 1980; West & Prinz, 1987). Alcoholism in the family is also associated with child psychopathology, including hyperactivity and conduct disorder; substance abuse, delinquency, and truancy; social inadequacy; somatic problems; anxiety and depression; and dysfunctional family interactions (West & Prinz, 1987). It has taken some time to demonstrate that alcohol by itself can be a teratogen because ingestion of alcohol is sometimes confounded with lifestyles that include other potentially teratogenic conditions, for example, poor medical care, high stress, and other drugs. However, with careful epidemiological and experimental work, alcohol itself has been implicated.

The question of how much alcohol is dangerous has not yet been answered completely. Apparently a small amount (equivalent to one glass of beer) may not harm a nonpregnant women. But, for pregnant women, alcohol must be regarded as a risk factor that increases with the amount of alcohol consumed (Cooper, 1987).

The "hard drugs" (e.g., heroin, methadone) are most certainly harmful to infants. Mothers who are addicted to these drugs during pregnancy pass on the addiction to their newborn infants because these drugs can penetrate the placenta from the mother's blood stream. Soon after birth, these babies are ordinarily treated for their addiction. However, they remain at risk for later problems because of factors confounded with taking hard drugs. One example of such confounded factors is the resources available to the mother.

Thus, whether maternal use of addictive drugs by itself has a long-term effect on the child is not yet clear, even though it is true that mothers who take drugs are more likely to have children with behavioral problems (Jeremy & Bernstein, 1984).

Therapeutic medications also can have undesirable side effects on unborn children. The most notorious of these is thalidomide. Thalidomide is a tranquilizing medication that has clear teratogenic effects when it is ingested by a pregnant woman. It produces malformations of the arms and legs. However, it apparently has little or no effect on cognitive development or on social attachment. On the other hand, other agents have been shown to have more general effects, including significant consequences on behavior. Included among these agents are dilantin, the anticonvulsant used to control epileptic seizures. In general, it is best for pregnant women to avoid ingesting nonfood substances. For those who must take medication for a health problem, they should do so with careful supervision of an obstetrician.

A more controversial area has to do with the behavioral consequences of certain food additives eaten by children. Examples of such additives are simple sugars and food dyes. According to the rationale for the view that such foods may have a detrimental effect on behavior, they may induce an allergic reaction in at least some children. The main symptom that has been related to ingestion of food additives is "hyperactivity," which we noted in the previous chapter is a poorly defined category. Although all cases of hyperactivity cannot be explained by the nature of the food the child takes in (Milich & Pelham, 1986), apparently some children do become more easy to deal with when certain food additives are removed from their diet (Thorley, 1983). Thus, modification of diet is an option for some (probably a few) children, but cannot be regarded as a general solution for any behavioral disorder.

Research on the relationship between parasitical, viral, or bacterial infections and behavioral disorders is scarce. However, it is known that such infections can have profound behavioral effects. For instance, if a mother contracts german measles (rubella) early in pregnancy, visual disorders and mental deficiency in the baby can result. School children may recover if they contract a virus that attacks the nervous system. However, other children may have depressed intellectual functioning (Chamberlain et al., 1983; Quart, Cruickshank, & Sarnaik, 1985). Thus, whereas infections may have no effect on behavior at all, there may be profound and generalized effects in some cases. Research on the sequelae of infections, particularly with respect to subtle defects, is badly needed.

Particularly important at this time would be research on pediatric human immunodeficiency virus-1 (HIV-1) and acquired immunodeficiency syndrome (AIDS). The first case of pediatric AIDS was diagnosed in 1982, and

AIDS has become the ninth leading cause of death in children. Neurological involvement characterizes some cases, and highly individual behavioral effects are also found. There has not yet been much research on the behavioral sequelae of HIV and AIDS. However, a multivariate, individual change model has been suggested (J. M. Fletcher et al., 1991).

Overall, then, many alterations of the chemical environment in the prenatal and postnatal periods can produce specific and general consequences on behavior. Further understanding of the influence of chemical factors on the development of behavior is needed. Prevention of developmental disorders is most easily accomplished by control of chemical environments, as compared with heredity and experiential environments. However, even control of chemical factors depends on altering lifestyles.

EXPERIENTIAL CAUSES

Experiential sources of developmental disorders begin at or soon after birth as the infant learns about its environment. We have shown in previous sections of this chapter that hereditary and chemical factors interact with experience to determine whether a child's development is more or less normal. In this section, and in other chapters of this book, we center our attention more on environments that specifically determine a child's experience and learned behaviors. As with heredity and chemical environments, the effects of experiences ordinarily are quite widespread because environments that affect learning tend to be confounded with other factors and because experiences interact in complex ways with one another. On the whole therefore, it is difficult to find any one experience that will determine behavioral abnormality. The more usual case is a complex set of experiences that build on one another over months and years to produce a deficit that is cumulative (Saco-Pollitt, Pollitt, & Greenfield, 1985).

The complexity of environments makes it especially difficult to locate any specific environmental effect that produces a disability. Moreover, (except with animal studies) it is difficult to point to specific traumatic instances as etiological agents. In specific cases of childhood disorders the clinician uses the retrospective method to locate the causative agent. As mentioned previously, the retrospective method, used in single cases, does not separate confounded variables very well. Therefore, it might seem impossible to make any definite statements about the role of experience in the development of childhood behavioral disorders. However, there are reports of cases of children who have experienced generalized extreme experiential deprivation. The extreme cases attest to the fact that generalized abnormal experience can have deleterious effects on a child's development (M. A. Murphy & Vogel, 1985; Tamaroff, Nir, & Straker, 1986). In addition, there are a few correlational studies, using the simultaneous method, that point to some reasonably specific environmental factors that can produce behavioral abnormalities.

Educational and social alterations from normal are the types of experiential factors reviewed here. Educational and social factors tend to be confounded with each other and are separated only for purposes of discussion. Educational deprivation refers to lack of appropriate objects or activities in the home or school; traumatic events; and unreasonably high expectations for achievement that occurs in some families. Social factors include deprivation of parents; abnormal social attachment; inappropriate social models; cultural factors; and neglect and abuse. These conditions are widespread and contribute importantly to the prevalence of various disorders.

As children grow older, they take on characteristics of the people around them. Their social behavior and their concepts of themselves become a kind of average of the behavior of the important people in their lives. This process is called *social learning,* and one form of it is a specific copying or modeling of these parents, siblings, and friends. When one of these significant people in the child's life is in some way abnormal, there is a chance that the child will model on this abnormality. For instance, a child with a very anxious parent may learn to be anxious through a social learning process. Children do not model the behavior of all people in the social environment equally. Of course, the amount of exposure the child has to the person will be one determinant of the amount of social learning. At least as important is the quality of the relationship the child has with the model. Modeling is most strong on people who are powerful in the family and who are loving. Thus, as with the other factors we have considered, the determinants of social learning are complex, but definable.

Social learning may either accentuate or moderate the reflection of a family member's characteristics in the child. It is the child's perception of the family member's abnormal characteristic that mediates the modeling process, thus the child's behavior can be an exaggeration of the parent's abnormality if the child's perception of the abnormality magnifies it. On the other hand, if the child does not perceive the abnormality as a very important aspect of the parent's behavior, the child may not be very abnormal at all. There may also be less abnormality in the child than in a particular adult because the child is usually exposed to many family members and friends, models on many of them, and therefore develops a personality that represents social learning from several sources. This not only tends to moderate abnormality, but provides a unique combination of social behaviors and concepts of self. The result is individuality of personality.

Social factors are probably at work in the effects of parental depression, excessive aggression in the family, and other psychopathology of the family on children's problems. Children of depressed parents have a higher rate of psychopathology than do comparison groups (S. B. Campbell, 1987; Downey & Coyne, 1990; Kazdin & Kolko, 1986; Orvaschel, Walsh-Allis, & Ye, 1988). This could be attributed to hereditary factors but also is probably the result of a lower level and different patterns of social interactions between the parents and children (Breznitz & T. Sherman, 1987).

Children who recently had been exposed to family violence have been reported by their mothers as having fewer interests, fewer social activities, and lower school performance than a comparison group (D. A. Wolfe, Zak, S. Wilson, & Jaffe, 1986). In an unique longitudinal study, boys who had presumably been exposed to family stress leading up to a divorce were rated as having less impulse control and excessive energy and aggression. Girls were apparently less affected (J. H. Block, J. Block, & Gjerde 1986; see also Lahey et al., 1988). Not all homes are nurturing places that promote normal cognitive and social growth. Some environments include a significant and surprising amount of sexual abuse, physical abuse, or neglect leading to hospitalization or even death. The high prevalence of child abuse is a relatively recent discovery. It stands as evidence that not all parents innately know how to rear children with attention to their best interests. Not very much is known about sexual abuse, perhaps because its manifestations are not always apparent and because families can and do hide its existence (Browne & Finkelhor, 1986). However, the correlates of neglect and physical abuse are becoming increasingly understood. Predictors include character-istics of both parents and the child. Different characteristics of fathers and of mothers predict child abuse (M. A. Perry, Wells, & Doran, 1983). On the other hand, there are some general characteristics of families that are apparently important. Child abuse occurs at all SES levels, but tends to be higher in families with low cohesiveness, that are under stress, and have relatively few resources to deal with the stress. There is some tendency for parents who were abused themselves to abuse their children (Webster-Stratton, 1985).

Characteristics of the child also are predictors of whether it is abused. Children who have a chronic illness (Sherrod, O'Connor, Vietze, & Alte-meier, 1984) or who are disabled in other ways are apparently more subject to abuse than are nonhandicapped children (Nesbit & Karagianis, 1982; R. White, Benedict, Wulff, & Kelley, 1987). Perhaps this occurs in families that are otherwise under stress or in which the child's disability challenges the coping resources of the family beyond its resources for coping allow. In sum, as with the other etiological agents we discussed before, the causes of child abuse are complex, and the results are tragic.

Educational Deprivation

Some children experience postnatal environments that fail to support normal cognitive growth. The most obvious of these are extended experiential deprivations. Among these are the relatively specific deprivations accompanying severe hearing and visual handicap. Sensory handicaps may be more or less severe, and they are amenable to correction. However, in a few cases, the disability is substantial and prevents the child from receiving experiences through the impaired organ. In this case the experiences necessary for development in a specific cognitive realm are not available. Children who are deaf from birth do not hear the language sounds on which their own language would normally be based. As a result, they are severely handicapped in language and in the cognitive skills for which language is necessary. This is a handicap in school that is difficult, though not impossible, to overcome.

The impairment in blind children is not as great. Children born with major visual handicaps are developmentally delayed in infancy when vision is the major sensory route for adaptation (Adelson & Fraiberg, 1974). At this time, their motor and cognitive development are delayed, and they may retain a deficit in spatial perception and cognition (Millar, 1988). However, unless there are other handicaps, blind children learn language normally and their subsequent school performance is at grade level, if they do not have other handicapping conditions, and if they receive schooling that compensates for their blindness.

Experiential deprivation also occurs in those homes in which there are no toys for the child to play with and in which the main caretaker does not interact with the child very much. The most obvious examples of this kind of deprivation occur in those rare cases in which children are reared in a small room or closet isolated from normal objects and experience. Such unfortunate children are the victims of psychotic parents. The children generally are mentally retarded and have little language. Fortunately, these cases are rare, but they do exist in modern society.

Less obvious is the child who is neglected by its main caregiver and whose environment includes few toys. Contrary to popular belief, such conditions are not necessarily closely associated with poverty. M. Lewis and C. D. Wilson (1972) observed infants and their mothers in families who lived at different SES levels. They showed that lower-class babies played no less than upper-class babies. Moreover, if anything, lower-class mothers had more behaviors encouraging social behavior than mothers in higher SES families. On the other hand, across SES classes, children from homes with few toys and little maternal control of the environment tend to perform less well in school than children who have toys in well-organized homes (Bradley & Caldwell, 1977).

At the other extreme are children who receive more attention than they need for normal development. These children have more toys and other possessions than they need, coupled with parenting that emphasizes much higher expectations than the child possibly can achieve (Elkind, 1981). The anxiety about achievement reflected in the parents' behavior is passed on to the children, often with the result that they avoid situations in which they could achieve well. The most successful parent is the one who avoids the extremes of deprivation and overexpectation and who creates an atmosphere in which learning is an attractive activity. This involves estimating what one's particular child is capable of learning at any particular time and constructing the situation as well as one can to promote that learning.

The previous examples of experiential factors have emphasized those environments that occur over a period of time and have a fairly general effect on the child's cognitive and personal development. What about those single, intense experiences that may produce a lasting effect on the child's development? In other words, what is the role of traumatic experiences on child development? Do, for instance, brief hospitalizations involving painful surgery have an enduring effect on the child's psychological development. In answering this question, one must take care that one actually is dealing with a situation that is limited in time. One hospitalization that follows a long period of illness and precedes an extended convalescence in an anxious family would not be an example of a single traumatic experience.

The life of an average child is filled with painful events that are experienced and then forgotten quickly. Later experiences, if they are positive tend to cancel the effects of the painful ones. There is little scientific evidence that a single experience by itself has the power to alter the general direction a child's life is taking, although the matter has not been studied adequately. However, it seems likely that the overall pattern the child's environment impresses on the child will be far more important than a single, even intense, event. Short-term hospitalizations do have short-term effects. But if these effects are not reinforced in the home after the child returns home, these effects will probably be temporary. However, repeated hospitalizations can be detrimental (Elander, Nilsson, & Lindberg, 1986).

Social Factors

Abnormal social environments certainly can produce developmental disorders. Extreme maternal deprivation, abnormal social attachment, inappropriate social models in the home, and extreme forms of neglect and abuse are common sources of later problems. As with the other causes of developmental disorders, these types of pathological experiences can be confounded with each other; their effects may cumulate to affect various aspects of behavior; or the effects may be temporary.

Baby monkeys who are reared without their mothers become fearful adults whose behavior in groups is inappropriate. They are overaggressive, they do not breed normally, and they do not take care of any infants they might bear (Harlow & Zimmerman, 1958). As pointed out earlier, gross isolation of human children produces major behavioral abnormalities. However, there are ways in which these major effects can be moderated. Baby monkeys who are reared with other babies develop abnormally intense attachments with each other, but are essentially normal in their social behavior when they are older (H. F. Harlow, M. K. Harlow, & Hansen, 1963). Human children, born in a concentration camp and who never had a permanent mother but did have the companionship of children of their own age, were more than usually fearful. However, their social behavior was surprisingly normal (A. Freud & Dann, 1951). Thus, being raised by a loving mother is optimum for children, and rearing in total social isolation produces severe psychopathology. However, rearing with peers with adequate caretaking by adults moderates the effects of isolation.

Otherwise normal children who are reared in barren environments with other children with a minimum of adult caregiving develop tendencies toward self-isolation and superficial sociability. Such children tend to engage in self-directed stereotyped activities and gather around a stranger seeking social contact (Provence & Lipton, 1962). Institutions are less common than they were a generation ago, but they still exist, especially for children who have other disabilities than those produced by their abnormal social rearing (e.g., severely retarded children).

Abnormality of social attachment of the child to members of its family, especially its primary caregiver, is a source of later psychopathology. The process of attachment of children to their mother has been carefully studied lately (Ainsworth, 1979). Especially important in this work has been the finding that children differ in the way they are attached to their mother. They may be securely attached, anxiously attached, or a mixture of several modes of attachment. It is not clear yet what causes these individual differences, but the differences do predict later behavior. Thus, for instance, anxiously attached 2 year olds tend to become anxious 7 year olds. There is the presumption that the abnormality of attachment produces the later anxiety. Of course, it is also possible that both the anxious attachment and the later anxiety are caused by a third factor.

More severe forms of psychopathology can result from disturbances of the early mother–infant relationship. Severe disturbance in that relationship (for instance, when there is essentially no nurturing by any adult) prevents the normal development of any coherent personality. The child grows physically, but without a unified self to organize its behavior. Milder forms of this disorder are "narcissism" in which the child seeks its self in other people; more intense forms may even include "schizophrenia," a total lack of a personality that results in major disorders of the way the child thinks. Theories about the severe consequences of abnormalities of maternal attachment are derived from retrospective analyses of clinical cases. The general approach probably is valid, but there have not been extensive systematic studies to support it. Especially in the case of childhood schizophrenia, there is reason to believe that genetic and biochemical factors rather than abnormality of maternal attachment are the critical etiological factors. In this case, a problem in attachment might be a result, rather than a cause of the childhood schizophrenia.

SUMMARY AND IMPLICATIONS

Behavior disorders are determined by hereditary, chemical, and experiential factors. There are hundreds of causes of development, working in complex interaction with each other to produce unique patterns of normal and abnormal behavior. Not only are interactions complex, but confounded variables having pleiotropic effects add obstacles to placing etiological categories and their effects into neat categories. Moreover, the effects of various intensities of teratogenic agents and the timing of their action provide additional dimensions determining individuality of result.

The effect of this complex of interactions is a continuum of reproductive casualty that expresses itself as a bimodal distribution of severity of behavioral disabilities. The two general factors represented by the bimodal distribution are, first, a deviation from average functioning and, second, frankly pathological processes. The two distributions overlap, so it is sometimes not possible to determine whether any single handicapped person is a representative of normal deviation or pathology. Sometimes it is possible to make the distinction by referring to other measures of functioning such as the electroencephalogram, biochemical measures, or some other nonbehavioral measures. However, behavioral measures do not by themselves permit a clear distinction between the two types.

Behavioral assessment also does not by itself indicate the cause of a behavioral disorder. Partly, this is because of the intertwining of causes and the pleiotropic effect mentioned earlier. Also, the retrospective methods that are characteristic of clinical diagnosis cannot decisively separate confounded etiological variables. Sometimes an excellent case history does allow the clinician to be confident that the onset of behavioral disabilities followed a particular event. However, this is difficult to do and is rare. Retrospective assessments are often speculative.

On the other hand, behavioral assessments are very important in determining whether an important problem in adaptation exists. They also are critical in defining the nature of the adaptive difficulty. Precise definition of the behavioral problem, whereas it does not point clearly to the cause of the difficulty, certainly is critical for adequate treatment.

The most important purpose of relating behavioral disabilities to etiology is for prevention. We have seen that abnormal physiological conditions in infancy do not necessarily result in behavioral disorders later on and that seemingly normal children may behave abnormally later. This means that a major criterion of whether an important disorder exists is whether there is a behavioral problem affecting adaptation in later childhood and adulthood. In other words, the major test of whether there is a behavioral disorder is not so much whether an early physiological abnormality existed but whether there is a significant behavioral problem later on. As a consequence of this principle, careful assessment of the long-term behavioral consequences of hereditary, chemical, or experiential agents should be part of any study that claims to have consequences for the understanding and prevention of behavioral disabilities.

Knowing that a factor or group of factors causes behavioral disability may or may not lead to prevention of the disability. In the case of highly specific conditions that are well understood, prevention is possible. For instance, knowing that ingestion of large amounts of lead produces brain damage and severe mental retardation led to government action that has reduced the amount of lead in the environments of young children. The diet for pheny-lketonuria prevents the major symptoms of the disorder, although there may be residual problems (Pennington, Doorninck, L. L. McCabe, &. E. R. B. McCabe, 1985). Even when the etiological conditions are complex, it is possible to reduce disabilities. Compensatory early education, when gener-ously funded and adequately managed, can reduce disabilities that result from deprived experience.

However, there are many things that militate against prevention pro-grams. The most important is lack of knowledge about what to prevent. For instance, whereas some forms of thyroid deficiency can be combated by feeding thyroid pills, others cannot, so there are still cases of cretinism, a type of mental deficiency. Furthermore, behavioral disabilities are not pre-vented because although knowledge is available, the cost of preventing it is great either in terms of money or personal convenience. This is because prevention programs must be carried out for a significant amount of time in the life of the individual child. It is known that use of addictive drugs by pregnant women is not good for the babies they are carrying. This knowl-edge is available, but there still are many cases of children who are born addicted to heroin, often because obtaining cooperation with prevention programs can be difficult (Brooks-Gunn, McCormick, &. Heagarty, 1988; Offord, 1987).

There are many types of programs that do prevent behavioral disorders. In what follows, some of them are reviewed. These programs are complex and require a significant expenditure of financial and personal resources. What makes these expenditures worthwhile is the contribution these pro-grams make to later care and happiness of the children and families involved.

The first group of programs deal with hereditary disorders and are called genetic counseling services. In these services, there is first a determination of whether a specific hereditary factor is involved in a child's disorder. Family histories, biochemical tests, and karyotypes are taken with a view to determining the risk of having another child in the family with the same condition. Once the risk has been determined, the family decides whether to have more children. This decision is aided by a counselor (usually a psychologist or social worker) who is specially trained about hereditary disorders.

Prenatal and perinatal screening for hereditary and hormonal disorders is a second approach to prevention of behavioral disorders of development (Rowley, 1984). Once the child has been conceived, it is possible to detect an abnormality by testing for biochemical abnormalities, malformations, or chromosomal defects. Such abnormalities can be detected between 2 and 4 months after conception. Methods of doing this include viewing the fetus visually with ultrasound, analyzing for biochemical abnormalities, doing karyotypes of the cells in the amniotic fluid (amniocentesis), or (less well investigated) by analyzing samples of chorionic villi (Modell, 1985). If an abnormality is found that may later involve severe disability, some families choose to terminate the pregnancy. Ordinarily, these prenatal tests are not considered routine but are done only with women considered to be at risk for a certain disorder. For example, because women over 35 years of age are somewhat more likely to have infants with chromosomal disorders, they frequently elect to have these tests (Berg, 1986; Finegan, Quarrington, H. E. Hughes, & Doran, 1987).

Screening for disorders is also accomplished soon after birth. In this case, tests of body fluids sometimes reveal a condition that has not yet become apparent in behavior. Phenylketonuria and cretinism can be detected with simple chemical tests done shortly after birth. In the case of PKU, a special diet sustained through a major portion of childhood can essentially prevent the severe mental retardation associated with the biochemical abnormalities. Giving thyroid hormone to the thyroid-deficient child can prevent the development of at least some cases of cretinism.

Although screening programs like these have succeeded dramatically in preventing many cases of developmental disorders of behavior, it must also be said that screening has so far worked well mainly for low-prevalence conditions. Therefore, although these programs are very important pioneering efforts, much more work must be done in this area.

At least as important as screening of the mother and the infant for hereditary and hormonal disorders are programs directed at removing potential teratogens from the environment. Examples are the legislation that has removed lead from paint that babies can put in their mouths and drug testing programs that removed thalidomide from the U.S. market. These programs are a complex cooperative effort of environmental medicine researchers, public health officials, and legislators. The two main ways in which these programs are carried out are education about the possible harmful effects of chemical agents in the environment and legislation when education alone is not effective.

The barriers to complete elimination of teratogens from the environment are complex. We do not know the potential teratogenic effects of many of the hundreds of new chemical substances that are developed each year. Second, many and perhaps most of these substances have beneficial as well as harmful effects. So the choice about whether or not to ban a chemical from the environment is not always a simple one to make. It is important, however, to distinguish between hesitation to ban a teratogen when its effects are not clear and the sluggishness in responding to protect children that results from ignorance, governmental inefficiency, or unrestrained profit motive.

Less difficult to defend are programs for eliminating infectious diseases and supplementing food for malnourished children. In industrialized nations, it is not so much a question of whether to provide additional sustenance when a child is not getting enough to eat. Most people are willing to feed hungry children. There is a problem, however, in knowing exactly what components of a diet are necessary for normal behavioral development. In most subpopulations of industrialized societies, children do get all they wish to eat, but may be missing protein, rare metals (e.g., zinc) or vitamins that are necessary for a balanced diet. The minimum daily requirements of the various components of diet for adequate behavioral development are not known. Here the essential solution is more research and distribution of knowledge so that adequate food supplementation programs can be perfected.

In other subpopulations of industrialized societies and widespread in undeveloped countries, food is scarce. In this case too, knowing what components of the diet are most important is necessary so that government planning for aid and for agriculture can be based on a policy motivated by adequate understanding of children's needs.

In addition to genetic counseling programs, mother and infant screening, and environmental management, there are educational programs that significantly reduce behavioral disorders. There is now little question that excellent early education programs carried out over a long period of time and reinforced by later schooling do reduce cumulative deficits and later adaptive problems. Questions have been raised about the cost of such programs and about their general effectiveness. When the programs are not managed properly, when they are brief and/or when there is no adequate follow-up, there should be little surprise that they have little beneficial effect. However, when the experiences of a deprived child are significantly enriched or when the child is removed from an abusing environment, it should also not be surprising that the effects are beneficial and important.

Although the effects on the child's behavior and later adaptation are well demonstrated, there are beneficial effects of the early intervention on the family. At the simplest level, the early education program provides time for the primary caregiver (usually the mother) to be free from her child. This is appropriate because handicapped children often have special health and disciplinary needs that require much more of parents than is generally expected. The free time provides them with time to work, shop, take care of the house, and to be part of the community. With chores accomplished, they can once more return to the child with energy.

The school provides a more direct support function as well. Often the parent participates in school and support group activities. There parents learn techniques for the special care of their child and also learns that they are not the only people with a handicapped child. These activities in the school (and often by school staff in the home) provide education to the family that supports them in their relationship with their child. Finally, the school can provide counseling for the parents about planning for the future of their child. Having a general idea of what to expect in their child's development and what medical, educational, and financial services will be available is often a critical determinant of the subsequent adaptation of handicapped children and their families. Much more is said about these experiential influences on behavioral development in subsequent chapters.

4

Identification and Diagnosis

An ecological view of the development of children emphasizes the relationship between characteristics of the child and the specific environment in which the child develops. A difficult child may do well with a sensitive and competent teacher. A mentally retarded adult who can succeed in an appropriate community setting may be unhappy and unproductive in another. A hearing-impaired youngster may succeed in one peer group but may be persecuted in another. Successful adaptation, in other words, is described in terms of the person's characteristics *and* the nature of the environment.

The central purpose of this chapter is to outline ways in which characteristics of children and environments are described. General concepts of normal and abnormal adaptation are reviewed, and typical steps in identification and referral of children with handicaps are described. Then, factors affecting identification are set forth, general principles of psychological measurement are reviewed, and the chapter closes with a section on types of description. Throughout, the chapter emphasizes that outcome depends on both individual and environmental characteristics.

ADAPTATION

Previously, we have seen how the concept of adaptation developed through evolutionary and educational theories in the 19th century. The idea that the behavioral development of animals and people is not fixed, but that they adapt to the world around them, became an important part of thinking in the Western world. The focus in the study of behavior began to shift from description of individuals to description of individuals living in specific environments. The dynamic relationship between people and the families and communities in which they lived increasingly became the reality that society has emphasized.

One perspective on adaptation saw it as one-sided. According to one simplistic view of the theory of natural selection, environments are stable and organisms who have the characteristics appropriate for living in that environment survive and reproduce, whereas animals and people who are not adaptive do not survive. Another one-sided concept of adaptation sees the environment as an active agent molding the person. For instance, the children become what an essentially static family made them.

These unidirectional concepts of adaptation see the environment as static, stable, and permanent. In the 20th century, environments came to be viewed as dynamic and molded by the individuals living in them. Families and communities not only help children to grow, but they respond to individual differences and react to changes in children as the children develop.

This more recent concept of the relationship between people and the environments in which they live has been termed *transactional* (Sameroff, 1982). The transactional view emphasizes that, throughout development, children not only are influenced by their environments, but they also powerfully affect them. A family with a severely retarded child changes its living style to incorporate the child into the family structure. Teachers respond to individual differences in their students and are themselves educated by the children with which they deal.

The transactional nature of adaptation also implies that what constitutes adaptation may change with particular times and places. Social scientists (e.g., Edgerton, 1975) emphasize that what is normal or abnormal is defined in terms of the values of each society. In Western industrial societies, development of the intellect; honesty; and both individualism and ability to conform are valued. As a result, these characteristics are emphasized in judging whether or not a child is adapting normally.

Although cultural variation in deviance is recognized, there are characteristics that are seen as abnormalities in all cultures. Severely deviant behaviors are recognized as unusual in any human culture (Kanner, 1949). Severe mental retardation, mental illness, and sensory and motor impairments are universally recognized as abnormalities in the sense that people with these severe disorders are seen as different from others in societies. Thus, recognition of severe handicaps is universal.

What differs is how the society responds to the disorders. Some societies do not distinguish between certain of the severe disorders. For instance, among the Semai of Malaya, retarded people are called deaf (Dentan, 1967). In Western societies, hearing-impaired people are sometimes mistakenly regarded as retarded.

Beyond their classification, even while severely handicapped people are identified as different, they may be treated in different ways. Deviant people may become shamans, they may be protected, they may be isolated from the general society, or they may even be killed (Edgerton, 1970).

People with handicaps also have effects on the society in which they live. They require major changes in the day-to-day life of their families (Blacher, 1984). Special education and rehabilitation have been transformed to include children with chronic handicapping conditions. Handicapped people and their advocates have produced changes in laws that allow them greater access to buildings, public transportation, health care, and jobs.

All of this shows that the relationship between handicapped children and their family and community is complex and dynamic. It is no wonder that classification systems vary; goals for education are in flux; and the status of handicapped people changes.

THE IDENTIFICATION PROCESS

Identifying children as different from others is the first step toward helping them live a reasonably normal, happy, and productive life. This help may involve changing the children so that they behave more like the norms of the culture, changing the environment so that it adapts appropriately to the child's handicaps, or most usually, changing both the child and the environment to make the transaction between them most adaptive. Identification involves *recognition, verification,* and *revision.*

Recognition

A disorder may be recognized first through informal or formal means. Informal methods include self-recognition of a problem. Or another person may perceive that something is wrong. People may note that they do not feel well and report the fact to a member of the family or a professional. Ordinarily, however, handicaps in children are noticed by a family member or a professional person.

Abnormal conditions can be detected prenatally through formal examinations such as chorionic villi screening, amniocentesis, and potentially, prenatal behavioral assessments like simple learning (Madison et al., 1986). However, behavioral abnormalities are usually detected after the child is born. Severe disabilities may be reflected in lethargy soon after birth or delayed development in infancy, but often may not be evident until much later, even school age.

More severe behavioral deviances are generally detected earlier than are milder conditions. Severe mental deficiency may be detected in the first 2 years during a routine pediatric neuromotor screening. Milder general cognitive and behavioral disorders may not become evident until the school years when the child begins to have difficulty learning school subjects and adapting to the discipline of the classroom.

Informal Recognition. Perhaps the most important people involved in informal recognition of handicapping conditions are members of the child's family, that is, the people who are in closest contact with the child (Masterson, 1985). An observant mother, especially one who has had previous experience with children, may be the first one to see how her child differs from others in ways that go beyond what would be expected from ordinary individual differences.

In addition, teachers and pediatricians are important in recognizing handicapping conditions. There is variation, however, in the rates of referral by these professionals based on their individual beliefs about the handicapping condition and about presumed effects on the child and the family (J. F. Goodman & Cecil, 1987).

Screening Tests. In addition to informal methods, there are formal procedures called screening tests that initially identify handicaps in children. There are screening tests for sensory disorders, motor development delay, neurological abnormalities, speech disorders, cognitive delay, various types of academic problems, and behavioral disorders. All of these screening procedures are intended only for a first look at the problem, not as a thorough diagnosis.

Screening procedures may reveal problems that were not apparent to the informal observer. Thus, hearing handicaps, muscle weakness, and early evidence of cognitive problems may all be discovered with formal screening procedures. But screening procedures are sometimes associated with false positives and false negatives. A false positive is a case in which the screening test suggests that a disorder is present when it really is not there. A false negative is an instance in which a real problem is not revealed by the test.

Ordinarily false positives and false negatives occur at unacceptably high rates with screening examinations (Sciarillo, M. M. Brown, Robinson, Bennett, & Sells, 1986). So, screening examinations are never intended to serve by themselves as the basis for decisions about the child's future. Instead, a screening test is intended as a supplement to informal observations to detect possible problems.

There has been much interest recently in the early identification of handicaps in children for the purpose of preventing them or reducing their effects. Some identification programs have focused on the school years, for instance to prevent suicide (Blumenthal & Kupfer, 1988). However, the largest amount of work has been concerned with the preschool period, mainly infancy. A notable recent feature of the work has been the use of multiple measures for prediction, sometimes with multivariate analyses (Kochanek, Kabacoff, & Lipsitt, 1987; Nicol, Stretch, Fundudis, I. Smith, & Davison, 1987). Single measures can differentiate groups of handicapped children (Meisels, Cross, & Plunkett, 1987), but use of a variety of biological, behavioral, and environmental measures seems better.

Verification

Both informal observations and screening procedures are appropriately followed by formal diagnostic procedures that attempt to verify the results of the screening. This more complex verification is accomplished under carefully controlled conditions by trained clinical diagnosticians. Diagnosis usually employs several levels of testing with well-standardized clinical procedures. These tests are interpreted by individuals who have had training and experience in the area of the diagnosis. Thus, a hearing screening may be conducted in a school room in a group-testing environment with a technician using primitive equipment, or a pediatrician may conduct an informal test of hearing in the office. However, once a hearing disorder is suspected, the child then is seen by an audiologist, who provides a detailed examination of the child's hearing by testing in a controlled environment. This detailed examination, not only tests the child in a controlled environment with several methods, but also includes a consideration of factors in the child's history and current situation that may be relevant to the etiology of the disorder and how it affects the child's functioning in everyday life.

The full diagnosis does not stop with a description of the child's problem. It also includes a detailed prescription for what should be done about it. This prescription may be a detailed treatment plan and may include a recommendation of where the treatment might best be carried out. Sometimes, the diagnosis suggests further tests, perhaps in other areas of functioning. A full diagnosis of a hearing loss thus would not only include an exact description of the loss. But it would also give an indication of the etiology, a specific prescription for treatment, and an indication of any other problems meriting examination by another clinician.

Often the areas covered by the diagnosis are broad. They certainly include an assessment of the health of the child. A thorough physical examination will either identify a cause that is producing the behavioral difficulty or exclude physiological factors as important. Subtle biochemical imbalance may have a profound effect on the child's learning in school. Medical examination can also turn up sensory or motor abnormalities such as unusual problems in coordination that may be signs of abnormalities that may be manifest later. Pediatric neurologists may then find abnormalities of the nervous system that can have pervasive effects on adaptation.

Psychological examination will emphasize detailed study of such things as sensorimotor functioning and perception, intellectual patterns, adjustment difficulties, and family behavior patterns. The sensorimotor tests include screening for sensory disorders that may then be followed up by vision and audition specialists. Screening for motor disorders that may influence later cognitive development is also done. Tests of perception and perceptual motor coordination emphasize close examination of initial information processing that can be important in both specific and more pervasive learning disabilities.

The psychologist may administer a standard intelligence test or more specialized tests of intellectual performance. The purpose of this testing is to identify general or specific cognitive problems that may underlie difficulties in academic achievement that a teacher has detected. If the child's problem seems to center on difficulty in social adaptation with peers, with the family, in school, or in the community, the psychologist may choose to interview the child and the parents and teachers, or perhaps observe the child in an appropriate context.

The social worker investigates the child's family adjustment and any potential difficulties in the school or community. The social worker also assesses the personal and financial resources that the family has available for dealing with their problem.

At the same time, teachers, parents, and specialized clinicians contribute to the analysis of the situation, providing the expertise they are most capable of giving. In the end, the group of clinicians communicate with one another and ultimately develop a short-term plan of treatment.

Ordinarily the full diagnostic examination is carried out by more than one professional. A team consisting of a number of professionals see the child individually and then discuss the case and plan treatment together. This is believed to be more efficient than one professional working alone. Indeed, federal law in the United States (PL 94-142) requires that educational planning for handicapped children is accomplished by teams that include a parent and a range of professional staff.

Revision

Diagnosis is always subject to revision. As the child matures, as the environment changes, or as treatment proceeds, regular reassessments will keep track of progress. Reassessment is an essential feature of treatment.

The full identification process therefore involves initial recognition of a problem through informal or formal screening procedures. This initial identification is appropriately verified by an elaborate diagnostic procedure that leads to a treatment plan. Then, as treatment is carried on, the child is reassessed regularly in order to track the changing character of the problem.

FACTORS AFFECTING IDENTIFICATION

There are several factors that determine if and when a condition is identified. The severity of the condition is an important factor. Definitions of the disorder and cultural and context factors must also be considered. In addition, the familiarity of the observer or tester, bias, and the well-known "labeling" effect, situational factors, and certain special problems in evaluating performance of children with handicaps come into play. All of these factors determine whether a condition is recognized in the first place and then whether it is verified and what kind of treatment is recommended.

Severity

Severity of a disorder refers to the extent that characteristics of an individual interfere with adaptation (Furlong & Yanagida, 1985; Weller, Strawser, & Buchanan, 1985). Individual disabilities vary in severity or a child may be afflicted with more than one disability. In either case, adaptation is more difficult. To the extent that disabilities interfere with adaptation, they become evident earlier in the child's life. Biological signs are detected earlier than behavioral symptoms, and more severe disorders are detectable in the first months or years of life (Lock, Shapiro, A. Ross, & Capute, 1986).

Severity also determines the nature of treatment. There are, of course, differences in treatment of different types of disability. Sensory disorders are dealt with differently from cerebral palsy or from emotional disorders. However, to the extent that each of these disabilities is severe, it becomes associated with other problems, and treatment becomes more uniform. A person with a profound visual impairment sometimes ends up in a supervised work situation similar to the supervised workshop for moderately retarded or psychotic people. Sheltered workshops for blind and for mentally retarded people may be run by different agencies, and they may be organized differently, but they are sheltered workshops rather than competitive employment.

Cultural and Situational Factors

Although the characteristics of the child with handicaps are important determinants of identification, the social environment also influences the time and the outcome of identification. Cultural differences, including various forms of bias and situational factors, may be factors of the environment that can influence the identification process. Social stereotypes are part of everyday life. When people are confronted with subcultural groups different from their own, but when they do not have experience with them, they still attribute specific characteristics to them. These attributions are often only partially correct, and they sometimes may be inaccurate (Caruso & Hodapp, 1988).

Stereotypes of people with handicaps generally are negative (Horsley & FitzGibbon, 1987; Lane, 1988). The idea that negative stereotypes or labels are harmful to children with handicaps is widely accepted. However, the labeling effect is not as strong as generally believed (Graham & Leone, 1987; Stanley & Comer, 1988; Yeates & Weisz, 1985). Thus, whereas stereotypes of children with handicaps may be inaccurate and negative, they are not necessarily detrimental.

Cultural Variables. The nature of handicapping conditions can vary according to cultural variables that challenge children in different ways (L. B. Leonard, Sabbadini, J. S. Leonard, & Volterra, 1987). However, cultural factors include national and subcultural differences in the way a handicap is viewed and how it is assessed and treated. For instance, for some time, it was believed that hyperactivity did not exist in Europe or in China (O'Leary, Vivian, & Cornoldi, 1984). It is now acknowledged that this disorder does exist universally. However, professionals in different countries take different approaches to its assessment and treatment. In one study of responses to a case description (O'Leary et al., 1984), Americans endorsed an organic view of hyperactivity and recommended many assessment methods and a variety of treatment procedures. Italians emphasized environmental and labeling concepts more emphatically. They were as likely to recommend psychodynamic therapy as were Americans but used other treatment methods less.

Cultural differences within a country are also important. Native Americans have different standards of what is normative behavior than the Anglo majority culture around them. This can result in Native Americans being seen as abnormal when they actually are not, or the person making the identification may fail to detect an abnormality when it is actually there (G. A. Harris, 1985).

These are only some examples of many types of cultural bias that may exist in the identification process (K. Kavale & Andreassen, 1984; Lambert & Hartsough, 1984; G. M. Morrison, MacMillan, & K. Kavale, 1985; Scruggs, Mastropieri, Tolfa, & Jenkins, 1985). When identification is done by using the standards and assessment procedures for the majority subculture, both false positives and false negatives for minority cultures are the consequence. Most evidence indicates that, proportional to their numbers in the population, Hispanic children were overenrolled in classes for mentally retarded children as recently as 15 years ago. Since that time, assessment has increasingly included Hispanic professionals and a variety of testing procedures that consider cultural and linguistic variation. As a result, at this time, Hispanic children are no longer overrepresented in classes for mentally retarded children. However, there are still more Hispanic children than one would expect in classes for children with learning disabilities (Mick, 1984–1985).

Cultural factors are also evident from misconceptions that people have of children with handicaps. Knowing that a child has one type of handicap can bias a person's judgment about the child's other behavioral characteristics. For instance, teacher expectations of a child's test scores depend, not only on the objective performance of the child, but also on knowledge that the child has a hearing-impairment. Children with severe hearing impairments are expected to do less well, despite evidence that they may fare well in a testing situation (Wolk, 1985). People are thought less likely to suffer from psychopathology if they are labeled mentally retarded or deaf than if they are not (Alford & Locke, 1984; L. Goldsmith & Schloss, 1986; Reiss, Levitan, & McNally, 1982). This "overshadowing effect" (Reiss & Syzszko, 1982) means that the stereotypes, whether about cultural characteristics, race, or handicapping condition, can influence identification, independent of the child's actual performance.

Situational Factors. In addition to cultural factors, characteristics of the situation can also influence the outcome of the identification process. General factors, such as stress in the family and availability of services, influence identification. Even specific situational factors, like the presence of toys in a testing room and item format of a test, may influence test scores (J. Benson & Ellison-Bidwell, 1984; T. Field, 1981).

The nature of the relationship with the specific child being evaluated is also important. A child who is familiar to the examiner may receive a different score than a child who is new. It is not clear whether familiarity increases scores or depresses them, but it is clear that familiarity is related to other variables such as the experience of the examiner or whether the child is handicapped (L. S. Fuchs & D. Fuchs, 1984; D. Fuchs, L. S. Fuchs, Power, & Dailey, 1985).

Thus, it is clear that there are many determinants of identification processes (Hoffman-Plotkin & Twentyman, 1984; Horn & Packard, 1985). Recognition, verification, and revision of the picture of individual children are the result of a dynamic mutual influence of the child and the community in which they live.

PRINCIPLES OF PSYCHOLOGICAL ASSESSMENT

The psychologist aids the family in determining whether the child needs special services. Psychologists may also provide some of those services, but in their role as diagnostician, they draw on a large range of methods for describing behavior. This section first discusses general considerations in testing or observing behavior. Reliability and validity concepts are reviewed. The distinction is drawn between norm- and criterion-referenced assessment, and the importance of individuation and use of multiple assessment approaches is emphasized.

Then, examples of specific types of procedures are demonstrated. Qualitative description; interviews; checklists; formal observation; rating scales; standardized tests; controlled laboratory procedures; and descriptions of the environment are discussed.

In reviewing these procedures, the reader should keep three things in mind. First, the purpose of assessment is to obtain a valid picture of the child's life situation. Insofar as possible, a clear and valid picture of the child, the family, and the community is one aim of the formal assessment process. Test scores provide part of this picture, and unbiased description is essential.

Moreover, although psychologists are experts at testing, and well-developed tests and other assessment procedures are necessary for a valid picture, it is the integration of the total picture of the child that is the essential character of a diagnosis.

Finally, a description of the child and the situation is useful only if it is part of a significant plan for treatment. Classification and general referral are sterile activities by themselves. Helping the child and the family improve their lives are the main purpose of a thorough description of the child (Keogh & Daley, 1983).

Reliability and Validity

Reliability and validity were considered in chapter 2. Here it is sufficient to say that assessment procedures with high reliability and validity contribute to fewer false positives and negatives. In order for a procedure to be valid, that is, to measure what it is intended to measure, it must first be reliable. It must give approximately the same results each time it is administered.

Assessment procedures vary widely in reliability. Well-standardized tests of intelligence that are administered in an appropriate manner tend to give essentially the same score if given again within a short time. Of course, the scores may vary by a few points. This means that there is error in even the best tests. IQ tests typically have reliability quotients of around .85. On the other hand, checklists of behavioral disorders may have significantly lower reliabilities for infrequently occurring and poorly defined items. When reliabilities are low there is no chance that they can measure anything consistently. That is, their validity must be low. In other words, if a psychological measure cannot measure something consistently, it cannot measure anything useful for diagnostic purposes. And if validity is low, there will be a high incidence of false positives and false negatives. Thus, procedures with low reliability produce errors in identification.

There has been substantial interest lately in the reliability of information from different sources. Parents and teachers, parents and children, and mothers and fathers have all been compared. Overall, reliability between different sources is moderately high, mothers are more sensitive to their children's problems than are fathers or the children themselves, and reliability differs for different measures (E. Clark, 1987; Edelbrock, Costello, Dulcan, Conover, & Kala, 1986; Kolko & Kazdin, 1988; L. A. Rosenberg, J. C. Harris, & Reifler, 1988; Soyster & Ehly, 1987).

Whereas low reliability means low validity, high reliability does not guarantee high validity. Sometimes it is possible to measure behavior consistently, but the measure does not mean much in relation to the child's future functioning. It may be possible to obtain reliable estimates of general developmental rate from testing of infant motor development in normal children. However, infant developmental rate measured with these motor developmental tests do not predict school success or even school-age IQ very well, unless extreme scores are taken into account. Thus, although baby tests of motor development can be reliable, they are not valid for predicting later development. On the other hand, when other measures are used or when developmentally disabled children are studied, baby tests can be more predictive (Aylward, Gustafson, Verhulst, & Colliver, 1987; Fewell, 1984; Maisto & German, 1986; Rose & Wallace, 1985).

Norm- and Criterion-Referenced Testing

There are two general approaches to assessment: norm- and criterion-referenced evaluation. These two approaches are only differences in emphasis, rather than clear alternatives. However, they do represent two rather different orientations and are therefore worth discussing separately.

Norm-Referenced Testing. Norm-referenced testing refers to those procedures in which a child's scores on formal tests are compared with scores of other children. The most common norm-referenced tests are school achievement tests, intelligence tests, and behavior checklists. In achievement and intelligence tests, a child answers several questions already answered by other children. Then the child's score is compared with the distribution of scores of these other children. Children who score poorly relative to others are judged to have a significant problem.

There are two major dimensions on which children are compared in norm-referenced tests. The first is degree of deviance. On behavior problem checklists, children who are seen by parents, teachers, and others to have significantly more disturbing behaviors than other children are considered to have a degree of deviance requiring treatment.

A second major dimension that norm-referenced procedures evaluate is status in development. Children who score poorly on neuromotor (Farber, Shapiro, Palmer, & Capute, 1985) or cognitive tests relative to other children of the same age are considered to be significantly delayed in development. Developmental delay is an important concept in the description of mental retardation, learning disabilities, and emotional immaturity.

Sometimes it is not possible to compare a child with other children of the same age because their handicaps are so unique or because there has been no standardization of a test with a comparable group (D. Fuchs, L. S. Fuchs, Benowitz, & Barringer, 1987; However, also see Bennett, Rock, & Jirele, 1987; Curry, D. R. Anderson, Zitlin, & Guise, 1987). Some autistic children do not cooperate fully in standardized tests of intelligence (Shah & N. Holmes, 1985); children with cerebral palsy cannot manage the items that require motor skills; IQ tests are not very sensitive at the lower extremes (Whiteley & Krenn, 1986). In such cases, the validity of the assessment is always in question.

However, because some information is often better than none, an effort is made to get scores on less well-standardized tests, sometimes with modifications of scoring (Centra, 1986) and from tests appropriate with other similar groups of children. Profoundly retarded older children are sometimes tested with procedures developed for testing normal babies. The assumption in doing this is that the profoundly retarded person functions at the mental level of an infant (Whitely & Krenn, 1986). These stop-gap measures are never entirely satisfactory, and the results must be interpreted with a great deal of care by experienced clinicians.

Criterion-Referenced Testing. The alternative to norm-referenced diagnosis is criterion-referenced evaluation. With this approach comparison with other children is not a necessary feature and evaluation is closely tied to treatment of specific problems. There is general agreement that four features distinguish the criterion-referenced approach (Powers, 1985; Strain, Sainto, & Maheady, 1984). The first is a detailed specification of the problems that need treatment (such as body-rocking; poor use of fork and knife; high activity during academic subjects; low scores in particular school subjects). This emphasis on specific behaviors contrasts with approaches that involve description of general problems that interfere in general with adaptation (Marston, Mirkin, & Deno, 1984).

The second characteristic of criterion-referenced procedures is an exploration of the characteristics of the environment or of the child that can affect the important "target" behavior. Characteristics of the environment might include such things as the noise level that can affect the amount of body-rocking or activity level; the number and type of other people in the environment that affect the proper use of table utensils; or the reinforcing conditions that increase or decrease the behaviors. Characteristics of the child might be such organismic variables as hunger level; amount and nature of drugs taken; or even the presence of another handicap.

Once the target behaviors have been identified and a good idea has been obtained of the things that affect it, the diagnostician is ready to go on to plan a treatment program. This is the third aspect of the criterion-referenced examination. The treatment program is a specific statement of the goals of treatment and the procedure that will be followed to reach that goal.

Finally, the criterion-referenced approach evaluates the efficacy of the planned treatment in terms of amount of positive, or even negative, change in the target behavior. Thus, if a specific reinforcement schedule in low-noise conditions is prescribed for reducing body-rocking, the diagnostician will wish to know whether body-rocking is reduced or even whether it might be inadvertently increased.

This emphasis on treatment and evaluation of treatment as part of the diagnostic process emphasizes that diagnosis is a continuing process that does more than place children in a general classification and refer them to an appropriate program. It follows them along, prescribing and assessing change as an essential part of the process.

In practice, combinations of the norm-referenced and the criterion-referenced approaches are often used. A family or teacher identifies a problem because of a specific behavior or behaviors that are causing a problem. A diagnostician identifies the general nature of the child's adaptive problem by applying norm-referenced tests, classifying the child as a member of a general group (such as Conduct Disordered), and then referring that child to an appropriate program for that group. Then, the family and the professionals in the program focus on the specific problems to be treated, and in so doing, employ criterion-referenced procedures.

Planning by a Team for the Individual Child

All of this emphasizes that planning for the child's treatment requires cooperation by the family and at least one professional person (Bagnato, 1984). It also means that a plan is unique for any individual at any particular time. The plan involves a clear description of the child's current abilities and skills and also a detailed and explicit educational or treatment plan on which day-to-day medical, psychological, and educational services are based.

Most of us have experienced consultation with a single professional person such as a physician or a psychological counselor. Planning for the child with handicaps is quite a different process. In the first place, parents are intimately involved in the actual decisions about their child's education and treatment. This is regarded as important, not only because it is their basic right and because parents generally know their children better than any other person does, but also because it is recognized that success of education and medical care depends heavily on whether parents understand and support the procedures.

Second, many children with handicaps have multiple handicaps or a single handicap may have multiple aspects. Thus, more than one professional person is generally involved in the assessment of children and planning for their treatment. Ordinarily, a psychologist, social worker, teacher, and physician and/or nurse participate along with a member of the family. In addition, when a specialized disorder such as a sensory problem, a speech difficulty, or motor disability is part of the picture, the appropriate professional person also participates.

Each professional person examines the child, and then the team meets to establish a plan. At the meeting, each professional person and the family member describes the child, and they then suggest appropriate short-term goals and procedures for education and treatment. The plan guides treatment for the ensuing year, and the team meets once a year to evaluate the child's progress and modify the plan, as necessary.

TYPES OF DESCRIPTION

When a psychologist encounters a new child, the psychologist must make several sequential decisions regarding the most appropriate ways of description. There are no firm rules about how to go about making these decisions, but it probably is a good idea first to interview the parent, teacher, or other person who knows the child best to obtain a picture of the child's current strengths and problems and to get a history of factors that may be relevant to the child's current difficulties. Then, if the child seems to have special difficulties with learning or thinking, tests of cognitive performance such as developmental tests, intelligence tests, or specific tests of cognitive performance may be administered. At the same time, if social difficulties seem to be part of the picture, perhaps one of the many behavior problem checklists, rating scales, or direct observation procedures may be used. The purpose of these testing procedures is to validate some of the statements made by the person who knows the child best and to turn up other aspects of the case that this person has not had the opportunity to observe.

Deciding which assessment procedure to use is obviously a complex procedure. This is partly because the number of assessment "instruments" is vast. There are hundreds—perhaps thousands—of tests, rating scales, checklists, and other procedures available. In this section, the various types of interviewing, rating, and testing procedures are described first. Then, standardized testing, laboratory examination, and description of environments are covered.

Interviewing

The central purpose of interviewing is to collect basic information from the people who know the child best. This information includes, not only the problems the child is having, but also a description of the situations in which the problems are most prevalent. In addition to a description of the current problem, information about the child's history is also sought. Medical and social information, and special experiences that might have influenced the current problems are of interest.

The people who know the child most closely are those who make the best informants. Ordinarily, these are the parents, the teachers, peers, and the child (Bierman & McCauley, 1987). Relatives, neighbors, and friends sometimes are helpful informants.

No one is a perfect informant. Even parents sometimes remember events incorrectly. They may emphasize some problems beyond their actual importance, and they may not realize the significance of other events. Children, especially when they are young, may not understand the interviewer's questions and may distort the meaning of events.

One partial solution to these problems is to structure the interview rather than leave it open-ended. That is, the clinician asks the informant a set of preestablished questions relevant to the child rather than simply asking the informant to talk about the child. The structured interview focuses the questions in such a way that appropriate information is most ready elicited. Several forms of structured and semistructured interview formats are available (Eyberg, 1985). One of them is role playing, in which informants are asked how they would respond to specific situations that the interviewer presents (J. N. Hughes & D. M. Hall, 1985).

Furthermore, the interviewer's questions themselves can structure the information. In other words, either in a structured interview or when the informant is not responsive, attempts by the interviewer to elicit answers might produce a pattern of responses that do not so much reflect the informant's views of the situation as the interviewer's preconceived ideas about the situation (D. Hughes & May, 1985).

Nevertheless, interviewing is an essential aspect of diagnosis. It produces mainly qualitative information that must be interpreted informally by the clinician. This means that it provides data that are often not very reliable or valid. On the other hand, the information is obtained from people who know the child best. Therefore, the interviews with parents, teachers, children, and others who know the child well provide information that could not be obtained in another way.

Checklists and Rating Scales

More quantitative information can be obtained from checklists or rating scales (the terms are often used interchangeably). There are hundreds of these scales available (Boyle & S. C. Jones, 1985; Eyberg, 1985; R. J. Thompson, 1985). A person who knows the child well is asked to respond to a list of characteristics by indicating which, and perhaps how much, of the characteristics the child shows. Then, the information may be used directly by indicating which problem, and perhaps how much of it, a child shows. Or the various problems may form patterns that can be revealed through statistical analysis. Cut-off points can aid clinical decision making, and the scales may be used in comparing a child with other children.

Rating scales have the advantage that they provide structured interviewing, with a statement of the degree of various problems. Rating scales are usually used to describe adjustment problems that are within the normal range or that may be regarded as abnormal if they occur too often or in inappropriate situations. Examples of such behaviors are hyperactivity (Edelbrock & Rancurello, 1985), aggression, and somatic complaints (Eyberg, 1985). Rating scales are not usually used for the detailed measurement of school achievement or cognitive disorders.

Rating scales tend to have moderately high reliability. Different instruments that are intended to measure roughly the same thing tend to agree moderately with one another (Edelbrock & Rancurello, 1985), and some of the same factors seem to describe the behavior of different clinical groups (Eason, Finch, Brasted, & Saylor, 1985; Schnittjer & Hirshoren, 1984). On the other hand, children can receive different ratings by different people and in different situations (Soyster & Ehly, 1986; Zentall, 1984). Overall, then, rating scales constitute an improvement over the qualitative approach of the interview method, but checklists and ratings must be seen as only one of many approaches to diagnosis.

Behavioral Observations

Interviews and rating scales have the advantage that they summarize behavior patterns that occur infrequently or have occurred over a long period of time. However, the quality of the data summarized in interviews depends on the (sometimes questionable) accuracy of the informant. A more direct approach is to observe the behavior and situational events as they are occurring. Direct observation, when done in an unbiased manner, can produce a picture of what the nature of the difficulties are, when they occur, and how frequent a problem they may be.

There are several approaches to clinical behavioral observation (Eyberg, 1985). Children may observe themselves and record the nature and frequency of events that trouble them. Children who are fearful of animals may systematically record instances of encounters with animals in everyday life, describe the situation, the type of animal, and the degree of fear. Then, the clinician and the child may review the child's data to determine the nature of the situations that evoke fear. Parents or teachers may systematically record the behavior that is of concern, again with a view to determining how much and in what situations the problem is occurring.

Direct observations are oriented to determining the frequency of problems in various situations in the everyday life of the child. It is also possible to obtain observations in a standard setting, with the observations done in a standard manner. Standardized observations may be done at home, in schools, or at the clinician's office in a small room that has things to play with or even in the waiting room of the office (Bush & Cockrell, 1987; Drotar & Crawford, 1987; Gresham, Reschly, & Carey, 1987). The child or the child and a parent are observed unobtrusively using a standard checklist of the types of behavior that are of interest. What emerges is a picture of the child's behavior or of the relationship between the child and its parent. Remarkably, even 15 minutes of observation in such standard situations can provide meaningful information about the child or the relationship with parents. Hyperactivity can be assessed (M. A. Roberts, Ray, & R. J. Roberts, 1984); differences of patterns of deviance in the presence of the mother and the father; and complex interaction of conduct disordered males and females all have been revealed with brief observations.

Thus, direct observation of behavior in naturally occurring or standard situations is a valuable source of information about the child. There are, however, some problems with the direct observation procedures. In the first place, they require a significant amount of time in regular and careful observation to produce meaningful information. Second, if the observer is not adequately trained or is careless in performing the observations, the information may be faulty. Third, the choice of what to observe is important. If an important situation is neglected or more emphasis is given to one behavior and a more important one is neglected, the observations may produce distorted information. Nevertheless, the direct observation of behavior has proved to be a useful source of information that, in combination with the various interview and rating procedures, provides most of the preliminary information about the child's history and current situation.

Standardized Tests

All of the diagnostic procedures discussed up to this point are useful, but their reliability and validity are, at best, moderate. More carefully designed and extensively validated are standardized tests. These standardized tests include measurement of motor development, various aspects of cognitive functioning, achievement in school subjects, and adaptive behavior.

There are two main properties of a standardized test. First, it is given in essentially the same way to all children who take it. Thus, group tests of school achievement involve asking the same questions in the same way to all children who take the tests, usually in a paper-and-pencil format. In individual intelligence tests, an examiner asks questions and presents verbal and nonverbal problems to an individual person and does so in essentially the same way to all people who are examined.

Second, the score that the person achieves on each component of the test can be compared with the scores of other people on the same component (i.e., it is norm-referenced). These other people are members of the standardization sample, a group carefully selected to represent a cross-section of the population. Thus, scores of an 8 year old on an intelligence test are compared with scores from the same test achieved by a large number of other 8 year olds.

In order for a standardized test to be valid, both of these properties must be present. The test must be given in a standard manner, and the standardization sample must be representative of the population. If either of these conditions is not fulfilled, the results probably will not be useful for treatment planning and may even be harmful to the person.

The widespread popular view that intelligence tests are not valid turns partly on the idea that, with some groups of children, intelligence tests are not given in a standardized manner. In fact, this can be true in some cases. If the child is an immigrant; comes from a minority ethnic group that has not had experiences required by the major tests; and/or suffers from a sensory or motor disability that prevents interacting with the test material, it may not be possible to test the child in a standardized manner.

On the other hand, some immigrants do very well on tests of intelligence; not all members of ethnic minorities are handicapped by their membership in their minority culture, and sensory and motor disabilities affect performance on some subtests more than others. It is therefore possible to use intelligence tests for treatment planning in certain cases if the test is given from the perspective of improving the child's opportunities for education. Unfortunately, standardized tests are often given in a mechanical way that results in the exclusion of children from the program that would be best for them. Under those circumstances, the tests may become instruments of ignorance and prejudice rather than aids to planning.

The solution is not to eliminate the standardized tests. Improving the methods of administering the test, changing scoring methods, broadening the standardization sample, clarifying what is the appropriate standardization sample, and perhaps changing some of the people who administer and interpret the test are all aspects of a more positive solution.

Laboratory Examinations

The previously covered methods of describing the child are all relatively crude. Even well-standardized tests use items that are chosen for their stability across situations and the ability to describe the person in a general way. The laboratory methods emphasize refined measurement, a quantitative approach, and analysis of response change as a function of change in the stimulus situation.

Most of the laboratory tests use traditional psychophysical methods. In tests of sensation, perception, or learning, these are several procedures for determining threshold levels for different stimuli. In tests of hearing, the interest is in finding out the intensity of a sound that the person can just hear, and this threshold is determined for different frequencies of sound. The result is a profile of thresholds for different sound frequencies.

Threshold determination is done with one of several psychophysical methods. The examiner or the child may vary the stimulus gradually from a point below which it can be heard until the child indicates that the sound can be heard or from above the threshold of hearing until the sound can no longer be hear (Lancioni, Coninx, & Smeets, 1989). With another method, the stimulus is not changed gradually. Instead, brief sounds or visual stimuli are presented above and below threshold at different intensities randomly, and children are asked to indicate whether they have heard the sound. The threshold is then said to be that intensity that divides the perceived from the unperceived stimuli. It is also possible to use similar methods to determine whether two stimuli are perceived as different from each other. All of these methods have even been used with children who cannot respond verbally (e.g., Hertz, 1987; Fagan, 1984).

More recently it has been recognized that thresholds can vary because there is a background level of stimulation that varies with different environments. This is true, so it is important to evaluate the background level of stimulation as well as the stimulus or signal, in the assessment of this signal detection.

Describing Environments

Environments are generally described informally. Planning for treatment may indicate that a child needs foster care or should be placed in a group home. A referral statement may indicate that the child performs poorly in a group classroom situation. These statements about the environment do provide information, but the information tends to be very general. Partly this is because our classification of environments has not been developed very clearly.

There are, however, a number of exceptions. There are anthropological studies that describe physical and social environments in great detail (Edgerton, 1975). There are theoretical statements that seek to guide the development of research into the description of environments and how they change throughout the life span (Bronfenbrenner, 1977). There also are explicit attempts to describe environments in standardized ways (Moos, 1974). There are pioneering studies that have assessed household resources and match person to environment characteristics (Dunst & Leet, 1987; Silverstein, Olvera, & Schalock, 1987). However, these attempts are only preliminary at this time. The scientific description of environments remains a task for the future.

SUMMARY

Children's handicaps are defined by the characteristics of the children, but also by the characteristics of the environments that the children live in. It is the relationship between children and their environments that define handicaps. Thus, assessments involve descriptions of the ways in which children and their environments adapt to one another.

Handicaps are recognized informally by people who know the child well or more formally as a result of screening examinations. Recognition is only the first of several steps in describing the child and in providing educational, medical, and social services. The relatively casual process of first recognition is followed by verification of a diagnosis. This verification is formal, and it is done by a team of professionals together with a member of the family. This team often includes a psychologist, a medical professional, and a social worker. It also includes other professionals, as appropriate to the child's clinical picture.

When and how a disability is recognized is determined by several factors. Perhaps the most important of these is the severity of the problem. More severe problems are more obvious and become manifest earlier. Thus, there is a clear relationship between the severity of the child's difficulties and the time it is discovered. Other factors influencing the time of diagnosis and the nature of the diagnosis are cultural and context effects, the definitions of disorders that people use, various forms of bias and labeling effects, and the nature of the diagnostic procedures used. Of special importance in this regard is the fact that some forms of disability are not easily amenable to standard descriptions.

Several standards are used to evaluate whether or not a diagnostic procedure is adequate. The most important are the reliability and validity of the procedures being used. These affect the rates of false positives and negatives. In addition, one wishes to know whether the child is being evaluated on norm- or criterion-referenced standards. Either approach may be appropriate, depending on the general purpose of the diagnosis. And combinations are common. It is also important to determine whether the child is seen by only one professional who provides a limited view of the case, or whether a number of people study the child and together provide as individual a picture of the child as possible.

During the verification of the diagnosis, a great many procedures may be used. These range from informal procedures providing qualitative information to highly controlled laboratory tests that result in quantitative information. These procedures and tests include open-ended and structured interviews; role playing; checklists and rating scales; formal observations of the child's behavior in appropriate contexts; standardized tests of academic, intellectual, and adaptive behavior; and laboratory tests of physiological, sensory, perceptual, motor, and cognitive functioning. All of these classes of procedures are important, though some are emphasized more than others, depending on the child.

Finally, recognition and verification have no meaning unless the information gained is employed for something useful. Ordinarily, a treatment plan emerges from the meetings of the family and professionals. We deal with this planning more fully in later chapters on treatment. However, at this point, it may be said that these plans ordinarily are short-term plans. That is, the team generates a plan intended to guide services for a few months to a year. Then, after that time, the team reviews the situation again on the assumption that the diagnostic picture has changed as a result of treatment and the child's maturation. In other words, the diagnostic treatment process is dynamic, with verification and reverification and planning proceeding with changes in the children and their environment.

II

Individual Psychology

5

Sensorimotor Processes

We have now reached the end of the first part of this book. Up to this point, we have discussed history, causes, classification, and diagnosis in a general way. The overall point has been that, through a democratic ideology and scientific study, our understanding of disorders of development has become more refined, and treatment programs have become more active and increasingly informed by the facts.

We now turn to a more detailed consideration of the nature of handicapping conditions by a review of various individual and social processes. In five chapters, current concepts about sensorimotor processes; attention, learning, and memory; thinking, play, and communication; motivation, personality, and psychopathology; and social relationships are reviewed. In all of these chapters, emphasis is placed on normal, as well as abnormal, development, and examples from the various types of handicap discussed in chapter 2 are used to show that all people share the same basic processes.

In this chapter, we deal with sensation and perception, brain organization, and motor organization. There is always a danger in oversimplifying basic sensorimotor processes. The idea that sensations are converted to responses in a linear series of steps is, perhaps, a convenient way of thinking about these processes. However, the situation is actually much more complex. Many processes can occur simultaneously. Sensations are part of an ongoing transaction between the children and the environment around them. Some sensory input affects the child's behavior, whereas most does not. Readiness states, motivation, and learning history are only a few of the determinants of which sensations do and do not affect the child.

The same sensations can have effects that vary from time to time and from individual to individual. What the person is like at the moment is critical in determining the effectiveness of stimulus events. The same general principle can be applied to the way that the brain processes information and motor systems are organized. They are all part of an integrated and dynamic system whose parts cannot be separated from each other and whose action in time has no beginning or end. Despite the fact that basic sensorimotor processes are integrated and dynamic, it is convenient to separate them for expository purposes.

SENSATION AND PERCEPTION

The relationship between difficulties in perception and abnormalities in more complex behaviors has been mentioned before in this book and is widely recognized among professionals. A problem in receiving information must affect children because, as we have shown, development does depend significantly on experience.

Even subtle perceptual deficits have important effects. Richards (1985), for instance, noted that visual-motor problems are very prevalent in the classroom and teachers who ignore them may be wasting their time attempting to teach many children if they do not take those difficulties into account. Tonge, Lipton, and Crawford (1984) stated that strabismus, a condition in which the eyes cross or deviate from each other, is associated with psychiatric disorder, mental retardation, educational difficulties, and even emotional problems in the family. Strabismus affects more than 5% of children who are 5 to 6 years old, so this condition needs early treatment.

In general then, the importance of sensory and perceptual disorders is recognized, and early diagnosis and treatment are important. Procedures are well-established for determining whether a child has a problem in sensory or perceptual function (Cattey, 1985; Dreschler, 1988; L. K. Miller, 1987). In using these methods, decisions must be made about what aspects of sensory function should be tested (Wharry & Kirkpatrick, 1986). Is it most appropriate, for instance, to test hearing with presentation of pure tones in a controlled setting or speech stimuli in relatively natural conditions (Salomon & Parving, 1985)?

Moreover, the role of attentional and motivational factors cannot be ignored (Zentall & Kruczek, 1988). We deal with attention and motivation in more detail in later chapters. However, for now, it should be clear that the results of sensory and perceptual tests depend on factors other than the person's input functions. As a result, sometimes children appear to have a perceptual disorder when they do not. With some, testing is difficult or impossible (Lennerstrand, Axelsson, & Andersson, 1983), and children differ with respect to their use of cues in visual stimulation (Millar, 1986).

Problems in testing sometimes preclude easy conclusions about sensory abilities. Almost everyone reading this chapter has experienced a screening test in school. Such screening tests are ordinarily superficial examinations that are adequate for their purpose of alerting parents and teachers to the existence of sensory disorders. However, some children and adults have very subtle but important perceptual deficits that are revealed only with extensive and repeated examination over a long period of time.

Intensive testing is necessary only in rare cases, but in those cases they are important, and they reveal the subtlety of sensory and perceptual functioning. Children with reading disabilities may show a difficulty in processing brief tones and visual stimuli (Reed, 1989; Slaghuis & Lovegrove, 1986). An even more dramatic example comes from a paper by Campion and Latto (1985). They reported on a case of a person who had a visual agnosia (a deficit in perception without any concomitant sensory impairment) resulting from carbon monoxide poisoning. The agnosia was manifested by the inability to recognize simple shapes or to perceive the orientation of lines or grating patterns. At first sight, his sensory systems appeared intact. He could negotiate obstacles in a room, reach out and grasp objects, and could comment on the color and texture of things. However, with special testing over a long period of time, it was revealed that, not only did the person have difficulties in color and brightness discrimination, but brain responses to relatively simple stimuli were also abnormal.

Some Dimensions of Sensory and Perceptual Disorders

Thus, a picture of the complexity of sensory and perceptual processes was revealed in this case. In what follows, some of the dimensions of sensory and perceptual handicaps are described. These processes can be affected in children of many clinical categories. That is, a specific perceptual handicap is not necessarily attributable to any one of the clinical categories, although categories may differ from one another in general (Dahle & McCollister, 1986; D. E. Smith, S. D. Miller, Stewart, Walter, & McConnell, 1988; L. L. Elliott, Hammer, & Scholl, 1989).

Children do not respond to all of the stimuli around them. All people respond to only a few things at a time. Their attention limits the scope of the stimuli that affect them. We deal with attentional mechanisms in more detail in the next chapter. However, for now, it is important to note that the range of stimuli to which some handicapped children respond is different. For some, it is increased (Millar, 1986), for others it is limited. Some hearing-

impaired, autistic, learning-disabled, or young normal children are overselective. They respond to only a severely limited set of stimuli (Fairbank,
Powers, & Monaghan, 1986). W. K. Bickel, Stella, and Etzel (1984) pointed out
that overselectivity is not an all or none thing. Children are not either
overselective or not. As with most other behavioral factors, we are talking
about a quantitative dimension rather than a condition that does or does not
exist.

Simple Stimuli.   The most conventional conception of the stimulus is a
simple one. We talk about pure tones, color discrimination, and touch
intensity thresholds. All of these simple stimuli have an important role in the
estimation of sensory abilities of children with handicaps. As indicated
earlier, suspected deficits in simple sensory losses can be assessed and
corrected.

However, in the real world, stimuli are rarely simple. Sensory events
occur against a background of other sensations. Perception of sounds may
be obscured by noises that are occurring at the same time. The ability to
distinguish a sound from background noises or a visual pattern from other
markings around the pattern is an important feature of perception with
which some children with handicaps have difficulties. The importance of the
background to the perception of a stimulus or signal has been recognized,
and the relationship of stimulus to background is evaluated with procedures
called signal detection. Hypoxic and hyperactive groups of children have
shown deficits in signal detection as compared with nonhandicapped groups
of children (Bylsma & Pivik, 1989; O'Dougherty, Neuchterlein, & Drew,
1984).

Temporal Organization.   In addition to the background as a factor in
the perception of stimuli, the way stimuli are organized in time is also
important. At the simplest level, children become more acute in detection of
gaps in bands of noise as they grow older (Irwin, Ball, Kay, Stillman, &
Rosser, 1985). This increasing acuity with age may be related to improved
speech perception, and delays in the development of temporal acuity may be
related to more complex disabilities.

Some children with hearing impairments may have problems not only
with simple pure tone thresholds, but they may also have difficulty in more
complex processes that involve temporal integration of sound signals. Bacon
and Viemeister (1985) showed that hearing-impaired listeners were less
sensitive than unimpaired children to amplitude modulation of the signals
when temporal modulation was involved. Some people who stutter are
different from normal in the point at which a sound, perceived as fused,
separates and is heard as two sounds (Bonin, Ramig, & Prescott, 1985).

Intrasensory Integration. Perceptual processes also include the integration of stimuli from different sense organs. One application of this idea is the dichotic listening situation in which different auditory stimuli are fed through earphones to each ear. Among other things, the test looks for abilities to distinguish between the stimuli from each ear and for capacity to integrate the different stimuli when appropriate. Poor readers sometimes have difficulties in identifying stimuli when the stimuli are presented simultaneously to different ears, though the readers have no such problem when the sounds are presented successively to a single ear (Dermody, Mackie, & Katsch, 1983).

Intersensory Integration. Integration of stimuli is also important between senses. Learning to read, for instance, involves the integration of visual and auditory stimuli (Ryckman & Nolen, 1985). Infants associate visual and auditory stimuli early in the sensorimotor period. Mentally retarded children are relatively more accurate on intrasensory than intersensory tasks, whereas the same discrepancy in normal children is not as great (Botuck, Turkewitz, & Moreau, 1987). Children with handicaps in intersensory integration may have difficulty in learning the things that involve the combining of information from two or more senses.

Pattern Perception. The complexity of perception is also revealed in visual pattern recognition. Full-term and low birth weight babies at 40 weeks of conceptional age (i.e., normal birth age) look at patterned stimuli and can distinguish them from one another by looking at one more than another. In addition, low birth weight babies look at these patterned stimuli for a longer time than do normal babies, perhaps indicating that they are taking longer to process the information that the patterned stimuli are providing (Spungen, Kurtzberg, & Vaughan, 1985). Mentally retarded people have important deficits in depth perception (R. Fox & Oross, 1988) and visual space perception (Rieser, Guth, & Weatherford, 1987), but not in memory for spatial information (Nigro & Roak, 1987).

Perception of Faces. One type of pattern that babies look at is schematic faces. During the first year, there are age changes in the amounts of information that are used in face recognition. Increasing amounts of information are integrated by older children (Pedelty, Levine, & Shevell, 1985). Autistic children have difficulty in perceiving the orientation of faces (Hobson, Ouston, & Lee, 1988b).

More complex types of perception involve conceptual abilities. Apparently, some deaf children, autistic children, mentally retarded children, and people with Turner's syndrome have difficulty in asessing emotional expression, with the degree of deficit depending on the particular emotion and the degree to which the child likes the other person (Hobson, Ouston, & Lee, 1988a, 1989; McCauley, Kay, Ito, & Treder, 1987; B. J. Wilson, Cantor, Gordon, & Zillman, 1986). But, in some instances, perceiving the emotions of others can be taught (Pietrzak, 1981). Autistic children sometimes fail to distinguish those characteristics of people that inform about whether the people are children or adults. This impairment in detecting age-related features is more severe than any difficulty that autistic children might have in detecting geometric figures, and it may be related to the social impairments that autistic children have (Hobson, 1987).

Self-recognition. Another example of person-perception is self-recognition. A common current test of self-recognition is a test of whether children recognize themselves in a mirror. Normal children and children with Down syndrome demonstrate self-recognition by the time their mental age is 2 to 3 years (Loveland, 1987). Most autistic children recognize themselves in mirrors, others do not. Self-recognition in autistic children is related to overall level of functioning, communicative speech abilities, medication use, and performance on a Piagetian object permanence test (Dawson & McKissick, 1984; Spiker & Ricks, 1984).

Overall then, the stimulus dimensions studied in the sensation and perception of children with handicaps range from relatively simple pure tones to complex social stimuli. Most stimuli are auditory or visual, although there is some interest in other modes (e.g., Benton, 1984). Perception involves not only processing of information within one stimulus modality, but also integration of different stimuli in space, time, and from different modalities. In all of these processes, individual children may have problems that can be identified.

Sensory Feedback. Before we leave this section on sensation and perception, something should be said about the role of perception in motor activity. All motor activity involves some sensory feedback from muscles as well as guidance from the visual and auditory environments. Children with handicaps often have problems in motor coordination that may be in part related to sensory and perceptual problems (R. Lord & Hulme, 1988a, as 1988b). At least some children who stutter apparently have tactile perception problems that are specific to the back of their tongue. Perhaps this specific problem is related to problems in motor coordination that children who stutter experience during speech (Fucci, Petrosino, Gorman, & D. Harris, 1985).

Likewise, some children with handicaps show various problems in copying visual figures. Problems in reproducing the figures may be seen in accuracy of shape and size approximation, orientation, and movement control. The problems, in turn, may be affected by the way the figures are presented. If they are presented by having the child copy the figures with a delay after the figures are presented, then visual memory is involved. If the child is permitted to trace the figure with his fingers, kinesthetic, and tactual input are added to visual input as determinants of drawing. Anwar (1983) showed that children with Down syndrome generally use kinesthetic information rather than visual information in drawing figures and they have a special problem in drawing only when memory is involved in the task. Otherwise, their drawing is comparable to other retarded children.

Thus, analysis of sensorimotor organization can be accomplished in people with handicaps. When they are tested on various sensorimotor tasks, groups of children with handicaps may be different from unimpaired children and from each other. However, differences between groups are not great, are not always consistent, and may depend on the measure used. Individual differences within groups are sometimes substantial.

BRAIN ORGANIZATION

The integration of perceptual and motor processes is carried on in the brain. Thus, any abnormal sensorimotor process must have its reflection in an abnormal brain process. This does not mean that the brain abnormality is the ultimate cause of the behavioral abnormality. It merely means that, because brain and behavior are aspects of one another, both are affected simultaneously.

Not surprisingly, it is often possible to detect a physiological or anatomical abnormality in children with behavioral abnormalities (Coble et al., 1984; Galaburda, 1985; C. Gillberg, Matousek, Petersen, & Rasmussen, 1984; Ornitz, Atwell, Kaplan, & Westlake, 1985; M. Sherman, Nass, & Shapiro, 1984; Shibagaki & Kiyono, 1985; Torello & Duffy, 1985).

On the other hand, it often happens that biological measures fail to differentiate normal from abnormal children (Denckla, LeMay, & Chapman, 1985; Grontved, Walter, & Gronberg, 1988; Hardle, Gasser, & Bacher, 1984; Hynd & Semrud-Clikeman, 1989). This is probably due to two factors. First, it is likely that not all biological processes are affected in all children with handicaps. Second, it may be that some measures of biological function are not as sensitive as behavioral measures. In such cases, it would be possible to detect a behavioral abnormality without, at the same time, seeing its physiological or structural parallel.

Much research has been devoted to detecting biological abnormalities that are specific to certain classes of abnormality. Thus, specific biological deviations have been sought for reading disabilities, minimal brain damage, and so forth. To some extent, this effort has not been very successful. Perhaps this is partly due to the fact that the classifications are not discrete, that is, that they overlap. Or possibly, transactional processes and multiple causation during development produce unique patterns of biological and behavioral abnormalities for individuals that preclude simple associations between behavioral classifications and specific biological abnormalities.

Sometimes the search for biological correlates of behavioral abnormalities has been very successful. This occurs especially when the behavioral abnormality is carefully defined and when the biological correlate is specific and related in some sensible way to the behavioral abnormality. Thus, when a generalized biological measure is related to a generalized behavioral measure, not much more is obtained than a generalized association. When the behavioral measure is somewhat specific (e.g., a disturbance in space perception) and the biological measure is also somewhat specific (e.g., a localized lesion in the right cerebral hemisphere), then more satisfying results are expected and obtained (Meerwaldt & Van Dongen, 1988; Murakami, Courchesne, Press, Yeung-Courchesne, & Hesselink, 1989).

In this section, we consider the range of biological characteristics that have been studied in children with handicaps. We continue our look at perceptual mechanisms by examining the effect of various stimuli on autonomic nervous system responding and on brain activity measured directly by examination of sensory evoked brain potentials. Then we look at organization of brain function more directly by considering the more intensively studied area of laterality of brain organization. The section on brain organization concludes with the general idea that demonstrable abnormalities of brain organization are found in at least some, but not all, children with handicaps. The study of brain function can be accomplished with handicapped children and such study is promising at this time.

Autonomic Nervous System Functioning

There have not been many recent studies of autonomic nervous system functioning of children with handicaps. Those that exist are often done in the context of the theory that these children may have abnormalities in behavioral arousal. Cardiac responsiveness and measures of electrical response of the skin are typical examples of the measures used. There is some evidence that these measures are related to maturity of adaptive behavior (Berntson, Ronca, Tuber, Boysen, & Leland, 1985; Shibagaki, Kiyono, & Matsuno, 1985).

Mentally retarded, autistic, and undersocialized aggressive children all have been shown to be underresponsive to stimulation. However, some studies show them to be overresponsive, and some studies show no difference at all. Even when there is a difference between handicapped and unimpaired groups, the differences are not generally dramatic and there can be individual exceptions to a general tendency (Berntson et al., 1985; Van Engeland, 1984; Schmidt, Solant, & Bridger, 1985; S. Stevens & Gruzelier, 1984). Thus, group comparisons suggest that there are autonomic abnormalities among children with handicaps, but the differences are not dramatic, and individual differences within groups are important.

Event-Related Brain Responses

Sensory and motor events are mirrored by changes in the electrical activity of the brain. These "evoked" or "event-related" responses can be measured from electrodes placed on various parts of the surface of the scalp. Changes in brain electrical activity are evident in various places on the surface of the brain and patterns of activity that depend on the nature of the event are picked up through amplification by the scalp electrodes.

Activity at various levels of the nervous system are detected in the record. Brain stem responses appear very soon after the stimulus (less than 10 ms), whereas responses reflecting activity in the cortex of the brain that are associated with cognitive processes occur much later (200–300 ms after the stimulus).

Studies of event-related potentials done with children with handicaps have tended to compare brain stem responses or activity in comparable electrode sites between the two halves of the brain. They have also compared responses to different stimuli in children having various types of handicap.

Brain stem response to auditory stimuli in newborns can predict behavioral development (Murray, 1988). Transmission time from onset of a simple auditory stimulus to the brain stem may be longer than normal in children with central language disturbance (Piggott & T. Anderson, 1983; but see Mason & Mellor, 1984), shorter than normal in autistic children (Rumsey, Grimes, Pikus, Duara, & Ismond, 1984), and no different from normal in people who stutter (Newman, Bunderson, & Brey, 1985) or who have been classified as learning disabled (Tait, Roush, & Johns, 1983).

An important study shows that direction of the difference between handicapped and normal groups can depend on the intensity of a stimulus (Widen, Folsom, G. Thompson, & W. R. Wilson, 1987). This suggests that comparisons of children with handicaps that use a restricted range of stimulation may not have results that are general. It also suggests that comparisons of the way the brain processes a variation in stimulation is perhaps more important than are statements of general sensitivity.

More consistency is seen when the longer latency cortical responses to more complex stimulation are studied. Autistic children are not generally abnormal when simply listening or looking at auditory or visual stimuli.

However, when they are asked to do something in response to a stimulus and when unexpected and novel stimuli are intermixed with expected and familiar stimuli, differences between autistic and age-matched controls are revealed. These differences depend on the nature of the stimulus with a different spatial distribution of abnormal brain responses for visual and auditory stimulation (Courchesne, Lincoln, Kilman, &. Galambos, 1985; Pritchard, Raz, &. August, 1987). Children with ADD have larger brain responses associated with psychological expectancy states (Aydin, F. Idiman, &. E. Idiman, 1987).

Children with language disorders have abnormal brain responses in the left temporal cortex, but children with speech disorders do not (Mason &. Mellor, 1984). Asymmetrical responses in the brain areas subserving language processing are also seen in dyslexic and some autistic children, though the exact nature of the abnormality varies from study to study (J. Cohen &. Breslin, 1984; Dawson, Finley, S. Phillips, &. Galpert, 1986; Johnstone et al., 1984; Shucard, Cummins, &. McGee, 1984). Suclassification has been espoused in studies of nonverbal learning disabilities (Semrud-Clikeman &. Hynd, 1990).

Patterns of integration of electrical activity between brain areas have also been studied. In general, with development and increasing skill, activity in different areas of the brain becomes more mature, specialized, and coordinated (Chisholm &. Karrer, 1988; Karrer &. C. Johnson, 1986; Warren &. Karrer, 1984). Among learning-disabled children, there is altered patterning of synchrony between brain areas (Sutton, Whiton, Topa, &. Moldofsky, 1986). Another study showed that auditory evoked response patterns changed after pairing a light with a sound stimulus repeatedly. Such changes occur in normal and autistic children but not as readily in mentally retarded children (Martineau, Garreau, Roux, &. Lelord, 1987).

The studies of event-related potentials are very promising. This is especially true when sharply defined groups of children are used; when the groups are defined in terms of specific psychological processes rather than the general classes; when stimuli are appropriate for the relevant processes; and when electrode placements are over brain areas that subserve the specific processes thought to be deficit.

Brain Lateralization

The two halves of the brain have become specialized to process different types of information. There is evidence for this in that people tend to be either left- or right-handed; spoken language is processed mainly on the left side in most people; and brain lesions have different effects, depending on their localization to the right or left lobes of the brain.

This lateralization of brain function certainly exists and is present at birth (Hahn, 1987). However, there has sometimes been a tendency to oversimplify the functions of the two halves of the brain. Educational curricula have been developed to emphasize left (verbal and abstract) activities versus right brain (spatial and artistic) functions. In fact, the left and right halves of the brain communicate and supplement each other so that the brain works as a whole, despite the tendency toward specialization that it shows under laboratory conditions. The distinction between left and right halves of the brain is a useful one for understanding brain function but practical applications of this knowledge will come from detailed understanding of the relationships between the various brain areas.

There is evidence that children with various types of handicap show various lateralization problems (Blood, 1985; J. E. Obrzut, A. Obrzut, Bryden, & Bartels, 1985) and that some do not (Pipe, 1988). Although there is an historical tradition associating laterality with reading problems, the real situation is more complex. For instance, it is possible that some types of reading disability may be associated with left-handedness, but others are not, and by no means do all left-handed children have problems in reading (Galaburda, 1985; Leong, 1984; Satz & J. M. Fletcher, 1987).

Perhaps more significant papers have questioned the idea that a laterality defect in any particular measure represents a general problem in lateralization or that even children with relatively well-defined groups of disabilities in lateralization can be characterized simply as having reversed lateralization (D. Elliott, Weeks, & C. L. Elliott, 1987; Pipe, 1988).

Physiological Evidence. There is not much *direct* evidence of abnormal brain lateralization in children with handicaps (Hiscock & Kinsbourne, 1987). However, three sources of such evidence are apparent in studies of children with localized brain lesions; studies of lateralization of electroencephalographic patterns under testing conditions; and blood flow studies. One recent study showed that children who have brain lesions lateralized either to one hemisphere or the other tended to have behavior problems. Those with lesions in their dominant hemisphere tended to show externalizing behavior problems, whereas children with lesions in their nondominant hemisphere had more internalizing problems (Sollee & Kindlon, 1987).

The alpha or resting wave of the electroencephalogram seems to be somewhat less in the left hemisphere of children who stutter than in a comparable normal sample (Fitch & Batson, 1989), whereas the degree of asymmetry for dyslexic children appears to be normal with this measure (Galin, Herron, Johnstone, Fein, & Yingling, 1988) and only possibly different with a measure of blood flow during a demanding cognitive task (Rumsey et al., 1987). As indicated in the previous section, some children with reading disorders demonstrate alterations in the asymmetry of evoked potentials when verbal material is presented. Perhaps most interesting, these unusual patterns can be made more normal if reading is improved through training (Bakker & Vinke, 1985).

Less direct tests of lateralization differences between normal children and various groups of children with handicaps are more common than are direct anatomical or physiological measures. These include dichotic listening tests, finger tapping tests, and correlates of laterality preference (e.g., handedness).

Dichotic Listening.   In studies of dichotic listening, different syllables or other sounds are fed through microphones to each ear, and children are asked to identify which of the two syllables they heard. Ordinarily, people identify the syllable to the right ear, so they are said to have a right ear advantage. This is also true of children who are dyslexic, learning disabled, or mentally retarded. That is, their dichotic listening laterality is not reversed. However, in general, for these groups, the right ear advantage is less accentuated than it is in normal children, with the group differences being attributed to attentional or other information-processing deficits (Dermody, Mackie, & Katsch, 1983; Hornstein & Mosley, 1986; J. E. Obrzut et al., 1985; K. Smith & Griffiths, 1987).

Finger Tapping.   Another indirect test of brain lateralization is speed of right and left finger tapping while processing language material. In one study of children with a hearing impairment (Marcotte & LaBarba, 1985) the children tapped a finger of either their left or right hand as quickly as they could. If they were not speaking, unimpaired children tapped at the same rate with each hand. However, if they spoke while tapping, one of their hands slowed, thus indicating laterality of language processing.

When the hearing-impaired children were compared with the unimpaired children, the degree of difference between the two hands in tapping suppression was less. In other words, evidence for a diminished lateralization of language (but not reverse laterality) comes from this study of deaf children. Similar results have been obtained with children who stutter and from young adults with Down syndrome (Brutten & Trotter, 1986; D. Elliott, Edwards, Weeks, Lindley, & Carnahan, 1987).

Handedness.   One aspect of lateralization is hand preference. Handedness may be assessed by self-report, using a checklist method, asking the child to manipulate objects, and by having the child tap a finger and measuring the tapping rate. Moreover, in addition to hand preferences, there are preferences for using one foot over the other, one eye over the other, and so forth. These various measures are correlated with each other but the correlations are not perfect. The best studies use multiple measures.

In the general population, 4% to 16% are left-handed (Batheja & Mc-Manus, 1985), about 85% are right-handed and the remainder are ambidextrous. Groups of children with handicaps often have a smaller percentage of right-handed individuals. For instance, among mentally retarded children the range of left-handed people in different studies is 6% to 33% (Batheja & McManus, 1985), and the proportion of left-handedness and mixed-handedness increases with severity of mental retardation (Soper, Satz, Orsini, Van Grop, & Green, 1987).

There has been some interest in the determinants of handedness in mentally retarded and autistic children. Certainly, there are several correlates: Age, brain damage, intelligence, language skills, and visuospatial abilities are all predictors (Tsai, 1984). Of most interest have been hereditary and pathological variables. One approach has been to look at the distribution of handedness in matched groups of retarded people with and without Down syndrome. The premise of these studies has been that if there is a different proportion of right- and left-handers in the Down and non-Down group, one could begin to look for a hereditary determinant of handedness on the 21st chromosome (i.e., the chromosome that is affected in Down syndrome). Unfortunately, the proportion of right- and left-handed people seems to be about the same in individuals with Down syndrome and appropriate comparison groups (Batheja & McManus, 1985; D. Elliott, Weeks, & R. Jones, 1986).

Perhaps more promising is an approach that correlates the handedness of children with the handedness of members of their family. A strong correlation would point to a hereditary factor influencing handedness. There is some correlation between mother's handedness and that of her children. However, this correlation is not very strong, and there is a weaker correlation of father's handedness with that of his children. Thus, in the general population, there is evidence for a sex-related hereditary factor associated with handedness, but the evidence is weak (Harkins & Michel, 1988).

Among mentally retarded people, there is an increase of left-handedness with severity and some association between their handedness and that of their family that is greater for mildly than for severely retarded people (Bradshaw-McAnulty, Hicks, & Kinsbourne, 1984; Pipe, 1987; Searleman, T. F. Cunningham, & Goodwin, 1988). There is a general conclusion that both heredity and undetermined pathological factors influence the elevated left-handedness in mentally retarded people. Similar conclusions come from studies of children with autism (Fein, Waterhouse, Lucci, Pennington, & Humes, 1985; C. Gillberg, 1983) and people who stutter (Christensen & Sacco, 1989).

Overall then, there is evidence for reduced brain laterality, but not reversed lateralization of children with handicaps. It appears at this time, however, that general statements about lateralization in children need to be qualified because there are few studies that ask whether different measures of lateralization are related to one another. Those that exist suggest that whereas general statements about group differences in lateralization can be made, statements about individuals and about specific processes wait on further study.

MOTOR ORGANIZATION AND DEVELOPMENT

Handedness is only one aspect of motor organization and motor development. The way specific responses are organized and how this organization develops with age is the subject of this next section. The topic of motor organization includes its description and the extensive study of reaction time. The study of motor development includes two main topics: assessment of level of motor development and the effects of experience and training.

Motor Organization

Three aspects of motor organization have been delineated by Bernstein: coordination, control, and skill (cited in Newell, 1985). Coordination is the definition of aspects of motor behavior as a functioning unit. Control refers to the process of organizing the unit. Skill acquisition maximizes control.

Some handicapping conditions are defined mainly in terms of motor handicaps. There are children whose motor coordination is exceptionally poor and whose condition is defined by their clumsiness (Henderson & D. Hall, 1982). Other children have clear motor disabilities that are caused by an injury to the brain. These children with cerebral palsy may or may not have other handicaps (e.g., Neilson & O'Dwyer, 1984).

Abnormal motor function is also characteristic of most other groups of children with handicaps. In fact, difficulties of coordination, control, and skill, although perhaps not universal in children with handicaps, are common, even in children with sensory (Brunt & Broadhead, 1982; Butterfield, 1986) and attentional disorders (Denckla, Rudel, Chapman, & Krieger, 1985). On the other hand, not all measures of motor performance distinguish clinical groups, and children who are clumsy may have little else wrong with them (Holland, 1987; Hulme & R. Lord, 1986; R. K. Stone, May, Alvarez, & Ellman, 1989). Thus, as with many measures of behavior, the diagnostic significance of motor deficits is imperfect.

Refined examination of specific motor skills seems to show greater promise for analysis of the nature of the motor problem. In one recent study of people with Down syndrome, a problem in gripping and lifting objects was traced to a deficit in using changes in sensory information (K. J. Cole, Abbs, & Turner, 1988). Likewise, poor performance of clumsy children on a motor task seemed to be attributable to impaired visual feedback rather than a problem with developing a program for motor action (R. Lord & Hulme, 1988a, 1988b).

Coordination and control problems may be manifest at the level of reflexes rather than at the brain level. Cutaneous reflexes show muscle response abnormalities in various clinical groups. These abnormalities can be useful in early detection of the disorders and to characterize the motor disorder more precisely. However, the form of the disorder is not necessarily specific to the type of disorder (Minderaa et al., 1985; Rowlandson & Stephens, 1985).

The intimate relation between sensory integration and motor organization is very evident in the study of control of static and dynamic postural control. Static postures are controlled by vestibular, muscular, skeletal, and visual inputs, with the relative importance of the sources of sensory control changing with age (Woollacott, 1986). The difficulty that blind children sometimes have in maintaining postures and their delays in motor maturation are attributable to the poverty of their visual input. They must use their remaining inputs to guide sitting and standing postures. As a result, their postures may be unstable (Sugden, 1986). The difficulty that some deaf children have in maintaining posture may be related to vestibular deficiencies that some of them have (Brunt, Layne, Cook, & Rowe, 1984).

Postural control may also be affected by cognitive variables. Children who have learning problems may have difficulties in developing the cognitive patterns that form the basis for motor control (G. Reid, 1986). Poor motor control in some mentally retarded individuals may be related not only to disorders of muscular input (Woollacott, 1986; Woollacott & Shumway-Cook, 1986) but also to their general learning problems (Sugden, 1986).

The same general principles apply in considering control of dynamic movements such as locomotion, prehension, throwing, and drawing. Visual inputs, as well as feedback from the vestibular system and muscles are important (W. E. Davis, 1986b; H. Williams et al., 1986), and complex motor programs must be learned. Among these programs are the qualitative organization of the movement and their timing (Ferrandez & Pailhous, 1986; Hulstijn & Mulder, 1986; Jeannerod, 1986; Roberton, 1986; Tsukahara, Aoki, Mita, & Yabe, 1985; Wann, 1986). Whereas the general organization and timing of these movements ordinarily follow the same principles in handicapped and normal children, their control in space and time may have different parameters and may be delayed in development (W. E. Davis, 1986a).

Perhaps the most widely studied aspect of motor performance is speed of reaction or reaction time. This experimental paradigm has been in existence for more than a century to evaluate information processing at different levels of complexity. Reaction time studies have been used to study the organization of simple responses to simple stimuli and also in the study of higher mental processes such as memory and decision making. In this chapter, we review simple reaction time. Complex reaction time is covered in the next chapter.

In simple reaction time, people are asked to respond as quickly as they can to a stimulus such as a sound or light. Then, the stimulus is presented repeatedly and an overall estimate of speed of reaction to the stimulus is obtained. The interest is to determine, first, whether the reaction time is generally slower in children with handicaps. Perhaps more interesting, an assessment is made of what component of the reaction time is different. That is, do children with handicaps differ from normal in input, central, or motor aspects of the stimulus–response organization?

In general, groups of people with handicaps are slower in reaction time than are people without handicaps. This statement applies to mentally retarded, learning-disabled, and emotionally handicapped groups of children (Brunt & Distefano, 1982; Martinius, 1984; Poretta, 1987). This does not mean that all handicapped children are slower than all normal children. In fact, there is substantial overlap between the groups. Thus, although there is a general slowness in the responses of children with handicaps, the difference is not sufficient to present the case for a diagnostic procedure.

On the other hand, speed differences do represent differences in the way that information is processed. Are certain children with handicaps slower in taking in information and coding it (input); processing the information (central processes); and/or organizing and performing responses (response)? One would like to know whether the motor system being measured is important. Importance of input systems is demonstrated in studies that vary aspects of the input in reaction time tasks. Children with problems in language development are less efficient in distinguishing the conditions of the warning that normally precedes most reaction time tasks (Martinius, 1984). The importance of motor systems may be seen from studies that compared the reaction times of normal children with those of children who stutter with respect to manual and phonatory response systems (Till, Reich, Dickey, & Seiber, 1983; Cross & Luper, 1983). These studies have shown that the children who stutter are slower than normal when both motor systems are assessed. This means that a general disability in processing information or organizing and executing a motor response may be implicated.

The most direct approach to assessing the components of reaction time is to look at sensory and motor evoked brain potentials that occur during performance of a reaction time task. There are not many such studies. However, one has compared children of different ages and mentally retarded adults with normal children (Karrer, 1986). This study showed that input speed did not differ for children of different ages or unimpaired children and mentally retarded people. However, the slower reaction time of the younger and the mentally retarded people was reflected in slower central and motor response components. At least as interesting, Karrer (and also Galbraith, 1986) showed that the patterning of brain potentials is different in mentally retarded people. Thus, it is not only slowness of reaction time, but also the different organization of the brain responses, that demonstrates less efficient processing of information.

If motor control depends at least partly on motor and cognitive programs that integrate sensory information with motor actions, one can ask whether efficiency of motor movements can be improved with motivational and training procedures. Anyone who has engaged in competitive sports and has trained for them will answer yes to that question. The issue is whether this is also true of children with handicaps and, if so, what conditions are most effective with which behaviors (G. Reid, 1986).

There have been very few studies of this kind with children with handicaps. However, there have been some. For instance, information feedback can improve reaction time performance (Wade, Hoover, & Newell, 1984); competition increases motor performance (Karper, Martinek, & Wilkerson, 1985); and extended practice made performance of children with Down syndrome almost normal in a complex motor task (Kerr & Blais, 1987).

Thus, motor action involves central programming that integrates sensory information with motor patterns. Many children with handicaps have more or less obvious problems in motor action that are evident at different levels from reflex action to complex motor skills and in the coordination and timing of the actions. These difficulties can be significantly overcome by training, but residual handicaps often remain.

Motor Development

The study of motor control and motor development have traditionally dealt with different issues. Although the field of motor control deals with ways of defining how movements are coordinated, motor development is concerned with ways that control processes change with age and what determines these changes (Sugden, 1986). The more recent literature has tended to see these approaches as more similar. As intensive studies of motor control have been applied to children of different ages, and as studies of individual differences have come to be emphasized as an aspect of motor control, the science of motor control has taken on developmental and individual aspects. Moreover, as motor learning has become important in the study of motor control, the determinants of changes in motor control have become a focus of interest. Thus, what were once two separate areas of endeavor are now unified into a more general movement science. This section emphasizes the two developmental aspects of the field: changes in motor control with age and determinants of those changes.

Age Changes. Describing changes in motor control with age can be done at three levels. The first is the general description of changes of posture that typically occur during the first 5 years of life. The newborn baby spends most of its time on its back, looking up and from side to side. When at rest, it tends to look to one side with its arms and legs in a typical posture known as the tonic leg reflex. This early indication of lateralization is just one piece of evidence that the nervous system is specialized very early in development.

In the first few months of life, children begin to turn to a prone position, then move gradually to all-fours and, toward the beginning of the second half of its first year, pull themselves to a standing position. Likewise, locomotion and also prehension go through predictable stages of development based on flexion and extension mechanisms that can plausibly be used in early training programs (Mishima, 1986).

Standardized Tests. During the 1930s and 1940s, these stages of motor development were studied and described intensively. These studies became the basis of several standardized tests of motor development (e.g., Henderson, Morris, & Ray, 1981), which form the basis for estimates of developmental rate. These tests are widely used, but two things are significant about them. First, they do not predict later intellectual development well at all. Second, they are still the main tests of development in the first 6 months, and are useful for early screening for severe disabilities.

Analysis of Development. Aside from general descriptions of motor development and standardized tests of motor development, the third approach to describing motor development is the analysis of the development of motor control. This third approach involves not only the description of what postural changes occur but also what is occurring during the transitions from stage to stage and how the processes of motor control change as the child matures. This involves the study of the influence of environmental factors and sophisticated ways of describing the behaviors: topology of the movements (Newell & Scully, 1988) and descriptions of coordination and timing (Ferrandez & Pailhous, 1986; Roberton, 1986; Wann, 1986).

One example of recent work in this area is the study by Henderson (1986) showing that the motor development of children with Down syndrome is not only delayed, but it also proceeds through sequences that are not typical. Likewise, Woolacott and Shumway-Cook (1986) and Haley (1987) showed that at least some children with Down syndrome have abnormalities in maintaining posture that are not merely the consequence of their retardation of development.

As important as the detailed description of what changes occur with age, and how they occur, is the analysis of the determinants of these changes. That is, what factors influence the course of development? According to the most common view, motor development proceeds through a series of stages determined by an unfolding of a genetically determined program. In other words, maturational factors determine motor development. Undoubtedly, a major determinant of the sequence and timing of motor development is heredity and is reflected in the universal sequencing and timing that is common to all humans.

However, there is variation in sequencing and timing that is especially noticeable in some children with handicaps. As we have made clear, sensory factors are important in motor control (W. E. Davis, 1986a). Thus, individual differences and the importance of sensory factors in motor control make plausible the idea that sensory or experiential factors may also determine the motor development.

There are several general classes of experience, including culture (Bril, 1986), that have been demonstrated to affect motor development. Sensory loss and the environmental deprivation of traditional residential institutions adversely affect motor development. Early general or specific stimulation programs can accelerate motor development. The effects are sometimes temporary, and they may be most effective at specific ages and with specific behaviors. In general, early stimulation is most effective when a new behavior is emerging (Henderson, 1986; MacLean, Arendt, & Baumeister, 1986; Sugden, 1986).

Overall then, the study of motor development has changed during the last 20 years from a simple descriptive approach, emphasizing the major "milestones" of motor maturation, to a more complex analysis of the nature and determinants of transitions in motor development. The description of coordination, including studies of timing have become important, and specific sensory and more general environmental effects have been added to maturational factors as determinants of the development of the motor programs underlying action.

SUMMARY

Sensorimotor processes are the most fundamental aspects of behavior. Children with handicaps often have problems in sensing and perceiving information from the outside world and in transforming that information into adaptive response. Although it would be a mistake to assume that all handicapped children have problems at the sensorimotor level or that the problems are always the same, the possibility must be considered in the individual case.

As with all the behavioral classes to be considered, individual differences in the patterning of sensorimotor processes are significant, and they tend to obscure differences between the major clinical categories.

The central nervous system mediates sensorimotor processes, as it does all behaviors. There is specialization in the nervous system, for instance in the lateralization of brain processes. This specialization can best be discerned if behaviors are clearly and specifically defined and if procedures for measuring brain function are exact. However, even then, it is clear that the brain acts as a dynamically integrated organ, and brain localization of handicaps in children tends to be more general and diffuse.

Motor control is mediated by more or less automatic complex processes called programs. These programs all involve sensory feedback, and many of them have learned components. Children with handicaps often have difficulty in organizing their motor movements. The programs underlying motor coordination often have learned components, so skill can often be improved with training.

Motor development is determined partly by genetically determined sequences in motor programs. However, because experience is also important, motor development is also affected by environmental deprivation.

The study of sensorimotor processes shows that experience, learning, and even cognitive processes are involved in perception and action. As we move to the next chapter, the role of these factors becomes even more important.

6 _____

Attention, Learning, and Memory

In the last chapter, it became clear that psychological processes cannot neatly be separated from each other. Sensory inputs are controlled by motor movements, and motor actions have sensory components. The same is true for attention, learning, and memory.

The information to which children are exposed may or may not become part of the permanent store of information they use in dealing with everyday life. Whether they have this information available to them depends on several things like the efficiency of the focus of their attention; how well they remember the information they actually attend to; and their ability to retrieve the information that is stored. As becomes evident in the next two chapters, simply having the memories available does not guarantee the abstract and complex thinking that is necessary for adaptation. Higher order problem solving requires complex intellectual strategies, and the use of these, in turn, depends on motivational variables.

From the moment that information is first received, cognitive processes are engaged in a complex and dynamic set of reactions. What one attends to is determined by what one already knows. What one remembers is dependent on one's interests. Problem-solving strategies depend on attention. Thus, the separation of psychological processes is to a certain extent a fiction that serves mainly to make their description convenient.

In addition to the complexity of cognitive processes, there is a central problem in this field because there is not always agreement on definitions. Attention problems, for instance, may for some people, be synonymous with hyperactive behavior, poor school learning, inability to concentrate for an extended period of time, underreacting or overreacting to stimulation, or merely with not doing what a teacher thinks is appropriate.

On the other hand, the terms, attention, learning, and memory do mean different things. *Attention* determines whether information is processed; *learning* is a change in behavior that is the result of experience; *memory* refers to the retention of processed information for short or long periods of time.

This chapter covers the basic aspects of information processing. It begins with a discussion of attention. Learning is then exemplified by a review of studies of discrimination learning and generalization. Various approaches to information processing are then defined, and studies of memory from those perspectives are reviewed. Finally, the efficiency of information processing ends this chapter and introduces the next.

ATTENTION

Failure to pay attention is perhaps the most common complaint that parents and teachers have about children. Whether the problem is attributed to lack of interest, too much television, hyperactivity, or just plain laziness, many people are satisfied with the explanation that their children's poor performance is caused by an attention deficit.

The attention of children does sometimes wander in a way that interferes with learning and, in a small number of cases, this problem may be pathological. However, rather than being a cause of problems, attention deficits are part of the problems themselves.

Keep in mind that attention is a poorly defined concept (Krupski, 1987; Posner & Petersen, 1990; Samuels, 1987). There is no single thing that we call attention. When a person changes physiologically in response to some stimulus, we say that the person's attention is aroused or alerted. When the person's eyes or ears are turned toward a sound, this orienting is called attention. Attention is also present when a child works at a task; when the child focuses on one part of an array of events; when some information is taken in and some is filtered out; and when the child is vigilant for some coming event or concentrates on a task for some time (Tomporowski & Allison, 1988). Some investigators (e.g., T. H. Carr, 1984) even think of attention as a complex mental process that is involved in goal selection for a task, controls information, selects input, and maintains short-term memory.

These phenomena express the range of things that are seen when one looks carefully at attention. Despite the sometimes bewildering complexity of the concept, there are some common features on which most people agree. As Boring (1933) said, "There has been so much controversy about what attention is and is not . . . that one is apt to lose sight of the truth that there really is a fundamental fact of attention" (p. 194).

Actually there are many definitions of attention. However, perhaps the most important one for our purposes states that attention is a limited capacity mental process involved in processing sensory input. That is, attention is the cognitive act that selects important from unimportant things happening around the child. When it is functioning normally, attention selects a limited range of events for further cognitive processing. This means that attention is involved in ignoring unimportant events and in admitting important things for further cognitive processing.

The selective aspect of the concept also means that attention is focused on only a limited portion of the environment and this focus may shift. Normally, attention is focused on that aspect of the environment containing the information necessary for adaptation, but attention can also involve several alterations. For instance, more or less information than necessary may be admitted for further processing (Rincover & Ducharme, 1987). Or, the focus of attention may shift more rapidly than is appropriate for best adaptation and may be more than usually susceptible to distraction by unimportant events.

Measuring Attention

In the laboratory, various aspects of attention may be measured in ways that reflect the complexity of the concept. Physiological arousal has been measured with heart rate changes (Raine & F. Jones, 1987), galvanic skin responses, and changes in the electroencephalogram. Focusing has been measured by careful observation of eye-fixations. The degree to which attention is sustained can be measured in tasks that ask the person to detect signals that occur infrequently (O'Dougherty, Neuchterlein, & Drew, 1984). Attention in complex information processing has been assessed with tasks involving necessary information and distractors presented simultaneously.

Paper-and-pencil tests have also been used to measure attention (Lunzer & Stratford, 1984). Impulsive children may respond more quickly to an assigned task (such as finding their way through a paper-and-pencil maze). In the course of the speedier, impulsive responses, they may make more errors. In other words, there may be a trade-off between speed of response and errors.

Observational studies in natural settings also reflect the basic ideas that we have about attention (e.g., Dienske, DeJonge, & Sanders-Woudstra, 1985; Prinz, Tarnowski, & Nay, 1984). These studies involve the measurement of such things as general activity level; attention to specific toys or school tasks; changes from toy to toy; responsiveness to requests by other people; and response to distractors. Measuring the relationship between general activity and specific attention is especially important because of a suspected relationship between hyperactivity and poor attention span in children.

Correlates of Attention

Attention depends not only on the characteristics of a person, but it is heavily dependent on the situation or the tasks that are set for the child. Distractions, difficulty of the learning material, duration of the task, and the salience of the stimuli are only some of the many situational factors that affect attention (B. P. Ackerman, 1987; Krupski, 1987; Tomporowski, Hayden, & Applegate, 1990).

It is also common knowledge that children vary the focus of their attention according to their motivation. If a child is not interested in something, attention may "wander," giving parents and teachers reason to believe that poor performance is related to motivational variables (however, see Kistner, 1985). Other variables correlated with attention are maturation and, less dependably, clinical category.

Development.   Young infants respond preferentially to some things in their environment. At least some measures of responsiveness seem to be related to mental age (not chronological age). That is, when it is possible to separate these two measures, it is mental age, rather than chronological age, that seems more important (M. Lewis & Brooks-Gunn, 1984). The idea that attention is related to intellectual maturation is reinforced by the idea that more intellectually mature severely retarded people attend more efficiently to the stimuli necessary to solve learning problems than do less intellectually developed severely retarded people (Zeaman & House, 1963).

Classification.   Mentally retarded children increase errors over several minutes on a paper-and-pencil task that requires maintenance of attention. Children with Down syndrome do not differ from other retarded children in this respect, although they do differ with respect to other task characteristics, such as work rate (Lunzer & Stratford, 1984). Premature infants who have had a history of intraventricular hemorrhage respond more slowly to the onset of a visual stimulus than do comparable children who have not had such hemorrhages (Landry, Leslie, J. M. Fletcher, & Francis, 1985; see also Rose, Feldman, McCarton, & Wolfson, 1988).

But on the whole, responsiveness to visual stimulation does not clearly differentiate categories of infants with handicap. For instance, infants of different clinical categories hold their attention to visual stimuli for equal amounts of time and habituate their eye fixation responses to repeated stimuli equally (Landry et al., 1985; M. Lewis & Brooks-Gunn, 1984; see Sigman, S. E. Cohen, Beckwith, & Parmelee, 1986 for a different result). And groups of emotionally disturbed children did not differ from normal children on selective attention tasks (Unruh & Gilliam, 1986). Thus, although there are some differences between diagnostic and etiological categories on attentional measures, the differences are not consistent.

Hyperactivity. Besides maturation and category differences, there has also been much interest in the relationship of attention to hyperactivity and to learning disabilities. The suspected relationship between hyperactivity and attention comes from the perception that some abnormal children engage in behaviors that prevent their attending to a task for the time necessary to complete it. These children are constantly on the move, shift their attention, and never seem to focus on anything for a significant time.

Attentional aspects of hyperactivity are so well accepted that the motor aspects of hyperactivity (i.e., the activity level) now seem less important than the attention deficits. It is not the hyperactivity itself that is important in the learning of "hyperactive children." Instead, some kind of attentional deficit is thought to be the focus of classification. In fact, children who were once classified as hyperactive are now said to have an Attention Deficit Disorder, although the practice has been criticized (Prior & Sanson, 1986).

The picture of low attention in very highly active children produced the idea that there is a negative relationship between attention and activity level in all children. As a result, normally active children were sometimes also seen as having attentional problems. However, the general relationship between activity level and attentional problems is not significant. In other words, although some abnormally hyperactive children may have attentional deficits, normally active boys and girls do not typically have attentional problems (Dienske, DeJonge, & Sanders-Woudstra, 1985).

In considering possible attentional abnormalities in hyperactive children, there are several possibilities. First, there may be no attentional difficulties at all. That is, what is apparently an attentional problem might be something else, such as a memory disorder. Apparently, this is not the case. Several studies have come up with the result that some aspect of attention is a problem in children who are abnormally hyperactive. However, Prior, Sanson, Freethy, and Geffen (1985) pointed out that many hyperactive children also have learning disabilities and when the learning disabilities are taken into account some aspects of the attention problems become minimal. Thus, the possibility remains that if learning disabilities can be separated from hyperactivity, hyperactive children may ultimately be shown to have no important attention deficits.

However, most studies do point to an attentional problem in children who are hyperactive. Although there is widespread agreement that hyperactive children have problems with attention, there is less agreement about the nature of the attention deficit, and there are recent careful studies that contradict the generalization (van der Meere & Sergeant, 1988a, 1988b, 1988c; Schachar, Logan, Wachsmuth, & Chajczyk, 1988). Problems with control of impulses; abnormal arousal of attention; excessive shifting of attention; distractibility; problems with maintenance of attention during an assigned task; inefficient selective attention; and excessive diffusion of attention are all aspects of attention that have been shown to be characteristics that differentiate groups of hyperactive children from unimpaired children (R. T. Brown & Wynne, 1984a, 1984b; Ceci & Tishman, 1984; Draeger, Prior, & Sanson, 1986; Prinz, Tarnowski, & Nay, 1984; Prior et al., 1985; Sergeant & Scholten, 1985a, 1985b; Zentall, 1985).

Learning Disorders. The problem of attention in children with learning disorders is at least as controversial. At one level, there is no question that learning-disabled children attend less well than do unimpaired children. Teachers often believe that learning-disabled children suffer from deficits in attention, and there is some evidence that supports this view (Beale, Matthew, Oliver, & Corballis, 1987; Eliason & Richman, 1987). However, it appears that any attentional problem that learning-disabled children show is minor, is related to the cognitive demands of tasks (Krupski, 1985), and has a significant but minor relationship to their school performance (Sinclair, Guthrie, & Forness, 1984).

On the other hand, there are studies that fail to demonstrate an attentional deficit in children with learning disabilities (Fleisher, Soodak, & Jelin, 1984), whether the studies are done in the laboratory or in the classroom (Kistner, 1985; Samuels & N. L. Miller, 1985).

Situational and Task Effects. It is worth finding out what exactly the attentional deficit is, because a specific understanding of the defect in the process leads to development of ways of reducing the effects of the problem. For instance, Zentall (1985) supported the idea that hyperactive children are less tolerant of situations that involve minimal stimulation and that addition of color stimulation to attention tasks should improve performance, at least in simpler tasks.

Ceci and Tishman (1984) predicted that hyperactive children, who they think underfocus their attention during learning, should be better than normal comparison children in remembering information that is not central to an assigned task. They found that this is true without any sacrifice of performance in the central task if the central task was easy, but not if it was difficult. In other words, by making the "required task" easier and putting desired information into aspects of the situation that are not apparently part of the material to be learned, one might improve the overall performance of children whose attention tends to be diffuse.

This kind of study carries the general implication that if one understands the nature of the attention processing of children who are hyperactive, one can design tasks to maximize the performance of children who have difficulty with conventional school work (see also Garkusha, 1984; Locher, 1985; Morrow, Burke, & Buell, 1985; Morton & Kershner, 1984; M. O. Smith et al., 1985).

Summary

Attention constitutes a set of poorly defined processes involved in selecting the information that may be processed further. Disagreements about the deficits in attention partly depend on the complexity of the concept, but attention also depends on maturation, category of handicap, and situational and tasks aspects. Situation effects on attention are the source of attempts to increase attention when the attentional problem is actually causing poor performance.

LEARNING AND MEMORY

Difficulty in benefiting from experience is one of the most important topics in the individual psychology of children with handicaps. This is so because much of a child's day is spent in school, with the family, or with peers where learning new things is the main activity. However, it is also important because learning and memory are central to all adaptation. Many handicaps are defined by difficulties in learning. This is obviously true with the cognitive disabilities, that is, learning disabilities and mental retardation. However, it should not be forgotten that sensory and chronic health disorders interfere with opportunities to learn and that emotional handicaps turn a child away from adaptive learning.

It is no surprise, therefore, that there is a large literature on the learning and memory of children with handicaps, much of it about children with cognitive problems. Most of these studies have been concerned with the nature of difficulties in learning and memory based on recent theories of conditioning, discrimination learning, and information processing. However, there also have been some studies of the influence of what a child knows on learning. An understanding of both the processes of acquisition of knowledge and the influence of what the child already knows may be important for a comprehensive theory of learning and memory handicaps.

There are two general approaches to the study of learning and memory.

The psychology of habituation, conditioning, and discrimination learning is concerned with factors involved in associating particular stimuli with particular responses; in finding out that two or more stimuli are different from each other and associating the differences with different responses; and in generalizing the impact of the stimuli to other similar stimuli and situations.

A somewhat different way of seeing learning deals with the processing of information. The information-processing approach views learning as the coding, storing, and retrieving of information. Coding, storing, and retrieving may be composed of subprocesses, and there may be feedback loops between them. Moreover, the nature of the information processed may be important, and the depth of processing at each stage may also influence the likelihood that any experience will actually end up being remembered.

The associative and information-processing approaches should be seen as general approaches to the study of learning and memory rather than as confirmed pictures of how learning takes place. Each is actually composed of many competing theories. Association and information-processing approaches are probably ultimately compatible, and both have contributed in important ways to our understanding of handicaps in learning and memory.

Habituation, Conditioning, and Discrimination Learning

Habituation.   One of the most important characteristics of the environment that a person responds to is whether or not something is new. Novel stimuli evoke attention, but as one becomes accustomed or *habituated* to them, the response gradually declines unless the stimulus becomes important in some way. Children are constantly meeting up with new situations and habituating to them, so that habituation is taking place all day, every day. Habituation therefore has a potential for affecting everything the child learns (Greenfield, 1985).

Learned responses also decline when they are no longer rewarded. This decline of a learned response is called *extinction.* In considering habituation and extinction, it is important not to confuse them with overall responsiveness. That is, habituation and extinction refer to the rate of change in response, rather than either initial responsiveness or overall responsiveness. Overall responsiveness may be affected by rate of decline in response to a novel or learned stimulus, but it is not necessarily the cause of the rate of decline.

Are children with handicaps abnormal in habituating to novel things and learning to ignore situations that are no longer important? One could imagine, for instance, that habituation might be slower. If that were true, a child would remain abnormally responsive to things that are really not significant.

Or someone might habituate too quickly. In that case, they might not be adequately attentive to what might be important events.

There is some evidence that habituation and extinction rates are different for children with handicaps (e.g., Gandhavadi & Melvin, 1985, 1989; Mullins & Rincover, 1985) In general, it appears that habituation and extinction rates are slower in children with handicaps, especially for those children with more severe handicaps. However, this literature is far from clear. A lack of recent studies and problems in interpretation of the studies that there are make any general statement about habituation in children with handicaps premature. However, it is clear that habituation deficits are possible.

Conditioning. The literature on simple conditioning is also not large. One form of this learning, classical conditioning, has a previously neutral stimulus coming to evoke a response that it did not previously stimulate. Even very young babies are capable of classical conditioning (Blass, Ganchrow, & Steiner, 1984). However, there are no recent studies of classical conditioning in children with handicaps. Older studies (L. E. Ross, 1966) suggest that classical conditioning even of severely retarded people is surprisingly normal. However, this issue would benefit from further study.

More suggestive is the comparison of intramodal and crossmodal conditioning. In intramodal conditioning, stimuli from the same sense class are connected during conditioning. Perhaps two auditory stimuli are paired. In crossmodal conditioning the stimuli come through different sense modes. A visual stimulus may be paired with an auditory stimulus.

There have been a few comparisons of intramodal and crossmodal conditioning, especially in infants. Crossmodal learning seems to require a more mature processing system than does intramodal conditioning. It is therefore not surprising that, in general, infants with handicaps have more difficulty learning crossmodal than intramodal connections (Rose, Feldman, McCarton, & Wolfson, 1988). Crossmodal processing increases with age, and older learning-disabled children may be delayed in this development (Snow, J. H. Barnett, K. Cunningham, & Ernst, 1988).

The other major form of simple learning, instrumental conditioning, has also been studied in babies. In this form of learning, a response gradually increases when the child is rewarded after performing the desired response. In one study, preterm infants took a longer time to learn a rewarded response and did not retain the response as long as did full-term babies. This group difference was related to measures of medical risk (Gekoski, Fagen, & Pearlman, 1984).

Discrimination Learning. Of much greater interest has been the immensely important area of discrimination learning. This general class of learning involves coming to respond one way to one stimulus and another way to another stimulus. For instance, walk when you see a green light, but do not walk when you see a red light.

Early studies of discrimination learning emphasized the role of attention in discrimination learning. In learning to differentiate stimuli, a child is learning to attend to the features of the stimuli that differentiated their important characteristics (Zeaman & House, 1963). In learning to distinguish red from green traffic lights, a person must learn that the important differentiating feature between them is color and not, for instance, form or texture. For an intelligent adult, this is an obvious distinction. However, for young children and for adults who are severely retarded, the important difference may be very difficult to learn (Bryant et al., 1988).

Since the early studies, scientists have demonstrated many ways of teaching these discriminations. Illuminating the "correct" stimulus after the person has made a choice is one typical way of focusing the person's attention on it (Meador, 1984; Meador, Rumbaugh, Tribble, & S. Thompson, 1984). Fading procedures are particularly effective. In fading, the stimuli are changed so that an initially obvious discrimination gradually becomes more difficult, but so that the child makes no errors (Strand & Morris, 1986, 1988).

Training methods such as these can efficiently improve the simple learning of people with severe learning disorders. However, in real life, stimulus situations are not always as simple as differentiating between two simultaneously presented stimuli. More often there are multiple or compound stimuli to respond to; one has to respond one way or another to a stimulus, depending on the occurrence of a third event (conditional discrimination); the stimuli are not always exactly the same as they were when the discrimination was first learned; and the learning may not transfer to a new situation.

Even two-choice discriminations can involve compound stimuli. Several dimensions may be included in even simple stimuli. Traffic lights differ, not only according to color, but also intensity and position in a vertical display. This redundancy makes it easier to tell the difference between the lights. As indicated earlier, discrimination learning sometimes involves attending to those aspects of the stimuli that actually differentiate between them. Most real-life discrimination learning involves taking advantage of the redundancy in stimuli, and so can teaching procedures (Strand & Morris, 1986).

Some children cannot take advantage of this redundancy because they focus on only a limited aspect of the stimuli, perhaps on only one dimension when three or four characteristics differentiate them. This tendency for overselection was first reported in autistic children, but also exists in retarded children and is negatively related to mental age. Several teaching methods have been shown to be effective in diminishing this overselectivity (K. D. Allen & Fuqua, 1985; Smeets, Hoogeveen, Striefel, & Lancioni, 1985).

In addition, children with handicaps may have difficulty in conditional discrimination learning. It is ordinarily true that green means go and red means stop, but it is also true that a person driving a car must stop at a green sign when a person is in the crosswalk. Young children are capable of learning conditional discriminations, employing complex classes of stimuli, and it is possible that even severely and profoundly retarded people can learn reasonably complex conditional discriminations. However, these accomplishments depend on careful and gradual training (DeRose, McIlvane, Dube, Galpin, & Stoddard, 1988; R. R. Saunders, K. J. Saunders, Kirby, & Spradlin, 1988; Sidman, Kirk, & Willson-Morris, 1985).

Generalization, Transfer, and Relational Learning. One particularly important aspect of more complex discrimination learning is concerned with generalization and transfer. Once a person has learned something, the question is whether that person can apply the knowledge in a new situation. If the child learns appropriate responses to red and green in the classroom, can the knowledge be applied when crossing the street? The general answer to this question is that learning is not necessarily automatically transferred to new situations. Transfer depends on the person responding to the relationship between stimuli and classes of stimuli (Green, Mackay, McIlvane, R. R. Saunders, & Soraci, 1990). Relational learning and transfer are individually determined and depend on the nature of the stimulus and on developmental level of the child (Green, 1990; Hupp, 1986; Kelman & Whiteley, 1986; Scott, Greenfield, & Partridge, 1989; Soraci, Deckner, Baumeister, & Carlin, 1990; Umetani, Kitao, & Katada, 1985).

In some children with handicaps, learning tends to be specific unless special attention is given to generalization training, so this training must be done in such a way that generalization is assured. Most importantly, this involves careful training where the relationships between stimuli and stimulus classes are connected (Mackay & Ratti, 1990; McIlvane, Dube, Kledaras, Iennaco, & Stoddard, 1990). When this is done, one can expect that the learning of the relationships will be retained for a long time in a range of situations (R. R. Saunders, K. J. Saunders, & Spradlin, 1990).

Other procedures have also been demonstrated to be successful in promoting generalization. Presenting many instances of unrewarded stimuli, rather than only one instance, as is done in the two-choice training situation, seems to improve generalization, at least initially (Griffiths, Boggan, Tutt, & Dickens, 1985). Presenting many instances of rewarded stimuli definitely makes generalization more likely than if only one instance is taught. For instance, if a child is taught to put one shirt on, generalization to a new shirt will not be as likely as if many shirts were used in the training (Day & Horner, 1986).

Verbal self-instruction has been more effective than a modeling procedure in encouraging generalization (Gow, Ward, & Balla, 1985). Manual signs can be generalized by profoundly retarded children if taught by verbal instruction or by visual stimuli, as long as the instruction is careful. However, there are individual differences in the success of these procedures (Duker & Morsink, 1984).

Summary

Conditioning and discrimination learning are pervasive aspects of the everyday learning of children with handicaps. Therefore, it is important to understand these kinds of associative learning and to ask whether training procedures are effective in practical situations. Some children with handicaps have difficulties with learning, but many procedures have been shown to be effective in helping even severely handicapped children to learn. However, simple training of one response does not guarantee its generalization to new situations. Here too, several general procedures have been shown to enhance transfer.

INFORMATION PROCESSING

The second general approach to the study of learning and memory is a group of information-processing theories. An older version of this approach sees learning and memory as a sequence of processes. A person is thought always to be living in the midst of a mass of stimuli. Some of these stimuli are processed by the person, but most are ignored. If a stimulus is effective, it may enter a very short sensory memory store, where it lasts no more than a few seconds. Most of the information in this very short sensory (or iconic memory) store dissipates and is not processed further.

The information that is processed then enters a short-term memory store. In short-term memory, several processes come into play. These processes, called *strategies*, include rehearsal, clustering the information into groups, or relating the new information to some well-learned information. If one of these strategies maintains the information in short-term memory for long enough, the information automatically enters a long-term memory store. Then, the information stays in long-term memory indefinitely and can be retrieved as needed, employing strategies similar to those used to organize the information for long-term storage.

Not many people agree with the details of this picture, but there is agreement on certain things. First, not all information is processed. Second, something like short-term memory (where information dissipates) and long-term memory (where information is held for a very long time) seem to represent the way information is processed and stored. Third, if there are such memory stores, there must be one or more processes for retrieving the information so that it can be used. Fourth, there is general agreement that what one already knows is very important in how efficiently each aspect of the memory systems work. That is, information in the long-term memory storage provides one critical basis for encoding and retrieving information.

In addition to these basic agreements, there are some disagreements about the processing and storing of information. The relatively simple picture presented previously portrays learning and memory as a sequence of separate processing stages. However, some theories see these processes occurring simultaneously with parallel processing. Even the sequential process theories include elaborate feedback loops between the various stages. Some people disagree on whether the stages are separate from one another, with some thinking that short-term memory is actually an aspect of long-term memory in an active state. Deemphasizing the stages, other theorists believe that what is important in getting a piece of information into a single stage of memory is effortful versus automatic processing, thoroughness or depth of processing of information, or attentional processes (Cowan, 1988).

Further complication derives from the fact that these general theories of information processing are applied to different types of learning material. Motor skills involve memory that integrates feedback stimuli from muscles (Horgan, 1985). Memory can be for events that are simultaneous or organized in a series. It can be for episodes in everyday life (e.g., images) or for material organized semantically, like words in stories.

Given the variety of the theories of information processes and memory, one should not be surprised that concepts of the development of memory are likewise complex. In fact, the major concepts of development of learning and memory have been applications of the findings with adults who do not have any significant memory problem.

Children do not process information as efficiently as do adults. For instance, they do not use some learning strategies as readily. In one sense, then, normal children can be said to be handicapped in processing information. It seems likely that people who are delayed in their development may also be handicapped in processing information. The central questions are: What processes are impaired? To what do we attribute the impairment? And what do we do about any impairment?

There has been much research into these questions, and certain processes have been shown to be impaired in children with handicaps. In fact, one leading researcher in the field has concluded that mentally retarded people manifest an "everything deficit," that is, a disability in all processes that have been studied (Detterman, 1987; see also Gutowski & Chechile, 1987). Even children with relatively specific disabilities such as reading disabilities, have problems in more general aspects of information processing (Torgesen, 1985). However, the situation is even more difficult than this conclusion about generality of deficits implies.

For one thing, not all aspects of memory have been studied equally. Handicaps in short-term memory are studied much more intensively than is long-term memory. Second, whereas it may be true that a group of children may, on average, show one kind of handicap or another, this does not mean that all, or even the majority, of the children in the group have the same pattern of handicaps (Kirchner & Klatzky, 1985; Lorsbach & Worman, 1989). Third, the overwhelming amount of research on learning and memory impairments in children has been done with mentally retarded and learning-disabled children.

This is reasonable, because mental retardation and learning disabilities are the cognitive disorders in which school problems in learning are most dramatically observed. However, there is reason to believe that children who are deprived of experience because of some sensory disorder, like visual or auditory impairments, might also have information-processing deficits and that attentional deficits should also clearly be related to the amount of information that is processed. The few studies of these categories of children suggest that such a conclusion is plausible and more research on information processing with children having sensory and attentional handicaps would be informative about specific determinants of disabilities (Bebko, 1984; Lufi & A. Cohen, 1985; Pring & Rusted, 1985; Ronnberg & Nilsson, 1987).

Sensory Store, Short-Term Memory, and Encoding

The sections that follow are organized according to a sequential stage of information processing: processing through a sensory store, coding into short-term memory, and encoding and retrieval of information in long-term memory. This organization is simple and convenient for exposition. However, remember that things are actually more complex. Information processing almost certainly involves feedback loops and parallel processing at various depths.

There is general agreement that mentally retarded children and children with reading disabilities have problems in short-term memory. When information is first processed it either does not enter the short-term memory store, or it dissipates more quickly. Beyond agreement on this general principle, there is discussion about more specific issues, and it is at these more specific levels that things become more interesting. For instance, is the deficit evident at the early stages of short-term memory as well as later? To what types of learning material does the short-term deficit apply? What subprocesses are responsible for the short-term memory deficit, and are these subprocesses similar to those of retrieval from long-term memory? Finally, given a short-term memory deficit, what can one do about it?

Sensory Storage. Given its importance, it is surprising that there has been little study of the very earliest stage of information processing, variously called sensory storage, iconic memory, or very short-term memory. The sensory storage stage is important because it determines the total amount of information available to be processed at later stages. Those studies that have been done suggest that retarded people have a problem in iconic memory (Hornstein & Mosley, 1987). This deficit depends somewhat on the type of material presented (words or pictures), and it is not helped much by intensive practice (Baumeister, Runcie, & Gardepe, 1984; Ellis & Wooldridge, 1985).

Short-Term Memory. The majority of studies of information processing in children with handicaps have been done to elucidate the deficits in short-term memory. That there are such deficits is revealed in a child's more-than-usual difficulty in recalling information immediately after it is presented. For instance, in the digit span test, children are asked to repeat a series of numbers immediately after they are read to them. Mentally retarded and learning-disabled children make more errors in doing this than do unimpaired children (see R. L. Cohen, Netley, & M. A. Clarke, 1984 for a broader picture).

At least two things are important in the digit span test (Das, 1985). Children must identify the elements that have been presented, and they must retain the order in which they have been presented. Both of these aspects of the list must be retained in short-term memory long enough (a few seconds) for the children to reproduce the list when the tester asks for the response.

It is possible that the difficulty children have with retaining material in short-term memory is based at least partly on a structural deficit. That is, automatic, noncognitive, neurophysiological processes could be less active in some children with handicaps, thereby producing lower impact of all stimuli that the child receives. There is some evidence in favor of this structural approach (Ellis & Meador, 1985; Ellis, Deacon, & Wooldridge, 1985), but other evidence does not support it (Ceci, 1984).

More prominent than structural deficits are problems in the cognitive strategies that maintain information in short-term memory and encode it into long-term memory. One of the common cognitive strategies is rehearsal (Greene, 1987). Imagine looking up a number in a telephone book and then keeping it in mind while you are dialing the number. Frequently, people will repeat the number sequence, that is, rehearse it, until they have finished dialing the number. In this way, they retain the number in short-term memory until it is no longer needed. While they rehearse, people may apply other strategies such as grouping or clustering the items (Moe & J. D. Harris, 1983), associating the items with well-known events, creating images, and elaborating the simpler items (Bauer & Emhert, 1984).

Many young children and children with learning disabilities and mental retardation are limited in rehearsing as a way of keeping material in short-term memory (D. Elliott & Grundy, 1984; Kirchner & Klatzky, 1985). That is, they may be motivated to remember the information, but they do not generally apply the appropriate strategy efficiently to do so. As a result, their performance on the digit span test and, presumably, their memory for all rapidly occurring events are faulty. This has implications for the total information they remember in the long run.

To say that many children with cognitive deficits are limited in rehearsal strategy does not say that they do not have such strategies or that the deficit is unmodifiable. When the materials are presented in certain ways, for instance, mentally retarded children have been shown to rehearse (Turner & Bray, 1985). Also, it is clear that rehearsal strategies can be trained. When they are, short-term memory improves, at least in limited testing situations (Butterfield, Wambold, & Belmont, 1973). It is even possible that it may not be so much a problem of not having a strategy available as it is of not knowing how and when to use it. That is, it is possible that a production deficiency may be the problem (Bray & Turner, 1987; Ferretti, 1989; see also Griswold, Gelzheiser, & Shepherd, 1987).

In addition to rehearsal, clustering or grouping of information is helpful in storage. There is some evidence that children with learning disabilities and mental retardation have problems in clustering, but the effect is not very general (Shepherd, Gelzheiser, & Solar, 1985; Lindgren & Richman, 1984; Todman & File, 1985).

Beyond relatively simple memory strategies like rehearsal and clustering, more complex intellectual processes like elaboration, imaging, planning, and association with known information and rules become important (Belmont & Mitchell, 1987; Borkowski, M. Carr, & Pressley, 1987; Kerr & Blais, 1985; Lorsbach & Gray, 1985; Turnure, 1987). These are dealt with in more detail in the next chapter.

Depth of Processing and Effortful Versus Automatic Processing.

Other dimensions have also been suggested as important determinants of memory. One of these is depth of processing. Limited depth of processing has been suggested as one factor that produces the memory problems of children with learning disabilities and mental retardation. If children only name a picture when they see it rather than saying what it is used for, the processing may be said to be more superficial. Boyd and Ellis (1986) found that mentally retarded people remembered stimuli more if they processed them more deeply. But this was also true of normal groups, and there was no statistical interaction between the depth of processing and intelligence variables. In other words, although deeper processing increases memory, the short-term memory deficit of mentally retarded people is not necessarily attributable to more superficial processing (see also Stan & Mosley, 1988).

A similar concept is the distinction between effortful and automatic processing. Effortful processing is voluntary, requires attention, and is affected by instruction, practice, and feedback. Automatic processing may be involuntary and does not require attention. Most important for our concerns, automatic processing should not change much as a function of age and should not differentiate between normal children and children with handicaps.

Most of the research dealt with in this chapter is concerned with effortful processing. However, there are a few studies of automatic processing. They deal with spatial memory (Ellis, Woodley-Zanthos, & Dulaney, 1989) and frequency processing (Ellis & Allison, 1988; Ellis, Palmer, & Reeves, 1988). Spatial memory does not improve with age after 5 years of age (Ellis, E. Katz, & J. E. Williams, 1987), and most people with Down syndrome remember spatial information normally (if they perceive it in the first place). Accuracy of memory for frequency estimates differs somewhat between normal and retarded groups, but the differences are minimal and perhaps not generally significant (Woodley-Zanthos & Ellis, 1989; see Borcherding et al., 1988 for a similar finding with children with ADD-H).

Semantic Encoding

In addition to processes like rehearsal, clustering, and effortful processing, the nature of the material to be remembered is also important. There has been some recent interest in semantic memory. Semantic memory refers to the encoding and storage of encyclopedic knowledge, independent of time and space (as contrasted with episodic knowledge images, pictures, and events that are context-specific).

There can be differences in semantic memory between groups of children with handicaps. Reading-disabled boys recall verbal items less efficiently than do boys with ADD-H (Benezra & Douglas, 1988), although the latter group recalls poorly organized semantic material under instruction (August, 1987). Some, but not all, children with learning disabilities have difficulties in phonological coding that impact on word identification and spelling skills (Torgesen, 1988).

Reading-disabled children organize items according to their sounds (phonologically) rather than their meaning (semantically) to a greater degree than do nondisabled children (Swanson, 1987), perhaps because the semantic memory of reading-disabled children may not be well-organized (Swanson, 1986). A semantic representation deficit may also be characteristic of mentally retarded children (Merrill & Bilsky, 1990).

Retrieval from Long-term Memory

The organization of semantic memory and an emphasis on what one already knows shifts our attention to long-term memory and retrieval of information from it. The concept of long-term memory includes all of the information that is stored for more than a few minutes. Long-term memory has a very large capacity, and it is thought to be a permanent store. That is, the amount of information that can be stored in long-term memory is very large, and once there, the information is assumed to be stored permanently.

The simplest retrieval process is the search of the stored material that occurs when a person has recognized something. In order to answer a multiple choice examination question correctly, for instance, one must attempt to match each of the answers that are provided in the exam question with information that is in the long-term memory store. This involves searching the memory store.

In addition to searching the memory store, children may be asked to organize and produce a response. That is, they may be asked to recall the material. An example of a test of recall is an essay examination, which is more difficult than a multiple choice recognition test.

There is a central problem with the long-term memory concept because there is no direct way of determining what is stored in long-term memory. The only way that the long-term memory store can be surveyed is to engage one or more retrieval processes. If children seem to be different in long-term memory (i.e., they forget more over a long period of time), it could either be that they have less information stored, the information dissipates more quickly, or they have problems in retrieving the information that may be there.

One general solution is simply to assume that long-term memory has an infinite capacity and duration in everyone and if there are memory problems, they are not in the long-term memory store itself. As a consequence of this "solution," if a child can remember something, it means that the information was contained in the child's long-term memory store. On the other hand, if something is not remembered, we do not know with certainty whether we are dealing with a storage problem (i.e., the information never did get in long-term memory), with abnormal rate of fading from long-term storage, or with a retrieval deficit.

Another complicating question is whether retrieval processes are the same as storage processes into short-term memory. They are not the same, although they have some components in common, such as rehearsal (Ornstein, Medlin, B. P. Stone, & Naus, 1985) or the spontaneous use of strategies (Moe & J. D. Harris, 1983). Some of the evidence that storage and retrieval are different comes from studies of their normal development and of their development in learning-disabled children.

Both storage and retrieval improve with age. However, the normal development of storage and of retrieval have different courses (Brainerd, Kingma, & M. L. Howe, 1985). Storage and retrieval are different for learning-disabled children as compared with unimpaired children and the differences may depend on the dimension assessed (M. L. Howe, Brainerd, & Kingma, 1985; Stelmack, Saxe, Noldy-Cullum, K. B. Campbell, & Armitage, 1988; Swanson & Rathgeber, 1986). Moreover, there are subgroup differences among learning-disabled children such that some children have both a storage and a retrieval deficit, whereas others have a problem only with storage (J. M. Fletcher, 1985). Thus, there seems to be little question that storage and retrieval share some characteristics, but they are different.

Forgetting

Perhaps the most important approach to the study of long-term memory is the study of forgetting. Certainly, people remember significant things in their lives for very long periods of time. Childhood memories, especially pleasant ones, are remembered. Even events that have probably not been retrieved and rehearsed for decades may be recalled.

Although information may exist in long-term memory for a very long time, forgetting also occurs. If people are asked to produce information that they once knew well, they may remember part of it, but the time it takes to relearn the information increases as a function of time. This general pattern is clear and is part of everyday experience. Whether children with handicaps forget more, how to interpret such a finding, and what to do about it are more controversial.

A concept of forgetting assumes that information is in the long-term store in the first place. Teachers who provide brief experience with learning material and then complain that the child cannot retain information do not take into account the possibility that the brief experience was not adequate for encoding the material into long-term memory. This is possible even if the child recites the material perfectly once or twice. In the laboratory, the comparison of two groups with respect to forgetting assumes that initial learning of the material was equivalent in the two groups (Belmont, 1966).

On the whole, it is not clear whether forgetting is greater than normal in learning-disabled or mentally retarded children. Some studies show that, if care is taken to see that material is well-learned initially or if tasks that use simple storage and retrieval are tested, forgetting curves are not steeper in these groups (McCartney, 1987). On the other hand, other workers do find a specific problem in the retention of information (Winters &. Semchuk, 1986).

Even if there is a problem in retention, should we interpret the problem as dissipation of information from the long-term memory store (so that the information is no longer there), or is it a retrieval deficit (the information is there, but it cannot be recognized or recalled)? As indicated earlier, it is difficult or impossible to decide between these two possibilities. If one assumes that the nature of long-term memory includes an infinite capacity and that information stored there stays indefinitely, then forgetting must be due to a retrieval deficit. This, of course, is a logical, not an empirical solution.

Whatever one believes about the exact mechanisms, the implications for practice are clear. First, one should have a precise idea of what a child already knows, including rules, spatial concepts, stories, songs, and information directly related to information that is to be processed. Using that information as a set of individually designed mnemonic supports, the teacher can use rehearsal, clustering, and other strategies to assure that new information is encoded into long-term memory.

Second, to reduce forgetting the instructor will assure that the material is practiced rigorously so that retrieval strategies are learned, and the material is overlearned. This will maximize the strength of the new learning in long-term memory. Third, review of the material will reduce forgetting by connecting this newly stored information with still other memories, by maintaining retrieval strategies, and/or by preventing possible dissipation of the information from long-term memory.

Executive Function, Central Processing, and Metamemory. Another basic approach in the study of complex information processing has been to look at metamemory or executive functions (e.g., Horgan, 1985; Lawson, 1985). There are intellectual processes that the child can bring into play to determine in any specific situation what strategy will be most efficient for maintaining information in memory and storing it. For instance, sometimes it is appropriate to rehearse a telephone number and sometimes it is best to write it down. Deciding which to do involves a higher order strategy. These metamemorial or executive function concepts are dealt with in more detail in the next chapter.

However, there is one major concept that is worth mentioning here. Metamemory depends on stored information. One strategy for maintaining memory in short-term memory and encoding it for storage in long-term memory is relating the new material to information that one already has (Siegler, 1983). Several studies have shown that if one relates information that is to be learned to material that has already been learned well, the performance of children with handicaps improves. Examples are relating the new information to stories, rules, and known organizational features. (Glidden & Warner, 1985; Lukose, 1987; Manis et al., 1987; Recht & Leslie, 1988). In some cases, the improvement is not permanent (Glidden & Warner, 1985). However, the use of mnemonics generally is regarded as an aid to memory (Mastropieri, Scruggs, & Levin, 1985) and may also help with transfer (Gelzheiser, 1984). Perhaps, these aids must be practiced in order to be retained.

Up to this point, we have shown that many children with handicaps have defects in processing information. These defects may reside at least partly in the fact that the children are delayed in their development. But deficits in attention, encoding information from short-term memory, and retrieving information are all demonstrable, at least in some children.

The case with long-term memory is not as clear. There have not been as many studies of possible differential decay of information in long-term memory, despite the obvious practical importance of the question. Perhaps this is due to the logical problems inherent in the long-term memory concept. Or the technical problems in studying long-term memory without including encoding or retrieval processes may be difficult to accomplish. In any case, when such studies have been done, it seems that any problems that there are reside more in encoding and retrieval than in the actual maintenance of information in memory.

This is very encouraging because it implies that if we can teach a child methods for storing and retrieving material, then we can depend on the memory remaining as intact in handicapped children as it is in unimpaired children. Such training procedures have involved a variety of strategies including rehearsal, grouping, and relating the new information to information that the child already has in memory.

SPEED OF PROCESSING

All of this discussion has neglected another very important dimension in the processing of information, the speed or efficiency with which the various processes can take place. In everyday life, a person moves in a constantly changing environment that requires sifting of stimuli, rapid encoding of information, speedy scanning of already present memories, and efficient retrieval of the information that is appropriate for the situation. How efficiently this is done determines how well the child adapts in any one situation and whether the child will be able to store information for future use.

There is often a speed-accuracy tradeoff. That is, a person may accomplish something correctly, but may be so slow in doing it as to lose the next set of information that must be dealt with. Alternatively, speed may be emphasized so that much information is processed, but some of it is processed incorrectly. None of us processes information both very rapidly and very accurately. All of us must balance speed and accuracy for an optimum tradeoff.

Given that some children with handicaps have problems in encoding and retrieval, we might expect that they would also be generally less efficient than unimpaired children in processing information (Maisto & Baumeister, 1984). One important issue has to do with whether efficiency of processing information is related to general intelligence. It could be that more intelligent people process information more efficiently. Perhaps they store more information and retrieve it more efficiently so that they adapt better. Although plausible, this idea has only weak support. There is some evidence that there is a relationship between intelligence and information-processing speed, but speed of processing accounts for only a small part (0%–25%) of the variability of intelligence in unimpaired people (P. Barrett, Eysenck, & Lucking, 1986).

The hypothesis is more promising among handicapped children because children with handicaps are ordinarily slower in their response to stimuli than are unimpaired people (Nettlebeck & Kirby, 1983a, b). The slowness has been demonstrated for input phases (Nettlebeck, Robson, Walwyn, Downing, & N. Jones, 1986; Whyte, Curry, & Hale, 1985); scanning from memory (Elbert, 1984; Merrill, 1985; Mosley, 1985; C. K. Varnhagen, Das, & S. Varnhagen, 1987); and motor performance (e.g., Leslie, Davidson, & Batey, 1985; P. H. Wolff, C. Cohen & Drake, 1984). Todman and Gibb (1985) presented a somewhat more complex picture in which information processing is slower but memory scanning appears to be normal. Perhaps this is because there are several aspects of processing speed (M. Anderson, 1988).

On the whole then, information processing of at least some children with handicaps is slower than normal. This slowness is probably one of the causes of a cumulative deficiency in the information stored (i.e., achievement) and therefore in the ability to adapt. On the other hand, this deficiency in processing information probably is not the same for all kinds of material. Semantic material, for instance, may be more subject to this processing deficit than nonverbal stimuli (Todman & Gibb, 1985).

It is also clear that something can be done to improve various aspects of information processing. Perceptual scanning (Lyon & L. E. Ross, 1984) and reaction and movement times (Wade, Hoover, & Newell, 1984; Kerr & Blais, 1987) have been improved through training. Accuracy and speed training have improved speed and accuracy, respectively (Eisenberger, Mitchell, McDermitt, & Masterson, 1984). Even drugs can improve information processing (M. K. Reid & Borkowski, 1984). Overall, some aspects of information-processing efficiency can be problematic in at least some children, but there are procedures for correcting them.

SUMMARY

Understanding how a child takes in, processes, and stores information is essential to understanding the learning that is essential to adaptation. The first stage of learning involves focusing and maintenance of attention. Attention has a long history of study, and though it can be defined and measured in many ways, there is general agreement that it selects sensory processes and it has a limited capacity. Many children with handicaps have attention deficits of various kinds, including problems with arousal of attention, with the range of attention focusing, and with vigilance of the maintenance of attention.

Children with hyperactivity are also sometimes thought to have an attentional deficit disorder. Although this may be true of abnormally active children, it is not true of normal children who are lively. Thus, the relationship between activity level and attention deficit is not simple. Moreover, the relationship is confused by the possibility that hyperactive children may also be learning disabled, and the real problem may be associated with the learning disability rather than the hyperactivity.

Once the child has attended to the information, it is processed and stored. Studies fall into two large groups, associative learning and information processing. The studies of associative learning include a large literature on habituation and extinction, conditioning, discrimination learning, and generalization and transfer. There are few recent studies of habituation, extinction, or conditioning. Those that there are suggest there may be an inhibition deficit in some children with disabilities, but on the whole these processes are remarkably intact even in severely disabled children.

There has been intensive study of discrimination learning and generalization, especially for purposes of practical training. Training children to focus on the essential stimulus dimensions has been a dominant theme of the literature, and this has been accomplished, taking into account a usual redundancy of information that is part of everyday life. Training discriminations can be accomplished quite easily with careful planning of the teaching, but training on one task does not guarantee that what has been learned will be transferred to a new task. Transfer and generalization, using, for instance, fading procedures and the teaching of relationships between stimuli, have been remarkably successful even with severely retarded people.

Besides associative learning, the other approach to the study of learning and memory has been one that analyzes the processing of information in sensory and short- and long-term memory stores. This processing involves maintenance of the information, encoding it for storage and retrieval of the information once it has been stored. The great majority of studies of children with handicaps have been concerned with processes that occur in short-term or working memory.

There have been few studies of the initial stages of processing or of long-term memory. Those that exist suggest there may be deficits in a sensory store, but perhaps none in long-term memory. There are definitely problems in short-term or working memory in many children with handicaps. These memory deficits can be attributed to some deficiency in the processes or strategies that maintain information in memory and encode it for permanent storage. These strategies may be as simple as rehearsal or may include more complex strategies such as elaboration of the material being processed. Information processing definitely depends on the knowledge that a child already has available.

Children with disabilities often are less efficient in processing and storing information. Recent work has shown that this reduction in speed of processing may not necessarily be a general one. However, when it exists, it could add to a cumulative deficit in adaptation.

7 ———————————

Intelligence, Play, and Language

A central assumption in this book has been that adaptation is the main focus when considering the psychology of children with handicaps. We turn now to the most human of adaptations, the varied and complex processes that we call intelligence, play, and language. If one wishes, it would be easy to start an argument about the definition of intelligence. Is intelligence a general characteristic of which people have a lot or a little? Is it one or more special abilities or talents? Or is it only what intelligence tests measure? In this chapter, we show that intelligence is all of these and much more.

Like most other general psychological concepts, such as emotions, perception, social behavior, and psychotherapy, intelligence is a very general idea having many facets, levels, and applications. It is true that one can characterize a person's general intelligence with a single number, the IQ score. However, this does not mean that the score completely characterizes the person's thinking. Although the IQ score is a pretty good predictor of children's success in school, it does not do as well in predicting their income and the likelihood that they will have friends. Moreover, the general IQ score does not predict specific delays in academic performance such as those seen in children with learning disabilities who have normal intelligence but who have specific problems in reading or arithmetic. Nor does it account for special talents in music, chess-playing, and mathematics that are found in otherwise normal, or even mentally retarded, people.

Perhaps most important, even when the IQ score predicts academic performance, it says nothing about how thinking is carried on or what to do about difficulties. In the last chapter, we showed that such things as the store of knowledge one already has and the awareness of coding and retrieval processes are important factors in memory. These "higher processes" are examples of the things that are important in thinking.

In this chapter, we examine more fully these higher processes and their importance for the understanding of children with handicaps. First we describe different aspects of intelligence and the major concepts that pertain to them. Then, several examples of research on cognition are reviewed. The possibility that there are cognitive differences specific to classes of handicaps are reviewed, and applications of research on cognition to educational treatment are considered. The large literature on exploration and play is then reviewed, followed by the research on language. Language is important for the elaboration of ideas and for social communication. In this chapter, we review its relation to cognition; the study of language in a social context is left until a later chapter on social behavior.

Cognition and language have a complex relationship. Language and basic cognitive processes are apparently separate systems, but they interact with one another. Information is stored and retrieved as language just as it is in cognitive processes, and language expresses ideas that are already present in cognition. Thus, cognition is necessary, but not sufficient for language. At the same time, language serves to elaborate ideas, so that complex cognition depends on language. This transactive relationship is especially important in handicapping conditions, and many disorders are expressed as disorders of communication: nonverbal, verbal, oral, and written.

INTELLIGENCE

General Intelligence or Specific Abilities?

Is intelligence dominated by a general factor, by a larger number of general factors (Kolligian & Sternberg, 1987), or is it made up of several more specific processes? This question has been asked for more than a century, but it has not yet been settled to everyone's satisfaction. On the one hand, tests of what we call intellectual processes tend to be correlated with one another. This points to a general factor that underlies all intelligent behavior. There are people who excel in almost everything they put their hand to, and there are others who have difficulty in almost everything. The behavior of such people is evidence for a general factor in intelligence.

On the other hand, although tests of intellectual abilities correlate with one another, they often do not correlate very highly (Scruggs & Mastropieri, 1983). Moreover, there are many children with special talents and others who have specific learning disabilities. This specificity points to the conclusion that intelligence is made up of separate abilities.

This conflict between the views that intelligence represents a single general factor and is made up of separate abilities has been resolved with the elegant idea that intelligence is indeed made up of separate abilities, but in the ordinary person, these abilities tend to be correlated with one another (Detterman, 1987). This theory accounts both for specific abilities and disabilities and for any correlation between intellectual tests.

Context Effects

Aside from the question of whether a general factor dominates behavior or whether specific factors are primary, there is the question of the contexts and conditions of testing. Intelligence tests do not completely describe the person's behavior. The context of testing is an important contributor to the person's performance, and the knowledge the person has about that context probably also is a factor. Thus, especially with the milder handicaps, the interaction between process, context, and knowledge seems to be the best descriptor of intelligence (Ceci & Baker, 1989).

Different contexts are represented in the various tests that are useful for practical purposes. For instance, measures of adaptive behavior are widely used (e.g., Giller, Dial, & Chan, 1986). In addition, modifying the mode of test administration, perhaps by providing extra time, also can have a significant impact on performance (Centra, 1986). An emphasis on the interaction of process, context, and knowledge leads to an approach to intellectual assessment and special education that sees description of intellect as a dynamic interaction between the teacher and student during learning (Campione, 1989). Thus, seeing intelligence as a dynamic interaction of context and individual is quite different from viewing it as a single stable characteristic of an individual.

Operations and Strategies

The notion that intelligence is made up of specific abilities is also consistent with the view that intelligence may be characterized as sets of mental operations. An operation is a mental process that selects and modifies information that the person receives or already has stored. Operations may be relatively simple, as when two events are discriminated from one another. Or they may be complex, for example, when a long mathematical formula is applied to information. In other words, from this view, intelligence is composed of a large set of mental operations. This way of putting it is represented in the theories of Jean Piaget and of Lev Semenovich Vygotsky (C. A. Stone, 1985).

Mental operations are sometimes called strategies. In the last chapter on learning and memory, relatively simple strategies such as rehearsal and grouping were described. In this chapter, we emphasize more complex strategies such as planning (Spitz, Minsky, & Bessellieu, 1985), analogical thinking (Nippold, Erskine, & Freed, 1988; Tzuriel & Klein, 1985), and metacognition (Belmont & Mitchell, 1987; Swanson, 1985).

Metacognition refers to two components: knowledge about the strategies one has available and regulation of those strategies. In other words, thinking refers both to awareness of ideas and to manipulation of them. Children with learning disabilities seem to have problems in both of these aspects of metacognition (Slife, J. Weiss, & Bell, 1985). Mentally retarded children and hyperactive children are deficient in general strategy use, which is at least partly a result of inadequate knowledge about how to go about using strategies (Belmont & Mitchell, 1987; Borkowski, M. Carr, & Pressley, 1987).

Developmental Delay

Strategy use increases with age in normal children, and it also becomes increasingly complex. Thus, development is a major predictor of thinking. Less obvious is the idea that delay in development is the major concept used to explain problems in use of strategies or operations. Delay of development is one of the main concepts used to explain problems in thinking.

However, there are also thinking problems that are better characterized as deviant. In other words, they represent thinking that does not occur in normal children at any age. The thinking processes are different, not merely delayed in development. Examples would be obsessive or paranoid thinking (Baron, 1982).

The distinction between disability manifest as a delay of development or as a deviation in development is probably oversimple and discussions about it have probably generated unnecessary heat. The "similar sequence hypothesis," which states that all people pass through the same cognitive stages, may not be true in detail even for the children with mild mental retardation it originally set out to describe. It certainly does not apply to children with severe mental handicaps, with autism, or even those with severe motor disabilities (Berninger, 1988; Morgan, 1986; B. Weiss, Weisz, & Bromfield, 1986).

Characteristics of Intellectual Disorders

Intelligence can be characterized as delayed or as different, but there are also more detailed ways of describing disorders of intellect, emphasizing performance on standardized intelligence tests, measures of everyday adaptation, specific abilities, and the importance of stored knowledge and how it is stored, retrieved, and used.

Standardized Tests. The most common way of describing intellectual processes is with standardized intelligence tests. Examples are the Stanford-Binet or the Wechsler Intelligence Scale for Children, which are administered to a single child at a time, and the Scholastic Aptitude Test, which is a group test. These scales are composed of several subtests, each of which assesses a complex psychological ability. For instance, the digit span test on the Wechsler scales tests children's attention and short-term memory by having them repeat a string of numbers.

Different IQ tests are made up of different subtests and they are often standardized on different populations, so it is not surprising they do not always result in the same score. This does not mean they are useless, but interpretation of IQ scores requires care (Spitz, 1986).

The different subtests in the IQ scales reflect different aspects of intelligence. Scores on the subtests correlate positively with one another, but to different degrees. If all subtests were almost perfectly correlated with each another, one could conclude that they are measuring only one thing, that is, general intelligence. However, the positive correlations between subtests are not only imperfect, but also variable. This means they not only measure general intelligence and assess factors specific to the subtests, but also reflect factors common to only some of the subtests but not others.

This complicated situation can be sorted out with a statistical procedure known as factor analysis that seeks common factors by summarizing the relationships between the scores of individual subtest scores. Through factor analysis, general intelligence and factors specific to an individual test, as well as intermediate factors such as verbal ability, are revealed. One study that can serve as an example was a factor analysis of the Wechsler Intelligence Scale for Children, which identified verbal comprehension and perceptual organization factors in the performance of children with learning disabilities (P. C. Fowler, 1986).

At least as useful as descriptions of groups, factor analysis provides the possibility of comparing factor structures between groups. Sex differences among learning-disabled children (Lawson & Inglis, 1985; C. D. Elliott & Tyler, 1987) and group differences between schizophrenic and autistic children (Asarnow, Tanguay, Bott, & Freeman, 1987) have been studied in this way.

Standardized tests of intelligence in children were developed to predict need for special services in school. Other scales are intended to measure adaptive behavior at home and in the community by assessing maturity of such skills as self-feeding, dressing, and use of money. The correlation between these adaptive behavior scales and the standardized intelligence tests is only moderate, although children with intellectual handicaps are also delayed on adaptive behavior scales. This means that intelligence tests and adaptive behavior scales measure different, but related things (Keith, Fehrmann, Harrison, & Pottebaum, 1987; Leigh, 1987).

Descriptions of Processes. More common than factor analyses are controlled studies that examine intellectual processes in detail. A recent development is the consideration of ways in which children with handicaps understand and produce stories. One study showed that reading-disabled children seem to have less difficulty in comprehending narratives than in producing them (Feagans & Short, 1984). Compositions written by normal and disabled students can be classified according to their cohesion, degree of expressiveness, and fluency. Many disabled readers and learners showed less understanding of a story in their compositions, and their writing tended to show a less mature expressiveness. Problems in fluency are related partly to learning and reading disabilities and in part to lower intelligence (Liles, 1985; Nodine, Barenbaum, & Newcomer, 1985). In picture stories, autistic children apparently have difficulty in understanding and expressing specific concepts, such as the mental states of the characters (Baron-Cohen, Leslie, & Frith, 1986). Learning-disabled children do not comprehend proverbs, cartoons, or other humor very well (Bruno, J. M. Johnson, & Simon, 1987; Lutzer, 1988; E. Pickering, A. Pickering, & Buchanan, 1987) Thus, in story material, comprehension and production problems can be defined. This understanding has implications for teaching procedures (Nodine, Barenbaum, & Newcomer, 1985).

Mathematics. Complex mental processes are also involved in mathematics, and children with learning disabilities and mental retardation have difficulties in solving arithmetic problems. To some extent, this is because they do not have the necessary concepts. For instance, there is reason to believe that these children are delayed in their ability to count, in memory for numbers and number combinations, and in acquisition of the idea that quantities are conserved when they change form (P. T. Ackerman, Anhalt, & Dykman, 1986; Baroody, 1986; Derr, 1985; Geary, Widaman, Little, & Cormier, 1987; Shalev, Weirtman, & Amir, 1988; see also R. T. Brown, Borden, Schleser, Clingerman, & Orenczuk, 1985). These basic cognitive problems may underlie some of the problems the children have in computation. Moreover, when computation is taken into account, there are additional problems in encoding and retrieving arithmetic information efficiently (Swanson & Rhine, 1985). This seems to be particularly true when the problem is presented to the children in story form (Bilsky & Judd, 1986).

Classification and Problem Solving. Classification and problem solving are other basic aspects of intelligent behavior. Seeing the similarities and differences between objects is important at both nonverbal and verbal levels and is at least partly based on perceptual processes (Burns, 1986; Greenfield & Scott, 1986). General mental level is probably more important than clinical category in determining verbal classification (Tager-Flusberg, 1985; Winters & Hoats, 1985).

Executive Function. Another important aspect of intelligence is the adaptation of such strategies as planning and evaluation to specific situations (i.e., executive activity). Levine and Langness (1985) called for the study of thinking in everyday situations. They studied the intellectual organizational techniques that mentally retarded people use in shopping in a supermarket. Although there were individual differences among the retarded people, all of the people they studied were able to buy their supplies and used a variety of metacognitive skills in doing so. Thus, mentally retarded people demonstrate executive activity when shopping. However, their executive activity is different from that of nonhandicapped people (Lawson, 1985), and this is also true of hyperactive children and children with learning disabilities (Cherkes-Julkowski, Gertner, & Norlander, 1986; Hamlett, Pellegrini, & C. K. Conners, 1987; Swanson, 1988a, 1988b). Moreover, it seems likely that a person's belief about the efficacy of a strategy will determine its use (Borkowski, Estrada, Milstead, & Hale, 1989).

Social Cognition. Cognition is also important in social situations. In fact, there is reason to believe that cognition in object and in social skill domains share common features (Seibert, Hogan, & Mundy, 1986). One study indicated that mentally retarded people may understand social situations but may not be able to apply the knowledge adequately (Soodak, 1990).

A most important aspect of social intelligence is the ability to see things from another person's point of view. This perspective-taking skill increases with mental age in nonhandicapped children, and mental age is also an important correlate of perspective taking in mentally retarded children. Social experience that mentally retarded children have because they are older can influence their tendency to take someone else's perspective, at least at some ages (Bliss, 1985). There is also evidence that a problem with perspective taking may be quite specific, and it may be independent of general mental age in some autistic children (Baron-Cohen, 1989).

Cognitive Style. Another aspect of cognition not determined simply by developmental level is cognitive style. Children differ with respect to the degree to which they evaluate answers before responding. Children who are typically reflective tend to respond slowly and to consider their answers, whereas other children respond more impulsively. This reflective–impulsive dimension is related to aggression and motivation for academic work, with impulsive children judged to be more aggressive and less motivated than more reflective children (Bernfeld & Peters, 1986). The dimension is also related to the manner of making moral judgments (Gargiulo, 1984). Cognitive style is related to some aspects of reading in hearing-handicapped children (Davey & LaSasso, 1985), whereas mentally retarded children are not different from normal children who have been matched for mental age. Thus, independent of developmental level, cognitive style seems to be an important aspect of cognition in children with handicaps.

Another dimension of cognitive style is field dependence or independence. Field dependent people are likely to be influenced by authority figures or peers, and they may be dependent on external opinions. Field independent people tend to be less affected by others, perhaps even socially detached. The studies of this dimension of cognitive style suggest there is a weak tendency for some children with handicaps to be field dependent (Bice, G. Halpin, & G. Halpin, 1986; Stoner & Glynn, 1987).

Still a third categorization of cognitive style divides people into three groups who organize incoming information differently, that is, descriptive-analytic, categorical, and relational. The information about this classification is meager, and it is controversial with respect to whether children with handicaps differ from normal (Knutson, 1986; Shinn-Strieker, 1986).

In sum, different aspects of intelligence can be described, and children with cognitive handicaps can be compared with nonhandicapped children. Sometimes there is a specific cognitive problem associated with a clinical category. More often a general handicap is described as a pervasive delay in intellectual development.

Clinical Categories and Intelligence

Level of maturational development is the best predictor of a child's complexity of thinking, and many children with handicaps have some sort of maturational delay, but there is also the question of whether children with specific categories of disability show qualitatively different patterns of thinking.

On the whole, they do not. That is, although many children with handicaps are delayed in their cognitive development, and although there are special patterns to this delay, there is no simple relationship between clinical category and pattern of cognitive development. In many studies, there are no differences between children with handicaps and children without handicaps. In others, there are differences, but there is substantial overlap between groups. Sometimes the differences exist in comparison with normal children, but groups of children with handicaps do not differ (Candler, D. L. Johnson, & Green, 1983; M. Gordon, Post, Crouthamel, & Richman, 1984; Swicegood & Crump, 1984).

These ideas are illustrated in the few recent studies of children with chronic health disorders. In general, children with chronic health handicaps, such as diabetes or myelomeningocele, score within the average range of intelligence, although they may have specific deficits associated with motor deficits or a general slowness in responding (C. S. Holmes & Richman, 1985; Shaffer, Friedrich, Shurtleff, & L. Wolf, 1985). Low birth weight children or children who have undergone tracheostomy are intellectually normal unless their illness is associated with neurological problems. Despite their normal general intelligence, however, they may be subject to specific skill deficits and emotional impairments (Holwerda-Kuipers, 1987; L. T. Singer, Wood, & Lambert, 1985). Thus, cognitive disorders in children with chronic health disorders are associated with physical problems and are individually determined. The individual differences between children in patterning of physical and mental problems points to an individual rather than a group approach to diagnosis and treatment (Shaffer et al., 1985).

From a practical point of view, it therefore seems as though assessing a specific child's pattern of intellectual performance, rather than inferring cognition from clinical category, seems most realistic. On the other hand, there are several worthwhile comparisons between groups. In general, these comparative studies seek to find some specific cognitive problem associated with a clinical category. The diagnostic categories included in these studies have been sensory disorders, reading and learning disabilities, mental retardation (including Down syndrome), and childhood autism and schizophrenia.

Sensory Disorders.   The question of the relationship between congenital sensory disorders and cognitive development has been around since at least the 17th century. An empiricist perspective predicts that a sensory disorder will limit experience, so that the cognition that depends on the affected sense will be delayed. It would be no surprise to find that congenitally blind children would have difficulty imagining what a color is like or that deaf children would have difficulty in learning spoken language. Children born with a visual handicap cannot use sight for the development of basic concepts about what the visual world is like. Moreover, some blind children are delayed in motor development, so that to the extent that basic concepts are dependent on motor action, they will be handicapped in early concept development such as object permanence. Nevertheless, they do learn through tactual and auditory experience that objects are permanent, and the sequencing of stages in this development apparently is normal (Bigelow, 1986). When they are older, these children can use tactual information to improve memory for auditorily presented text material, though they are not as efficient in doing this as are blind children whose visual handicap was incurred after birth (Pring & Rusted, 1985). Finally, blind children are delayed in moral reasoning and this is partly related to their cognitive delay (Markoulis, 1988).

Hearing handicapped children show delayed (Bracken & Cato, 1986) and perhaps different (F. X. Gibbons, 1985; Zwiebel & Mertens, 1985) cognitive development, especially if the children are not given special education. However, this applies more to cognition that depends on language than to nonverbal cognitive skills (Bond, 1987). These deficits are more pronounced if the handicapped children have lost their hearing early in infancy. Moreover, the extent of the handicap varies with the mode of communication. The cognitive problem is less apparent with nonverbal material and when the child has been taught the specific concepts being tested.

Learning Disabilities. Thus, children who are born with a sensory disorder may be specifically affected in some aspect of cognition. Children with learning disabilities are thought to have specific disabilities in school performance associated with specific islands of cognitive delay. Actually, the cognitive problems of children with learning disabilities are more general than this. Groups of children who have been classified as learning disabled have, for instance, been shown to have difficulty in time estimates and in problem solving on some tasks but not others (Dodd, Griswold, G. H. Smith, & Burd, 1985; Ludlow & Woodrum, 1985). On intelligence tests, there is even evidence that whereas the profiles of groups of subtests show more unevenness in learning-disabled groups than in mildly mentally retarded children, this may be a statistical artifact of selection of children who have difficulties in regular classes (Van der Wissel, 1987). This reinforces the idea mentioned in the previous chapter that mentally retarded and learning-disabled groups share difficulties in the coding and retrieval of information.

Mental Retardation. Mental retardation is a delay in development, perhaps characterized by low efficiency in the action of general and specific cognitive processes (M. Anderson, 1986). In mentally retarded people, the cognitive problems are pervasive, although in a very few, surprisingly special outstanding skills such as musical, artistic, and calendar calculation abilities have been reported (A. L. Hill, 1978; L. K. Miller, 1987, 1989; N. O'Connor & Hermelin, 1989).

Ordinarily, subgroups of mentally retarded people do not differ from each other in important ways. However, there is an exception with Down syndrome. It may be remembered from a previous chapter that Down syndrome is associated with an abnormality of the 21st chromosome. This has led to the expectation of some association with dementia alzheimer type, especially premature aging. There is indeed some evidence for such association because although the mental growth of people with Down syndrome increases until they are 30 or 40 years of age, they do seem to decline more rapidly than other mentally retarded people, especially after they are 50 (Berry, Groeneweg, Gibson, & R. I. Brown, 1984; Thase, Tigner, Smeltzer, & Liss, 1984). There is also some evidence that they have special difficulty with expressive language early in life (C. C. Cunningham, Glenn, Wilkinson, & Sloper, 1985). It should be emphasized, however, that these differences between people with Down syndrome and other retarded people are statistically significant but not dramatic, and there is now even some question about the basic finding (Fenner, Hewwitt, & Torpy, 1987). In any case, there certainly is overlap between the various types of mental retardation.

Autism and Schizophrenia.   The overlap of cognitive disorders is also evident in the study of childhood autism and schizophrenia. The two groups do differ somewhat on measures of cognitive performance in that groups of schizophrenic children are somewhat less delayed than children who have been diagnosed as autistic. However, both groups show similar patterns of cognitive problem and are characterized as being delayed in all skills (Waterhouse & Fein, 1984).

More attention has been given to the nature of the cognitive deficits in autistic children. About 75% of children with autism are also mentally retarded. This is consistent with Rutter's (1983) concept that a central cognitive deficit is basic to the social and language problems that are characteristic of autism. It is also consistent with Wing's view (1981) that autistic children have problems in three areas: producing and monitoring normal species-specific preverbal sounds, drives to explore the environment and explain experiences, and recognition of other human beings who are of special significance to them.

Some of these hypothesized special deficits are intended to differentiate autistic children from sociable mentally retarded children of the same mental level. It is not yet clear whether they are successful in doing so. Autistic children are apparently no more egocentric than other children of the same mental level (Hobson, 1984), and they have no special problem in self-recognition, that is, distinguishing themselves from others (Dawson & McKissick, 1984). Thus, although we know that autistic children are delayed in cognitive, language, and social areas, we do not yet know whether these delays are themselves specific to childhood autism. The best guess now seems to be that there is incomplete overlap between the cognitive and language deficits of children with autism and with mental retardation, but autistic children seem to have an as yet unspecified problem in social interaction.

From all this, it seems clear that there is much overlap in the cognitive processes of the various categories of handicap. This overlapping can exist in the efficiency of the general cognitive processes as well as more specific operations. In turn, these processes depend on the knowledge that the child already has. We turn now to a consideration knowledge structures, how they affect intellectual activity, and methods of training to improve intelligence.

Training Cognition

People sometimes think intelligence determines the limits of how much a person can know. However, it is also true that what people know determines the efficiency of their cognitive processes. This point was made in the last chapter when we noted that the nature and amount of stored information affects coding and retrieval processes. We now apply this principle to higher processes and relate it to training methods.

The interpretation of what an IQ score means has always been controversial and continues to be so. On the one hand, it is possible to regard the IQ as a rough measure of how well a person will be able to learn and think in the future. This is the basis of the use of the IQ score as a practical predictor of grade placement in school. On the other hand, there is general agreement that how well a person scores on an IQ test is a result of both a person's ability to learn and the degree to which that person has had the opportunity to learn the skills tested on conventional intelligence tests.

This emphasis on the opportunity to learn as a determiner of IQ scores is consistent with the idea that knowledge is an important aspect of intelligent behavior. In order to act in an intelligent manner (or to succeed on an item in an IQ test), one must be acquainted with the structure of the problem one is dealing with and the necessary facts for solution of the problem.

Learning Potential.   Some children have not had adequate opportunity to learn the skills necessary to answer the questions on IQ tests, but they have no intrinsic difficulty in learning those skills, given the opportunity. Making a distinction between children who *have not* learned and children who *cannot* learn has been made through an approach to testing called *learning potential testing* or *dynamic assessment.*

In this case, one tests performance on a subtest, trains the person how to do the test, and then retests that person's performance. If low initial performance is mainly a consequence of experiential deprivation, then training should provide the child with the necessary experience to accomplish the task, and the score should be significantly elevated. On the other hand, if initial performance is not mainly the result of experiential deprivation, but is more due to a problem in learning, this improvement in scores should be more difficult. These predictions have been tested by Budoff (1969). He showed that, among children who already have a low IQ, a learning potential procedure can distinguish between children who are more likely to benefit from education and children who have a more difficult time with academic work, as well as that children who gain more tend to come from lower socioeconomic and immigrant homes. An application of the learning potential principle has also been shown to improve performance of deaf children who, of course, may also be regarded as suffering from experiential deprivation that depresses verbal cognitive functioning (Keane & Kretschmer, 1987).

The learning potential approach is reasonable and has been available for many years. However, it is not used in everyday practice very often. Perhaps it is too difficult to standardize the training procedures that are part of the overall method. Perhaps it is merely a case of cultural lag that prevents its acceptance.

On the other hand, it may be that whereas the learning potential procedure is useful in demonstrating that certain children can learn better than a biological deficit concept of the IQ would lead one to expect, in fact the short training procedures of the learning potential procedure cannot compensate for the loss in experience associated with either a biological or a long-term experiential deficit. That is, if one believes that all disabilities, by their very nature, involve at least some deprivation of experiences important for normal cognitive development, then neither the conventional IQ test nor the learning potential procedure can be regarded as totally satisfactory for identifying whether poor performance is due to either an experiential factor or to some other factor that is independent of experience.

The alternative is to shift the emphasis away from general questions of diagnosis toward more specific questions about the nature of cognitive problems and what to do about them. This shift does not deny the importance of diagnosis, but it emphasizes very specific descriptions, and it relates these descriptions to the application of well-defined procedures for training done as a consequence of dynamic assessment (Campione, 1989). Thus, IQ tests and Learning Potential can be useful for general planning for school systems and for determining school placement for individuals, but minimizing the effects of experiential deprivations, whatever the source, can best be accomplished with well-defined educational programs.

Training Cognitive Skills. We discuss general educational treatment programs more fully in chapter 10. At this point, it should be sufficient to say that education programs that begin early (early intervention) have proven to be effective in preventing a cumulative deficit in cognition. Also successful have been individualized planning of education programs that take into account the child's current cognitive level and motivation.

The focus of the programs that train cognition is on general skills that are applicable in many contexts. Thus, planning, thinking with analogies, skill transfer, locating the main idea in texts, and coordinating social cues with what one already knows are all examples of the higher order skills that are important for training of intelligence. These skills are examples of the kinds of metacognition we have discussed earlier as important for promoting generalization.

As with all other behavioral training, a most important aspect of the training of intellectual skills is the clear definition of the skill that is to be taught. Second, the procedure itself must be set out so that the teacher knows what it is. The procedure is well-defined, but is flexible enough so that it adapts to the differences that most certainly occur between children. The procedure also involves several repetitions of the correct performance with different materials in different contexts to be quite sure that the child has learned the skill well and can apply it reliably.

Finally, successful training includes evaluation. Simply teaching a skill is no guarantee that it is learned. Moreover, a single correct repetition of a principle does not necessarily mean that the principle will be remembered later on. Instead, continual testing to determine whether the cognitive skill is learned and remembered is a necessary feature of the training programs in this area.

There have been several successful attempts to teach specific cognitive skills to children with handicaps. McConaghy and Kirby (1987) broke down analogy problems into five components (encoding, inference, mapping, application, preparation of the response). Using these concepts, they demonstrated that mentally retarded adults performed better after training that used these concepts than after simply being asked to solve a series of analogies. Minsky, Spitz, and Bessellieu (1985) showed that training involving a combination of modeling, giving information on how to organize the problem, and a step-by-step helping procedure increased performance on a laboratory planning task. J. A. Barton (1988) taught metacognitive strategies on a problem-solving task, and Larson and Gerber (1987) trained impulse control to learning-disabled and low-achieving youthful offenders through metacognitive strategies.

These experiments, among many others (Palincsar & D. A. Brown, 1987; Swanson, 1989), show that cognitive skills can be trained with complex procedures. However, there are certain features about them that raise other questions. First, they are laboratory experiments and do not by themselves demonstrate that the kind of cognitive skills important in the classroom are also trainable. That training of intellectual skills is also possible in the classroom has, however, been demonstrated with learning-disabled children who have been taught to identify the main ideas and story lines in reading passages (Idol, 1987; J. P. Williams, 1986), to study (D. F. Alexander, 1985), and to induce skill transfer through training for appropriate strategy selection (Gelzheiser, Shepherd, & Wozniak, 1986). Thus, the experimental studies probably reflect general processes that are also happening in the classroom.

The experimental studies also showed that although, in general, performance can increase as a result of careful and extended training, some aspects of performance may not change and other aspects that have not been trained do increase. For instance, in the training of analogies, encoding time may be increased at the beginning of training but not thereafter. This means that it is worthwhile assessing, not only overall performance, but also components of performance in order to evaluate the basis of general improvement in performance.

The laboratory studies also point out that training can affect, not only cognitive skills, but also motivation. In fact, the increase in cognition might even be interpreted as resulting from motivational improvement. In the study of planning by Minsky and colleagues (1985), the most impressive change in the trainees was increased confidence in their own ability and improved persistence at the task. Thus, because of the refinement in their procedures, the laboratory studies were able to demonstrate important details about the effectiveness of training.

Taken as a group, the studies of training of cognitive skills are consistent in showing improvement of intellectual skills with training. However, they are inconsistent in what is perhaps their most important criteria, the degree to which improvements in performance are retained for long periods and transfer to other situations.

Retention and Transfer.   According to recent opinion, retention and transfer can be promoted if one recognizes that successful learning of cognitive skills most often occurs in a social context where the interaction between the teacher and several students is reciprocal (Reeve & A. L. Brown, 1985; Turnure, 1987). In contrast to an approach in which limited strategies are taught through a formula whose structure and purpose the student does not understand is a teaching method in which the student is an active participant in the learning process. This approach depends on the assumption that children generally are active in learning about their environment. In teaching reading to children who are delayed in reading skills, the goals and structure of the lesson are clear to the teacher and become clear to the students as they are given the opportunity to ask about them, to assume the role of the teacher in the group, and to evaluate others as well as themselves.

As a result, the students' ability to engage in these activities increases. They also gain in feelings of self-competence, and scores on tests of reading comprehension increase and remain higher over at least several months (Reeve & A. L. Brown, 1985). Thus, the assumption that the child is an active learner in a reciprocal social situation has been the basis for efficient training in children with handicaps. Not only are complex intellectual skills increased with this approach, but feelings of self-competence that increase the child's motivation to learn are also affected. The overall result is a more intelligent, more active learner.

PLAY AND COGNITIVE DEVELOPMENT

The preceding section points out that intellectual skills develop as a result of experience and that it is possible to teach them in formal educational settings. However, many concepts are not learned in school or by formal teaching at home. Active children who are curious about the world learn things from informal observation during the course of everyday life. One such aspect is play. In this section, we review the rather large literature on the play of handicapped children.

To begin with, it is important to understand the complexity of the concept of play. It is possible that some of the contradictions in the literature on play of children with handicaps is at least partly a result of the different meanings the concept has for different people.

Although everyone can recognize instances of play when they occur, there is little agreement on the definition of the concept of play. When a kitten chases a ball, when a baby bangs a rattle, when two children pretend to be a "mommy" and a "daddy," and when a group of children are running a race, most people would agree that play is occurring. However, defining the common attributes of these behaviors is more difficult.

Moreover, it is sometimes difficult to differentiate play activities from other behaviors. For instance, play and exploration are sometimes believed to be related phenomena. But as you can see from the examples in the previous paragraph, many play behaviors are not simply exploration, and one would not regard the activities of the explorers of the South Pole as play.

Perhaps the most ambiguous aspect of the concept of play has to do with its adaptive function. There are several formal theories of the function of play, but the most important purports that children learn about their physical and social world when they play and this learning prepares them for adulthood. The idea that the function of play is to learn is a widely held point of view, and its acceptance is the basis of the organization of curriculum in early education.

Although the idea that play fosters learning probably is correct, there are two related questions that have emerged recently to complicate the issue. First, does a child always learn something when playing? Second, is it the play itself that is the basis of learning or does play merely form one occasion, among a variety of experiences, that teach a child about the world? In other words, does play provide a unique experience, or even a better experience, than, for example, modeling the behavior of an older person or direct tuition?

Asking these more refined questions about play requires testing procedures that contrast the effects of play, observation, directed practice, and perhaps other types of nonplay experience on an activity like problem solving. There have not been many studies that do this. However, those that do (e.g., Vandenberg, 1981) indicate that children do not always learn from playing and whether they do or not depends on their developmental level in combination with the nature of the material to be learned.

Types of Play

This more complex view of the nature of play leads to the consideration of specific types of play rather than to the discussion of play in general. In the literature on children with handicaps, distinctions have been made between various types of play (Rubin & N. Howe, 1985; Yawkey & Toro-Lopez, 1985). Level of cognitive development is one basis for classification. Thus, (a) sensorimotor play, constructive play, dramatic play, and games-with-rules or (b) presymbolic play, autosymbolic play, single scheme games, multiple scheme games, and planned symbolic games are two sequences thought to be correlates of developmental level.

Typologies that categorize toys and play activities into functional groupings are also available. One of these is the distinction between instructional, constructional, realistic replicas, and real objects. It is important to note that there are subclassifications of play behavior and they are the basis for design of toy materials.

In addition, different types of toys and situations elicit different types of play (Pellegrini, 1985; Rubin & Howe, 1985). Art materials elicit solitary and constructive play. Realistic representational toys stimulate pretend play in younger children, whereas more abstract toys may encourage pretend play in older children.

Furthermore, when we compare handicapped with nonhandicapped children or assess the effects of play, are we dealing with the amount of play or its organization? How much a child plays is necessary condition for determining its effects. The organization of play is also important. The number of toys children can be interested in, whether they construct something when they play, or whether they play alone or with others are all aspects of the organization of play.

Play of Children with Handicaps

There are two central issues emphasized in the scientific literature on play of children with handicaps. First, is the play of children with handicaps different from play behavior of nonhandicapped children? The second deals with ways of increasing the amount and maturity of play behavior.

Almost all children engage in play, so it would be an error to say that children with handicaps do not play (McConkey, 1985). However, some differences have been found. At least some measures of play behavior have been found to show differences from normal in mentally retarded, autistic, language-disordered, hearing-impaired, and high risk, but not low risk, preterm children (Cannella, Berkeley, Constans, & Parkhurst, 1987; Casby & McCormack, 1985; Li, 1985; Loveland, 1987; McCune & Ruff, 1985; Roth & D. M. Clark, 1987; Udwin & Yule, 1983; Wulff, 1985). In most studies, however, important measures do not differentiate clinical groups (MacTurk, Vietze, McCarthy, McQuiston, & Yarrow, 1985), and sometimes the differences disappear when developmental age is taken into account (e.g., Casby & Ruder, 1983; Vandenberg, 1985). As might be expected, play behavior is correlated with both intelligence and language development (Lombardino & Sproul, 1984), but sometimes these relationships are not as strong in handicapped children as they are in nonhandicapped children (C. C. Cunningham, Glenn, Wilkinson, & Sloper, 1985; Wulff, 1985).

There has been special interest in the symbolic play of children with autism. Symbolic play is important because it may indicate the child's capacity for mental representation. This capacity is thought to mediate the relation between play and language that is deficit in autistic children (Mundy, Sigman, Ungerer, & T. Sherman, 1987). Play is, in fact, correlated with language development in autistic children (Atlas & Lapidus, 1988), and autistic children show a low level of play (Baron-Cohen, 1987). However, it is possible that their low amount of play can be attributed to motivational factors as well as to cognitive variables (V. Lewis & Boucher, 1988). Thus, its significance is not yet certain.

Use of Play in Treatment

There are several uses of play in treatment of children with handicaps. Perhaps the most widely known are play diagnosis and play therapy. Both of these clinical methods deal primarily with symbolic play in which complex fantasy is reflected in the play behavior. There is very little recent research on either of these approaches (Lentz, 1985). In diagnosis, standard toys representing human beings are presented to the children, and they are encouraged to play with them. The diagnosis assumes that important psychological issues that concern the children, will be reflected in the social situations that they construct as they engage in play with the dolls. In the play therapy, the therapist and the children talk about the children's conceptions of the relationships between the dolls.

Increasing Toy Play

There is somewhat more study of ways of encouraging toy play. Some of this research evaluates whether play has actually been increased, but not much has been devoted to determining whether there actually is an effect of play on cognitive processes. The play of even profoundly retarded children can be increased rather easily by providing appropriate toys. Playing with such toys has immediate beneficial effects (G. Murphy, J. Carr, & Callias, 1986). In the case of children at the sensorimotor or prelinguistic level of development, sensory feedback such as vibration, lights, and sounds can be important. In some children, modification of the toys for easier manipulation, and matching toys to cognitive levels can be helpful. Langley (1985) listed criteria for appropriateness of toys, including safety; durability; appropriateness for the sensory, motor, and cognitive characteristics of the child; and the nature of the environment in which the toy will be used. In addition to physical factors, social influences can also be important. For example, parents encourage play behavior and do so differently for 12-month-old children who were born prematurely (Landry, Chapieski, & Schmidt, 1986).

The research on play in handicapped children may be summarized as follows: Almost all children play. There are some differences between handicapped and nonhandicapped groups in both amount and organization of play. However, individual differences are great, and whether or not there are differences depends on the measure of playing that is used. Play can be encouraged, primarily by appropriate selection and modification of toys. It is widely believed that play is beneficial for cognitive development, but the nature of this benefit is not yet known.

LANGUAGE

Cognition and Language

Communication is the transmission of ideas from one individual to another (Lloyd & Karlan, 1984). Language is the medium of this communication and involves the perception or transmission of more or less abstract symbols through informal gestures, and manual, oral, and written formal signs. The exact connection between nonlinguistic cognition and language has received much discussion, and it is clear that the two are related in important ways (Rice, 1983). Current views suggest that cognition and language are both "cognitive" (i.e., they represent abstract thinking processes).

Nonlinguistic and linguistic systems are different but incompletely overlapping. Nonlinguistic ideas ordinarily map onto linguistic forms, but the reverse might not be true, and language and nonlanguage systems may not be strongly related in development (Petitto, 1987). There are some ideas that cannot be expressed well in language (e.g., colors), and some linguistic forms (e.g., grammar) have no nonlinguistic parallels.

Language communicates ideas, but it also elaborates them. Formation of nonlinguistic concepts precedes their expression in language, but having words for objects and events also aids in the formation of new and more refined concepts. This transactional relationship between the overlapping systems applies to later childhood and adulthood, but there is discussion about whether it also holds true of early childhood. Possibly, babies and toddlers develop nonlinguistic concepts before their linguistic parallels and the nonlinguistic ideas are necessary for the linguistic ones. Or possibly, the two systems develop in parallel, but separately. The literature on this issue is mixed. Overall, the transactional relationship between the two systems is emphasized here.

In addition to its relationship to nonlinguistic cognition, there are other general features of language that are important for understanding children with handicaps. One is the distinction between verbal and nonverbal communication. We ordinarily think of oral or written verbal speech when we think of language communication. However, pictures, facial expressions, and sign language are also forms of linguistic communication that are especially important for some children with handicaps.

Another important distinction is between comprehension and expression of language. Children generally comprehend a linguistic concept before they express it. They have the information stored, but retrieving it and putting it into communicable form are additional processes that are necessary for expression. This distinction is important in language training studies because receptive and expressive training can have different effects (Hupp, Mervis, Able, & Conroy-Gunter, 1986).

Language Handicaps. The transactional relationship between cognition and language, the distinction between verbal and nonverbal communication, and the difference between comprehension and expression are all ideas that have been important for the understanding of language of children with handicaps. A positive but incomplete association between language and intellectual handicaps is an important feature of the literature and is understandable from the idea that cognition and language are separate but related cognitive systems.

It is also true that children with handicaps such as learning disabilities, mental retardation, autism, and sensory disorders may have language problems (e.g., Paul & D. J. Cohen, 1985). This is consistent with the concept that nonlinguistic and linguistic systems are overlapping, but are at least somewhat separate, cognitive processes.

A most important idea relating cognition and language handicaps is that language involves the learning and processing of arbitrary symbols for objects and events. Some children with handicaps are thought to have global or more specific problems in symbolic-representational functioning (Ohta, 1987). Delays in such skills as memory or categorization of function, form, and color may predict receptive language ability. This suggests again that there is an intimate relationship between cognition and language, and it has been the basis of studies in which individual differences in language learning and performance are accounted for at least partly by differences in cognitive tasks (F. A. Conners & Detterman, 1987; Torgesen, Rashotte, & Greenstein, 1988). On the other hand, in specific groups, such as children with autism, these types of categorization do not necessarily predict receptive language very well (Ungerer & Sigman, 1987). Thus, although cognitive and language measures may be correlated, the connection between them is not always clear.

Development and Delay. Perhaps the most commonly stated concept in the study of language handicaps is the description of language development as delayed. This implies that language is proceeding normally but at a slower rate than normal. There is good evidence that this is true, but the situation is actually more complicated (Rondal, 1988). Children with visual disorders, hearing impairments, autism, language impairments, or Down syndrome may all show development of language that proceeds at a slower rate than normal and that follows the same sequencing of development (Bigelow, 1987; Bishop & Edmundson, 1987; Schirmer, 1985; L. Smith & Von Tetzchner, 1986; Tager-Flusberg et al., 1990).

On the other hand, whereas sequencing appears basically intact, such aspects of language as babbling (Oller & Eilers, 1988), the specific words a child learns (Bigelow, 1987), or the relationship of specific aspects of language development to other forms of physical, cognitive, and socioemotional development may show significant deviations in children with handicaps (Abbeduto, Furman, & Davies, 1989; Cardoso-Martins, C. B. Mervis, & C. A. Mervis, 1985; Cromer, 1987; Mundy, Sigman, Kasari, & Yirmiya, 1988; Schery, 1985; L. Smith & Von Tezchner, 1986; Willich, Prior, Cumming, & Spanos, 1988). Therefore, knowing that a child's language is delayed may be an important, but incomplete, description.

Process Analysis. Aside from characterizing language as delayed and/or deviant, another approach is to find out what processes are deficit in language disorders and to attempt to normalize handicaps by modifying these processes. At any specific level of language development, groups of children with language disorders may have deficits in perception and attention (T. F. Campbell & McNeil, 1985; L. L. Elliott, Hammer, & Scholl, 1989; Martinius, 1984). They also have difficulties in storing words and stories in memory and retrieving and using them (Crais & Chapman, 1987; Kail, Hale, Leonard, & Nippold, 1984), and they may have problems in general symbolic representation (J. R. Johnston & Weismer, 1983). It is not yet clear whether the perceptual, attentional, memory, and representational problems are the causes of the language disorders. They could be parallel, but independent impairments. However, it is obvious from these examples that children with language handicaps may have other problems besides their language disorder.

Looking at linguistic systems more closely, one can ask whether children with language disorders who are at a particular level of language development process linguistic information any differently than normal children. In general, language processing is done in a similar way in all human beings. On the whole, there is little reason to believe that children with handicaps are different in any fundamental way. On the other hand, there are some exceptions to this generalization also worth considering.

Take lateralization in reception of language information, for instance. When two different simultaneously spoken phrases strike each ear separately, the person hears only one of them, usually the one that is loudest. However, if the intensity of the two phrases is exactly equal, the phrase to the right ear is the one that is identified and processed by the left cerebral hemisphere. This lateralization of perception of linguistic information is usually interpreted as evidence that the two sides of the brain are specialized to process different types of information. The left hemisphere specializes in segmental, analytic, and time dependent processing, whereas the right hemisphere ordinarily is involved in nonsegmental, time-independent processing. Language is segmental and occurs sequentially over time, thus the left hemisphere is thought to process language in most people.

Studies of normal people show the right ear (left hemisphere) advantage, and this is also true of most handicapped people. However, groups of retarded people with Down syndrome reliably have a left ear advantage. If the left ear (right cerebral hemisphere) advantage of people with Down syndrome reflects the fact that they are processing linguistic information with the hemisphere that is specialized for processing nonsegmental, time-independent information, they should have more of a problem with processing verbal instructions than in processing pictures. Apparently, this is the case. Hartley (1985) showed that, when matched with retarded people who did not have Down syndrome, people with Down syndrome had more difficulty with syntactic material than with spatial information.

Nonverbal Communication

We turn now to a consideration of nonverbal communication, which includes the perception and expression of emotions, gestures that accompany oral speech, and at least certain aspects of sign languages. Nonverbal communication is important for a number of reasons: It includes some of the cognitive precursors of language, it can involve information that words do not transmit, and it has been used extensively in communication training for children who have language problems.

Perception of Emotions. A focus on nonverbal communication, in addition to verbal communication, can lead one to look at the way children perceive the emotions of others. When there is a problem in perceiving the emotions of others, difficulties in social adjustment may ensue. Some children have little or no expressive speech. This does not necessarily mean they do not understand. When they can be shown to comprehend, they often can be taught special ways of communicating.

The study of the perception and expression of emotions in children with handicaps is not very well advanced. What is available suggests that children with handicaps do identify vocal expressions of emotion. Like nonhandicapped children, they are more sensitive to negative than to positive emotions. However, overall they are less sensitive to these cues, and their sensitivity is related to their general language development (J. A. Courtright & I. C. Courtright, 1983; Marcell & Jett, 1985).

Gestures. Gestures and sign languages, on the other hand, have been the subject of more intensive study because of their importance in communication of hearing-impaired, mentally retarded, and autistic children. Lloyd and Karlan (1984) listed 16 factors that are important in considering nonspeech communication systems. For example, nonspeech communication is usually through the visual mode, it can be slower than speech, its symbols are often similar to their visual referent, and the symbols are generally less abstract. These factors make nonspeech systems appropriate for communication of children with auditory problems.

Gesture communication declines in normal babies as spoken language increases (Goldin-Meadow & Morford, 1985), but gestures remain part of communication acts of hearing children throughout life. Children with disabilities may have deficits in this area though some aspects of gestural communication can be normal (Attwood, Frith, & Hermelin, 1988; Grogan, 1988; Mundy, Sigman, Ungerer, & T. Sherman, 1986). For instance, children with hearing impairments can develop communication systems that have all the features of natural spoken languages. Deaf babies develop gestural languages that have the same linguistic characteristics as the gestures of normal babies. As they grow older, the gesture systems of hearing-impaired children increase, elaborate, and become creative (Marschak, West, Nall, & Everhart, 1986).

Sign Languages. Sign languages for hearing-impaired people have been generally available since the 18th century. However, in the last generation, teaching sign languages has also been used to increase the communication of hearing children with language handicaps (e.g., Keogh, Whitman, Beeman, Halligan, & Starzynski, 1987; Konstantareas, 1987; Yoder & Layton, 1988). It has been argued (Deuchar & James, 1985) that the various sign languages (e.g., British sign language and American sign language) are actually different from each other and they are certainly different from spoken English. For instance, people who understand British sign language do not necessarily understand American sign language.

Thus, conceiving of sign languages as conversions of spoken language into manual form is not as correct as seeing them as different languages. This has important implications for training. One can consider sign language as if it were a first language and training could begin earlier than it ordinarily begins now (on average, at 2 years).

Early intervention in sign language instruction is also supported by the early advantage of signs in language learning. As indicated earlier, infants use gestural systems. They also learn and use formal signs more easily than they do spoken words. This sign advantage is characteristic of young children and also of certain children whose speech is delayed. Older unimpaired children of deaf parents encode phonologically in preference to signs when they are fluent in both speech and American sign language (Abrahamsen, Cavallo, & McCluer, 1985; E. G. Carr, Pridal, & Dores, 1984; Guttentag & Schaefer, 1987).

Not only hearing-impaired, but even severely retarded children can be taught to communicate in everyday situations (Romski, Sevcik, & Rumbaugh, 1985), as long as individual differences are taken into account (P. Friedman & K. A. Friedman, 1980). Although there is a long history of controversy over whether it is desirable to teach a sign or oral speech system of communication, in fact use of both together is most common (French-St. George & Stoker, 1988). In addition, pictures, microcomputers, visual symbols, and written material are all used to increase the efficiency of the communicative act (Abrahamsen, Romski, & Sevcik, 1989; Romski, Sevcik, & Joyner, 1984; Romski, Sevick, & Pate, 1988).

Written Communication

Although most of the literature on written communication has been concerned with the normal and abnormal development of reading, there has also been some work on spelling (Gerber & Hall, 1987; Pennington et al., 1986) and on various aspects of writing (Giordano, 1983; Graham & K. R. Harris, 1988). These have been very recent developments, and the study of spelling and of writing is still only beginning.

Reading Problems. The most important aspect of the field is the analysis of dyslexia (reading disability), which is perhaps the most prevalent of the learning disabilities. However, it is worth noting that reading problems are also important with other clinical categories. In order to understand and reconstruct a story, one must decode the word sounds, understand the meaning of the words, perceive the grammar that makes up a sentence, be able to follow the gist of the story, and then analyze and reconstruct the narrative. Groups of children with handicaps (hearing-impaired, language-delayed, learning-disabled, and mentally retarded children) have been shown to have difficulties at one or more of these levels (Abbeduto, Davies, & Furman, 1988; L. Davenport, Yingling, Fein, Galin, & Johnstone, 1986; Fujiki, Brinton, & Dunton, 1987; Meline & Brackin, 1987; Merrill & Mar, 1987; Payne & Quigley, 1987; Ripich & Griffith, 1988). Children who stutter display more eye fixations and eye regressions during reading, though they do not err more or comprehend less when they read (Brutten, Bakker, Janssen, & Van der Meulen, 1984). Children with behavior problems sometimes have reading problems, and when they do, prognosis for adjustment in adulthood is less favorable (Maughan, Gray, & Rutter, 1985). Reading braille is challenging for blind children because the letters in braille print are more easy to confuse with one another than are those of script (Pring, 1984). Hearing-impaired adolescents show reading performance that is correlated with their cognitive profiles, such that poorer verbal and sequential skills are associated with their reading problems (Craig & H. W. Gordon, 1988; Geers & Moog, 1989). And, of course, mentally retarded children are delayed in reading, as they are in other cognitive activities (Rom, 1985).

On the other hand, reading is perhaps the easiest form of receptive communication for children with hearing handicaps because it does not suffer from the low signal-to-noise ratio and the short-term memory load of lip-reading (Grove & Rodda, 1984). There are a number of children with autism who read the written word unusually well for their age and do so compulsively. These hyperlexic children may not comprehend what they read very well, but they can read aloud appropriately (T. E. Goldberg, 1987; Whitehouse & J. C. Harris, 1984). All of this means that reading is not a field of study that is restricted to children with dyslexia.

Dyslexia. Nevertheless, most interest has been focused on studies of the processes involved in reading in dyslexic children. To study reading in dyslexic children, it is necessary to have a notion about the processes involved in reading and also to have a concept of what one means by dyslexia. There seems to be some confusion in the literature on dyslexia. If there is, it is partly because neither our understanding of reading nor our concept of dyslexia is complete. Nevertheless, it is possible to draw some general conclusions based on recent work.

Reading involves, first an awareness that the printed word is a special stimulus and that it is organized in a special way in space (from left to right in English). Associating a letter or group of letters (graphemes) with a sound (phoneme) that may or may not have meaning is also necessary. That is, decoding the visual stimulus to sounds and words is also part of the process. Attending to written letters or words by looking at them reasonably efficiently is part of reading quickly. Relating the unique written materials and their associated sounds to meaning of the single words and to the whole organization of the written passage is the most complex group of cognitive processes involved. Dyslexic children are delayed or deficit in some of these processes and not others (Szeszulski & Manis, 1987).

The disorder or disorders called dyslexia involve an unusual difficulty in reading in a person who is otherwise generally average or above average intellectually (Baddeley, Logie, & Ellis, 1988; Shaywitz & Waxman, 1987). Dyslexia does not mean the same thing as the term "illiterate." There are many people who are illiterate because they have not had an opportunity to learn to read. Others cannot read well because they do not learn anything very well, and reading is only one of the skills they have difficulty in developing. Still other people may be competent in reading skills but fail to the develop the skill to a very high level because they never use it. None of these groups is properly called dyslexic. Most studies of dyslexia use children who score normal or above normal on an intelligence test but who also are at least 2 years behind their school grade level in reading.

Until recently this general definition of dyslexia was characteristic of the literature. However, in the last 10 years, it has become clear that there are subgroups and significant individual differences among the reading-disabled population (Bialystok & Mitterer, 1987; Lieberman, Meskill, Chatillon, & Schupack, 1985; M. W. Lovett, 1987; M. W. Lovett, Ransby, & Barron, 1988; Pennington et al., 1986; Seymour & MacGregor, 1984; Watson & Goldgar, 1988; but see van den Bos, 1984 for an exception). Thus, although the pioneering research on reading disability treated children with dyslexia as a homogeneous group, it is now becoming clear that problems with specific aspects of reading may characterize the deficits of different children. Although the subclassification is not yet agreed on, this major refinement of the concept of dyslexia (or if you will, dyslexias) will surely have a major impact on the diagnosis and remedial education of these children.

In order for this progress to occur, more will have to be known about their reading processes. In what follows, different aspects of reading are reviewed with an indication of whether there is reason to believe that at least some children with dyslexia have problems with that process. Preschool-age children realize that print is a particular way of representing objects. That is, they can distinguish between printing and drawing. It is not clear whether children with specific reading disabilities have problems in this area, but language-disordered preschoolers are less able in this respect (Gillam & J. R. Johnston, 1985). In addition to awareness of the special properties of printing, differentiation of left from right, and the recognition that printing is organized from left to right (at least in English) are necessary conditions for efficient reading. Each of these characteristics may be a problem for some children with dyslexia (Fisher, Bornstein, & Gross, 1985; Penso, 1984). On the other hand, whereas efficient eye movements may be important in reading, and children with reading disabilities show longer eye fixations, more fixations, and more eye regressions during reading, these problems are the result but not the cause of difficulties in processing textual materials (Rayner, 1985).

Children with reading disabilities are sometimes thought to have problems in visual perception, manifested for instance in the reversal of letters like *b* and *d*. Young children and children with reading disabilities do reverse letters. However, they make other errors as well, and errors by reversal and inversion of letters by dyslexic children are no more common relative to other types of errors than they are in children who have no difficulties in reading. Moreover, these errors are probably not due as much to a disorder in visual perception as they are to applying name codes to the letters (Bigsby, 1985; Corballis, Macadie, Crotty, & Beale, 1985; G. Richardson, 1984).

If reading problems are not a result of abnormal eye movements or visual perception, what are they related to? There is general agreement now that one central problem in dyslexia is in phonological processing, that is in accessing, blending, and segmenting sounds (e.g., Bruck & Treiman, 1990). This represents a general difficulty in decoding sounds because it affects not only the translation of graphemes to phonemes as in reading but apparently also may be the basis of a difficulty in differentiating audible sounds and in repeating words when they are spoken.

If language sounds are processed less efficiently by disabled readers, they may not remain in memory as long as is the case with normal readers. Thus, naming objects, reading and comprehending sequential information, and dealing with long sentences will be difficult (R. B. Katz, 1986; Kirby & Robinson, 1987; Tallal, 1984). This would be true even if there were no specific memory deficit for phonological material in disabled readers. However, there is evidence that over and above the phonological processing difficulty, there is also a specific problem in memory for verbal material, in retrieving verbal information from long-term memory, and in understanding grammatic structure of sentences. That is, initial processing, storing and retrieval of phonological information of language symbols is deficit in children with dyslexia (Catts, 1986; German, 1985; Gough & Tunmer, 1986; R. S. Johnston, Rugg, & Scott, 1987; Liberman & Shankweiler, 1985; Manis, 1985; L. A. Murphy, Pollatsek, & Well, 1988; L. Siegel & Ryan, 1988; Snowling, Goulandris, Bowlby, & Howell, 1986; Stanovich, 1985; Torneus, 1984; Wood, Richman, & Eliason, 1989).

Going beyond decoding, memory, and retrieval of verbal material, we consider syntax and semantics. Dyslexic children have less problem with using rules for the succession of letters in a word or in using the context of a sentence to derive the meaning of the words in it (C. M. Fletcher & Prior, 1990). In fact, it appears that in order to compensate for their phonological problem they use these orthographic regularities and the context at least as much as do normal readers to extract the meaning of words (Horn & Manis, 1985). Moreover, once the sounds are analyzed, children with dyslexia have no problem with meaning because at least in some contexts they perform normally with frequent and familiar words that they have already analyzed.

All of this suggests that rule-based reading and comprehension processes are different from phonological decoding. This separation is dramatized in those cases of hyperlexia in which children can read very well, but cannot understand what they read. In other words, they can decode very efficiently but those who have low verbal ability do not comprehend what they read (T. E. Goldberg, 1987; Snowling & Frith, 1986; Whitehouse & J. C. Harris, 1984).

The distinction between phonological decoding and retrieving deficits, on the one hand, and comprehension deficits point to the separation of these two general processes. Actually, however, they interact with each other. Decoding a written passage is necessary (though not sufficient) for its comprehension. On the other hand, the motivation to understand what is in magazines and books leads one to read (i.e., to practice decoding skills). If one cannot decode, there is usually not much motivation to read. Thus, the two general processes are intertwined, and it is therefore not surprising that many children with dyslexia do show problems in both decoding and comprehending (Gough & Tunner, 1986). Or possibly this complex picture comes from the mixing of different types of dyslexia within heterogeneous groups of children with dyslexia.

Treatment.   Whatever the cause of the complexity of the picture, it is clear that the treatment of reading disorders might benefit from attention to both decoding processes and those things involved in understanding of text. Those treatment programs that do so are reasonably successful. That is, procedures that emphasize both analysis of phonics and of meaning have done better than either approach by itself (Vellutino & Scanlon, 1986; see also D. E. Wolff, Desberg, & Marsh, 1985). Most studies, however, use different approaches. That is, whereas they do not necessarily specify the exact problem that the child has prior to planning of training, they may still be successful (Brailsford, Snart, & Das, 1984; B. C. Holmes, 1985; Rashotte & Torgesen, 1985).

Speech

The distinction between language and speech is most important. That is, the coding of thoughts into verbal form is believed to constitute a separate group of processes from the organization of the group of motor acts that we call speech.

Perhaps the most important method for studying the organization of words and the structure of sentences is to examine errors in natural speech. This is done by recording the speech of a person in a natural or semicontrolled situation and then looking for patterns of errors in the formation of words or in the structure of sentences in the language samples. Thus, repeated errors in use of tenses, in placement of words in a sentence, or of sounds in words reveal the ways that the speech is organized. Most of this research is done with normal adults, with adults with aphasia (Stemberger, 1984), and with young children. Rather little has been done with children with handicaps.

On the other hand, the organization of speech has been intensively studied, especially in children with speech disorders. There are many forms of speech disorders. They include mutism, hesitations, problems in formation or sounding of words, and stuttering. They can be classified in many ways (Locke, 1983; Pannbacker, 1984).

To some extent, these disorders have a more cognitive base. For instance, some children with conduct and anxiety disorders hesitate before speaking, and this has been interpreted as a sign of reflection and cognitive planning of sentences (Kotsopoulos & Mellor, 1986). Articulation disordered subgroups of language-impaired children differ with respect to imitation, but not on other perceptual or developmental language measures (Isaacs & Haynes, 1984; Smit & Bernthal, 1983).

The auditory feedback from speaking is important for the normal production of speech. Young children are disrupted by alterations in the feedback from speech to a greater extent than are adults, indicating that the sensorimotor organization of speech is part of normal development (G. M. Siegel, Pick, & Garber, 1984). Very likely this is an experiential effect because the abnormal speech sounds of many congenitally deaf children seem to be based on a lack of the normal auditory feedback from speaking (Boothroyd, 1985).

Other forms of speech defect, such as athetoid dysarthria, are related to problems in the control of the muscles of the motor apparatus. Apparently, this is a problem with abnormal voluntary activity rather than involuntary activity because articulation is interrupted more in the intervals between syllables than in enunciating the syllables themselves (Neilson & O'Dwyer, 1984).

Stuttering. The most widely studied speech disorder is stuttering. Stuttering is characterized by elemental repetitions and prolongations in speech that are involuntary (St. Louis, Hinzman, & Hull, 1985; Perkins, 1983; Wingate, 1983). The group of children who stutter is actually composed of a number of subgroups (Rentschler, 1984), but subgrouping has not been an important feature of recent research. Perhaps this is one of the reasons that no clear picture about the etiology, processes, and treatment of stuttering has yet emerged.

There are, however, some facts about which there is general agreement (Wingate, 1983). Most stuttering begins gradually before 6 years of age, and in these cases, many children spontaneously improve. However, improvement is more difficult after the childhood period. Males are much more likely to stutter than are females, and there is a tendency for stuttering to run in families. Stuttering is more prevalent among individuals with low intelligence, and delayed language and articulation disorders are more common in children who stutter. There is no clear scientific basis for the commonly held view that experiential or personality variables are associated with the development of initiation of stuttering (Cox, Seider, & Kidd, 1984; Peters & Hulstijn, 1984).

Theories about the nature of stuttering have changed with time. Psychoanalytic and behaviorist theories that emphasized the critical importance of learning in the development of stuttering are no longer very influential. An older emphasis on stuttering as reflecting a problem in motor coordination of speech has reasserted itself. One source of this emphasis is the sudden onset of stuttering in certain adolescents who have a neurological problem. There is a suggestion, as yet only a suggestion, that brain lateralization is affected in children who stutter (Brutten & Trotter, 1985).

If stuttering involves a problem in coordination of speech, there still is a question of what aspect or aspects of speech coordination are the problem. The idea that auditory feedback from speaking is important draws strength from a lower prevalence of stuttering in severely deaf children and from the fact that normal speech disruptions in the presence of delayed auditory feedback are very like stuttering. However, an authoritative review by Garber and G. M. Siegel (1982) concluded that perceptual studies provide no evidence of a defect in auditory self-monitoring of speech in stuttering.

Garber and Siegel did point to the possibility that a problem in tactile and proprioceptive feedback might be involved in stuttering, but they indicated there were too few studies for any conclusions. Although this is still true, a recent study has shown that sensitivity of the tongue was relatively lower than for the hand in a stuttering group than a group of fluent speakers. Thus, tactile sensitivity of the tongue may be lower children who stutter (Fucci, Petrosino, Gorman, & D. Harris, 1985). Whether this lower sensitivity is a cause of stuttering or merely a correlate of it remains to be seen.

At the other end of the stimulus-response dimension, there has traditionally been interest in whether a disorder of the muscles of the larynx can lie at the basis of stuttering. One study in this tradition (Conture, Schwartz, & Brewer, 1985) showed that there was such a problem when a person stuttered, but the problem was better characterized as one in the interaction among laryngeal, articulatory, and respiratory systems.

This complex result points to an intricate set of mechanisms at fault in stuttering. That there is such a complex mechanism involved in stuttering is suggested by the fact that reaction times for vocal responses are lower in children who stutter, and perhaps more important, that reaction time for vocal responses and a finger response were highly correlated. That is, attentional (Arends, Povel, & Kolk, 1988), prosodic (Bergmann, 1986), and a general factor of timing of motor responses (Cross & Luper, 1983) seem to have been implicated. The latter point has been emphasized further by Kent (1983) by expressing the view that the central disturbance in stuttering is a reduced ability to generate temporal patterns that are essential for the normal flow of speech. That is, temporal schema or strategies are necessary for fluent speech, and it is possible that children who stutter have a problem in their smooth organization. (However, see Caruso, Conture, & Colton, 1988 for a different view.)

Whatever the basic process or processes involved in stuttering, it is a simple matter to alter stuttering patterns. Stuttering can be reduced by having the child sing, speak in rhythm, participate in choral reading, slow down speech, speak alone, or whisper. In general, asking the children to alter their usual method of speaking will reduce stuttering (Wingate, 1983).

More enduring effects are sought in speech therapy for stuttering. Psychoanalytic therapy is not an effective method, but behavioral procedures, for instance, various forms of operant conditioning, have been shown to be effective. The duration and generality of these effects still need study (Nittrouer & Cheney, 1984). More generally, the best predictor of success with stuttering is simply the amount of therapy in which the person engages (Wingate, 1983).

SUMMARY

The most important and unique aspect of human adaptation is intelligence. Whether it is best to describe intelligence as a single general attribute or as a number of more or less specific abilities continues to be controversial. Basically, intelligence involves specific abilities that are ordinarily highly correlated with one another and therefore seem to represent a single general factor. This would account for the existence of unusual talent, as well as specific disabilities, in the presence of a general level of intelligence.

Intellectual processes are described psychometrically, naturalistically, and in controlled laboratory studies. Whatever the approach, it is clear that the diagnostic category of children with handicaps is helpful only sometimes in predicting how children think.

The development of children's intellectual skills depends on both their ability to learn and the opportunities for relevant learning that they have had. The relationship between experience and learning ability is reciprocal rather than additive, with the result that it is not usually possible to determine whether a child's intellectual performance is due completely to ability or to experience. This means that intellectual ability is partly made up of what the child knows already. As a practical matter, therefore, a distinction between basic ability and what the child already knows cannot be made easily.

Perhaps more fruitful is an approach that attempts to teach all children how to think. This has been accomplished in many studies, with many forms of thinking. The most successful of these teaching methods assumes that most children are motivated to learn, that promoting understanding of the purposes and structure of the problem being dealt with is important, and that learning takes place in a social context where the relationship among the students and between the students and the teacher is reciprocal and active. Successful training programs not only increase intellectual skills, but also motivation.

Most learning of intellectual skills occurs in informal situations that people identify as play, and play is generally regarded as important for the development of intellectual skills. What is not so clear is whether play is more efficient than other forms of learning or exactly what it is that children learn when they play. Answering these questions requires carefully controlled studies. A few of these have been done with nonhandicapped children. The studies suggest that what is learned by playing depends on the developmental level of the child, the play experience, and the testing situation. There have been no studies like this with handicapped children.

Research on play with children with handicaps has shown that almost all children engage in play. Amount of play and the structure of play is sometimes different between handicapped and nonhandicapped groups of children, but there is much overlap between the groups. Providing appropriate toys increases the amount of play, but it is not yet clear whether doing this has any long-term effects.

Cognition and language are overlapping systems. Handicaps in either can be described as delayed or different and can be manifest at nonverbal and verbal levels. Children with other handicaps also can be impaired in language. Reading and speech impairments are particularly common, and scientific analysis has partly clarified the processes involved in these two areas of disability.

Sign language has been used to increase communication in hearing-handicapped individuals and severely retarded people. However, it is now most common to use manual signs in association with several other visual, auditory, and even tactual modes to maximize total communication.

8 _____

Motivation and Personality

The cognitive processes reviewed in the last three chapters are not a complete description of how information is received, processed, stored, and applied. Perhaps they represent the machine. However, what factors determine whether this machine operates at all? What drives it? Psychology points to motivation and personality variables to explain this dynamic aspect of behavior.

It is possible to overemphasize the distinction between the dynamic principles of motivation and those that describe cognition. In fact, ability and motivational variables interact constantly to determine competent performance. However, at the levels of common sense and of formal science, the separation of cognition and motivation has been useful.

In this chapter, we also review deviations of personality that are so great as to be regarded as pathological. In doing so, the mainly philosophical question of the relationship between personality and psychopathology is considered. Also, we review recent studies of the more empirically based question of the nature of personality structure and its deviations.

As in other chapters, we ask about the extent to which categories of disorders of development account for motivation, personality, and psychopathology. We show that much of the literature about children with handicaps is devoted to comparisons of groups of children having various categories of handicapping condition but that, although useful in describing personality differences, the conventional categories provide only incomplete prediction.

In the context of these larger issues, several topics are discussed: temperament; incentive motivation; attributions about success and failure; response to stress; self concepts; and self-control. A number of active research areas under the general headings of eating disorders, self-stimulatory behaviors, mood, anxiety and depression, activity level, impulsiveness, and aggression behaviors are also included.

You may have noted that some of these topics are associated with conventional categories of handicap. For instance, depression, activity level, and aggression are commonly associated with the clinical categories Depression, Hyperactivity, and Conduct Disorders. However, discerning students know from their own experience that depression, activity level, and aggression are concepts that describe the behaviors of normal children. One of the general purposes of this chapter is to emphasize again that children with handicaps are best described in terms of concepts that describe all of us.

GENERAL CONCEPTS

How is it best to describe the dynamic factors involved in everyday activities? Using a general way to describe them certainly is not enough. Saying that people are well-motivated or that they have lots of personality gives some sense that the they are active or that you are attracted to them. However, such general descriptors have had limited usefulness. It is not so much that psychologists reject such concepts as general drive, arousal, libido, or attractiveness. Psychologists accept these concepts and use them actively. However, they find it necessary to go beyond them. Ideas such as specific motivators, dysphoric mood, and aggression then becomes the level at which psychologists work. In this sense personality is similar to intelligence in that it is useful to approach it at a somewhat specific level.

Specific Description

If general descriptions of motivation and personality are not enough, how do we describe their structure? In other words, what is the nature of personality? A know-nothing approach might assert that motivation and personality are such complex features of the unique human spirit that it is not possible to describe them. In fact, the situation is not simple, but most investigators feel that personality can be described in terms of, at most, five or six general dimensions, each of which is a composite of several characteristics (Digman & Inouye, 1986). Examples would be surgency (described by such words as talkative, silent, sociable, reclusive, adventurous, caution) and agreeableness (good-natured, irritable, mild and gentle, headstrong, cooperative, negativistic, jealous).

On the other hand, although there may be only a few fundamental personality constructs, most of the literature on motivation and personality has to do with more specific concepts such as incentives, temperament, mood, self-efficacy, and aggression. It is at this more specific level of description that much of the remainder of this chapter focuses.

Personality Classes and Dimensions

On the whole, motivation and personality characteristics are regarded as dimensions rather than classes. That is, a person is more correctly described as more or less agreeable rather than as an agreeable or disagreeable person. (See Gangestad & Snyder, 1985 for a possible exception.) This point is important to emphasize in this discussion because the force of common usage and of much clinical practice often involves placing people into classes. This chapter points out that the placement of people into discrete categories of personality is no longer supported by current thinking.

Less clear is whether psychopathology represents the extreme form of a personality dimension or whether it is best to consider it as a qualitatively different psychological state. Is clinical depression an extreme expression of the blue periods we all experience, or is it a different phenomenon? There is no clear answer to this question. The classification systems that we discussed in the chapter on categories of childhood disorder take either a dimensional or a class approach. For the purposes of this chapter (which emphasizes process analyses), we assume that most pathological states are extreme forms of normal behavior patterns. However, where the evidence indicates that a pathological condition is qualitatively different in addition to being quantitatively different from normal, the recent evidence is presented.

Traits and Situational Determinants

The next general question is whether motivation and personality factors transcend situations or are closely tied to environmental variables. This issue is solved primarily by definition. Motivation is seen as tied to specific incentives (for instance, food can define hunger, response to a monster can define fear). Likewise, personality can be defined as only those dynamic factors that are present in many situations (anxiousness, aggressiveness, depressiveness). Situational factors, different observers, and different measures do bring out some aspects of personality relative to others, and the effects of these environmental conditions are sometimes powerful (J. Kagan, 1988). But there is at least a degree of stability in measures of personality that transcends environmental conditions (Achenbach, McConaughy, & Howell, 1987; Fergusson & Horwood, 1987). It is these common factors that are emphasized in the study of normal and abnormal personality. (See Levine, 1985, summarized later for a different emphasis.)

Continuity and Discontinuity

Somewhat similar to this personality versus situation issue is the continuity--discontinuity question. To what extent do children's personalities or psychopathologies vary as they develop? Do children who score high on a test of infant irritability also score high on tests of irritability when they are adults? Do signs of behavioral disturbance change or remain stable as the children grow older (Breslau & Marshall, 1985)? To some extent, this continuity–discontinuity issue is difficult to answer because measures of personality and psychopathology change with age. One assesses irritability in an infant in different ways than in an older child or adult. Nevertheless, especially in the area of temperament, there has been substantial interest in the stability of personality.

In summary, then, the study of dynamic aspects of behavior involves several basic concepts, some of which are assumptions and some of which have scientific empirical support. Issues centering around the appropriate level of description and around stability and change dominate these concepts, with multiple perspectives characteristic of the discussions.

Categories of Childhood Disorder

Perhaps the most active research area in the study of dynamic factors in the behavior of children with handicaps is the search for unique patterns of personality or psychopathology associated with the standard categories of childhood disorder. According to a central expectation, there are unique factors that define at least some of the disorders, and there have been dozens of recent studies. Two central questions are asked in these studies: First, are personality disorders associated with specific categories of handicap? Second, do the various types of handicap differ from one another?

In reference to the answer to the first question, children with handicaps do indeed have a higher likelihood than normal children of showing personality deviations. This generalization applies to all categories of handicap that have been studied, that is, children with hemophilia, spina bifida, epilepsy, orthopedic problems, sickle cell disease, visual or auditory handicaps, speech or language disorders, specific (but perhaps not general) reading disabilities, learning disabilities, mental retardation, and emotional handicaps (Bender, 1987a, 1987b; Cantwell & Baker, 1985; Chess & Fernandez, 1981; Handford, Mayes, Bixler, & Mattison, 1986; Cullinan & M. H. Epstein, 1985; Hurtig & L. S. White, 1986; Jorm, Share, Matthews, & Maclean, 1986; Leudar, Fraser, & Jeeves, 1984; Perrin, Ramsey, & Sandler, 1987; Schnittjer & Hirshoren, 1984; Tew & Laurence, 1985).

Once it is said that children with handicaps are more likely than normal to have deviations in personality, the statement must be qualified. Although some individuals within these groups do show deviations, the majority do not. Statistical comparisons do show significantly elevated levels of personality deviations when groups of children with handicaps are compared with groups of average children, but the prevalence of abnormality does not exceed 75% and usually is much lower.

Sometimes personality deviations are characteristic of children with only the most severe handicaps (Handford, Mayes, Bixler, & Mattison, 1986). Often they are characteristic of some measures, but not others, and the presence of a personality deviation depends on who is rating the child's behavior. For instance, one study showed that children from different category groups do not rate themselves differently (Burden & Parish, 1983).

Furthermore, the difference between handicapped and nonhandicapped groups may be attributable to other correlated factors. For instance, the difference between children with sickle cell disease and healthy children may be less attributable to the repeated periods of pain that the child experiences (the obvious explanation) but more to factors associated with the social class from which the children come (Lemanck, Moore, Gresham, Williamson, & Kelley, 1986).

One may conclude that children with handicaps, no matter which category they come from, may be especially susceptible to personality deviations. However, these differences from normal are not universal within the handicapped groups, and they may not even be common.

Categories of children may differ from each other with respect to the levels of various dimensions. However, there is question whether the dimensions that describe them are the same or different. Are differences between groups of children quantitative or qualitative? The way to answer this question is to compare groups with respect to the factors that summarize the correlations between items on a test or rating scale. This procedure is known as *factor analysis*. There have been several factor analyses of scores for individual groups, and these studies suggest that the dimensions describing the different categories of handicapping conditions and normal children are the same. However, the only way really to test the similarity–difference issue is to compare factor analyses of different groups in the same study.

Among the dozens of studies of group differences, there are only a few that compare the factor structures of scores on the same rating scale, given to more than one group. These studies confirm that, on the whole, the same personality dimensions describe the behavior of all children (M. H. Epstein, Cullinan, & Polloway, 1986; Schnittjer & Hirshoren, 1984).

We can conclude from all of this that, whereas handicapped children are at greater risk for personality disorders than are normal children, having one handicap does not necessarily mean the child will also have a personality disorder. Moreover, if children do deviate on a personality dimension, they are most likely to be quantitatively, not qualitatively, different. In other words, with respect to motivation and personality, children with handicaps are essentially normal.

TEMPERAMENT

Definition

We begin with the concept of temperament. Its definition is not yet very clear. Major workers in the field take rather different perspectives on what to include and what not to include in its study. Does temperament include cognitive variables or is temperament a separate, but interacting domain of psychological functioning? What elements should one include? Modern pioneers such as Chess and Thomas (cited in Goldsmith et al., 1987) defined nine elements of temperament: rhythmicity of biological functioning, activity level, approach and withdrawal from new stimuli, adaptability, sensory threshold, predominant quality of mood, intensity of mood expression, distractibility, and persistence/attention span. Buss and Plomin saw temperament as composed of three qualities: emotionality or distress, activity defined in terms of tempo and vigor, and degree of sociability. Rothbart (cited in Goldsmith et al., 1987) also saw three components, but they are somewhat different: negative reactivity, positive reactivity, and behavioral inhibition in the face of novel or intense stimuli.

Are we talking about behavioral tendencies or about emotional behaviors themselves? Is high heritability a prerequisite for including an element, or is heritability irrelevant? Is temperament characteristic of the person who interacts with the environment so that we look for a match between the environment and the child's temperament. Or does the character of temperament reside in the person-environment interaction itself? What happens with age? Do temperamental traits remain stable over age, do they change, do new ones develop and some drop out with maturation and interaction with the environment?

All of these issues are controversial. However, a unifying perspective has been presented by McCall (cited in Goldsmith et al., 1987). Categories of temperament refer more to inclinations or tendencies to respond than to specific behaviors. Activity, reactivity, emotionality, and sociability are tendencies that most workers would agree exist. These tendencies are most easily seen in their simplest form during early infancy, and this may account for the fact that the literature on temperament concentrates on studies of infants.

There may be stability in temperaments as children develop, but it is also possible that new ones emerge and some drop out. Certainly, those that remain will be elaborated in interaction with the environment, and this accounts for the fact that there is also a literature on older children. The most interesting studies are longitudinal follow-ups of children from infancy into late childhood and even older (H. H. Goldsmith et al., 1987).

Of special interest to us is the concept of temperamental difficulty. Some theorists (e.g., Chess and Thomas) center their interest in temperament on an attempt to describe difficult temperament in babies and to determine whether difficult babies grow into older children who are at higher risk for behavioral difficulties. Other theorists do not use the concept of "difficulty" in their consideration about temperament, or they believe that the concept is too complex to be useful. For those who find the concept useful, it refers to fussy and irritable babies, those who withdraw, and children with irregular biological functions. That is, children who are difficult to take care of are thought to be difficult babies. This means that the definition of "difficult" inheres not only in the behavioral characteristics of the baby, but also in the ability of the caregiver to cope with the behavior.

Measurement

In the earliest studies of temperament, parents were interviewed about the characteristics of their children. More recently the relatively informal interviews have been replaced with several rating scales, each of which is designed with a particular concept of temperament in mind. Although these scales are widely used for clinical and research purposes, their reliability and validity are at best moderate. This is true of temperament in general (Gibbs, Reeves, &. C. C. Cunningham, 1987; Windle, 1988) and temperamental difficulty in particular (Daniels, Plomin, &. Greenhalgh, 1984; Maziade, Boutin, Cote, &. Thivierge, 1986; Zeanah, Keener, Anders, &. Levine, 1986).

The basis of this low reliability and validity almost certainly derives from several factors. The most important is the complexity of the concept of temperament and difficult temperament. Second, the fact that different people having different experiences with children are describing them must contribute a significant amount of variability to the description. Finally, and most important, there are real changes in temperament that occur across situations and with development (Korn &. Gannon, 1983; Peters-Martin &. Wachs, 1984; R. P. Martin et al., 1986).

These factors work against stable measures of temperament and must be kept in mind when considering the recent literature. Nevertheless, there have been several studies with handicapped children that are interesting and meaningful. These studies have been accomplished with premature and low birth weight babies, with infants with Down syndrome, and with school-age learning-disabled children (see also Prior, Glazner, Sanson, &. Debelle, 1988).

Premature Babies

Interest in the temperament of premature babies comes from the impression that they may be difficult to care for and they have difficulties in social adaptation. It is possible that mothers of premature babies may see them as more difficult in temperament than others do (Spungen &. Farran, 1986). However, in most studies this is not true, and there is little evidence that the temperament of premature babies is different or that these premature babies are more difficult than appropriate control groups (Riese, 1988). On the other hand, it is possible that children who have suffered perinatal respiratory distress are different on some temperament measures. For babies who were born prematurely certain aspects of temperament may be associated with behavior during developmental testing and with scores on an infant scale of cognitive development (Oberklaid, Prior, &. Sanson, 1986; G. Ross, 1987; Roth, Eisenberg, &. Sell, 1984; Spungen &. Farran, 1986; Stiefel, Plunkett, &. Meisels, 1987; Watt, 1987). Thus, the general level of dimensions of temperament probably is not different in premature children, but it is possible that future studies will turn up biological risk factors that are associated with temperament. It is also possible that the organization of the development of temperament, as revealed in correlational studies, is different in premature babies.

Down Syndrome

The studies of children with Down syndrome are partly motivated by a social stereotype. Children with Down syndrome are sometimes thought of as being more placid and easier to take care of than normal children of the same developmental or chronological age level. It is possible that, on some measures, children with Down syndrome are easier than other groups of delayed children (Marcovitch, S. Goldberg, MacGregor, &. Lojkasek, 1986). However, in studies employing adequate methodology, there are no temperament differences between children with Down syndrome and normal children (Huntington & Simeonsson, 1987). In other words, the stereotype is apparently incorrect.

One study of children with Down syndrome compared the ratings of temperament made by mothers and fathers (Marcovitch et al., 1986). Mothers scored their children as more active and distractible and less withdrawn than did the children's fathers.

Learning-disabled Children

This difference in ratings by different people also is an aspect of the literature with school-age learning-disabled children. In these studies, teachers do the ratings of temperament. Three aspects of temperament are rated. Resource room teachers viewed the learning-disabled children as more task-oriented but also more negative in their behavior than did the regular teachers of the same individuals. There was no difference in the teachers' estimates of the children's adaptability. These results were interpreted as suggesting that, in regular classes, learning-disabled children may be more likely to withdraw and behave in a passive manner (Pullis, 1985).

Passivity, lack of involvement, and low task orientation is regarded as a characteristic of children with learning disabilities (Bender, 1985, 1987a, 1987b). It is not, however, a strong effect, perhaps partly because of variations in the environments the children are in and who is doing the rating.

In summary, then, studies of temperamental differences between handicapped and nonhandicapped children do not show very powerful general differences. Rater effects and situation variability may be more important. Perhaps the weakness of the effects results from the imperfect rating instruments used to assess temperament. However, for now, it is possible to conclude that the stereotypes about the temperament of premature children, children with Down syndrome, and learning-disabled children are not powerful descriptors.

Specific aspects of temperament will become important to us later in this chapter and also in the next one on social behavior. Activity level, aggression, and sociability are all concepts that become part of the discussion. However, for now, the general concept of temperament or of the difficult child, have not proven very useful in describing groups of children with handicaps.

It is possible that specific aspects of temperament can be useful for describing the behavior of individual children. Before concluding that a specific child is characterized by deviant temperament, however, it is useful to consider other factors that may be important in the rating. Such factors might include other characteristics of the child, the nature of the environment the child is in, and the perspective of the person who is doing the rating.

INCENTIVE MOTIVATION

Up until this point, the more stable features of motivation and personality have been the focus of the discussion. Now, we turn to a consideration of the factors in the environment that motivate and reward behavior. First of all, behavioral scientists take it as an assumption that all complex behavior is motivated. This principle is more of an assumption than a proven finding because it is not always possible to identify all of the motivators for behavior. However, it is almost a cliche that identification of someone's unique interests is a key to teaching that person something efficiently.

There is a corollary to this central assumption that all behavior is motivated: People generally come to a learning situation with different patterns of preference for motivators and rewards. Certain students are influenced strongly by grades, and others prefer the pleasure of accomplishment associated with a job well done.

Most students are influenced by both grades and the pleasure of their own accomplishment, and it is possible to talk about generalized rewards, that is, motivators that influence almost everyone. Such generalized rewards include candy for most children, food when the child is hungry, and opportunity to play. However, the fact that a reward may be generally applicable does not mean that it has the same effect with all children at all times. Thus, teaching that depends on a single reward such as a candy, a bit of breakfast cereal, or a pat on the head cannot hope to be maximally successful for all children in the class.

Teachers know the individual likes and dislikes of children (Dewhurst & Cautela, 1980). However, this knowledge is ordinarily arrived at casually and may not be as deep as the teacher may wish. An easy way to discover the hierarchy of motivations for any young (or developmentally young) child is to use some variant of a paired comparison procedure. In a paired comparison test, two choices are provided (for instance, a piece of candy corn and a bit of chocolate). If a child chooses one over the other consistently, it is likely that the one the child has chosen will be more effective as a motivator in a learning situation (Pace, Ivancic, Edwards, Iwata, & Page, 1985). Such an individualized motivation map is part of any well-designed teaching procedure.

A hierarchy is also characteristic of more complex motivations such as overall values, motivation for academic success, the helplessness that results from repeated failure, and even the increased motivation consequent on not engaging in a response. With these motivational concepts, the procedures for establishing motivational levels may be somewhat more complex, but are not too difficult to be practical (e.g., J. Arnold, 1984; Hayes-Scott & Dowaliby, 1984; Koegel & Mentis, 1985; Konarski, 1987; Schwethelm & Mahoney, 1986).

Sometimes motives are not obvious, or they are difficult to demonstrate. A case in point is stereotyped or autistic behaviors. These are bizarre and endlessly repeated patterns such as body-rocking, gazing at hands, or stereotyped play with objects. The behaviors are common in some autistic, severely retarded, and visually impaired children. There have been several theories about the motivational basis for these behaviors. Recently, it has been shown that the sensory feedback from these behaviors is important for their maintenance (Lovaas, Newson, & Hickman, 1987; Rincover, 1986; Winnega & Berkson, 1986). Perhaps as important as the feedback itself is the opportunity to control the feedback. That is, control appears to be rewarding for the child (Buyer, Berkson, Winnega, & Morton, 1987)

This discussion has focused on the intimate relationship between motivation as something that the parent and teacher can affect and different hierarchies of motivational preferences as a stable individual difference (personality) variable. Taking the individual differences into account while maximizing the motivating characteristics of the environment is not all that successful teachers and therapists do. But it is one of the most important things. Consequently, we turn to a further consideration of some of the motivational constructs that have been important in the recent literature on motivation and personality of children with handicaps.

MASTERY, SUCCESS, AND FAILURE

The search to describe the nature of individual differences in motivation has centered on the motivation for mastery, achievement, and control of the environment in the face of success and failure in everyday life. Various aspects of self-concept, the attribution of reasons for degree of achievement, and locus of control are part of this area of study. Response to stress, anxiety, learned helplessness, and depression are also relevant here (Dweck, 1986; Sabatino, 1982).

Children with learning disabilities, autism, and mental retardation sometimes engage less in learning for the fun of it. Their motivation may be reduced or unrealistically high, and this is often attributed to the fact that they have experienced a history of failure or have learned that their behavior is unrelated to any rewards they do receive (Koegel & Mentis, 1985).

However, some groups with handicaps show no problem in achievement motivation (Hayes-Scott & Dowaliby, 1984), and there are large individual differences among those groups when there is such a tendency. In this section, the group differences and the individual differences are described and the basis of these individual differences are explored. This section concludes that dimensions of motivation that are reviewed are important and can be used in the course of planning education for children with handicaps. However, because of the interaction of several individual differ- ence variables, the results reported in the literature tend to be inconsistent.

Failure and Stress

The context for most of the research on motivation is the environment of schools, though there has been some interest in motivation for work in adult mentally retarded people, and the relevance of social situations has also been pointed out (Gresham, 1984). In all these situations, there is the general assumption that children with handicaps have experienced repeated failure, which exceeds significantly the everyday frustrations that normal people encounter.

In addition to more failure, handicapped people are also thought to be more exposed to stress. The concept of stress is related to the concept of failure, but it is somewhat broader. Stress refers to the stream of potentially threatening and challenging situations requiring action and adaptation that any person experiences from birth onward (Compas, 1987). In discussing stress, it is important to distinguish between differences in life events and in the response to them. In other words, one can distinguish between objective and subjective stress. There is some evidence that children with handicaps are exposed to more stressors than nonhandicapped children, that the nature of the stressor differs for different groups of children with handicaps (Hodges, Kline, Barbero, & Flanery, 1984), and that the number of stressors is correlated with amount of symptomatology (Wertlieb, Weigel, Springer, & Feldstein, 1987). On the other hand, there is also evidence that children's perceptions of the nature and intensity of a stressor are mediated by cognitive level (J. M. Brown, O'Keeffe, Sanders, & Baker, 1986) and perhaps by temperamental variables or coping styles (Band & Weisz, 1988; Cowen, 1988). It is particularly important to note that there are some children who seem to be invulnerable to a history of extreme stressors (Compas, 1987; W. P. Smith & Rossman, 1986; Wertlieb et al., 1987).

Although children with handicaps often experience failure and stress in regular classrooms, it is possible to conceive of environments in which children with handicaps do not fail as much. Supportive families, special education classes, sheltered workshops, active employment, and participa- tion in an active social life probably reduce the amount of failure that children experience (Compas, 1987; Levine, 1985).

Successes provide a sense of mastery or self-efficacy, and in turn, confi- dence that the person can regulate life events. Repeated failure over a period of years predicts different academic and work performance and negatively affects the person's attitudes about performance. It is possible that this history of failure can begin even in the earliest relationship between the mother and newborn infant (W. L. Donovan & Leavitt, 1985).

Self-esteem

These effects tend to be different for different individuals and specific to the disability, the type of task, the measure, and to what the person attributes success or failure (Cooley & Ayres, 1988; A. H. Gordon, Lee, Dulcan, & Finegold, 1986). Perhaps the most obvious effect of chronic failure is reduced self-esteem. This seems to be a general finding. However, the statement that children with disabilities generally view themselves negatively must be qualified. In the first place, standard measures of self-concept often have limited validity. Second, people with disabilities do not spend much of their time thinking about their failures. They have other agendas as well (Jahoda, Markova, & Cattermole, 1988). Finally, positive social support that exists in some families, classrooms, and in psychotherapy can limit the effects of failure on feelings of self-esteem, self-efficacy, and self-competence (DeFrancesco & J. Taylor, 1985; C. W. Hall & Richmond, 1985; Grant & Fodor, 1986; E. E. Jones, 1985; Leon, Lucas, Colligan, Ferdinande, & Kamp, 1985; Mallick, Whipple, & Huerta, 1987; Omizo, Amerikaner, & Michael, 1985; Omizo, Cubberly, & Longano, 1984; Zetlin & Turner, 1988; however, see also Wagner & Geffken, 1986).

Persistence

An alternative to inventories of self-concept are more behaviorally based measures. In our discussion of temperament, we discussed the concept of persistence. Persistence at a task is also one important measure of motivation. Children who persist longer when given the opportunity to work as long as they wish are thought to be more highly motivated to work at that task. Infants who interact with more complex toys for a longer time are thought to be showing their motivation to achieve mastery over the problem that the toy represents.

This simple concept of persistence needs to be qualified, however. Normal children engage in at least two forms of activities with objects. One is goal-directed behavior oriented to solving the problem inherent in the object. The other form of activity is simple exploration. No children persist very long at either exploration or problem solving with toys or other tasks that are very complex for them. Normal children do explore and attempt mastery of toys that are somewhat complex and therefore interesting. Retarded children may explore more complex toys, but do persist mainly with toys that they already have the skills to deal with. On the other hand, recent evidence with infants denies an earlier assertion from research with older retarded people that retarded people perseverate on or repeat low complexity behaviors (Schwethelm & Mahoney, 1986).

Persistence must take into account the complexity of the task in relation to the person's cognitive abilities. It is also important to distinguish persistence as goal-oriented behavior and as exploration. When one restricts oneself to goal-oriented problem solution with a task, the idea that persistence reflects motivation to master a more complex task than the child is already familiar with seems to apply to normal children but may not be general enough to apply to all children with handicaps.

Success and Failure

With this warning in mind, it should be said that persistence remains a main measure of motivation to work at a task. Persistence, however, is not the only measure of motivation. The attributions of the reasons for success or failure are also important, and the study of these attributions is a major feature of the recent literature.

The character of the goals of a task influences children's interpretation of success or failure and their performance. Dweck (1986) distinguished between learning goals and performance goals. With learning goals, people seek to increase their competence. Mastery tasks are oriented toward learning goals. On the other hand, children emphasizing performance goals seek to gain favorable judgments about their competence.

Which of these goals children emphasize in a task is related to their attribution of the things that are important for success or failure. Learning goals generally are tied up with explanations that emphasize effort. That is, if children see a task as one requiring high performance, the effort involved in accomplishing the task will be emphasized in explanations about why they have succeeded or failed on a task. On the other hand, if they saw the goal of the task as one of improving their skills, they will emphasize ability as an explanation.

Locus of Control and Learned Helplessness

In addition to the factors of complexity, the nature of the goals the children have, and the attribution of success or failure to ability, effort, or task characteristics, success or failure may be attributed to their own characteristics (their ability or effort) or to something outside themselves (luck, the conditions of testing, or the actions of others). That is they may see the *locus of control* of their actions more in themselves or more outside themselves.

A concept related to the concept of locus of control is *learned helplessness*.

People may learn, with experience, that the rewards or punishments that they receive in the course of everyday life are a direct consequence of their actions or more independent of what they do. That is, they may be in control of what happens to them or they may learn how to be helpless.

Various combinations of complexity, the nature of goals, attributions to ability or effort, locus of control, and the relationship between action and reward all describe the psychology of different children. They reflect how children conceive of the situation. But their conception of the nature of the causes of success and failure may differ from the way others see it. Thus, a judgment about whether children have succeeded or failed on a task may differ markedly from the way their parent or teacher perceives the situation. Nevertheless, it is thought that how children view their performance along these dimensions will be an important determinant of the way they respond to their learning environment, whether they persist or give up on a task, or whether they are pleased or disappointed with their performance.

With these basic concepts in mind, we can now turn to a review of the recent literature on persistence, attributions of success and failure, locus of control, and learned helplessness of children with handicaps. First of all, it is worth pointing out again that the literature tends to be inconsistent (e.g., Friedman & Medway, 1987; Licht, Kistner, Ozkaragoz, Shapiro, & Clausen, 1985). Perhaps this is because the results in this field depend on age and sex (Kistner, K. White, Haskett, & Robbins, 1985; Licht et al., 1985) of the child and also on the conditions of the study and the particular measures used.

In general, though, success experiences increase persistence and ratings of self-efficacy, and failure experiences lower them (Lyman, Prentice-Dunn, D. R. Wilson, & Bonfilio, 1984). Consistent with this is that groups of children who probably have experienced a history of chronic failure, for example learning-disabled and mentally retarded children, differ from nonhandicapped children on at least some of their attributions of the basis of their success and failure (Jacobsen, Lowery, & DuCette, 1986; Gargiulo & O'Sullivan, 1986).

Lower self-perceptions of ability in learning-disabled children develop before the middle-school years. They continue thereafter, and they are an important predictor of low achievement (Chapman, 1988; N. L. Stein, 1987). Learning-disabled children who attribute failure to controllable causes perform better in school than those who think that they can do nothing about the causes of school failure (Kistner, Osborne, & LeVerrier, 1988). Programs that demonstrate during skill training that success comes with effort increase performance of children with learning disabilities (Borkowski, Weyhing, & M. Carr, 1988; Schunk & Cox, 1986). Thus, there is a clear relationship between internal locus of control and achievement.

At least as important, there sometimes are no group differences between children with and without handicaps, the differences are minimal, or they apply to only certain measures (D. E. Friedman & Medway, 1987; Unruh, Cronin, & Gilliam, 1987). This means that there may be very important heterogeneity within the groups of children with handicaps.

Haywood and Switzky (1985) took advantage of an understanding that this heterogeneity exists by varying reward conditions in accordance with the motivational orientation of individuals within a group of mentally retarded adults. They found that if the motivational conditions were consistent with the perceived locus of control of a person (internal or external), work productivity was maximized relative to conditions that ignored these individual differences.

One can conclude from all of this that it is important to recognize that motivation is important for learning and that attributions about the reasons for success and failure are highly individual. Age, sex, and type of handicap do influence these attributions. But more important, the individual differences are most significant. At this time, it is possible to go beyond the obvious statement that there are individual differences between children. The dimensions of success and failure, complexity of task, persistence of effort, the perceived goals of learning and performance, attribution to ability and to effort, locus of control, and the relation between action and reward are all the interacting ways that these individual differences can be described.

ANXIETY AND DEPRESSION

With these motivational concepts in mind, we can now turn to a consideration of anxiety and depression. These two concepts are related to each other, but they do not overlap completely. Anxiety and depression are both avoidant coping strategies that in milder forms can be adaptive. Milder levels of anxiety can improve performance (Levine, 1985), and mild depressions can prevent the overcommitment that comes with unrealistic considerations of what is possible (i.e., grandiose thinking). However, in more severe forms, the avoidance that comes with anxiety or depression may interfere with positive actions that are the mark of successful problem solving in social and work situations.

Anxiety

On the other hand, anxiety and depression are not exactly the same thing. We know this because anxiety is sometimes accompanied by an elevated rather than depressed mood, and severe depressions sometimes occur without perception of any emotion, including anxiety. Anxiety may be defined by historical factors, by the stimuli that evoke it, by the nature of the response, and by response to specific treatments. Children who have been exposed to early depriving, unpredictable, or abusive rearing situations may be rated as more anxious or socially withdrawn (e.g., J. H. Block, J. Block, & Gjerde, 1986; A. L. Dean, Malik, Richards, & Stringer, 1986; Francis, Last, & C. C. Strauss, 1987). School phobias and fears that are not age-appropriate (e.g., Ferrari, 1986; H. J. Jackson, 1983; Sparks, 1986) are examples of anxious behaviors defined by situations. Obsessive ideas and compulsive ritualistic behaviors that interfere with adaptation are examples of behavioral manifestations that have defined anxiety (Vitiello, Spreat, & Behar, 1989). Finally, response to certain behavior therapies and to certain psychopharmacological agents are sometimes regarded as ways of defining anxiety disorders (J. B. Murray, 1986).

This means that anxiety is a diffuse concept with broad application. It is surprising, therefore, that there has not been much recent literature on the subject in children generally and handicapped children in particular. Levine (1985) argued for a distinction between situational and trait anxiety. There is reason to believe that children with visual and learning handicaps can show evidence of increased anxiety (Dollinger, Horn, & Boarini, 1988; Matson, Manikam, Heinze, & Kapperman, 1986). An older literature argues for greater anxiety in mentally retarded people that is accompanied by poor task performance. However, Levine showed that mentally retarded people who are engaged in work and social life showed less anxiety than did mentally retarded people who were not so engaged. He also showed that more anxious people were more, not as one might expect, less productive.

All of this is consistent with the idea that anxiety is a diffuse dimension defined in various ways. The core of the concept includes the idea that anxiety may be activating, and at this level, it might promote successful coping. On the other hand, when anxiety is very severe and chronic, the best coping involves avoidance of the stressful situation. Avoidance precludes application of skills that promote success and therefore feelings of the self-efficacy that can compete with anxiety.

Depression

There are four approaches to the study of depression. These approaches are sometimes seen as competing views, but probably are best viewed as complementary to one another. The biological view seeks biochemical and hereditary causes for depression. The psychoanalytic approach looks to early social relationships as important in the development of depression. The behaviorist theories of depression believe that the social reinforcement history of the children is important, particularly a lack of association between the children's actions and the rewards they receive. Finally, the cognitive approach proposes that the way different people explain the events in their lives may help account for individual differences in the likelihood of developing depression in people who otherwise have objectively similar histories of success and failure and degree of control over their environments.

All of these approaches are currently believed to be useful in describing depression and its causes (Digdon & Gotlib, 1985). Partly this is because it is doubtful whether depression is a unitary syndrome derived from a single etiology. More likely, a range of symptoms derived from the interaction of several possible causes defines a general concept that we call depression.

Furthermore, depression means different things at different ages. At one time, it was thought that young children are incapable of being depressed because their cognitive development did not permit the kinds of concepts thought to be inherent in depression. More recently, it has been recognized that even very young children are capable of becoming depressed, but the processes involved in causing a child's depression and the manifestations of depression may be very different in children of different ages and between adolescents and adults (Stehouwer, Bultsma, & Blackford, 1985).

Nevertheless, we use a single word to describe the collection of symptoms that define depression. What are some of these symptoms in children? It is possible to answer this question in a number of ways. We can look at children who are believed by clinicians to be depressed or we can look at children in a nonclinic population who score extremely high on tests that are said to describe depression. We can ask the children about how they feel; ask their age peers, parents, and teachers; and even observe them. All of these methods have been used, and because they tend to look at different groups of children and tap different areas of the child's life, they tend to emphasize different characteristics (Kerr, Hoier, & Versi, 1987).

However, it is sadness (dysphoric mood) that most clearly defines depression. Children who are chronically sad are those who are most generally regarded as depressed. That is, depression is tied up with a dimension of mood. Of course, everyone is sad at one time or another, and at some ages sadness is common. It is only when this sadness is severe, chronic, and obviously not age appropriate that clinicians identify a child as depressed (Digdon & Gotlib, 1985).

It is also true that while feeling or being judged by others as sad is a necessary condition for diagnosis of depression in children, it is not a sufficient condition. There are several other characteristics that are significantly associated with ratings of depression that further define the complex of associated symptoms. These characteristics include low self-esteem, different attributions of locus of control, increased levels of subjective and objective life stress, anxiety, low assertiveness, social withdrawal and social rejection, poor interpersonal problem solving, low achievement, attention problems, appetite and sleep disturbance, thoughts about suicide, low and high activity, lower motor proficiency, and some biochemical abnormalities (B. P. Allen, 1987; Birleson, Hudson, Buchanan, & S. Wolff, 1987; Bodiford, Eisenstadt, J. H. Johnson, & Bradlyn, 1988; Faust, Baum, & Forehand, 1985; Humphries, Gruber, J. Hall, & Kryscio, 1985; Kashani, Carleson, Horwitz, & J. C. Reid, 1985; Koenig, 1988; Mullins, L. J. Siegel, & Hodges, 1985; Nolen-Hoeksema, Girgus, & Seligman, 1986; C. C. Strauss, Forehand, Frame, & K. Smith, 1984; C. C. Strauss, Last, Hersen, & Kazdin, 1988; Wright, 1985).

Thus, like anxiety, the concept of depression is diffuse. It is possible to distinguish a few very severe, chronic, easily identifiable cases from the much larger group whose depression is episodic and related to environmental stressors (Hodgman, 1985). However, beyond these few cases, a definitive diagnosis of depression as a restricted entity is often difficult in practice.

Nevertheless, depression certainly exists in children, and it is related to stress and lack of social support. From all that has been said in this section about the effects of chronic failure on motivation, one might expect that children who often experience failure might be more likely to feel and be rated as depressed. There are several studies that confirm this expectation. Groups of children with learning disabilities, attention-deficit disorders, and mental retardation all have elevated levels of perceived depression (Bohline, 1985; Borden, R. T. Brown, Jenkins, & Clingerman, 1987; D. Goldstein, Paul, & Sanfilippo-Cohn, 1985; Prout & Schaefer, 1985; W. M. Reynolds & K. L. Miller, 1985; Wright & Stimmel, 1984). Thus, it is important to be sensitive to the possibility that children with cognitive disorders may also be afflicted with feelings of depression.

On the other hand, depression is by no means universal among children with disabilities. The elevated levels in the studies cited previously are not very large differences, and some studies fail to show a significant difference between handicapped and nonhandicapped children (D. T. Stevenson & Romney, 1984). This means that simple comparisons between the major categories of handicaps are not adequate to account for the individual differences within or between them.

A more analytic strategy has been helpful. One approach has been to form subgroups within a general category and take a correlational strategy. D. Goldstein and colleagues (1985) studied four subgroups of children with learning disabilities. One was a group with hyperactivity, another was composed of children who also had socioemotional difficulties, a third had low IQs and the fourth was learning disabled but had none of these other characteristics. All four of these groups had higher than average levels of depression, but the average depression score of the four groups did not differ from each other. However, whereas the average depression scores did not distinguish the groups from each other, the groups were very different when their depression scores were correlated with IQ and with achievements tests in reading and mathematics. The learning-disabled children with no other handicaps showed negligible correlations between depression and either IQ or reading and math scores. The children who also had low IQs showed significant correlations of depression and various aspects of intelligence. The depression scores of the group with socioemotional handicaps were correlated significantly with the achievement, but not with any IQ measure. And the hyperactive children tended to be more depressed only when their IQ and achievement scores were low. D. Goldstein and colleagues interpreted these group differences as reflecting different manifestations of depression in the different groups. For instance, the children with learning disabilities and no other handicap were thought to become unhappy as a consequence of transitory events following frustration or loss, whereas the depression of the learning-disabled children with socioemotional disorders was characterized as chronic or stable depression.

Other studies (e.g., B. A. Benson, Reiss, D. C. Smith, & Laman, 1985; Laman & Reiss, 1987) reported that the mentally retarded people who are more likely to feel depressed are those who have poor social skills and who also receive less social support. Despite what one might expect from common sense, depression is not related to the amount of stigmatization the person feels. However, reduced social skills and social support are related in an important way to feelings of depression.

These studies go beyond a comparison of the major categories of handicap. Both looked at patterns of correlations between variables that were chosen on the basis of a conception of the relationship between depression, other characteristics of the person, and life events. This approach seems to be a most important way of discovering the determinants of individual differences between children.

In summary, the concept of depression is a diffuse one that includes many of the same ideas that are used in describing response to success and failure and to stress. The children's perceptions of their experiences as well as the experience as viewed by others are central features of the analyses. Variables associated with biology, early social history, a continuing pattern of success and failure, and current social and work requirements interact to determine the children's perception of themselves, their willingness to engage the world, and the degree to which they will succeed in the future.

IMPULSIVENESS, HYPERACTIVITY, AND AGGRESSION

Concepts such as self-esteem and attribution describe the way children account for success and failure in their lives. Another aspect of personality is concerned with the control of action. Controlling impulses, delaying gratification, and concepts of self-efficacy are all aspects of the control of action, and these concepts have been used in the description of impulsiveness, hyperactivity, and aggression.

Children are capable of managing their emotions to some degree at least (Terwogt, Schene, & P. L. Harris, 1986). However, controlling their impulses or delaying gratification of their desires are aspects of a problem that all children have in adapting to the adult world. When this limitation in control is very extreme, it may be recognized as abnormal.

Impulsiveness, hyperactivity, and unsocialized aggression have all been viewed as resulting from a limitation in one control mechanism or another. Impulsiveness is part of the reflective–impulsive dimension of cognitive style discussed in a previous chapter. Everyone is more or less reflective or impulsive at one time or another. That is, people respond without much thought to a situation, or they may be more likely to consider the consequences of their actions with care. Children whose behavior is generally impulsive to an extent that interferes with their general adaptation are thought to be abnormal in this dimension. Children who are overreflective are called obsessive and are usually classified as part of an anxiety disorder, that is, as an instance of overcontrol.

The concept of hyperactivity may include impulsive responding, but ordinarily it is reserved for the case in which a child moves around excessively. In a previous chapter, we distinguished between hyperactivity as an abnormal rate of shifting attention and as motor action. These two concepts are still commonly confused, but hyperactivity is most properly restricted to an excess of general motor activity level rather than to abnormal shifting of attention.

Impulsiveness and hyperactivity may be unrelated to social behavior, but aggression is defined in social terms. Even unsocialized aggression is defined in terms of its effect on others. Behaviors that intentionally cause injury to others are said to be aggressive behaviors. Such behaviors may include direct physical assaults, verbal behavior, and behaviors with indirect effects such as fire setting and vandalism. The definition of aggression is somewhat confusing because aggression can result from an organized action of a group or a seemingly purposeless act by an individual. In this section, we consider only unsocialized aggression.

Each of these general classes of behavior, impulsiveness, hyperactivity, and unsocialized aggression are extremes of dimensions that describe normal behavior and they may all be seen as resulting from imperfect development of the behaviors that control them.

Although the concept of inadequate control ties these three concepts together, it is also true that impulsiveness, hyperactivity, and aggression are not identical in concept, and though there may be a relationship between them, they may not be correlated very highly (Hinshaw, 1987). That is, whereas there is a tendency for hyperactive children also to be impulsive or aggressive, this tendency may not be very strong.

Likewise, the concept of self-control as a general personality trait is too simple. Different measures of self-control by different people do not correlate highly with one another. For instance, the judgment of whether a child is deviant in control mechanisms depends on the context of the judgment and who (the child, peers, teacher, or parent) is making the estimate (W. M. Reynolds & K. D. Stark, 1986). Moreover, self-control mechanisms are only one determinant of impulsiveness, hyperactivity, and unsocialized aggression (e.g., Frankel & Simmons, 1985).

Although the concept of self-control is complex, it is clear that deviations in impulsiveness, hyperactivity, and aggression do exist and can be part of a person's personality for a long time. Children who are regarded as inhibited or uninhibited at 21 months of age are different socially at 5 years. Hyperactivity and aggression at 3 years of age predicts problems at 6 years old, and temper tantrums in childhood that are frequent are related to adaptive problems at 30 and 40 years of age (S. B. Campbell, Breaux, Ewing, & Szumowski, 1986; Caspi, Elder, & Bem, 1987; Rapport, Tucker, DuPaul, Merlo, & Stoner, 1986; Reznick et al., 1986).

Thus, impulsiveness, hyperactivity, and unsocialized aggressiveness are real, enduring characteristics of some children, and these behavior patterns may or may not be related to one another. The correlates and determinants of their development are also complex. For instance, general self-esteem is apparently not related to aggression (Schaughency, Frame, & C. C. Strauss, 1987), but certain aspects of self-efficacy may be. Specifically, aggressive children find it easier to perform aggressive acts than do nonaggressive children, and they see aggression as instrumental in obtaining certain desired rewards and avoiding aversive experience. That is, aggressive children find it more efficacious to commit aggressive acts than do nonaggressive children (D. G. Perry, L. C. Perry, & Rasmussen, 1986). This suggests that aggressive patterns are at least partly learned. The effects of parents, siblings, friends, past school programs, and even television viewing have all been implicated, at least for some children, though television viewing may have variable effects on aggression (Eron, 1987; Haskins, 1985; Frankel & Simmons, 1985; Sprafkin & Gadow, 1988; Sprafkin, Gadow, & Grayson, 1988).

In summary, several things may be said about impulsiveness, hyperactivity, and aggression. Each of them is a complex dimension. The dimensions overlap in the sense that some children may be abnormal in more than one at a time and the dimensions are correlated. Nevertheless, these three dimensions mean very different things, and although they are correlated, they do not overlap completely. The concepts of self-control, delay of gratification, and self-efficacy have been used with some success in explaining various aspects of impulsive behavior, hyperactivity, and aggression. However, at this time, these concepts need refining.

SUMMARY

The dynamic aspects of behavior have at their base concepts related to personality and specific incentives. Two issues are specially important. Are motivational factors specific to certain situations or are they reflected in all contexts? Is it best to characterize motivational variables and personality factors as dimensions or as discrete classes?

In general, groups of children with handicaps are more likely to show personality deviations than are normal children. However, the prevalence of these deviations is low, and all children can be described by the same personality dimensions.

Temperament is a diffuse concept denoting inclinations to behave in one way or another. There are social stereotypes about the temperament of premature children, learning-disabled children, and children with Down syndrome. Studies have not confirmed the validity of these stereotypes.

More successful has been the assessment of specific incentives that motivate behavior in learning situations. There are clear differences in what rewards different children, and these incentive patterns can be assessed in a valid manner.

Children with handicaps, like other children, strive for mastery of their environment. Although they often succeed, they also experience more failure than do normal children. They make attributions of the causes of their success and failure in the same way as do normal children. But they tend to have lower self-esteem, patterns of learned helplessness, and greater attribution of external control of success. These group differences can produce more failure. On the other hand, the group differences are not very great and attribution differences can be diminished with appropriate instruction and social support.

The concepts of anxiety and depression are complex, and they are overlapping categories. Likewise, impulsiveness, hyperactivity, and aggression are related, but independent. Groups of children with handicaps may be more anxious, depressed, impulsive, hyperactive, and/or aggressive than normal children, but the differences between groups are not impressive.

III

Social Psychology

9 _____ · _____

Social Interactions

The first part of this book dealt with basic concepts: history, causes, classification, and diagnosis. Then, we turned to the psychology of the individual: perception, learning, intelligence, language, and personality. The last part of the book is concerned with the person living in society: social interactions in family and school, education and treatment methods, and life in the community.

In thinking about the person, our central concept of adaptation again comes to the fore. However, instead of thinking of adaptation as a process in which a person adapts to an unchanging society in family and school, adaptation is regarded as mutual, transactional, dialectic. That is, although it is true that children with disabilities must learn to adapt to their family, neighborhood, school, and workplace, it is also true that society adapts to individual differences between people.

This conception of a mutual relationship between the individual and society has always been a part of the relationship between human societies and the disabled people within them. However, it was not until recently that this idea became an important part of psychological theory and research. Traditionally, it was thought that the goal of education and treatment is to normalize behavior so that the person could adapt more easily to a standard conception of society. Such a perspective is exemplified, for instance, in conventional psychoanalytic and behavioristic treatment methods. However, more recently, it has become clear that, when a family or a society provides education and care for a disability, they are themselves changing in important ways in response to the disabled person. This has been evident in a changing legal system that has guaranteed basic civil rights to people with handicaps, in improved physical access to public buildings, and even in the recent inclusion of handicapped people as parts of groups in television dramas and commercials.

The relationship between people is therefore mutual. It is best to see this mutual relationship as basically dyadic. That is, whereas families and communities are complexes of relationships that sometimes defy precise analysis, it is what happens between two people that describes the fundamental nature of relationships. Thus, most psychological research on social relationships of people with disabilities is done on two-person relationships.

Relationships may be basically dyadic, but they are determined to some extent by factors outside of the dyad. Remember, for instance, the last time that you were telling someone a secret and a third friend entered the room. Perhaps you changed the subject of the conversation or stopped talking abruptly.

The point is that dyadic relationships are determined partly by other relationships. A person's network of relationships can be vast, so social behavior is sometimes regarded as too complex to study scientifically. In fact, this is not true. The level of description broadens from the analysis of the dyad to that of complex networks like families and communities. Analyses of dyads can be precise and elegant. As more people are brought into consideration, general attitudes, cultural factors, and institutions become aspects of the analysis. They are not as precise, but because they take into consideration more of the situation, they can be equally valid. It would be nice, of course, if we could be both precise and general. However, social psychology has not yet reached that point.

In previous chapters, we have considered the social behavior of individual children with handicaps. For instance, we have mentioned that some children have difficulties in perceiving the meaning of the facial expressions of others. Cognitive factors may also be involved because children with cognitive problems have problems not only in thinking about academic material, but they may also have difficulties in construing social situations. Motivational and personality factors are also involved. In fact, personality characteristics like shyness or aggressiveness are often defined in terms of social interactions. Given these deficiencies in the social skills of some children with handicaps, it is no surprise that many of them experience difficulties in acceptance from others or that they are downright rejected.

However, the social difficulties that children with handicaps often have are based not only on their lack of social skills, but also on the behavior patterns of others. Culturally transmitted negative social stereotypes, rigidity in response to individual differences, and tendencies to sentimentalize and overprotect people with handicaps are also major sources of the social difficulties of children with handicaps.

These characteristics of others are assessed through several well-developed methods. Surveys of specific attitudes toward people with handicaps are particularly common, for instance, in studies of the attitudes of caregivers and teachers. Sociometric ratings in which all children in a classroom are asked to rate all of their classmates with respect to specific characteristics are also used to assess relative popularity and dominance of children having specific personal characteristics.

In general, these studies show that attitudes toward children with handicaps are sometimes negative, sometimes protective, and sometimes neutral, so that the task of recent research has been to determine the conditions under which specific attitudes and sociometric ratings occur in the social environments of children with handicaps.

The relationship between specific handicapped children and individual parents, adult caregivers, teachers, siblings, or peers has received much attention lately because it is the most important focus of social behavior. One way in which the relationship between children with handicaps and others is studied is to compare their attitudes with respect to particular issues. Probably the most valid way of doing this is through participant observation procedures in which researchers live and work with the people they are studying for long periods of time. This allows a more intimate perception of the perspectives of the members of a family or other social group than is possible with any other methodological approaches. However, even the proponents of this approach (e.g., Edgerton, 1984) acknowledge that it is very costly and perhaps subjective. Other approaches are more common.

Formal surveys of opinions or attitudes are an alternative. One aspect of survey analysis involves the comparison of the scores of the child and of another person. If the scores are similar, it is concluded that their relationship is closer or better, at least with respect to the characteristics measured by the device.

Another approach is to rate the social situation. For instance, the Home Observation Measurement of the Environment (HOME) scale evaluates various aspects of the home environment such as degree of organization and the extent that the home is child-centered. Other examples include rating scales that evaluate various types of environment from the perspective of the caregiver and others that estimate the degree to which an institutional environment is homelike.

Far more frequent in recent research are observational studies. Most commonly children are observed with their mother during eating, play, or solving a problem. These observations are not casual. They involve recording the behavior of both members of the dyad in great detail, looking

especially at who initiates which behavior and how the other person typically responds to that initiation. The specific behaviors recorded in such
observations depend on the purpose of the study, the developmental level of
the child, and the situation used. Examples of typical behaviors are eye
fixations and specific types of words. These observations are often accomplished by repeated review of audio or video recordings of the observation
sessions.

These then are the general methods used to study the social life of
children with handicaps. In the sections that follow, we consider the individual social skills of children with handicaps, the psychology of families,
more specific focus on mother–child relationships, child abuse, the relationships between handicapped children and their siblings, and nonfamily peer
relationships.

SOCIAL SKILLS DEFICITS

In previous chapters, we have shown that generic problems in behaving
appropriately in social situations can accompany perceptual, cognitive, language, and personality disorders. In this section, individual personality and
social skills deficits and their treatment are described further, this time in
the social context of this chapter.

Descriptive Studies

The literature on individual social deficits has become less influential than it
was 20 years ago. Social handicaps in children have their source in deficits in
those children themselves. There is now less emphasis in the research
literature on identifying those deficits and providing corrective treatment
for them. Instead, the mutual adjustment of handicapped children and their
community is receiving the greatest attention.

Although groups of children with handicaps are generally believed to
have problems in social adaptation, sometimes these problems are not very
apparent. If one asks handicapped and normal children themselves about
the personal characteristics that describe them, differences in self-
perception may be minimal. In one study, children with handicaps rated
themselves differently than children without handicaps on only 5 out of 48
characteristics. Moreover, whereas on 4 of these (dumb, foolish, honest, and
wise) the handicapped children rated themselves less positively, they did
regard themselves as more jolly. Thus, not all measures of personality
predict problems in social adaptation (Burden & Parish, 1983).

This point is reinforced by follow-up studies. J. G. Parker and Asher (1987) reviewed the literature on the relationship between peer acceptance, aggressiveness, and shyness/withdrawal in childhood and later personal adjustment. They cited the pervasive concept that children who are deviant in these factors are at risk for dropping out, criminal behavior, and psychopathology in adulthood. They concluded from an extensive review that there is general support for the idea that poor peer adjustment predicts later difficulties, but the evidence is stronger for low acceptance and aggressiveness than for shyness/withdrawal and for dropping out and criminal behavior than for psychopathology.

The case may vary not only for the source of the information and the type of measure, but results may also depend on the situation. G. M. Morrison (1985) studied learning-handicapped children and nonhandicapped children in school classes organized in various ways. Children may realistically estimate their actual social status in a class, or they may underestimate or overestimate it. Unrealistic estimations may characterize handicapped or nonhandicapped individuals. Morrison found that the proportion of children who demonstrate unrealistic estimations can vary with the environment. Berkson and Romer (1980) also showed that social interactions depend, not only on personal characteristics of mentally retarded people, but also on the place that they are in.

Thus, the social behavior that people engage in depends not only on their handicap, but at least as important, on the measure of social behavior, their personality, and the situation they are in. Nevertheless, it is possible to describe social behavior and some of its deficits in terms of specific aspects of behavior.

The traditional approach to describing social deficits of individuals is to use a trait approach. That is, general factors, such as sociability, that summarize social characteristics of individuals are used to predict their behavior in most or all social situations. Such prediction has not been very successful. Ways of measuring social skills may be more important than abstract classifications, and the use of social traits to predict or explain social behavior has given way to another, more molecular approach (Gresham, 1986; Gresham & Reschly, 1987a, 1987b).

The central ideas here are social competence and social skills. The concept of social competence includes a consideration of the outcome of social behaviors and may involve an evaluative component. Thus, to describe how competent people are in introducing themselves to others, ask others about how well they perform this set of behaviors. As indicated earlier, there may be several different pictures of the competence of one individual, depending on whether parents, teachers, caregivers, or peers are asked and whether an informal interview or more standardized procedures are used.

Skills are part of what makes up competence. The skills people demonstrate in introducing themselves to others are, of course, complex. However, they can be described: wait until others are finished talking, smile, ask the other person his name, and so forth. Skills can be described in precise terms or more generally, and they may apply to only specific situations or to many situations.

In talking about skill deficits, it is important to distinguish competence and skill from performance. That is, in determining what the nature of social skill training is to be for children, it is important to know whether they know the skills but are not performing them appropriately or whether they have not learned the skills well enough. It is not possible to tell from lack of performance if it is a competence or performance problem. However, by observing children carefully, one can see whether they ever perform the skills appropriately. If they do, then it is clear that one needs to motivate or teach the children to apply the skills rather than to teach the skills. Examples of performance deficits that are common in all children but are especially common in some children with handicaps include problems with self-control, lack of flexibility in responding to changes in social situations, and shyness.

Most of the research on social skill deficits of individuals can be divided into descriptive studies and treatment studies. The descriptive studies are either comparisons of groups of normal children with groups of children with various classes of handicaps or they may also attempt to differentiate various classes.

In general, it is clear that groups of children with handicaps have social skills deficits. Aside from the obvious problems of those groups whose main disabilities are defined in social terms (e.g., autism and the various conduct disorders), other types of handicapping conditions are also associated with social deficits. Hearing handicapped, mentally retarded, and learning-disabled groups have been shown to have social skill problems, and these may even be apparent in the behavior of infants (Gallagher, Jens, & O'Donnell, 1983; Yoder, 1987).

Problems are not often specific to the clinical category. They include such general categories of behavior as aggression, disruptiveness, insensitivity, difficulty in imitation, and withdrawal. The problems do not necessarily characterize all members of the group, and group differences may be minor. That is, although there is a tendency for groups of handicapped people to be different socially from groups of nonhandicapped children, this may not apply to all of the handicapped children, and the nature of the social skill deficit can only be statistically predicted from group membership (Cheney & Foss, 1984; Dawson & Adams, 1984; S. C. Jackson, Enright, & Murdock, 1987; Macklin & Matson, 1985; Saloner & Gettinger, 1985; A. P. Thomas, Bax, & Smyth, 1988).

The lack of specificity for individuals is characteristic of the more interesting studies in this area. These studies compare classes of disability with each other. For instance, one study showed that learning-disabled boys show more hyperactivity and (less depression and social withdrawal) than other clinic-referred groups. Another study showed that emotionally handicapped children are especially characterized by deficits in social-cognitive problem solving when they were compared with average learners, students with developmental learning delays, or children who are accelerated academically. Again, it must be emphasized that these characterizations are not necessarily specific to one category or all the individuals in it and the characteristics of the groups overlap substantially. It is also true that these comparisons are quite crude. However, they represent a useful direction in clarifying possible differences between the categories of handicaps, to the extent that they exist (Elias, Gara, Rothbaum, Reese, & Ubriaco, 1987; McConaughy & Ritter, 1986).

Training

The most explicit studies of individual social skills deficits are training studies. This is not surprising because one must specify deficits in detail if one is to improve the person's performance and evaluate the degree of improvement. There have been a large number of studies of social skills training with mentally retarded, learning-disabled, or other groups. These have focused for example on nonverbal motoric behaviors (facial expressions, gestures, body contact, appearance); verbal behaviors (asking questions, making small talk, performing social rituals like shaking hands); affective behaviors (expressing attitudes or feelings, recognizing internal emotional cues, referential communication, empathic responding); and social cognitive skills (interpersonal problem solving, role taking, thinking emphatically, discrimination of social cues, understanding social norms). Training involves separating each of these general skills into subskills and using modeling and social rewards to establish them. On the whole, the experience with training procedures has been positive, although once learned the skills are not necessarily used in all situations, and generalization training may be required (Davies & Rogers, 1985; Schneider & B. M. Byrne, 1987; Schumaker & Hazel, 1984; Strain, Odom, & McConnell, 1984; Tisdelle & St. Lawrence, 1988). We discuss skill training further in the next chapter.

Pragmatics

Before leaving the subject of individual social skills, a discussion of linguistic interaction rules (pragmatics) can serve as a transition to our consideration of social behavior as relationship. Pragmatics is the study of the rules used in communication. The emphasis in this aspect of the study of language is on social appropriateness rather than on syntax or grammar. Common examples of these rules include appropriate taking of turns in conversation, asking questions when one does not understand something, and maintaining the topic of conversation.

Research on disabilities in pragmatics has suffered from methodological faults and from lack of theoretical rigor. Small sampling, inconsistent and sometimes incorrect use of categories, failure to repeat studies, and a disagreement about whether to study pragmatics of natural conversation or of more standardized settings are only some of the contributors to a somewhat ambiguous picture (McTear, 1985).

Most of the studies have been carried out with children with learning disabilities, language disorders, or mental retardation. These have shown that children with disabilities do seem to have a deficit in pragmatic skills, though the deficit is not necessarily pervasive. It is likely that as a group, children with disabilities interrupt more, maintain topics less, provide less information, and need greater repetition (Dudley-Marling, 1985; Hargrove, Straka, & Medders, 1988; McCord & Haynes, 1988; Peskett & Wooton, 1985).

The situation is more clear with autistic children in whom the intention to communicate is not only delayed, but actually abnormal. This abnormality has been attributed to the child's language learning environment as well as factors inherent in the child. However, in these studies of children with autism, adequate comparison groups of mentally retarded and normal children are not always used (Wetherby, 1986).

In language interaction, it is not only the children's pragmatic skills that must be taken into account. The person with whom they communicate is also important. Parents attribute meaning to a child's vocal utterances and respond according to these attributions (Yoder & Feagans, 1988). Parents, and even retarded children, adjust their own speech to the language ability of their communicating partner (Bliss, 1984; H. Davis, Stroud, & Green, 1988), but this adjustment does not seem to affect the verbal output of their partner much (Moellman-Landa & Olswang, 1984). Lay people judge others as retarded or not retarded on the basis of their speech and language ability, with voice quality a major criterion for judgment (Kernan, Sabshay, & Shinn, 1989).

Summary

Research on social skill deficits in children with handicaps can be summarized briefly. If there are general social traits, they do not predict social behavior of children with handicaps very well. On the other hand, a very large set of social behaviors can be defined for any individual, and important problems in one or more of them can be defined and sometimes corrected. It is unlikely that many skill deficits are specific to any of the standard classifications of handicap. On the other hand, it is likely that some handicapped individuals do have specific difficulties. These difficulties derive from unknown factors but are probably related to social learning history.

FAMILIES AND OTHER CAREGIVERS

The families of children with handicaps are essentially like those of all children. Caregiving and companionship in families are especially obvious early in life, but they continue well into adulthood and often throughout life. Maternal care in nuclear families is the modal relationship covered in the research literature. However, especially recently, the importance of fathers, siblings, various forms of single-parent families, and the role of other members of the extended family have been studied.

Sometimes families cannot retain responsibility for the child with handicaps. This is relatively rare, but well-publicized, and occurs when the child's handicap is severe, when the family perceives it as more severe than others might, or when the families' resources are limited. Then, the child is placed out of the natural home with a relative, through adoption, or in a group-living environment. Often there are combinations of these home and out-of-home placements through temporary arrangements. In all of these supplementary or substitute forms of care, the natural family rarely loses contact with the child.

Going to school and then to work is normative as children grow older. In those environments, teachers and friends provide caregiving, instruction, and intimacy that overlaps with the care, instruction, and intimacy the child receives at home.

These social features that are common to all environments are emphasized here. To be sure, families, schools, and institutions are different in many ways. For instance, schools may employ formal curricula for teaching, whereas families tend to be less formal in their teaching. Friendships are different from sibships in that they tend to be less enduring. However, committed caregiving is one aspect of the social behavior of good parents, of teachers, and of caregivers in an institution. Intimacy that results in mutual understanding, caregiving, and fighting are characteristics of friendships and sibling relationships. Thus, the less formal aspects of the relationship are discussed in the remainder of this chapter. More formal educational and treatment approaches are dealt with later.

Three Theories and Their Applications

We continue with a review of three approaches to the study of families of children with handicaps: the *stage-loss theory*, the *stress-resource theory*, and the *family-systems approach.* These approaches should not be seen as mutually exclusive because they have features in common. However, they do represent points of view with different implications.

The loss theory of family response to children with handicaps is an application of a more general view that loss of anything that one values (such as a loved one through death, or a limb, or even such a trivial thing as one's keys) results in a sequence of grief and mourning responses that are universal and predictable. The first stage is recognition of the disability or loss. The second is emotional disorganization that may be accompanied by feelings of grief, anxiety, anger, and search for explanations of the cause of the disability. In the third stage, the person accepts and adjusts to the disability or loss (Blacher, 1984).

This loss theory has had broad appeal. It is intuitively reasonable and has been applied in a wide variety of situations. Its application to responses to children with handicaps involves the notion that before a child is born, parents have an ideal of what that child will be. An imperfect child represents a loss of that ideal. If the imperfection is very evident, recognition (the first stage) can be expected to be dramatic and to have dramatic effects. A stage of denial of the handicap follows, sometimes accompanied by protest, anger, and guilt. Finally, there is the third stage, adaptation. The paradigmatic example is a family who initially denies the existence of a handicap but then comes to accept the fact of the disability and the responsibility for planning for, caring for, and educating the child.

Although this theory is intuitively reasonable and has had broad application in treatment programs, it has been criticized. The theory has problems because the concepts that describe the stages are so general they are regarded as too vague for specific predictions. In addition, the idea that there is a sequence that is universal does not seem to be consistent with the facts. Families of children with handicaps do not necessarily go through all of the stages, and some families may not manifest any of them. Certainly, the specific manifestations of each of the stages is so variable that the general statement of the three stages is an inadequate descriptor of what is happening to specific families. Furthermore, it is not always possible to assign a response definitely to one behavior or to another. Thus, grief and anger are sometimes seen as part of the second, mourning stage and sometimes are viewed as part of adaptation. Thus, although the loss-stage theory has popular appeal because it is simple and often generally describes the facts, it does not go much beyond the most obvious characteristics of response to loss (Blacher, 1984; Kupst et al., 1984).

Another account is stress-resource theory. This approach proposes that several factors associated with a handicapping condition place stress on the members of a family and their community. The amount of stress that a family experiences depends on several factors such as the severity of the handicap, the vulnerability of the family, and the resources at the family's disposal to deal with the stress.

The most mature form of stress-resource theory is the Double ABCX model of McCubbin and Patterson (Bristol, 1987). This model states that degree of family crisis (X) is predicted by the other family stresses a family is exposed to, the coping strategies a family uses in managing potential crises, and the meaning the family assigns to having a child with handicaps.

The stress-resource theory is different from the universal loss theory because it leads one to look for differences between families in their response to stress and to attempt to account for those differences. For instance, it certainly is the case that different families vary dramatically in their response to children with handicaps. These family differences are reviewed here and are due to several major factors in the child, in the family, and in the environment. This point of view emphasizes the multiplicity of events that influence the family's response (Dadds, 1987; Morgan, 1988).

The stress-resource approach views the family of children with disabilities in the same general terms as families in general. That is, all families are subject to stresses at one time or another, and the families find ways of coping with those stresses with more or less success. Disability in a family may present various stressful situations, and depending on the psychological and physical resources that the family has at its disposal, the family finds ways of coping with the stressor. Thus, three general factors are considered: those that mediate vulnerability to stress, the material resources of the family and coping and adaptive behaviors of the family (E. A. Byrne & C. C. Cunningham, 1985).

The third approach is the family systems approach. It focuses on individual differences within a family and the ways in which the members of a family interact. Mothers, fathers, grandparents, individual siblings, aunts and uncles, and other people who are close to the family are factors in the life of the child with handicaps, as they are with any child. This statement, once made, is so obvious that it may seem unnecessary. However, tradition as reflected in the recent research literature so clearly emphasizes mother- -child relationships in the period prior to school age that it probably is worth pointing out that there are many people in the family, they respond differently, and their interactions form the focus of study.

The family systems approach has the strength that it goes beyond differences between families to a consideration of the relationships between people within families. Unfortunately, it tends not to be very explicit. Although loss theory has some general predictions and the stress-resource approach has several specific ones, the family systems approach does not make many explicit general predictions, perhaps because of its emphasis on the dynamic quality of the relationships between different people. It does have some general ideas underlying it, however, and the emphasis on differences within the family is very important.

The three approaches should not be seen as competing theories. Handicaps, by definition, provide challenges that can be stressful. Responses to that stress can include denial, guilt, anger, and also adaptation in its various forms. The degree and type of stress and the nature of responses to it depend on many factors that include the severity of the handicapping condition, the original relationship among family members, attitudes about handicap, and financial resources available to the family, among many other things. Thus, an integrated understanding of the relationship between members of the family, using the concepts from loss theory and stress-resource theory seems to be an approach that is useful now.

More on the Stress-Resource Approach

In the course of life in the real world, all families encounter stresses that they must cope with, and all families do cope or adapt more or less successfully. The success of their adaptation to the stressor depends on factors in the family. These include the degree of cohesiveness and communication between the family members and the extent to which they support one another.

This account is satisfactory for an initial understanding of what families in general encounter, including families that include a child with handicaps. However, the perspective is not very specific and therefore does not account for individual differences between families very well. For instance, it does not say much about why some families that have a handicapped child dissolve in an acrimonious divorce, whereas others raise all of their children in a harmonious atmosphere, dealing with the problems that a handicapped child may present in the practical way that they deal with any of life's problems.

The stress-resource approach has attempted to define the characteristics of children and parents that account for these individual differences. At this time, the approach can hardly be called complete. However, our knowledge is well ahead of where it was even a decade ago, and the consequences are practical. Instead of emphasizing only the difficulties that a family has in responding to a child with a handicapping condition and being vague about the factors that differentiate between families, more recent literature seems to be taking a more philosophical approach, showing sensitivity to the strengths a family and helping it to plan specific strategies for solving the practical problems that may be associated with handicapping conditions.

One major advance has been the definition of the major factors. For instance, stress can be defined in terms of characteristics of the handicapped child or in terms of the family members' perception of those characteristics. As indicated previously, the stress can be specific to the type of handicap such that it works on the family only for medical situations or for social situations. Furthermore, in general, a severe disability that requires much care will be more stressful than a mild disability (Bebko, Konstantereas, & Springer, 1987; C. E. Cunningham, Benness, & L. S. Siegel, 1988; Erickson & Upshur, 1989; Gowen, Johnson-Martin, Goldman, & Appelbaum, 1989; V. S. Harris & McHale, 1989; Jessop, Riessman, & R. E. K. Stein, 1988).

However, the objective aspects of the stressor are not the only predictors of the success of adaptation. The way the family perceives the objective stress is also important. Some families perceive an objectively minor handicap as a major tragedy. For them, it is one, and this must be appreciated. Other families are able to experience even the most threatening conditions in their children with a relatively low degree of distress. For instance, in one study of families of children who were in the early stages of cancer, parents scored between 25 and 57 on a scale of subjective distress whose scores could range from 15–60 (Blotcky, Raczynski, Gurwitch, & K. Smith, 1985).

Social Support

Accounting for this discrepancy between objective and subjective aspects of stress has been accomplished by the concept that certain attitudes or social factors mediate or modulate between the objective and subjective stress. The most important modulator has been social support. That is, members of families experience less stress when they experience more social support from each other (B. McKinney & Peterson, 1987; Minnes, 1988; Stoneman & Crapps, 1988).

Social support is a broad concept that has been defined primarily by the person who is receiving it. That is, in practice, research on social support measures the support, not by the behavior of the person or who may be providing it, but by the person who is its object.

There are some difficulties from defining support this way, because it may confound support with perceived stress. That is, people who feel that they are under high stress may report that they are not receiving "enough" support. It is not clear in this case whether support and stress are, in fact, independently defined concepts.

Despite the dangers to valid interpretation that are inherent in asking the same person to evaluate stress and support, there are some studies that do not fall into this trap. That is, they do look at perceived stress and perceived support by the same person, but they also take at least indirect objective measures of these factors by having others make judgments about objective stress and the amount of support that the person receives. More important, even those studies that do assess perceived stress and perceived support can be useful because they do look at the nature of the relationship between these two subjective factors (Black, Cohn, Smull, & Crites, 1985; Blotcky et al., 1985; Dunst, Leet, & Trivette, 1988; Dunst, Trivette, & Cross, 1986; B. McKinney & Peterson, 1987).

In general, then, although there are some potential problems of interpretation, it probably is safe to say that there is an important inverse relationship between amount of support that a person receives and the stress that one feels. Support, in turn, has to do with the amount of cohesion and the type of communication that goes on in a family. Members of families differ in their involvement with and sensitivity to one another. One major way of assessing this involvement and sensitivity is to ask parents to describe their handicapped children and to ask the children to describe themselves. Then, the responses on the same questionnaire are compared. Although there are usually major sources of agreement, there may also be important differences in their perspectives. For instance, as compared with the perspectives of their children, parents may underestimate the depressive symptoms of their depressed children or may overestimate the failures of their learning-disabled children. One study has classified families according to their degree of cohesion (disengaged-enmeshed) and adaptability (chaotic-rigid). They found that families of nondelinquent adolescents seem to be intermediate on both of these dimensions. Families of delinquent children tend to be both chaotic and enmeshed and not, for instance, chaotic and disengaged. This means that both how close families are and how they solve problems together are independent and important measures of family functioning (Angold et al., 1987; McLoughlin, F. L. Clark, Mauck, & Petrosko, 1987; G. M. Morrison & A. Zetlin, 1988; Rodick, Henggeler, & Hanson, 1986).

Up until now, we have described the relationship between stress, family support, and communication. That parents should experience less stress is important in its own right, and knowing the specific factors that contribute to a reduction of stress is also important. However, it is also good to ask whether it makes any difference to the children. Here, the literature is clearly affirmative. Whether one is dealing with school achievement or psychosocial variables, positive results are most common in supportive and cohesive families whose behavior is directed toward fostering their child's development (Bodner-Johnson, 1986; P. L. Johnson & O'Leary, 1987; Nihira, Mink, & C. E. Meyers, 1985).

Before we leave the triad of stress, support, and communication, we should emphasize that although we have been talking about family factors, it is on individuals that these effects work. Support is effective because it enables a mother to be more flexible. A relationship based on promoting growth, while assuring protection, permits children to have experiences that increase their learning. Thus, the relationships that we have summarized are not only correlation coefficients between questionnaire measures. It is important to think about how they affect each person in the family.

When we do this we come to recognize that these family factors interact with the characteristics of the individuals. If we take these individual characteristics into account, we have a more effective understanding than if we are satisfied with the general statement that support is a good thing. For instance, whereas adequacy of the support system was important in a follow-up study of coping with pediatric leukemia, so were previous experiences coping with illnesses and an attitude of living in the present. Even more impressive is a study that showed an interaction of support and locus of control. Mothers with internal locus of control and less spouse support experienced more stress (Kupst et al., 1984; B. McKinney and Peterson, 1987).

Methods

There are several methods for describing the family as a whole and individual dyadic relationships. In clinical practice, informal interview of one or more members of the family is common, but this approach is not used widely in the research literature. Two factors account for this difference. Perhaps the most important is economic. Research is expensive, even more than clinical practice. Thus, research studies must be brief and therefore must depend on more reliable and standardized procedures than is possible in treatment or educational environments.

Open-ended interviewing offers the possibility of revealing more information about the family than is possible with closed-ended interviews, brief observations, and rating scales, all of which tap limited categories. However, open-ended interviewing tends to be less reliable and the information obtained must be checked. This is possible in clinical environments, but it is not ordinarily possible with research studies because of financial considerations.

Interviewing is discouraged as the main research method also because most scientific statements tend to be quantitative due to the precision that quantification allows. Open-ended interviewing can produce quantitative information if the responses are coded into categories. However, this is a very laborious procedure, and it has not been used very much in this field. Ordinarily, predetermined scales or other systems that produce quantitative scores are the basis of the data collection and reporting.

All of this said, interviewing, especially over a long period of time, can provide descriptive qualitative information that is important for understanding families (Masterson, 1985). The method is often used at the initial stages of a research project, and most behavioral scientists continue to collect informal information through informal interviews and observations as part of their overall research strategy. The information they obtain from these informal sources is used to guide them in the planning of their future work.

More formal methods include observations, closed-ended interviews, and a variety of rating scales. Brief observations of life in the family, employing predetermined behavior categories, is one approach. The behavioral observation method is sometimes remarkably useful, considering the brief amounts of time that are ordinarily used. Also, one would expect that the observer would affect the behavior of the family. Despite these possible limitations, behavioral observations do have the advantage of direct observation rather than obtaining the picture through the eyes of family members or through less direct measures.

Observation has been used successfully in studies of families of aggressive children. For instance, in one study, members of families of four groups of children were observed for a total of 10 minutes during each of 6 to 10 days. Observation results were analyzed into five factors: verbal emotionality, physical dependency, social involvement, hostile-controlling, and hostile-impulsive. Differences between the four groups depended on the behavioral factor studied. Hostility of either kind was lower in families of normal children than in families of stealers, social-aggressive, or hyperactive-aggressive children, but families of these three groups of troubled children were similar to each other. On the other hand, patterns between the four groups were not as obvious for the three other factors. The hyperactive-aggressive group was more socially involved, but the stealers and normal children were less involved and did not differ from one another (W. J. Carlson, W. B. Williams, & Davol, 1984).

Far more common than observational methods are close-ended interviews, checklists, and rating procedures. One group of researchers uses several standardized scales that tap different aspects of family life. Combining the results from these scales statistically has allowed them to characterize families in a number of ways and relate these characterizations to cultural variables and to the development of children. In one study, homes of Japanese and American children with mental retardation were studied. The study showed that, although there were differences in the things emphasized in parenting in the two countries, the relationships between parenting and measures of child development were similar across cultures (Nihira, Tomiyasu, & Oshio, 1987; Nihira, Webster, Tomiyasu, & Oshio, 1988).

The studies also related characteristics of the family to child development in slow-learning and retarded children. As might be expected, a great number of factors in the home were related to the child's development, and these factors were differentially important at different developmental levels.

Perhaps most important for our consideration here, it was possible to learn these things from a 2-hour session in the home by observing the environment and having the family fill out forms.

Moreover, these studies found that families can be classified into different groups and family characteristics are related to child behavior in a bidirectional manner. From cluster analysis, a taxonomy of seven family lifestyles has been derived for families of children who are slow learners. These seven groups represent different patterns on factors derived from the various tests. They are not completely distinct from one another. However, they do predict different patterns of child development.

The relationship between the family and child development characteristics can be bidirectional, with the direction depending on the developmental level of the child and the behavior considered. Ordinarily, one thinks that family characteristics cause the child to develop more or less quickly. However, these studies show that the direction of the relationship depends on the nature of the family, as well as the specific measure of child development being looked at. Thus, in learning-oriented families the child influenced the family with respect to community participation, achievement orientation, provision of learning materials, harmony, quality of the residential environment, but not expressiveness. In achievement-oriented families, parents influenced the child on all variables. In outer-directed families, effects were more bidirectional. This perspective certainly supports the idea that the relationship between children and their families are specifiable and mutual (C. E. Meyers, Nihira, & Mink, 1984; Mink, Blacher, & Nihira, 1988; Mink, C. E. Meyers, & Nihira, 1984; Mink & Nihira, 1986).

These two programs of study, one using observation procedures and the other multiple standardized tests with sophisticated statistical analysis, are notable because they are programmatic and innovative methodologically. Another methodological approach is one that is common with studies of infants and preschool children. In these studies the HOME rating scale is used. It is a rating scale with forms appropriate for homes of infants and for preschoolers. The rating scale includes items that, when factor analyzed, produce three factors: emotional and verbal responsivity; avoidance of punishment; and a factor reflecting items that measure the availability of concept-development toys, maternal involvement in children's play, and story reading activities. Much has also been made of items that tap the degree of organization of the home.

The HOME predicts intellectual development in normal children in low income homes. Their development is related to the learning materials present in the home and the support of the mother for developmental advance. Among children with handicaps, children from low income families that show a failure-to-thrive syndrome seem to come from less organized homes. On the other hand, the HOME shows no difference in families of normal children and developmentally disabled babies or children with Down syndrome (D. A. Allen, G. Affleck, McGrade, & McQueeny, 1983; Bradley, Casey, & Wortham, 1984; Bradley, Rock, Caldwell, & Brisby, 1989; L. Smith & Hagen, 1984; J. H. Stevens & Bakeman, 1985).

These three methodological approaches are exemplary because they use consistent and relatively well standardized procedures. However, it must be said that a consistent approach is not a general characteristic of the recent literature on families of children with handicaps. For the most part, different studies employ different procedures, many of which are closed-ended interviews that are not well standardized. This situation is not all bad. Useful information, closely tied to diagnostic and treatment programs, often does emerge. However, the use of poorly standardized procedures does make the validity of information and the comparability of studies difficult to assess.

Another general problem of method in studies of families of children with handicaps has to do with the groups used (Stoneman, 1989). Most studies fail to use appropriate comparison groups. The first studies to be summarized have as their goal the description of characteristics of families of children with handicaps. This is certainly a useful thing to do. However, if one is describing the characteristics of families of children with handicaps, this implies that one is interested in knowing how those families differ from families of children without handicaps. Or if one is describing the families of children with specific disorders (as most studies of this kind do), then one would wish to know whether the characteristics of the family are unique to the specific handicap or are a response to disability in general.

Thus, it would seem that the ideal research design in studies of this kind would be a comparison of the group one is specifically interested in with properly matched groups of families of children with other handicaps and families without handicaps. Some of the first group of studies to be reviewed are designed in this way, but most are not.

Comparisons Between Families

In most studies, groups of families of children with handicaps are different from groups of families without such children. However, there are studies that show no difference (Abbott & Meredith, 1986; Cox, Seider, & Kidd, 1984; Spaulding & Morgan, 1986; Wertleib, Hauser, & Jacobson, 1986). This means that a generalized stereotype of an abnormal family resulting from a handicapped child is not valid. Instead, the evidence is strong that some families of some children are different on some measures. The appropriate attitude toward families with handicapped children, therefore, is a sensitivity toward the possibility of difficulties in certain areas while retaining the attitude that families of children with handicapped children are fundamentally normal.

The most common stereotypes about the effect of having a child with handicaps are that stress is increased, depression is more probable, and marital difficulties increased in families with children with handicaps. The evidence is not consistent for any of these factors. Studies that appropriately compare families of children with handicaps with families of nonhandicapped children sometimes find mothers, but not fathers, more subject to depression. Other studies show no difference at all. The same is true with perceived marital adjustment. Some studies do find a negative effect of a child with handicaps on marital adjustment. Again, adequately designed studies are conflicting in their results. Although stress may be greater in some families, it is not necessarily perceived as greater. It is still possible that there are general effects of a handicapped child that increase stress, depression, and marital difficulty, but it is unlikely that these effects are powerful or general (Bristol, Gallagher, & Schopler, 1988; Kazak, 1987; Spaulding & Morgan, 1986).

It seems unlikely that effects of having a handicapped child are obvious or general, but there are some factors that have emerged from studies of specific groups. It has been shown, for instance, that families of children with cystic fibrosis are far more concerned about factors associated with hospitalization than any other factors. Intellectually handicapped children evoked less positive attitudes about creativity, control, play, and teaching interactions from parents than nonhandicapped children. Parents of depressed children reward their children at much lower rates than do parents of nondepressed or nonclinic children. In other words, although one cannot be confident about general family effects associated with disability, there do seem to be specific effects associated with the specific problems of a child (D. A. Cole & Rehm, 1986; S. Phillips, Bohannon, Gayton, & S. B. Friedman, 1985; Strom, Daniels, Wurster, Rees, & Goldman, 1984).

Learning That the Child Is Disabled

Parents first learn about their child's disability at any time from immediately after birth until well into the school years. Parents generally respond with shock when first told that their child is handicapped. In some families, the news is accepted calmly because the parents already suspected there was something wrong. In a few, the final diagnosis comes after a long series of tests, during which time nothing definite has been revealed. In these few families, the news is accepted with feelings of relief to know what the disorder involves and to receive information about what to do for the child (Cella, S. W. Perry, Poag, Amand, & Goodwin, 1988).

How the information is presented to the parents is very important to them. They wish to be told the full truth by a supportive person. Prognosis, implications for the future, and information about what they can do are most important. Unfortunately, even recent studies (e.g., Quine & Pahl, 1987) indicate that the majority of parents of children with handicaps report that they were told about the child's handicap by a person (usually a physician) who was uncomfortable with the situation and who was not very informative about what their child's handicap involved and what to do about it.

After the initial shock, most parents proceed to a process of reorganization and adaptation. Obtaining the best information helps them to integrate the child with handicaps into the family. There is evidence that parents do not always get this information because professionals judge the information needs of parents incorrectly. For instance, one study showed that physicians overestimated parents' concern with medical needs of children with epilepsy and underestimated their concern with basic child-rearing issues such as the child's dependence on parents, use of spare time, and arguments (Coulter & Koester, 1985).

Continuing Adaptation

Families adapt in one way or another to their child's handicap. However, it should not be thought that this adaptation is necessarily permanent and stable. Predictable life changes that accompany growing older as well as unforeseen environmental events provide new challenges to adaptation. For instance, perceived stress of parents can increase during early adolescence and also early adulthood when their mentally retarded children reach adolescence and leave school. Thus, stress and coping should be seen as dynamic and continuing processes in the lives of all families, including those with handicapped children (Damrosch & L. A. Perry, 1989; Wikler, 1986).

Descriptions of Families

Although it is appropriate to conceive of family response to their child's handicap as dynamic and variable, it is also possible to be more specific about characteristics of the family that enable one to predict whether they will cope or adapt successfully to any stress involved. These factors include, among other things, the structure of the family, the nature of its organization, and the typical mode of the family in responding to life's challenges.

Before turning to the family itself, however, factors outside of the family should be emphasized. Despite their probable importance, cultural factors, financial influences, and the organization of services have not been studied very often. Examples of recent studies that have looked into these factors are studies showing differential understanding of, and participation in, special education programs by three ethnic groups, lack of caregiving patterns for diabetic children as a function of income level, and higher perceived stress in parents of children at risk for sudden infant death syndrome whose respiration is monitored at home rather than in the hospital. A number of studies do measure factors like these but exclude their effect in statistical analysis (Blacher, Nihira, & C. E. Meyers, 1987; Lyman, Wurtele, & D. R. Wilson, 1985; Lynch & R. C. Stein, 1987; Marteau, Bloch, & Baum, 1987).

The most obvious structural characteristic of the family is the social role of its members. We are accustomed to thinking in terms of a nuclear family, that is, mother, father, and children. However, it is clear that most of the recent literature is concerned with the relationship between mothers and their handicapped child, and there is also a literature on siblings of children with handicaps. We review these studies of mother–child relationships and of siblings of children with handicaps later. However, it is appropriate to point out that fathers, extended families, single parent families, and adoptive families have also been studied and there have been several studies of the family as a whole.

The few studies of fathers, of members of extended families, of adoptive families, and of single-parent families show that although these parents and grandparents share many characteristics with mothers, they are also somewhat different. As a group fathers engage in more physical play with their handicapped children than do mothers. Differences in reported anxiety, marital conflict, and amount of involvement in caretaking have been reported in some studies. These differences are minor and except for physical play may not be consistent across studies. More important, the differences between fathers and mothers of children with handicaps are also seen when fathers and mothers of nonhandicapped children are compared. In other words, differences between fathers and mothers are not attributable to having a child with handicaps because the same differences (or lack of difference) also exist in families of nonhandicapped children (Bristol et al., 1988; Damrosch & L. A. Perry, 1989; S. Goldberg, Marcovitch, MacGregor, & Lojkasek, 1986; Levy-Schiff, 1986; MacDonald, 1987; Margalit & Heiman, 1986; Milgram & Atzil, 1988).

This pattern of minor but significant differences between family members is also reflected in the few studies of grandparents, adoptive, and single-parent families. Grandparents do not differ from parents on many aspects of a questionnaire assessing their view of their autistic children. However, on those items on which they do differ, grandmothers, but not grandfathers, are more positive.

Despite the importance of the issue, studies of families who have adopted children with disabilities are rare. The research that is available provides a generally positive picture. Mother–infant attachment is essentially normal in nonhandicapped adoptive babies. Reports are also positive for families who have adopted mentally retarded children, and adoption of even emotionally

disturbed children reaches a success rate of 70% (Glidden, 1989; Glidden &.
Pursley, 1989; Glidden, Valliere, &. Herbert, 1988; R. M. Kagan &. W. J. Reid,
1986; L. M. Singer, Brodzinsky, Ramsay, Steir &. Waters 1985).

Mothers who raise their handicapped child alone are typically under
more financial stress and are less likely to have emotional support from
another person than are mothers who raise their handicapped children with
another person. When their baby is 9 months of age, mothers in single-
parent families have more negative perceptions of the temperament of their
handicapped babies, and the environments the mothers provide for the child
appear to be less stimulating (D. A. Allen, G. Affleck, McGrade, &. McQueeney, 1984a, 1984b; S. L. Harris, Handleman, &. Palmer, 1985).

Taken together, these studies done outside of the context of the mother–
infant and sibling relationships in nuclear families contribute to the idea that
families of children with handicaps are essentially like families of nonhandicapped children, and the studies suggest that, as with families of nonhandicapped children certain environmental and structural or role differences
must be taken into account in considering the family as a whole. It is not so
much that these factors are dramatic or necessarily consistent. However, it is
more valid to view families as differentiated structures that are ecologically
determined rather than as homogeneous groups uninfluenced by their
environments.

MOTHERS AND CHILDREN

Some of the general concepts reviewed earlier have guided the research on
mother–child relationships. According to the central idea in the field,
mothers respond to children with handicaps differently than they do to
normal children, but the nature of their response is dependent on environmental factors, on characteristics of both the child and of the mother
interacting with each other, and on the specific situation in which they find
themselves. Of special interest has been their mutual behavior in feeding and
play situations, when they are separated from each other briefly, and when
they talk.

Focus on mothers with their infants is based on the general understanding that mothers have the greatest responsibility for care of infants
(Feiring &. M. Lewis, 1987). Fathers, other relatives, neighbors, and community agencies also participate, in the United States at least, but it is the mother
who has the greatest commitment and spends most of the time with the child
with handicaps (Bristol et al., 1988; Cooke &. Lawton, 1984). Whether this is
the case in all cultures is not clear because cross-cultural studies are rare
(Mary, 1990). However, it is likely that this focused responsibility will follow
the general care patterns found in the culture at large. It is also important to
note that the literature on mothers and children may also be relevant to the

relationships with their charges of other caregivers like institution and nursing home staff. However, there is little study of this possibility.

Factors that determine the interaction of parents with their children with handicaps include the environment, enduring characteristics of the parent, and the temperament of the child. What is happening in the environment is perhaps the most obvious determinant of how the mother and the child with handicaps interact. Cultural beliefs such as the idea that sin of the parents is related to the child's impairment may or may not be a determinant of behavior toward the child (Rodgers, 1987; Stern & Karraker, 1988; Tollison, Palmer, & Stowe, 1987). A relationship between a mother's friends and her family can predict her sensitivity toward her premature child. Behavior is different in a clinic setting than it is at home, and what the mother is asked to do in the clinic with her child also transforms the interaction. If the mother has experienced aggression from others in her life, she may act more aggressively toward her child. All of these are examples of environmental effects (Dumas, 1986; Togonu-Bickersteth & Odebiyi, 1985; Webster-Stratton, 1985b; Zarling, Hirsch, & Landry, 1988).

The direct experience a mother has had with her handicapped baby is at least as important as what her doctor says. Mothers begin to respond differently to their children before they are given a formal diagnosis, and they respond no differently from normal if their high-risk baby turns out to be developing normally. On the other hand, people are affected in their response toward babies if they are told incorrectly that the baby is premature, whereas inexperienced people are less accurate in their assessment of a child's facial expressions than are the child's mother or teacher (Maurer & Newbrough, 1987; Minde, Perrotta, & Hellmann, 1988; Scheiner, Sexton, Rockwood, Sullivan, & H. Davis, 1985; Stern & Hildebrandt, 1986). The person who knows the child best therefore is a good guide to the accurate description of the child.

On the other hand, parents tend to see the problems of their handicapped children more negatively than do the children themselves (Margalit, 1986; McLoughlin, F. L. Clark, Mauck, & Petrosko, 1987; Treiber & Mabe, 1987). Perhaps this is related to the fact that, although they hold the same general values about development as do parents of children who are developing normally, they do place emphasis on somewhat different things. For instance, mothers of handicapped preschoolers attach greater importance to their children's physical development than do mother's of nonhandicapped preschoolers (Quirk, Sexton, Ciottone, Minami, & Wapner, 1984).

Differences Between Families

Aside from differences between parents of handicapped children and parents of normally developing children, there are substantial individual differences among parents of children with handicaps, and these differences may be related to development. A maternal behavioral style that emphasizes maternal pleasure and child orientation is positively related to mental development, whereas one that emphasizes quantity of stimulation and control is negatively related to development. A belief by the mother in her ability to effect behavioral change (internal locus of control) does seem to predict amount of involvement in caregiving and reduced mood disturbance (G. Affleck, McGrade, D. A. Allen, & McQueeney, 1985; M. Fox, 1985; Mahoney, 1988; Mahoney, Finger, & Powell, 1985).

Thus, it is clear that specifiable characteristics of the parent determine the nature of her response to her handicapped child. Of course, the characteristics of the child are also important. Among the child factors that predict the nature of the relationship between the parent and the children are the children's developmental status, the nature of the handicap, and the behavioral characteristics of the children independent of their clinical classification. However, beyond these general factors it is important to understand that the level of specific behaviors best characterizes the relationship between parents and their children.

The most obvious developmental factor predicting mother–child relationships is chronological age. Mothers of infants with handicaps do respond more to their handicapped infants as they grow older, even taking into account that their infants become more active. However, this apparent relationship with chronological age is accounted for by correlated increases in physical maturity and behavioral maturation. That is, the maturity of a child's physique and behavior are better predictors of relationship with its parents than is simple chronological age (Bendersky & M. Lewis, 1986; Brooks-Gunn & M. Lewis, 1984; Maier, D. L. Holmes, Slaymaker, & Reich, 1984; Yoder, 1987).

The importance of specifying exact predictors is also evident in studies comparing maternal responsiveness to children of different classes of handicaps. That parental experience is important here is indicated by a birth order effect such that first-born preterm infants receive more stimulation than later born preterm infants, whereas such a birth order effect is not evident in normal term births (Bendersky & M. Lewis, 1986).

Differences between categories of handicaps are sometimes accounted for by correlated differences in developmental maturity. For instance, one study (Brooks-Gunn & M. Lewis, 1984) showed that mothers responded more to developmentally delayed infants, but this difference was due not to a difference in clinical category but to the fact that the delayed children were more mature mentally than the normal comparison group. Another study set out to ask whether mothers might respond less to children who had disfiguring craniofacial anomalies (T. M. Field & Vega-Lahr, 1984). They found that at 3 months of age, the mothers looked at their babies no less, but they did smile and play less with their babies. However, this difference was attributed, not to the babies' facial disfigurement, but to the lower level of social behavior the babies engaged in. That is, a mother responds largely to the behavior of her baby.

This is true not only of mothers' relationships with infants but also of the relationship between parents and their older children with handicaps. Mothers respond more negatively to children who are classified as hyperactive or conduct-disordered and who tend to respond in a noncompliant manner. It is not clear from these correlational studies whether the parents' behavior causes the child's noncompliance or whether it is a response to the child's difficult behavior. One way of clarifying this ambiguity is to change the child's behavior through treatment and then ask whether there is a concomitant change in the response of the parents. One example of this "experimental" approach involved the reduction of noncompliance behavior in hyperactive children by administering a stimulant drug, Ritalin. When this was done parental controlling reactions to the child were also reduced. This study tests one direction of the interaction and supports the notion that parents respond to changes in children's behavior (K. E. Anderson, Lytton, & Romney, 1986; Barkley, Karlsson, Pollard, & J. V. Murphy, 1985; Befera & Barkley, 1985).

The focus on specific interactions, rather than on general variables such as age or clinical category, has characterized recent research on parental interactions with children with handicaps, and the mutual influence of mothers and babies has been emphasized (Crnic & Greenberg, 1987; Jacobvitz & Sroufe, 1987).

Observational studies of mothers and babies in the first 6 months show that initial relationships between mothers and premature babies or babies with Down syndrome are different from normal in that their emotional responses to each other in face-to-face situations are less well integrated (Berger & C. C. Cunningham, 1986; Lester, Hoffman, & Brazelton, 1985; Malatesta, Grigoryev, Lamb, Albin, & Culver, 1986). Depending on the study that one looks at, these initial differences may or may not dissipate. Certainly mothers of premature children have different concerns than do mothers of normal children. Parents of children with problems are more affected by considerations of health of the baby than by the mothers' previous life experiences. This is understandable because some premature children have health problems and are difficult to feed. Consequently, mothers of infants with handicaps tend to give their children more caregiving attention, but spend less time with them in pleasurable activities, especially if the children do in fact have health problems. Whether or not this effect dissipates with age of the child over the first 6 months depends on the study, which in turn probably reflects the sample being used (Coates, & M. Lewis, 1984; Landry, 1986; Minde, Perrotta, & Marton, 1985; Mullen, Coll, Vohr, Muriel, & Oh, 1988).

Social Attachment

By 2 years of age, patterns of social relationships between mothers and children are well-established. Some children with handicaps (for instance, iron-deficient children and mentally retarded, motorically handicapped children) stay closer to their mothers than do other groups of handicapped or normal children. Some children are not very responsive to their mothers, and the mothers respond by asking questions, issuing instructions to the children, or by ignoring them rather than playing with them. Thus, one can conclude that, although the patterns are by no means universal, there is a greater tendency for the social relationships of parents with their handicapped children to be unusual because the more prevalent health problems and behavioral deviations of some handicapped children evoke different patterns of responding (Hanzlik & Stevenson, 1986; Lozoff, Klein, & Prabucki, 1986; Sigman, Mundy, T. Sherman, & Ungerer, 1986; Wasserman & R. Allen, 1985).

The social attachment of the child at this age has been vigorously studied in the laboratory. The response of the infant to its mother when she leaves and when the infant is exposed to a strange person are thought to reflect the character of the social attachment that exists between the pair. At 1 to 2 years of age, the child is observed playing with toys with the mother present. Then, a stranger enters the room. Does play cease, and does the child go to its mother? Then, the mother leaves the room, and after a while, she returns. Does the infant continue to play quietly? Or cry?

Children respond very differently, and although the evidence is conflicting, response in this attachment test sometimes predicts later behavior. For instance, securely attached (as compared with avoidant or resistant) infants have higher IQs in kindergarten (Van Ijzendoorn & Van Vliet-Visser, 1988).

Comparison of children with handicaps with normal children in the attachment situation is complicated by the fact that some children differ on emotional expressivity independent of the quality of their attachment. Children with Down syndrome seem to cry less than normal, but otherwise they do respond normally to the departure of their mother and to a stranger's presence. That is, they come closer to their mother when a stranger enters the room, and they seem disturbed when their mother leaves. The basic normality of the attachment responses of handicapped infants is also seen in preterm infants, neurologically impaired infants, and even autistic children, although in some cases their attachment is more difficult to classify as secure, avoidant, or resistant or they seem like chronologically younger children (S. Goldberg, Perrotta, Minde, & Corter, 1986; Shapiro, M. Sherman, Calamari, & Koch, 1987; Sigman & Mundy, 1989; Sigman & Ungerer, 1984; Stahlecker & M. C. Cohen, 1985; R. A. Thompson, Cicchetti, Lamb, & Malkin, 1985).

This attachment testing situation describes the nature of the young child's relationship with the mother. Attachment is also assessed in situations in which the mother feeds the baby and they play together. However, in this case the behavior of the mother is also described. Interactions during the first 6 months are important because the nature of these social behaviors can be correlated with school achievement. In fact, there is evidence that these relationships are better predictors of cognitive measures at 6 years of age than are the conventional developmental tests done in the first 2 years (Coates & M. Lewis, 1984).

Some of the same principles are evident in the play interactions of older children with their mothers. However, chronic noncompliance by older children becomes a new factor that can further increase the negative quality of the relationship between the mother and her handicapped child. This kind of noncompliance seems to be especially pronounced in children with attention deficit disorder with hyperactivity (Barkley, Karlsson, & Pollard, 1985; Tarver-Behring, Barkley, & Karlsson, 1985).

There is clear evidence, therefore, that although the basic character of social relationships between mothers and infants is normal in most children with handicaps, there are some differences. From the beginning, emotional responsiveness of some babies is patterned differently, and integration of responses between mothers and infants may be less as the mother attempts to adapt to her child's characteristics (Landry & Chapieski, 1989). In some children, these abnormalities become less, but in others they become more of a problem. Parents may attempt to compensate for abnormalities in the child's behavior by increasing caregiving activities, and they may grow to respond less to the child, especially in the relaxed situations in which much cognitive growth occurs.

These general principles of mutual adaptation are particularly evident when one looks at studies of verbal interactions that have been done during the last 15 years. Earlier studies showed that maternal responses to children with handicaps tend to be more instructional, controlling, and supportive than to normal children of the same chronological age. This result applied to deaf, language-delayed, behavior-disordered, autistic, and mentally retarded children. More recent studies, however, have shown that these differences are reduced when account is taken of the children's lower mental age, language development, or verbal initiations. In other words, the mother is adjusting her speech patterns to what she perceives to be the language processing abilities of her child, although this adaptation is not always perfect (Conti-Ramsden & Friel-Patti, 1984; Crowell, Feldman, & Ginsberg, 1988; Garrard, 1989; Henggeler, Watson, & Cooper, 1984; Kasari, Sigman, Mundy, & Yirmiya, 1988; Langlois, Hanrahan, & Inouye, 1986; Maurer & Sherrod, 1987; Milne & E. G. Johnson, 1985; Nienhuys, Horsborough, & Cross, 1985; Tannock, 1988; Wasserman, R. Allen, & Linares, 1988).

That this is not a unidirectional process is also clear. The mother has other things that occupy her so that, for instance, she may make more changes in conversational topic and may not be infinitely sensitive to the things that the child is attending to (M. Harris, D. Jones, Brookes, & Grant, 1986). If children stutter, the mother may interrupt them, although mothers are less likely to do this than are mothers of nonstuttering children (S. C. Meyers & Freeman, 1985).

In response, the children adjust their responses. Autistic children may be more responsive to communications that they can understand than to more complex information (Curcio & Paccia, 1987). As a result, although the basic processes of communication between mother and child are the same in all mother–child dyads, communication may be less perfectly integrated in some children with handicaps than they typically are in normal children.

CHILD ABUSE

Positive communication breaks down dangerously in cases of child abuse. Although it is possible to conceive of child abuse as qualitatively different from the normal interactions of mothers and children, it is probably more valid to consider abusive behavior as the extreme manifestation of the negative features of communication that can occur in any family.

There is great variation in definitions of child abuse that results in a somewhat confused literature. However, three general kinds of child abuse are recognized: physical abuse, neglect, and sexual abuse. The sources and manifestations of these forms of abuse may be quite different, but they all represent a disruption in a healthy parent–infant relationship, and they can have long-term detrimental effects on the child's psychological development that can reach into the next generation (Emery, 1989; S. White, Halpin, Strom, & Santilli, 1988).

The physical consequences of child abuse may include injury as severe as death. The psychological consequences include more anxiety and less readiness to learn in the company of adults when the child is young. Abused and neglected children have lower scores on cognitive tests than comparison groups, abused children tend to be more aggressive and have more accidents when they are older. Neglected children are less social and have lower self-esteem. In adulthood, there may be problems in sexual relationships. The concept that there is a tendency for adults with a history of abuse to abuse their own children is widely accepted, but the scientific evidence for it is not clear, perhaps because this intergenerational effect is moderated by other variables such as social support (Aber & J. P. Allen, 1987; Browne & Finkelhor, 1986; Egeland, Jacobvitz, & Sroufe, 1988; A. L. Dean, Malik, Richards, & Stringer, 1986; Dubowitz, Hampton, Bithoney, & Newberger,

1987; Hoffman-Plotkin & Twentyman, 1984; H. M. Hughes, 1988; Kashani, Shekim, Burk, & Beck, 1987; Ney, 1988; Webster-Stratton, 1985a; Widom, 1989; D. A. Wolfe, 1985).

The stress-resource and family perspectives have been the most helpful in promoting an understanding of the causes of violence toward children. Several stressors have been identified as predisposing a family to child abuse. Unemployment, financial burdens, single-parenting, teenage parenting, and having many young children are important. In addition, patterns of violence within the family, having been abused as a child, and lack of satisfaction with and participation in child rearing have also been identified (Newberger, Hampton, Marx, & K. M. White, 1986; H. Parker & S. Parker, 1986; Porter, 1986; Sack, Mason, & Higgins, 1985; Zuravin, 1988).

Some studies of mothers with their maltreated children show that they interfere with their child's goal-directed behavior and are more hostile to their child than is the case in comparison groups (Kavanagh, Youngblade, J. B. Reid, & Fagot, 1988; Lyons-Ruth, Connell, Zoll, & Stahl, 1987; Oldershaw, Walters, & Hall, 1986). Other studies show no such behavioral difference, but they do find that parents of abused children perceive their children as difficult to care for (e.g., more aggressive and hyperactive). Parents of abused children also have difficulty in correctly identifying the emotions of their children (Camras et al., 1988; Kropp & Haynes, 1987; J. B. Reid, Kavanagh, & Baldwin, 1987; Trickett & Susman, 1988).

The current literature therefore focuses on the parent contribution to child abuse. This is appropriate because it is parents who are the main active force in child abuse. However, the family perspective also leads one to look for the child's contribution. For one thing, children may perceive abuse differently as a function of age (Wurtele & C. L. Miller, 1987). However, when children are, in fact, hyperactive, noncompliant, aggressive, or difficult to care for, a susceptible parent may be more likely to respond with hostility and ultimately neglect (Zirpoli, Snell, & Loyd, 1987). The studies of lower parental response to infants and children with handicaps are consistent with this, and so are studies of the higher prevalence of child abuse in children with disabilities. However, it should be emphasized that the studies relating childhood handicaps to being abused are rare and are often not adequately designed (R. White, Benedict, Wulff, & Kelley, 1987). Sometimes, there is no such effect (Caplan & Dinardo, 1986). It is likely that any higher level of abuse toward children with handicaps comes mainly from families of children who are difficult to care for and whose parents are less skilled in child rearing.

Psychological treatment of families in which child abuse occurs depends on an understanding of the dynamics within the family. Here, the systems perspective has been seen as most useful. However, perhaps because our understanding of family dynamics is still limited, short-term effects are limited, and the recidivism rate is high (Emery, 1989). On the other hand, there is some evidence that mothers who do not abuse their children, despite a history of themselves being abused, feel they have dependable support from someone else in the family or from psychotherapy (Egeland et al., 1988).

The last resort is to have the child removed from the home to foster care. Although this might seem to be a good solution to protect the child while the family is being treated, it also has its drawbacks. Different criteria are used to remove children of lower class families than from wealthy families. Moreover, the quality of foster care is not always high, children are shifted from placement to placement, and this unstable arrangement often may last for years (M. H. Katz, Hampton, Newberger, Bowles, & Snyder, 1986).

At this time, there are no satisfactory practical ways of resolving the dilemma of violence toward children, and one can only be pessimistic about simplistic solutions.

SIBLINGS

The idea that presence of a handicapped child in a family may increase the stress within the family brings with it the prediction that handicapped children put their siblings at risk for emotional harm (Cadman, Boyle, & Offord, 1988; Daniels, J. J. Miller, Billings, & Moos, 1986; Dyson, Edgar, & Crnic, 1989). There is some evidence that, in adulthood, some siblings of mentally retarded people do resent their handicapped brothers or sisters and have broken contact with them. However, many others feel affection and responsibility for their handicapped siblings (Zetlin, 1986).

This means that the effect of handicapped children on their siblings may be variable, that is, similar to effects of the interaction of nonhandicapped siblings. This can only be determined by adequately controlled comparisons of siblings of handicapped and of nonhandicapped children. There are not many of these adequately designed studies. But there are a few that have been done recently.

Observational studies of mentally retarded children with their siblings show that they interact socially (Stoneman, Brody, C. H. Davis, & Crapps, 1987). The siblings adapt to the lower competence of their retarded brothers and sisters and are more prosocial and less imitative. They report their relationship as positive, no less positive than the relationship to normal siblings, whereas mothers rate the relationship as more negative (McHale & Gamble, 1989) and focus on the nurturance of the disabled child (Begun, 1989).

As with normal siblings there is variability in the relationship between handicapped and normal siblings. There is some thought that normal older sisters of children with handicaps may show negative or positive effects of having a handicapped brother or sister. The idea is that mothers with a handicapped child use their daughters to aid in the management of the family and therefore put their daughters under stress, which in turn affects the sibling relationship. There is some evidence for the idea that older sisters do more work in families with a handicapped child, and the mothers in those families do not do any less work. However, there seems to be no relationship between siblings' estimates of their relationship with their handicapped brother or sister and either age or gender (Gath & Gumley, 1987; McHale, Sloan, & Simeonsson, 1986; Stoneman, Brody, C. H. Davis, & Crapps, 1988). Some studies (e.g., Israelite, 1986) show a few differences between siblings of handicapped children and siblings of normal children on measures of self-concept, whereas other studies do not show such differences (e.g., Lobato, Barbour, L. J. Hall, & C. T. Miller, 1987). However, differences in ratings of aggression may appear if the mothers rather than the children are making the estimates.

Overall, then, the relationship between handicapped children and their siblings are largely normal. Although, some siblings may be vulnerable to psychological injury as a result of having a sibling with handicaps, such consequences are highly individual and their predictors are still obscure.

PEERS

There have been many studies of handicapped children and their age peers. This research has been done in the context of the movement to mainstream children with handicaps, (i.e., to educate children in regular rather than special classes). What follows is a review of this literature on peer relationships. A consideration of mainstreaming is included in the next chapter.

Sociometric Status

Many of the studies of peer relationships have been studies of sociometric status. In a hierarchy of stated social preference, where do children with handicaps stand? If one asks the members of a school class to rate their classmates, each child will have a definite preference for some members of their class over others. This preference is an instance of the process of social comparison that people regularly engage in. The determinants of preference are a resultant of the evaluations and attributions made on many separate personal dimensions. Among these dimensions are degrees of aggression, social withdrawal, physical attractiveness, and skill that the other children are perceived to have (Aboud, 1985; Younger & Boyko, 1987).

This suggests correctly that the concept of social status may be complex. Estimates of sociometric status can be quite stable even in groups of kindergarten children. But the meaning of social status is surprisingly complex. It is known that the meaning of low acceptance is not quite the same as active rejection. The attributes used by children to evaluate their peers change with age. Social status is defined not only by peer rating or nomination procedures. Teachers may do the rating of who likes whom, and observations of children in groups may also be used (Dygdon, Conger, & Keane, 1987; Ray, 1985; Wasik, 1987).

Children with handicaps that differ in social status from normal children are generally found to be lower or less popular. They are accepted less and often are socially rejected more. This generalization applies to mentally retarded children, children with learning disabilities, emotionally disturbed children, depressed children, hyperactive children, and even children who are wearing a hearing aid. However, this answer should not be taken to mean that all children with disabilities are rejected or less accepted than their normal peers. Even in the groups that are generally rejected, some children are as popular as normal. It is probably better to say that children with disabilities are at risk for low social status rather than that the groups are characteristically lower (Bierman & McCauley, 1987; Dudley-Marling & Edmiaston, 1985; C. Johnston, Pelham, & H. A. Murphy, 1985; Peterson, Mullins, & Ridley-Johnson, 1985; Sabornie & Kauffman, 1985; Silverman & Klees, 1989).

The complexity of the concept of social status and the individual differences found for children with handicaps has led investigators to ask about the correlates or predictors of rated social status in children with handicaps. One determinant of the way children rate their handicapped peers is their understanding of the nature of the handicap. Children rate more favorably if they see the child with handicaps as more similar to themselves and if they attribute the handicap to factors that the handicapped child cannot control (Bak & Siperstein, 1987a; Sigelman & Begley, 1987). There is cultural variation in the understanding of the causes of handicapping conditions, so cultural variation in sociometric ratings of handicapped children might be expected, but are not universal (Bierman, 1987; Gresham & Reschly, 1987b; Payne, 1985). Teachers' perceptions of the child may also be important (G. M. Morrison, Forness, & MacMillan, 1983).

Age and gender also correlate with the way that children understand and rate handicapping conditions. In general, older children are more tolerant of differences, although this is less true of aggression than of physical handicaps. Perhaps this is because older children can see that the cause of the disability lies outside of the intentions of the handicapped child. With respect to gender, girls tend to be more accepting of handicapping conditions than are boys (Cowardin, 1986; Graffi & Minnes, 1988; Royal & M. C. Roberts, 1987; J. S. Safran & S. P. Safran, 1985; Sigelman & Begley, 1987).

The clinical category that a child is in does not necessarily help predict social status. For instance, one study showed that learning-disabled, mildly retarded, and low achieving children were all lower than normal in sociometric status, but these handicapped groups did not differ from one another (Bender, Wyne, Stuck, & Bailey, 1984; C. G. Johnson, Sigelman, & Falkenberg, 1986; Landau, Milich, & McFarland, 1987; Van Bourgondien, 1987).

On the other hand, many specific behaviors have been associated with higher social status and others with lower status. Competence, playing well with toys, sharing, athletic skill, affection, and tactful verbal exchanges are all related positively to social attractiveness. Hyperactivity, externalizing behaviors (such as screaming, hitting, biting, and whining) and internalizing behaviors (such as moodiness, shyness, depression, and social withdrawal) are all associated with lower status. In general, antisocial behavior is associated with rejection, whereas shyness and social withdrawal lead to neglect (J. R. Asarnow, 1988; Bak & Siperstein, 1987a; C. L. Carlson, Lahey, Frame, Walker, & Hynd, 1987; Flicek & Landau, 1985; French, 1988; Hagborg, 1987; Hoyle & Serafica, 1988; Johnson et al., 1986; Pearl, M. Donahue, & Bryan, 1985; Peterson, Mullins, & Ridley-Johnson, 1985; Strain, 1985; A. R. Taylor, Asher, & G. A. Williams, 1987; Whalen, Henker, Castro, & Granger, 1987).

All of the foregoing studies have looked at social status of handicapped children from the perspective of the nonhandicapped peers and sometimes from that of the teacher. However, there are a few studies that also consider the situation from the point of view of the child or adult with handicaps. Physically handicapped children rate physical attractiveness differently than do nonhandicapped children (Harper, Wacker, & Cobb, 1986).

One might suppose that rejected and socially neglected children and mentally retarded and learning-disabled people might not perceive the fact that they are not socially accepted. However, there is no evidence for this. It is, in fact, clear that people with disabilities are socially sensitive and they take their lower social status seriously, sometimes but not always seeing the behavior of others in negative terms. They feel lonely and turn to other handicapped people for their social needs. When they do, the social structure of the groups of handicapped people is essentially normal (Emler, Reicher, & A. Ross, 1987; Foster, 1989; Lederberg, Rosenblatt, Vandell, & Chapin, 1987; J. S. Murphy & Newlon, 1987). In general, people with handicaps rate the social status of others more negatively than do nonhandicapped people. However, this effect may be stronger in women than in men and in shy and withdrawn people rather than in those who are boisterous or aggressive (Bichard, Alden, Walker, & McMahon, 1988; C. I. Carlson, 1987; F. X. Gibbons, 1985; T. J. Lewis & Altman, 1987; C. T. Miller et al., 1989; Sabornie, 1987; Sabornie & Kauffman, 1987; Siperstein & Bak, 1989; Waas, 1988; E. Weiss, 1984).

Studies of ways to increase the rated acceptance of handicapped children by nonhandicapped peers have increased recently. The most influential of the ideas underlying such studies purports that simply having children together with their nonhandicapped peers will have the effect of increasing acceptance rate. This idea follows from the theory that mere exposure increases affection. This theory is generally true when initial response is neutral or positive and when subsequent interactions are not negative. However, merely placing handicapped children in contact with normal peers would not be expected to work if initial attitudes or subsequent interactions are negative. Nevertheless, there are examples in which it can be successful, though in at least some cases, more than simple contact is involved (Carsrud et al., 1984; Esposito & Reed, 1986).

Attitudes can be made more positive by attempts to change the peers' attributions about the handicapping condition. Peers may be negative toward a person who engages in poor social behavior. But telling the peers that the child is mentally retarded can improve their attitude. However, this effect seems to work better if the children are behaving in a withdrawn manner than if they are aggressive. Likewise, peers are harder on hyperactive children whom they see as causing their own annoying behavior than if the peers attribute that behavior to a failure of the child's medication. In general, then, to what people attribute behavior is important in their evaluations of it, so that when it is possible to change attributions about the behavior of children with handicaps, it may also be possible to improve social status ratings (Bak & Siperstein, 1986; Sigelman & Shorokey, 1986).

Perhaps attitudes can best be changed through positive personal interaction between the normal peer and the handicapped child. There have been several studies showing that such interactions as peer-tutoring improve the attitudes between the specific normal and handicapped children. However, these studies demonstrate only limited generalization to other handicapped children (Acton & Zarbatany, 1988; Armstrong, Rosenbaum, & King, 1987; D. W. Johnson & R. T. Johnson, 1984; Rosenbaum, Armstrong, & King, 1986; Shisler, Osguthorpe, & Eiserman, 1987).

These studies of social status of children with handicaps have assessed the attitudes of specific people toward others. They can be summarized briefly. Although the concept of sociometric status is complex, people with disabilities are at greater risk for lower social status than are nonhandicapped people. The predictors of this lower status depends on characteristics of the nonhandicapped children such as age, gender, but more particularly on the way they perceive the behavior of the handicapped child relative to that of others. Observational studies confirm that certain behaviors of handicapped children, such as aggression, incompetence, and social withdrawal increase the probability that these children will be rejected or unpopular. Children with handicaps are sensitive to their lower social status, and particularly if they withdraw from social contact, view their social interactions negatively. All of this can be changed, but there may be limits to doing it that lie in the behavior of the handicapped child and the perceptions of the nonhandicapped peer.

Reviewing the literature on peer relationships leaves one wondering about what actually happens in the everyday interaction of handicapped and nonhandicapped people. The studies using rating scales that we have already reviewed has been supplemented recently by several investigations in which the interaction of handicapped and nonhandicapped children have been observed directly (Siperstein, Bak, & O'Keefe, 1988).

As in rating studies, groups of children with handicaps are different socially from normal children. This applies to depressed, conduct-disordered, hyperactive, learning-disabled, deaf, autistic, and abused children, and the differences are manifest in a higher rate of aggression and also relatively greater isolation. However, the things that influence playmate choice (such as choosing to be with someone similar with respect to age and ethnicity) may not be different (Altmann & Gotlib, 1988; Van Engeland, Bodnar, & Bolhuis, 1985; Dawson & Fernald, 1987; Gard, Turone, & Devlin, 1985; B. W. Gottlieb, J. Gottlieb, Berkell, & Levy, 1986; Grenell, Glass, & K. S. Katz, 1987; Main & George, 1985; E. E. Jones, 1985; Lederberg, Chapin, Rosenblatt, & Vandell, 1986; Schneider, Ledingham, B. M. Byrne, Oliver, & Poirier, 1985).

There are fewer studies that compare different groups of children with disabilities in an effort to differentiate them socially. Those that exist indicate that it is possible to differentiate some clinical groups with direct observations of social behavior. However, the results are conflicting. One study showed minimal differences between conduct-disordered and anxious-withdrawn groups, although both groups were different from normal. Another study showed that emotionally disturbed boys exhibited more aggression and noncompliance than learning-disabled boys (Panella & Henggeler, 1986; Sprafkin & Gadow, 1987). The observational studies therefore generally support the rating studies of social status. However, they tend to be more specific in their statements about any differences between groups and do show the extent to which differences are age-, gender-, and situation-specific.

Perhaps more interesting are studies that emphasize the nature of interpersonal interaction rather than describing general rates of various social behaviors. Children with handicaps have problems when observed in groups with normal children. They receive fewer responses that are prosocial, they may be relatively passive in initiating social interactions, their responses to aggression may be excessive and although they are involved in normal dominance hierarchies, their hierarchies may be less than normally stable (Blackman & Dembo, 1984; Howes & Eldredge, 1985; Konstantareas & Homatidis, 1985; L. S. Siegel, C. E. Cunningham, & Van der Spuy, 1985).

Some of the studies that we have reviewed take into account the differences in developmental level of handicapped and in normal children. In some of them, there is a confounding of developmental level in comparisons of groups of children with handicaps and normal children. However, most of the current studies take into account those differences and some make them the focus of the research.

Children who are developmentally closer to each other interact more easily. When mental development is homogeneous in groups, interaction increases, although problems in social interaction remain. However, interaction also becomes more positive when mentally retarded children are paired with normal children of the same chronological age, perhaps because the normal children take a more active role in organizing the play activities. This suggests that the problems that exist in heterogeneous groups of handicapped and nonhandicapped children can be reduced by making the groups more homogeneous with respect to developmental level and by creating special temporary pairing arrangements. These ideas have found application in improving the social interaction rates of disabled children who have been mainstreamed into regular classes (D. A. Cole, Vandercook, & Rynders, 1987; Guralnick, 1980; Guralnick & Groom, 1987).

In addition to developmental level, there are other personal factors that influence social interaction of children with handicaps. There are few observational studies of the influence of physical attractiveness. Those that there are suggest that physical impairments result in less social response from nonhandicapped children (Cole, 1988). Also, mentally retarded people who are rated as less physically attractive may receive fewer services. We deal with effects of drugs in the next chapter. However, it can be noted here that methylphenidate reduces objectionable behavior of younger ADD or hyperactive children without producing social withdrawal (C. E. Cunningham, L. S. Siegel, & Offord, 1985; S. A. Richardson, Koller, & M. Katz, 1985a; Whalen et al., 1987).

In addition to the characteristics of handicapped children, those of normal peers are also important. Social behavior of autistic children increased when playing with younger nonhandicapped children. One particularly interesting study tested the influence of characteristics of a playmate on the social play of deaf preschool and kindergarten children. When deaf children played with other deaf children they used more visual communication than when they played with hearing children. More important, a deaf child played more with a hearing child who was a neighborhood friend than with a stranger, and this was a stronger effect than was the experience of the hearing child with deaf children (Lederberg, Ryan, & Robbins, 1986; C. Lord

& Hopkins, 1986). Friendships occur within groups of children with handicaps, and they serve to reduce conflict (Howes, 1985; Panella & Henggeler, 1986).

A third general influence on interactions of handicapped with nonhandicapped children is their situation. Toys that evoke cooperative play in younger children and tasks that require cooperation tend to promote social behavior of handicapped and nonhandicapped children. However, there is some variation in the effectiveness of cooperative tasks. Sometimes it seems to have detrimental effects. Nevertheless, this approach is consistent with the generally positive peer tutoring programs reviewed in the next chapter (M. A. Anderson, 1985; Beckman & Kohl, 1984; Brady, Shores, McEvoy, Ellis, & J. J. Fox, 1987; Cosden, Pearl, & Bryan, 1985; C. E. Cunningham & L. S. Siegel, 1987; D. W. Johnson, R. T. Johnson, Warring, & Maruyama, 1986; Kreimeyer & Antia, 1988; Putnam, Rynders, R. T. Johnson, & D. W. Johnson, 1989; N. Rao, Moely, & Lockman, 1987).

Teacher intervention can also be effective in increasing the positive social interaction of children with and without handicaps. When a teacher attempts to regulate what is going on in cooperative play situations, the effect can be positive, especially if their intervention is kept at a low level. However, this effectiveness may be limited to the early phases of the relationship between the two children. Afterward, it may decrease the social play (D. A. Cole, Meyer, Vandercook, & McQuarter, 1986; Meyer et al., 1987).

SUMMARY

The social interactions of handicapped children with their family and with their peers has often been oversimplified to a caricature of the real situation. There are common stereotypes that children with disabilities place unbearable stress on families, that siblings are harmed psychologically, and that children with handicaps are rejected by their age peer groups.

Like most stereotypes, one can find cases that are examples. However, there are also plenty of exceptions, so that the actual case is better described as variable and multidetermined. There can be so much stress in a family that it breaks up and the siblings bear emotional scars for life. Or the challenge of having a handicapped child may prove to be an integrating force in the family, and the siblings may learn to take responsibility and grow to be unusually mature adults. It is also possible that a disability may have no special perceptible effect on the family beyond that of any child.

Children with disabilities are often less popular than are normal children. However, some groups of children with disabilities do not differ at all, and when they do, it can be as much a result of their own aggressive or shy behavior as it is a natural rejection of all handicaps.

As with most of the other topics in this book, the appropriate way of thinking about the social interactions of children with handicaps is in terms of the factors that determine sociability in all people. A multivariate predictive and descriptive stance seems most useful to account for individual variability.

There have been some useful theoretical approaches that have guided much of the recent research in the field. Perhaps the most useful now is a stress-resource approach that sees the social manifestation of a handicapping condition as a consequence of any of a number of specifiable challenges to adaptation interacting with one or many resources that the individual or group has working on it. The consequences are highly individual, but they can be analyzed for any individual case or for groups.

One important predictor is the type of handicap. To the extent that type of handicap is associated with specific behaviors that are important to social adjustment, classification can be important. On the other hand, when categories overlap significantly, as they often do, the conventional classifications are not very helpful. More useful is the development of an understanding of what factors influence social integration of any person and then applying that understanding to the description and prediction for the individual child, family, and peer group.

In this chapter, we have listed a great many factors that influence the social life of children with disabilities. They include characteristics of the disabled child (e.g., aggressive behavior, severity of medical difficulties, clarity of communication), family, and peer characteristics (e.g., personal history, current personality, attitudes, financial resources, social structure). All of these and many more are determinants of the consequences for such factors as the integration of the family, child abuse, out-of-home placement, success of mainstreaming, and the happiness and ultimate social effectiveness of all members of society.

10 _____

Educational Programs and Treatment Methods

Knowledge about what children and their families are like can determine the rational organization of educational programs and specific treatment methods. Often, however, things do not work out quite that way. Ideological and fiscal considerations are also important components of all practical planning, and sometimes these are all that is involved because so little is known about children. It is also often true that these ideological and fiscal factors sometimes drive the scientific effort rather than the reverse. However, in the long run, education and treatment are validated or rejected through the test of experience. Thus, a combination of ideology, budget, and knowledge inform the best programs.

In this chapter, we review factors important in educational programs and treatment methods. We emphasize first the importance of family participation and the attitudes of teachers and caregivers because they are perhaps the most important factors in determining the long-term success or failure of any specific treatment program. Then we review some general programmatic approaches in schools, such as early education, the use of computers in instruction, mainstreaming, and peer instruction.

The heart of the chapter is a review of recent evaluations of specific treatment methods that we have not covered before, that seem to be significant, and for which there is reasonably substantial formal assessment with children with handicaps. The review leaves out widely used treatment methods such as some rehabilitation programs, activity therapy, art therapy, most medical procedures, most speech therapy, and physical therapy. This is not because these approaches do not work or are not significant, but only because there has been little scientific work of a psychological nature reported recently in these fields on children with handicaps. The section concerns itself with specific treatment procedures that have received recent study with children with handicaps. Psychotherapy in its various forms, behavioral programs that focus on specific behaviors, and assessments of specific pharmacological agents are examples.

The reader should remember that this is not a manual of techniques for dealing with their own problems or even those of children with handicaps. It is intended, instead, to cover some of the general issues involved in choosing, applying, and assessing some procedures and to give an idea of what has been emphasized in recent literature.

EDUCATION AND TREATMENT AS AN ART

It is sometimes said that teaching and clinical work are an art as much as a science. What does this mean? Although it may mean different things to different people, perhaps the heart of its meaning can be found in the principle of individual variation emphasized throughout this book. It means that no single program or technique will have highly predictable results with all children at all times. Not only are teacher and context effects important, but differences within and between individual children present different problems for teachers and clinicians.

Dealing with all of this variation is what makes teaching and clinical work an art. From this point of view, an art is not a mysterious ability that one is born with or that one automatically learns with experience. Rather, an art involves having learned a wide range of techniques or skills and also learned in what situation to apply any particular skill or group of skills.

This emphasis on the learning of a wide range of skills and use of sophistication in applying them implies that experience with a range of children with handicaps is important. However, the amount of experience is not sufficient for making a competent teacher or clinician. There are great differences between master teachers and more mediocre practitioners, despite an equal number of years of service. On the other hand, having had more opportunity to learn the skills involved in practice is undoubtedly beneficial.

The emphasis on the importance of sophistication also blurs the distinction between art and science. There may be differences between the skills involved in clinical work and in research (G. M. Siegel & Spradlin, 1985). However, to the extent that having learned skills that help and do not cause harm is a matter of sharing knowledge with others, clinical art and science are similar. Both involve sizing up situations and accounting for variability in behavior. With this spirit in mind, this chapter summarizes the recent scientific work on educational programs and treatment methods.

FAMILIES, PROFESSIONALS, AND CAREGIVERS

It would be incorrect to think that there is a sharp separation between the general categories of people who help children with handicaps to grow. Families, professionals, and other caregivers, teachers, clinicians, and advocates share several characteristics. Commitment to a particular child may vary between individuals, but members of these three groups share a commitment to growth of the children with whom they work. This commitment may be mainly to specific individuals, as in the case of parents, caregivers in a residential program, teachers, and certain clinicians, like speech therapists. Or the focus of commitment may be to a broader group. Lawyers, administrators, and disabled people in an advocate role may not involve themselves with any one individual, but they may have an effect on thousands of people.

None of the categories of caregivers has a priority on quality of the effect. There is potential for help and for harm from any who represent themselves as committed to helping people with disabilities. As in any walk of life, there are saints and there are charlatans in the service systems for people with handicaps. However, also typically, most parents and teachers are decent and imperfect.

They vary in the commitment, time spent, and quality of the effect they have, and in turn, their effect is related to the interrelated factors of ideology, understanding, and learning. Moreover, these people who work with handicapped children are subject to the pleasures and annoyances that one encounters with any person. They often experience motivational changes, as reflected in the common human phenomenon called burnout. In this section, we consider some of these factors that make for individual differences between the people who work with people with handicaps.

Parents

Parents come first in this review because parents ordinarily have the most intense and enduring commitment to people with handicaps. We have reviewed much of the recent literature on families in the last chapter, and we return to the topic in the next one. In this chapter, two things are emphasized. First, parents have the most fundamental role in the education and treatment of their children. Second, parents vary in their effectiveness as caregivers, teachers, and therapists. Describing that variation is a first step toward supporting parents in these roles, when necessary.

When the disabled person is a young child, families provide most of the physical care and the learning environment during the preschool years, though some young children can be in early education programs for part of the week. Even some parents who are themselves mentally retarded take on these duties successfully (Budd & Greenspan, 1985). Families are the educators and caregivers of last resort for children who are dependent and when services are unavailable. When school systems exclude children with handicaps, when residential programs become unavailable, when disabled adults are unemployed, society turns to families to take responsibility.

In many instances, people with disabilities become independent as they grow older. However, when disabilities are more severe, the person may continue to be dependent. When that happens, there are several things that can handicap the family in coping: For example, consider the extra time required, changes that the family must make in its lifestyle, and alterations of roles within the family. If the parents are elderly, the illnesses associated with age can make things difficult. Some experts urge that clinicians and educators take some of these difficulties into account in planning family-based intervention programs (Rodger, 1986).

Parents have been the main advocates for the development of medical and educational services when these programs are not available for their children. They participate, either formally or informally, in the practical education of other families of children with disabilities, and they frequently become professionals in human services because of their special interest.

Parents often have clear ideas about appropriate and inappropriate educational procedures and treatments for their children. For instance, parents of autistic and severely retarded children prefer nonpunitive procedures in the treatment of self-injurious behaviors. By law in the United States at this time, parents participate in the educational planning for their children. However, there are several possible impediments to such participation, including inadequate knowledge and skills by both parents and teachers, lack of confidence on the part of parents, their informal exclusion from discussions, and power struggles between parents and teachers. However, when parents do participate, they ordinarily express considerable satisfaction with the school, the teacher, and the services received (D. W. Barnett, Zins, & Wise, 1984; C. E. Meyers & Blacher, 1987; D. Pickering & Morgan, 1985; Singh, Watson, & Winton, 1987).

Families can be helped to reduce the handicaps of their children. Most parent-centered programs have been oriented to children in the preschool years. We review some of the studies later in this chapter. However, it may be said here that the involvement of both parents of children with conduct problems is more effective than when only one participates, programs oriented to helping discordant families to increase communication and solve problems together help to reduce the conduct disorder, and the ADD-H children of mothers who perceive that they have familial and community support show greater improvement on a number of measures than those whose parents do not have such support (Dadds, Schwartz, & Sanders, 1987; Horn, Ialongo, Popovich, & Peradotto, 1987; Webster-Stratton, 1985c).

Professionals, Advocates, and Caregivers

The number of people engaged in educating, treating, caring for, and advocating on behalf of people with handicaps is very large. This is an expression of society's commitment to helping people with handicaps become happy and productive members of the general community. As a rule, these teachers, medical workers, therapists, advocates, direct care staff, and administrators carry out their tasks in a sensitive and competent manner without much fanfare. However, sometimes their work does not meet the highest standards. Then they are properly accused of being bureaucratic, unmotivated, incompetent, or worse. To a certain extent, these problems are based on psychological and organizational factors that can be altered.

Expectations. A unique study compared parents and clinicians about their expectations for children with handicaps. It showed that, to some extent, parents and clinicians emphasize different things when they think about their children. Parents place greatest value on achievement of mobility and self-care skills in the present and on normal functioning in later years. Clinicians, on the other hand, rate the mood of the child and family functioning as most important. Although these differences are not great, they can form the basis for problems in communication between parents and clinicians (Cadman, C. Goldsmith, & Bashim, 1984).

Pediatricians. Most studies of knowledge and attitudes about handicapping conditions have been done with physicians and teachers. As a group, physicians who have had little experience with children with disabilities tend to underestimate the differences between children from the same family. Pediatricians who have had no training about behavior during medical school or residencies do not know as much about behavioral pediatrics as do physicians who have been trained in programs funded to provide such training. This is important because diagnosis and referral of children's disabilities involve a judgment about behavioral characteristics, and pediatricians are often the first step in identification of children with disabilities.

Pediatricians are conservative about referring mildly retarded children for services, and they also are less optimistic than other clinicians about the prognosis for mentally retarded people. Although they believe that early intervention can be effective, they also believe that its benefits may be greater for the families than they are for the children themselves. Few pediatricians are aware of the special education programs of their current patients. All of this may be due to an emphasis in the traditional training of pediatricians on anatomy and physiology, with almost no training in developmental psychology or education. Supplementing the training of pediatricians with information relevant to the behavior of children with handicaps seems desirable at this time (J. F. Goodman & Cecil, 1987; Guralnick et al., 1988; Palfrey, Sarro, J. D. Singer, & Wenger, 1987; S. Phillips, S. B. Friedman, Zebal, & Parrish, 1985; Schachter & R. K. Stone, 1985; Wolraich & Siperstein, 1986).

Teachers. Federal legislation in the United States has recently mandated the mainstreaming of children with handicaps. In the 19th century and first half of the 20th century, special education meant education of children with handicaps in special classes and schools separate from those of normal children. Since then, however, the move to educate all children in regular classes has taken force as a result of professional, parental, and legislative pressure. We review the mainstreaming movement later in this chapter. Here it is appropriate to cite recent research on the attitudes of teachers of both special and regular classes toward children with handicaps.

The instruction goals of teachers of children with handicaps tend to emphasize either achievement of cognitive skills or training of social competence. Although one might expect pupils of teachers with an orientation toward social competence to be more advanced in this area, actually their students are less competent in self-care, communication, socialization, and occupation. It might appear that teachers with a social orientation are less successful in their goals than those with a cognitive orientation (Tzuriel & Golinsky, 1985). However, because this study by Tzuriel and Golinsky was a correlational study, the causal direction of the relationship is not clear. It is possible that teachers with a social orientation worked with less able children.

There are clear cultural differences in teachers' expectations of students. Whereas special education teachers tend to be more tolerant of deviation than are teachers of children in regular classes in both Australia and the United States, there are also differences, including a higher rating by U.S. teachers of characteristics that facilitate class management and less emphasis on promoting peer-to-peer social processes (Walker & Lamon, 1987).

In studies of teachers' perceptions, attitudes, and expectations, there is a focus on factors associated with discipline in the classroom. Most of these studies are concerned with the nature of behavior disorders in the school setting. These studies are not limited to children with a diagnosis of conduct disorder or behavior disorder. Children with learning disabilities are perceived by teachers as engaging in fewer prosocial acts and more antisocial acts than normal children, and there are also differences between different settings, ages, and sex of the child. However, there is general agreement that behavior disorders in the school are characterized by such behaviors as severe and mild physical aggression toward teachers, toward other students, toward themselves and objects; hyperactivity; inattentiveness and relative lack of responsibility (Bullock, Zagar, Donahue, & Pelton, 1985; Center & Wascom, 1986; 1987; Cullinan, M. H. Epstein, & Kauffman, 1984; Ruhl & C. A. Hughes, 1985).

Teachers also have clear perceptions of the ways that they deal with disciplinary problems. They report that the most effective, easiest to use, and most frequently used methods include redirection of the student toward appropriate behavior and manipulation of rewards. Removing children from the classroom and interventions that involve physical contact, especially severe corporal punishment, are not regarded as effective and are not thought to be frequently used (Martens, Peterson, Witt, & Cirone, 1986).

In addition to studies that ask teachers what they do in the classroom, there also are some that observe teacher interactions with students. Teachers' judgment about hyperactivity and aggression may be more accurate in large classrooms than in small group or individual settings. The teachers may respond more negatively to less popular children and children who are at risk for educational problems, but they may also give more unsolicited praise to children with handicaps. Teachers may not be aware of these patterns of response, but the pattern can be changed by increasing their awareness (Milich & Landau, 1988; Siperstein & Goding, 1985; Stipek & Sanborn, 1985).

Caregivers. There are also a few observational studies of caregivers in residential programs. Feeding takes up much of the time of staff in nursing homes for severely handicapped people, and social interactions may be limited. In those institutions and small group homes where social interaction is more frequent, appropriate behavior is often ignored whereas inappropriate behaviors produce caregiver attention. This pattern tends to be more true in institutions and large community units than in small community units. When caregivers talk to hospitalized children, the children are more or less responsive depending, not only on individual factors, but also on how sick the children are (Felce et al., 1987; Ohwaki & Zingarelli, 1988; Susman & Hollenbeck, 1984; Walbran & Hile, 1988).

Supervision. Caregiving improves when supervision improves. Most studies of the effects of supervision have been done with caregivers in residential programs rather than with teachers in classrooms. Many of the studies are inadequately designed in that they do not specify the treatments exactly, they evaluate effects only on the teaching or caregiving staff, they do not provide for tests in real-life situations or for follow-ups, or appropriate control conditions are not included in the design of the study.

Nevertheless, some things can be concluded from the literature. Simply adding staff or giving instruction to them seems to have minimal effect. Training programs can change attitudes of supervisory staff, but the effect of changing attitudes on teaching has not been adequately evaluated. Role playing may be more effective than lectures. However, most effective are contingency management procedures. When caregivers are told specifically what to do, when their performance is observed and formally noted, and when they are rewarded for engaging in training, training by staff does indeed increase (Demchak, 1987; Maher, 1985; M. B. Parsons, Schepis, D. H. Reid, McCarn, & Green, 1987; Seys & Duker, 1988).

Stress and Burnout. Supervision may also be important to reduce feelings of stress on the job. Teachers who report that they receive support from supervisors and peers feel less job stress. In turn, at least certain aspects of stress may be related to job burnout, a phenomenon that is common in human service industries (Cope, Grossnickle, Covington, Durham, & Zaharia, 1987). Subjective aspects of burnout include feelings of emotional exhaustion, depersonalization, lack of accomplishment, negativism, inflexibility, and powerlessness. Objective aspects of burnout include absenteeism, job turnover, complaining, lowered resistance to illness, and a number of other characteristics incompatible with good performance in human services occupations (Caton, Grossnickle, Cope, Long, & Mitchell, 1988; Cherniss, 1988; Fimian, 1986).

Job stress is related to burnout in some people. However, it is also true that jobs one might at first sight consider to be stressful, such as caring for severely disabled people, do not seem to have higher burnout rates than other jobs. Furthermore, work overload, lack of ability in the job, family pressure, management relations, and lack of career progression, all of which may be regarded as stress factors, do not correlate with aspects of burnout. The only job stress measure that does seem to be related to a measure of burnout is a relationship between underutilization and emotional exhaustion. In other words, if work does not utilize the person's skills adequately, the work may be perceived as not meaningful and burnout tends to be more common (Bersani & Heifetz, 1985; Caton et al., 1988; Hildebrand & Seefeldt, 1986; E. J. Silver, Lubin, & Silverman, 1984).

This completes our review of recent research on parent and professional and other caregiver factors in determining whether a handicapped child or adult receive exemplary services. These factors are not always considered when school, residential, and sheltered work programs are managed. The result is less than optimal management of programming with its resultant mediocrity of effect and high human and financial cost.

FOLLOW-UP STUDIES

In the next section, we begin to consider school programs for children with handicaps. For convenience, we take them in rough chronological age order, beginning with programs for infants. However, before doing that, it is important to review some of the many follow-up studies that seek to assess what happens to infants and children if one looks at them over time. This is important because given no special educational intervention at all, children mature if reared in reasonably normal environments. A main problem in evaluating studies of the effectiveness of early intervention and special education programs is to show that they do a better job in maintaining maximum growth than does normal rearing. (No one believes that rearing in educationally deprived environments is good enough.) We show that educational intervention is indeed important, but also that certain conditions must be fulfilled in order for them to be effective. However, first, follow-up studies are reviewed.

Follow-up studies of children with handicaps fall into three types, roughly grouped according to age. First, there are investigations of what happens to children who are found to have some problem at birth or in their first year. Then, there are studies of the development of handicapping conditions during the school years. Finally, there are longitudinal studies of what happens to children with handicaps as they grow into adulthood. The first two of these are covered in this chapter, and long-term follow-ups are discussed in the next chapter.

There is a central idea that runs through all of these longitudinal studies: There are many paths possible in development, so multiple factors influence the outcome of even severe disabilities. This means that, although it is possible to say with some certainty that a group found to have a handicapping condition early may also have some disability later on, the nature of the later disability may not be so easily predictable. Also, variability within the group may depend not only on the initial variability but also on what has happened to each individual in the intervening time. In other words, statements of general risk for groups seem possible at this time, but the more specific future of the individual child is less predictable.

Infancy to School Years

Several studies have shown that infants with severe problems in infancy may have problems as long as 5 years later. This statement applies, for example, to children who were born prematurely and with very low birth weight, those who failed to thrive, those with neurological problems at birth, or those whose mothers were on methadone maintenance programs when the babies were born (Chikovani, Mirimova, Mirzoyan, Znamenskaya, & Khodakova, 1984; Coolman et al., 1985; H. L. Johnson, Diano, & Rosen, 1984; Klein, 1988, L. T. Singer & Fagan, 1984).

On the other hand, there are some studies in which no difference between disabled infants and comparison groups is found on follow-up. Often, there are effects but they are limited to only a small proportion of the children. Sometimes, the behaviors affected are quite specific, and the age at which these differences are seen is also specific. This individual specificity implies that both research and treatment in follow-up studies can benefit from a multivariate approach and a focus on individual life histories rather than simple categories and group designs and methods (Barnard, Bee, & Hammond, 1984; Bozynski et al., 1984; S. B. Campbell, 1987; S. E. Cohen, Parmelee, Sigman, & Beckwith, 1988; Elliman, Bryan, & Elliman, 1986; M. Field, 1984; Hoy, Bill, & Sykes, 1988; Mali, Tyler, & Brookfield, 1989; G. Ross, 1987; Ruff, McCarton, Kurtzberg, & Vaughan, 1984; Tramontana, Hooper, & Selzer, 1988).

There are a few studies that have taken this multivariate approach by examining variables that predict behavioral handicaps in children. One of these compared the developmental histories of children who were judged to be hyperactive at 6 years of age. These children and a comparison group were subsamples of a larger group of children who had been judged to be at risk for later disabilities because of their negative family social history. All of these children had not only been judged as hyperactive or not hyperactive at 6 years of age, but also had been given a test measuring distractibility at 42 months of age. In addition, assessments were taken of neonatal status, of temperament in the newborn period and 3, 6, and 30 months, and of social behavior with their mothers at home and in a laboratory. Moreover, behavior of their mothers when the infants were 6, 24, and 42 months were also taken.

The most general result of the study indicated that, whereas motor maturity and social experience scores predicted hyperactivity, there was little overlap in the cases the measures predicted. More specifically, intrusive care at 6 months, overstimulating care at 42 months, motor maturity at 7 and 10 days, and distractibility at 42 months were all associated with later hyperactivity. The remainder of the 38 early child variables, including temperament measures and the reflex and arousal measures taken in the newborn period did not predict hyperactivity at all. This study demonstrates the specificity of prediction that is possible with the use of a longitudinal approach with specific measures and concepts. Many more of this kind of study are needed (Jacobvitz & Sroufe, 1987).

School Year Follow-ups

There have also been follow-up studies from the preschool years to school age or during the school years. Some of these include studies of language impairment (Forell & Hood, 1985; Paul & D. J. Cohen, 1984; Shriberg & Kwiatkowski, 1988), mental retardation (Vig, Kaminer, & Jedrysek, 1987), hyperactivity (R. T. Brown & Borden, 1986; I. C. Gillberg & C. Gillberg, 1988; Lambert, 1988), neurodevelopmental disorders (I. C. Gillberg, C. Gillberg, & Groth, 1989) and childhood autism (Cantwell, Baker, Rutter, & Mawhood, 1989; C. Gillberg & Steffenberg, 1987). All of these studies show at least a significant degree of stability over the years of follow-up.

Particularly impressive are long-term follow-up studies that correlate behavior in the preschool years with maladaptive behavior in adolescence. Some studies focus on particular child behaviors like early aggression, whereas others show complex interactions of factors like child gender, early childhood behavior, and family factors in predicting later maladaptive behavior (J. Block, J. H. Block, & Keyes, 1988; J. V. Lerner, Hertzog, Hooker, Hassibi, & A. Thomas, 1988).

One of the most sophisticated studies has been a 7-year follow-up of reading achievement during the school years (Butler, Marsh, M. J. Sheppard, & J. L. Sheppard, 1985). It went beyond simply correlating early reading achievement scores with later achievement. It tested a model of what accounted for the maintenance of low or high reading achievement. It showed that reading scores in kindergarten did not directly influence later reading scores. Rather, kindergarten performance was related to reading in the primary grades, which in turn was related to more mature reading. That is, reading skills are gradually evolving developmental phenomenon rather than a fixed trait (R. E. Stark et al., 1984; Vig et al., 1987).

EARLY INTERVENTION

Early intervention programs are predicated on the general assumption that some children do not receive experiences in their natural home and community environment adequate to maintain physical, cognitive, emotional, or social development. This can occur when the environment is lacking in some way and/or when a disabled child cannot benefit easily from a normally stimulating environment.

When conditions for normal growth are lacking, the child may begin life relatively normal, but environmental and personal deficits may combine so that the child's development is increasingly delayed. This compounding of the effects of experiential deprivation over time produces what is known as a cumulative deficit. Later deficits build on earlier ones so that the overall deficit accumulates (Breitmayer & Ramey, 1986; Saco-Pollitt, Pollitt, & Greenfield, 1985).

The general solution to the problem of cumulative deficits is to prevent them by providing the needed compensatory experiences in nursery, home, and school settings. Support has grown for the concept of education in the infancy and preschool periods, beginning soon after the child has been identified as being at risk or having a disability (Garber, 1988). Such compensatory education once focused on early school programs (that is center-based programs). However, now early intervention ordinarily includes participation of a member of the family and often focuses on training the family at home (Odom, Yoder, & G. Hill, 1988).

The general theory that deprivation of appropriate experiences can produce a cumulative deficit is plausible, and compensatory education makes sense, but there are several sources of opposition to these ideas. First, early intervention does not work for everyone. Normal children from homes that do provide adequate learning environments would not be expected to benefit very much from programs that enrich their already stimulating environments. Second, whereas early education programs that have been tested adequately seem to meet the goals of reducing cumulative deficits, at least some of the gains are lost if the child subsequently is placed in a normal school program that does not maintain these gains (Gibson & A. Harris, 1988).

Furthermore, although there have been several successful demonstrations of the efficacy of early education programs, no one yet knows what components account for the success and which are irrelevant. Finally, although early studies of compensatory education have shown positive effects, these studies were ordinarily carried out in university settings with an adequate number of highly trained personnel, good physical facilities, and cooperative families. Efficacy studies in more general communities are being reported only now.

All of these objections point to the need to specify more exactly the optimum conditions for accomplishing the goal of reducing cumulative deficits. We can expect that these conditions will be related to the nature of the home or community, the characteristics of the child that change with age, and the variable nature of educational components. Certainly we know that parental interest is one contributor to their participation in early intervention programs and that parental interest, in turn, depends on their personal well-being and the social support they have available to them. The time that intervention begins is also significant, with earlier intervention generally more effective (Musselman, Lindsay, & A. K. Wilson, 1988). As becomes evident, the nature of the intervention varies greatly from study to study so that the very meaning of the term "early intervention" can be puzzling (Bailey & Simeonsson, 1988; Dunst, Leet, & Trivette, 1988; Fenske, Zalenski, Krantz, & McClannahan, 1985).

Our review of studies of early intervention concentrates on nonmedical interventions done after the child is born. Some children and their parents have begun socialization programs almost immediately after birth when the child's disability is manifested by extreme prematurity or a failure to thrive. In those cases, the child stays in the hospital perhaps for months, and socialization between the infant and the family relationships do not have an opportunity to develop normally. The few studies of socialization programs in the hospital have emphasized the importance of the continuity between hospital and later home intervention. When designed with appropriate contrast groups, these studies show that all measures are not affected, but maintenance of cognitive and social growth are improved during the first year as a consequence of socialization experiences during the period in the hospital nursery, of support of the family, and of home visits by a nurse after the child has been sent home (Resnick, Armstrong, & Carter, 1988).

In-Home Programs.   Most early intervention programs include at least a component of parent participation. In the first year or two, programs are concentrated in the home. These programs vary considerably in their approach. Some teach the parent to teach the child developmental skills, others focus on increasing the mutual social interaction of the parent and the child, whereas still others are oriented toward certain skills and use highly specific measures. Whatever the procedure used, positive effects of the intervention are ordinarily found, although there are major design problems in many of the studies, the effects may be limited to some measures and not others, and the long-term effects are not usually studied. Sometimes effects on parent well-being are as important as are the effects on the child (Barrera, Rosenbaum, & C. E. Cunningham, 1986; Brown-Gorton & Wolery, 1988; Girolametto, 1988; Mahoney & Powell, 1988; Shonkoff, Hauser-Cram, Krauss, & Upshur, 1988).

Day Care.   The simplest form of early education done out of the home is accomplished in day-care centers where the major intent is to provide caregiving to the child when its mother is at work. None of the recent studies of day care have focused on children with handicaps. However, the literature is relevant to children with handicaps who are cared for out of their home by people other than a parent.

Day care refers to any method of out-of-home care that is at least custodial. This includes not only care in centers where there are many children, but also care in private homes and by relatives of the parents. The discussion of the benefits and risks of day care can easily be oversimplified.

Recent work has shown that consequences depend on factors in the child interacting with the parent and home characteristics and the quality of the care that the child receives.

Everyone agrees, however, that many parents whose children are in day-care programs are forced by their economic circumstances to find a place for their children. There is also general agreement that poor care has detrimental effects and there is a need for improved supervision of day-care centers (Gamble & Zigler, 1986).

Center-Based Programs.   Most studies of early intervention evaluate effects of formal educational programs in center-based programs. A significant number of these evaluations involve long-term assessments. Some consider the effects on the parents as well as on their children, whereas others consider cultural variables promoting or impeding such programs (D. A. Allen, G. Affleck, McGrade, & McQueeney, 1984b; Ramey & F. A. Campbell, 1984; Mastropieri & Scruggs, 1985).

The most important recent development in early intervention research has been a recognition that, to be most useful, evaluation of these prevention programs requires greater precision than has been typical up to now. The most valuable of the recent studies are those that have contrasted various approaches to early intervention. Generally, they have shown that different kinds of programs produce different effects (but see Musselman et al., 1988). As an instance, one program with older preschool children emphasized direct instruction by maximizing the time children spent with academic materials to be learned, whereas another program facilitated general cognitive processes that were hoped to serve the basis for more efficient learning. Both programs were effective. However, there were dramatic differences between the curricula in promoting the use of language, with the program that facilitated cognitive processes more effective (Dale & K. N. Cole, 1988; Shonkoff et al., 1988).

The recent literature on early intervention has shown that, in general, intervention programs have been shown to be beneficial to the children and to their families. Several questions remain concerning cost-effectiveness of various approaches and concerning the specific nature of the consequences of early intervention. However, it is clear that parent involvement has become a crucial factor in most early intervention programs, whether home-based or center-based.

SCHOOL PROGRAMS

Education for children with handicaps became institutionalized as part of the growing universal education movement during the 19th century. However, it was not until 1975 that special education for all handicapped children became required by law in the United States. Internationally, there is great variation in the degree and manner that education of children with handicaps is provided, and the impact of public legislation in the United States is still variable.

Nevertheless, school programs for handicapped children have grown in sophistication and amount. The recent literature on school programs is vast, and some of it is scientific. Much of the literature is concerned with fundamentally political issues such as the impact of legislation, the excess of children from minority ethnic groups in special education classes, and the significance of an increase of learning-disabled children and simultaneous reduction of educable mentally retarded children in special education.

Although societal variables are fundamental to an understanding of special education, we concentrate on the recent scientific literature that investigates the processes that characterize effective special education. School and classroom organization, the nature of curricula in special programs, evaluation methods, the impact of technology, mainstreaming, and peer-tutoring are the process variables that are the focus of the discussion. Studies of more specific treatment procedures are covered later in the chapter.

The characteristics of effective schools have been studied intensively and are generally understood. Educational leadership, orderly school climate, high achievement expectations, systematic monitoring of school performance, and an emphasis on basic skills are all features of good school programs. An active teacher who organizes material and provides feedback is an effective teacher (W. E. Bickel & D. D. Bickel, 1986).

These same principles should also apply to special education of children with handicaps. It is possible to be more specific about factors associated with better performance in students with special needs. Clinical category is not a simple predictor. Although questionaire studies asking teachers what they do in the classroom may find differences between categories of children with handicaps, research that actually looks at what is happening in the classroom finds that, when activities are only generally specified, within clinical category variation is large relative to any differences between categories (Hundert, Cassie, & N. Johnston, 1988; Lovitt, Rudsit, Jenkins, Pious, & Benedetti, 1985; Westling, 1985; Ysseldyke, Thurlow, Christenson, & J. Weiss, 1987).

More promising are studies of specific procedures that influence various kinds of learning. Even such simple environmental modifications such as teaching some things in the morning and others in the afternoon or having children sit in rows to decrease distractions and at tables to increase discussion have been shown to be effective. At this level of specific analysis, clinical category differences have sometimes emerged (Morton & Kershner, 1985; Wheldall & Lam, 1987).

Planning for Individuals. Public legislation not only requires universal education for all children with handicaps, but it also mandates a specific plan for the child's education called an Individualized Educational Plan (IEP). This planning is accomplished by a committee that includes school personnel and members of the child's family. There has been little study of the participation by parents in the planning for their children, and the research that has been done suffers from limited sampling. However, what there is suggests that parent participation is incomplete, that parents are satisfied with teachers of their children, but that they are dissatisfied with the services that they receive from other professionals (C. L. Barton, L. E. Barton, Rycek, & Brulle, 1984; O'Hagan, Sandys, & Swanson, 1984; Vaughn, Bos, Harrell, & Lasky, 1988).

Approaches to planning for the individual child can come from parents and from the children themselves. Ordinarily, however, such plans are based on a curriculum that has been established for the school. Such curricula can be embodied in a formal program plan for the school as a whole or for the class. However, they are not universally available. In one study of the availability of program plans, it was shown that schools for children with severe behavioral disturbance almost always provide a statement of criteria for student admission to the program. But only half of schools state goals for programs or indicate the nature of the design of the program, and only one-third describe instructional methods, curricula, or methods of evaluation of progress (F. Brown, Weed, & I. M. Evans, 1987; Grosenick, N. L. George, & M. P. George, 1988).

Surveys of curricular sources indicate that program planning originates from many ideas. Some of these are general. Proceeding from normal developmental sequences and beginning at the child's current developmental level; using the individual interactions between the teacher and the child as a guide for program planning, or analyzing natural settings such as normal mother–child interactions can be general sources. Other approaches include particular theoretical perspectives as a guide. Examples would be analysis of specific behaviors, encouragement of self-regulated learning, or the use of cognitive models to promote transfer of learning.

All of these sources have been shown to be effective in promoting learning when compared with no special program. However, this could merely mean that organizing learning in some way is better than having no plan. This principle is useful, but perhaps more useful are comparisons of different curricular approaches. Not many of such comparisons have been done, but some are available. When comparisons between plausible approaches are done, they tend to show that different procedures have different effects, but that the effects are specific to the group affected and the behavioral measure used (Cosden, Pearl, & Bryan, 1985; Darch & Carnine, 1986; Waldron, Diebold, & Rose, 1985).

These studies imply that many approaches can be useful with any specific group of children. The well-educated and experienced teacher will have access to many approaches that can be tailored to individual children in the IEP. They must ascertain that goals for the teaching and methods for evaluating progress for any particular child should be made explicit.

Resources. Adding to the resources that any teacher has available from education and experience, there are also the program resources available in any particular school. The greater the range of program options available, the more flexible the individual teacher can be. A great many programs have been described lately. Most involve familiar curricular concepts involving sensory discrimination and cognitive skills, quantitative skills, and communication skills important for verbal and nonverbal social interaction and reading and writing. There is reason to believe that some curricular areas like social issues and formal physical education may be deemphasized in programs for children with handicaps. There is interest in music, the visual arts, and poetry. But quality research in art education is lacking relative to that in many other areas. There is also much interest in sex education, but here again, well-designed research is sparse compared to other areas (Aarons & Dixon, 1988; Fine, 1987; Haight & Fachting, 1986; Lagomarcino, D. H. Reid, Ivancic, & Faw, 1984; S. E. Miller, 1987).

Technology. The impact of technology on education has become very evident in the literature on special education. Man-made objects have been used to compensate for handicapping conditions for at least 800 years, and the development of such technology has accelerated since the industrial revolution. Eyeglasses, hearing aids, wheelchairs, prosthetic limbs, and medications are all familiar examples. Electronic technologies, particularly, have allowed miniaturization and increasingly sensitive and complicated applications. Typewriters and hand-held calculators are examples of devices that have been used to increase the efficiency of teaching with children who have difficulty learning (D. Byrne, 1986; Calhoun, 1985; Horton, 1985).

The most recent development, and it is a vigorous one, has been the use of computers. Computers are available for enhancing and clarifying sensory input. Some computers act as an aid to locomotion or to communication for people who cannot speak clearly. In the classroom, microcomputers add to the teacher's range of materials for instruction without replacing the teacher. They can individualize instruction and give immediate feedback about success or lack of success. In doing this they can provide the student with an accurate account of previous performance and efficiently summarize trends in the individual student's performance (Blamey, Cowan, Alcantara, & G. M. Clark, 1988; R. D. Clark, 1984; Wacker, Wiggins, M. Fowler, & Berg, 1988).

Microcomputers allow individualized pacing, learning with a minimum of errors, and provide opportunities for extended practice without taking an inordinate amount of the teacher's time. Instruction can occur in private so that the self-esteem of the student is not challenged inappropriately. Or group work on computers is possible. Computers have been used with hearing or visually handicapped children, children with articulation and language handicaps, learning-disabled, mentally retarded, and even autistic children.

There are, however, some problems that limit the use of microcomputers in the classroom at this time. Some children have difficulty with the complex keyboard or in understanding the rules involved in some software. The software is not always appropriate for children with handicaps, and sometimes the material in computer programs is not adequately integrated with the rest of the curriculum.

Perhaps less easy to correct are attributes of teachers. Microcomputers involve a shift in role on the part of a teacher from information purveyor to organizer of the relationship between the computer and the student. This requires not only a change in teaching style by some teachers, but also familiarity and interest in computers that some teachers do not as yet possess. It is likely, however, that as computers become a more familiar part of the home and school environment, these difficulties will diminish (Ager, 1985; Goldman & Pellegrino, 1987; Lieber & Semmel, 1985; Panyan, 1984).

Evaluation.   Federal legislation, besides establishing universal education for children with handicaps and requiring a formal curricular planning process, also espouses accountability. Evaluation depends on the point of view of the person doing the evaluation. For instance, parents and certain teachers emphasize the goals of integration into regular schooling somewhat more than do behavior therapists. On the other hand, everyone agrees that professional practices, staff development, data-based instruction, and the ultimate functioning of the child are important things to consider in evaluating school programs (Meyer, Eichinger, & Park-Lee, 1987).

Follow-up of the IEP can be conducted with more or less formal methods. There is evidence that if the teacher keeps a systematic data base concerning adequacy of the student's performance, goal setting by teachers and student performance are perceived by the teacher as improved relative to the more usual less formal approaches (L. S. Fuchs, D. Fuchs, & Stecker, 1989).

There are dilemmas involved in grading students with handicapping conditions. Norm-referenced grading in which a handicapped child is compared with other children is one approach. Self-referenced grading compares the child's current performance with previous levels. Criterion-referenced grading indicates the child's achievement with respect to defined standards of performance. Carpenter (1985) espoused use of a combination of these approaches to communicate to parents, other professionals, and the child in the most complete way.

MAINSTREAMING

The democratic ideal of equality of opportunity nowhere has had greater influence in school programming for children with handicaps than in the movement to educate all children in regular classes. This movement has been called *mainstreaming*. Before the 1960s, equality of educational opportunity for children with handicaps was thought to be fulfilled through special education in classes that were separated from the mainstream. However, by the end of the 1960s, opinion had begun to shift to the view that special education in separate classes and schools was not accomplishing its goals. It appeared that children did not learn any better in separate schools than they would have in regular classes, and separate education was more expensive and tended to isolate handicapped children from their nonhandicapped peers.

The mainstreaming movement was at first characterized by optimism. People who have espoused the ideals of mainstreaming have been confident that all children with handicaps could learn as well in regular classes, would ultimately be more accepted socially than they would be in isolated special classes, and would increase in their self-esteem from succeeding in regular classes. In addition, it was believed that elimination of special classes would reduce the costs of educating children with handicaps.

Complexity of the Concept. Simple ideals can be forceful agents for social change. But sometimes unexpected factors complicate the outcome. Perhaps most basic of all has been problems in the conceptualization of the concept of mainstreaming. Originally, two levels of integration were conceived. A child was placed either in special or in regular classes. Pretty quickly, however, it became clear that a continuum of mainstreaming characterizes the concept. That is, several educational options are available. In the United States, about 25% of children with handicaps are served exclusively in regular classes. Somewhat less than 25% are educated in completely separate classes within the same school, and another 5% are in separate schools or residential programs. Almost 50% of children with handicaps receive part of their education in regular classes and spend part of their day in resource rooms that are adapted to the special educational needs that the children have. These percentages are averages for the United States, but there are major variations among the 50 states (Danielson & Bellamy, 1989).

When looked at more closely, the mainstreaming concept becomes even more elaborate. Children who are mainstreamed are often placed in class-rooms that are appropriate for them. But sometimes mainstreaming consists of assignment to grades that are not age-appropriate for the child, and they may be assigned to more than one group of regular classes, or to only a portion of a sequence of instruction in a regular class. Moreover, there seems to be little difference in the actual time spent in group or individual instruction. Category of handicap is not an important predictor of the amount of individualized instruction. Individualized instruction occurs in resource rooms, but less in segregated special classes or regular classes (Sansone & Zigmond, 1986; Ysseldyke, Thurlow, Christenson, & McVicar, 1988).

Effectiveness.   Given the complexity of the concept of mainstreaming, it is perhaps not too surprising that comparisons of the effectiveness of various forms of placement have shown no major differences in academic achievement in the various forms. It appears that background of the child and the quality of instruction are more important predictors than is type of placement (J. Q. Affleck, Madge, Adams, & Lowenbraun, 1988; Kluwin & Moores, 1989). Peers of children with learning handicaps respond to the fact that the children with handicaps are in a special class rather than a resource room, even if the children have not been formally labeled as learning disabled or mentally retarded (Bak, Cooper, Dobroth, & Siperstein, 1987).

Factors that Promote Success.   Thus, to evaluate whether or not the mainstreaming movement has been successful seems to be too simple a question. Perhaps a more tangible question is the definition of the factors that might be important in increasing integration of children with handicaps into regular schooling. Looking at it from this perspective, several definite factors have emerged recently.

The first of these is developmental age. Several studies have shown that integration of normal and handicapped children is possible and effective in the preschool period. When integrated with mildly handicapped individuals, nonhandicapped children are not impaired in their development, and their parents perceive no detrimental effect on their child. This is important because some parents of nonhandicapped children are initially afraid that the development of their normal child may be impaired by association with a handicapped child. Apparently there is no evidence for this fear.

The social and play behavior of preschool children with handicaps con-tinues to be delayed relative to that of normal children when they are in groups with normal children. However, the degree of delay depends on the situation they are in and the maturity of the nonhandicapped children. Moreover, the handicapped children are generally improved in the main-streamed situation over the case in the segregated class. In the regular class, organization of the class to increase social behavior is successful. Although all of this points to a beneficial effect of mainstreaming on children with handicaps, without a detrimental effect on nonhandicapped children, there are as yet few satisfactory generalization or follow-up studies (Burstein, 1986; M. Dean & Nettles, 1987; Guralnick & Groom, 1988a,b; Jenkins, Odom, & Speltz, 1989; Travis, A. R. Thomas, & Fuller, 1985).

Older handicapped children feel apprehensive about being moved from a segregated class to a mainstreamed environment. These worries include apprehension about various aspects of academic and social interactions. The children are also concerned about factors inherent in moving back and forth between regular and special class placements, and the majority of children prefer to be taught by their classroom teacher than by a specialist. Taking these fears and preferences into consideration in managing the transition to mainstreaming would probably be useful in decreasing that apprehension, but the issue has not been studied further (Jenkins & Heinen, 1989; Tymitz-Wolf, 1984).

The social status of children with handicaps tends to be less than that of normal children in mainstreamed classes, and the children with handicaps also continue to have problems related to academic achievement. Children in segregated classes are generally unknown to normal peers in regular classes, but the handicapped children in the regular classes are less accepted socially. However, they may also be less rejected. In other words, whereas main-streaming provides the opportunity to be part of the normal group, in fact children with handicaps generally participate less than the average normal child. The children with handicaps are seen as more shy, less cooperative, and less likely to have leadership skills. They, themselves, experience more dissatisfaction and feel more anxiety about their peer relations.

With respect to academic skills, children with learning disabilities are no different on several measures such as on-task behavior, compliance to requests, and asking questions. However, on average, they do not come to class equipped, they attend less, and they do not volunteer comments or questions as often. Children with Down syndrome make better progress in the mainstreamed class (Casey, D. Jones, Kugler, & Watkins, 1988; Coben & Zigmond, 1986; A. R. Taylor, Asher, & G. A. Williams, 1987; Zigmond, Kerr, & Schaeffer, 1988).

Organized programs for increasing the skills of the child with handicaps and for increasing the knowledge of normal peers apparently can be suc-cessful even with autistic children and has been espoused as a general approach. As agents of change, parents and school administrators are probably important, and their role has been recognized. However, most of the literature has been focused on teachers and peers, an indication that it is believed that major changes occur in the classroom (Gresham, 1984; Sasso, Simpson, & Novak, 1985).

Teachers. Although there have been almost no recent studies of parents and administrators, there have been a number of studies of regular class teachers. There are exceptions, but many regular classroom teachers fail to make the adjustments necessary to compensate for what they perceive to be reading problems, behavior problems, and poor participation and attendance. They do grade children with disabilities using a lower standard. This relative lack of response to children with handicaps has been viewed partly as the response of an already overburdened teacher to additional work. More frequently it is conceived also as a lack of the specialized training or a question of attitudes (Brady & R. D. Taylor, 1989; Bender & Ukeje, 1989; Ivarie, Hogue, & Brulle, 1984; Slate & Saudargas, 1987; Ward & Center, 1987; Webster & M. M. Johnson, 1987; Zigmond, Levin, & Laurie, 1985).

There are cultural differences in support of mainstreaming. Although there is a movement toward mainstreaming in Australia, teachers in Australia are less confident that mainstreaming will be effective for the child with disabilities or for the normal children in their class than are Canadian teachers. Within the United States, there are clear differences between teachers of regular classes and special educators in their response to several questions, most important of which was the variety of handicapping conditions that the respondent was willing to teach. These studies suggest that programs oriented to selection of teachers with positive attitudes toward mainstreaming and focusing on educating teachers of regular classes about handicapping conditions might be helpful in fostering maximum adjustment of the child with handicaps to the mainstreamed environment (Ansu-Kyeremeh, 1987; Gans, 1987; Gow, Ward, Balla, & Snow, 1988).

Peer-Tutoring. There has also been keen interest in peer relationships (Brinker & Thorpe, 1986) and peer-tutoring as a way of improving the behavior, academic skills, and self-concept of children with handicaps. Peer-tutoring is also thought to be helpful for the peer-tutors themselves (Lazerson, Foster, S. I. Brown, & Hummel, 1988). The many studies of peer-tutoring include approaches in which a normal child tutors a handicapped child, a handicapped child tutors a normal child (for instance, in sign language), the normal and handicapped children tutor each other, children with handicaps tutor one another, and also major reorganizations of the class in which all children monitor the performance of everyone else (S. A. Fowler, 1986; Osguthorpe & Scruggs, 1986; Realon, Favell, Stirewalt, & Phillips, 1986).

The studies almost always show that that peer-tutoring increases academic skills, improves speech, decreases maladaptive behaviors like truancy, and increases the social relationship between the tutor and the person being tutored. Less definite are effects on self-esteem. Positive effects are seen, not only for the person receiving instruction, but also for the one who gives it. These positive effects are seen for learning-disabled, mentally retarded, behavior-disordered, and even some autistic children (Mowrer & Conley, 1987; Osguthorpe & Scruggs, 1986).

The results of peer-tutoring studies are impressive and encouraging, but many of them are done with small samples and most do not test for generalization or duration of the effects. On the whole, most studies are concerned with the simple question of whether peer-tutoring is effective. There has been little interest in determining the factors that might be important in having peer-tutoring become a routine aspect of mainstreamed education. Nor has there been much interest in asking why peer-tutoring works or what attributes work best (but see Schunk, Hanson, & Cox, 1987).

Peer-tutoring therefore seems to be one procedure for promoting mainstreaming. Added to selection and training of supportive teachers, the ideal of mainstreaming can be fostered. However, there is a third factor that is important for successful integration of children with handicaps. That factor is to help the handicapped children themselves to behave as normally as possible.

BEHAVIORAL TREATMENT

A scientific approach has perhaps nowhere had more impact than in the study of treatment procedures. Whether one is considering behavioral or medical treatments, the development of general knowledge and the acceptance of the need for scientific evaluation of the efficacy of treatment procedures have combined to provide an array of procedures that can be used to ameliorate disabilities of children.

In this section and the next, we consider the extensive literature on treatment procedures that influence the behavior of children with handicaps. In several previous chapters, we have included brief reviews of treatment methods that emerged from the study of various psychological processes. The purpose of the next two sections is to consider more general issues that most treatments share.

One of these general issues is the distinction between a specific treatment procedure and the more general curricular and organizational issues that were covered in the first part of this chapter. The application of a particular reinforcement schedule for the reduction of aggressive behavior or the use of a specific medication to increase attention in the classroom are examples of specific treatment procedures. Mainstreaming or a general curriculum for the teaching of beginning reading are more general. Intermediate between specific treatments and more general approaches are programs that emphasize a reasonably definable approach to therapy. Aerobic exercise, reduction of food additives, or cognitive behavior therapy are examples here. It is probably fair to say that the more specific we can be in describing a treatment and its effects, the more useful the information.

Evaluation and Implementation

We have already seen that almost any organized activity can affect the behavior of a group of children significantly. This might lead one to expect that many treatment methods can be effective, and there is evidence that this is true (Frankel & Simmons, 1985; Rutter, 1985b). It is also true that certain popular treatment regimes have been tested and shown not to have the effects advertised. The public acceptance of a treatment program can be a result of its ideological attractiveness or of the effectiveness in the media on the part of its proponents (L. B. Silver, 1987). Careful evaluations of treatment claims based on accepted scientific procedures are the way to distinguish actual effectiveness from false claims.

Making the consideration of the acceptability of a procedure difficult are individual differences in response to the same treatment. That there should be individual differences in response to treatment is inevitable and probably is obvious to the reader. It can even happen that, whereas a treatment may be generally ineffective, it can prove to be important for a few children. It is also possible for the same procedure to be helpful for one child and harmful for another. Moreover, a treatment may be ineffective for the child it is directed to, but it may have an important impact on the family of the child (L. B. Silver, 1987).

Assessment of the effectiveness of the treatment therefore comes down to evaluation of a carefully defined procedure with specific behaviors of individual children and their families. As we shall see, procedures are available for doing this. However, adequate procedures are not always applied, and the research literature on treatment effectiveness must be read with care. Studies suffer from inadequate description of procedures and measurement, from small and nonrandom sampling of subjects, from inadequate control conditions, and from failure to test for generalization of effects. Any one of these errors can limit or distort the information, and sometimes no study would be better than an inadequate one. However, it is possible to review a large number of studies. When this is done, the plausibility of using most treatment approaches for at least some children is clear (Skiba & Casey, 1985).

Demonstrating the possibility of using a treatment is one thing. It is another to account for its implementation. There is not much research on treatment implementation. However, it is clear that there are definite preferences by professionals and consumers for some treatment modalities over others. There is a general rejection of restrictive and punitive practices, although in the case of self-injurious and aggressive behaviors, such procedures are accepted as necessary by some. For hyperactive children the use of medication with a combination of behavioral strategies is preferred by both school psychologists and child clinical psychologists, though they differ in their preference for diagnostic procedures. Parents, teachers, and behavior therapists of children with autism differ to some extent with respect to therapy goals for the children (Morgan, 1989; P. P. Rosenberg & Beck, 1986; Runco & Schreibman, 1987).

These similarities and differences in accepting therapeutic strategies may be independent of the demonstrated effectiveness of the procedures. The social roles of the parent or professional in relation to the child, their training and specific experiences, and their philosophies of treatment and views about ethics are all undoubtedly important. Whatever the factors, they need far more study because they are probably as important for implementation of treatments as are demonstrations of effectiveness.

Before proceeding to the treatment procedures themselves, perhaps it would be good to remind the reader that the most desirable treatment is prevention (e.g., Reber, Kazak, & Himmelberg, 1987). Prevention can mean the elimination of a condition before it begins, the reduction of multiple risk factors, or the reduction of an increase of disabilities that can accompany any disorder of development. Programs that accomplish these aims are probably less expensive and are certainly more appropriate than are programs that focus on reducing the maximum expression of a handicapping condition after it has emerged.

Actually, when we are talking about behavioral approaches, the distinction between prevention and treatment is sometimes difficult to make. Arranging environments, scheduling reinforcements, and assuring generalization across situations and time are the general approaches used for any behavioral procedure. Whether they are applied to preventing pathology or reducing existing problems is probably a distinction that is less important.

More significant is the increasing use of formal procedures for the evaluation of the effectiveness of treatment. If a teacher or therapist engages in an educational or treatment procedure, there is an assumption that the treatment will be effective and the effect will be beneficial. There is no assurance that either of these assumptions, effectiveness or benefit, are guaranteed either for the group as a whole or for the individual case.

For one thing, the child may improve without instruction or treatment because of factors in the situation other than the formal treatment. There may be no improvement in a specific child or for a group as a whole despite extended treatment. Under such circumstances, if those people providing treatment believe they are maximally effective, they may be fooling themselves.

To eliminate errors of interpretation like these, teachers often use informal baselines of behavior against which to evaluate the success of what they do. Either they compare what the children were like prior to the treatment program, or they compare the children's posttreatment performance with that of children who have not had the program. This informal approach can be useful, but it is subject to errors in memory on the part of the teacher or inadequate sampling of comparison groups.

More formal assessments of baseline performance before treatment begins and comparisons of one treatment with another are the basic methods used in the scientific evaluation of effectiveness of treatment. These formal methods involve, not only sampling of baseline performance or comparison between groups who have received different types of treatment, but they also require a clear and repeatable description of what actually is done during the treatment. This may involve formal description of the curriculum, the lesson plans, the environment, an outline of the reinforcement schedule, a script for the psychotherapy session, and so forth. Some treatment procedures are more simple to describe than others. There is understandable scepticism about the possibilities of evaluating complex procedures such as psychotherapy. However, evaluation of complex, as well as more simple procedures, have been accomplished.

A particularly important aspect of evaluation is long-term follow-up. Most studies of effectiveness are concerned only with the efficacy of a treatment in the situation and time period in which the treatment is done. However, long-term follow-up is desirable because, even if treatment is effective, it is important to know whether it will be necessary to maintain a level of treatment in other situations over time. Such generalization and follow-up studies are sometimes inconvenient and expensive to do but they have also been accomplished (Andrews & Craig, 1988; S. L. Harris, 1986; Hurford & Webster, 1985).

Equally important, but even less common, are assessments of the harm that a treatment might be causing. Most teachers and psychologists assume that what they are doing is at least innocuous and may be doing some good. Although this is plausible most of the time, there are situations when it may not be true. An obvious example includes some of the punishment procedures that are used to decrease objectionable behaviors.

Clinical Category Effects

The research on psychological treatments is voluminous. One question that we may ask of it is the one that we have been asking throughout this book and which is perhaps most critical here. Does the children's diagnosis make much difference in their treatment, or is treatment independent of category? At this time, this question cannot be answered with assurance because the recent literature has not been concerned with this question. Surprisingly, there are no satisfactory studies in which children in different categories are provided with the same treatment and success evaluated (see Sack, Mason, & Collins, 1987 for a possible exception).

Instead, the efficacy of various treatment procedures is evaluated with more or less specific groups of children. For, instance, with children who are obese, the influences of diet, exercise, and various forms of behavior modification for maintaining diet are assessed. With severely retarded children, there has recently been emphasis on training of specific social skills. With children who are antisocial, training of parents to train their children, family therapy, cognitive problem solving, and community-based interventions seem to have some success, whereas pharmacotherapy, training of specific behaviors, and residential treatment seem less successful (L. H. Epstein & Wing, 1987; Foxx & McMorrow, 1985; Kazdin, 1987; Lovaas, 1987; Spence, 1986; Varni & Banis, 1985).

Several treatment approaches are available, each of which is made up of a number of more specific methods. There may be a tendency to concentrate some approaches with some of the clinical categories. However, because of wide individual differences within diagnostic categories, any one child within a category is a candidate for one or a combination of the treatment approaches.

There are several implications of this overlap of treatment to diagnostic category. First, a simple concept that associates diagnostic category with a specific treatment probably is not valid (at least on the basis of the type of studies that have been done up to now). Second, it means that instead of focusing on diagnostic category, the parent, teacher, or clinician normally concentrates on the needs of a particular child at any moment in time and applies that combination of treatment procedures that seems most appropriate for those needs (Campione, 1989).

Third, the person who delivers treatment needs to be broadly trained to deliver a wide range of procedures, and perhaps as important, must decide which combination of procedures is appropriate for the individual child at any time and place. Fourth, research on treatment needs to focus on the interaction between the specific procedure, the characteristics of the child and the family, and the environment in which they exist.

General category differences in the focus of treatment therefore do seem to exist as predictors of the type of treatment provided. But the same treatment may be used for people in any category, various treatments may be applied to the different individuals within any category, and individual differences in the patterning of treatments are substantial. The focus of the description of treatments therefore will be on the treatment approaches themselves, with the understanding that any approach is potentially of use with any particular child.

General Treatment Approaches

Residential Programming. We begin with procedures that are widely used but are only generally defined. Residential programming and psychotherapy are important aspects of therapeutic intervention. They share important features but also a certain difficulty of definition.

In one sense, placement of a child out of the home can be regarded as a kind of treatment. Much has been written about residential treatment, and we review some of the more recent literature in the next chapter. However, here it is sufficient to say that it is not so much the residential placement itself that is or is not therapeutic. Whatever happens in the program relative to what might happen in the natural home or community school is the determinant of the child's behavior. Thus, although there have been descriptions of therapeutic programs in residential treatment programs, some of these descriptions do not include evaluations of their efficacy (D. P. Harris, Cote, & Vipond, 1987; L. I. Siegel, 1987).

Psychotherapy. Psychotherapy, on the other hand, is a general form of treatment. It has been defined loosely as the systematic use of a human relationship to effect enduring changes in a person's cognition, feelings, and behavior (Strupp, 1986). Defined this very general way, there is no question that psychotherapy can be effective. However, the question has been about what types of psychotherapy are effective and what behaviors are affected. Behavioral therapies seem to be more effective than nonbehavioral approaches such as client-centered and dynamic therapies. However, this difference is only apparent because outcome measures for behavioral therapies are more like behaviors dealt with in therapy than is the case with nonbehavioral therapies.

There are also no important differences between play therapy and non-play therapies, group therapy versus single person therapies, and therapy that treats parents and therapy administered only to children. Overall then, psychotherapy is effective, but there are few general differences in the consequences of various types of therapy (Casey & Berman, 1985).

More important may be the type of behaviors that are treated. As mentioned earlier, there are no adequate studies of relative effectiveness of psychotherapy between children who are assigned to different clinical categories. At first sight, there are differences in the type of measures assessed. Fear and anxiety, cognitive skills, global adjustment, social adjustment, and school achievement are improved, whereas measures of personality and self-concept are affected less. However, this difference may also be due to the fact that those measures that show an improvement are used mainly in behavioral therapies. When this confounding of treatment method with measure used is taken into account, there may be no important difference in the measure taken. In other words, behavioral methods that use assessments similar to the behaviors treated do show a larger effect, and this effect is on certain outcome measures that the behavioral studies focus on. When this confusion between method and measure is sorted out, the conclusion is that effects of all types of psychotherapy are positive, and all measures of children's behaviors are affected. However, if one insists that impact be general, that is, behaviors be different from those treated, the effects of the different psychotherapies are small (Casey & Berman, 1985).

It is not clear whether this is an optimistic or a pessimistic set of results. It is optimistic in that it indicates that psychotherapies can have the generalized and enduring positive influence for which they are intended. It is pessimistic in that they do not always have that influence. Clearly, it is important to try to find out what factors maximize success. At this point in time it looks as though clear definition of the process, focus on general behaviors, and use of generalization procedures are all being pursued in attempts to improve success rates.

Sensorimotor Therapies.   In what follows, we describe concepts and procedures that are used to build desirable behaviors and to reduce undesirable ones. We begin with several groups of studies whose intent it was to ask whether a particular complex procedure can be effective in increasing appropriate behaviors or decreasing inappropriate ones. Then, we focus on studies whose purpose it is to build a complex set of skills that are needed in everyday living.

Some types of therapy focus on sensory and motor procedures for influencing development and behavior (Ottenbacher et al., 1987). Body massage and passive movement of limbs of premature infants in high risk nurseries increases rate of weight gain, increases amount of time awake, and accelerates behavioral development. In older children and adults who are hyperactive, learning disabled, or mentally retarded, vestibular stimulation is widely used by occupational therapists and is believed to be effective. However, the demonstrations of efficacy are controversial because of unexplained contradictory results in the literature and defects in the studies. Vestibular stimulation and the more general sensory integration approach may be effective in promoting development and making behavior more normal, but the scientific basis for it must be described as controversial at this time (Arendt, MacLean, & Baumeister, 1988; L. E. Arnold, D. L. Clark, Sachs, Jakim, & Smithies, 1985; Carte, D. Morrison, Sublett, Uemura, &

Setrakian, 1984; Huff & S. C. Harris, 1987; D. C. Morrison & Sublett, 1986; Pothier & Cheek, 1984; Scafidi et al., 1986).

Another approach that has been taken with a number of clinical groups lately is short sessions of physical exercise. There is no evidence that physical exercise like jogging affects intelligence, adaptive behavior, school achievement, or self-concept as measured on standardized tests. But exercise has at least a short-term beneficial effect on maladaptive behaviors such as talking inappropriately in class or autistic stereotyped behaviors. How these beneficial effects are produced is not understood, but it is known that in order to be effective, the exercise must be vigorous (W. H. Evans, S. S. Evans, Schmid, & Pennypacker, 1985; Jansma & Combs, 1987; Kern, Koegel, & Dunlap, 1984; MacMahon & Gross, 1987; McGimsey & Favell, 1988; Tomporowski & Ellis, 1984).

Other General Approaches.   There are also studies of complex treatment packages that are intended to develop complex practical skills. Many of these have been studies of training of self-help skills in severely and profoundly retarded people. These studies have improved in quality as defined by such factors as report of reliability of measures, use of a design that permits assessment of treatment effects, clarity of description of subjects, sample size, and measures of generalization and follow-up (Konarski & Diorio, 1985).

Other studies have concerned themselves with a wide range of behaviors in various populations. For instance, one study reported training of recreational behavior in mentally retarded children in which maintenance of training was achieved by using a fading procedure. Another evaluated assertiveness training in highly anxious adolescents. It showed specificity of effect in that assertiveness increased and anxiety decreased as a result of training, but mathematics performance was not influenced. Still another study showed that training produced more alternatives in social problem solving in emotionally and behaviorally disturbed children, but it also produced more antisocial responses. These studies show that complex treatments can be, and usually are, effective. However, the effect is not always general or enduring, it does not always influence all desired measures, its effect can sometimes be detrimental, and because the procedure is complex, it is not always possible to tell which aspect of it is producing the effect. This points to the desirability of clear description of behavior treatments, as well as evaluation of specific results and their generality (Amish, Gesten, J. K. Smith, H. B. Clark, & C. Stark, 1988; R. C. Katz & Singh, 1986; Wehr & Kaufman, 1987).

More informative are those studies that compare the effectiveness of more than one treatment procedure. One example is a study of training dating skills that compared three complex treatment procedures. This study showed that two procedures emphasizing problem solving produced increases, whereas one that focused on relaxation and tension reduction produced no increase in social behavior. Another study of anger management training for mentally retarded adults showed an apparent effect of four methods, but no differences between the methods. However, lack of a no-treatment comparison group made it difficult to draw any definite conclusions about the effectiveness of the four methods (B. A. Benson, Rice, & Miranti, 1986; Mueser, Valenti-Hein, & Yarnold, 1987). Treatment procedures that are defined in general terms can therefore have their effects evaluated. It is best to compare a number of treatments in the same study and to determine whether the effects are general and enduring. It is also desirable to be sensitive to the possibility that the treatment may have negative effects.

Besides evaluating general approaches to treatment, it is also possible to define treatments more explicitly. The common feature to all approaches to therapy is, as we have said, the social element. That is, at least two people are involved in the therapeutic relationship. Characterizing the things that they do together that are beneficial and not detrimental to the child with handicaps has been the purpose of much recent research.

Specific Treatments

It is appropriate to evaluate two general classes of events before proceeding to a complex training or behavioral treatment procedure. The first is a medical examination to determine whether a medical procedure might easily correct a specific behavioral disability. As is pointed out later in this chapter, drug intervention may be a powerful determinant of a child's behavior. In some circumstances, it is preferable either alone, or in combination with behavioral treatment to modify behavior in the desired direction.

Another simple approach is to determine whether a relatively simple change in the environment might correct a problem or develop a desired behavior. Research using this natural ecological approach has not been very common recently. However, there have been good examples. One dramatic one has to do with the reduction of rumination. Rumination is the chronic regurgitation, chewing, and swallowing of previously ingested food. It can result in a life-threatening loss of body weight. Medical interventions and punitive behavioral approaches have not been very effective. Instead, one group of studies has shown that encouraging chewing before a meal or feeding a low-calorie diet to satiation are effective in dramatically reducing rumination. Another study has shown that simply withdrawing attention at the time that the rumination occurs can also decrease its occurrence. Therefore, analysis of why a person is doing something and what in the environment is maintaining the behavior seems to be a sensible approach to modifying a specific behavior before more complex and invasive procedures are attempted (M. B. Kelly & Heffner, 1988; Rast, J. M. Johnston, Lubin, & Ellinger-Allen, 1988).

Reinforcement. Once medical and environmental analyses are done there are several procedures available for increasing desired behaviors. The most familiar is to provide positive reinforcement for the desired behavior. Learning is clearly improved with reward compared with nonreward conditions. A wide range of reinforcements are available, including the familiar rewards of food and praise. However, not all children are responsive to food and social rewards, and other classes of reinforcement such as vibration, vestibular stimulation, music, tokens for reward, and daily report cards have been of interest lately. Most significant, it is clear that different children are responsive to specific reinforcers. That is, there are no completely general reinforcers. What is most rewarding must be evaluated for each child separately (Dolliver, A. F. Lewis, & McLaughlin, 1985; Gaughan & Axelrod, 1989; K. Ottenbacher & Altman, 1984; Sandler & McLain, 1987).

A particularly interesting reinforcement procedure is response deprivation. In this procedure, children are deprived of the opportunity to perform an activity in which they ordinarily engage. Then, they are allowed to perform that activity as a reward for increasing performance of the desired activity. If a child normally engages in both math and writing activity, improvement in writing can be achieved simply by reducing opportunity to engage in math and then using the opportunity to do math as a reward for increasing writing performance (Konarski, Crowell, & Duggan, 1985).

Prompts. Not only is reinforcement important, but procedures for presenting the material to be learned can also be specified. Recently, there has been interest in prompts and in related methods of presentation of what is to be learned. Prompts are essentially instructions of what the child should do. These may include words, gestures, pictures, physical guidance, and modeling or demonstration prompts. In the literature on prompts, the instructions and the conditions under which they are given are carefully specified. The system of least prompts in which the child is given the opportunity to make the correct response before the prompt is given is desirable and is generally successful (Doyle, Wolery, Ault, & Gast, 1988; Omizo, W. E. Cubberly, & R. D. Cubberly, 1985).

Time Delay and Errorless Learning. The system of least prompts is similar to time-delay methods and to errorless learning. In time-delay, the system of least prompts is applied for a specific time interval, perhaps for 10 seconds. In errorless learning, the sequence of training is such that the child never fails to make a correct response. All of the procedures have the strength of beginning with a response that the child already knows well and gradually shifting control of that response to conditions that prior to training would not have evoked the desired response. For instance, in one study, young, blind, retarded children who had never reached for objects before were trained to reach and grasp for objects. Another study demonstrated training of spontaneous expressions of affection in echolalic autistic children after first having trained the children to give hugs on request. Then, using a time-delay procedure, the tendency of the children to repeat words was paired with the hug by training so that when a person asked for a hug, the child responded with a hug and the verbal expression of affection (Charlop & Walsh, 1986; Correa, Poulson, & Salzberg, 1984).

Chaining. Still another approach is breaking up the material into smaller sections and teaching each of the smaller pieces until each is mastered. The procedure is called *chaining* if this is done either in a forward or a backward sequence. Although this partial task training can be effective, its effect is not necessarily general, and it sometimes is less effective than teaching the whole task at once (Cipani, 1985; Spooner, 1984).

One can conclude from the literature on procedures for teaching desired behaviors that it is possible to describe such procedures in detail and to evaluate their effectiveness with each individual to which they are applied. This is a real advance over the views that teaching procedures are so complex they cannot be analyzed and because there are individual differences, there is not much point in trying to evaluate the effects of teaching approaches. In fact, an excellent teacher describes procedures used in teaching and evaluates their effects for each child. Similar general principles are also applicable to decreasing undesirable behaviors.

Reducing Undesirable Behaviors. It is important to note that whereas it is often possible, and even easy, to decrease undesirable behaviors with a variety of means, it is rarely possible to eliminate them completely. As indicated earlier, prevention is probably a more efficient strategy in the long run than is treatment for an undesirable behavior that has been practiced for months or even years. However, prevention is not yet a well worked out approach, so most research has to do with reducing behaviors that are already a part of the child's everyday life.

Ideally, one can reduce undesirable behaviors by determining which factors maintain them and by eliminating those factors. There has been relatively little research that focuses on natural reinforcements that maintain undesirable behavior. One example is the *sensory extinction* procedure used with autistic children who manipulate objects in the same way for months or even years. These stereotyped behaviors are maintained by specific feedback from the behaviors themselves. By masking the feedback, one can sometimes eliminate the stereotyped behaviors completely. However, sensory extinction does not have wide application for two main reasons. First, the natural reinforcers may be difficult to assess, and, second, even if it is possible to determine what the natural reinforcers are, it may not be possible to control them (Aiken & Salzberg, 1984).

These objections also apply to another promising approach. This one has to do with schedules of reinforcement. It is possible that the amount of stereotypic behavior or of hyperactivity that a person engages in is adjunctive to the rate of reinforcement for other behaviors. As an instance, the amount of abnormal stereotyped behavior has an inverse relationship to how often a person is rewarded for engaging in an adaptive behavior. Frequent reinforcement produces a lower rate of abnormal stereotyped behaviors. The results are less clear with hyperactivity, and this issue needs more study (Prior, Wallace, & Milton, 1984; Wieseler, Hanson, Chamberlain, & T. Thompson, 1988).

Better established is the principle that other activities can compete with undesirable behaviors. There are dozens of studies showing that undesirable behaviors will decrease when the child engages in another behavior. This principle applies to behaviors that are incompatible or even just different from the undesired behavior. Examples are presenting sensory stimulation to reduce self-injurious behaviors and aberrant vocalizations, training polite behavior to reduce behavior problems in the classroom, and providing environments that promote interpersonal contact to reduce autistic behaviors (E. G. Carr & Durand, 1985; Dadds, Schwartz, Adams, & Rose, 1988; Gunter et al., 1984; C. R. Taylor & Chamove, 1986).

When targeted undesired behaviors are reduced, it often happens that other undesired behaviors appear in their place. This is sometimes used as an argument against reducing the targeted behavior. However, it is possible to apply treatment until all of the undesired behaviors have been reduced to a satisfactory level. It is true also that unexpected positive behaviors, like play, also emerge. This emphasizes the importance of a focused and continuing treatment regime (Fellner, LaRoche, & Sulzer-Azaroff, 1984).

Aversive Approaches. Building alternative behaviors is generally regarded as the first thing to try when attempting to reduce undesirable behaviors. However, these positive procedures do not work with all children, and sometimes they are not effective at all. People who have responsibility for care of children then often turn to punishment as a way of solving their problem. Aversive or punitive procedures are very common in modern society. In the past they have been sanctioned for the management of various levels of misbehavior. Now, however, there is much controversy over the use of aversive procedures by professional psychologists (e.g., Butterfield, 1990), and the approval of punishment procedures has become tightly limited in law, if not always in practice (Egelston, Sluyter, Murie, & Hobbs, 1984; G. S. Singer & Irvin, 1987).

In this discussion, we are not concerned so much with the use of punishment for minor problems. One solution for them is greater tolerance for minor deviations. Behaviors such as whining do not require intrusive punishment. When a change in the child's behavior is necessary, it is likely that attention to causes of the problem and application of some of the principles we have already discussed will solve the problem.

However, there are serious behavioral problems, like aggression or self-injurious behaviors of severely disabled children, that are dangerous to others or threaten the health of the child who engages in the behaviors. This is where the current controversies about the use of punishment procedures have been focused. The discussion can be heated. There has been much discussion about the ethics of using such procedures. Ethical issues generally cannot be resolved with scientific procedures. However, scientific studies can inform ethical issues and perhaps help in their resolution.

Two central scientific issues dominate the controversies about aversive procedures. The first has to do with relative acceptability of different treatments, the second deals with treatment effectiveness. In one group of studies, staff members of community programs rated more restrictive procedures as less favorable, but severity of the problem was also a factor making aversive procedures more acceptable (Miltenberger, Lennox, & Erfanian, 1989; see also Morgan, 1989 and Tarnowski, Rasnake, Mulick, & Kelly, 1989). In another study, special educators were asked to rate 18 approaches to treatment with respect to efficacy, acceptability, intrusiveness, and restrictiveness. When a treatment was rated as intrusive, it was also regarded as restrictive. Perhaps more important, treatments that were rated as efficacious were also regarded as acceptable. This relationship between effectiveness and acceptability is a general finding in the literature. There is less agreement about which treatments are effective, and there is also a difference between parent and child ratings about relative acceptability of different procedures (Irvin & Lundervold, 1988; Kazdin, 1984).

Thus, the judgment about acceptability of a treatment procedure seems to be related to the answer to the second issue. That is, what in fact are the consequences of different aversive treatment procedures? What are their benefits, and what are their negative side effects? In considering the studies of efficacy of aversive treatments, the reader should note that many of the studies are poorly conducted. Many of them use just one or two subjects, and they often fail to provide adequate baseline controls (Lundervold & Bourland, 1988). As might be expected from the previous discussion about treatments, results of studies of treatment effects can be highly individual. For one thing, not all procedures are studied to the same degree. Less intrusive procedures, such as social disapproval and increasing response cost, are evaluated more frequently than are more intrusive and restrictive procedures like time-out and corporal punishment.

Moreover, not all treatments are used for the same problems. Intrusive treatments are not ordinarily used for managing social behavior, although they are common with stereotyped and self-injurious behaviors. In addition to variation in the use of the large number of procedures that are available, different procedures are effective for different problems. Time-out seems to be effective for aggression and disruption/destruction, although these procedures are ineffective for self-injurious and stereotyped behaviors (Lennox, Miltenberger, Spengler, & Erfanian, 1988).

There is no reason that only one intrusive aversive procedure need be used. Aversive procedures can be weaker and still effective if several are used. Sometimes weaker aversive procedures can be more effective, as when a brief reprimand is more effective than a long one. Perhaps more commonly, reinforcement for positive behaviors is combined with an aversive procedure to provide an effective treatment regime (Abramowitz, O'Leary, & Futtersak, 1988; Charlop, Burgio, Iwata, & Ivancic, 1988).

In summary, then, aversive procedures are used with severe disorders when other procedures have not been effective. Certain ethical issues cannot be dealt with in the scientific literature, but the facts can inform the discussion of ethical issues. Acceptability of aversive procedures is related to their perceived effectiveness in reducing undesired behaviors. Design of most of the research on effectiveness of aversive procedures suffers from poor control and limited sampling. Nevertheless, it appears that at least some aversive procedures can be effective, though different procedures are used with different problems and in different combinations with each other.

Self-Instruction.   In the treatment methods that have been described up to now, emphasis has been placed on the parent, teacher, or therapist applying some program for changing the child's behavior. An important theme of research in the last 10 years also includes examination of treatments that foster the abilities that children have for organizing the material to be learned. Ultimately, the child must master the strategies necessary for adaptive behavior if behavior change is to generalize to a number of situations and if it is to endure. Procedures for doing this include approaches to increase the cognitive skills that we have covered in previous chapters, for example, strategies for learning specific skills, metacognitive skills for relating strategies to the goals of the class, and self-efficacy training. In particular, they emphasize those strategies that permit the child to participate as fully as possible in learning.

There have been many demonstrations that treatment packages incorporating self-instruction are effective in changing behavior. Work productivity can be increased and disruptive behavior can be reduced with such packages (C. L. Cole, Gardner, & Karan, 1985; McNally, Kompik, & G. Sherman, 1984).

There are fewer comparisons of self-instruction with other approaches. Those that exist suggest that self-instruction is effective, but is not necessarily superior to other methods. To some extent, this is due to the fact that self-control and other behavioral procedures have common elements. For instance, in one study of therapy for depression in children, both a self-control and a behavioral problem-solving therapy were more successful than a control condition, but both involved self-monitoring of behavior (Bowers, Clement, Fantuzzo, & Sorensen, 1985; Graham & Freeman, 1985; K. D. Stark, W. M. Reynolds, & Kaslow, 1987).

Therefore, insofar as possible, it is worthwhile to specify the components of each treatment procedure. Self-monitoring and various forms of self-instruction are two techniques that have been used successfully. In self-monitoring, a person records the instances of behaviors that the teacher has specified. Undesirable behaviors, like emotional outbursts or instances of inattention, or desirable behaviors, such as on-task behaviors, may be recorded. Recording may be prompted by the teacher, a peer, or the children themselves, and recording may be reinforced with a token system. When these things are done the specified behavior change ordinarily occurs as a consequence (Christie, Hiss, & Lozanoff, 1984; McLaughlin, Krappman, & Welsh, 1985; Reese, J. A. Sherman, & Sheldon, 1984; Snider, 1987).

Self-instruction programs teach children to ask themselves relevant questions that may help them to learn important things. To aid comprehension of written material, children with a learning disability may be taught to ask "WH" questions, that is, who, what, where, when, and why? To reduce inappropriate anger, children may be taught to ask themselves questions and give themselves instructions like, "What is the problem?", "Focus in," and "What is my answer?" (F. L. Clark, Deshler, Schumaker, Alley, & Warner, 1984; Lochman & Curry, 1986).

Self-instruction procedures can have a positive effect on the behaviors they were intended to improve. However, there are also factors that can moderate their influence. Perhaps the most obvious is the developmental level of the child. Self-monitoring, self-reinforcing, and self-instructional procedures do not work with children who are not ready for them. They are not necessary with children who are mature enough so that these behavioral patterns are already functioning. It is only with children who can learn to self-instruct but who have not yet done so that these procedures can be most effective (T. L. Whitman, 1987).

At least as important, attribution of success and failure by any particular child can be taken into account in the training. When the negative attributions are countered in the training of children with learning disabilities, strategy utilization and self-instruction are made more effective (M. K. Reid & Borkowski, 1987).

MEDICAL TREATMENTS

The principles of medical treatment are the same for children with handicaps as they are for any person. Consequently, this is not a treatise on medicine and only those aspects of medical treatment specifically related to the behavior of children with handicaps is of interest here. These treatments, which include surgery, dietary management, and especially behavior management with pharmacological agents, are used together with behavioral procedures or when interpersonal procedures are not believed to be indicated or have proven ineffective.

This can happen under a number of circumstances. Perhaps there are no known educational or psychological approaches that take care of the child's problem. More commonly, interpersonal approaches are available and they do help, but they may not be completely effective. Then, it becomes reasonable to consider a medical approach to supplement the educational program. However, there are also times when effective educational and behavioral treatments are available but parents, teachers, or staff members are not aware of them or are unwilling to use them. When that occurs, medical procedures may be used unnecessarily in place of interpersonal treatments.

Predicting degree of cooperation with long-term medical treatment, providing cosmetic facial surgery to increase social acceptance, and modifying diet to normalize behavior are all areas in which some of research has been done recently. However, the interest in these areas is minor, compared with an intense interest in certain aspects of psychopharmacology.

Analysis of the effect of pharmacological agents on problem behaviors has been very active lately and has been accomplished at two levels. The first has to do with deciding the relative effectiveness of behavioral treatments versus pharmacological treatment in the management of behavior. The second level of research assesses the effectiveness of various agents on specific behaviors. Most of the research on treatment effectiveness has focused on the action of methylphenidate with ADD-hyperactivity or on various psychotropic drugs in controlling self-injurious behaviors of autistic and severely retarded children and adults.

Cooperation with Medical Procedures

The issue of cooperation or compliance with medical treatment is always significant but is especially important in life-threatening disorders. The lives of children with cystic fibrosis can be prolonged significantly with appropriate administration of antibiotics and nutritional supports. Although most children and their families follow the medical procedures, about 20% to 30% do not. More adolescents than would be expected by chance avoid complying so that age is one predictor of noncompliance. However, there is also variability within age classes. Compliance can be predicted by a scale that has the child respond to stories about compliance with medical procedures. Thus, by taking both age and responses on the scale into consideration, counseling resources for promoting compliance can be made more responsive (Czajkowski & Koocher, 1987).

Cosmetic Surgery

Plastic surgery of the face and tongue has recently been developed for children with Down syndrome to foster social acceptance and to help correct breathing problems, drooling, and speech defects. Initial impressions suggested that this approach would be helpful. Studies using more adequate controls showed that the main benefit has been on the perception by parents that there has been an improvement. However, there are physical, emotional, and social risks to the surgery that must be balanced with this benefit (S. Katz & Kravetz, 1989; May, 1988; C. L. Parsons, Iacono, & Rozner, 1987).

Nutrition

Despite its obvious importance, research on nutrition and its relation to behavior is scarce and confusing. There is some reason to believe that severely disabled individuals in institutions suffer from deficiencies in riboflavin and folic acid. The causes of these deficiencies are only suspected and their consequences on behavior unknown. Although children with autism are thought to have deficient diets, the evidence for this is not strong. Some autistic children do have peculiar dietary preferences, but their dietary intakes are apparently balanced and complete, perhaps because their parents believe that diet is important (H. S. Cole, Lopez, Epel, Singh, & Cooperman, 1985; Raiten & Massaro, 1986).

Megavitamin therapies and food-additive free diets have been controversial in the popular press, and they have received extensive evaluation. These therapies have no general effect on learning ability, hyperactivity, attention, or behavior disorders. It is possible that the effect on a few children is beneficial. However, in evaluating such individual effects, a considerable placebo effect must be taken into account (Aman, Mitchell, & Turbott, 1987;

Menaloscino, Donaldson, Gallagher, Golden, & J. E. Wilson, 1988; Wender, 1986).

Facial surgery and dietary studies emphasize that initial enthusiasms about the efficacy of a treatment sometimes are moderated when the treatment is examined with adequate sampling and appropriate controls. The scientific examination of treatment procedures takes time and financial resources, and the inevitable delays and costs may be seen as unnecessary obstacles to the amelioration of what are often desperate situations. However, as these two instances show, procedures that seem to a clinician or parent to be effective may after all merely represent a placebo effect or may be harmful. The resolution of this dilemma comes from the speedy evaluation of new procedures, using well-accepted scientific procedures.

Psychopharmacology

Most research on medical approaches to behavior of children with handicaps has been on the use and effectiveness of pharmacological agents in behavioral management. Various psychotropic agents are used widely in schools and institutions, most importantly for management of hyperactivity, aggression, and self-injurious behavior. Although pharmacological treatment is widespread, it is ordinarily prescribed empirically, that is, without a clear understanding of how the treatment is working and sometimes whether it is working at all. Satisfactory research is available only for the use of methylphenidate on hyperactivity, and even there the picture of the action of the drug is not yet clear. Sometimes published information is available, but the information is defective because of problems in research design (Aman & Singh, 1986; Forness & K. A. Kavale, 1988; Werry, 1988; Zametkin & Rapoport, 1987).

Some of the older research pitted behavioral against pharmacological approaches, asking whether one is more effective than the other. This competitive attitude is still evident in some recent studies. Perhaps a more productive idea is the proper combination of an effective interpersonal treatment with an appropriate pharmacological regime to produce more beneficial effects than either can alone. However, this idea has yet to be investigated fully (Aman & Singh, 1986; Schalock, Foley, Toulouse, & J. A. Stark, 1985).

Several general factors may influence drug effects. Of course, individual differences in response to treatment are as obvious here as they are for interpersonal treatments. In addition, drug effects may be different in different situations. Changes evident in the laboratory, for instance, may or may not be apparent in the classroom. Third, dose effects are obvious. Perhaps it is less obvious that the maximal effect of a drug can be different for different response classes, for example, dose-response curves are different for learning than for social behavior (Werry, 1988).

What follows is a consideration of patterns of use of pharmacological treatment in different populations, mainly mentally retarded people. Then, recent research on some of the major drugs is considered. The use of particular pharmacological agents changes with time. Therefore, the main point here deals not so much with the effectiveness of particular drug classes, but with the more general considerations of what procedures are typically used to evaluate drugs, what behaviors have been altered, and the interactions of pharmacological with interpersonal treatments (L. C. Sheppard, Ballinger, & Fenton, 1987).

Drug Usage. Statistical descriptions of drug use have definitely focused on drug treatment of people with mental retardation. These descriptions reveal that a greater proportion of mentally retarded people in institutions than in community placements receive psychotropic medication and, within the community, more restrictive settings are associated with greater use of medication. Depending on other factors, between one-third and two-thirds of people in these programs receive psychotropic medication, in addition to other forms of medication such as anticonvulsants.

This high level of medication may be due to the fact that the people in restrictive environments actually need more psychotropic medication. But it is also possible that a significant amount of medication is prescribed inappropriately and/or that medication is used as an unnecessary form of behavior control in institutions or institutionlike living environments. At this time the studies are not adequate to decide whether either or both of these possibilities hold (Aman, C. J. Field, & Bridgman, 1985; Bates, Smeltzer, & Arnoczky, 1986; Huessy & Ruoff, 1984; J. E. Martin & Agran, 1985).

Within the population of people who are mentally retarded, individual differences are correlated with use of medication. Psychotropic drugs are prescribed for young adults more than for children or elderly people, medication is more common in more severely retarded people, and high use rates are more common with some clinical subgroups (Fischbacher, 1987; Jacobson, 1988).

Less well studied are comparisons between mentally retarded people and other groups. One project compared mildly retarded, learning-disabled, and seriously emotionally disturbed school children. Overall, learning-disabled children received less medication than either mentally retarded or emotionally disturbed children, although learning-disabled children received more stimulants for hyperactivity and fewer anticonvulsants than did the retarded children (Cullinan, Gadow, & M. H. Epstein, 1987).

Methylphenidate. The drug that has been studied most completely is methylphenidate (Ritalin). This agent and other stimulants have been used widely with children, mainly those with attention deficit disorder with hyperactivity. This wide use is a reflection of the demonstrated effectiveness of this drug and other stimulants on many children with ADD-H. The reliability of the effect of methylphenidate has stimulated more in-depth study of this drug than of any other psychotropic pharmaceutical agent used with children. Many of these studies are well-designed, employing adequate sampling and appropriate controls, including double-blind procedures (Henker & Whalen, 1989).

Although many of the studies are satisfactory, most of them are assessments of the action of short-term administration of methylphenidate. Long-term studies are afflicted with problems of attrition of subjects and the cost of doing such studies, and there are not many of them. Those that exist indicate that methylphenidate continues to be effective over a period of more than a year for some clinically significant measures, at least for those children who respond to the drug in the first place (Safer & Allen, 1989). Moreover, effectiveness is limited to the time that methylphenidate is actually being administered, that is, there have been no demonstrated effects that endure after methylphenidate is withdrawn. The literature on the effectiveness in adulthood is mixed (R. T. Brown, Borden, Wynne, Schleser, & Clingerman, 1986; Gauthier, 1984; Hechtman, G. Weiss, & Perlman, 1984; McBride, 1988).

The effects of methylphenidate depend on the individual child, the dose level, and the behavioral measure used to assess effectiveness. Situational factors and premedication behavioral levels may also be important, but have not been studied enough to characterize. The question is not so much whether methylphenidate works, but with whom and under what conditions the drug is effective.

Earlier studies suggested that as many as 40% of ADD-H children do not respond to methylphenidate. However, this conclusion was based on using only one dependent measure as the test of effectiveness. If a battery of measures is used, 80% to 100% of ADD-H children respond favorably on at least some measures. Why one child responds favorably on one measure and a second child responds favorably on another measure is not known and has actually not been considered (Barkley, Fischer, Newby, & Breen, 1988; Douglas, Barr, Amin, O'Neill, & Britton, 1988).

In general, effectiveness increases with amount of methylphenidate given until side effects are encountered. The exact dose-effectiveness relationship probably also varies with the behavior studied, although there is controversy about whether maximum effectiveness is the same or different for different behaviors. Clearly, studies are needed that look systematically at dose–effect curves for different behaviors over the full safe range of methylphenidate. Such studies are being done (Douglas et al., 1988; Pelham, Bender, Caddell, Booth, & Moorer, 1985; Rapport, Stoner, DuPaul, Birmingham, & Tucker, 1985).

Methylphenidate is rarely used alone. Ordinarily it is given to a child who is attending school and who may be involved in some interpersonal therapy. There have been some studies that compare the effectiveness of methylphenidate with interpersonal procedures of various kinds or ask whether the effect of this drug plus a behavioral treatment is better than either alone. In general, these studies suffer from design problems, such as ceiling effects, small samples, or behavioral approaches that may not adequately take into account the child's developmental level. It is not surprising therefore that the results from these studies are mixed (see Hinshaw, Henker, & Whalen, 1984 for an exception).

More promising are studies of the specific behaviors affected by methylphenidate. First of all, whereas the case is weak for an important effect of this agent on scores on intelligence tests, methylphenidate does reduce hyperactivity, off-task behaviors, and disruptive behavior, and it increases compliance, information processing, learning, and academic performance (Douglas, Barr, O'Neill, & Britton, 1986; Malone, Kershner, & L. Siegel, 1988; M. K. Reid & Borkowski, 1984; Vyse & Rapport, 1989).

This improvement in behavior occurs more in structured situations than free-play situations, and it applies to interactions with both adults and other children. There is no indication that methylphenidate affects certain social behavior in informal situations, that is, by increasing approaches to others or producing social withdrawal (Barkley, 1988; C. E. Cunningham, L. S. Siegel, & Offord, 1985; Wallander, Schroeder, Michelli, & Gualtieri, 1987; Whalen et al., 1987).

Methylphenidate is an effective drug with known behavioral consequences. If used below toxic levels with children who clearly have attention deficit disorder with hyperactivity, beneficial effects are demonstrable. There are not enough studies to determine whether beneficial effects are also seen in other groups. Also, one must remember that the focusing of attention that comes with methylphenidate can be overdone, with the result that the child's perception can become limited in scope and thinking becomes rigid.

Other Psychotropic Drugs.   Although the situation is quite satisfactory with methylphenidate, the situation is not at all satisfactory with other psychotropic drugs (anticonvulsants are not reviewed here). Despite the fact that a large number of psychotropic drugs are used widely, none has such clear beneficial effects as methylphenidate.

Two problems are evident. Most commonly, initial enthusiasm and widespread acceptance of an agent may be unwarranted because later tests of effectiveness do not confirm the earlier clinical findings. A case in point is the recent use of fenfluramine to diminish the symptoms of autism and autistic-like symptoms in other populations. Although early reports of the use of fenfluramine were promising, tests done in the mid-1980s produced conflicting evidence. As these studies improved in design, the picture of the effect became more controversial. For instance, it appears now that at best, a small proportion of children with autism respond favorably to fenfluramine. These studies also exemplify the second problem: Behavioral (and of course physical) toxic effects may accompany the administration of any drug. In the case of fenfluramine, discrimination learning may decline.

Administration of neuroleptics is only variably effective and can produce motor abnormalities (Aman, Teehan, A. J. White, Turbott, & Vaithianathan, 1989; R. Perry et al., 1989). Some tranquilizers not only reduce abnormal behaviors, but may also reduce desirable ones like social interaction. In short, assessment of drug effectiveness appropriately includes, not only the target behavior, but also other potential problems that might emerge (Altmeyer et al., 1987; M. Campbell, 1988; R. K. Stone, Alvarez, & May, 1988; Verglas, Banks, & Guyer, 1988).

At this time there are several lines of investigation that seem promising. One of these is an effort to determine which individual factors may predict the development of motor abnormalities in people receiving antipsychotic drugs. Another is the focus on drug management of self-injurious behavior.

The treatment of life-threatening, self-injurious behaviors such as head-hitting or self-biting seems to have no general solution at this time. One ingenious theory about them holds that the pain resulting from self-injurious behaviors may release brain opiates, which, in turn, maintain the behaviors. According to this idea, administration of nalaxone (or Naltrexone), an opiate antagonist, might break this circle and result in the reduction of self-injurious behaviors. At this time the tests of this theory are mixed, but the idea is worth following up (J. M. Rao, Cowie, & Mathew, 1987; Sandman, Barron, & Colman, 1990; Szymanski, Kedesdy, Sulkes, Cutler, & Stevens-Our, 1987).

There is yet another promising possibility: Piracetam may increase information processing for words in dyslexic children. This has already been demonstrated in studies of reading verbal learning and evoked brain responses. However, further examination is needed. There are also studies of the effectiveness of the agents used for treating depression on depressive mood disorders of children. These are important because, as we saw with methylphenidate, agents that are effective with adults may not always have similar effects in children (C. K. Conners et al., 1987; DeLong & Aldershof, 1987; Rudel & Helfgott, 1984).

SUMMARY

Research on treatment for children with handicaps involves more than the analysis of individual procedures. Treatment begins with the person providing the care and treatment, that is, a parent, a professional, or a caregiver.

The attitudes of these people is a crucial feature of the overall treatment plan.

Treatment is done in the context of the general development of the child. Follow-up studies have shown that, no matter what the specific disability, adaptive difficulties are part of the life of disabled children, if the disability is significant in the first place. The predictors of disabilities typically are complex interactions of individual, family, and experiential factors.

To some extent the cumulative deficit that accompanies disabilities can be reduced with early intervention programs that usually are a combination of center-based and home-based education. Such programs are not very well defined at this time. Treatment programs throughout the school years can be general or specific. Greater specification of these programs is desirable, and study designs that contrast treatments are desirable but not yet common. Nevertheless, behavioral treatments tend to be effective at least for some children, and individual response is characteristic. This implies that teachers and therapists should have at their disposal a range of procedures that they can apply in the individual case.

Reliable behavioral procedures for increasing desirable behaviors are available. They are based on a great number of positive reinforcement and scheduling methods. Procedures for reducing undesirable behaviors are controversial. In general, aversive methods are avoided unless the undesirable behavior is health threatening and the procedure has been demonstrated as clearly effective.

There are few studies of medical procedures for behavioral treatment. The one big exception is psychopharmacology, especially the demonstration that methylphenidate reduces hyperactivity. However, all drugs have the potential for side effects and even the successful ones can have complex effects. In general, a combination of appropriate drug administration with sophisticated behavioral procedures is the preferred approach.

11 _____

Life in Adulthood

Up to now, we have reviewed the factors that influence the adaptation of children with handicaps while they are growing up. Now, we consider what happens to them as adults. First, longitudinal studies are considered. These studies show that several factors predict whether a child with handicaps adapts successfully as an adult. Then, we consider what living as an adult is like for severely disabled adults and review the factors that determine the quality of adult life in the community. In the past, much of the literature was concerned with residential programs, perhaps because where one sleeps and eats are basic to life. However, in the last 10 years, increasing recognition of how one spends one's day has been apparent in studies of adaptation to work. New programs for supporting adults with handicaps in competitive employment have been the main focus of this new research. A description of these active work programs concludes the chapter and this book.

FOLLOW-UP STUDIES

One might expect that the difficulties that can occur in childhood would signify further difficulties in adulthood. Although this is sometimes true, it is not universal. Variability is once again the central idea in considering outcome of handicaps in children, as it has been with most of the topics considered up to now (Baker & Cantwell, 1987b). Many children with handicaps grow up to be adults who have no special adjustment problems. As many as 75% of mentally retarded children grow up to have jobs and families and require no special services (A. M. Clarke & A. D. B. Clarke, 1988). Two thirds of children with learning disabilities have plans to continue their education beyond secondary school and many can be expected to succeed if colleges provide them with diagnostic and instructional support services (Dalke & Schmitt, 1987).

If a correlation does exist between handicaps in childhood and difficulties of adjustment in adulthood, how are we to interpret the correlation? Does the same problem continue over time? Are the problems clearly different in nature, but the childhood disorder causes the adult problem? Or are both the childhood disorder and the adult problem simply indicated by a third factor that is not itself pathological but is a sign of pathology and produces the correlation?

A reading problem that continues into adulthood and interferes with adaptation both in school and at work would be an example of a problem continuing over time. Early deprivation of nurturance that produces unhappiness in childhood and antisocial behavior in adulthood might be an example of different, but related problems in childhood and adulthood. In this case, one might say that the early deprivation caused the adult antisocial behavior, perhaps mediated by the unhappiness of childhood (see S. A. Richardson, Koller, & M. Katz, 1985). Finally, school failure and difficulty in maintaining a job may not be the heart of the pathological condition, but they can be indicators that something is wrong. Analyzing the nature of correlations and the reason for them seems to be a task for the future. Doing so is particularly important, not only to clarify the nature of the relation between handicaps in childhood and later adjustment, but also perhaps to prevent childhood disorders from continuing into adulthood.

To accomplish these analyses, refinements in method and interpretation are necessary. Prospective longitudinal research, rather than retrospective studies, certainly is indicated. Retrospective studies are less expensive than following the same children into adulthood. But sampling problems and potential bias are a problem of retrospective studies, and retrospective studies do not allow the detailed analysis of the child's actual life history that longitudinal studies permit.

The use of adequate comparison groups should be more common than it has been recently. Comparisons with well-matched normal groups or with other groups of children with handicaps allow more meaningful interpretations of adult outcome rates than are possible with a follow-up of only a single group of children with handicaps (e.g., Parham, S. Reid, & Hamer, 1987).

A look at multiple predictors characterizes recent research in this area. Most studies begin with a follow-up of children who have been identified as representing specific clinical classifications such as dyslexia or hyperactivity. Because this is so, the review of studies is organized according to clinical classification. However, within these studies, it has been found that other variables like general intelligence, antisocial behavior, social acceptance, and financial support are significant predictors of outcome in adulthood. These other variables have also been the main predictors in studies not restricted to a single clinical classification. This means that prediction of adult outcome must take into consideration, not only clinical classification, but perhaps even more importantly, other variables.

To complicate the situation even further, the measures in adulthood are often different in the various published studies. Work success, marital adjustment, criminal behavior, and referrals for psychotherapy are only some of the things that have been used to define adjustment in adulthood. These variables are not necessarily defined in similar ways across studies, and they may not be correlated with one another, so the picture from all of these studies is not necessarily coherent.

Finally, in different studies, the same variable may sometimes be a predictor variable and sometimes a measure of later adjustment. Thus, school dropout has been used as a predictor in some studies and as a measure of adult adjustment in others.

In summary, the recent research on correlates of adjustment of adults who were handicapped when they were children goes well beyond the simple statement that some of these children have later difficulties. The specificity of the questions asked and the multiplicity of the variables used for prediction and for measurement of adjustment have resulted in a reasonably explicit picture of the nature of the correlates.

General Predictors

Severity. The most important variable predicting whether a child will have difficulties in adulthood is the severity of the child's adaptive problem. Severe disabilities such as severe mental retardation, childhood autism, or profound deafness continue to afflict the person as an adult, whereas mild or transient learning or behavioral disorders may have few implications for later life (S. A. Richardson, Koller, M. Katz, & McLaren, 1984).

As manifestations of severity, general factors such as cognitive problems or antisocial behavior can predict problems in adulthood (Kohlberg, Ricks, & Snarey, 1984). General intelligence predicts subsequent achievement, at least to some extent. Chronic behavior problems that are not typical for the child's chronological age can also be a sign of later difficulties, although many individual children with behavior disorders do not show them later on (Mulvey & LaRosa, 1986). Some variables that might seem plausibly to be connected with later adjustment (e.g., shyness) have turned out not to be significant predictors (J. G. Parker & Asher, 1987).

Environment. Variations in the environment of adults also are important. Studies of the work adaptation of adults who were educated in special classes have shown generally that 50% to 70% are employed, but that their employment is often in part-time and lower paying jobs. Mildly retarded individuals are somewhat less successful than are learning-disabled or behaviorally disturbed children, which confirms the predictive role of severity (Edgar, 1987; Hasazi, L. R. Gordon, & Roe, 1985).

The importance of employment is highlighted in a follow-up of children who left school early. This study showed that those children who ultimately found jobs and were working reported a greater subjective sense of well-being than did those children who remained unemployed (A. Donovan, Oddy, Pardoe, & Ades, 1986). This means that not only child characteristics, but also adult environments are important determinants of adult adaptation.

Developmental Factors. The intricacy of developmental factors that determine adult adjustment is demonstrated in an exemplary study of women who had been reared in residential children's homes. This group of women was compared with a well-matched group of women who had been reared in the homes of their natural families. This study revealed that the adult adjustment of the institution-reared women was substantially worse than that of the women reared in their families. Despite this difference, many of the institution-reared women were well adjusted. The central question of the study involved analyzing which factors made for the good adjustment of those women who had had an unfavorable early rearing history. Systematic checking of several hypotheses showed that disruptive early parenting was correlated with poor outcome, and favorable experiences in school and being married to a nondeviant spouse were factors that correlated with better adjustment in adulthood. That is, individual factors, early rearing, school experiences and adult environments all were correlated with adult adaptation (Rutter & Quinton, 1984).

Classification

Dyslexia. We turn now to a further delineation of predictive factors, first with a consideration of follow-up studies of children with dyslexia. These studies found that children who have difficulty with reading in the school years generally also have reading difficulties as adults, and this is true not only in terms of general reading scores, but also is characteristic of particular aspects of reading such as word recognition and phonic analysis (Scarborough, 1984).

Despite the continuing problem with reading, children with dyslexia enter and complete college at a high rate. It takes many of them somewhat longer to complete a college program, and they tend to major in business rather than in professional or technical programs. Their academic major predicts their vocational choice because a greater proportion than average find their way into managerial and sales jobs rather than professional or technical positions (Finucci, Gottfredson, & Childs, 1985).

Children with reading problems sometimes also have behavior disorders. When they do, the behavior disorders are associated with early school leaving, indications of unstable work records, and depressed job skill levels. However, because these same factors are characteristic of normal readers with behavior disorders in early adulthood, these problems cannot be attributed to the association of dyslexia with behavior disorders. This result demonstrates the importance of including appropriate comparison groups in follow-up studies in this area (Maughan, Gray, & Rutter, 1985).

Learning Disabilities. There have been several follow-up studies of children with the broader classification of learning disabilities (e.g., Rogan & Hartman, 1990). One study compared women who had been learning disabled when they were children with their normal sisters. As adults, a large percentage of both groups were employed and were also married. They were equally successful in their occupation in that about half were in professional or technical jobs. There was no difference between the groups in their self-esteem or their feelings of mastery of their environment.

There were differences between the learning-disabled women and their sisters with respect to the type of employment they had chosen. The learning-disabled group chose education and human services, whereas their sisters chose science, mathematics, and writing. They also differed in that the learning-disabled women remembered their education as being more difficult and less enjoyable. In fact, however, there was little evidence that the nature of their education influenced their ultimate success (N. C. Goodman, 1987).

These results come, perhaps, from the fact that the samples were drawn from families from higher socioeconomic status (SES) levels. One study has shown that SES is a major predictor of occupational outcome of adults who were learning disabled as children (S. C. O'Connor & Spreen, 1988). It is apparently second only to IQ in its power. Intelligence, severity of learning disability, and perhaps presence of neurological disorder are also predictors. At this time, treatment does not influence outcome very strongly. In any case, all of these prediction studies of children with learning disabilities are merely statistical. That is, they do not predict the individual case very well, because taken together, the predictors do not account for more than 50% of the variability in the outcome scores (Spreen, 1988).

Attention Deficit Disorder. The importance of considering several factors besides diagnostic classification is also apparent in follow-up studies of children who were rated as hyperactive when they were in school. Several studies have shown that young adults who were rated as hyperactive or ADD-H as children were at significant risk for impulsive behavior, antisocial acts, and substance abuse. Moreover, the degree of risk is related to the severity of the original symptoms. Children rated as mildly hyperactive showed none of these problems in adulthood, whereas those rated as severely hyperactive did have them (Gittelman, Mannuzza, Shenker, & Bonagura, 1985; Greenfield, Hechtman, & G. Weiss, 1988; Klinteberg, Magnusson, & Schalling, 1989; Mannuzza, Klein, Bonagura, Konig, & Shenker, 1988).

However, this relatively simple picture is made more complex when the IQ of the children and adults is considered. In some studies, intelligence of the ADD-H children is slightly lower than that of the normal comparison group. In one study, when adequate account of the IQ difference and a drinking problem of the child's father were taken into account, a difference between the groups in their record of arrests was eliminated. This means that, simply stated, ADD-H children are at risk for later social problems and the risk may be a consequence of other factors besides their hyperactivity. It also means that measures of severity, general intelligence, and social background should be part of follow-up studies (Wallander, 1988).

Mild Mental Retardation. Studies of mentally retarded children reveal other important factors. These studies are among the most extensive and detailed of all follow-up studies of children with handicaps. Whereas most of the studies reviewed here examined young adults no more than 10 years after they were first seen, there are studies of mentally retarded children well into adulthood, with one detailed study following up children 40 years after they were first contacted.

In these studies, not only severity and social background, but also sex differences, age, and multiple measures in adulthood are considered. It is clear that these variables interact. Severity is clearly indicated as a variable in that the life course of mildly retarded people is quite different from that of severely retarded children. As they grow older most mildly retarded individuals live essentially normal lives, whereas severely retarded people live and work in protected environments. Among mildly retarded people, men work almost as much and they earn almost as much as their normal siblings and as unrelated normal men from their social class. They are more likely to be employed if they have worked during high school, but vocational education does not seem to influence the probability of their finding work. Jobs are found through informal social networks of friends more importantly than through social agencies. Mildly retarded women do not work as much as men, and this lower rate of employment is greater proportionally than the same effect in comparable normal populations (Hasazi et al., 1985; R. T. Ross, Begab, Dondis, Giampiccolo, & C. E. Meyers, 1985).

The rate of marriage is somewhat less in mildly retarded people than in their siblings or comparable unrelated normal people, and the married retarded people have fewer children. On an open-ended self-evaluation test, mildly retarded people were essentially normal in evaluating themselves on such characteristics as interpersonal relations and life achievements. Some mildly retarded people were higher in specifying their faults, but at the same time more of them indicated that they had no faults at all. In contrast with the open-ended self-evaluation, the mildly retarded group was lower on an extensive personality inventory that assessed such factors as poise, socialization, achievement, and measures of interest.

Overall, whereas mildly retarded people live essentially normal lives, somewhat fewer of them are employed, they earn lower salaries, the women do not work as much as would be expected, fewer are married, they have fewer children, and their lifestyle is more passive (R. T. Ross et al., 1985). This means that although most mildly retarded individuals are well adjusted, there is reason to believe that some of them are in need of psychological services.

Severe Mental Retardation and Autistic Disorders.   The situation is quite different for severely retarded individuals and for children with pervasive developmental disorders (autism and autism-related disorders). It is likely that many children with severe psychological disabilities like these will always need to live in protected environments. The three major factors that determine whether they will live at home or in an institution are health problems, intellectual level, and maladaptive behaviors that make them difficult to care for.

There are not many follow-up studies of people with severe disabilities. Those that do exist show clearly that there is a relationship between intellectual level and place of residence in adulthood. Children with relatively high IQs remain in their own homes, and a few live in independent and semi-independent apartments. Moderately retarded people may be found in foster care, small group homes, or nursing homes. Profoundly retarded children and autistic children with lower IQs generally are sent to state-operated or community institutions (Eyman & Widaman, 1987).

Maladaptive behaviors and severe chronic health problems also predict earlier and continuing out-of-home placement. That is, retarded and autistic children and adults who are difficult to care for are placed in more restrictive environments earlier and for a continuing period. There are many individual exceptions to these general rules. A few parents devote their whole lives to caring for a severely retarded child with life-threatening illnesses until they are too old to provide such care. However, as pointed out in the next section, this lifestyle is statistically less common (L. Wolf & B. Goldberg, 1986).

Children with handicaps grow up to be adults and most live satisfying and productive lives. As a group, they are at higher risk for vocational and personal problems that are a consequence of their early history, their current situation, and their personal characteristics. Personal characteristics have been studied most frequently, and severity of the childhood disorder seems to be the strongest correlate with later problems. However, the importance of early and current environments have also been demonstrated. These are emphasized somewhat more in the next sections on residential and work environments.

COMMUNITY LIVING

People spend most of their time in the places in which they live, where they work, and where they receive extra help and engage in recreational activities (Brimblecombe, 1985). This is true not only of normal people but also of people with disabling conditions. As we have tried to show in the last section, the situation with mildly disabled people is essentially the same as with normal people and will not concern us further. However, there has been intense discussion and research about the lives of more severely disabled people who require special support. Overwhelmingly, the research is concerned with living environments and with supported and sheltered employment, with less interest in recreational environments.

The distinction between these three classes of environment should not be overdrawn, because activities that are typical of each environment also occur in all three types of environment. Recreational activities occur in living environments and in sheltered workshops, people take their meals in all environments, and people may work for wages in their homes. However, the intimate aspects of life such as sleeping, eating, and long-term committed relationships with family or family-substitutes are characteristic of living environments. Productive activities that involve the community are aspects of work, and social interactions with friends are the main characteristic of out-of-home recreational environments.

Prior to the 16th century, most people with disabilities lived in their natural home as part of an extended family, working in cottage industries and agriculture. With the industrial revolution and urbanization came the development of alternative living environments. During the 19th century and through the first half of the 20th century, placement in increasingly large institutions was the most obvious characteristic of this development. By the 1950s, the two main alternatives for a severely disabled person were life in the natural home or life in an institution.

However, by that time dissatisfaction with both of these alternatives had become widespread. The natural home was often a satisfactory solution for many disabled adults, but in certain circumstances it was impossible for parents to provide the best care for the disabled person. Perhaps the parents became too old, the financial burden was too great, the medical requirements were too stringent, or the relationship of the parents and their adult disabled child became strained.

The alternative, placement in an institution, often was unsatisfactory. Institutions were afflicted with many problems. Most institutions were isolated in rural areas. Staffing was inadequate, with respect to both number and quality. Programs were primarily custodial, often caring but sometimes abusive. People were placed inappropriately and sometimes even lost. The cost to the government, despite inferior services, was burdensome.

Beginning in the 1950s, society's response was to provide a greater range of alternatives and to reduce the size and function of the state-operated institutions. Currently, people with severe disabilities live in a range of residences that receive their financial support from a combination of private and governmental sources. A large number of severely disabled people live with their immediate family or a relative. Many live in homes of friends, in foster care, or independently with occasional home visits by someone who can provide professional or other support service (Seltzer & Krauss, 1984; Sherman, Frenkel & Newman, 1984).

Others live in groups with other people with disabilities in a variety of situations. Included are group homes of less than 10 people, larger community residences of up to 150 people, convalescent or nursing homes for short- or long-term stay associated with medical needs, city-, county-, or state-operated institutions, and prisons (C. Smith, Algozzine, Schmid, & Hennly, 1990). Still other disabled people have no permanent homes. They live transitory lives with relatives, in shelters, and on the streets (Rowitz, 1987).

Deinstitutionalization

These are not necessarily all stable residential solutions. The options have continued to change during the last 50 years. The most obvious change has been the deinstitutionalization movement. The number of people in state-operated programs in rural areas has declined. Many institutions have been closed, and those that remain are now reserved for the most severely disabled people. At the same time, the possibilities in the community have expanded and continue to grow, and with those changes has come a certain amount of instability (B. K. Hill, Bruininks, Lakin, Hauber, & McGuire, 1985).

Several factors have contributed to a small, but significant, tendency to a "reinstitutionalization" movement, that is, to place certain people in institutions. The deinstitutionalization movement occurred very rapidly, without time for adequate preparation of community programs. The growing number of people living on the street and instances of abuse and neglect in some community programs have generated a call to return people to what are perceived to be safer living environments (Elpers, 1987). At the same time, bureaucratic changes that have included changes in funding mechanisms and governmental and private reorganizations have eliminated community residences that were actually reasonably satisfactory.

Besides these organizational shifts there is also residential instability brought on by such things as deaths in a family or changes in the needs of the disabled person. Thus, whereas the living environment of many disabled people is as stable as that of anyone else, major change is a reality for a significant number.

The history of residential care of severely handicapped children is, therefore, first one of increasing options for placement. This positive change has been accompanied by a tendency toward instability of placement that is a consequence of organizational factors in the service system and the family.

We turn now to a review of the extensive literature on what life is like in state-operated and community placements. This literature has been characterized by the development of a reasonably clear statement about the many factors that influence placement decisions and life in residential programs. Ten years ago, characteristics of the disabled person were thought to be the main factors worth looking at in predicting out-of-home placements and the nature of life in residential programs. Now, specific factors in the community and the family have been added.

Out-of-Home Placement. A family's decision to separate from severely disabled children by placing them into an institution or community residential program is one of the most difficult any parent can make. The literature does not yet adequately describe the anguish associated with this decision. However, the many factors related to such a decision have been studied recently, and a clearer picture has emerged during the last 10 years.

Stress-resource theories, as described in an earlier chapter on social processes, emphasize three factors: the child's characteristics, the family's perspective on the situation they are confronted with, and the resources available to the family (D. A. Cole, 1986). This perspective is useful for thinking about out-of-home placement.

The most obvious characteristic related to out-of-home placement is chronological age. As with normal children, there is a decline with age in the probability that a child will be in the home. In less severely disabled people, separation may be essentially normal, but it may be delayed. However, in profoundly retarded children, out-of-home placement generally occurs much earlier than normal. Fifty percent of profoundly retarded children are out of their natural home by the time they are 10 years old, and more than 80% have been placed by age 18. The processes involved in separation have not been studied adequately. But it is likely that the factors involved in separation change with age. An extreme example would be the comparison of early separation in handicapped children, where early placement is primarily the decision of the parents, whereas with the more normal, but perhaps delayed, separation of less handicapped young adults, the child's initiation is more important (Cattermole, Jahoda, & Markova, 1988).

Other child factors that influence out-of-home placement are intellectual level, maladaptive behavior, greater financial cost, major medical problems, ambulation, toileting, speech, and visual impairment. More severely retarded and autistic children tend to be placed earlier, and children who are aggressive either to others or to themselves are also at greater risk. The other factors are less consistently demonstrated. However, in general, children who are more difficult and expensive to care for are more likely to be placed earlier (Borthwick-Duffy, Eyman, & J. F. White, 1987; Chetwynd, 1985; B. R. Sherman, 1988).

At least as important as the characteristics of the child are several factors that describe the family and the community in which the family lives. Some of these factors are covered by stress resource theories, and some are not. Those that are included are lack of availability and/or use of respite care and other services within the home, greater cost of maintaining a handicapped child, disruption of the family (including a perception of low support within the family), single parent and small families, and lower family income. Factors not covered by stress resource theory include ethnicity and degree of religious preferences. Whites and less religious families opt for out-of-home placement more than do nonwhites and more religious people (Ayer, 1984; Borthwick-Duffy et al., 1987; Buckle, 1984; D. A. Cole & Meyer, 1989; Russell, 1984; B. R. Sherman, 1988; Wynne & Rogers, 1985).

The decision to place a person is based partly on which residential programs are available. Where a child or adult goes when placed out of the home also depends on the matching of their characteristics with the characteristics of the program. Ideally, a child with chronic, severe medical needs will go to a program that has well-trained medical staff and modern medical facilities. An adult who has no special medical needs, but who is able to participate in groups and work at simple tasks, may be in a group home and work in sheltered employment. A shy child from a disruptive home may benefit from a short-term residential program that emphasizes intensive group therapy.

When the many individual, family, and community factors involved in placement are taken into consideration, the prediction of whether any particular child will be placed out of the home can potentially be accomplished with a high degree of accuracy. In addition, it is also possible to predict whether the child will be retained at home, placed in an institution, or sent to a community program. However, because there have been few studies that match the person's characteristics to the characteristics of the residential program and no prospective studies of differential placement (as opposed to concurrent correlational studies) such prediction seems now as only a very likely possibility (Jacobson, 1987; Schalock & Jensen, 1986).

After the children have been placed in an institution or community residence, the family usually maintains contact with them. But contact varies from outright neglect to parent participation in therapy and care. Ordinarily, the family visits the residential program, and children may be brought home for weekend visits and vacations. The stay in the residential program may not be permanent, and this is particularly true of out-of-home respite care or short-term therapeutic residential programs. The determinants of the nature of the relationship that the family maintains with the child include such factors as the proximity of the residential program and the degree of faith that the parents have that their participation can make a difference (M. Fox, 1985; Russell, 1984). In general, the relationship is a continuing one that changes as the child grows older in the alternative living environment. However, not much is known about these shifts in the relationships with time because there have been no longitudinal studies of the issue.

Institutions and the Community System.   On the other hand there have been a great many studies attempting to characterize the dimensions that significantly differentiate residential settings. There is an assumption that quality of life and psychological growth differ in various programs. No social group is identical with any other, so the general statement that residential programs differ should come as no surprise to the reader. The question is whether it is possible to characterize those differences, and once that is done, to relate those characterizations to quality of life and personal growth measures. Ideally, one would then go further and show that specific characteristics of a program not only are correlated with higher quality of life and faster growth, but also that they cause these changes.

At this time, the way one characterizes residential programs is somewhat confused. The major distinction current is the difference between an institution and a community program. An institution is usually a large organization, operated by a state government, and located at the outskirts of a city or in a rural area. Ideally, a community program is a small apartment or house, operated by a private organization, and located close to the family and generic services of a town or city.

A significant distinction between institution and community that is confusing is the variability of community programs. State-operated institutions are large and located outside of large urban areas. Community programs generally are operated by private organizations, but they may be operated by the state and do ordinarily receive a significant proportion of their funding from governmental sources. Community programs may also be large, housing as many as 150 people, but they often are small and may be like a normal home. Finally, community programs ordinarily are established in towns and cities, reasonably close to generic services like libraries, parks, and general hospitals, though some people who live in the community programs may use these facilities differently than does the general population or may rarely use them because they are inaccessible (Welch, Nietupski, & Hamre-Nietupski, 1985).

Although the general distinction between institutions and community programs therefore sometimes can be confusing, a few things can be said. The purpose of state-operated institutions is somewhat different from that of the community programs. The institutions serve as a backup resource that the state provides for people who do not succeed in community placement. This difference results from the principle that most people espouse, that is, that all people should live in an environment that is as normal as possible. In most cases, this means life in a community residence. However, in the case of a few people who are profoundly disabled and require intensive custodial care, who are chronically subject to medical emergencies, and/or who have maladaptive behaviors that prevent them from living in the community, institution life may be the most normal that is possible.

As we have said, state-operated and community programs are in flux. However, the instability is reflected somewhat differently in the two service systems. The number of people served in institutions and the number of institutions have declined since the late 1960s. Residents of state-operated programs have often been moved to other institutions. At the same time, the number of people and programs in the community system have increased, and community placements have generally been more unstable than institutional placements. Many institutions have remained and are essentially the same as were there before, whereas others have been closed or replaced. New programs and types of programs in the community have been established, and as many as 40% of the community residences in existence in 1977 were no longer there in 1982.

This instability in the state-operated and community systems has been an important part of the deinstitutionalization movement. It is not clear at this time whether residential programs will become more stable in the future. However, it can safely be said that, for many severely disabled people, residential instability is an important fact of life (B. K. Hill et al., 1985; Sumpton, Raynes, & Thorp, 1987).

This is important because moving around can have important physical and psychological consequences. Negative effects seem to be limited to certain groups under some conditions. People who are in poor condition to begin with can show evidence of stress, manifested in such things as poorer health, increased mental confusion, depression, social withdrawal, and decreased language functioning. On the other hand, there can be positive effects, especially if functioning was depressed in the first environment and the quality of the second environment is more fitting for the particular characteristics of the person involved. Thus, moving to small community placements or to redesigned institutional environments sometimes improve the fit between the person and the environment manifested in greater interaction with the physical environment and with other clients and staff (Braddock & Heller, 1985; Felce, M. Thomas, De Kock, Saxby, & Repp, 1985; Mallory & Herrick, 1987; Schumacher, Qvammen, & Wisland, 1986).

Financial Cost. One of the main motivations for building the community system was financial. If community programs used generic community services rather than similar services as the special hospitals, fire departments, and security staffs that were necessary in the institutions, community service programs should be less expensive for the state. The situation has actually turned out to be ambiguous. The original estimates of cost indeed showed that if one simply divides the total cost of a program by the number of people served, state-operated institutions are more expensive. However, doing this comparison does not take into consideration such factors as the generally higher staff ratios required for dealing with residents who are more difficult to care for, the problems associated with costing the use of generic services in community programs, and the great differences in patterns of costs between different institutions and between community programs. When such factors are considered, differential costs between institution and community living are not so clear (Bensberg & J. J. Smith, 1984; Epple, Jacobson, & Janicki, 1985).

Quality of Life. Another motivation for building the community system was improvement of the quality of life for people with severe disabilities. The picture of life in the community here is generally positive, but not without disappointment and challenge. It can be viewed from several perspectives, including the nature and amount of services provided, comparative rates of personal development in community and institution care, quality of life in the place of residence, and degree of participation in the surrounding community. There have been several descriptive and comparative studies of these factors and some useful analytic studies of characteristics of individuals and environments that predict them.

Services differ in institution and community programs. However, there are some unexpected findings that reveal the complexity of the institution–

community distinction. In general, when institutions and community programs are compared, several factors can be confounded in the comparison. For instance, size, architecture, rural-urban cultures, and characteristics of the people living in the programs all differ simultaneously. The best studies attempt to separate these factors statistically, but there are not many of such studies (T. Thompson, Robinson, Graff, &. Ingenmey, 1990).

Characteristics of individuals can be controlled if the same people are followed from institution to community placements in studies of the effects of deinstitutionalization. These follow-up studies are available, but controls for the simple effects of moving are not always available. Thus, conclusions about the relative benefits of institutional and community placements must be regarded with care.

In general, more professional services are provided in large rather than in small facilities, and in state-operated rather than in community programs. To some extent, this may be due to the fact that people who reside in small community programs are in good physical health, as compared with people in institutions. However, medical needs do not account completely for the difference because statistical procedures that remove the influence of individual characteristics still show that larger programs provide more professional services. Perhaps this is also because smaller programs in the community do not need to provide professional services as much because they use generic community programs to a greater extent (Gothelf, 1985; Jacobson, E. J. Silver, &. Schwartz, 1984; McDonald, 1985).

It seems that there are more professional services in larger programs, but it also seems that staff of small programs interact more with their clients than do direct-service staff of large programs. Again, this may not be so much size as other factors that are important in determining this social interaction, for example, behavior problems, and ambulation (M. Thomas et al., 1986).

Given the complexity of the comparison between institution and community programs, it is perhaps not too surprising that differences in development as a function of locus of placement are not impressive. Nutritional status of fragile severely disabled people is not adversely affected in foster care placements. Adaptive behavior growth is not different in a moderately sized facility as compared with a small community program. Wariness of others is not different for various residence types, although it increases over time in large programs and decreases in small programs (K. Alexander, Huganir, &. Zigler, 1985; Silverman, E. J. Silver, Sersen, Lubin, &. Schwartz, 1986; Springer, 1987; Zigler, Balla, &. Kossan, 1986).

Differences in development are not impressive, but the nature of the lifestyle can be different in institutions and small community programs. Again, however, the differences between programs within these residence types are dramatic and should be kept in mind. As we have seen, staff contact is generally higher in small programs, and generic services in the community are used more. Staff have more autonomy in small programs, their activities are oriented to care and leisure pursuits of the residents, and clients take more initiative in going to community environments. Among these leisure pursuits are more active involvement with the physical environment of the home and visits to shops and restaurants. These visits are met with acceptance by proprietors and the community at large, even for severely disabled people.

On the other hand, the relationship of people in small group homes with their community is limited to relatively superficial contacts. With the exception of some relationships with family members, connections with neighbors and with other members of the community tend to be superficial. It is important to note that some clients may be socially isolated, and degree of social support (for instance by the person's family) predicts failure or success in the community placement (Aveno, 1989; Crapps, Langone, & Swaim, 1985; Dalgleish, 1985; Felce, 1988; Heal & Chadsey-Rusch, 1985; Rawlings, 1985; Rock, 1988; Schalock & Lilley, 1986).

Although the greater autonomy in smaller programs provides the positive effect of more client-oriented activities and more initiative by clients, freedom brings with it potential dangers. Medical incidents and involvement with the police occurs in community programs, although these incidents are focused on only a few people. There have also been warnings about abuse of clients, and as many as 40% of staff do not understand or support the concept of normalization. However, the literature about accidents, instances of law violation, abuse, and acceptance of the basic philosophy underlying community placement is inadequate, so that not much that is definitive can be said about the problems of community living (Anstey & Gaskin, 1985; Aveno & Renzaglia, 1988; Hewitt, 1987; Spangler & Gilman, 1985).

Aside from the influence of institutional and small community environments on the residents themselves, these placements have their influence on the family and the community at large. Parents tend, overwhelmingly, to express satisfaction with their child's placement, whether it is in an institution or the community. This satisfaction has produced resistance to the deinstitutionalization movement by parents. Parent resistance combines with staff resistance to impede deinstitutionalization (Heller, Bond, & Braddock, 1988; Rudie & Riedl, 1984; Spreat, Telles, Conroy, Feinstein, & Colombatto, 1987). Partly, parent satisfaction is dependent on the perception by families that their children have medical needs that are satisfied in an institutional environment. As a matter of fact, parents tend to perceive that the medical needs of their children are greater than do the caregivers of the children (Conroy, 1985). Perception of medical needs becomes less influential if the parents receive a training program when their child is moved to a community program, and then the characteristics of the community program become more important than medical needs in forming their attitudes (Grimes & Vitello, 1990). In short, then, sensitivity to parents' concerns about medical needs are an important factor to consider in moving their children from one residence to another.

In community placements, parents feel more relaxed in talking with staff than they did when the child was in the institution, and they may spend more time doing so. On the other hand, seeing their child in a more homelike environment may rekindle some of the guilt feelings that they experienced when they first placed their child out of the home. Some parents continue to take their children home for weekend visits, as they did when the child was in the institution, but they rarely bring the child home permanently (Halliday, 1987).

On the whole, it is clear that small residential programs in the community are different from larger programs, not so much in their size, but with respect to such things as the nature of the individual client needs, the organization of the program, and the character of access to the community. It is also clear that the ideals that motivated the deinstitutionalization movement, that is, less expensive care and enriched quality of life, have only partially been fulfilled. Nevertheless, for many less severely disabled people who were moved from institutions, life in the community has represented a release from a custodial lifestyle that was, to say the least, not appropriate for them.

Response of the Community.   With respect to the wider community, there is a major stereotype that introduction of a community living facility to a community will reduce property values. This stereotype results in vigorous opposition to such homes in certain communities. The issue has been studied several times. None of the studies have produced any evidence that introduction of a small community living program for severely disabled people has any influence at all on property values (Gelman, Epp, Downing, Twark, & Eyerly, 1989). On the other hand, some landlords also have had difficulty in renting apartments to retarded individuals for independent living arrangements. This difficulty is partly due to prejudice against them from other tenants and the landlords themselves. But it may also be due to inappropriate behavior of some individuals who are not ready for independent living (Salend & Giek, 1988).

General responses of normal community members to introduction of a living facility to their neighborhood have been empirically classified into four categories: active support, passive opposition, active opposition, and illegal opposition. General attitudes (e.g., a concept of disabled people as inferior in social functioning) could lead to specific attitudes such as expectations about the impact disabled people would have in the community into which they move. These specific attitudes, might, in turn, trigger specific behaviors that represent the general response types. In other words, knowing both general and specific attitudes of a member of the community, employing empirically derived categories of attitudes, is perhaps the most useful way of preparing members of the community to accept their neighbors with disabilities (Cnaan, Adler, & Ramot, 1986).

Leisure Skills. Before we leave the topic of living in the community, there are a few more specialized issues that can be reviewed. These include leisure skills, self-help groups, sexuality, parenting, and the special issues associated with aging.

When they are not engaged in work or school activities, children and adults with disabilities have free time to engage in leisure activities. Children with learning disabilities have fundamentally the same preferences for leisure activities as do nonhandicapped children. Playing ball games, riding bicycles, playing outside, playing with friends, and watching television are all listed by both groups. A greater proportion of children with learning disabilities prefer to play alone, they feel lonely, they are passive in play, and substantially fewer watch television. However, overall, their preferences for playing are substantially normal (Margalit, 1984; Swift & R. B. Lewis, 1985).

Other children are perceived as needing training to play appropriately. Activities that are challenging are thought to increase self-esteem of juvenile offenders, and there is some evidence that this is true. Teaching leisure activities has been thought to decrease boredom that could plausibly lead to delinquency, drug abuse, and inappropriate interpersonal behaviors. However, good studies that show this are not yet available (Munson, 1988).

Normal and mildly handicapped people play spontaneously, but severely retarded people are thought to lack leisure and recreational skills as a consequence of their retardation in development. There are many studies available that show that play can be increased by providing appropriate play materials, but that training procedures that focus on the development, maintenance, and generalization of these skills can be more effective (Nietupski, Ayres, & Hamre-Nietupski, 1983).

Self-Help Groups. Self-help groups for people with handicaps have developed as part of a larger movement toward the development of self-help groups for increasing self-identity and self-advocacy. There has not been much formal research in this field. However, self-help groups exist for hearing-impaired and also mentally retarded people. These groups engage in many activities including meetings, social functions, training nonhandicapped people, and advocacy. These groups have definable values and goals (Keys & Foster-Fishman, 1991). At meetings, discussions center on the desire for independence, feelings of loneliness, interest in romantic relationships, and developing a sense of self-worth (Browning, Thorin, &. Rhoades, 1984; Finisdore, 1984; Hoshmand, 1985).

Many of these self-help groups have advisors that aid in the organization of the group. Some advisors are more active than is appropriate and suppress the initiative of members of the group, whereas others stay in the background and ultimately withdraw so that the groups truly are self-help groups (Worrell, 1987).

Sexuality and Parenting.   There has been general interest in sexuality and parenting by adults with disabilities, but again good empirical research is sparse. What research there is suggests that mildly retarded individuals have friends, they are sexually expressive, and they are capable of sexual discretion. Nevertheless, they are perceived as sexually incompetent. As a result, they do not receive adequate sex education. More severely retarded people can also have friends, but this is less likely, especially when they are nonverbal. They may engage in inappropriate masturbation and nonvolitional homosexuality, perhaps because of their severe cognitive deficiencies, but it may be due partly to the fact that they reside in atypical environments such as institutions (Abramson, T. Parker, &. Weisberg, 1988; Chapman &. Pitceathly, 1985; Cuvo, Gonzalez, &. O'Brien, 1985; Mueser, Valenti-Hein, &. Yarnold, 1987; Koller, Richardson, &. M. Katz, 1988; Krauss &. Seltzer, 1989).

The perception of mentally retarded people as sexually incompetent stems partly from a fear that they will have children and they will be inadequate parents. Good information on this issue would be important to have, but the few studies that exist suffer from inadequate sampling and lack of appropriate comparison groups. In general, people who work in the field believe that, although mentally retarded people can be competent parents, children of retarded people with lower IQ are at risk for neglect and physical abuse. This effect can be moderated because retarded parents often receive help from normal family members and professionals in rearing their children (Budd &. Greenspan, 1985; Chapman &. Pitceathly, 1985; Gath, 1988; Seagull &. Scheurer, 1986; Tymchuk, Andron, &. Rahbar, 1988; Whitman, Graves, &. Accardo, 1987).

Later Life.   Services for elderly people with handicaps are growing, but the research about their lives has just begun. The information that is available focuses on the nature of a person's changing social life. One study of formerly institutionalized retarded people indicates that they became less dependent on benefactors as they grew older. At an average age of 62, they had become more independent, more socially competent, and had a greater zest for life than earlier (Edgerton, 1988). This picture is consistent with the general finding for people of average intelligence that intellectual functioning does not generally decline dramatically until after the sixth decade.

Even after that time, there is variability in intellectual functioning that is predicted by social factors such as social participation and absence of dissolution of the family. In general, continued intellectual functioning among nonhandicapped people seems to be related to continued involvement in life's activities (Schaie, 1984).

The situation with people with other handicaps is somewhat more complicated. The quality of life of women with hearing-impairments seems to be predicted positively by social support, but also negatively by degree of communication handicap in relation to their reference group and by their perceived health status. Thus, social factors but also health factors are implicated (Magilvy, 1985).

Ordinarily, elderly people with handicaps associate with their families. However, this may not always be optimal for either the family or the elderly handicapped person. At least for some families, especially siblings with whom the elderly handicapped person lives, the elderly person is perceived as being a burden. On the other hand, studies of informal social networks show that elderly handicapped people who live in community residences or institutions seem to have more, rather than fewer, friends than if they live at home. Of course, these statements are preliminary, and are statistical. In any individual case, family living can be mutually beneficial for all of the individuals involved (Krauss & Erickson, 1988; Seltzer, 1985).

When the family is not adequate to provide the social support, there are several options including foster care, various options in independent and group community living, nursing homes that are fitted to attend primarily to the increasing medical needs of the older population, and institutions. These options are growing, both in their variety and the number of people served. Most of them are not specialized for the elderly population, and there is some question about whether age-specialized services are appropriate (Krauss & M. M. Seltzer, 1986; M. M. Seltzer, 1988; G. B. Seltzer, Finaly, & Howell, 1988).

WORK

Many people with handicaps spend most of their time in the place that they live. Restriction of life to their home is partly a result of a lack of appropriate work opportunities. Sometimes it can be due to an overprotective attitude on the part of the person's family or fear of the outside world by the handicapped person.

Although many people with handicaps do have a job, between 30% and 70% of learning-disabled, mentally retarded, hearing-handicapped and other adults with handicaps are at greater risk for unemployment. They may be employed part-time, their average income is lower, and they move from job to job more often (Cartledge, 1987; Phillippe & Auvenshine, 1985; Wehman, 1988).

For those people who are not in the employment mainstream, the situation has improved during the last decade. The improvement is partly a result of a healthy economy and partly due to vigorous federal programs that have fostered an active stance resulting in training, supported employment programs (Inge, Banks, Wehman, J. W. Hill, & Shafer, 1988) and equal access to employment (J. Stark & Goldsbury, 1988). One study showed that, of people having developmental disabilities that interfered significantly with adaptation, almost 20% had been placed in transitional training, supported employment, or competitive employment during a 1-year period, and this constituted a marked increase in the rate of placement as compared with the previous year. Job placement was mainly in food and beverage preparation, janitorial, assembly, and lodging occupations (Kiernan, McGaughey, & Schalock, 1988).

Whether these persons are employed depends on the severity of their cognitive and social disabilities, where they live, and the amount and nature of the services they receive. Upon leaving school, many mildly disabled people find jobs and live essentially normal lives. However, some do not, and more severely disabled people have even more difficulty with employment. Some studies show that no one with an IQ less than 50 is employed. Other research is more optimistic, showing that even severely retarded people can work in competitive employment if they are carefully selected and well-supervised in the work situation. The success of these supported employment demonstrations shows itself in a low worker turnover rate, greater employer satisfaction, and a fiscal saving for governmental support programs. Retarded workers are not absent more than nonhandicapped workers, they work less overtime, but they also take fewer vacations (Brickey, K. M. Campbell, & Browning, 1985; Gibson, Rogers, & Fields, 1987; M. L. Hill et al., 1987; Kregel, M. H. Hill, & Banks, 1988; J. E. Martin, Rusch, Tines, Brulle, & D. M. White, 1985; S. A. Richardson, Koller, & M. Katz, 1988; Wehman, J. W. Hill, Wood, & Parent, 1987).

Employers, vocational rehabilitation professionals, teachers, and the clients themselves agree on what it takes to succeed in competitive employment. Specific job skills, appropriate work-related skills like punctuality and responsiveness to safety requirements, basic communication with supervisors, and good grooming are regarded as fundamental to being hired for the job and being retained (Alper, 1985; D. L. Lovett & M. B. Harris, 1987; Minskoff, Sautter, Hoffmann, & Hawks, 1987; Mueller, Wilgosh, & Dennis, 1987; Salzberg, Agran, & Lignugaris/Kraft, 1986; Shafer, Kregel, Banks, & M. L. Hill, 1988).

Although many people with severe disabilities work in supported or competitive employment, most are clients in sheltered workshops. Ideally, these sheltered workshops are transitional placements that provide vocational and socialization training in preparation for work in competitive environments. However, this ideal is not always fulfilled. Clients are most often satisfied with the friends they have in the workshop. Participating in work activities is not particularly important for them. At the same time, their parents (and probably also many staff members) prefer sheltered over competitive placements, especially for more severely disabled clients (Dudley & Schatz, 1985; Schuster, 1990; J. W. Hill, Seyfarth, Banks, Wehman, & Orelove, 1987).

Moreover, if their attitudes were changed and their skills increased, there is no guarantee that jobs would be available to them. The few studies of the economics of employment of handicapped people suggests that they compete, often unsuccessfully with nonhandicapped people for a limited range of relatively unskilled service jobs (R. Brown, Hibbard, & Waters, 1986; Hirst, 1987; Schuster, 1990).

Certainly, research can and should be devoted to solving these problems. Meanwhile, the more restricted goal of increasing the skills of the person with handicaps has received attention, whether it is in transitional programs from school to adulthood or with adults themselves. In addition to teaching specific job skills, increased assertiveness in the job interview, a variety of other job interview skills, and training in filling out employment applications have been demonstrated with people who stutter, with mentally retarded people and with people who have learning disabilities. Increasing work initiative, task maintenance, and more general job maintenance skills have been accomplished with learning-disabled and mentally retarded people, and inappropriate behaviors have been reduced in people with autism (Duran, 1985; J. A. Kelly & Christoff, 1985; M. Martin & Horsfall, 1987; Mathews & Fawcett, 1984; McCuller, Salzberg, & Lignugaris/Kraft, 1987; Roessler & V. A. Johnson, 1987; Schloss, Espin, M. A. Smith, & Suffolk, 1987; M. D. Smith & Coleman, 1986; Srikameswaran & G. L. Martin, 1984; Trach & Rusch, 1989).

CONCLUSIONS

Children with mild disabilities grow up to live reasonably normal lives. Although they may continue to have some problems, they find jobs, have families if they want to, and can be happy. Adults with mild disabilities represent the majority of those who required special services when they were children. The prognosis for the smaller proportion of individuals who have severe disabilities is less favorable. Those with severe cognitive and social disorders are especially at risk to be dependent in adulthood on their families, the government, or more usually, both.

Out-of-home placement may occur very early in the lives of severely disabled children, especially when they exceed the emotional or financial resources of their family. Most severely and profoundly retarded children are placed out of the home by the time they reach adulthood, either in foster care or in some group-living situation.

From the beginning of the 19th century until the end of World War II, group living for people with severe disabilities meant life in a state-operated institution separated from general society. During the last 50 years, the movement to integrate severely disabled people into general society has encouraged placement into generally smaller residences in their home community managed by private organizations that receive funding from the government. This deinstitutionalization movement has had complex effects. It probably has not saved the money that was once hoped for, and some people are placed into jeopardy of physical harm and social exclusion when they do not have adequate supervision. On the other hand, for many—perhaps most—living in the community has brought with it a more normal lifestyle.

Included in this more normal lifestyle is the opportunity to work at regular jobs. Federal legislation in the United States and the results of research have worked against some of the stereotypes fostering the idea that disabled people cannot compete in the marketplace. While severely disabled people still often work in sheltered workshops, recent studies have shown that at least some of them can work in competitive industry if their interpersonal skills allow it, if they have intensive training, if management and co-workers are accepting, and if the worker is supported in the work environment for a transitional period.

References

Aarons, L., & Dixon, E. M. (1988). Poetry recitation with persons who are mentally retarded. *Mental Retardation, 26,* 103–104.

Abbeduto, L., Davies, B., & Furman, L. (1988). The development of speech act comprehension in mentally retarded individuals and nonretarded children. *Child Development, 59,* 1460–1472.

Abbeduto, L., Furman, L., & Davies, B. (1989). Relation between the receptive language and mental age of persons with mental retardation. *American Journal on Mental Retardation, 93,* 535–543.

Abbott, D. A., & Meredith, W. H. (1986). Strengths of parents with retarded children. *Family Relations, 35,* 371–375.

Abel, E. L. (1980). Fetal alcohol syndrome: Behavioral teratology. *Psychological Bulletin, 87,* 29–50.

Aber, J. L., & Allen, J. P. (1987). Effects of maltreatment on young children's socioemotional development: An attachment theory perspective. *Developmental Psychology, 23,* 406–414.

Aboud, F. E. (1985). Children's application of attribution principles to social comparisons. *Child Development, 56,* 682–688.

Abrahamsen, A., Cavallo, M. M., & McCluer, J. A. (1985). Is the sign advantage a robust phenomenon? From gesture to language in two modalities. *Merrill-Palmer Quarterly, 31,* 177–209.

Abrahamsen, A. A., Romski, M. A., & Sevcik, R. A. (1989). Concomitants of success in acquiring an augmentative communication system: Changes in attention, communication, and sociability. *American Journal on Mental Retardation, 93,* 475–496.

Abramowitz, A. J., O'Leary, S. G., & Futtersak, M. W. (1988). The relative impact of long and short reprimands on children's off-task behavior in the classroom. *Behavior Therapy, 19,* 243–247.

Abramson, P. R., Parker, T., & Weisberg, S. R. (1988). Sexual expression of mentally retarded people: Educational and legal implications. *American Journal on Mental Retardation, 93*, 328–334.

Achenbach, T. M., & Edelbrock, C. S. (1978). The classification of child psychopathology: A review and analysis of empirical efforts. *Psychological Bulletin, 85*, 1275–1301.

Achenbach, T. M., & Edelbrock, C. S. (1981). Behavioral problems and competencies reported by parents of normal and disturbed children aged 4 through 16. *Monographs of the Society for Research in Child Development, 46*, Whole No. 188.

Achenbach, T. M., & Edelbrock, C. S. (1984). Psychopathology of childhood. *Annual Review of Psychology, 35*, 227–256.

Achenbach, T. M., McConaughy, S. H., & Howell, C. T. (1987). Child/adolescent behavioral and emotional problems: Implications of cross-informant correlations for situational specificity. *Psychological Bulletin, 101*, 213–232.

Achenbach, T. M., Verhulst, F. C., Baron, G. D., & Althaus, M. (1987). A comparison of syndromes derived from the Child Behavior Checklist for American and Dutch boys aged 6–11 and 12–16. *Journal of Child Psychology and Psychiatry, 28*, 437–453.

Ackerman, B. P. (1987). Attention and memory in children and adults in context-interactive and context-independent situations. *Journal of Experimental Child Psychology, 44*, 192–221.

Ackerman, P. T., Anhalt, J. M., & Dykman, R. A. (1986). Arithmetic automatization failure in children with attention and reading disorders: Association and sequela. *Journal of Learning Disabilities, 19*, 222–232.

Acton, H. M., & Zarbatany, L. (1988). Interaction and performance within cooperative groups: Effects on nonhandicapped students' attitudes toward their mildly mentally retarded peers. *American Journal on Mental Retardation, 93*, 16–23.

Adelman, H. S., & Taylor, L. (1986). The problems of definition and differentiation and the need for a classification schema. *Journal of Learning Disabilities, 19*, 514–520.

Adelson, E., & Fraiberg, S. (1974). Gross motor development in infants blind from birth. *Child Development, 45*, 114–126.

Affleck, G., McGrade, B. J., Allen, D. A., & McQueeney, M. (1985). Mothers' beliefs about behavioral causes for their developmentally disabled infant's condition: What do they signify? *Journal of Pediatric Psychology, 10*, 293–303.

Affleck, J. Q., Madge, S., Adams, A., & Lowenbraun, S. (1988). Integrated classroom versus resource model: Academic viability and effectiveness. *Exceptional Children, 54*, 339–348.

Ager, A. (1985). Recent developments in the use of microcomputers in the field of mental handicap: Implications for psychological practice. *Bulletin of the British Psychological Society, 38*, 142–145.

Aiken, J. M., & Salzberg, C. L. (1984). The effects of a sensory extinction procedure on stereotypic sounds of two autistic children. *Journal of Autism and Developmental Disorders, 14*, 291–299.

Ainsworth, M. D. (1979). Infant–mother attachment. *American Psychologist, 34*, 932–937.

Alexander, D. F. (1985). The effect of study skill training on learning disabled students' retelling of expository material. *Journal of Applied Behavior Analysis, 18,* 263–267.

Alexander, K., Huganir, L. S., & Zigler, E. (1985). Effects of different living settings on the performance of mentally retarded individuals. *American Journal on Mental Deficiency, 90,* 9–17.

Alford, J. D., & Locke, B. J. (1984). Clinical responses to psychopathology of mentally retarded persons. *American Journal of Mental Deficiency, 89,* 195–197.

Allen, B. P. (1987). Youth suicide. *Adolescence, 22,* 271–290.

Allen, D. A., Affleck, G., McGrade, B. J., & McQueeney, M. (1983). Characteristics of the Home Observation for measurement of the environment inventory in a sample of high-risk/developmentally disabled infants. *Infant Behavior and Development, 6,* 53–60.

Allen, D. A., Affleck, G., McGrade, B. J., & McQueeney, M. (1984a). Effects of single-parent status on mothers and their high-risk infants. *Infant Behavior and Development, 7,* 347–359.

Allen, D. A., Affleck, G., McGrade, B. J., & McQueeney, M. (1984b). Factors in the effectiveness of early childhood intervention for low socioeconomic status families. *Education and Training of the Mentally Retarded, 19,* 254–260.

Allen, K. D., & Fuqua, R. W. (1985). Eliminating selective stimulus control: A comparison of two procedures for teaching mentally retarded children to respond to compound stimuli. *Journal of Experimental Child Psychology, 39,* 55–71.

Alper, S. (1985). Comparing employer and teacher identified entry-level job requisites of service occupations. *Education and Training of the Mentally Retarded, 20,* 89–96.

Altmann, E. O., & Gotlib, I. H. (1988). The social behavior of depressed children: An observational study. *Journal of Abnormal Child Psychology, 16,* 29–44.

Altmeyer, B. K., Locke, B. J., Griffin, J. C., Ricketts, R. W., Williams, D. E., Mason, M., & Stark, M. T. (1987). Treatment strategies for self-injurious behavior in a large service delivery network. *American Journal of Mental Deficiency, 91,* 333–340.

Aman, M. G., Field, C. J., & Bridgman, G. D. (1985). City-wide survey of drug patterns among non-institutionalized mentally retarded persons. *Applied Research in Mental Retardation, 6,* 159–171.

Aman, M. G., Mitchell, E. A., & Turbott, S. H. (1987). The effects of essential fatty acid supplementation by Efamol in hyperactive children. *Journal Abnormal Child Psychology, 15,* 75–90.

Aman, M. G., & Singh, N. N. (1986). A critical appraisal of recent drug research in mental retardation: The Coldwater studies. *Journal of Mental Deficiency Research, 30,* 203–216.

Aman, M. G., Teehan, C. J., White, A. J., Turbott, S. H., & Vaithianathan, C. (1989). Haloperidol treatment with chronically medicated residents: Dose effects on clinical behavior and reinforcement contingencies. *American Journal on Mental Retardation, 93,* 452–460.

Ames, L. B. (1985). Learning disability—very big around here. *Research Communications in Psychology, Psychiatry, and Behavior, 10,* 17–35.

Amish, P. L., Gesten, E. L., Smith, J. K., Clark, H. B., & Stark, C. (1988). Social problem-solving training for severely emotionally and behaviorally disturbed children. *Behavioral Disorders, 13,* 175–186.

Anderson, K. E., Lytton, H., & Romney, D. M. (1986). Mothers' interactions with normal and conduct-disordered boys: Who affects whom? *Developmental Psychology, 22,* 604–609.

Anderson, M. (1986). Understanding the cognitive deficit in mental retardation. *Journal of Child Psychology and Psychiatry, 27,* 297–306.

Anderson, M. (1988). Inspection time, information processing and the development of intelligence. *British Journal of Developmental Psychology, 6,* 43–57.

Anderson, M. A. (1985). Cooperative group tasks and their relationship to peer acceptance and cooperation. *Journal of Learning Disabilities, 18,* 83–86.

Andrews, G., & Craig, A. (1988). Prediction of outcome after treatment for stuttering. *British Journal of Psychiatry, 153,* 236–240.

Angold, A., Weissman, M. M., John, K., Merikangas, K. R., Prusoff, B. A., Wickramaratne, P., Gammon, G. D., & Warner, V. (1987). Parent and child reports of depressive symptoms in children at low and high risk of depression. *Journal of Child Psychology and Psychiatry, 28,* 901–915.

Anstey, T. J., & Gaskin, M. (1985). Service providers understanding of the concept of normalization. *Australia and New Zealand Journal of Developmental Disabilities, 11,* 91–95.

Ansu-Kyeremeh, K. (1987). Community education for the development of a rural Ghanaian village. *Alberta Journal of Educational Research, 33,* 43–61.

Anwar, F. (1983). The role of sensory modality for the reproduction of shape by the severely retarded. *British Journal of Developmental Psychology, 1,* 317–327.

Arends, N., Povel, D-J., & Kolk, H. (1988). Stuttering as an attentional phenomenon. *Journal of Fluency Disorders, 13,* 141–151.

Arendt, R. E., MacLean, Jr., W. E., & Baumeister, A. A. (1988). Critique of sensory integration therapy and its application in mental retardation. *American Journal on Mental Retardation, 92,* 401–411.

Armstrong, R. W., Rosenbaum, P. L., & King, S. M. (1987). A randomized controlled trial of a 'Buddy' programme to improve children's attitudes toward the disabled. *Developmental Medicine and Child Neurology, 29,* 327–336.

Arnold, J. (1984). Values of exceptional students during early adolescence. *Exceptional Children, 51,* 230–234.

Arnold, L. E., Clark, D. L., Sachs, L. A., Jakim, S., & Smithies, C. (1985). Vestibular and visual rotational stimulation as treatment for attention deficit and hyperactivity. *American Journal of Occupational Therapy, 39,* 84–91.

Asarnow, J. R. (1988). Peer status and social competence in child psychiatric inpatients. *Journal of Abnormal Child Psychology, 16,* 151–162.

Asarnow, R. F., Tanguay, P. E., Bott, L., & Freeman, B. J. (1987). Patterns of intellectual functioning in non-retarded autistic and schizophrenic children. *Journal of Child Psychology & Psychiatry, 28,* 273–280.

Atlas, J. A., & Lapidus, L. B. (1987). Patterns of symbolic expression in subgroups of the childhood psychoses. *Journal of Clinical Psychology, 43,* 177–188.

Atlas, J. A., & Lapidus, L. B. (1988). Symbolization levels in communicative behaviors of children showing pervasive developmental disorders. *Journal of Communication Disorders, 21,* 75–84.

Attwood, A., Frith, U., & Hermelin, B. (1988). The understanding and use of interpersonal gestures by autistic and Down's syndrome children. *Journal of Autism and Developmental Disorders, 18,* 241–257.

August, G. J. (1987). Production deficiencies in free recall: A comparison of hyperactive, learning-disabled, and normal children. *Journal of Abnormal Child Psychology, 15,* 429–440.

Aveno, A. (1989). Community involvement of person with severe retardation living in community residences. *Exceptional Children, 55,* 309–314.

Aveno, A., & Renzaglia, A. (1988). A survey of attitudes of potential community training site staff toward persons with severe handicaps. *Education and Training in Mental Retardation, 23,* 213–223.

Aydin, C., Idiman, F., & Idiman, E. (1987). Contingent negative variation in normal children and in children with attention deficit disorder. *Advances in Biological Psychiatry, 16,* 178–190.

Ayer, S. (1984). Community care: Failure of professionals to meet family needs. *Child: Care, Health and Development, 10,* 127–140.

Aylward, G. P., Gustafson, N., Verhulst, S. J., & Colliver, J. A. (1987). Consistency in the diagnosis of cognitive, motor, and neurologic function over the first 3 years. *Journal of Pediatric Psychology, 12,* 77–98.

Bacon, S. P., & Viemeister, N. F. (1985). Temporal modulation transfer functions in normal-hearing and hearing impaired listeners. *Audiology, 24,* 117–134.

Baddeley, A. D., Logie, R. H., & Ellis, N. C. (1988). Characteristics of developmental dyslexia. *Cognition, 29,* 197–228.

Bagnato, S. J. (1984). Team congruence in developmental diagnosis and intervention: Comparing clinical judgment and child performance measures. *School Psychology Review, 13,* 7–16.

Bailey, Jr., D. B., & Simeonsson, R. J. (1988). Assessing needs of families with handicapped infants. *Journal of Special Education, 22,* 117–127.

Bak, J. J., Cooper, E. M., Dobroth, K. M., & Siperstein, G. N. (1987). Special class placements as labels: Effects on children's attitudes toward learning handicapped peers. *Exceptional Children, 54,* 151–155.

Bak, J. J., & Siperstein, G. N. (1986). Protective effects of the label 'Mentally retarded' on children's attitudes toward mentally retarded peers. *American Journal of Mental Deficiency, 91,* 95–97.

Bak, J. J., & Siperstein, G. N. (1987a). Effects of mentally retarded children's behavioral competence on nonretarded peers' behaviors and attitudes. *American Journal of Mental Deficiency, 92,* 31–39.

Bak, J. J., & Siperstein, G. N. (1987b). Similarity as a factor effecting change in children's attitudes toward mentally retarded peers. *American Journal of Mental Deficiency, 91,* 524–531.

Baker, L., & Cantwell, D. P. (1987a). Factors associated with development of psychiatric illness in children with early speech/language problems. *Journal of Autism and Developmental Disorders, 17,* 499–510.

Baker, L., & Cantwell, D. P. (1987b). A prospective psychiatric follow-up of children with speech/language disorders. *Journal of the American Academy of Child and Adolescent Psychiatry, 26,* 546–553.

Bakker, D. J., & Vinke, J. (1985). Effects of hemisphere-specific stimulation on brain activity and reading in dyslexics. *Journal of Clinical and Experimental Neuropsychology, 7,* 505–525.

Baldwin, J. M. (1894). *Mental development in the child and the race.* New York, NY: MacMillan.

Band, E. B., & Weisz, J. R. (1988). How to feel better when it feels bad: Children's perspectives on coping with everyday stress. *Developmental Psychology, 24,* 247–253.

Barkley, R. A. (1987). The assessment of attention deficit-hyperactivity disorder. *Behavioral Assessment, 9,* 207–233.

Barkley, R. A. (1988). The effects of methylphenidate on the interactions of preschool ADHD children with their mothers. *Journal of the American Academy of Child and Adolescent Psychiatry, 27,* 336–341.

Barkley, R. A., Fischer, M., Newby, R. F., & Breen, M. J. (1988). Development of a multimethod clinical protocol for assessing stimulant drug response in children with attention deficit disorder. *Journal of Clinical Child Psychology, 17,* 13–24.

Barkley, R. A., Karlsson, J., & Pollard, S. (1985). Effects of age on the mother–infant interactions of ADD-H and normal boys. *Journal of Abnormal Child Psychology, 13,* 631–637.

Barkley, R. A., Karlsson, J., Pollard, S., & Murphy, J. V. (1985). Developmental changes in the mother–child interactions of hyperactive boys: Effects of two dose levels of Ritalin. *Journal of Child Psychology and Psychiatry, 26,* 705–715.

Barnard, K. E., Bee, H. L., & Hammond, M. A. (1984). Developmental changes in maternal interactions with term and preterm infants. *Infant Behavior and Development, 7,* 101–113.

Barnett, D. W., Zins, J. E., & Wise, L. (1984). An analysis of parental participation as a means of reducing bias in the education of handicapped children. *Special Services in the Schools, 1,* 71–84.

Barnett, W. S. (1986). Definition and classification of mental retardation: A reply to Zigler, Balla, and Hodapp. *American Journal of Mental Deficiency, 91,* 111–116.

Baron, J. (1982). Personality and intelligence. In R. J. Sternberg (Ed.), *Handbook of human intelligence* (pp. 308–351). Cambridge: Cambridge University Press.

Baron-Cohen, S. (1987). Autism and symbolic play. *British Journal of Developmental Psychology, 5,* 139–148.

Baron-Cohen, S. (1989). The autistic child's theory of mind: A case of specific developmental delay. *Journal of Child Psychology and Psychiatry, 30,* 285–297.

Baron-Cohen, S., Leslie, A. M., & Frith, U. (1986). Mechanical, behavioural and intentional understanding of picture stories in autistic children. *British Journal of Developmental Psychology, 4,* 113–125.

Baroody, A. J. (1986). Counting ability of moderately and mildly handicapped children. *Education and Training of the Mentally Retarded, 21,* 289–300.

Barrera, M. E., Rosenbaum, P. L., & Cunningham, C. E. (1986). Early home intervention with low birth-weight infants and their parents. *Child Development, 57,* 20–33.

Barrett, D. E., Radke-Yarrow, M., & Klein, R. E. (1982). Chronic malnutrition and child behavior: Effects of early caloric supplementation on social and emotional functioning. *Developmental Psychology, 18,* 541–556.

Barrett, P., Eysenck, H. J., & Lucking, S. (1986). Reaction time and intelligence: A replicated study. *Intelligence, 10,* 9–40.

Barton, C. L., Barton, L. E., Rycek, R. F., & Brulle, A. R. (1984). Parents and information: What they receive and what they need. *Mental Retardation and Learning Disability Bulletin, 12,* 98–104.

Barton, J. A. (1988). Problem-solving strategies in learning disabled and normal boys: Developmental and instructional effects. *Journal of Educational Psychology, 80,* 184–191.

Bates, W. J., Smeltzer, D. J., & Arnoczky, S. M. (1986). Appropriate and inappropriate use of psychotherapeutic medications for institutionalized mentally retarded persons. *American Journal of Mental Deficiency, 90,* 363–370.

Batheja, M., & McManus, I. C. (1985). Handedness in the mentally handicapped. *Developmental Medicine and Child Neurology, 27,* 63–68.

Bauer, R. H., & Emhert, J. (1984). Information processing in reading-disabled and nondisabled children. *Journal of Experimental Child Psychology, 37,* 271–281.

Baumeister, A. A., Runcie, D., & Gardepe, J. (1984). Processing of information in iconic memory: Differences between nonretarded and retarded subjects. *Journal of Abnormal Psychology, 93,* 433–447.

Beach, R. S., Gershwin, M. E., & Hurley, L. S. (1982). Gestational zinc deprivation in mice: Persistence of immunodeficiency for three generations. *Science, 218,* 469–471.

Beale, I. L., Matthew, P. J., Oliver, S., & Corballis, M. C. (1987). Performance of disabled and normal readers in the Continuous Performance Test. *Journal of Abnormal Child Psychology, 15,* 229–238.

Bearison, D. J., & Pacifici, C. (1984). Psychological studies of children who have cancer. *Journal of Applied Developmental Psychology, 5,* 263–280.

Bebko, J. M. (1984). Memory and rehearsal characteristics of profoundly deaf children. *Journal of Experimental Child Psychology, 38,* 415–428.

Bebko, J. M., Konstantereas, M. M., & Springer, J. (1987). Parent and professional evaluations of family stress associated with characteristics of autism. *Journal of Autism and Developmental Disorders, 17,* 565–576.

Beckman, P. J., & Kohl, F. L. (1984). The effects of social and isolate toys on the interactions and play of integrated and nonintegrated groups of preschoolers. *Education and Training of the Mentally Retarded, 19,* 169–174.

Befera, M. S., & Barkley, R. A. (1985). Hyperactive and normal girls and boys: Mother–child interaction, parent psychiatric status and child psychopathology. *Journal of Child Psychology and Psychiatry, 26,* 439–452.

Begun, A. L. (1989). Sibling relationships involving developmentally disabled people. *American Journal on Mental Retardation, 93,* 566–574.

Beitchman, J. H., Hood, J., Rochon, J., & Peterson, M. (1989). Empirical classification of speech/language impairment in children: 2. Behavioral characteristics. *Journal of the American Academy of Child and Adolescent Psychiatry, 28,* 118–123.

Beitchman, J. H., Hood, J., Rochon, J., Peterson, M., Mantini, T., & Majumdar, S. (1989). Empirical classification of speech/language impairment in children: 1. Identification of speech/language categories. *Journal of the American Academy of Child and Adolescent Psychiatry, 28,* 112–117.

Beitchman, J. H., Nair, R., Clegg, M., Ferguson, B., & Patel, P. G. (1986). Prevalence of psychiatric disorders in children with speech and language disorders. *Journal of the American Academy of Child Psychiatry, 25,* 528–535.

Beitchman, J. H., Wekerle, C., & Hood, J. (1987). Diagnostic continuity from preschool to middle childhood. *Journal of the American Academy of Child and Adolescent Psychiatry, 26,* 694–699.

Belmont, J. M. (1966). Long-term memory in mental retardation. In N. R. Ellis (Ed.), *International review of research in mental retardation* (Vol. 1, pp. 219–255). New York: Academic Press.

Belmont, J. M., & Mitchell, D. W. (1987). The general strategies hypothesis as applied to cognitive theory in mental retardation. *Intelligence, 11,* 91–105.

Bender, W. N. (1985). Differences between learning disabled and non-learning disabled children in temperament and behavior. *Learning Disabilities Quarterly, 8,* 11–18.

Bender, W. N. (1987a). Behavioral indicators of temperament and personality in the inactive learner. *Journal of Learning Disabilities, 20,* 301–305.

Bender, W. N. (1987b). Secondary personality and behavioral problems in adolescents with Learning Disabilities. *Journal of Learning Disabilities, 20,* 280–285.

Bender, W. N., & Ukeje, I. C. (1989). Instructional strategies in mainstream classrooms: Prediction of the strategies teachers select. *Remedial and Special Education, 10,* 23–30.

Bender, W. N., Wyne, M. D., Stuck, G. B., & Bailey, D. B. (1984). Relative peer status of learning disabled, educable mentally handicapped, low achieving, and normally achieving children. *Child Study Journal, 13,* 209–216.

Bendersky, M., & Lewis, M. (1986). The impact of birth order on mother–infant interactions in preterm and sick infants. *Journal of Developmental and Behavioral Pediatrics, 7,* 242–246.

Benezra, E., & Douglas, V. I. (1988). Short-term serial recall in ADDH, normal, and reading-disabled boys. *Journal of Abnormal Child Psychology, 16,* 511–525.

Bennett, R. E., Rock, D. A., & Jirele, T. (1987). GRE score level, test completion, and reliability for visually impaired, physically handicapped, and nonhandicapped groups. *Journal of Special Education, 21,* 9–21.

Bensberg, G. J., & Smith, J. J. (1984). Comparative costs of public residential and community residential facilities for the mentally retarded. *Educational and Training of the Mentally Retarded, 19,* 45–48.

Benson, B. A., Reiss, S., Smith, D. C., & Laman, D. S. (1985). Psychosocial correlates of depression in mentally retarded adults: 2. Poor social skills. *American Journal of Mental Deficiency, 89,* 657–659.

Benson, B. A., Rice, C. J., & Miranti, S. V. (1986). Effects of anger management training with mentally retarded adults in group treatment. *Journal of Consulting and Clinical Psychology, 54,* 728–729.

Benson, J., & Ellison-Bidwell, W. (1984). The effect of item format on the validity of achievement tests for the learning disabled. *Child Study Journal, 14,* 301–307.

Benton, A. L. (1984). Dyslexia and spatial thinking. *Annals of Dyslexia, 34,* 69–85.

Berg, J. M. (1986). Prenatal diagnosis of mental retardation and its implications. *Psychiatric Clinics of North America, 9,* 625–634.

Bergeman, C. S., & Plomin, R. (1988). Parental mediators of the genetic relationship between home environment and infant mental development. *British Journal of Developmental Psychology, 6,* 11–19.

Berger, J., & Cunningham, C. C. (1986). Aspects of early social smiling by infants with Down's syndrome. *Child: Care, Health and Development, 12,* 13–24.

Bergmann, G. (1986). Studies in stuttering as a prosodic disturbance. *Journal of Speech and Hearing Research, 29,* 290–300.

Berkson, G. (1974). Social responses of animals to infants with defects. In M. Lewis & L. E. Rosenblum (Eds.), *The effect of the infant on its caregiver* (pp. 239–249). New York: Wiley.

Berkson, G., & Landesman-Dwyer, S. (1977). Behavioral research on severe and profound mental retardation. *American Journal of Mental Deficiency, 81*, 428–454.

Berkson, G., & Romer, D. (1980). Social ecology of supervised communal facilities for mentally disabled adults: 1. Introduction. *American Journal of Mental Deficiency, 85*, 219–228.

Bernfeld, G. A., & Peters, R. De V. (1986). Social reasoning and social behavior in reflective and impulsive children. *Journal of Clinical Child Psychology, 15*, 221–227.

Berninger, V. W. (1988). Development of operational thought without a normal sensorimotor stage. *Intelligence, 12*, 219–230.

Berntson, G. G., Ronca, A. E., Tuber, D. S., Boysen, S. T., & Leland, H. (1985). Cardiac reactivity and adaptive behavior. *American Journal of Mental Deficiency, 89*, 415–419.

Berry, P., Groeneweg, G., Gibson, D., & Brown, R. I. (1984). Mental development of adults with Down syndrome. *American Journal of Mental Deficiency, 89*, 252–256.

Bersani, Jr., H. A., & Heifetz, L. J. (1985). Perceived stress and satisfaction of direct-care staff members in community residences for mentally retarded adults. *American Journal of Mental Deficiency, 90*, 289–295.

Bialystok, E., & Mitterer, J. (1987). Metalinguistic differences among three kinds of readers. *Journal of Educational Psychology, 79*, 147–153.

Bice, T. R., Halpin, G., & Halpin, G. (1986). A comparison of the cognitive styles of typical and mildly retarded children with educational recommendations. *Education and Training of the Mentally Retarded, 21*, 93–97.

Bichard, S. L., Alden, L., Walker, L. J., & McMahon, R. J. (1988). Friendship understanding in socially accepted, rejected, and neglected children. *Merrill-Palmer Quarterly, 34*, 33–46.

Bickel, W. E., & Bickel, D. D. (1986). Effective schools, classrooms, and instruction: Implications for special education. *Exceptional Children, 52*, 489–500.

Bickel, W. K., Stella, E., & Etzel, B. (1984). A reevaluation of stimulus overselectivity: Restricted stimulus control or stimulus control hierarchies. *Journal of Autism and Developmental Disorders, 14*, 137–157.

Bierman, K. L. (1987). The clinical significance and assessment of poor peer relations: Peer neglect versus peer rejection. *Journal of Developmental and Behavioral Pediatrics, 8*, 233–240.

Bierman, K. L., & McCauley, E. (1987). Children's descriptions of their peer interactions: Useful information for clinical child assessment. *Journal of Clinical Child Psychology, 16*, 9–18.

Bigelow, A. (1987). Early words of blind children. *Journal of Child Language, 14*, 47–56.

Bigelow, A. E. (1986). The development of reaching in blind children. *British Journal of Developmental Psychology, 4*, 355–366.

Bigsby, P. (1985). The nature of reversible letter confusions in dyslexic and normal readers: Misperception or mislabeling? *British Journal of Educational Psychology, 55*, 264–272.

Bilsky, L. H., & Judd, T. (1986). Sources of difficulty in the solution of verbal arithmetic problems by mentally retarded and nonretarded individuals. *American Journal of Mental Deficiency, 90,* 395–402.

Birleson, P., Hudson, I., Buchanan, D. G., & Wolff, S. (1987). Clinical evaluation of a self-rating scale for depressive disorder in childhood (Depression self-rating scale). *Journal of Child Psychology and Psychiatry, 28,* 43–60.

Bishop, D. V. M., & Edmundson, A. (1987). Specific language impairment as a maturational lag: Evidence from longitudinal data on language and motor development. *Developmental Medicine and Child Neurology, 29,* 442–459.

Blacher, J. (1984). Sequential stages of parental adjustment to the birth of a child with handicaps: Fact or artifact? *Mental Retardation, 22,* 55–68.

Blacher, J., Nihira, K., & Meyers, C. E. (1987). Characteristics of home environment of families with mentally retarded children: Comparison across levels of retardation. *American Journal of Mental Deficiency, 9,* 313–320.

Black, M. M., Cohn, J. F., Smull, M. W., & Crites, L. S. (1985). Individual and family factors associated with risk of institutionalization of mentally retarded adults. *American Journal of Mental Deficiency, 90,* 271–276.

Blackman, A. A., & Dembo, M. H. (1984). Prosocial behaviors in a mainstreamed preschool. *Child Study Journal, 14,* 205–215.

Blair, E., & Stanley, F. (1985). Interobserver agreement in the classification of cerebral palsy. *Developmental Medicine and Child Neurology, 27,* 615–622.

Blamey, P. J., Cowan, R. S. C., Alcantara, J. I., & Clark, G. M. (1988). Phonemic information transmitted by a multichannel electrotactile speech processor. *Journal of Speech and Hearing Research, 31,* 620–629.

Blashfield, R. K., & Draguns, J. G. (1976a). Evaluative criteria for psychiatric classification. *Journal of Abnormal Psychology, 85,* 140–150.

Blashfield, R. K., & Draguns, J. G. (1976b). Toward a taxonomy of psychopathology: The purpose of psychiatric classification. *British Journal of Psychiatry, 129,* 574–583.

Blass, E. M., Ganchrow, J. R., & Steiner, J. E. (1984). Classical conditioning in newborn humans 2–48 hours of age. *Infant Behavior & Development, 7,* 223–235.

Bliss, L. S. (1984). The development of listener-adapted communication by educable mentally impaired children. *Journal of Communication Disorders, 17,* 371–384.

Bliss, L. S. (1985). The development of persuasive strategies by mentally retarded children. *Applied Research in Mental Retardation, 6,* 437–447.

Block, J., Block, J. H., & Keyes, S. (1988). Longitudinally foretelling drug usage in adolescence: Early childhood personality and environmental precursors. *Child Development, 59,* 336–355.

Block, J. H., Block, J., & Gjerde, P. F. (1986). The personality of children prior to divorce: A prospective study. *Child Development, 57,* 827–840.

Blood, G. W. (1985). Laterality differences in child stutterers: Heterogeneity, severity levels, and statistical treatments. *Journal of Speech and Hearing Disorders, 50,* 66–72.

Blotcky, A. D., Raczynski, J. M., Gurwitch, R., & Smith, K. (1985). Family influences on hopelessness among children early in the cancer experience. *Journal of Pediatric Psychology, 10,* 479–493.

Blumenthal, S. J., & Kupfer, D. J. (1988). Overview of early detection and treatment strategies for suicidal behavior in young people. *Journal of Youth and Adolescence,* 17, 1–23.

Bodiford, C. A., Eisenstadt, T. H., Johnson, J. H., & Bradlyn, A. S. (1988). Comparison of learned helplessness cognitions and behavior in children with high and low scores on the Children's Depression Inventory. *Journal of Clinical Child Psychology,* 17, 152–158.

Bodner-Johnson, B. (1986). The family environment and achievement of deaf students: A discriminant analysis. *Exceptional Children, 52,* 443–449.

Bohline, D. S. (1985). Intellectual and affective characteristics of attention deficit disordered children. *Journal of Learning Disabilities, 18,* 604–608.

Bond, G. G. (1987). An assessment of cognitive abilities in hearing and hearing-impaired preschool children. *Journal of Speech and Hearing Disorders, 52,* 319–323.

Bonin, B., Ramig, P., & Prescott, T. (1985). Performance differences between stuttering and nonstuttering subjects on a sound fusion task. *Journal of Fluency Disorders, 10,* 291–300.

Boothroyd, A. (1985). Evaluation of speech production of the hearing impaired: Some benefits of forced-choice testing. *Journal of Speech and Hearing Research, 28,* 185–196.

Borcherding, B., Thompson, K., Kruesi, M., Bartko, J., Rapoport, J. L., & Weingartner, H. (1988). Automatic and effortful processing in attention deficit/hyperactivity disorder. *Journal of Abnormal Child Psychology, 16,* 333–345.

Borden, K. A., Brown, R. T., Jenkins, P., & Clingerman, S. R. (1987). Achievement attributions and depressive symptoms in attention deficit-disordered and normal children. *Journal of School Psychology, 25,* 399–404.

Borges-Osorio, M. R., & Salzano, F. M. (1987). Frequencies of language disabilities and their family patterns in Porto Alegre, Brazil. *Behavior Genetics, 17,* 53–69.

Boring, E. G. (1933). *The physical dimensions of consciousness.* New York: Century Company.

Borkowski, J. G., Carr, M., & Pressley, M. (1987). "Spontaneous" strategy use: Perspectives from metacognitive theory. *Intelligence, 11,* 61–76.

Borkowski, J. G., Estrada, M. T., Milstead, M., & Hale, C. A. (1989). General problem-solving skills: Relations between metacognition and strategic processing. *Learning Disability Quarterly, 12,* 57–70.

Borkowski, J. G., Weyhing, R. S., & Carr, M. (1988). Effects of attributional retraining on strategy-based reading comprehension in learning-disabled students. *Journal of Educational Psychology, 80,* 46–53.

Bornstein, M. (1989). Sensitive periods in development: Structural characteristics and causal interpretations. *Psychological Bulletin, 105,* 179–197.

Borthwick-Duffy, S. A., Eyman, R. K., & White, J. F. (1987). Client characteristics and residential placement patterns. *American Journal on Mental Deficiency, 92,* 24–30.

Botuck, S., Turkewitz, G., & Moreau, T. (1987). Auditory-visual equivalence by mentally retarded and intellectually average older children. *American Journal of Mental Retardation, 92,* 318–321.

Bowers, D. S., Clement, P. W., Fantuzzo, J. W., & Sorensen, D. A. (1985). Effects of teacher-administered and self-administered reinforcers on learning disabled children. *Behavior Therapy, 16,* 357–369.

Boyage, S., Collins, J. K., Maberly, G. F., Morris, J. G., Jupp, J. J., & Eastman, C. J. (1987). Congenital iodine deficiency disorders (endemic cretinism): History and description. *Australia and New Zealand Journal of Developmental Disabilities, 13*, 3–11.

Boyd, B. D., & Ellis, N. R. (1986). Levels of processing and memory in mentally retarded and nonretarded persons. *Intelligence, 10*, 1–8.

Boyle, M. H., & Jones, S. C. (1985). Selecting measures of emotional and behavioral disorders of childhood for use in general populations. *Journal of Child Psychology and Psychiatry, 26*, 137–159.

Bozynski, M. E. A., Nelson, M. N., Rosati-Skertich, C., Genaze, D., O'Donnell, K., & Naughton, P. (1984). Two year longitudinal follow-up of premature infants weighing < 1,200 grams at birth: Sequelae of intracranial hemorrhage. *Journal of Developmental and Behavioral Pediatrics, 5*, 346–352.

Bracken, B. A., & Cato, L. A. (1986). Rate of conceptual development among deaf preschool and primary children as compared to a matched group of nonhearing impaired children. *Psychology in the Schools, 23*, 95–99.

Braddock, D., & Heller, T. (1985). The closure of mental retardation institutions: 2. Implications. *Mental Retardation, 23*, 222–229.

Bradley, R. H., & Caldwell, B. M. (1977). Home observation for measurement of the environment: A validation study of screening efficiency. *American Journal of Mental Deficiency, 81*, 417–420.

Bradley, R. H., Caldwell, B. M., Rock, S. L., Casey, P. M., & Nelson, J. (1987). The early development of low-birthweight infants: Relationship to health, family status, family context, family processes, and parenting. *International Journal of Behavioral Development, 10*, 301–318.

Bradley, R. H., Casey, P. H., & Wortham, B. (1984). Home environments of low SES non-organic failure-to-thrive infants. *Merrill-Palmer Quarterly, 30*, 393–402.

Bradley, R. H., Rock, S. L., Caldwell, B. M., & Brisby, J. A. (1989). Uses of the HOME Inventory for families with handicapped children. *American Journal of Mental Retardation, 94*, 313–330.

Bradshaw-McAnulty, G., Hicks, R. E., & Kinsbourne, M. (1984). Pathological left-handedness and familial sinistrality in relation to degree of mental retardation. *Brain and Cognition, 3*, 349–356.

Brady, M. P., Shores, R. E., McEvoy, M. A., Ellis, D., & Fox, J. J. (1987). Increasing social interactions of severely handicapped autistic children. *Journal of Autism and Developmental Disabilities, 17*, 375–390.

Brady, M. P., & Taylor, R. D. (1989). Instructional consequences in mainstreamed middle school classes: Reinforcement and corrections. *Remedial and Special Education, 10*, 31–36.

Brailsford, A., Snart, F., & Das, J. P. (1984). Strategy and reading comprehension. *Journal of Learning Disabilities, 17*, 287–290.

Brainerd, C. J., Kingma, J., & Howe, M. L. (1985). On the development of forgetting. *Child Development, 56*, 1103–1119.

Bray, N. W., & Turner, L. A. (1987). Production anomalies (not strategic deficiencies) in mentally retarded individuals. *Intelligence, 11*, 49–60.

Breitmayer, B. J., & Ramey, C. T. (1986). Biological nonoptimality and quality of postnatal environment as codeterminants of intellectual development. *Child Development, 57*, 1151–1165.

Breslau, N., & Marshall, I. A. (1985). Psychological disturbance in children with physical disabilities: Continuity and change in a 5-year follow-up. *Journal of Abnormal Child Psychology, 13*, 199–215.

Breznitz, Z., & Sherman, T. (1987). Speech patterning of natural discourse of well and depressed mothers and their young children. *Child Development, 58*, 395–400.

Brickey, M. P., Campbell, K. M., & Browning, L. J. (1985). A 5-year follow-up of sheltered workshop employees placed in competitive jobs. *Mental Retardation, 23*, 67–73.

Bril, B. (1986). Motor development and cultural attitudes. In H. T. A. Whiting, & M. G. Wade (Eds.), *Themes in motor development* (pp. 297–314). Dordrecht: Nijhoff.

Brimblecombe, F. S. W. (1985). The needs of young intellectually retarded adults. *British Journal of Psychiatry, 146*, 5–10.

Brinker, R. P., & Thorpe, M. E. (1986). Features of integrated educational ecologies that predict social behavior among severely mentally retarded and nonretarded students. *American Journal of Mental Deficiency, 91*, 150–159.

Bristol, M. M. (1987). Mothers of children with autism or communication disorders: Successful adaptation and the Double ABCX model. *Journal of Autism and Developmental Disorders, 17*, 469–486.

Bristol, M. M., Gallagher, J. J., & Schopler, E. (1988). Mothers and fathers of young developmentally disabled and nondisabled boys: Adaptation and spousal support. *Developmental Psychology, 24*, 441–451.

Broman, S. H., Nichols, P. L., & Kennedy, W. A. (1975). *Preschool IQ: Prenatal and early developmental correlates.* Hillsdale, NJ: Lawrence Erlbaum Associates.

Bronfenbrenner, U. (1977). Toward an experimental ecology of human development. *American Psychologist, 32*, 513–531.

Brooks-Gunn, J., & Lewis, M. (1984). Maternal responsivity in interactions with handicapped infants. *Child Development, 55*, 782–793.

Brooks-Gunn, J., McCormick, M. C., & Heagarty, M. C. (1988). Preventing infant mortality and morbidity: Developmental perspectives. *American Journal of Orthopsychiatry, 58*, 288–296.

Brown, F., Weed, K., & Evans, I. M. (1987). Perceptions of handicapped and nonhandicapped students of the importance and utility of their high school curricula. *Education and Training in Mental Retardation, 22*, 185–196.

Brown, J. M., O'Keeffe, J., Sanders, S. H., & Baker, B. (1986). Developmental changes in children's cognition to stressful and painful situations. *Journal of Pediatric Psychology, 11*, 343–357.

Brown, R., Hibbard, M., & Waters, B. (1986). The transition of the mentally retarded from school to work: The implications of structural unemployment. *Children and Youth Services Review, 8*, 227–241.

Brown, R. T., & Borden, K. A. (1986). Hyperactivity at adolescence: Some misconceptions and new directions. *Journal of Clinical Child Psychology, 15*, 194–209.

Brown, R. T., Borden, K. A., Schleser, R., Clingerman, S. R., & Orenczuk, S. (1985). The performance of attention-deficit-disordered and normal children on conservation tasks. *Journal of Genetic Psychology, 146*, 535–540.

Brown, R. T., Borden, K. A., Wynne, M. E., Schleser, R., & Clingerman, S. R. (1986). Methylphenidate and cognitive therapy with ADD children: A methodological reconsideration. *Journal of Abnormal Child Psychology, 14*, 481–497.

Brown, R. T., & Wynne, M. E. (1984a). Attentional characteristics and teachers' ratings in hyperactive, reading disabled, and normal boys. *Journal of Clinical Child Psychology, 13,* 38–43.

Brown, R. T., & Wynne, M. E. (1984b). An analysis of attentional components in hyperactive and normal boys. *Journal of Learning Disabilities, 17,* 162–166.

Brown-Gorton, R., & Wolery, M. (1988). Teaching mothers to imitate their handicapped children: Effects on maternal mands. *Journal of Special Education, 22,* 97–107.

Browne, A., & Finkelhor, D. (1986). Impact of child sexual abuse: A review of the research. *Psychological Bulletin, 99,* 66–77.

Browning, P., Thorin, E., & Rhoades, C. (1984). A national profile of self-help/self-advocacy groups of people with mental retardation. *Mental Retardation, 22,* 226–230.

Bruck, M., & Treiman, R. (1990). Phonological awareness and spelling in normal children and dyslexics: The case of initial consonant clusters. *Journal of Experimental Child Psychology, 50,* 156–178.

Bruno, R. M., Johnson, J. M., & Simon, J. (1987). Perception of humor by regular class students and students with learning disabilities or mild mental retardation. *Journal of Learning Disabilities, 20,* 568–570.

Brunt, D., & Broadhead, G. D. (1982). Motor proficiency traits of deaf children. *Research Quarterly for Exercise and Sport, 53,* 236–238.

Brunt, D., & Distefano, E. A. (1982). The effect of movement uncertainty on reaction and movement times of learning disabled and normal boys. *Canadian Journal of Applied Sport Sciences, 7,* 138–141.

Brunt, D., Layne, C. S., Cook, M., & Rowe, L. (1984). Automatic postural responses of deaf children from dynamic and static positions. *Adapted Physical Activity Quarterly, 1,* 247–252.

Brutten, G. J., Bakker, K., Janssen, P., & Van der Meulen, S. (1984). Eye movements of stuttering and nonstuttering children during silent reading. *Journal of Speech and Hearing Research, 27,* 562–566.

Brutten, G. J., & Trotter, A. C. (1985). Hemispheric interference: A dual-task investigation of youngsters who stutter. *Journal of Fluency Disorders, 10,* 77–85.

Brutten, G. J., & Trotter, A. C. (1986). A dual-task investigation of young stutterers and nonstutterers. *Journal of Fluency Disorders, 11,* 275–284.

Bryant, J. T., Deckner, C. W., Soraci, Jr., S. A., Baumeister, A. A., & Blanton, R. L. (1988). Oddity learning in developmentally delayed children: Facilitation by means of familiar stimuli. *American Journal on Mental Retardation, 93,* 138–143.

Buckle, J. R. (1984). The extra costs of mentally handicapped living. *International Journal of Rehabilitation Research, 7,* 78–80.

Budd, K. S., & Greenspan, S. (1985). Parameters of successful and unsuccessful interventions with parents who are mentally retarded. *Mental Retardation, 23,* 269–273.

Budoff, M. (1969). Learning potential: A supplementary procedure for assessing the ability to reason. *Seminars in Psychiatry, 1,* 278–290.

Bullock, L. M., Zagar, E. L., Donahue, C. A., & Pelton, G. B. (1985). Teachers' perceptions of behaviorally disordered students in a variety of settings. *Exceptional Children, 52,* 123–130.

Burd, L., Fisher, W., & Kerbeshian, J. (1987). A prevalence study of pervasive developmental disorders in North Dakota. *Journal of the American Academy of Child and Adolescent Psychiatry, 26*, 700–703.

Burden, P. R., & Parish, T. S. (1983). Exceptional and normal children's descriptors of themselves. *Education, 104*, 204–205.

Burns, B. (1986). Relationship of perceived stimulus structure and intelligence: Further tests of a separability hypothesis. *American Journal of Mental Deficiency, 91*, 196–200.

Burstein, N. D. (1986). The effects of classroom organization on mainstreamed preschool children. *Exceptional Children, 52*, 425–434.

Bush, J. P., & Cockrell, C. S. (1987). Maternal factors predicting parenting behaviors in the pediatric clinic. *Journal of Pediatric Psychology, 12*, 505–518.

Butler, S. R., Marsh, H. W., Sheppard, M. J., & Sheppard, J. L. (1985). Seven-year longitudinal study of the early prediction of reading achievement. *Journal of Educational Psychology, 77*, 349–361.

Butterfield, E. C. (1990). The compassion of distinguishing punishing behavioral treatment from aversive treatment. *American Journal on Mental Retardation, 95*, 137–141.

Butterfield, E. C., Wambold, C., & Belmont, J. M. (1973). On the theory and practice of improving short-term memory. *American Journal of Mental Deficiency, 77*, 654–669.

Butterfield, S. A. (1986). Gross motor profiles of deaf children. *Perceptual and Motor Skills, 62*, 68–70.

Buyer, L. S., Berkson, G., Winnega, M. A., & Morton, L. (1987). Stimulation and control as components of stereotyped body-rocking. *American Journal of Mental Deficiency, 91*, 543–547.

Bylsma, F. W., & Pivik, R. T. (1989). The effects of background illumination and stimulant medication on smooth pursuit eye movements of hyperactive children. *Journal of Abnormal Child Psychology, 17*, 73–90.

Byrne, D. (1986). Recent advances in acoustic hearing aids. *Volta Review, 88*, 31–43.

Byrne, E. A., & Cunningham, C. C. (1985). The effects of mentally handicapped children on families: A conceptual review. *Journal of Child Psychology and Psychiatry, 26*, 847–864.

Cadman, D., Boyle, M., & Offord, D. R. (1988). The Ontario Child Health Study: Social adjustment and mental health of siblings of children with chronic health problems. *Journal of Developmental and Behavioral Pediatrics, 9*, 117–121.

Cadman, D., Boyle, M., Szatmari, P., & Offord, D. R. (1987). Chronic illness, disability, and mental and social well-being: Findings of the Ontario Child Health Study. *Pediatrics, 79*, 805–812.

Cadman, D., Goldsmith, C., & Bashim, P. (1984). Values, preferences, and decisions in the care of children with developmental disabilities. *Journal of Developmental and Behavioral Pediatrics, 5*, 60–64.

Calhoun, M. L. (1985). Typing contrasted with handwriting in language arts instruction for moderately mentally retarded students. *Education and Training of the Mentally Retarded, 20*, 48–52.

Campbell, A. (1987). Self-reported delinquency and home life: Evidence from a sample of British girls. *Journal of Youth and Adolescence, 16*, 167–177.

Campbell, M. (1988). Fenfluramine treatment of autism. *Journal of Child Psychology and Psychiatry, 29,* 1–10.

Campbell, S. B. (1985). Hyperactivity in preschoolers: Correlates and prognostic implications. *Clinical Psychology Reviews, 5,* 405–428.

Campbell, S. B. (1987). Parent-referred problem 3-year-olds: Developmental changes in symptoms. *Journal of Child Psychology and Psychiatry, 28,* 835–845.

Campbell, S. B., Breaux, A. M., Ewing, L. J., & Szumowski, E. K. (1986). Correlates and predictors of hyperactivity and aggression: A longitudinal study of parent-referred problem preschoolers. *Journal of Abnormal Child Psychology, 14,* 217–234.

Campbell, T. F., & McNeil, M. R. (1985). Effects of presentation rate and divided attention on auditory comprehension in children with an acquired language disorder. *Journal of Speech and Hearing Research, 28,* 513–520.

Campion, J., & Latto, R. (1985). Apperceptive agnosia due to carbon monoxide poisoning: An interpretation based on critical band masking from disseminated lesions. *Behavioural Brain Research, 15,* 227–240.

Campione, J. C. (1989). Assisted assessment: A taxonomy of approaches and an outline of strengths and weaknesses. *Journal of Learning Disabilities, 22,* 151–165.

Camras, L. A., Ribordy, S., Hill, J., Martino, S., Spaccarelli, S., Stefani, R. (1988). Recognition and posing of emotional expressions by abused children and their mothers. *Developmental Psychology, 24,* 776–781.

Candler, A. C., Johnson, D. L., & Green, C. (1983). The differences among children with learning problems. *Education, 104,* 219–223.

Cannella, G. S., Berkeley, T. R., Constans, T. M., & Parkhurst, S. A. (1987). Cognitive processes of at-risk and typically developing infants: Comparison of exploration, play, and problem-solving. *Child Study Journal, 17,* 269–286.

Cantwell, D. P., & Baker, L. (1985). Psychiatric and learning disorders in children with speech and language disorders: A descriptive analysis. *Advances in Learning and Behavioral Disabilities, 4,* 29–47.

Cantwell, D. P., & Baker, L. (1987). Prevalence and type of psychiatric disorder and developmental disorders in three speech and language groups. *Journal of Communication Disorders, 20,* 151–160.

Cantwell, D. P., Baker, L., Rutter, M., & Mawhood, L. (1989). Infantile autism and developmental receptive dysphasia: A comparative follow-up into middle childhood. *Journal of Autism and Developmental Disorders, 19,* 19–31.

Caplan, P. J., & Dinardo, L. (1986). Is there a relationship between child abuse and learning disability? *Canadian Journal of Behavioural Science, 18,* 367–380.

Cardoso-Martins, C., Mervis, C. B., & Mervis, C. A. (1985). Early vocabulary acquisition by children with Down syndrome. *American Journal of Mental Deficiency, 90,* 177–184.

Carey, W. B., & McDevitt, S. C. (1981). Minimal brain dysfunction and hyperkinesis: A clinical viewpoint. *Annual Progress in Child Psychiatry and Child Development, 33,* 589–597.

Carlson, C. I. (1987). Social interaction goals and strategies of children with learning disabilities. *Journal of Learning Disabilities, 20,* 306–311.

Carlson, C. L., Lahey, B. B., Frame, C. L., Walker, J., & Hynd, G. W. (1987). Sociometric status of clinic-referred children with attention deficit disorders with and without hyperactivity. *Journal of Abnormal Child Psychology, 15,* 537–547.

Carlson, W. J., Williams, W. B., & Davol, H. (1984). A factor structure of child home observation data. *Journal of Abnormal Child Psychology, 12,* 245–260.

Carpenter, D. (1985). Grading handicapped pupils: Review and position statement. *Remedial and Special Education, 6,* 54–59.

Carr, E. G., & Durand, V. M. (1985). Reducing behavior problems through functional communication training. *Journal of Applied Behavior Analysis, 18,* 111–126.

Carr, E. G., Pridal, C., & Dores, P. A. (1984). Speech vesus sign comprehension in autistic children: Analysis and prediction. *Journal of Experimental Child Psychology, 37,* 587–597.

Carr, T. H. (1984). Attention, skill, and intelligence: Some speculations on extreme individual differences in human performance. In P. H. Brooks, R. Sperber, & C. McCauley (Eds.), *Learning and cognition in the mentally retarded* (pp. 189–216). Hillsdale, NJ: Lawrence Erlbaum Associates.

Carsrud, A. L., Carsrud, K. B., Dodd, B. G., LeUnes, A., Rhine, J., & Trout, S. (1984). Effects of institutional tours on attitudes toward the mentally retarded and their institutional settings. *Applied Research in Mental Retardation, 5,* 99–105.

Carte, E., Morrison, D., Sublett, J., Uemura, A., & Setrakian, W. (1984). Sensory integration therapy: A trial of a specific neurodevelopmental theory for the remediation of learning disabilities. *Journal of Developmental and Behavioral Pediatrics, 5,* 189–194.

Cartledge, G. (1987). Social skills, learning disabilities, and occupational success. *Journal of Reading, Writing, and Learning Disabilities International, 3,* 223–239.

Caruso, A. J., Conture, E. G., & Colton, R. H. (1988). Selected temporal parameters of coordination associated with stuttering in children. *Journal of Fluency Disorders, 13,* 57–82.

Caruso, D. R., & Hodapp, R. M. (1988). Perceptions of mental retardation and mental illness. *American Journal on Mental Retardation, 93,* 118–124.

Casby, M. W. (1989). National data concerning communication disorders and special education. *Language, Speech, and Hearing Services in Schools, 20,* 22–30.

Casby, M. W., & McCormack, S. M. (1985). Symbolic play and early communication development in hearing-impaired children. *Journal of Communication Disorders, 18,* 67–78.

Casby, M. W., Ruder, K. F. (1983). Symbolic play and early language development in normal and mentally retarded children. *Journal of Speech and Hearing Research, 26,* 404–411.

Casey, R. J., & Berman, J. S. (1985). The outcome of psychotherapy with children. *Psychological Bulletin, 98,* 388–400.

Casey, W., Jones, D., Kugler, B., & Watkins, B. (1988). Integration of Down's syndrome children in the primary school: A longitudinal study of cognitive development and academic attainments. *British Journal of Educational Psychology, 58,* 279–286.

Caspi, A., Elder, Jr., G. H., & Bem, D. J. (1987). Moving against the world: Life-course patterns of explosive children. *Developmental Psychology, 23,* 308–313.

Caton, D. J., Grossnickle, W. F., Cope, J. G., Long, T. E., & Mitchell, C. C. (1988). Burnout and stress among amployees at a state institution for mentally retarded persons. *American Journal on Mental Retardation, 93,* 300–304.

Cattermole, M., Jahoda, A., & Markova, I. (1988). Leaving home: The experience of people with a mental handicap. *Journal of Mental Deficiency Research, 32,* 47–57.

Cattey, T. J. (1985). The bivariate plotting procedure for hearing assessment of adults who are severely and profoundly mentally retarded. *Mental Retardation, 23,* 283–287.

Catts, H. W. (1986). Speech production/phonological deficits in reading-disordered children. *Journal of Learning Disabilities, 19,* 504–508.

Ceci, S. J. (1984). A developmental study of learning disabilities and memory. *Journal of Experimental Child Psychology, 38,* 352–371.

Ceci, S. J., & Baker, J. G. (1989). On learning . . . more or less: A knowledge × process × context view of learning disabilities. *Journal of Learning Disabilities, 22,* 90–99.

Ceci, S. J., & Tishman, J. (1984). Hyperactivity and incidental memory: Evidence for attentional diffusion. *Child Development, 55,* 2192–2203.

Cederblad, M. (1988). Behavioural disorders in children from different cultures. *Acta Psychiatrica Scandinavica, Suppl. No. 344, 78,* 85–92.

Cella, D. F., Perry, S. W., Poag, M. E., Amand, R., & Goodwin, C. (1988). Depression and stress responses in parents of burned children. *Journal of Pediatric Psychology, 13,* 87–99.

Center, D. B., & Wascom, A. M. (1986). Teacher perceptions of social behavior in learning disabled and socially normal children and youth. *Journal of Learning Disabilities, 19,* 420–425.

Center, D. B., & Wascom, A. M. (1987). Teacher perceptions of social behavior in behaviorally disordered and socially normal children and youth. *Behavioral Disorders, 12,* 200–206.

Centra, J. A. (1986). Handicapped student performance on the Scholastic Aptitude Test. *Journal of Learning Disabilities, 19,* 324–327.

Chamberlain, R. N., Christie, P. N., Holt, K. S., Huntley, R.M.C., Pollard, R., & Roche, M. C. (1983). A study of school children who had identified virus infections of the central nervous system during infancy. *Child: Care, Health and Development, 9,* 29–47.

Chapman, J. W. (1988). Cognitive-motivational characteristics and academic achievement of learning disabled children: A longitudinal study. *Journal of Educational Psychology, 80,* 357–365.

Chapman, J. W., & Pitceathly, A. S. (1985). Sexuality and mentally handicapped people: Issues of sex education, marriage, parenthood, and care staff attitudes. *Australia and New Zealand Journal of Developmental Disabilities, 11,* 227–235.

Charlop, M. H., Burgio, L. D., Iwata, B. A., & Ivancic, M. T. (1988). Stimulus variation as a means of enhancing punishment effects. *Journal of Applied Behavior Analysis, 21,* 89–95.

Charlop, M. H., & Walsh, M. E. (1986). Increasing autistic children's spontaneous verbalizations of affection: An assessment of time delay and peer modeling procedures. *Journal of Applied Behavior Analysis, 19,* 307–314.

Cheney, D., & Foss, G. (1984). An examination of the social behavior of mentally retarded workers. *Education and Training of the Mentally Retarded, 19,* 216–221.

Cherkes-Julkowski, M., Gertner, N., & Norlander, K. (1986). Differences in cognitive processes among handicapped and average children: A group learning approach. *Journal of Learning Disabilities, 19,* 438–445.

Cherniss, C. (1988). Observed supervisory behavior and teacher burnout in special education. *Exceptional Children, 54*, 449–454.

Chess, S., & Fernandez, P. (1981). Do deaf children have a typical personality? *Annual Progress in Child Psychiatry and Child Development*, 295–305.

Chetwynd, J. (1985). Some costs of caring at home for an intellectually handicapped child. *Australia and New Zealand Journal of Developmental Disabilities, 11*, 35–40.

Chikovani, M. I., Mirimova, T. D., Mirzoyan, N. S., Znamenskaya, E. I., & Khodakova, I. I. (1984). Characteristics of the neuropsychological development of premature children with perinatal brain damage. *Soviet Neurology and Psychiatry, 17*, 3–11.

Chisholm, R. C., & Karrer, R. (1988). Movement-related potentials and control of associated movements. *International Journal of Neuroscience, 42*, 131–148.

Christensen, J. M., & Sacco, P. R. (1989). Association of hair and eye color with handedness and stuttering. *Journal of Fluency Disorders, 14*, 37–45.

Christie, D. J., Hiss, M., & Lozanoff, B. (1984). Modification of inattentive classroom behavior: Hyperactive children's use of self-recording with teacher guidance. *Behavior Modification, 8*, 391–406.

Ciadella, P., & Mamelle, N. (1989). An epidemiological study of infantile autism in a French department (Rhone): A research note. *Journal of Child Psychology and Psychiatry, 30*, 165–175.

Cipani, E. (1985). An analysis of a partial task training strategy for profoundly retarded institutionalized clients. *Journal of Behavior Therapy and Experimental Psychiatry, 16*, 49–55.

Clark, E. (1987). Responses of mothers and fathers on the personality inventory for children: Are they significantly different? *Journal of Psychoeducational Assessment, 2*, 138–148.

Clark, F. L., Deshler, D. D., Schumaker, J. B., Alley, G. R., & Warner, M. M. (1984). Visual imagery and self-questioning: Strategies to improve comprehension of written material. *Journal of Learning Disabilities, 17*, 145–149.

Clark, R. D. (1984). Handicapped children and computers. *School Psychology Review, 13*, 461–468.

Clarke, A. D. B., & Clarke, A. M. (1987). Research on mental handicap, 1957–1987: A selective review. *Journal of Mental Deficiency Research, 31*, 317–328.

Clarke, A. M., & Clarke, A. D. B. (1988). The adult outcome of early behavioural abnormalities. *International Journal of Behavioral Development, 11*, 3–19.

Cnaan, R. A., Adler, I., & Ramot, A. (1986). Public reaction to establishment of community residential facilities for mentally retarded persons in Israel. *American Journal on Mental Deficiency, 90*, 677–685.

Coates, D. L., & Lewis, M. (1984). Early mother–infant interaction and infant cognitive status as predictors of school performance and cognitive behavior in 6-year-olds. *Child Development, 55*, 1219–1230.

Coben, S., & Zigmond, N. (1986). The social integration of learning disabled students from self-contained to mainstream elementary school settings. *Journal of Learning Disabilities, 19*, 614–618.

Coble, P. A., Taska, L. S., Kupfer, D. J., Kazdin, A. E., Unis, A., & French, N. (1984). EEG sleep 'abnormalities' in preadolescent boys with a diagnosis of conduct disorder. *Journal of the American Academy of Child Psychiatry, 23*, 438–447.

Cohen, J., & Breslin, P. W. (1984). Visual evoked responses in dyslexic children. *Annals of the New York Academy of Sciences, 425,* 338–343.

Cohen, R. L., Netley, C., & Clarke, M. A. (1984). On the generality of the short-term memory/reading ability relationship. *Journal of Learning Disabilities, 17,* 218–221.

Cohen, S. E., Parmelee, A. H., Sigman, M., & Beckwith, L. (1988). Antecedents of school problems in children born preterm. *Journal of Pediatric Psychology, 13,* 493–508.

Cole, C. L., Gardner, W. I., & Karan, O. C. (1985). Self-management training of mentally retarded adults presenting severe conduct difficulties. *Applied Research in Mental Retardation, 6,* 337–347.

Cole, D. A. (1986). Out-of-home child placement and family adaptation: A theoretical framework. *American Journal on Mental Deficiency, 91,* 226–236.

Cole, D. A. (1988). Difficulties in relationships between nonhandicapped and severely mentally retarded children: The effect of physical impairments. *Research in Developmental Disabilities, 9,* 55–72.

Cole, D. A., & Meyer, L. H. (1989). Impact of needs and resources on family plans to seek out-of-home placement. *American Journal on Mental Retardation, 93,* 380–387.

Cole, D. A., Meyer, L. H., Vandercook, T., & McQuarter, R. J. (1986). Interactions between peers with and without severe handicaps: Dynamics of teacher intervention. *American Journal of Mental Deficiency, 91,* 160–169.

Cole, D. A., & Rehm, L. P. (1986). Family interaction patterns and childhood depression. *Journal of Abnormal Child Psychology, 14,* 297–314.

Cole, D. A., Vandercook, T., & Rynders, J. (1987). Dyadic interactions between children with and without mental retardation: Effects of age discrepancy. *American Journal of Mental Deficiency, 92,* 194–202.

Cole, H. S., Lopez, R., Epel, R., Singh, B. K., & Cooperman, J. M. (1985). Nutritional deficiencies in institutionalized mentally retarded and physically disabled individuals. *American Journal of Mental Deficiency, 89,* 552–555.

Cole, K. J., Abbs, J. H., & Turner, G. S. (1988). Deficits in the production of grip forces in Down syndrome. *Developmental Medicine and Child Neurology, 30,* 752–758.

Colombo, J. (1982). The critical period concept: Research, methodology and theoretical issues. *Psychological Bulletin, 91,* 260–275.

Compas, B. E. (1987). Coping with stress during childhood and adolescence. *Psychological Bulletin, 101,* 393–403.

Conners, C. K., Reader, M., Reiss, A., Caldwell, J., Caldwell, L., Adesman, A., Mayer, L., Berg, M., Clymer, R., & Erwin, R. (1987). The effects of Piracetam upon visual event-related potentials in dyslexic children. *Psychophysiology, 24,* 513–521.

Conners, F. A., & Detterman, D. K. (1987). Information-processing correlates of computer-assisted word learning by mentally retarded students. *American Journal of Mental Deficiency, 91,* 606–612.

Conroy, J. W. (1985). Medical needs of institutionalized mentally retarded persons: Perceptions of families and staff members. *American Journal of Mental Deficiency, 89,* 510–514.

Conti-Ramsden, G., & Friel-Patti, S. (1984). Mother–child dialogues: A comparison of normal and language-impaired children. *Journal of Communication Disorders, 17,* 19–35.

Conture, E. G., Schwartz, H. D., & Brewer, D. W. (1985). Laryngeal behavior during stuttering: A further study. *Journal of Speech and Hearing Research, 28,* 233–240.

Cooke, K., & Lawton, D. (1984). Informal support for the carers of disabled children. *Child: Care, Health and Development, 10,* 67–79.

Cooley, E. J., & Ayres, R. R. (1988). Self-concept and success-failure attributions of nonhandicapped students and students with learning disabilities. *Journal of Learning Disabilities, 21,* 174–178.

Coolman, R. B., Bennett, F. C., Sells, C. J., Swanson, M. W., Andrews, M. S., & Robinson, N. M. (1985). Neuromotor development of graduates of the neonatal intensive care unit: Patterns encountered in the first 2 years of life. *Journal of Developmental and Behavioral Pediatrics, 6,* 327–333.

Cooper, S. (1987). The fetal alcohol syndrome. *Journal of Child Psychology and Psychiatry, 28,* 223–227.

Cope, J. G., Grossnickle, W. F., Covington, K. B., Durham, T. W., & Zaharia, E. S. (1987). Staff turnover as a function of performance in a public residential facility. *American Journal of Mental Deficiency, 92,* 151–154.

Coplin, J. W., & Morgan, S. B. (1988). Learning disabilities: A multidimensional perspective. *Journal of Learning Disabilities, 21,* 614–622.

Corballis, M. C., Macadie, L., Crotty, A., & Beale, I. L. (1985). The naming of disoriented letters by normal and reading-disabled children. *Journal of Child Psychology and Psychiatry, 26,* 929–938.

Correa, V. I., Poulson, C. L., & Salzberg, C. L. (1984). Training and generalization of reach-grasp behavior in blind, retarded young children. *Journal of Applied Behavior Analysis, 17,* 57–69.

Cosden, M., Pearl, R., & Bryan, T. H. (1985). The effects of cooperative and individual goal structures on learning disabled and nondisabled students. *Exceptional Children, 52,* 103–114.

Coulter, D. L., & Koester, B. S. (1985). Information needs of parents of children with epilepsy. *Journal of Developmental and Behavioral Pediatrics, 6,* 334–338.

Courchesne, E., Lincoln, A. J., Kilman, B. A., & Galambos, R. (1985). Event-related brain potential correlates of the processing of novel visual and auditory information in autism. *Journal of Autism and Developmental Disorders, 15,* 55–76.

Courtright, J. A., & Courtright, I. C. (1983). The perception of nonverbal vocal cues of emotional meaning by language-disordered and normal children. *Journal of Speech and Hearing Research, 26,* 412–417.

Cowan, N. (1988). Evolving conceptions of memory storage, selective attention, and their mutual constraints within the human information-processing system. *Psychological Bulletin, 104,* 163–191.

Cowardin, N. W. (1986). Adolescent characteristics associated with acceptance of handicapped peers. *Adolescence, 21,* 931–940.

Cowen, S. E. (1988). Coping strategies of university students with learning disabilities. *Journal of Learning Disabilities, 21,* 161–188.

Cox, N. J., Seider, R. A., & Kidd, K. K. (1984). Some environmental factors and hypotheses for stuttering in families with several stutterers. *Journal of Speech and Hearing Research, 27,* 543–548.

Craig, H. B., & Gordon, H. W. (1988). Specialized cognitive function and reading achievement in hearing-impaired adolescents. *Journal of Speech and Hearing Disorders, 53,* 30–41.

Crais, E. R., & Chapman, R. C. (1987). Story recall and inferencing skills in language/learning disabled and nondisabled children. *Journal of Speech and Hearing Disorders, 52,* 50–55.

Crapps, J. M., Langone, J., & Swaim, S. (1985). Quantity and quality of participation in community environments by mentally retarded adults. *Education and Training of the Mentally Retarded, 20,* 123–129.

Cravens, H. (1978). *The triumph of evolution: American scientists and the heredity-environment controversy.* Philadelphia: University of Pennsylvania Press.

Crnic, K. A., & Greenberg, M. T. (1987). Transactional relationships between perceived family style, risk status, and mother–child interactions in 2-year-olds. *Journal of Pediatric Psychology, 12,* 343–362.

Cromer, R. F. (1987). Word knowledge acquisition in retarded children: A longitudinal study of acquisition of a complex linguistic structure. *Journal of Speech and Hearing Disorders, 52,* 324–334.

Cross, D. E., & Luper, H. L. (1983). Relation between finger reaction time and voice reaction time in stuttering and nonstuttering children and adults. *Journal of Speech and Hearing Research, 26,* 356–361.

Crowell, J. A., Feldman, S. S., & Ginsberg, N. (1988). Assessment of mother–child interactions in preschoolers with behavior problems. *Journal of the American Academy of Child and Adolescent Psychiatry, 27,* 303–311.

Cullinan, D., & Epstein, M. H. (1985). Adjustment problems of mildly handicapped and nonhandicapped students. *Remedial and Special Education, 6,* 5–11.

Cullinan, D., Epstein, M. H., & Kauffman, J. M. (1984). Teachers' ratings of students' behaviors: What constitutes behavior disorder in school. *Behavioral Disorders, 10,* 9–19.

Cullinan, D., Gadow, K. D., & Epstein, M. H. (1987). Psychotropic drug treatment among learning-disabled, educable mentally retarded, and seriously emotionally disturbed students. *Journal of Abnormal Child Psychology, 15,* 469–477.

Cunningham, C. C., Glenn, S. M., Wilkinson, P., & Sloper, P. (1985). Mental ability, symbolic play and receptive and expressive language of young children with Down's syndrome. *Journal of Child Psychology and Psychiatry, 26,* 255–265.

Cunningham, C. E., Benness, B. B., & Siegel, L. S. (1988). Family functioning, time allocation, and parental depression in the families of normal and ADDH children. *Journal of Child Clinical Psychology, 17,* 169–177.

Cunningham, C. E., & Siegel, L. S. (1987). Peer interactions of normal and attention-deficit-disordered boys during free-play, cooperative task, and simulated classroom situations. *Journal of Abnormal Child Psychology, 15,* 247–268.

Cunningham, C. E., Siegel, L. S., & Offord, D. R. (1985). A developmental dose-response analysis of the effects of methylphenidate on the peer interactions of attention deficit disordered boys. *Journal of Child Psychology and Psychiatry, 26,* 955–971.

Curcio, F., & Paccia, J. (1987). Conversations with autistic children: Contingent relationships between features of adult input and children's response adequacy. *Journal of Autism and Developmental Disorders, 17,* 81–93.

Curry, J. F., Anderson, D. R., Zitlin, M., & Guise, G. (1987). Validity of academic achievement measures with emotionally handicapped children. *Journal of Clinical Child Psychology, 16,* 51–56.

Curry, J. F., & Thompson, Jr., R. J. (1985). Patterns of behavioral disturbance in developmentally disabled and psychiatrically referred children: A cluster analytic approach. *Journal of Pediatric Psychology, 10,* 151–167.

Cuvo, A. J., Gonzalez, P. A., & O'Brien, S. (1985). Social validation of heterosexual social behavior in community settings: A comparison of mentally retarded and non-mentally retarded adults. *Applied Research in Mental Retardation, 6,* 421–435.

Czajkowski, D. R., & Koocher, G. P. (1987). Medical compliance and coping with cystic fibrosis. *Journal of Child Psychology and Psychiatry, 28,* 311–319.

Dadds, M. R. (1987). Families and the origins of child behavior problems. *Family Process, 26,* 341–357.

Dadds, M. R., Schwartz, S., Adams, T., & Rose, S. (1988). The effects of social context and verbal skill on the stereotypic and task-involved behaviour of autistic children. *Journal of Child Psychology and Psychiatry, 29,* 669–676.

Dadds, M. R., Schwartz, S., & Sanders, M. R. (1987). Marital discord and treatment outcome in behavioral treatment of child conduct disorders. *Journal of Consulting & Clinical Psychology, 55,* 396–403.

Dahle, A. J., & McCollister, F. P. (1986). Hearing and otologic disorders in children with Down syndrome. *American Journal of Mental Deficiency, 90,* 636–642.

Dale, P. S., & Cole, K. N. (1988). Comparison of academic and cognitive programs for young handicapped children. *Exceptional Children, 54,* 439–447.

Dalgleish, M. (1985). Family contacts of mentally handicapped adults in different types of residential care. *British Journal of Mental Subnormality, 31,* 114–116.

Dalke, C., & Schmitt, S. (1987). Meeting the transition needs of college-bound students with learning disabilities. *Journal of Learning Disabilities, 20,* 176–180.

Damrosch, S. P., & Perry, L. A. (1989). Self-reported adjustment, chronic sorrow, and coping of parents of children with Down syndrome. *Nursing Research, 38,* 25–30.

Daniels, D., Miller, J. J., Billings, A. G., & Moos, R. H. (1986). Psychosocial functioning of siblings of children with rheumatic disease. *Journal of Pediatrics, 109,* 379–383.

Daniels, D., & Plomin, R. (1985). Origins of individual differences in infant shyness. *Developmental Psychology, 21,* 118–121.

Daniels, D., Plomin, R., & Greenhalgh, J. (1984). Correlates of difficult temperament in infancy. *Child Development, 55,* 1184–1194.

Danielson, L. C., & Bellamy, G. T. (1989). State variation in placement of children with handicaps in segregated environments. *Exceptional Children, 55,* 448–455.

Darch, C., & Carnine, D. (1986). Teaching content area material to learning disabled students. *Exceptional Children, 53,* 240–246.

Das, J. P. (1985). Aspects of digit-span performance: Naming time and order memory. *American Journal of Mental Deficiency, 89,* 627–634.

Davenport, J. W., & Dorcey, T. P. (1972). Hypothyroidism: Learning deficit induced in rats by early exposure to thiouracil. *Hormones and Behavior, 3,* 97–112.

Davenport, J. W., Gonzalez, L. M., Carey, J. C., Bishop, S. B., & Hagquist, W. W. (1976). Environmental stimulation reduces learning deficits in experimental cretinism. *Science, 191,* 578–579.

Davenport, L., Yingling, C. D., Fein, G., Galin, D., & Johnstone, J. (1986). Narrative speech deficits in dyslexics. *Journal of Clinical and Experimental Neuropsychology, 8,* 347–361.

Davey, B., & LaSasso, C. (1985). Relations of cognitive style to assessment components of reading comprehension for hearing-impaired adolescents. *Volta Review, 87,* 17–27.

Davidson, L. L. (1987). Hyperactivity, antisocial behavior, and childhood injury: A critical analysis of the literature. *Journal of Developmental and Behavioral Pediatrics, 8,* 335–340.

Davies, R. R., & Rogers, E. S. (1985). Social skills training with persons who are mentally retarded. *Mental Retardation, 23,* 186–196.

Davis, G. E., & Leitenberg, H. (1987). Adolescent sex offenders. *Psychological Bulletin, 101,* 417–427.

Davis, H., Stroud, A., & Green, L. (1988). Maternal language environment of children with mental retardation. *American Journal on Mental Retardation, 93,* 144–153.

Davis, W. E. (1986a). Development and coordination and control in the mentally handicapped. In H. T. A. Whiting & M. G. Wade (Eds.), *Themes in motor development* (pp. 143–158). Dordrecht: Nijhoff.

Davis, W. E. (1986b). Precise visual information and throwing accuracy of mentally handicapped subjects. In M. G. Wade (Ed.), *Motor skill acquisition of the mentally handicapped* (pp. 25–44). Amsterdam: Elsevier.

Dawson, G., & Adams, A. (1984). Imitation and social responsiveness in autistic children. *Journal of Abnormal Child Psychology, 12,* 209–226.

Dawson, G., & Fernald, M. (1987). Perspective-taking ability and its relationship to the social behavior of autistic children. *Journal of Autism and Developmental Disorders, 17,* 487–498.

Dawson, G., Finley, C., Phillips, S., & Galpert, L. (1986). Hemispheric specialization and the language abilities of autistic children. *Child Development, 57,* 1440–1453.

Dawson, G., & McKissick, F. C. (1984). Self-recognition in autistic children. *Journal of Autism and Development Disorders, 14,* 383–394.

Day, H. M., & Horner, R. H. (1986). Response variation and the generalization of a dressing skill: Comparison of a single instance and general case instruction. *Applied Research in Mental Retardation, 7,* 189–202.

DeFrancesco, J. J., & Taylor, J. (1985). Dimensions of self-concept in primary and middle school learning disabled and nondisabled students. *Child Study Journal, 15,* 99–105.

De La Cruz, F. (1985). Fragile X syndrome. *American Journal of Mental Deficiency, 90,* 119–123.

DeLong, R. G., & Aldershof, A. L. (1987). Long-term experience with lithium treatment in childhood: Correlation with clinical diagnosis. *Journal of the American Academy of Child and Adolescent Psychiatry, 26,* 389–394.

DeRose, J. C., McIlvane, W. J., Dube, W. V., Galpin, V. C., & Stoddard, L. T. (1988). Emergent simple discrimination established by indirect relation to differential consequences. *Journal of the Experimental Analysis of Behavior, 50,* 1–20.

Dean, A. L., Malik, M. M., Richards, W., & Stringer, S. A. (1986). Effects of parental maltreatment on children's conceptions of interpersonal relationships. *Developmental Psychology, 22,* 617–626.

Dean, M., & Nettles, J. (1987). Reverse mainstreaming: A successful model for interaction. *Volta Review, 89,* 27–34.

Decker, S. N., & Bender, B. G. (1988). Converging evidence for multiple genetic forms of reading disability. *Brain and Language, 33,* 197–215.

Demchak, M. (1987). A review of behavioral staff training in special education settings. *Education and Training in Mental Retardation, 22,* 205–217.

Denckla, M. B., Rudel, R. G., Chapman, C., & Krieger, J. (1985). Motor proficiency in dyslexic children with and without attentional disorders. *Archives of Neurology, 42,* 228–231.

Denckla, M. B., LeMay, M., & Chapman, C. A. (1985). Few CT scan abnormalities found even in neurologically impaired learning disabled children. *Journal of Learning Disabilities, 18,* 132–135.

Dentan, R. K. (1967). The response to intellectual impairment among the Semai. *American Journal on Mental Deficiency, 71,* 764–766.

Dermody, P., Mackie, K., & Katsch, R. (1983). Dichotic listening in good and poor readers. *Journal of Speech and Hearing Research, 26,* 341–348.

Derr, A. M. (1985). Conservation and mathematics achievement in the learning disabled child. *Journal of Learning Disabilities, 18,* 333–336.

Detterman, D. K. (1987). Theoretical notions of intelligence and mental retardation. *American Journal of Mental Deficiency, 92,* 2–11.

Deuchar, M., & James, H. (1985). English as the second language of the deaf. *Language and Communication, 5,* 45–51.

Dewhurst, D. L. T., & Cautela, J. R. (1980). A proposed reinforcement survey schedule for special needs children. *Journal of Behavior Therapy and Experimental Psychiatry, 11,* 109–112.

Diaz-Fernandez, F. (1988). Descriptive epidemiology of registered mentally retarded persons in Galicia (Northwest Spain). *American Journal on Mental Retardation, 92,* 385–392.

Dienske, H., DeJonge, G., & Sanders-Woudstra, J. A. R. (1985). Quantitative criteria for attention and activity in child psychiatric patients. *Journal of Child Psychology and Psychiatry, 26,* 895–915.

Digdon, N., & Gotlib, I. H. (1985). Developmental considerations in the study of childhood depression. *Developmental Review, 5,* 162–199.

Digman, J. M., & Inouye, J. (1986). Further specification of the five robust factors of personality. *Journal of Personality & Social Psychology, 50,* 116–123.

Dodd, J. M., Griswold, P. E., Smith, G. H., & Burd, L. (1985). A comparison of learning disabled and other children on the ability to make functional time estimates. *Child Study Journal, 15,* 189–197.

Dollinger, S. J., Horn, J. L., & Boarini, D. (1988). Disturbed sleep and worries among learning disabled adolescents. *American Journal of Orthopsychiatry, 58,* 428–434.

Dolliver, P., Lewis, A. F., & McLaughlin, T. F. (1985). Effects of a daily report card on academic performance and classroom behavior. *Remedial and Special Education, 6,* 51–52.

Donovan, A., Oddy, M., Pardoe, R., & Ades, A. (1986). Employment status and psychological well-being: A longitudinal study of 16-year-old school leavers. *Journal of Child Psychology and Psychiatry, 27,* 65–76.

Donovan, W. L., & Leavitt, L. A. (1985). Simulating conditions of learned helplessness: The effects of interventions and attributions. *Child Development, 56,* 594–603.

Douglas, V. I., Barr, R. G., Amin, K., O'Neill, M. E., & Britton, B. G. (1988). Dosage effects and individual responsivity to methylphenidate in attention deficit disorder. *Journal of Child Psychology and Psychiatry, 29,* 453–475.

Douglas, V. I., Barr, R. G., O'Neill, M. E., & Britton, B. G. (1986). Short term effects of methylphenidate on the cognitive, learning and academic performance of children with attention deficit disorder in the laboratory and the classroom. *Journal of Child Psychology and Psychiatry, 27,* 191–211.

Downey, G., & Coyne, J. C. (1990). Children of depressed parents: An integrative review. *Psychological Bulletin, 108,* 50–76.

Doyle, P. M., Wolery, M., Ault, M. J., & Gast, D. L. (1988). System of least prompts: A literature review of procedural parameters. *Journal of the Association for Persons with Severe Handicaps, 13,* 28–40.

Draeger, S., Prior, M., & Sanson, A. (1986). Visual and auditory attention performance in hyperactive children: Competence or compliance. *Journal of Abnormal Child Psychology, 14,* 411–424.

Dreschler, W. A. (1988). Dynamic-range reduction by peak clipping or compression and its effects on phoneme perception in hearing-impaired listeners. *Scandinavian Audiology, 17,* 45–51.

Drotar, D., & Crawford, P. (1987). Using home observation in the clinical assessment of children. *Journal of Clinical Child Psychology, 16,* 342–349.

Dubowitz, H., Hampton, R. L., Bithoney, W. G., & Newberger, E. H. (1987). Inflicted and noninflicted injuries: Differences in child and familial characteristics. *American Journal of Orthopsychiatry, 57,* 525–535.

Dudley, J. R., & Schatz, M. S. (1985). The missing link in evaluating sheltered workshop programs: The clients' input. *Mental Retardation, 23,* 235–240.

Dudley-Marling, C. C. (1985). The pragmatic skills of learning disabled children: A review. *Journal of Learning Disabilities, 18,* 193–199.

Dudley-Marling, C. C., & Edmiaston, R. (1985). Social status of learning disabled children and adolescents: A review. *Learning Disability Quarterly, 8,* 189–204.

Duff, R., & Campbell, A. (1973) Moral and ethical dilemmas in the special care nursery. *New England Journal of Medicine, 289,* 890–894.

Duker, P. C., & Morsink, H. (1984). Acquisition and cross-setting generalization of manual signs with severely retarded individuals. *Journal of Applied Behavior Analysis, 17,* 93–103.

Dumas, J. E. (1986). Indirect influence of maternal social contacts on mother–infant interactions: A setting event analysis. *Journal of Abnormal Child Psychology, 14,* 205–216.

Dunst, C. J., & Leet, H. E. (1987). Measuring the adequacy of resources in households with young children. *Child: Care, Health and Development, 13,* 111–125.

Dunst, C. J., Leet, H. E., & Trivette, C. M. (1988). Family resources, personal well-being, and early intervention. *Journal of Special Education, 22,* 108–116.

Dunst, C. J., Trivette, C. M., & Cross, A. H. (1986). Mediating influences of social support: Personal, family, and child outcomes. *American Journal of Mental Deficiency, 90,* 403–417.

Duran, E. (1985). Teaching janitorial skills to autistic adolescents. *Adolescence, 20,* 225–232.

Dutton, D. B. (1985). Socioeconomic status and children's health. *Medical Care, 23,* 142–156.

Dweck, C. S. (1986). Motivational processes affecting learning. *American Psychologist, 41,* 1040–1048.

Dygdon, J. A., Conger, A. J., & Keane, S. P. (1987). Children's perceptions of the behavioral correlates of social acceptance, rejection, and neglect in their peers. *Journal of Clinical Child Psychology, 16,* 2–8.

Dyson, L., Edgar, E., & Crnic, K. (1989). Psychological predictors of adjustment by siblings of developmentally disabled children. *American Journal on Mental Retardation, 94,* 292–302.

Eason, L. J., Finch, A. J., Brasted, W., & Saylor, C. F. (1985). The assessment of depression and anxiety in hospitalized pediatric patients. *Child Psychiatry and Human Development, 16,* 57–64.

Edelbrock, C., & Costello, A. J. (1988). Convergence between statistically derived behavior problem syndromes and child psychiatric diagnoses. *Journal of Abnormal Child Psychology, 16,* 219–231.

Edelbrock, C., Costello, A. J., Dulcan, M. K., Conover, N. C., & Kala, R. (1986). Parent–child agreement on child psychiatric symptoms assessed via structured interview. *Journal of Child Psychology and Psychiatry, 27,* 181–190.

Edelbrock, C., Costello, A. J., & Kessler, M. D. (1984). Empirical corroboration of attention deficit disorder. *Journal of the American Academy of Child Psychiatry, 23,* 285–290.

Edelbrock, C., & Rancurello, M. D. (1985). Childhood hyperactivity: An overview of rating scales and their applications. *Clinical Psychology Review, 5,* 429–445.

Edgar, E. (1987). Secondary programs in special education: Are many of them justifiable? *Exceptional Children, 53,* 555–561.

Edgerton, R. B. (1970). Mental retardation in non-Western societies: Toward a cross-cultural perspective on incompetence. In H. C. Haywood (Ed.), *Socio-cultural aspects of mental retardation* (pp. 523–559). New York: Appleton-Century-Crofts.

Edgerton, R. B. (1975). Issues relating to the quality of life among mentally retarded persons. In M. J. Begab & S. A. Richardson (Eds.), *The mentally retarded and society* (pp. 127–140). Baltimore: University Park Press.

Edgerton, R. B. (1984). The participant-observer approach to research in mental retardation. *American Journal of Mental Deficiency, 88,* 498–505.

Edgerton, R. B. (1988). Aging in the community—A matter of choice. *American Journal on Mental Retardation, 92,* 331–335.

Egeland, B., Jacobvitz, D., & Sroufe, L. A. (1988). Breaking the cycle of abuse. *Child Development, 59,* 1080–1088.

Egelston, J. D., Sluyter, G. V., Murie, S. S., & Hobbs, T. (1984). Trends in the use of restrictive and aversive procedures in a facility for developmentally disabled persons. *Education and Training of the Mentally Retarded, 19,* 306–311.

Ehrhardt, A. A., & Meyer-Bahlberg, H.F.L. (1981). Effects of prenatal sex hormones on gender-related behavior. *Science, 211,* 1312–1318.

Eisenberger, R., Mitchell, M., McDermitt, M., & Masterson, F. A. (1984). Accuracy versus speed in the generalized effort of learning-disabled children. *Journal of the Experimental Analysis of Behavior, 42,* 19–36.

Elander, G., Nilsson, A., & Lindberg, T. (1986). Behavior in four-year-olds who have experiences hospitalization and day care. *American Journal of Orthopsychiatry, 56,* 612–616.

Elardo, R., Solomons, H. C., & Snider, B. C. (1987). An analysis of accidents at a day care center. *American Journal of Orthopsychiatry, 57,* 60–65.

Elbert, J. C. (1984). Short-term memory encoding and memory search in the word recognition of learning-disabled children. *Journal of Learning Disabilities, 17,* 342–345.

Elias, M. J., Gara, M., Rothbaum, P. A., Reese, A. M., & Ubriaco, M. (1987). A multivariate analysis of factors differentiating behaviorally and emotionally dysfunctional children from other groups in school. *Journal of Clinical Child Psychology, 16,* 307–312.

Eliason, M. J., & Richman, L. C. (1987). The Continuous Performance Test in learning disabled and nondisabled children. *Journal of Learning Disabilities, 20,* 614–619.

Eliason, M. J., & Richman, L. C. (1988). Behavior and attention in LD children. *Learning Disability Quarterly, 11,* 360–369.

Elkind, D. (1981). *The hurried child: Growing up too fast too soon.* Reading, MA: Addison-Wesley.

Elliman, A. M., Bryan, E. M., & Elliman, A. D. (1986). Low birth weight babies at 3 years of age. *Child: Care, Health and Development, 12,* 287–311.

Elliott, C. D., & Tyler, S. (1987). Learning disabilities and intelligence test results: A principal components analysis of the British Ability Scales. *British Journal of Psychology, 78,* 325–333.

Elliott, D., Edwards, J. M., Weeks, D. J., Lindley, S., & Carnahan, H. (1987). Cerebral specialization in young adults with Down syndrome. *American Journal of Mental Deficiency, 91,* 480–485.

Elliott, D., & Grundy, S. B. (1984). Short-term memory for movement duration in mentally retarded and nonretarded adults. *Australia and New Zealand Journal of Developmental Disabilities, 10,* 191–195.

Elliott, D., Weeks, D. J., & Elliott, C. L. (1987). Cerebral specialization in individuals with Down syndrome. *American Journal of Mental Retardation, 92,* 263–271.

Elliott, D., Weeks, D. J., & Jones, R. (1986). Lateral asymmetries in finger-tapping by adolescents and young adults with Down syndrome. *American Journal of Mental Deficiency, 90,* 472–475.

Elliott, L. L., Hammer, M. A., & Scholl, M. E. (1989). Fine-grained auditory discrimination in normal children and children with language-learning problems. *Journal of Speech and Hearing Research, 32,* 112–119.

Ellis, N. R., & Allison, P. (1988). Memory for frequency of occurrence in retarded and nonretarded persons. *Intelligence, 12,* 61–75.

Ellis, N. R., Deacon, J. R., & Wooldridge, P. W. (1985). Structural memory deficits of mentally retarded persons. *American Journal of Mental Deficiency, 89,* 393–402.

Ellis, N. R., Katz, E., & Williams, J. E. (1987). Developmental aspects of memory for spatial localization. *Journal of Experimental Child Psychology, 44,* 401–412.

Ellis, N. R., & Meador, D. M. (1985). Forgetting in retarded and nonretarded person under conditions of minimal strategy use. *Intelligence, 9,* 87–96.

Ellis, N. R., Palmer, R. L., & Reeves, C. L. (1988). Developmental and intellectual differences in frequency processing. *Developmental Psychology, 24,* 38–45.

Ellis, N. R., Woodley-Zanthos, P., & Dulaney, C. L. (1989). Memory for spatial location in children, adults, and mentally retarded persons. *American Journal on Mental Retardation, 93,* 521–527.

Ellis, N. R., & Wooldridge, P. W. (1985). Short-term memory for pictures and words by mentally retarded and nonretarded persons. *American Journal of Mental*

Deficiency, 89, 622–626.

Elpers, J. R. (1987). Are we legislating reinstitutionalization? *American Journal of Orthopsychiatry, 57*, 441–446.

Emery, R. E. (1989). Family violence. *American Psychologist, 44*, 321–328.

Emler, N., Reicher, S., & Ross, A. (1987). The social context of delinquent conduct. *Journal of Child Psychology and Psychiatry, 28*, 99–109.

Enderby, P., & Phillipp, R. (1986). Speech and language handicap: Towards knowing the size of the problem. *British Journal of Disorders of Communication, 21*, 151–165.

Epple, W. A., Jacobson, J. W., & Janicki, M. P. (1985). Staffing ratios in public institutions for persons with mental retardation in the United States. *Mental Retardation, 23*, 115–124.

Epstein, L. H., & Wing, R. R. (1987). Behavioral treatment of childhood obesity. *Psychological Bulletin, 101*, 331–342.

Epstein, M. H., Cullinan, D., & Polloway, E. A. (1986). Patterns of maladjustment among mentally retarded children and youth. *American Journal of Mental Deficiency, 91*, 127–134.

Erickson, M., & Upshur, C. C. (1989). Caretaking burden and social support: Comparison of mothers of infants with and without disabilities. *American Journal on Mental Retardation, 94*, 250–258.

Eron, L. D. (1987). The development of aggressive behavior from the perspective of a developing behaviorism. *American Psychologist, 42*, 435–442.

Esposito, B. G., & Reed, II, T. M. (1986). The effects of contact with handicapped persons on young children's attitudes. *Exceptional Children, 53*, 224–229.

Esser, A. (1961). *Das Antlitz der Blindheit in der Antike.* Leiden: E. J. Brill.

Evans, W. H., Evans, S. S., Schmid, R. E., & Pennypacker, H. S. (1985). The effects of exercise on selected classroom behaviors of behaviorally disordered adolescents. *Behavioral Disorders, 11*, 42–51.

Eyberg, S. M. (1985). Behavioral assessment: Advancing methodology in pediatric psychology. *Journal of Pediatric Psychology, 10*, 123–139.

Eyman, R. K., & Widaman, K. F. (1987). Life-span development of institutionalized and community-based mentally retarded persons, revisited. *American Journal of Mental Deficiency, 91*, 559–569.

Fagan, III, J. F. (1984). The relationship of novelty preferences during infancy to later intelligence and later recognition memory. *Intelligence, 8*, 339–346.

Fairbank, D., Powers, A., & Monaghan, C. (1986). Stimulus overselectivity in hearing-impaired children. *Volta Review, 88*, 269–278.

Faraone, S. V., & Tsuang, Ming T. (1985). Quantitative models of genetic the transmission of schizophrenia. *Psychological Bulletin, 98*, 41–66.

Farber, J. M., Shapiro, B. K., Palmer, F. B., & Capute, A. J. (1985). The diagnostic value of the neurodevelopmental examination. *Clinical Pediatrics, 24*, 367–372.

Farrell, G. (1956). *The story of blindness.* Cambridge: Harvard University Press.

Faust, J. (1987). Correlates of the drive for thinness in young female adolescents. *Journal of Clinical Child Psychology, 16*, 313–319.

Faust, J., Baum, C. G., & Forehand, R. (1985). An examination of the association between social relationships and depression in early adolescence. *Journal of Applied Developmental Psychology, 6*, 291–297.

Feagans, L., & Appelbaum, M. I. (1986). Validation of language subtypes in learning disabled children. *Journal of Educational Psychology, 78*, 358–364.

Feagans, L., & Short, E. J. (1984). Developmental differences in the comprehension and production of narratives by reading disabled and normally achieving children. *Child Development, 55*, 1727–1736.

Fein, D., Waterhouse, L., Lucci, D., Pennington, B., & Humes, M. (1985). Handedness and cognitive functions in pervasive developmental disorders. *Journal of Autism Developmental Disorders, 15*, 323–333.

Feiring, C., & Lewis, M. (1987). The ecology of some middle class families at dinner. *International Journal of Behavioral Development, 10*, 377–390.

Felce, D. (1988). Evaluating the extent of community integration following the provision of staffed residential alternatives to institutional care. *Irish Journal of Psychology, 9*, 346–360.

Felce, D., Saxby, H., De Kock, U., Repp, A., Ager, A., & Blunden, R. (1987). To what behaviors do attending adults respond? A replication. *American Journal of Mental Deficiency, 91*, 496–504.

Felce, D., Thomas, M., De Kock, U., Saxby, H., & Repp, A. (1985). An ecological comparison of small community-based houses and traditional institutions: 2. Physical setting and the use of opportunities. *Behavior Research and Therapy, 23*, 337–348.

Fellner, D. J., LaRoche, M., & Sulzer-Azaroff, B. (1984). The effects of adding interruption to differential reinforcement on targeted and novel self-stimulatory behaviors. *Journal of Behavior Therapy and Experimental Psychiatry, 15*, 315–321.

Fenner, M. E., Hewitt, K. E., & Torpy, D. M. (1987). Down's syndrome: Intellectual and behavioural functioning during adulthood. *Journal of Mental Deficiency Research, 31*, 241–249.

Fenske, E. C., Zalenski, S., Krantz, P. J., & McClannahan, L. E. (1985). Age at intervention and treatment outcome for autistic children in a comprehensive intervention program. *Analysis and Intervention in Developmental Disabilities, 5*, 49–58.

Fergusson, D. M., & Horwood, L. J. (1987). The trait and method components of ratings of conduct disorder: 2. Factors related to the trait component of conduct disorder scores. *Journal of Child Psychology and Psychiatry, 28*, 261–272.

Ferrandez, A. M., & Pailhous, J. (1986). From stepping to adaptive walking: Modulations of an automatism. In H.T.A. Whiting, & M. G. Wade (Eds.), *Themes in motor development* (pp. 265–278). Dordrecht: Nijhoff.

Ferrari, M. (1986). Fears and phobias in childhood: Some clinical and developmental considerations. *Child Psychiatry and Human Development, 17*, 75–87.

Ferretti, R. P. (1989). Problem solving and strategy production in mentally retarded persons. *Research in Developmental Disabilities, 10*, 19–31.

Fewell, R. R. (1984). Assessment of preschool handicapped children. *Educational Psychologist, 19*, 172–179.

Field, M. (1984). Follow-up developmental status of infants hospitalized for nonorganic failure to thrive. *Journal of Pediatric Psychology, 9*, 241–256.

Field, T. (1981). Ecological variables and examiner biases in assessing handicapped preschool children. *Journal of Pediatric Psychology, 6*, 155–163.

Field, T. M., & Vega-Lahr, N. (1984). Early interactions between infants with cranio-facial anomalies and their mothers. *Infant Behavior and Development, 7,* 527–530.

Fimian, M. J. (1986). Social support and occupational stress in special education. *Exceptional Children, 52,* 436–442.

Fine, E. (1987). Are we preparing adolescents with learning disabilities to cope with social issues? *Journal of Learning Disabilities, 20,* 633–634.

Finegan, J. K., Quarrington, B. J., Hughes, H. E., & Doran, T. A. (1987). Infant development following midtrimester amniocentesis. *Infant Behavior and Development, 10,* 379–383.

Finisdore, M. (1984). Self-help in the mainstream. *Volta Review, 86,* 99–107.

Finucci, J. M., Gottfredson, L. S., & Childs, B. (1985). A follow-up study of dyslexic boys. *Annals of Dyslexia, 35,* 117–136.

Fischbacher, E. (1987). Prescribing in a hospital for the mentally retarded. *Journal of Mental Deficiency Research, 31,* 17–29.

Fisher, C. B., Bornstein, M. H., & Gross, C. G. (1985). Left-right coding and skills related to beginning reading. *Developmental and Behavioral Pediatrics, 6,* 279–283.

Fitch, J. L., & Batson, E. A. (1989). Hemispheric asymmetry of alpha wave suppression in stutterers and nonstutterers. *Journal of Fluency Disorders, 14,* 47–55.

Fleisher, L. S., Soodak, L. C., & Jelin, M. A. (1984). Selective attention deficits in learning disabled children: Analysis of the data base. *Exceptional Children, 51,* 136–141.

Fletcher, J. M. (1985). Memory for verbal and nonverbal stimuli in learning disability subgroups: Analysis by selective reminding. *Journal of Experimental Child Psychology, 40,* 244–259.

Fletcher, C. M., & Prior, M. R. (1990). The rule learning behavior of reading disabled and normal children as a function of task characteristics and instruction. *Journal of Experimental Child Psychology, 50,* 39–58.

Fletcher, J. M., Ewing-Cobbs, L., Miner, M. E., Levin, H. S., & Eisenberg, H. M. (1990). Behavioral changes after closed head injury in children. *Journal of Consulting and Clinical Psychology, 58,* 93–98.

Fletcher, J. M., Francis, D. J., Pequegnat, W., Raudenbush, S. W., Bornstein, M., Schmitt, F., Brouwers, P., & Stover, E. (1991). Neurobehavioral outcomes in diseases of childhood. *American Psychologist, 46,* 1267–1277.

Flicek, M., & Landau, S. (1985). Social status problems of learning disabled and hyperactive earning disabled boys. *Journal of Clinical Child Psychology, 14,* 340–344.

Folstein, S., & Rutter, M. (1977). Infantile autism: A genetic study of 21 twin pairs. *Journal of Child Psychology and Psychiatry, 18,* 297–321.

Folstein, S. E., & Rutter, M. L. (1988). Autism: Familial aggregation and genetic implications. *Journal of Autism and Developmental Disorders, 18,* 3–30.

Forell, E. R., & Hood, J. (1985). A longitudinal study of two groups of children with early reading problems. *Annals of Dyslexia, 35,* 97–116.

Forness, S. R., & Kavale, K. A. (1988). Psychopharmacologic treatment: A note on classroom effects. *Journal of Learning Disabilities, 21,* 144–147.

Forness, S. R., & Cantwell, D. P. (1982). DSM III psychiatric diagnoses and special education categories. *Journal of Special Education, 16,* 49–63.

Foster, S. (1989). Social alienation and peer identification: A study of the social construction of deafness. *Human Organization, 48,* 226–235.

Fowler, P. C. (1986). Cognitive differentiation of learning-disabled children on the WISC-R: A canonical model of achievement correlates. *Child Study Journal, 16,* 25–38.

Fowler, S. A. (1986). Peer-monitoring and self-monitoring: Alternatives to traditional teacher management. *Exceptional Children, 52,* 573–581.

Fox, M. (1985). Maternal involvement in residential day treatment. *Social Casework, 66,* 350–357.

Fox, R., & Oross, III, S. (1988). Deficits in stereoscopic depth perception by mildly mentally retarded adults. *American Journal on Mental Retardation, 93,* 232–244.

Foxx, R. M., & McMorrow, M. J. (1985). Teaching social skills to mentally retarded adults: Followup results from three studies. *Behavior Therapist, 8,* 77–78.

Fraiberg, S., & Freedman, D. A. (1964). Studies in the ego development of the congenitally blind child. *Psychoanalytic Study of the Child, 19,* 113–169.

Francis, G., Last, C. G., & Strauss, C. C. (1987). Expression of separation anxiety disorder: The roles of age and gender. *Child Psychiatry and Human Development, 18,* 82–89.

Frankel, F., & Simmons, III, J. Q. (1985). Behavioral treatment approaches to pathological unsocialized physical aggression in young children. *Journal of Child Psychology and Psychiatry, 26,* 525–551.

Frankenberger, W., & Harper, J. (1988). States' definitions and procedures for identifying children with mental retardation: Comparison of 1981–1982 and 1985–1986 guidelines. *Mental Retardation, 26,* 133–136.

French, D. C. (1988). Heterogeneity of peer-rejected boys: Aggressive and nonaggressive subtypes. *Child Development, 59,* 976–985.

French-St. George, M., & Stoker, R. G. (1988). Speechreading: An historical perspective. *Volta Review, 90,* 17–31.

Freud, A., & Dann, S. (1951). An experiment in group upbringing. *Psychoanalytic Study of the Child, 6,* 127–168.

Freud, S. (1938). *The basic writings of Sigmund Freud.* New York: Modern Library.

Friedman, D. E., & Medway, F. J. (1987). Effects of varying performance sets and outcome on the expectations, attributions, and persistence of boys with learning disabilities. *Journal of Learning Disabilities, 20,* 312–316.

Friedman, P., & Friedman, K. A. (1980). Accounting for individual differences when comparing the effectiveness of remedial language teaching methods. *Applied Psycholinguistics, 1,* 151–170.

Fucci, D., Petrosino, L., Gorman, P., & Harris, D. (1985). Vibrotactile magnitude production scaling: A method for studying sensory-perceptual responses of stutterers and fluent speakers. *Journal of Fluency Disorders, 10,* 69–75.

Fuchs, D., Fuchs, L. S., Benowitz, S., & Barringer, K. (1987). Norm-referenced tests: Are they valid for use with handicapped students? *Exceptional Children, 54,* 263–271.

Fuchs, D., Fuchs, L. S., Power, M. H., & Dailey, A. M. (1985). Bias in the assessment of handicapped children. *American Educational Research Journal, 22,* 185–198.

Fuchs, L. S., & Fuchs, D. (1984). Examiner accuracy during protocol completion. *Journal of Psychoeducational Assessment, 2,* 101–108.

Fuchs, L. S., Fuchs, D., & Stecker, P. M. (1989). Effects of curriculum-based measurement on teachers' instructional planning. *Journal of Learning Disabilities, 22,* 51–59.

Fujiki, M., Brinton, B., & Dunton, S. (1987). The ability of normal and language-impaired children to produce grammatical corrections. *Journal of Communication Disorders, 20,* 413–424.

Furlong, M. J., & Yanagida, E. H. (1985). Psychometric factors affecting multidisciplinary team identification of learning disabled children. *Learning Disabilities Quarterly, 8,* 37–44.

Gajar, A. H., Hale, R. L., Kuzovich, C., & Saxe, J. (1984). Profile analysis of a referral sample. *Journal of Psychology, 116,* 207–214.

Galaburda, A. M. (1985). Developmental dyslexia: A review of biological interactions. *Annals of Dyslexia, 35,* 21–33.

Galbraith, G. C. (1986). Evoked potentials, response timing, and motor behavior: A response. In M. G. Wade (Ed.), *Motor skill acquisition of the mentally handicapped* (pp. 213–226). Amsterdam: Elsevier.

Galin, D., Herron, J., Johnstone, J., Fein, G., & Yingling, C. (1988). EEG alpha asymmetry in dyslexics during speaking and block design tasks. *Brain and Language, 35,* 241–253.

Gallagher, R. J., Jens, K. G., & O'Donnell, K. J. (1983). The effect of physical status on the affective expression of handicapped infants. *Infant Behavior and Development, 6,* 73–77.

Galton, F. (1973). *Inquiries into the human faculty and its development.* New York: AMS Press. (Original work published 1883)

Gamble, T. J., & Zigler, E. (1986). Effects of infant day care: Another look at the evidence. *American Journal of Orthopsychiatry, 56,* 26–42.

Gandhavadi, B., & Melvin, J. L. (1985). Electrical blink reflex habituation in mentally retarded adults. *Journal of Mental Deficiency Research, 29,* 49–54.

Gandhavadi, B., & Melvin, J. L. (1989). Habituation of optically evoked blink reflex in mentally retarded adults. *Journal of Mental Deficiency Research, 33,* 1–11.

Gangestad, S., & Snyder, M. (1985). "To carve nature at its joints": On the existence of discrete classes in personality. *Psychological Review, 92,* 317–349.

Gans, K. D. (1987). Willingness of regular and special educators to teach students with handicaps. *Exceptional Children, 54,* 41–45.

Garber, H. L. (1988). The Milwaukee Project: Preventing mental retardation in children at risk. *Monograph of the American Association on Mental Retardation.* Washington, DC: American Association on Mental Retardation.

Garber, S. R., & Siegel, G. M. (1982). Feedback and motor control in stuttering. In D. K. Routh (Ed.), *Learning, speech, and the complex effects of punishment* (pp. 93–123). New York: Plenum.

Gard, G. C., Turone, R., & Devlin, B. (1985). Social interaction and interpersonal distance in normal and behaviorally disturbed boys. *Journal of Genetic Psychology, 146,* 189–196.

Gargiulo, R. M. (1984). Cognitive style and moral judgement in mentally handicapped and non-handicapped children of equal mental age. *British Journal of Developmental Psychology, 2,* 83–89.

Gargiulo, R. M., & O'Sullivan, P. S. (1986). Mildly mentally retarded and nonretarded children's learned helplessness. *American Journal of Mental Deficiency, 91,* 203–206.

Garkusha, Y. F. (1984). An experiment in developing voluntary attention in children with motor alalia. *Soviet Psychology, 22,* 76–88.

Garrard, K. R. (1989). Mothers' verbal directives to delayed and nondelayed children. *Mental Retardation, 27,* 11–18.

Garvar, A., & Schmelkin, L. P. (1989). A multidimensional scaling study of administrators' and teachers' perceptions of disabilities. *Journal of Special Education, 22,* 463–478.

Gath, A. (1988). Mentally handicapped people as parents. *Journal of Child Psychology and Psychiatry, 29,* 739–744.

Gath, A., & Gumley, D. (1987). Retarded children and their siblings. *Journal of Child Psychology and Psychiatry, 28,* 713–730.

Gaughan, E., & Axelrod, S. (1989). Behavior and achievement relationships with emotionally disturbed children: An applied study. *Psychology in the Schools, 26,* 89–99.

Gauthier, M. (1984). Stimulant medications in adults with attention deficit disorder. *Canadian Journal of Psychiatry, 29,* 435–440.

Geary, D. C., Widaman, K. F., Little, T. D., & Cormier, P. (1987). Cognitive addition: Comparison of learning disabled and academically normal elementary school children. *Cognitive Development, 2,* 249–269.

Geers, A., & Moog, J. (1989). Factors predictive of the development of literacy in profoundly hearing-impaired adolescents. *Volta Review, 91,* 69–86.

Gekoski, M. J., Fagen, J. W., & Pearlman, M. A. (1984). Early learning and memory in the preterm infant. *Infant Behavior and Development, 7,* 267–276.

Gelman, S. R., Epp, D. J., Downing, R. H., Twark, R. D., & Eyerly, R. W. (1989). Impact of group homes on the values of adjacent residential properties. *Mental Retardation, 27,* 127–134.

Gelzheiser, L. M. (1984). Generalization from categorical memory tasks to prose by learning disabled adolescents. *Journal of Educational Psychology, 76,* 1128–1138.

Gelzheiser, L. M., Shepherd, M. J., & Wozniak, R. H. (1986). The development of instruction to induce skill transfer. *Exceptional Children, 53,* 125–129.

Gerber, M. M., & Hall, R. J. (1987). Information processing approaches to studying spelling deficiencies. *Journal of Learning Disabilities, 20,* 34–42.

German, D. J. (1985). The use of specific semantic word categories in the diagnosis of dysnomic learning-disabled children. *British Journal of Disorders of Communication, 20,* 143–154.

Gibbons, C. L. (1985). Deaf children's perception of internal body parts. *Maternal-Child Nursing Journal, 14,* 37–46.

Gibbons, F. X. (1985). Stigma perception: Social comparison among mentally retarded persons. *American Journal of Mental Deficiency, 90,* 98–106.

Gibbs, M. V., Reeves, D., & Cunningham, C. C. (1987). The application of temperament questionnaires to a British sample: Issues of reliability and validity. *Journal of Child Psychology and Psychiatry, 28,* 61–77.

Gibson, D. (1978). *Down's syndrome: The psychology of mongolism.* Cambridge: Cambridge University.

Gibson, D., & Harris, A. (1988). Aggregated early intervention effects on Down's syndrome persons: Patterning and longevity of benefits. *Journal of Mental Deficiency Research, 32,* 1–17.

Gibson, D., Rogers, T. B., & Fields, D. L. (1987). The structure of habilitation. *International Journal of Rehabilitation Research, 10,* 115–126.

Gillam, R. B., & Johnston, J. R. (1985). Development of print awareness in language-disordered preschoolers. *Journal of Speech and Hearing Research, 28,* 521–526.

Gillberg, C. (1983). Autistic children's hand preferences: Results from an epidemiological study of infantile autism. *Psychiatry Research, 10,* 21–30.

Gillberg, C. (1988). The neurobiology of infantile autism. *Journal of Child Psychology and Psychiatry, 29,* 257–266.

Gillberg, C., Matousek, M., Petersen, I., & Rasmussen, P. (1984). Perceptual, motor and attentional deficits in 7-year-old children. *Acta Paedopsychiatra, 50,* 243–253.

Gillberg, C., & Steffenburg, S. (1987). Outcome and prognostic factors in infantile autism and similar conditions: A population-based study of 46 cases followed through puberty. *Journal of Autism and Developmental Disorders, 17,* 273–287.

Gillberg, I. C. (1985). Children with minor neurodevelopmental disorders: 3. Neurological and neurodevelopmental problems at age 10. *Developmental Medicine and Child Neurolology, 27,* 3–16.

Gillberg, I. C., & Gillberg, C. (1988). Generalized hyperkinesis: Follow-up study from age 7 to 13 years. *Journal of the American Academy of Child and Adolescent Psychiatry, 27,* 55–59.

Gillberg, I. C., Gillberg, C., & Groth, J. (1989). Children with preschool minor neurodevelopmental disorders: 5. Neurodevelopmental profiles at age 13. *Developmental Medicine and Child Neurology, 31,* 14–24.

Giller, V. L., Dial, J. G., & Chan, F. (1986). The Street Survival Skills Questionnaire: A correlational study. *American Journal of Mental Deficiency, 91,* 67–71.

Giordano, G. (1983). The pivotal role of grammar in correcting writing disabilities. *Journal of Special Education, 17,* 473–481.

Girolametto, L. E. (1988). Improving the social-conversational skills of developmentally delayed children: An intervention study. *Journal of Speech and Hearing Disorders, 53,* 156–167.

Gittelman, R., Mannuzza, S., Shenker, R., & Bonagura, N. (1985). Hyperactive boys almost grown up: 1. Psychiatric status. *Archives of General Psychiatry, 42,* 937–947.

Glidden, L. M. (1989). Parents for children, children for parents. *Monograph of the American Association on Mental Retardation, 11.*

Glidden, L. M., & Pursley, J. T. (1989). Longitudinal comparisons of families who have adopted children with mental retardation. *American Journal on Mental Retardation, 94,* 272–277.

Glidden, L. M., Valliere, V. N., & Herbert, S. L. (1988). Adopted children with mental retardation: Positive family impact. *Mental Retardation, 26,* 119–125.

Glidden, L. M., & Warner, D. A. (1985). Semantic processing and serial learning by EMR adolescents. *American Journal of Mental Deficiency, 89,* 635–641.

Goldberg, S., Marcovitch, S., MacGregor, D., & Lojkasek, M. (1986). Family responses to developmentally delayed preschoolers: Etiology and the father's role. *American Journal of Mental Deficiency, 90,* 610–617.

Goldberg, S., Perrotta, M., Minde, K., & Corter, C. (1986). Maternal behavior and attachment in low-birth-weight twins and singeltons. *Child Development, 57,* 34–46.

Goldberg, T. E. (1987). On hermetic reading abilities. *Journal of Autism and Developmental Disorders, 17,* 29–44.

Goldin-Meadow, S., & Morford, M. (1985). Gesture in early child language: Studies of deaf and hearing children. *Merrill-Palmer Quarterly, 31,* 145–176.

Goldman, S. R., & Pellegrino, J. W. (1987). Information processing and educational microcomputer technology: Where do we go from here? *Journal of Learning Disabilities, 20,* 144–154.

Goldsmith, H. H., Buss, A. H., Plomin, R., Rothbart, M. K., Thomas, A., Chess, S., Hinde, R. A., & McCall, R. B. (1987). Roundtable: What is temperament? Four approaches. *Child Development, 58,* 505–529.

Goldsmith, L., & Schloss, P. J. (1986). Diagnostic overshadowing among school psychologists working with hearing-impaired learners. *American Annals of the Deaf, 131,* 288–293.

Goldstein, D., Paul, G. G., & Sanfilippo-Cohn, S. (1985). Depression and achievement in subgroups of children with learning disabilities. *Journal of Applied Developmental Psychology, 6,* 263–275.

Goldstein, M. S. (1969). Human paleopathology and some diseases in living primitive societies: A review of the recent literature. *American Journal of Physical Anthropology, 31,* 285–294.

Goodman, J. F., & Cecil, H. S. (1987). Referral practices and attitudes of pediatricians toward young mentally retarded children. *Journal of Developmental and Behavioral Pediatrics, 8,* 97–105.

Goodman, N. C. (1987). Girls with learning disabilities and their sisters: How are they faring in adulthood? *Journal of Clinical Child Psychology, 16,* 290–300.

Gordon, A. H., Lee, P. A., Dulcan, M. K., & Finegold, D. N. (1986). Behavioral problems, social competency, and self perception among girls with congenital adrenal hyperplasia. *Child Psychiatry and Human Development, 17,* 129–138.

Gordon, M., Post, E. M., Crouthamel, C., & Richman, R. A. (1984). Do children with constitutional delay really have more learning problems? *Journal of Learning Disabilities, 17,* 291–293.

Gothelf, C. R. (1985). Variations in resource provision for community residences serving persons with developmental disabilities. *Education and Training of the Mentally Retarded, 20,* 130–138.

Gottfried, A. W. (1985). Measures of socioeconomic status in child development research: Data and recommendations. *Merrill-Palmer Quarterly, 31,* 85–92.

Gottlieb, B. W., Gottlieb, J., Berkell, D., & Levy, L. (1986). Sociometric status and solitary play of LD boys and girls. *Journal of Learning Disabilities, 19,* 619–622.

Gottlieb, G. (1983). The psychobiological approach to developmental issues. In P. H. Mussen (Ed.), *Handbook of child psychology* (4th ed., Vol. 2, pp. 1–26). New York: Wiley. 1–26.

Gough, P. B., & Tunmer, W. E. (1986). Decoding, reading, and reading disability. *Remedial and Special Education, 7,* 6–10.

Gould, S. J. (1977). *Ontogeny and phylogeny.* Cambridge, MA: Harvard University Press.

Gow, L., Ward, J., & Balla, J. (1985). The use of verbal self-instruction training (VSIT) to enhance learning in the mentally retarded. *Educational Psychology, 5,* 115–134.

Gow, L., Ward, J., Balla, J., & Snow, D. (1988). Directions for integration in Australia:

Overview of a report to the Commonwealth schools Commission: 2. *The Exceptional Child, 35,* 5–22.

Gowen, J. W., Johnson-Martin, N., Goldman, B. D., & Appelbaum, M. (1989). Feelings of depression and parenting competence of mothers of handicapped and nonhandicapped infants: A longitudinal study. *American Journal on Mental Retardation, 94,* 259–271.

Graffi, S., & Minnes, P. M. (1988). Attitudes of primary school children toward the physical appearance and labels associated with Down syndrome. *American Journal on Mental Retardation, 93,* 28–35.

Graham, S., & Freeman, S. (1985). Strategy training and teacher- vs student-controlled study conditions: Effects on LD students' spelling performance. *Learning Disability Quarterly, 8,* 267–274.

Graham, S., & Harris, K. R. (1988). Research and instruction in written language: Introduction to the special issue. *Exceptional children, 54,* 495–496.

Graham, S., & Leone, P. (1987). Effects of behavioral disability labels, writing performance, and examiner's expertise on the evaluation of written products. *Journal of Experimental Education, 55,* 89–94.

Grant, C. L., & Fodor, I. G. (1986). Adolescent attitudes toward body image and anorexic behavior. *Adolescence, 21,* 271–281.

Green, G. (1990). Differences in development of visual and auditory-visual equivalence relations. *American Journal on Mental Retardation, 95,* 260–270.

Green, G., Mackay, H. A., McIlvane, W. J., Saunders, R. R., & Soraci, Jr., S. A. (1990). Perspectives on relational learning in mental retardation. *American Journal on Mental Retardation, 95,* 249–259.

Greene, R. L. (1987). Effects of maintenance rehearsal on human memory. *Psychological Bulletin, 102,* 403–413.

Greenfield, B., Hechtman, L., & Weiss, G. (1988). Two subgroups of hyperactives as adults: Correlations of outcome. *Canadian Journal of Psychiatry, 33,* 505–508.

Greenfield, D. B. (1985). Facilitating mentally retarded children's relational learning through novelty-familiarity training. *American Journal of Mental Deficiency, 90,* 342–348.

Greenfield, D. B., & Scott, M. S. (1986). Perceptual and conceptual variants of the oddity task as a predictor of learning disability. *Journal of Abnormal Child Psychology, 14,* 135–148.

Gregory, J. F., Shanahan, T., & Walberg, H. (1985). A descriptive analysis of high school seniors with speech disabilities. *Journal of Communication Disorders, 18,* 295–304.

Grenell, M. M., Glass, C. R., & Katz, K. S. (1987). Hyperactive children and peer interaction: Knowledge and performance of social skills. *Journal of Abnormal Child Psychology, 15,* 1–13.

Gresham, F. M. (1984). Social skills and self-efficacy for exceptional children. *Exceptional Children, 51,* 253–261.

Gresham, F. M. (1986). Conceptual and definitional issues in the assessment of children's social skills: Implications for classification and training. *Journal of Clinical Child Psychology, 15,* 3–15.

Gresham, F. M., & Reschly, D. J. (1987a). Dimensions of social competence: Method factors in the assessment of adaptive behavior, social skills, and peer acceptance. *Journal of School Psychology, 23,* 367–381.

Gresham, F. M., & Reschly, D. J. (1987b). Sociometric differences between mildly handicapped and nonhandicapped black and white students. *Journal of Educational Psychology, 79,* 195–197.

Gresham, F. M., Reschly, D. J., & Carey, M. P. (1987). Teachers as 'tests': Classification accuracy and concurrent validation in the identification of learning disabled children. *School Psychology Review, 16,* 543–553.

Griffiths, P., Boggan, J., Tutt, G., & Dickens, P. (1985). Visual discrimination learning in mentally handicapped adults. *Journal of Mental Deficiency Research, 29,* 347–357.

Grimes, S. K., & Vitello, S. J. (1990). Follow-up study of family attitudes toward deinstitutionalization: Three to 7 years later. *Mental Retardation, 28,* 219–225.

Grinder, R. E. (1967). *A history of genetic psychology.* New York: Wiley.

Griswold, P. C., Gelzheiser, L. M., & Shepherd, M. J. (1987). Does a production deficiency hypothesis account for vocabulary learning among adolescents with learning disabilities? *Journal of Learning Disabilities, 20,* 620–626.

Grogan, S. C. (1988). Nonverbal communication in children with reading problems. *Journal of Learning Disabilities, 21,* 364–369.

Grontved, A., Walter, B., & Gronberg, A. (1988). Auditory brain stem responses in dyslexic and normal children: A prospective clinical investigation. *Scandinavian Audiology, 17,* 53–54.

Grosenick, J. K., George, N. L., & George, M. P. (1988). The availability of program descriptions among programs for seriously emotionally disturbed students. *Behavioral Disorders, 13,* 108–115.

Grossman, H. J. (1973). *Manual on terminology and classification in mental retardation.* Washington, DC: American Association on Mental Deficiency.

Grove, C., & Rodda, M. (1984). Receptive communication skills of hearing-impaired students: A comparison of four methods of communication. *American Annals of the Deaf, 129,* 378–385.

Gunter, P., Brady, M. P., Shores, R. E., Fox, J. J., Owen, S., & Goldzweig, I. R. (1984). The reduction of aberrant vocalizations with auditory feedback and resulting collateral behavior change of two autistic boys. *Behavior Disorders, 9,* 254–263.

Guralnick, M. J. (1980). Social interactions among preschool children. *Exceptional Children, 46,* 248–253.

Guralnick, M. J., & Groom, J. M. (1987). Dyadic peer interactions of mildly delayed and nonhandicapped preschool children. *American Journal of Mental Deficiency, 92,* 178–193.

Guralnick, M. J., & Groom, J. M. (1988a). Friendships of preschool children in mainstreamed playgroups. *Developmental Psychology, 24,* 595–604.

Guralnick, M. J., & Groom, J. M. (1988b). Peer interactions in mainstreamed and specialized classrooms: A comparative analysis. *Exceptional Children, 54,* 415–425.

Guralnick, M. J., Heiser, K. E., Eaton, A. P., Bennett, F. C., Richardson, H. B., & Groom, J. M. (1988). Pediatricians' perceptions of the effectiveness of early intervention for at-risk and handicapped children. *Journal of Developmental and Behavioral Pediatrics, 9,* 12–18.

Guskin, S. L. (1978). Theoretical and empirical strategies for the study of the labelling of mentally retarded persons. In N. R. Ellis (Ed.), *International review of research on mental retardation* (Vol. 9, pp. 127–158). New York: Academic Press.

Gutowski, W. E., & Chechile, R. A. (1987). Encoding, storage, and retrieval components of associative memory deficits of mildly mentally retarded adults. *American Journal of Mental Deficiency, 92*, 85–93.

Guttentag, R. E., & Schaefer, E. G. (1987). Phonological encoding by hearing children of deaf parents. *Cognitive Development, 2*, 169–178.

Hagborg, W. (1987). Hearing-impaired students and sociometric ratings: An exploratory study. *Volta Review, 89*, 221–228.

Hagerman, R. J., & Sobesky, W. E. (1989). Psychopathology in Fragile-X syndrome. *American Journal of Orthopsychiatry, 59*, 142–147.

Hahn, W. K. (1987). Cerebral lateralization of function: From infancy through childhood. *Psychological Bulletin, 101*, 376–392.

Haight, S. L., & Fachting, D. D. (1986). Materials for teaching sexuality, love and maturity to high school students with learning disabilities. *Journal of Learning Disabilities, 19*, 344–350.

Haley, S. M. (1987). Sequence of development of postural reactions by infants with Down syndrome. *Developmental Medicine and Child Neurology, 29*, 674–679.

Hall, C. W., & Richmond, B. O. (1985). Non-verbal communication, self-esteem and interpersonal relations of LD and non-LD students. *The Exceptional Child, 32*, 87–91.

Halliday, S. (1987). Parental attitudes to the community care of their mentally handicapped children, before and after they move into the community. *British Journal of Mental Subnormality, 33*, 43–49.

Hamlett, K. W., Pellegrini, D. S., & Conners, C. K. (1987). An investigation of executive processes in the problem-solving of attention deficit disorder-hyperactive children. *Journal of Pediatric Psychology, 12*, 227–240.

Handford, H. A., Mayes, S. D., Bixler, E. O., & Mattison, R. E. (1986). Personality traits of hemophilic boys. *Journal of Developmental and Behavioral Pediatrics, 7*, 224–229.

Hanson, M. J. (1981). Down's syndrome children: Characteristics and intervention research. In M. Lewis & Rosenblum L. (Eds.), *The uncommon child* (pp. 83–114). New York: Plenum.

Hanzlik, J. R., & Stevenson, M. B. (1986). Interaction of mothers with their infants who are mentally retarded, reared with cerebral palsy, or nonretarded. *American Journal of Mental Deficiency, 90*, 513–520.

Hardle, W., Gasser, T., & Bacher, P. (1984). EEG-responsiveness to eye opening and closing in mildly retarded children compared to a control group. *Biological Psychology, 18*, 185–199.

Hargrove, P. M., Straka, E. M., & Medders, E. G. (1988). Clarification requests of normal and language-impaired children. *British Journal of Disorders of Communication, 23*, 51–62.

Harkins, D. A., & Michel, G. F. (1988). Evidence for a maternal effect on infant hand-use preferences. *Developmental Psychobiology, 21*, 535–541.

Harlow, H. F., Harlow, M. K., & Hansen, E. W. (1963). The maternal affectional system of rhesus monkeys. In H. L. Rheingold (Ed.) *Maternal behavior in mammals* (pp. 254–281). New York: Wiley.

Harlow, H. F., & Zimmerman, R. B. (1958). The development of affectional responses in infant monkeys. *Proceedings of the American Philosophical Society, 102*, 501–509.

Harper, D. C., Wacker, D. P., & Cobb, L. S. (1986). Children's social preference toward peers with visible physical differences. *Journal of Pediatric Psychology, 11,* 323–342.

Harris, D. P., Cote, J. E., & Vipond, E. M. (1987). Residential treatment of disturbed delinquents: Description of a centre and identification of therapeutic factors. *Canadian Journal of Psychiatry, 32,* 579–583.

Harris, G. A. (1985). Considerations in assessing English language performance of Native American children. *Topics in Language Disorders, 5,* 42–52.

Harris, M., Jones, D., Brookes, S., & Grant, J. (1986). Relations between the non-verbal context of maternal speech and rate of language development. *British Journal of Developmental Psychology, 4,* 261–268.

Harris, S. L. (1986). Brief report: A 4- to 7-year questionnaire follow-up of participants in a training program for parents of autistic children. *Journal of Autism and Developmental Disorders, 16,* 377–383.

Harris, S. L., Handleman, J. S., & Palmer, C. (1985). Parents and grandparents view the autistic child. *Journal of Autism and Developmental Disorders, 15,* 127–136.

Harris, V. S., & McHale, S. M. (1989). Family life problems, daily caregiving activities, and the psychological well-being of mothers of mentally retarded children. *American Journal of Mental Retardation, 94,* 231–239.

Hartley, X. Y. (1985). Receptive language processing and ear advantage of Down's syndrome children. *Journal of Mental Deficiency Research, 29,* 197–205.

Hasazi, S. B., Gordon, L. R., & Roe, C. A. (1985). Factors associated with the employment status of handicapped youth exiting high school from 1979 to 1983. *Exceptional Children, 51,* 455–469.

Hasazi, S. B., Gordon, L. R., Roe, C. A., Finck, K., Hull, M., & Salembier, G. (1985). A statewide follow-up on post high school employment and residential status of students labeled, "Mentally Retarded." *Education and Training of the Mentally Retarded, 20,* 222–234.

Haskins, R. (1985). Public school aggression among children with varying day-care experience. *Child Development, 56,* 689–703.

Hayes-Scott, F. C., & Dowaliby, F. J. (1984). Academic motivation to improve writing skills: A comparison of normally hearing and hearing-impaired students. *American Annals of the Deaf, 129,* 431–434.

Haywood, H. C., & Switzky, H. N. (1985). Work response of mildly mentally retarded adults to self- versus external regulation as a function of motivational orientation. *American Journal of Mental Deficiency, 90,* 151–159.

Heal, L. W., & Chadsey-Rusch, J. (1985). The lifestyle satisfaction scale (LSS): Assessing individuals' satisfaction with residence, community setting, and associated services. *Applied Research in Mental Retardation, 6,* 475–490.

Hechtman, L., Weiss, G., & Perlman, T. (1984). Young adult outcome of hyperactive children who received long-term stimulant treatment. *Journal of the American Academy of Child Psychiatry, 23,* 261–269.

Heller, T., Bond, M. A., & Braddock, D. (1988). Family reactions to institutional closure. *American Journal on Mental Retardation, 92,* 336–343.

Hemmings, B. C. (1985). The gifted/handicapped: Some basic issues. *Exceptional Children, 32,* 57–62.

Henderson, S. E. (1986). Some aspects of the development of motor control in Down's syndrome. In H. T. A. Whiting & M. G. Wade (Eds.), *Themes in motor development* (pp. 69–92). Dordrecht: Nijhoff.

Henderson, S. E. (1987). The assessment of "clumsy" children: Old and new approaches. *Journal of Child Psychology and Psychiatry, 28,* 511–527.

Henderson, S. E., & Hall, D. (1982). Concomitants of clumsiness in young schoolchildren. *Developmental Medicine and Child Neurology, 24,* 448–460.

Henderson, S. E., Morris, J., & Ray, S. (1981). Performance of Down syndrome and other retarded children on the Cratty Gross Motor Test. *American Journal of Mental Deficiency, 85,* 416–424.

Henggeler, S. W., Watson, S. M., & Cooper, P. F. (1984). Verbal and nonverbal maternal controls in hearing mother–deaf child interaction. *Journal of Applied Developmental Psychology, 5,* 319–329.

Henker, B., & Whalen, C. K. (1989). Hyperactivity and attention deficits. *American Psychologist, 44,* 216–223.

Hertz, B. G. (1987). Acuity card testing of retarded children. *Behavioural Brain Research, 24,* 85–92.

Hewitt, S. E. (1987). The abuse of deinstitutionalised persons with mental handicaps. *Disability, Handicap and Society, 2,* 127–135.

Hildebrand, J., & Seefeldt, C. (1986). Teacher burnout and environmental quality in child care centers. *Child Care Quarterly, 15,* 90–97.

Hill, A. L. (1978). Savants: Mentally retarded individuals with special skills. In N. R. Ellis (Ed.), *International review of research in mental retardation* (Vol. 9, pp. 227–298). New York: Academic Press.

Hill, B. K., Bruininks, R. H., Lakin, K. C., Hauber, F. A., & McGuire, S. P. (1985). Stability of residential facilities for people who are mentally retarded, 1977–1982. *Mental Retardation, 23,* 108–114.

Hill, J. W., Seyfarth, J., Banks, P. D., Wehman, P., & Orelove, F. (1987). Parent attitudes about working conditions of their adult mentally retarded sons and daughters. *Exceptional Children, 54,* 9–23.

Hill, M. L., Banks, P. D., Handrich, R. R., Wehman, P. H., Hill, J. W., & Shafer, M. S. (1987). Benefit-cost analysis of supported competitive employment for persons with mental retardation. *Research in Developmental Disabilities, 8,* 71–89.

Hinshaw, S. P. (1987). On the distinction between attentional deficits/hyperactivity and conduct problems/aggression in child psychopathology. *Psychological Bulletin, 101,* 443–463.

Hinshaw, S. P., Henker, B., & Whalen, C. K. (1984). Self-control in hyperactive boys in anger-inducing situations: Effects of cognitive-behavioral training and methylphenidate. *Journal of Abnormal Child Psychology, 12,* 55–77.

Hirst, M. (1987). Careers of young children with disabilities between ages 15 and 21 years. *Disability, Handicap and Society, 2,* 61–74.

Hiscock, M., & Kinsbourne, M. (1987). Specialization of the cerebral hemispheres: Implications for learning. *Journal of Learning Disabilities, 20,* 130–143.

Hobbs, N. (1975). *The futures of children.* San Francisco: Jossey-Bass.

Hobson, R. P. (1984). Early childhood autism and the question of egocentrism. *Journal of Autism and Developmental Disorders, 14,* 85–104.

Hobson, R. P. (1987). The autistic child's recognition of age- and sex-related characteristics of people. *Journal of Autism and Developmental Disorders, 17,* 63–79.

Hobson, R. P., Ouston, J., & Lee, A. (1988a). Emotion recognition in autism: Coordinating faces and voices. *Psychological Medicine, 18,* 911–923.

Hobson, R. P., Ouston, J., & Lee, A. (1988b). What's in a face? The case of autism. *British Journal of Psychology, 79*, 441–453.

Hobson, R. P., Ouston, J., & Lee, A. (1989). Recognition of emotion by mentally retarded adolescents and young adults. *American Journal on Mental Retardation, 93*, 434–443.

Hodges, K., Kline, J. J., Barbero, G., & Flanery, R. (1984). Life events occurring in families of children with recurrent abdominal pain. *Journal of Psychosomatic Research, 28*, 185–188.

Hodgman, C. H. (1985). Recent findings in adolescent depression and suicide. *Journal of Developmental and Behavioral Pediatrics, 6*, 162–170.

Hoffman-Plotkin, D., & Twentyman, C. T. (1984). A multimodal assessment of behavioral and cognitive deficits in abused and neglected preschoolers. *Child Development, 55*, 794–802.

Holland, B. V. (1987). Fundamental motor skill performance of non-handicapped and educable mentally impaired students, *Education and Training in Mental Retardation, 22*, 197–204.

Holmes, B. C. (1985). The effects of a strategy and sequenced materials on the inferential comprehension of disabled readers. *Journal of Learning Disabilities, 18*, 542–546.

Holmes, C. S., & Richman, L. C. (1985). Cognitive profiles of children with insulin-dependent diabetes. *Journal of Developmental and Behavioral Pediatrics, 6*, 323–326.

Holwerda-Kuipers, J. (1987). The cognitive development of low-birthweight children. *Journal of Child Psychology and Psychiatry, 28*, 321–328.

Horgan, J. S. (1985). Control in memory for movement cues by mentally retarded children. *Perceptual and Motor Skills, 60*, 439–444.

Horn, C. C., & Manis, F. R. (1985). Normal and disabled readers' use of orthographic structure in processing print. *Journal of Reading Behavior, 17*, 143–161.

Horn, W. F., Ialongo, N., Popovich, S., & Peradotto, D. (1987). Behavioral parent training and cognitive-behavioral self-control therapy with ADD-H children: Comparative and combined effects. *Journal of Clinical Child Psychology, 16*, 57–68.

Horn, W. F., & Packard, T. (1985). Early identification of learning problems: A meta-analysis. *Journal of Educational Psychology, 77*, 597–607.

Hornstein, H. A., & Mosley, J. L. (1986). Dichotic-listening task performance of mildly mentally retarded and nonretarded individuals. *American Journal of Mental Deficiency, 90*, 573–578.

Hornstein, H. A., & Mosley, J. L. (1987). Iconic memory deficit of mildly mentally retarded individuals. *American Journal of Mental Deficiency, 91*, 413–421.

Horsley, I. A., & FitzGibbon, C. T. (1987). Stuttering children: Investigation of a stereotype. *British Journal of Disorders of Communication, 22*, 19–35.

Horton, S. (1985). Computational rates of educable mentally retarded adolescents with and without calculators in comparison to normals. *Education and Training of the Mentally Retarded, 20*, 14–24.

Hoshmand, L. T. (1985). Phenomenologically based groups for developmentally disabled adults. *Journal of Counseling and Development, 64*, 147–148.

Howe, M. L., Brainerd, C. J., & Kingma, J. (1985). Storage-retrieval processes of normal and learning-disabled children: A stages-of-learning analysis of picture-word effects. *Child Development, 56,* 1120–1133.

Howe, S. G. (1848). *Report of the Commission on Idiocy to the Commonwealth of Massachusetts.* Boston: Coolidge & Wiley.

Howes, C. (1985). The patterning of agonistic behaviors among friends and acquaintances in programs for emotionally disturbed children. *Journal of Applied Developmental Psychology, 6,* 303–311.

Howes, C., & Eldredge, R. (1985). Responses of abused, neglected, and nonmaltreated children to the behaviors of their peers. *Journal of Applied Developmental Psychology, 6,* 261–270.

Howie, P. M. (1981). Intrapair similarity in frequency of disfluency in monozygotic and dizygotic twin pairs containing stutterers. *Behavior Genetics, 11,* 227–238.

Hoy, E. A., Bill, J. M., & Sykes, D. H. (1988). Very low birthweight: A long-term developmental impairment? *International Journal of Behavioral Development, 11,* 37–67.

Hoyle, S. G., & Serafica, F. C. (1988). Peer status of children with and without learning disabilities—A multimethod study. *Learning Disability Quarterly, 11,* 322–332.

Huessy, H. R., & Ruoff, P. A. (1984). Towards a rational drug usage in a state institution for retarded individuals. *Psychiatric Journal of the University of Ottawa, 9,* 56–58.

Huff, D. M., & Harris, S. C. (1987). Using sensorimotor integrative treatment with mentally retarded adults. *American Journal of Occupational Therapy, 41,* 227–231.

Hughes, D., & May, D. (1985). Some limitations of the interview form in careers counselling for the mildly mentally handicapped. *British Journal of Guidance and Counselling, 13,* 178–190.

Hughes, H. M. (1988). Psychological and behavioral correlates of family violence in child witnesses and victims. *American Journal of Orthopsychiatry, 58,* 77–90.

Hughes, J. N., & Hall, D. M. (1985). Performance of disturbed and nondisturbed boys on a role play test of social competence. *Behavioral Disorders, 11,* 24–29.

Hulme, C., & Lord, R. (1986). Clumsy children: A review of recent research. *Child: Care, Health and Development, 12,* 257–269.

Hulstijn, W., & Mulder, T. (1986). Motor dysfunctions in children. Towards a process-oriented diagnosis. In H. T. A. Whiting & M. G. Wade (Eds.), *Themes in motor development* (pp. 109–126). Dordrecht: Nijhoff.

Humphries, L., Gruber, J., Hall, J., & Kryscio, R. (1985). Motor proficiency in depressed adolescent inpatients: Biochemical and clinical diagnostic correlates. *Journal of Developmental and Behavioral Pediatrics, 6,* 259–262.

Hundert, J., Cassie, J. B., & Johnston, N. (1988). Characteristics of emotionally disturbed children referred to day-treatment, special-class, outpatient, and assessment services. *Journal of Clinical Child Psychology, 17,* 121–130.

Huntington, G. S., & Simeonsson, R. J. (1987). Down's syndrome and toddler temperament. *Child: Care, Health and Development, 13,* 1–11.

Hupp, S. C. (1986). Effects of stimulus mode on the acquisition, transfer, and generalization of categories by severely mentally retarded children and adolescents. *American Journal of Mental Deficiency, 90,* 579–587.

Hupp, S. C., Mervis, C. B., Able, H., & Conroy-Gunter, M. (1986). Effects of receptive and expressive training of category labels on generalized learning by severely mentally retarded children. *American Journal of Mental Deficiency, 90,* 558–565.

Hurford, D. P., & Webster, R. L. (1985). Decreases in simple reaction time as a function of stutterers' participation in a behavioral therapy. *Journal of Fluency Disorders, 10,* 301–310.

Hurtig, A. L., & White, L. S. (1986). Psychosocial adjustment in children and adolescents with sickle-cell disease. *Journal of Pediatric Psychology, 11,* 411–427.

Hynd, G. W., & Semrud-Clikeman, M. (1989). Dyslexia and brain morphology. *Psychological Bulletin, 106,* 447–482.

Idol, L. (1987). Group story mapping: A comprehension strategy for both skilled and unskilled readers. *Journal of Learning Disabilities, 20,* 196–205.

Inge, K. J., Banks, P. D., Wehman, P., Hill, J. W., & Shafer, M. S. (1988). Quality of life for individuals who are labeled mentally retarded: Evaluating competitive employment versus sheltered workshop employment. *Education and Training in Mental Retardation, 23,* 97–104.

Irvin, L. K., & Lundervold, D. A. (1988). Social validation of decelerative (punishment) procedures by special educators of severely handicapped students. *Research in Developmental Disabilities, 9,* 331–350.

Irwin, R. J., Ball, A. K. R., Kay, N., Stillman, J. A., & Rosser, J. (1985). The development of auditory temporal acuity in children. *Child Development, 56,* 614–620.

Isaacs, L. D., & Haynes, W. O. (1984). Linguistic processing and performance in articulation-disordered subgroups of language-impaired children. *Journal of Communication Disorders, 17,* 109–120.

Israel, A. C., & Shapiro, L. S. (1985). Behavior problems of obese children enrolling in a weight reduction program. *Journal of Pediatric Psychology, 10,* 449–460.

Israelite, N. K. (1986). Hearing-impaired children and the psychological functioning of their normal-hearing siblings. *Volta Review, 88,* 47–54.

Itard, J. (1962). *The wild boy of Aveyron.* New York: Appleton-Century-Crofts.

Ivarie, J., Hogue, D., & Brulle, A. R. (1984). An investigation of mainstream teacher time spent with students labeled learning disabled. *Exceptional Children, 51,* 142–149.

Jackson, H. J. (1983). Current trends in the treatment of phobias in autistic and mentally retarded persons. *Australia and New Zealand Journal of Developmental Disabilities, 9,* 191–208.

Jackson, S. C., Enright, R. D., & Murdock, J. Y. (1987). Social perception problems in learning disabled youth: Developmental lag versus perceptual deficit. *Journal of Learning Disabilities, 20,* 361–364.

Jacobsen, B., Lowery, B., & DuCette, J. (1986). Attributions of learning disabled children. *Journal of Educationl Psychology, 78,* 59–65.

Jacobson, J. W. (1988). Problem behavior and psychiatric impairment within a developmentally disabled population: 3. Psychotropic medication. *Research in Developmental Disabilities, 9,* 23–28.

Jacobson, J. W. (1987). Individual program plan goal content in developmental disabilities programs. *Mental Retardation, 25,* 157–164.

Jacobson, J. W., Silver, E. J., & Schwartz, A. A. (1984). Service provision in New York's group homes. *Mental Retardation, 22,* 231–239.

Jacobvitz, D., & Sroufe, L. A. (1987). The early caregiver–child relationship and attention-deficit disorder with hyperactivity in kindergarten: A prospective study. *Child Development, 58,* 1488–1495.

Jahoda, A., Markova, I., & Cattermole, M. (1988). Stigma and the self-concept of people with a mild mental handicap. *Journal of Mental Deficiency Research, 32,* 103–115.

Jansma, P., & Combs, C. S. (1987). The effects of fitness training & reinforcement on maladaptive behaviors of institutionalized adults, classified as mentally retarded/emotionally disturbed. *Education and Training in Mental Retardation, 22,* 268–279.

Jeannerod, M. (1986). The formation of the finger grip during prehension: A cortically-mediated visuo-motor pattern. In H. T. A. Whiting & M. G. Wade (Eds.), *Themes in motor development* (pp. 183–206). Dordrecht: Nijhoff.

Jenkins, J. R., & Heinen, A. (1989). Students' preferences for service delivery: Pull-out, in-class, or integrated models. *Exceptional Children, 55,* 516–523.

Jenkins, J. R., Odom, S. L., & Speltz, M. L. (1989). Effects of social integration on preschool children with handicaps. *Exceptional Children, 55,* 420–428.

Jeremy, R. J., & Bernstein, V. J. (1984). Dyads at risk: Methadone-maintained women and their 4-month-old infants. *Child Development, 55,* 1141–1154.

Jessop, D. J., Riessman, C. K., & Stein, R. E. K. (1988). Chronic childhood illness and maternal mental health. *Journal of Developmental and Behavioral Pediatrics, 9,* 147–156.

Johnson, C. G., Sigelman, C. K., & Falkenberg, V. F. (1986). Impacts of labeling and competence on peers' perceptions: Mentally retarded versus nonretarded perceivers. *American Journal of Mental Deficiency, 90,* 663–668.

Johnson, D. W., & Johnson, R. T. (1984). Building acceptance of differences between handicapped and nonhandicapped students: The effects of cooperative and individualistic instruction. *Journal of Social Psychology, 122,* 257–267.

Johnson, D. W., Johnson, R. T., Warring, D., & Maruyama, G. (1986). Different cooperative learning procedures and cross-handicap relationships. *Exceptional Children, 53,* 247–252.

Johnson, H. L., Diano, A., & Rosen, T. S. (1984). Twenty-four-month neurobehavioral follow-up of children of methadone-maintained mothers. *Infant Behavior and Development, 7,* 115–123.

Johnson, P. L., & O'Leary, K. D. (1987). Parental behavior patterns and conduct disorders in girls. *Journal of Abnormal Child Psychology, 15,* 573–581.

Johnston, C., Pelham, W. E., & Murphy, H. A. (1985). Peer relationships in ADDH and normal children: A developmental analysis of peer and teacher ratings. *Journal of Abnormal Child Psychology, 13,* 89–100.

Johnston, J. R., & Weismer, S. E. (1983). Mental rotation abilities in language-disordered children. *Journal of Speech and Hearing Research, 26,* 397–403.

Johnston, R. S., Rugg, M. D., & Scott, T. (1987). Phonological similarity effects, memory span and developmental reading disorders: The nature of the relationship. *British Journal of Psychology, 78,* 205–211.

Johnstone, J., Galin, D., Fein, G., Yingling, C., Herron, J., & Marcus, M. (1984). Regional brain activity in dyslexic and control children during reading tasks: Visual probe event-related potentials. *Brain and Language, 21,* 233–254.

Jones, C. J. (1985). Analysis of the self-concepts of handicapped students. *Remedial and Special Education, 6,* 32–36.

Jones, E. E. (1985). Interpersonal distancing behavior of hearing-impaired vs. normal-hearing children. *Volta Review, 87,* 223–230.

Jorm, A. F., Share, D. L., Matthews, R., & Maclean, R. (1986). Behaviour problems in specific reading retarded and general reading backward children: A longitudinal study. *Journal of Child Psychology and Psychiatry, 27,* 33–43.

Jourdain, M. (1916). *Diderot's early philosophical works.* Chicago: Open Court Publishing.

Kagan, J. (1988). The meanings of personality predicates. *American Psychologist, 43,* 614–620.

Kagan, R. M., & Reid, W. J. (1986). Critical factors in the adoption of emotionally disturbed youths. *Child Welfare, 65,* 63–73.

Kail, R., Hale, C. A., Leonard, L. B., & Nippold, M. A. (1984). Lexical storage and retrieval in language-impaired children. *Applied Psycholinguistics, 5,* 37–49.

Kanner, L. (1949). *A miniature textbook of feeblemindedness.* New York: Child Care Publications.

Kanner, L. (1964). *A history of the care and study of the mentally retarded.* Springfield, IL: Charles C Thomas.

Karper, W. B., Martinek, T. J., & Wilkerson, J. D. (1985). Effects of competitive/non-competitive learning on motor performance of children in mainstream physical education. *American Corrective Therapy Journal, 39,* 10–15.

Karrer, R. (1986). Input, central and motor segments of response time in mentally retarded and normal children. In M. G. Wade (Ed.), *Motor skill acquisition of the mentally handicapped* (pp. 167–188). Amsterdam: Elsevier.

Karrer, R., & Johnson, C. (1986). Are correlations between leads of slow preparatory ERP components an index of neural organization? In W. C. McCallum, R. Zappoli, & F. Denoth (Eds.), *Cerebral psychophysiology: Studies in event-related potentials* (pp. 253–254). Amsterdam: Elsevier.

Kasari, C., Sigman, M., Mundy, P., & Yirmiya, N. (1988). Caregiver interactions with autistic children. *Journal of Abnormal Child Psychology, 16,* 45–56.

Kashani, J. H., Carlson, G. A., Horwitz, E., & Reid, J. C. (1985). Dysphoric mood in young children referred to a child development unit. *Child Psychiatry and Human Development, 15,* 234–242.

Kashani, J. H., Shekim, W. O., Burk, J. P., & Beck, N. C. (1987). Abuse as a predictor of psychopathology in children and adolescents. *Journal of Clinical Child Psychology, 16,* 43–50.

Katz, M. H., Hampton, R. L., Newberger, E. H., Bowles, R. T., & Snyder, J. C. (1986). Returning children home: Clinical decision making in cases of child abuse and neglect. *American Journal of Orthopsychiatry, 56,* 253–262.

Katz, R. B. (1986). Phonological deficiencies in children with reading disability: Evidence from an object-naming task. *Cognition, 22,* 225–257.

Katz, R. C., & Singh, N. N. (1986). Increasing recreational behavior in mentally retarded children. *Behavior Modification, 10,* 508–519.

Katz, S., & Kravetz, S. (1989). Facial plastic surgery for persons with Down syndrome: Research findings and their professional and social implications. *American Journal on Mental Retardation, 94,* 101–110.

Kavale, K., & Andreassen, E. (1984). Factors in diagnosing the learning disabled: Analysis of judgmental policies. *Journal of Learning Disabilities, 17,* 273–278.

Kavale, K. A., & Forness, S. R. (1984). The historical foundations of learning disabilities. *Remedial and Special Education, 6,* 18–24.

Kavale, K. A., & Forness, S. R. (1986). School learning, time and learning disabilities: The dissociated learner. *Journal of Learning Disabilities, 19,* 130–138.

Kavale, K. A., & Forness, S. R. (1987). The far side of heterogeneity: A critical analysis of empirical subtyping research in learning disabilities. *Journal of Learning Disabilities, 20,* 374–382.

Kavanagh, K. A., Youngblade, L., Reid, J. B., & Fagot, B. I. (1988). Interactions between children and abusive versus control parents. *Journal of Clinical Child Psychology, 17,* 137–142.

Kazak, A. E. (1987). Families with disabled children: Stress and social networks in three samples. *Journal of Abnormal Child Psychology, 15,* 137–146.

Kazdin, A. E. (1984). Acceptability of aversive procedures and medication as treatment alternatives for deviant child behavior. *Journal of Abnormal Child Psychology, 12,* 289–302.

Kazdin, A. E. (1987). Treatment of antisocial behavior in children: Current status and future directions. *Psychological Bulletin, 102,* 187–203.

Kazdin, A. E., & Kolko, D. J. (1986). Parent psychopathology and family functioning among childhood firesetters. *Journal of Abnormal Child Psychology, 14,* 315–329.

Keane, K. J., & Kretschmer, R. E. (1987). Effect of mediated learning intervention on cognitive task performance with a deaf population. *Journal of Educational Psychology, 79,* 49–53.

Keith, T. Z., Fehrman, P. G., Harrison, P. L., & Pottebaum, S. M. (1987). The relation between adaptive behavior and intelligence: Testing alternative explanations. *Journal of School Psychology, 25,* 31–43.

Keller, C. E., Ball, D. W., & Hallahan, D. P. (1987). Questioning the defense of different numbers: A reply to Algozzine and Ysseldyke. *Remedial and Special Education, 8,* 57–59.

Kelly, J. A., & Christoff, K. A. (1985). Job interview training. *Psychiatric Aspects of Mental Retardation Reviews, 4,* 5–8.

Kelly, M. B., & Heffner, H. E. (1988). The role of attention in the elimination of chronic, life-threatening vomiting. *Journal of Mental Deficiency Research, 32,* 425–431.

Kelman, W. P., & Whiteley, J. H. (1986). Habituation and generalization of habituation by nonambulatory, profoundly mentally retarded children. *American Journal of Mental Deficiency, 90,* 566–572.

Kent, R. D. (1983). Facts about stuttering: Neuropsychologic perspectives. *Journal of Speech and Hearing Disorders, 48,* 249–255.

Keogh, B. K., & Daley, S. E. (1983). Early identification: One component of comprehensive services for at-risk children. *Topics in Early Childhood Special Education, 3,* 7–16.

Keogh, D., Whitman, T., Beeman, D., Halligan, K., & Starzynski, T. (1987). Teaching interactive signing in a dialogue situation to mentally retarded individuals. *Research in Developmental Disabilities, 8,* 39–53.

Kerfoot, M. (1988). Deliberate self-poisoning in childhood and early adolescence. *Journal of Child Psychology and Psychiatry, 29,* 335–343.

Kern, L., Koegel, R. L., & Dunlap, G. (1984). The influence of vigorous versus mild exercise on autistic stereotyped behaviors. *Journal of Autism and Developmental Disorders, 14,* 57–67.

Kernan, K. T., Sabshay, S., & Shinn, N. (1989). Lay people's judgements of storytellers as mentally retarded or not retarded. *Journal of Mental Deficiency Research, 33,* 149–157.

Kernan, K. T., Sabshay, S., & Shinn, N. (1988). Discourse features as criteria in judging the intellectual ability of speakers. *Discourse Processes, 11,* 203–220.

Kerr, M. M., Hoier, T. S., & Versi, M. (1987). Methodological issues in childhood depression: A review of the literature. *American Journal of Orthopsychiatry, 57,* 193–198.

Kerr, R., & Blais, C. (1987). Down syndrome and extended practice of a complex motor task. *American Journal of Mental Deficiency, 91,* 591–597.

Kerr, R., & Blais, C. (1985). Motor skill acquisition by individuals with Down syndrome. *American Journal of Mental Deficiency, 90,* 313–318.

Keys, C. B., & Foster-Fishman, P. (1991, July). *National trends in advocacy in developmental disabilities.* Paper presented at the Third Biennial Conference on Community Research and Action, Tempe, AZ.

Kiernan, W. E., McGaughey, M. J., & Schalock, R. L. (1988). Employment environments and outcome for adults with developmental disabilities. *Mental Retardation, 26,* 279–288.

Kirby, J. R., & Robinson, G. L. (1987). Simultaneous and successive processing in reading disabled children. *Journal of Learning Disabilities, 20,* 243–252.

Kirchner, D. M., & Klatzky, R. L. (1985). Verbal rehearsal and memory in language-disordered children. *Journal of Speech and Hearing Disorders, 28,* 556–565.

Kistner, J., White, K., Haskett, M., & Robbins, F. (1985). Development of learning-disabled and normally achieving children's causal attributions. *Journal of Abnormal Child Psychology, 13,* 639–647.

Kistner, J. A. (1985). Attentional deficits of learning-disabled children: Effects of rewards and practice. *Journal of Abnormal Child Psychology, 13,* 19–31.

Kistner, J. A., Osborne, M., & LeVerrier, L. (1988). Causal attributions of learning-disabled children: Developmental patterns and relation to academic progress. *Journal of Educational Psychology, 80,* 82–89.

Klein, N. K. (1988). Children who were very low birthweight: Cognitive abilities and classroom behavior at 5 years of age. *Journal of Special Education, 22,* 41–54.

Kline, R. B., Lachar, D., & Gdowski, C. L. (1988). Convergence and concurrent validity of DSM-III diagnoses and the Personality Inventory for Children (PIC). *Canadian Journal of Behavioural Science, 20,* 251–264.

Klinteberg, B. A., Magnusson, D., & Schalling, D. (1989). Hyperactive behavior in childhood and adult impulsivity: A longitudinal study of male subjects. *Personality and Individual Differences, 10,* 43–49.

Kluwin, T. N., & Moores, D. F. (1989). Mathematics achievement of hearing impaired adolescents in different placements. *Exceptional Children, 55,* 327–335.

Knutson, G. G. (1986). Conceptualizing style differences of normally achieving and exceptional students. *Psychological Reports, 58,* 675–678.

Kochanek, T. T., Kabacoff, R. I., & Lipsitt, L. P. (1987). Early detection of handicapping conditions in infancy and early childhood: Toward a multivariate model. *Journal of Applied Developmental Psychology, 8,* 411–420.

Koegel, R. L., & Mentis, M. (1985). Motivation in childhood autism: Can they or won't they? *Journal of Child Psychology and Psychiatry, 26,* 185–191.

Koenig, L. J. (1988). Self-image of emotionally disturbed adolescents. *Journal of Abnormal Child Psychology, 16*, 111–126.

Kohlberg, L., Ricks, D., & Snarey, J. (1984). Childhood development as a predictor of adaptation in adulthood. *Genetic Psychology Monographs, 110*, 91–172.

Kolko, D. J., & Kazdin, A. E. (1986). A conceptualization of firesetting in children and adolescents. *Journal of Abnormal Child Psychology, 14*, 49–61.

Kolko, D. J., & Kazdin, A. E. (1988). Parent–child correspondence in identification of firesetting among child psychiatric patients. *Journal of Child Psychology and Psychiatry, 29*, 175–184.

Kolko, D. J., Kazdin, A. E., & Meyer, E. C. (1985). Aggression and psychopathology in childhood firesetters: Parent and child reports. *Journal of Consulting and Clinical Psychology, 53*, 377–385.

Koller, H., Richardson, S. A., & Katz, M. (1988). Peer relationships of mildly retarded young adults living in the community. *Journal of Mental Deficiency Research, 32*, 321–331.

Kolligan, Jr., J., & Sternberg, R. J. (1987). Intelligence, information processing, and specific learning disabilities: A triarchic synthesis. *Journal of Learning Disabilities, 20*, 8–17.

Konarski, Jr., E. A. (1987). Effects of response deprivation on the instrumental performance of mentally retarded persons. *American Journal of Mental Deficiency, 91*, 537–542.

Konarski, Jr., E. A., Crowell, C. R., & Duggan, L. M. (1985). The use of response deprivation to increase the academic performance of EMR students. *Applied Research in Mental Retardation, 6*, 15–31.

Konarski, Jr., E. A., & Diorio, M. S. (1985). A quantitative review of self-help research with the severely and profoundly mentally retarded. *Applied Research in Mental Retardation, 6*, 229–245.

Konstantareas, M. M. (1987). Autistic children exposed to simultaneous communication training: A followup. *Journal of Autism and Developmental Disorders, 17*, 115–131.

Konstantareas, M. M., & Homatidis, S. (1985). Dominance hierarchies in normal and conduct-disordered children. *Journal of Abnormal Child Psychology, 13*, 259–268.

Kopp, C. B. (1983). Risk factors in development. In P. H. Mussen (Ed.), *Handbook of child psychology,* (4th ed., Vol. 2, pp. 1081–1188). New York: Wiley.

Kopp, C. B., & Krakow, J. B. (1983). The developmentalist and the study of biological risk: A view of the past with an eye toward the future. *Child Development, 54*, 1086–1108.

Korn, S. J., & Gannon, S. (1983). Temperament, cultural variation and behavior disorder in preschool children. *Child Psychiatry and Human Development, 13*, 203–212.

Kotsopoulos, S., & Mellor, C. (1986). Extralinguistic speech characteristics of children with conduct and anxiety disorders. *Journal of Child Psychology and Psychiatry, 27*, 99–108.

Krauss, M. W., & Erickson, M. (1988). Informal support networks among aging persons with mental retardation: A pilot study. *Mental Retardation, 26*, 197–201.

Krauss, M. W., & Seltzer, M. M. (1986). Comparison of elderly and adult mentally retarded persons in community and institutional settings. *American Journal of Mental Deficiency, 91*, 237–243.

Krauss, M. W., & Seltzer, M. M. (1989). *The social networks of adults with mental retardation: Extensiveness, independence, and reciprocity.* Paper presented at the 113th meeting of the American Association on Mental Retardation, May 28–June 1, 1989, Chicago.

Kregel, J., Hill, M. H., & Banks, P. D. (1988). Analysis of employment specialist intervention time in supported competitive employment. *American Journal on Mental Retardation, 93,* 200–208.

Kreimeyer, K., & Antia, S. (1988). The development and generalization of social interaction skills in preschool hearing-impaired children. *Volta Review, 90,* 219–231.

Kropp, J. P., & Haynes, O. M. (1987). Abusive and nonabusive mothers' ability to identify general and specific emotion signals of infants. *Child Development, 58,* 187–190.

Krupski, A. (1985). Variations in attention as a function of classroom task demands in learning handicapped and CA-matched nonhandicapped children. *Exceptional Children, 52,* 52–56.

Krupski, A. (1987). Attention: The verbal phantom strikes again—A response to Samuels. *Exceptional Children, 54,* 62–65.

Kuo-Tai, T. (1988). Mentally retarded persons in the People's Republic of China: Review of epidemiological studies and services. *American Journal on Mental Retardation, 93,* 193–199.

Kupst, M. J., Schulman, J. L., Maurer, H., Honig, G., Morgan, E., Fochtman, D. (1984). Coping with pediatric leukemia: A 2-year follow-up. *Journal of Pediatric Psychology, 9,* 149–163.

Lagomarcino, A., Reid, D. H., Ivancic, M. T., & Faw, G. D. (1984). Leisure-dance instruction for severely and profoundly retarded persons: Teaching an intermediate community-living skill. *Journal of Applied Behavior Analysis, 17,* 71–84.

Lahey, B. B., Hartdagen, S. E., Frick, P. J., McBurnett, K., Connor, R., & Hynd, G. W. (1988). Conduct disorder: Parsing the confounded relation to parental divorce and antisocial personality. *Journal of Abnormal Psychology, 97,* 334–337.

Lahey, B. B., Shaughency, E. A., Hynd, G. W., Carlson, C. L., & Nieves, N. (1987). Attention deficit disorder with and without hyperactivity: Comparison of behavioral characteristics of clinic-referred children. *Journal of the American Academy of Child and Adolescent Psychiatry, 26,* 718–723.

Laman, D. S., & Reiss, S. (1987). Social skill deficiencies associated with depressed mood of mentally retarded adults. *American Journal of Mental Deficiency, 92,* 224–229.

Lambert, N. M. (1988). Adolescent outcomes for hyperactive children. *American Psychologist, 43,* 786–799.

Lambert, N. M., & Hartsough, C. S. (1984). Contribution of predispositional factors to the diagnosis of hyperactivity. *American Journal of Orthopsychiatry, 54,* 97–109.

Lancioni, G. E., Coninx, F., & Smeets, P. M. (1989). A classical conditioning procedure for the hearing assessment of multiply handicapped persons. *Journal of Speech and Hearing Disorders, 54,* 88–93.

Landau, S., Milich, R., & McFarland, M. (1987). Social status differences among subgroups of LD boys. *Learning Disability Quarterly, 10,* 277–282.

Landry, S. H. (1986). Preterm infants' responses in early joint attention interactions. *Infant Behavior and Development, 9,* 1–14.

Landry, S. H., & Chapieski, M. L. (1989). Joint attention and infant toy exploration: Effects of Down syndrome and prematurity. *Child Development, 60,* 103–118.

Landry, S. H., Chapieski, M. L., & Schmidt, M. (1986). Effects of maternal attention-directing strategies on preterms' response to toys. *Infant Behavior and Development, 9,* 257–269.

Landry, S. H., Leslie, N. A., Fletcher, J. M., & Francis, D. J. (1985). Visual attention skills of premature infants with and without intraventricular hemorrhage. *Infant Behavior and Development, 8,* 309–321.

Lane, H. (1984). *When the mind hears: A history of the deaf.* New York: Random House.

Lane, H. (1988). Is there a "Psychology of the deaf"? *Exceptional Children, 55,* 7–19.

Langley, M. B. (1985). Selecting, adapting, and applying toys as learning tools for handicapped children. *Topics in Early Childhood Special Education, 5,* 101–118.

Langlois, A., Hanrahan, L. L., & Inouye, L. L. (1986). A comparison of interactions between stuttering children, nonstuttering children, and their mothers. *Journal of Fluency Disorders, 11,* 263–273.

Largo, R. H., Molinari, L., Pinto, L. C., Weber, M., & Duc, C. (1986). Language development of term and preterm children during the first 5 years of life. *Developmental Medicine and Child Neurology, 28,* 333–350.

Larson, K. A. (1988). A research review and alternative hypothesis explaining the link between learning disability and delinquency. *Journal of Learning Disabilities, 21,* 357–369.

Larson, K. A., & Gerber, M. M. (1987). Effects of social metacognitive training for enhancing overt behavior in learning disabled and low achieving delinquents. *Exceptional Children, 54,* 201–211.

Lawson, J. S., & Inglis, J. (1985). Learning disabilities and intelligence test results: A model based on a principal components analysis of the WISC-R. *British Journal of Psychology, 76,* 35–48.

Lawson, M. J. (1985). Observing executive activity in a simple assembly task. *American Journal of Mental Deficiency, 89,* 642–649.

Lazerson, D. B., Foster, H. L., Brown, S. I., & Hummel, J. W. (1988). The effectiveness of cross-age tutoring with truant, junior high school students with learning disabilities. *Journal of Learning Disabilities, 21,* 253–255.

Lederberg, A. R., Chapin, S. L., Rosenblatt, V., & Vandell, D. L. (1986). Ethnic, gender, and age preferences among deaf and hearing preschool peers. *Child Development, 57,* 375–386.

Lederberg, A. R., Rosenblatt, V., Vandell, D. L., & Chapin, S. L. (1987). Temporary and long-term friendships in hearing and deaf preschoolers. *Merrill-Palmer Quarterly, 33,* 515–533.

Lederberg, A. R., Ryan, H. B., & Robbins, B. L. (1986). Peer interaction among young deaf children: The effect of partner hearing status and familiarity. *Developmental Psychology, 22,* 691–700.

Leigh, J. (1987). Adaptive behavior of children with learning disabilities. *Journal of Learning Disabilities, 20,* 557–562.

Lemanck, K. L., Moore, S. L., Gresham, F. M., Williamson, D. A., & Kelly, M. L. (1986).

Psychological adjustment of children with sickle cell anemia. *Journal of Pediatric Psychology, 11,* 397–410.

Lennerstrand, G., Axelsson, A., & Andersson, G. (1983). Visual testing with "preferential looking" in mentally retarded children. *Behavioural Brain Research, 10,* 199–202.

Lennox, D. B., Miltenberger, R. G., Spengler, P., & Erfanian, N. (1988). Decelerative treatment practices with persons who have mental retardation: A review of 5 years of the literature. *American Journal on Mental Retardation, 92,* 492–501.

Lentz, K. (1985). Fears and worries of young children as expressed in a contextual play setting. *Journal of Child Psychology and Psychiatry, 26,* 981–987.

Leon, G. R., Lucas, A. R., Colligan, R. C., Ferdinande, R. J., & Kamp, J. (1985). Sexual, body-image, and personality attitudes in anorexia nervosa. *Journal of Abnormal Child Psychology, 13,* 245–258.

Leonard, L. B., Sabbadini, L., Leonard, J. S., & Volterra, V. (1987). Specific language impairment in children: A cross-linguistic study. *Brain and Language, 32,* 233–252.

Leong, C. K. (1984). Confessions of a schoolman: On dyslexia and laterality. *Annals of Dyslexia, 34,* 15–27.

Lerner, J. V., Hertzog, C., Hooker, K. A., Hassibi, M., & Thomas, A. (1988). A longitudinal study of negative emotional states and adjustment from early childhood through adolescence. *Child Development, 59,* 356–366.

Lerner, R. M., & Hood, K. E. (1986). Plasticity in development: Concepts and issues for intervention. *Journal of Applied Developmental Psychology, 7,* 139–152.

Leslie, S. C., Davidson, R. J., & Batey, O. B. (1985). Purdue Pegboard performance of disabled and normal readers: Unimanual versus bimanual differences. *Brain and Language, 24,* 359–369.

Lester, B. M., Hoffman, J., & Brazelton, T. B. (1985). The rhythmic structure of mother–infant interaction in term and preterm infants. *Child Development, 56,* 15–27.

Leudar, I., Fraser, W. I., & Jeeves, M. A. (1984). Behaviour disturbance and mental handicap: Typology and longitudinal trends. *Psychological Medicine, 14,* 923–935.

Levi, G., & Piredda, M. L. (1986). Semantic and phonological strategies for anagram construction in dyslexic children. *Journal of Learning Disabilities, 19,* 17–22.

Levine, H. G. (1985). Situational anxiety and everyday life experiences of mildly mentally retarded adults. *American Journal of Mental Deficiency, 90,* 27–33.

Levine, H. G., & Langness, L. L. (1985). Everyday cognition among mildly mentally retarded adults: An ethnographic approach. *American Journal of Mental Deficiency, 90,* 18–26.

Levy, S., Zoltak, B., & Saelens, T. (1988). A comparison of obstetrical records of autistic and nonautistic referrals for psychoeducational evaluations. *Journal of Autism and Developmental Disorders, 18,* 573–581.

Levy-Shiff, R. (1986). Mother–father–child interactions in families with a mentally retarded young child. *American Journal of Mental Deficiency, 91,* 141–149.

Lewandowski, L. J. (1985). Clinical syndromes among the learning disabled. *Journal of Learning Disabilities, 18,* 177–178.

Lewis, M., & Brooks-Gunn, J. (1984). Age and handicapped group differences in infants' visual attention. *Child Development, 55,* 858–868.

Lewis, M., & Wilson, C. D. (1972). Infant development in lower-class American families. *Human Development, 15,* 112–127.

Lewis, T. J., & Altman, R. (1987). Attitudes of students with mental retardation toward their handicapped and non-handicapped peers. *Education and Training in Mental Retardation, 22,* 256–261.

Lewis, V., & Boucher, J. (1988). Spontaneous, instructed and elicited play in relatively able autistic children. *British Journal of Developmental Psychology, 6,* 325–339.

Li, A. K. (1985). Toward more elaborate pretend play. *Mental Retardation, 23,* 131–136.

Liberman, I. Y., & Shankweiler, D. (1985). Phonology and the problems of learning to read and write. *Remedial and Special Education, 6,* 8–17.

Licht, B. G., Kistner, J. A., Ozkaragoz, T., Shapiro, S., & Clausen, L. (1985). Causal attributions of learning disabled children: Individual differences and their implications for persistence. *Journal of Educational Psychology, 77,* 208–216.

Lieber, J., & Semmel, M. I. (1985). Effectiveness of computer application to instruction with mildly handicapped learners: A review. *Remedial and Special Education, 6,* 5–12.

Lieberman, P., Meskill, R. H., Chatillon, M., & Schupack, H. (1985). Phonetic speech perception deficits in dyslexia. *Journal of Speech and Hearing Research, 28,* 480–486.

Liles, B. Z. (1985). Production and comprehension of narrative discourse in normal and Language Disordered children. *Journal of Communication Disorders, 18,* 409–427.

Lindgren, S. D., & Richman, L. C. (1984). Immediate memory functions of verbally deficient reading-disabled children. *Journal of Learning Disabilities, 17,* 222–225.

Lindgren, S. D., deRenzi, E., & Richman, L. C. (1985). Cross-national comparisons of developmental dyslexia in Italy and the United States. *Child Development, 56,* 1404–1417.

Lloyd, L. L., & Karlan, G. R. (1984). Non-speech communication symbols and systems: Where have we been and where are we going? *Journal of Mental Deficiency Research, 28,* 3–20.

Lobato, D., Barbour, L., Hall, L. J., & Miller, C. T. (1987). Psychosocial characteristics of preschool siblings of handicapped and nonhandicapped children. *Journal of Abnormal Child Psychology, 15,* 329–338.

Locher, P. J. (1985). Use of haptic training to modify impulse and attention control deficits of learning disabled children. *Journal of Learning Disabilities, 18,* 89–93.

Lochman, J. E., & Curry, J. F. (1986). Effects of social problem-solving training and self-instruction training with aggressive boys. *Journal of Clinical Child Psychology, 15,* 159–164.

Lock, T. M., Shapiro, A., Ross, A., & Capute, A. J. (1986). Age of presentation in developmental disability. *Journal of Developmental and Behavioral Pediatrics, 7,* 340–345.

Locke, J. L. (1983). Clinical phonology: The explanation and treatment of speech sound disorders. *Journal of Speech and Hearing Disorders, 48,* 339–341.

Loeber, R., & Schmaling, K. B. (1985). Empirical evidence for overt and covert patterns of antisocial conduct problems: A metaanalysis. *Journal of Abnormal Child Psychology, 13,* 337–353.

Lombardino, L. J., & Sproul, C. J. (1984). Patterns of correspondence and non-correspondence between play and language in developmentally delayed preschoolers. *Education and Training of the Mentally Retarded, 19,* 5–14.

Lord, C., & Hopkins, J. M. (1986). The social behavior of autistic children with younger and same-age nonhandicapped peers. *Journal of Autism and Developmental Disorders, 16,* 249–262.

Lord, R., & Hulme, C. (1988a). Patterns of rotary pursuit performance in clumsy and normal children. *Journal of Child Psychology and Psychiatry, 29,* 691–701.

Lord, R., & Hulme, C. (1988b). Visual perception and drawing ability in clumsy and normal children. *British Journal of Developmental Psychology, 6,* 1–9.

Lorsbach, T. C., & Gray, J. W. (1985). The development of encoding processes in learning disabled children. *Journal of Learning Disabilities, 18,* 222–227.

Lorsbach, T. C., & Worman, L. J. (1989). The development of explicit and implicit forms of memory in learning disabled children. *Contemporary Educational Psychology, 14,* 67–76.

Lovaas, O. I., Newsom, C., & Hickman, C. (1987). Self-stimulatory behavior and perceptual reinforcement. *Journal of Applied Behavior Analysis, 20,* 45–68.

Lovaas, O. I. (1987). Behavioral treatment and normal educational and intellectual functioning in young autistic children. *Journal of Consulting and Clinical Psychology, 55,* 3–9.

Loveland, K. A. (1987). Behavior of young children with Down syndrome before the mirror: Exploration. *Child Development, 58,* 768–778.

Lovett, D. L., & Harris, M. B. (1987). Important skills for adults with mental retardation: The client's point of view. *Mental Retardation, 25,* 351–356.

Lovett, M. W. (1984). The search for subtypes of specific reading disability: Reflections from a cognitive perspective. *Annals of Dyslexia, 34,* 155–178.

Lovett, M. W. (1987). A developmental approach to reading disability: Accuracy and speed criteria of normal and deficient reading skill. *Child Development, 58,* 234–260.

Lovett, M. W., Ransby, M. J., & Barron, R. W. (1988). Treatment, subtype, and word type effects in dyslexic children's response to remediation. *Brain and Language, 34,* 328–349.

Lovitt, T., Rudsit, J., Jenkins, J., Pious, C., & Benedetti, D. (1985). Two methods of adapting science materials for learning disabled and regular seventh graders. *Learning Disability Quarterly, 8,* 275–285.

Lozoff, B., Klein, N. K., & Prabucki, K. M. (1986). Iron-deficient anemic infants at play. *Journal of Developmental and Behavioral Pediatrics, 7,* 152–158.

Ludlow, B. L., & Woodrum, D. T. (1985). Hypothesis testing and problem solving by learning disabled and nondisabled boys. *Perceptual and Motor Skills, 60,* 160.

Lufi, D., & Cohen, A. (1985). Attentional deficit disorder and short-term visual memory. *Journal of Clinical Psychology, 41,* 265–267.

Luk, S. (1985). Direct observation studies of hyperactive behaviors. *Journal of the American Academy of Child Psychiatry, 24,* 338–344.

Lukose, S. (1987). Knowledge and behavior relationships in the memory ability of retarded and non-retarded students. *Journal of Experimental Child Psychology, 43,* 13–24.

Lundervold, D., & Bourland, G. (1988). Quantitative analysis of treatment of aggression, self-injury, and property destruction. *Behavior Modification, 12,* 590–617.

Lunzer, E. A., & Stratford, B. (1984). Deficits in attention in young children with specific reference to Down's syndrome and other mentally handicapped children. *Early Child Development: Care, 17,* 131–154.

Lutzer, V. D. (1988). Comprehension of proverbs by average children and children with learning disorders. *Journal of Learning Disabilities, 21,* 104–108.

Lyman, R. D., Prentice-Dunn, S., Wilson, D. R., & Bonfilio, S. A. (1984). The effect of success or failure on self-efficacy and task persistence of conduct-disordered children. *Psychology in the Schools, 21,* 516–519.

Lyman, R. D., Wurtele, S. K., & Wilson, D. R. (1985). Psychological effects of parents of home and hospital apnea monitoring. *Journal of Pediatric Psychology, 10,* 439–448.

Lynch, E. W., & Stein, R. C. (1987). Parent participation by ethnicity: A comparison of Hispanic, Black, and Anglo families. *Exceptional Children, 54,* 105–111.

Lyon, S. R., & Ross, L. E. (1984). Comparison scan training and the matching and scanning performance of severely and profoundly mentally retarded students. *Applied Research in Mental Retardation, 5,* 439–449.

Lyons-Ruth, K., Connell, D. B., Zoll, D., & Stahl, J. (1987). Infants at social risk: Relations among infant maltreatment, maternal behavior, and infant attachment behavior. *Developmental Psychology, 23,* 223–232.

MacDonald K. (1987). Parent–child physical play with rejected, neglected, and popular boys. *Developmental Psychology, 23,* 705–711.

MacLean, Jr., W. E., Arendt, R. E., & Baumeister, A. A. (1986). Early motor development and stereotyped behavior: The effects of semi-circular canal stimulation. In M. G. Wade (Ed.), *Motor skill acquisition of the mentally handicapped* (pp. 73–100). Amsterdam: Elsevier.

MacMahon, J. R., & Gross, R. T. (1987). Physical and psychological effects of aerobic exercise in boys with learning disabilities. *Journal of Developmental and Behavioral Pediatrics, 8,* 274–277.

MacMillan, D. L. (1989). Equality, excellence and the EMR populations: 1970–1989. *Psychology in Mental Retardation and Developmental Disabilities, 15,* 1–10.

MacTurk, R. H., Vietze, P. M., McCarthy, M. E., McQuiston, S., & Yarrow, L. J. (1985). The organization of exploratory behavior in Down syndrome and nondelayed infants. *Child Development, 56,* 573–581.

Mackay, H. A., & Ratti, C. A. (1990). Position-numeral equivalences and delayed position recognition span. *American Journal on Mental Retardation, 95,* 271–282.

Macklin, G. F., & Matson, J. L. (1985). A comparison of social behaviors among nonhandicapped and hearing impaired children. *Behavioral Disorders, 11,* 60–65.

Madison, L. S., Adubato, S. A., Madison, J. K., Nelson, R. M., Anderson, J. C., Erickson, J., Kuss, L. M., & Goodlin, R. C. (1986). Fetal response decrement: True habituation? *Journal of Developmental and Behavioral Pediatrics, 7,* 14–20.

Madison, L. S., Mosher, G. A., & George, C. H. (1986). Fragile-X syndrome: Diagnosis and research. *Journal of Pediatric Psychology, 11,* 91–102.

Magilvy, J. K. (1985). Quality of life of hearing-impaired older women. *Nursing Research, 34,* 140–144.

Maher, C. A. (1985). Effects of training high school principals in problem solving with conduct disordered adolescents. *Journal of Child and Adolescent Psychotherapy, 2,* 21–25.

Mahoney, G. (1988). Maternal communication style with mentally retarded children. *American Journal on Mental Retardation, 92*, 352–359.

Mahoney, G., Finger, I., & Powell, A. (1985). Relationship of maternal behavior style to the development of organically impaired mentally retarded infants. *American Journal of Mental Deficiency, 90*, 296–302.

Mahoney, G., & Powell, A. (1988). Modifying parent–child interaction: Enhancing the development of handicapped children. *Journal of Special Education, 22*, 82–96.

Maier, Jr., R. A., Holmes, D. L., Slaymaker, F. L., & Reich, J. N. (1984). The perceived attractiveness of preterm infants. *Infant Behavior and Development, 7*, 403–414.

Main, M., & George, C. (1985). Responses of abused and disadvantaged toddlers to distress in agemates: A study in the day care setting. *Developmental Psychology, 21*, 407–412.

Maisto, A. A., & Baumeister, A. A. (1984). Dissection of component processes in rapid information processing tasks. In P. H. Brooks, R. Sperber, & C. McCauley (Eds.), *Learning and cognition in the mentally retarded* (pp. 165–189). Hillsdale NJ: Lawrence Erlbaum Associates.

Maisto, A. A., & German, M. L. (1986). Reliability, predictive validity, and interrelationships of early assessment indices used with developmentally delayed infants and children. *Journal of Clinical Child Psychology, 15*, 327–332.

Malatesta, C. Z., Grigoryev, P., Lamb, C., Albin, M., & Culver, C. (1986). Emotion socialization and expressive development in preterm and full-term infants. *Child Development, 57*, 316–330.

Mali, M., Tyler, P., & Brookfield, D. S. K. (1989). Developmental outcome of high-risk neonates in North Staffordshire. *Child: Care, Health and Development, 15*, 137–145.

Mallick, M. J., Whipple, T. W., & Huerta, E. (1987). Behavioral and psychological traits of weight-conscious teenagers: A comparison of eating-disordered patients and high- and low-risk groups. *Adolescence, 22*, 157–168.

Mallory, B. L., & Herrick, S. C. (1987). The movement of children with mental retardation from institutional to community care. *Journal of the Association for Persons with Severe Handicaps, 12*, 297–305.

Malone, M. A., Kershner, J. R., & Siegel, L. (1988). The effects of methylphenidate on levels of processing and laterality in children with attention deficit disorder. *Journal of Abnormal Child Psychology, 16*, 379–395.

Manis, F. R. (1985). Acquisition of word identification skills in normal and disabled readers. *Journal of Educational Psychology, 77*, 78–90.

Manis, F. R., Savage, P. L., Morrison, F. J., Horn, C. C., Howell, M. J., Szeszulski, P. A., & Holt, L. K. (1987). Paired associate learning in reading-disabled children: Evidence for a rule-learning deficiency. *Journal of Experimental Child Psychology, 43*, 25–43.

Mannuza, S., Klein, R. G., Bonagura, N., Konig, P. H., & Shenker, R. (1988). Hyperactive boys almost grown up. *Archives of General Psychiatry, 45*, 13–18.

Marcell, M. M., & Jett, D. A. (1985). Identification of vocally expressed emotions by mentally retarded and nonretarded individuals. *American Journal of Mental Deficiency, 89*, 537–545.

Marcotte, A. C., & LaBarba, R. C. (1985). Cerebral lateralization for speech in deaf and normal children. *Brain and Language, 26*, 244–258.

Marcovitch, S., Goldberg, S., MacGregor, D. L., & Lojkasek, M. (1986). Patterns of temperament variation in three groups of developmentally delayed preschool children: Mother and father ratings. *Journal of Developmental and Behavioral Pediatrics, 7,* 247–252.

Margalit, M. (1984). Leisure activities of learning disabled children as a reflection of their passive life style and prolonged dependency. *Child Psychiatry and Human Development, 15,* 133–141.

Margalit, M. (1986). Mothers' perceptions of anxiety of their diabetic children. *Journal of Developmental and Behavioral Pediatrics, 7,* 27–30.

Margalit, M., & Heiman, T. (1986). Family climate and anxiety in families with learning disabled boys. *Journal of the American Academy of Child Psychiatry, 25,* 841–846.

Markoulis, D. (1988). Moral and cognitive reasoning features in congenitally blind children: Comparisons with the sighted. *British Journal of Developmental Psychology, 6,* 59–69.

Marschak, M., West, S. A., Nall, L., & Everhart, V. (1986). Development of creative language devices in signed and oral production. *Journal of Experimental Child Psychology, 41,* 534–550.

Marston, D., Mirkin, P., & Deno, S. L. (1984). Curriculum-based measurement: An alternative to traditional screening, referral, and identification. *Journal of Special Education, 18,* 109–117.

Marteau, T. M., Bloch, S., & Baum, J. D. (1987). Family life and diabetic control. *Journal of Child Psychology and Psychiatry, 28,* 823–833.

Martens, B. K., Peterson, R. I., Witt, J. C., & Cirone, S. (1986). Teacher perceptions of school-based interventions. *Exceptional Children, 53,* 213–223.

Martin, J. E., & Agran, M. (1985). Psychotropic and anticonvulsant drug use by mentally retarded adults across community residential and vocational placements. *Applied Research in Mental Retardation, 6,* 33–49.

Martin, J. E., Rusch, F. R., Tines, J. J., Brulle, A. R., & White, D. M. (1985). Work attendance in competitive employment: Comparison between employees who are nonhandicapped and those who are mentally retarded. *Mental Retardation, 23,* 142–147.

Martin, M., & Horsfall, D. (1987). Training work skills for students with severe and multiple handicapping conditions. *Australia and New Zealand Journal of Developmental Disabilities, 13,* 151–159.

Martin, R. P., Wisenbaker, J., Matthews-Morgan, J., Holbrook, J., Hooper, S., & Spalding, J. (1986). Stability of teacher temperament ratings over 6 and 12 months. *Journal of Abnormal Child Psychology, 14,* 167–179.

Martineau, J., Garreau, B., Roux, S., & Lelord, G. (1987). Auditory evoked responses and their modifications during conditioning paradigm in autistic children. *Journal of Autism and Developmental Disorders, 17,* 525–539.

Martinius, J. (1984). Complex visual reaction time measurements under irregular and regular preparatory interval conditions in children with developmental language problems. *Acta Paedopsychiatrica, 50,* 111–118.

Mary, N. L. (1990). Reactions of Black, Hispanic, and white mothers to having a child with handicaps. *Mental Retardation, 28,* 1–5.

Mason, S. M., & Mellor, D. H. (1984). Brain-stem, middle latency and late cortical evoked potentials in children with speech and language disorders. *EEG and Clinical Neurophysiology, 59,* 297–309.

Masterson, J. (1985). Family assessment of the child with intractable asthma. *Journal of Developmental and Behavioral Pediatrics, 6,* 244–251.

Mastropieri, M. A., & Scruggs, T. E. (1985). Early intervention for socially withdrawn children. *Journal of Special Education, 19,* 429–441.

Mastropieri, M. A., Scruggs, T. E., & Levin, J. R. (1985). Mnemonic strategy instruction with learning disabled adolescents. *Journal of Learning Disabilities, 18,* 94–100.

Mathews, R. M., & Fawcett, S. B. (1984). Building the capacities of job candidates through behavioral instruction. *Journal of Community Psychology, 12,* 123–129.

Matousek, M., Rasmussen, P., & Gillberg, C. (1984). EEG frequency analysis in children with so-called minimal brain dysfunction and related disorders. *Advances in Biological Psychiatry, 15,* 102–108.

Matson, J. L., Manikam, R., Heinze, A., & Kapperman, G. (1986). Anxiety in visually handicapped children and youth. *Journal of Clinical Child Psychology, 15,* 356–359.

Maudsley, H. (1890). *The pathology of mind.* New York: D. Appleton & Co.

Maughan, B., Gray, G., & Rutter, M. (1985). Reading retardation and anti social behaviour: A follow-up into employment. *Journal of Child Psychology and Psychiatry, 26,* 741–758.

Maurer, H., & Newbrough, J. R. (1987). Facial expressions of mentally retarded and nonretarded children: 2. Recognition of nonretarded adults with varying experience with mental retardation. *American Journal of Mental Deficiency, 91,* 511–515.

Maurer, H., & Sherrod, K. B. (1987). Context of directives given to young children with Down syndrome and nonretarded children: Development over 2 years. *American Journal of Mental Deficiency, 91,* 579–590.

May, D. C. (1988). Plastic surgery for children with Down syndrome: Normalization or extremism? *Mental Retardation, 26,* 17–19.

Maziade, M., Boutin, P., Cote, R., & Thivierge, J. (1986). Empirical characteristics of the NYLS temperament in middle childhood: Congruities and incongruities with other studies. *Child Psychiatry and Human Development, 17,* 38–52.

McBride, M. C. (1988). An individual double-blind crossover trial for assessing methylphenidate response in children with attention deficit disorder. *Journal of Pediatrics, 113,* 137–145.

McCall, R. B. (1981). Nature-nurture and the two realms of development: A proposed interaction with respect to mental development. *Child Development, 52,* 1–12.

McCartney, J. R. (1987). Mentally retarded and nonretarded subject' long-term recognition memory. *American Journal of Mental Retardation, 92,* 312–317.

McCauley, E., Kay, T., Ito, J., & Treder, R. (1987). The Turner syndrome: Cognitive deficits, affective discrimination, and behavior problems. *Child Development, 58,* 464–473.

McConaghy, J., & Kirby, N. H. (1987). Using the componential method to train mentally retarded individuals to solve analogies. *American Journal of Mental Deficiency, 92,* 12–23.

McConaughy, S. H., & Ritter, D. R. (1986). Social competence and behavioral problems of learning disabled boys aged 6–11. *Journal of Learning Disabilities, 19,* 39–45.

McConkey, R. (1985). Changing beliefs about play and handicapped children. *Early*

Child Development and Care, 19, 79–94.

McCord, J. S., & Haynes, W. O. (1988). Discourse errors in students with learning disabilities and their normally achieving peers: Molar versus molecular views. *Journal of Learning Disabilities, 21,* 237–243.

McCuller, G. L., Salzberg, C. L., & Lignugaris/Kraft, B. (1987). Producing generalized job initiative in severely mentally retarded sheltered workers. *Journal of Applied Behavior Analysis, 20,* 413–420.

McCune, L., & Ruff, H. A. (1985). Infant special education: Interactions with objects. *Topics in Early Childhood Special Education, 5,* 59–68.

McDermott, P. A. (1984). Child behavior disorders by age and sex based on item factoring of the revised Bristol guides. *Journal of Abnormal Child Psychology, 12,* 15–36.

McDonald, E. P. (1985). Medical needs of severely developmentally disabled persons residing in the community. *American Journal of Mental Deficiency, 90,* 171–176.

McGee, R., Silva, P. A., & Williams, S. M. (1984). Behaviour problems in a population of 7-year-old children: Prevalence, stability and types of disorder. *Journal of Child Psychology and Psychiatry, 25,* 251–259.

McGimsey, J. F., & Favell, J. E. (1988). The effects of increased physical exercise on disruptive behavior in retarded persons. *Journal of Autism and Developmental Disorders, 18,* 167–179.

McGuire, J., & Richman, N. (1987). Outcome of behavior problems in the preschool setting. *Child: Care, Health and Development, 13,* 403–414.

McHale, S. M., & Gamble, W. C. (1989). Sibling relationships of children with disabled and nondisabled brothers and sisters. *Developmental Psychology, 25,* 421–429.

McHale, S. M., Sloan, J., & Simeonsson, R. J. (1986). Sibling relationships of children with autistic, mentally retarded, and nonhandicapped brothers and sisters. *Journal of Autism and Developmental Disorders, 16,* 399–413.

McIlvane, W. J., Dube, W. V., Kledaras, J. B., Iennaco, F. M., & Stoddard, L. T. (1990). Teaching relational discrimination to individuals with mental retardation: Some problems and possible solutions. *American Journal on Mental Retardation, 95,* 283–296.

McKinney, B., & Peterson, R. A. (1987). Predictors of stress in parents of developmentally disabled children. *Journal of Pediatric Psychology, 12,* 133–150.

McKinney, J. D. (1989). Longitudinal research on the behavioral characteristics of children with learning disabilities. *Journal of Learning Disabilities, 22,* 141–150.

McKinney, J. D., & Speece, D. L. (1986). Academic consequences and longitudinal stability of behavioral subtypes of learning disabled children. *Journal of Educational Psychology, 78,* 365–372.

McLaren, J., & Bryson, S. E. (1987). Review of recent epidemiological studies of mental retardation: Prevalence, associated disorders, and etiology. *American Journal of Mental Retardation, 92,* 243–254.

McLaughlin, T. F., Krappman, V. F., & Welsh, J. M. (1985). The effects of self-recording for on-task behavior of behaviorally disordered special education students. *Remedial and Special Education, 6,* 42–45.

McLoughlin, J. A., Clark, F. L., Mauck, A. R., & Petrosko, J. (1987). A comparison of parent–child perceptions of student learning disabilities. *Journal of Learning Disabilities, 20,* 357–360.

McNally, R. J., Kompik, J. J., & Sherman, G. (1984). Increasing the productivity of mentally retarded workers through self-management. *Analysis and Intervention in Developmental Disabilities, 4*, 129–135.

McNutt, G. (1986). The status of learning disabilities in the states: Consensus of controversy? *Journal of Learning Disabilities, 19*, 12–16.

McQueen, P. C., Spence, M. W., Garner, J. B., Pereira, L. H., & Winsor, E. J. T. (1987). Prevalence of major mental retardation and associated disabilities in the Canadian maritime provinces. *American Journal of Mental Deficiency, 91*, 460–466.

McTear, M. F. (1985). Pragmatic disorders: A question of direction. *British Journal of Disorders of Communication, 20*, 119–127.

Meador, D. M. (1984). Effects of color on visual discrimination of geometric symbols by severely and profoundly mentally retarded individuals. *American Journal of Mental Deficiency, 89*, 275–286.

Meador, D. M., Rumbaugh, D. M., Tribble, M., & Thompson, S. (1984). Facilitating visual discrimination learning of moderately and severely mentally retarded children through illumination of stimuli. *American Journal of Mental Deficiency, 89*, 313–316.

Meerwaldt, J. D., & Van Dongen, H. R. (1988). Disturbances of spatial perception in children. *Behavioural Brain Research, 31*, 131–134.

Meisels, S. J., Cross, D. R., & Plunkett, J. W. (1987). Use of the Bayley Infant Behavior Record with preterm and full-term infants. *Developmental Psychology, 23*, 475–482.

Meline, T. J., & Brackin, S. R. (1987). Language-impaired children's awareness of inadequate messages. *Journal of Speech and Hearing Disorders, 52*, 263–270.

Menolascino, F. J., Donaldson, J. Y., Gallagher, T. F., Golden, C. J., & Wilson, J. E. (1988). Orthomolecular therapy: Its history and applicability to psychiatric disorders. *Child Psychiatry and Human Development, 18*, 133–150.

Merrill, E. C. (1985). Differences in semantic processing speed of mentally retarded and nonretarded persons. *American Journal of Mental Deficiency, 90*, 71–80.

Merrill, E. C., & Bilsky, L. H. (1990). Individual differences in the representation of sentences in memory. *American Journal on Mental Retardation, 95*, 68–76.

Merrill, E. C., & Mar, H. H. (1987). Differences between mentally retarded and nonretarded persons' efficiency of auditory sentence processing. *American Journal of Mental Deficiency, 91*, 406–414.

Meyer, L. H., Eichinger, J., & Park-Lee, S. (1987). A validation of program quality indicators in educational services for students with severe disabilities. *Journal of the Association for Persons with Severe Handicaps, 12*, 251–263.

Meyer, L. H., Fox, A., Schermer, A., Ketelsen, D., Montan, N., Maley, K., & Cole, D. (1987). The effects of teacher intrusion on social play interactions between children with autism and their nonhandicapped peers. *Journal of Autism and Developmental Disorders, 17*, 315–332.

Meyers, C. E., & Blacher, J. (1987). Parents' perceptions of schooling for severely handicapped children: Home and family variables. *Exceptional Children, 53*, 441–449.

Meyers, C. E., Nihira, K., & Mink, I. T. (1984). Predicting retarded students' short-term growth from home environment. *Applied Research in Mental Retardation, 5*, 137–146.

Meyers, S. C., & Freeman, F. J. (1985). Interruptions as a variable in stuttering and disfluency. *Journal of Speech and Hearing Research, 28*, 428–435.

Mick, L. B. (1984–1985). Assessment procedures as related to enrollment patterns of Hispanic students in special education. *Educational Research Quarterly, 9*, 27–35.

Milgram, N. A., & Atzil, M. (1988). Parenting stress in raising autistic children. *Journal of Autism and Developmental Disorders, 18*, 415–424.

Milich, R., & Landau, S. (1988). Teacher ratings of inattention/overactivity and aggression: Cross-validation with classroom observations. *Journal of Clinical Child Psychology, 17*, 92–97.

Milich, R., & Pelham, W. E. (1986). Effects of sugar ingestion on the classroom and playgroup behavior of attention deficit disordered boys. *Journal of Consulting and Clinical Psychology, 54*, 714–718.

Millar, S. (1986). Aspects of size, shape and texture in touch: Redundancy and interference in children's discrimination of raised dot patterns. *Journal of Child Psychology and Psychiatry, 27*, 367–381.

Millar, S. (1988). Models of sensory deprivation: The nature/nurture dichotomy and spatial representation in the blind. *International Journal of Behavioral Development, 11*, 69–87.

Miller, C. T., Malcarne, V. L., Clarke, R. T., Lobato, D., Fitzgeral, M. D., & Br and, P. (1989). What mentally retarded and nonretarded children expect of one another. *American Journal on Mental Retardation, 93*, 396–405.

Miller, L. C., Hampe, E., Barrett, C. L., & Noble, H. (1971). Children's deviant behavior within the general population. *Journal of Consulting and Clinical Psychology, 37*, 16–22.

Miller, L. K. (1987). Developmentally delayed musical savant's sensitivity to tonal structure. *American Journal of Mental Deficiency, 91*, 467–471.

Miller, L. K. (1989). *Musical savants: Exceptional skill in the mentally retarded.* Hillsdale, NJ: Lawrence Erlbaum Associates.

Miller, S. E. (1987). Training personnel and procedures for Special Olympics athletes. *Education and Training in Mental Retardation, 22*, 244–249.

Milne, J., & Johnson, E. G. (1985). Modification of children's speech as a function of the perceived intellectual capacity of the listener. *Journal of Mental Deficiency Research, 29*, 225–231.

Miltenberger, R. G., Lennox, D. B., & Erfanian, N. (1989). Acceptability of alternative treatments for persons with mental retardation: Ratings from institutional and community-based staff. *American Journal on Mental Retardation, 93*, 388–395.

Minde, K. (1988). Behavioral abnormalities commonly seen in infancy. *Canadian Journal of Psychiatry, 33*, 741–747.

Minde, K., Perrotta, M., & Hellmann, J. (1988). Impact of delayed development in premature infants on mother–infant interaction: A prospective investigation. *Journal of Pediatrics, 112*, 136–142.

Minde, K., Perrotta, M., & Marton, P. (1985). Maternal caretaking and play with full-term and premature infants. *Journal of Child Psychology and Psychiatry, 26*, 231–244.

Minderaa, R. B., Volkmar, F. R., Hansen, C. R., Harcherik, D. F., Akkerhuis, G. W., & Cohen, D. J. (1985). Brief report: Snout and visual rooting reflexes in infantile autism. *Journal of Autism and Developmental Disorders, 15*, 409–416.

Mink, I. T., Blacher, J., & Nihira, K. (1988). Taxonomy of family life styles: 3. Replication with families with severely mentally retarded children. *American Journal on Mental Retardation, 93,* 250–264.

Mink, I. T., Meyers, C. E., & Nihira, K. (1984). Taxonomy of family life styles: 2. Homes with slow-learning children. *American Journal of Mental Deficiency, 89,* 111–123.

Mink, I. T., & Nihira, K. (1986). Family life-styles and child behaviors: A study of direction of effects. *Developmental Psychology, 22,* 610–616.

Minnes, P. M. (1988). Family resources and stress associated with having a mentally retarded child. *American Journal on Mental Retardation, 93,* 184–192.

Minskoff, E. H., Sautter, S. W., Hoffmann, F. J., & Hawks, R. L. (1987). Employer attitudes toward hiring the learning disabled. *Journal of Learning Disabilities, 20,* 53–57.

Minsky, S. K., Spitz, H. H., & Bessellieu, C. L. (1985). Maintenance and transfer of training by mentally retarded young adults on the Tower of Hanoi problem. *American Journal of Mental Deficiency, 90,* 190–197.

Mishima, J. (1986). Principle of development promotion: Proposition of flexion-extension hypothesis. *Journal of Human Development, 22,* 28–41.

Modell, B. (1985). Chorionic villus sampling: Evaluating safety and efficacy. *The Lancet, 1,* 737–740.

Moe, G. L., & Harris, J. D. (1983). Effects of encoding and retrieval strategies on the recall of learning disabled and normal children. *Journal of General Psychology, 109,* 233–246.

Moellman-Landa, R., & Olswang, L. B. (1984). Effects of adult communication behaviors on language-impaired children's verbal output. *Applied Psycholinguistics, 5,* 117–134.

Moos, R. H. (1974). Evaluating treatment environments. *Evaluating treatment environments.* New York: Wiley.

Morgan, R. L. (1989). Judgments of restrictiveness, social acceptability, and usage: Review of research on procedures to decrease behavior. *American Journal of Mental Retardation, 94,* 121–133.

Morgan, S. B. (1986). Autism and Piaget's theory: Are the two compatible? *Journal of Autism and Developmental Disorders, 16,* 441–457.

Morgan, S. B. (1988). The autistic child and family functioning: A developmental-family systems perspective. *Journal of Autism and Developmental Disorders, 18,* 263–280.

Morgan, S. B., & Brown, T. L. (1988). Luria-Nebraska Neuropsychological Battery-Children's Revision: Concurrent validity with three learning disability subtypes. *Journal of Consulting and Clinical Psychology, 56,* 463–466.

Morice, R., & Slaghuis, W. (1985). Language performance and reading ability at 8 years of age. *Applied Psycholinguistics, 6,* 141–160.

Morris, T., Blashfield, R., & Satz, P. (1986). Developmental classification of reading-disabled children. *Journal of Clinical and Experimental Neuropsychology, 8,* 371–392.

Morrison, D. C., & Sublett, J. (1986). The effects of sensory integration therapy on nystagmus duration, equilibrium reactions and visual-motor integration in reading retarded children. *Child: Care, Health and Development, 12,* 99–110.

Morrison, G. M. (1985). The social status-socioempathy relationship among mildly handicapped and nonhandicapped children: Analysis of the person × environment fit. *Applied Research in Mental Retardation, 6,* 1–14.

Morrison, G. M., Forness, S. R., & MacMillan, D. L. (1983). Influences on the sociometric ratings of mildly handicapped children: A path analysis. *Journal of Educational Psychology, 75,* 63–74.

Morrison, G. M., MacMillan, D. L., & Kavale, K. (1985). System identification of learning disabled children: Implications for research sampling. *Learning Disability Quarterly, 8,* 2–10.

Morrison, G. M., & Zetlin, A. (1988). Perceptions of communication, cohesion, and adaptability in families of adolescents with and without learning handicaps. *Journal of Abnormal Child and Psychology, 16,* 675–685.

Morrow, L. W., Burke, J. G., & Buell, B. J. (1985). Effects of a self-recording procedure on the attending to task behavior and academic productivity of adolescents with multiple handicaps. *Mental Retardation, 23,* 137–141.

Morton, L. L., & Kershner, J. R. (1984). Negative air ionization improves memory and attention in learning-disabled and mentally retarded children. *Journal of Abnormal Child Psychology, 12,* 353–365.

Morton, L. L., & Kershner, J. R. (1985). Time-of-day effects upon children's memory and analogical reasoning. *Alberta Journal of Educational Research, 31,* 26–34.

Mosley, J. L. (1985). High-speed memory-scanning task performance of mildly mentally retarded and nonretarded individuals. *American Journal of Mental Deficiency, 90,* 81–89.

Mowrer, D. E., & Conley, D. (1987). Effect of peer administered consequences upon articulatory responses of speech-defective children. *Journal of Communication Disorders, 20,* 319–326.

Mrazek, D. A. (1986). Childhood asthma: Two central questions for child psychiatry. *Journal of Child Psychology and Psychiatry, 27,* 1–5.

Mueller, C. W., & Parcel, T. L. (1981). Measures of socioeconomic status: Alternatives and recommendations. *Child Development, 52,* 13–30.

Mueller, H. H., Wilgosh, L., & Dennis, S. S. (1987). Employment survival skills: What vocational rehabilitation professionals believe to be most important. *Mental Retardation and Learning Disabilities Bulletin, 15,* 7–20.

Mueser, K. T., Valenti-Hein, D., & Yarnold, P. R. (1987). Dating-skills groups for the developmentally disabled. Social skills and problem-solving versus relaxation training. *Behavior Modification, 11,* 200–228.

Mullen, M. K., Coll, C. G., Vohr, B. R., Muriel, A. C., & Oh, W. (1988). Mother–infant feeding interaction in full-term small-for-gestational-age infants. *Journal of Pediatrics, 112,* 143–148.

Mullins, L. L., Siegel, L. J., & Hodges, K. (1985). Cognitive problem-solving and life event correlates of depressive symptoms in children. *Journal of Abnormal Child Psychology, 13,* 305–314.

Mullins, M., & Rincover, A. (1985). Comparing autistic and normal children along the dimensions of reinforcement maximization, stimulus sampling, and responsiveness to extinction. *Journal of Experimental Child Psychology, 40,* 350–374.

Mulvey, E. P., & LaRosa, J. F. (1986). Delinquency cessation and adolescent development: Preliminary data. *American Journal of Orthopsychiatry, 56,* 212–224.

Mundy, P., Sigman, M., Kasari, C., & Yirmiya, N. (1988). Nonverbal communication skills in Down syndrome children. *Child Development, 59,* 235–249.

Mundy, P., Sigman, M., Ungerer, J., & Sherman, T. (1986). Defining the social deficits of autism: The contribution of non-verbal communication measures. *Journal of Child Psychology and Psychiatry, 27,* 657–669.

Mundy, P., Sigman, M., Ungerer, J., & Sherman, T. (1987). Nonverbal communication and play correlates of language development in autistic children. *Journal of Autism and Developmental Disorders, 17,* 349–364.

Munson, W. W. (1988). Effects of leisure education versus physical activity or informal discussion on behaviorally disordered youth offenders. *Adapted Physical Activity Quarterly, 5,* 305–317.

Murakami, J. W., Courchesne, E., Press, G. A., Yeung-Courchesne, R., & Hesselink, J. R. (1989). Reduced cerebellar hemisphere size and its relationship to vermal hypoplasia in autism. *Archives of Neurology, 46,* 689–694.

Murphy, G., Carr, J., & Callias, M. (1986). Increasing simple toy play in profoundly mentally handicapped children: 2. Designing special toys. *Journal of Autism and Developmental Disorders, 16,* 45–58.

Murphy, J. S., & Newlon, B. J. (1987). Loneliness and the mainstreamed hearing impaired college student. *American Annals of the Deaf, 132,* 21–25.

Murphy, L. A., Pollatsek, A., & Well, A. D. (1988). Developmental dyslexia and word retrieval deficits. *Brain and Language, 35,* 1–23.

Murphy, M. A., & Vogel, J. B. (1985). Looking out from the isolator: David's perception of the world. *Journal of Developmental and Behavioral Pediatrics, 6,* 118–121.

Murray, A. D. (1988). Newborn auditory brainstem evoked responses (ABRs): Longitudinal correlates in the first year. *Child Development, 59,* 1542–1554.

Murray, J. B. (1986a). Psychological aspects of anorexia nervosa. *Genetic, Social and General Psychology Monographs, 112,* 5–40.

Murray, J. B. (1986b). Successful treatment of obsessive-compulsive disorders *Genetic, Social and General Psychology Monographs, 112,* 175–199.

Musselman, C. R., Lindsay, P. H., & Wilson, A. K. (1988). An evaluation of recent trends in preschool programming for hearing-impaired children. *Journal of Speech and Hearing Disorders, 53,* 71–88.

Muuss, R. E. (1986). Adolescent eating disorder: Bulimia. *Adolescence, 21,* 257–267.

National Institute of Handicapped Research. (1985). *Summary of data on handicapped children and youth* Washington, DC: U. S. Government Printing Office.

Needleman, H. L., Schell, A., Bellinger, D., Leviton, A., & Allred, E. N. (1990). The long-term effects of exposure to low doses of lead in childhood. *New England Journal of Medicine, 322,* 83–88.

Neiger, B. L., & Hopkins, R. W. (1988). Adolescent suicide: Character traits of high-risk teenagers. *Adolescence, 23,* 469–475.

Neilson, P. D., & O'Dwyer, N. J. (1984). Reproducibility and variability of speech muscle activity in athetoid dysarthria of cerebral palsy. *Journal of Speech and Hearing Research, 27,* 502–517.

Nesbitt, W. C., & Karagianis, L. D. (1982). Child abuse: Exceptionality as a risk factor. *Alberta Journal of Educational Research, 28,* 69–76.

Nettelbeck, T., & Kirby, N. H. (1983a). Measures of timed performance and intelligence. *Intelligence, 7,* 39–52.

Nettelbeck, T., & Kirby, N. H. (1983b). Retarded–nonretarded differences in speed of processing. *Australian Journal of Psychology, 35,* 445–453.

Nettelbeck, T., Robson, L., Walwyn, R. T., Downing, A., & Jones, N. (1986). Inspection time as mental speed in mildly mentally retarded adults: Analysis of eye gaze, eye movement, and orientation. *American Journal of Mental Deficiency, 91,* 78–91.

Newberger, E. H., Hampton, R. L., Marx, T. J., & White, K. M. (1986). Child abuse and pediatric social illness: An epidemiological analysis and ecological reformulation. *American Journal of Orthopsychiatry, 56,* 589–601.

Newell, K. M. (1985). Coordination, control and skill. In D. Goodman, R. B. Wilberg, & I. M. Franks (Eds.), *Differing perspectives in motor learning, memory, and control* (pp. 295–317). Amsterdam: Elsevier.

Newell, K. M., & Scully, D. M. (1988). Steps in the development of coordination: Perception of relative motion. In J. Clark & J. Humphrey (Eds.), *Advances in motor development research* (Vol. 1, pp. 153–170). New York: AMS Press.

Newman, P. H., Bunderson, K., & Brey, R. H. (1985). Brain stem electrical responses of stutterers and normals by sex, ears, and recovery. *Journal of Fluency Disorders, 10,* 59–67.

Ney, P. G. (1988). Transgenerational child abuse. *Child Psychiatry and Human Development, 18,* 151–168.

Nichols, P. L. (1984). Familial mental retardation. *Behavior Genetics, 14,* 161–170.

Nichols, R. C. (1981). Origins, nature, and determinants of intellectual development. In M. J. Begab, H. C. Haywood, & H. L. Garber (Eds.), *Psychosocial influences in retarded performance* (Vol. 1, pp. 127–154). Baltimore, MD: University Park Press.

Nicol, A. R., Stretch, D. D., Fundudis, T., Smith, I., & Davison, I. (1987). The nature of mother and toddler problems: 1. Development of a multiple criterion screen. *Journal of Child Psychology and Psychiatry, 28,* 739–754.

Nienhuys, T. G., Horsborough, K. M., & Cross, T. G. (1985). A dialogic analysis of interaction between mothers and their deaf or hearing preschoolers. *Applied Psycholinguistics, 6,* 121–140.

Nietupski, J., Ayres, B., & Hamre-Nietupski, S. (1983). A review of recreation/leisure skills research with moderately, severely and profoundly mentally handicapped individuals. *Australia and New Zealand Journal of Developmental Disabilities, 9,* 161–176.

Nigro, G. N., & Roak, R. M. (1987). Mentally retarded and nonretarded adults' memory for spatial location. *American Journal of Mental Deficiency, 91,* 392–397.

Nihira, K., Mink, T., & Meyers, C. E. (1985). Home environment and development of slow-learning adolescents: Reciprocal relations. *Developmental Psychology, 21,* 784–794.

Nihira, K., Tomiyasu, Y., & Oshio, C. (1987). Homes of TMR children: Comparison between American and Japanese families. *American Journal of Mental Deficiency, 91,* 486–495.

Nihira, K., Webster, R., Tomiyasu, Y., & Oshio, C. (1988). Child-environment relationships: A cross-cultural study of educable mentally retarded children and their families. *Journal of Autism and Developmental Disorders, 18,* 327–341.

Nippold, M. A., Erskine, B. J., & Freed, D. B. (1988). Proportional and functional analogical reasoning in normal and language-impaired children. *Journal of Speech and Hearing Disorders, 53,* 440–448.

Nirje, B. (1985). The basis and logic of the normalization principle. *Australia and New Zealand Journal of Developmental Disabilities, 11,* 65–68.

Nittrouer, S., & Cheney, C. (1984). Operant techniques used in stuttering therapy: A review. *Journal of Fluency Disorders, 9,* 169–190.

Nodine, B. F., Barenbaum, E., & Newcomer, P. (1985). Story composition by learning disabled, reading disabled, and normal children. *Learning Disability Quarterly, 8,* 167–179.

Nolen-Hoeksema, S., Girgus, J. S., & Seligman, M. E. (1986). Learned helplessness in children: A longitudinal study of depression, achievement, and explanatory style. *Journal of Personality and Social Psychology, 51,* 435–442.

O'Connor, N., & Hermelin, B. (1989). The memory structure of autistic idiot-savant mnemonists. *British Journal of Psychology, 80,* 97–111.

O'Connor, S. C., & Spreen, O. (1988). The relationship between parents' socio-economic status and education level, and adult occupational and educational achievement of children with L.D. *Journal of Learning Disabilities, 21,* 148–153.

O'Donnell, J. P., Leicht, D. J., Phillips, F. L., Marnett, J. P., & Horn, W. F. (1988). Stability of children's behavior problems: A $3\frac{1}{2}$-year longitudinal study. *Journal of Applied Developmental Psychology, 9,* 233–241.

O'Dougherty, M., Neuchterlein, K. H., & Drew, B. (1984). Hyperactive and hypoxic children: Signal detection, sustained attention, and behavior. *Journal of Abnormal Psychology, 93,* 178–191.

O'Hagan, F. J., Sandys, E. J., & Swanson, W. I. (1984). Educational provision, parental expectation and physical disability. *Child: Care, Health and Development, 10,* 31–38.

O'Leary, K. D., Vivian, D., & Cornoldi, C. (1984). Assessment and treatment of "hyperactivity" in Italy and the United States. *Journal of Clinical Psychology, 13,* 56–60.

Oberklaid, F., Prior, M., & Sanson, A. (1986). Temperament of preterm versus full-term infants. *Journal of Developmental and Behavioral Pediatrics, 7,* 159–162.

Obrzut, J. E., Obrzut, A., Bryden, M. P., & Bartels, S. G. (1985). Information processing and speech lateralization in learning-disabled children. *Brain and Language, 25,* 87–101.

Odom, S. L., Yoder, P., & Hill, G. (1988). Developmental intervention for infants with handicaps: Purposes and programs. *Journal of Special Education, 22,* 11–24.

Offord, D. R. (1987). Prevention of behavioral and emotional disorders in children. *Journal of Child Psychology and Psychiatry, 28,* 9–19.

Ohta, M. (1987). Cognitive disorders of infantile autism: A study employing the WISC, spatial relationship conceptualization, and gesture imitations. *Journal of Autism and Developmental Disorders, 17,* 45–62.

Ohwaki, S., & Zingarelli, G. (1988). Feeding clients with severe multiple handicaps in a skilled nursing care facility. *Mental Retardation, 26,* 21–24.

Oldershaw, L., Walters, G. C., & Hall, D. K. (1986). Control strategies and noncompliance in abusive mother–child dyads: An observational study. *Child Development, 57,* 722–732.

Oller, D. K., & Eilers, R. E. (1988). The role of audition in infant babbling. *Child Development, 59,* 441–449.

Omenn, G. S. (1976). Inborn errors of metabolism: Clues to understanding human behavioral disorders. *Behavior Genetics, 6,* 263–284.

Omizo, M. M., Amerikaner, M. J., & Michael, W. B. (1985). The Coopersmith Self-Esteem Inventory as a predictor of feelings and communication satisfaction toward parents. *Educational and Psychological Measurement, 45,* 389–395.

Omizo, M. M., Cubberly, W. E., & Longano, D. M. (1984). The effects of group counseling on self-concept and locus of control among learning disabled children. *Journal of Humanistic Education and Development, 23,* 69–79.

Omizo, M. M., Cubberly, W. E., & Cubberly, R. D. (1985). Modelling techniques, perceptions of self-efficacy, and arithmetic achievement among learning disabled children. *The Exceptional Child, 32,* 99–105.

Ornitz, E. M., Atwell, C. W., Kaplan, A. R., & Westlake, J. R. (1985). Brain-stem dysfunction in autism: Results of vestibular stimulation. *Archives of General Psychiatry, 42,* 1018–1025.

Ornstein, P. A., Medlin, R. G., Stone, B. P., & Naus, M. J. (1985). Retrieving for rehearsal: An analysis of active rehearsal in children's memory. *Developmental Psychology, 21,* 633–641.

Orvaschel, H., Walsh-Allis, G., & Ye, W. (1988). Psychopathology in children of parents with recurrent depression. *Journal of Abnormal Child Psychology, 16,* 17–28.

Osguthorpe, R. T., & Scruggs, T. E. (1986). Special education students as tutors: A review and analysis. *Remedial and Special Education, 7,* 15–26.

Ottenbacher, K., & Altman, R. (1984). Effects of vibratory, edible, and social reinforcement on performance of institutionalized mentally retarded individuals. *American Journal of Mental Deficiency, 89,* 201–204.

Ottenbacher, K. J., Muller, L., Brandt, D., Heintzelman, A., Hojem, P., & Sharpe, P. (1987). The effectiveness of tactile stimulation as a form of early intervention: A quantitative evaluation. *Journal of Developmental and Behavioral Pediatrics, 8,* 68–76.

Pace, G. M., Ivancic, M. T., Edwards, G. L., Iwata, B. A., & Page, T. J. (1985). Assessment of stimulus preference and reinforcer value with profoundly retarded individuals. *Journal of Applied Behavior Analysis, 18,* 249–255.

Palfrey, J. S., Sarro, L. J., Singer, J. D., & Wenger, M. (1987). Physician familiarity with the educational programs of their special needs patients. *Journal of Developmental and Behavioral Pediatrics, 8,* 198–202.

Palincsar, A. S., & Brown, D. A. (1987). Enhancing instructional time through attention to metacognition. *Journal of Learning Disabilities, 20,* 66–75.

Panella, D., & Henggeler, S. W. (1986). Peer interations of conduct-disordered, anxious-withdrawn, and well-adjusted black adolescents. *Journal of Abnormal Child Psychology, 14,* 1–12.

Pannbacker, M. (1984). Classification systems of voice disorders: A review of the literature. *Language, Speech, and Hearing Services in Schools, 15,* 169–174.

Panyan, M. V. (1984). Computer technology for autistic students. *Journal of Autism and Developmental Disabilities, 14,* 375–382.

Parham, C., Reid, S., & Hamer, R. M. (1987). A long-range follow-up study of former inpatients at a children's psychiatric hospital. *Child Psychiatry and Human Development, 17,* 199–209.

Paris, S. G., & Oka, E. R. (1986). Self-regulated learning among exceptional children. *Exceptional Children, 53,* 103–108.

Parker, H., & Parker, S. (1986). Father–daughter sexual abuse: An emerging perspective. *American Journal of Orthopsychiatry, 56,* 531–549.

Parker, J. G., & Asher, S. R. (1987). Peer relations and later personal adjustment: Are low-accepted children at risk? *Psychological Bulletin, 102,* 357–389.

Parsons, C. L., Iacono, T. A., & Rozner, L. (1987). Effect of tongue reduction on articulation in children with Down syndrome. *American Journal of Mental Deficiency, 91,* 328–332.

Parsons, M. B., Schepis, M. M., Reid, D. H., McCarn, J. E., & Green, C. W. (1987). Expanding the impact of behavioral staff management: A large-scale log-term application in schools serving severely handicapped students. *Journal of Applied Behavior Analysis, 20,* 139–150.

Pasamanick, B., & Knobloch, H. (1966). Retrospective studies on the epidemiology of productive casualty: Old and new. *Merrill-Palmer Quarterly, 12,* 7–26.

Paul, R., & Cohen, D. J. (1984). Outcomes of severe disorders of language acquisition. *Journal of Autism and Developmental Disorders, 14,* 405–421.

Paul, R., & Cohen, D. J. (1985). Comprehension of indirect requests in adults with autistic disorders and mental retardation. *Journal of Speech and Hearing Research, 28,* 475–479.

Payne, J. A., & Quigley, S. (1987). Hearing-impaired children's comprehension of verb-particle combinations. *Volta Review, 89,* 133–143.

Payne, M. A. (1985). Barbadian children's understanding of mental retardation. *Applied Research in Mental Retardation, 6,* 185–198.

Pearl, R., Donahue, M., & Bryan, T. (1985). The development of tact: Children's strategies for delivering bad news. *Journal of Applied Developmental Psychology, 6,* 141–149.

Pedelty, L., Levine, S. C., & Shevell, S. K. (1985). Developmental changes in face processing: Results from multidimensional scaling. *Journal of Experimental Child Psychology, 39,* 421–436.

Pelham, W. E., Bender, M. E., Caddell, J., Booth, S., & Moorer, S. H. (1985). Methylphenidate and children with attention deficit disorder: Dose effects on classroom academic and social behavior. *Archives of General Psychiatry, 42,* 948–952.

Pellegrini, A. D. (1985). Social-cognitive aspects of children's play: The effects of age, gender, and activity centers. *Journal of Applied Developmental Psychology, 6,* 129–140.

Pennington, B. F., & Bruce, S. D. (1988). Genetic influences on learning disabilities: An update. *Journal of Consulting and Clinical Psychology, 56,* 817–823.

Pennington, B. F., Doorninck, W. J. V., McCabe, L. L., & McCabe, E. R. B. (1985). Neuropsychological deficits in early treated phenylketonuric children. *American Journal of Mental Deficiency, 89,* 467–474.

Pennington, B. F., McCabe, L. L., Smith, S. D., Lefly, D. L., Bookman, M. O., Kimberling, W. J., & Lubs, H. A. (1986). Spelling errors in adultsa with a form of familial dyslexia. *Child Development, 57,* 1001–1013.

Pennington, B. F., & Smith, S. D. (1983). Genetic influences on learning disabilities and speech and language disorders. *Child Development, 54,* 369–387.

Penso, D. E. (1984). A study of horizontal directionality and difficulty with reading, writing and spelling. *International Journal of Rehabilitation Research, 7,* 427–429.

Perkins, W. H. (1983). The problem of definition: Commentary on "Stuttering."

Journal of Speech and Hearing Disorders, 48, 246–249.

Perrin, E. C., Ramsey, B. K., & Sandler, H. M. (1987). Competent kids: Children and adolescents with a chronic illness. *Child: Care, Health and Development, 13,* 13–32.

Perry, D. G., Perry, L. C., & Rasmussen, P. (1986). Cognitive social learning mediators of aggression. *Child Development, 57,* 700–711.

Perry, M. A., Wells, E. A., & Doran, L. D. (1983). Parent characteristics of abusing and nonabusing families. *Journal of Clinical Child Psychology, 12,* 329–336.

Perry, R., Campbell, M., Adams, P., Lynch, N., Spencer, E. K., Currenc, E. L., & Overall, J. E. (1989). Long-term efficacy of Haloperidol in autistic children: Continuous versus discontinuous drug administration. *Journal of the American Academy of Child and Adolescent Psychiatry, 28,* 87–92.

Peskett, R., & Wootton, A. J. (1985). Turn-taking and overlap in the speech of young Down's syndrome children. *Journal of Mental Deficiency Research, 29,* 263–273.

Peters, H. F. M., & Hulstijn, W. (1984). Stuttering and anxiety. *Journal of Fluency Disorders, 9,* 67–84.

Peters-Martin, P., & Wachs, T. D. (1984). A longitudinal study of temperament and its correlates in the first 12 months. *Infant Behavior and Development, 7,* 285–298.

Peterson, L., Mullins, L. L., & Ridley-Johnson, R. (1985). Childhood depression: Peer reactions to depression and life stress. *Journal of Abnormal Child Psychology, 13,* 597–609.

Petitto, L. A. (1987). On the autonomy of language and gesture: Evidence from the acquisition of personal pronouns in American Sign Language. *Cognition, 27,* 1–52.

Pfeffer, C. R., Zuckerman, S., Plutchik, R., & Mizruchi, M. S. (1987). Assaultive behavior in normal school children. *Child Psychiatry and Human Development, 17,* 166–176.

Phillippe, T., & Auvenshine, D. (1985). Career development among deaf persons. *Journal of the Rehabilitation of the Deaf, 19,* 9–17.

Phillips, C. J., Hon, Y., Smith, B., & Sutton, A. (1986). Severe mental retardation in children from socially disadvantaged families. *Child: Care, Health and Development, 12,* 69–91.

Phillips, S., Bohannon, W. E., Gayton, W. E., & Friedman, S. B. (1985). Parent interview findings regarding the impact of cystic fibrosis on families. *Journal of Developmental and Behavioral Pediatrics, 6,* 122–127.

Phillips, S., Friedman, S. B., Zebal, B. H., & Parrish, J. M. (1985). Residents' knowledge of behavioral pediatrics. *Journal of Developmental and Behavioral Pediatrics, 6,* 268–272.

Pickering, D., & Morgan, S. B. (1985). Parental ratings of treatments of self-injurious behavior. *Journal of Autism and Developmental Disorders, 15,* 303–314.

Pickering, E., Pickering, A., & Buchanan, M. L. (1987). LD and nonhandicapped boys' comprehension of cartoon humor. *Learning Disability Quarterly, 10,* 45–51.

Pietrzak, W. (1981). Perception of the emotions of others by deaf schoolchildren. *Defektologiya, 4,* 37–42.

Piggott, L. R., & Anderson, T. (1983). Brainstem auditory evoked response in children with central language disturbance. *Journal of the American Academy of Child Psychiatry, 22,* 535–540.

Pipe, M. (1987). Pathological left-handedness: Is it familial? *Neuropsychologia, 25,* 571–577.

Pipe, M. (1988). Atypical laterality and retardation. *Psychological Bulletin, 104,* 343–347.

Plomin, R., Loehlin, J. C., & DeFries, J. C. (1985). Genetic and environmental components of "environmental" influences. *Developmental Psychology, 21,* 391–402.

Polloway, E. A., Epstein, M. H., & Cullinan, D. (1985). Prevalence of behavior problems among educable mentally retarded students. *Education and Training of the Mentally Retarded, 20,* 3–13.

Poplin, M. S. (1988). The reductionistic fallacy in learning disabilities: Replicating the past by reducing the present. *Journal of Learning Disabilities, 21,* 389–400.

Porretta, D. L. (1987). Selected parameters of response organization in mildly mentally retarded children. *Perceptual and Motor Skills, 64,* 95–100.

Porter, S. J. (1986). Assessment: A vital process in the treatment of family violence. *Family Therapy, 13,* 105–112.

Posner, M. I., & Petersen, S. E. (1990). The attention system of the human brain. *Annual Review of Neuroscience, 13,* 25–42.

Pothier, P. C., & Cheek, K. (1984). Current practices in sensory motor programming with developmentally delayed infants and young children. *Child: Care, Health and Development, 10,* 340–348.

Powers, M. D. (1985). Behavioral assessment and the planning and evaluation of interventions for developmentally disabled children. *School Psychology Review, 14,* 155–161.

Preyer, W. (1973). *The mind of the child.* New York: Arno Press.

Pring, L. (1984). A comparison of the word recognition processes of blind and sighted children. *Child Development, 55,* 1865–1877.

Pring, L., & Rusted, J. (1985). Pictures for the blind: An investigation of the influence of pictures on recall of text by blind children. *British Journal of Developmental Psychology, 3,* 41–45.

Prinz, R. J., Tarnowski, K. J., & Nay, S. M. (1984). Assessment of sustained attention and distraction in children using a classroom analogue task. *Journal of Clinical Child Psychology, 13,* 250–256.

Prior, M., Sanson, A., Freethy, C., & Geffen, G. (1985). Auditory attentional abilities in hyperactive children. *Journal of Child Psychology and Psychiatry, 26,* 289–304.

Prior, M., & Sanson, A. (1986). Attention deficit disorder with hyperactivity: A critique. *Journal of Child Psychology and Psychiatry, 27,* 307–319.

Prior, M., Wallace, M., & Milton, I. (1984). Schedule-induced behavior in hyperactive children. *Journal of Abnormal Child Psychology, 12,* 227–244.

Prior, M. R., Glazner, J., Sanson, A., & Debelle, G. (1988). Research note: Temperament and behavioural adjustment in hearing impaired children. *Journal of Child Psychology and Psychiatry, 29,* 209–216.

Pritchard, W. S., Raz, N., & August, G. J. (1987). Visual augmenting/reducing and P300 in autistic children. *Journal of Autism and Developmental Disorders, 17,* 231–242.

Proshansky, H. M., & Kaminoff, R. D. (1981). Environmental quality and developmental outcomes for children. In M. J. Begab, H. C. Haywood, & H. L. Garber (Eds.), *Psychosocial influences in retarded performance* (Vol 1, pp. 219–254). Baltimore, MD: University Park Press.

Prout, H. T., & Schaefer, B. M. (1985). Self-reports of depression by community-based *mildly mentally retarded adults. American Journal of Mental Deficiency, 90,* 220–222.

Provence, S., & Lipton, R. C. (1962). *Infants in institutions: A comparison of their development with family-reared infants during the first year of life.* New York: International Universities.

Pullis, M. (1985). LD students' temperament characteristics and their impact on decisions by resource and mainstream teachers. *Learning Disability Quarterly, 8,* 109–122.

Putnam, J. W., Rynders, J. E., Johnson, R. T., & Johnson, D. W. (1989). Collaborative skill instruction for promoting positive interactions between mentally handicapped and nonhandicapped children. *Exceptional Children, 55,* 550–557.

Quart, E. J., Cruickshank, W. M., & Sarnaik, A. (1985). Prior history of learning disabilities in Reye's syndrome survivors. *Journal of Learning Disabilities, 18,* 345–349.

Quay, H. C. (1979). Classification. In H. C. Quay & J. S. Werry (Eds.), *Psychopathological disorders of childhood* (pp. 1–42). New York: Wiley.

Quay, H. C., Routh, D. K., & Shapiro, S. K. (1987). Psychopathology of childhood: From description to validation. *Annual Review of Psychology, 38,* 491–532.

Quine, L., & Pahl, J. (1987). First diagnosis of severe handicap: A study of parental reactions. *Developmental Medicine and Child Neurology, 29,* 232–242.

Quirk, M., Sexton, M., Ciottone, R., Minami, H., & Wapner, S. (1984). Values held by mothers for handicapped and nonhandicapped preschoolers. *Merrill-Palmer Quarterly, 30,* 403–418.

Raine, A., & Jones, F. (1987). Attention, autonomic arousal, and personality in behaviorally disordered children. *Journal of Abnormal Child Psychology, 15,* 583–599.

Raiten, D. J., & Massaro, T. (1986). Perspectives on the nutritional ecology of autistic children. *Journal of Autism and Developmental Disorders, 16,* 133–143.

Ramey, C. T., & Campbell, F. A. (1984). Preventive education for high-risk children: Cognitive consequences of the Carolina Abecedarian Project. *American Journal of Mental Deficiency, 88,* 515–523.

Rantakallio, P., & von Wendt, L. (1986). Mental retardation and subnormality in a birth cohort of 12,000 children in Northern Finland. *American Journal of Mental Deficiency, 90,* 380–387.

Rao, J. M., Cowie, V. A., & Mathew, B. (1987). Tardive dyskinesia in neuroleptic medicated mentally handicapped subjects. *Acta Psychiatrica Scandinavica, 76,* 507–513.

Rao, N., Moely, B. E., & Lockman, J. J. (1987). Increasing social participation in preschool social isolates. *Journal of Clinical Child Psychology, 16,* 178–183.

Rapport, M. D., Stoner, G., DuPaul, G. J., Birmingham, B. K., & Tucker, S. (1985). Methylphenidate in hyperactive children: Differential effects of dose on academic, learning, and social behavior. *Journal of Abnormal Child Psychology, 13,* 227–244.

Rapport, M. D., Tucker, S. B., DuPaul, G. J., Merlo, M., & Stoner, G. J. (1986). Hyperactivity and frustration: The influence of control over and size of rewards in delaying gratification. *Journal of Abnormal Child Psychology, 14,* 191–204.

Rashotte, C. A., & Torgesen, J. K. (1985). Repeated reading and reading fluency in learning disabled children. *Reading Research Quarterly, 20,* 180–188.

Rast, J., Johnston, J. M., Lubin, D., & Ellinger-Allen, J. (1988). Effects of premeal chewing on ruminative behavior. *American Journal of Mental Retardation, 93,* 67–74.

Rawlings, S. (1985). Behaviour and skills of severely retarded adults in hospitals and small residential homes. *British Journal of Psychiatry, 146,* 358–366.

Ray, B. M. (1985). Measuring the social position of the mainstreamed handicapped child. *Exceptional Children, 52,* 57–62.

Rayner, K. (1985). The role of eye movements in learning to read and reading disability. *Remedial and Special Education, 6,* 53–60.

Realon, R. E., Favell, J. E., Stirewalt, S. C., & Phillips, J. F. (1986). Teaching severely handicapped persons to provide leisure activities to peers. *Analysis and Intervention in Developmental Disabilities, 6,* 203–219.

Reber, M., Kazak, A. E., & Himmelberg, P. (1987). Phenylalanine control and family functioning in early-treated phenylketonuria. *Developmental and Behavioral Pediatrics, 8,* 311–317.

Recht, D. R., & Leslie, L. (1988). Effect of prior knowledge on good and poor readers' memory of text. *Journal of Educational Psychology, 80,* 16–20.

Reed, M. A. (1989). Speech perception and the discrimination of brief auditory cues in reading disabled children. *Journal of Experimental Child Psychology, 48,* 270–292.

Reese, R. M., Sherman, J. A., & Sheldon, J. (1984). Reducing agitated-disruptive behavior of mentally retarded residents of community group homes: The role of self-recording and peer-prompted self-recording. *Analysis and Intervention in Developmental Disabilities, 4,* 91–107.

Reeve, R. A., & Brown, A. L. (1985). Metacognition reconsidered: Implications for intervention research. *Journal of Abnormal Child Psychology, 13,* 343–356.

Reid, G. (1986). The trainability of motor processing strategies with developmentally delayed performers. In H. T. A. Whiting & M. G. Wade (Eds.), *Themes in motor development* (pp. 93–108). Dordrecht: Nijhoff.

Reid, J. B., Kavanagh, K., & Baldwin, D. V. (1987). Abusive parents' perceptions of child problem behaviors: An example of parental bias. *Journal of Abnormal Child Psychology, 15,* 457–466.

Reid, M. K., & Borkowski, J. G. (1984). Effects of methylphenidate (Ritalin) on information processing in hyperactive children. *Journal of Abnormal Child Psychology, 12,* 169–185.

Reid, M. K., & Borkowski, J. G. (1987). Causal attributions of hyperactive children: Implications for teaching strategies and self-control. *Journal of Educational Psychology, 79,* 296–307.

Reiss, S. (1990). Special section on dual diagnosis: Introduction. *American Journal on Mental Retardation, 94,* 577.

Reiss, S., Levitan, G. W., & McNally, R. J. (1982). Emotionally disturbed mentally retarded people. *American Psychologist, 37,* 361–367.

Reiss, S., & Syzszko, J. (1982). Emotional disturbance and mental retardation: Diagnostic overshadowing. *American Journal of Mental Deficiency, 86,* 567–574.

Rentschler, G. J. (1984). Effects of subgrouping in stuttering research. *Journal of Fluency Disorders, 9,* 307–311.

Rescorla, L. (1988). Cluster analytic identification of autistic preschoolers. *Journal of Autism and Developmental Disorders, 18*, 475–492.

Resnick, M. B., Armstrong, S., & Carter, R. L. (1988). Developmental intervention program for high-risk premature infants: Effects on development and parent–infant interactions. *Journal of Developmental and Behavioral Pediatrics, 9*, 73–78.

Reynolds, C. R. (1985). Measuring the aptitude-achievement discrepancy in learning disability diagnosis. *Remedial and Special Education, 6*, 37–48.

Reynolds, W. M., & Miller, K. L. (1985). Depression and learned helplessness in mentally retarded and nonmentally retarded adolescents: An initial investigation. *Applied Research in Mental Retardation, 6*, 295–306.

Reynolds, W. M., & Stark, K. D. (1986). Self-control in children: A multimethod examination of treatment outcome measures. *Journal of Abnormal Child Psychology, 14*, 13–23.

Reznick, J. S., Kagan, J., Snidman, N., Gersten, M., Baak, K., & Rosenberg, A. (1986). Inhibited and uninhibited children: A followup study. *Child Development, 57*, 660–680.

Ricciuti, H. N. (1981). Developmental consequences of malnutrition in early childhood. In M. Lewis & L. A. Rosenblum (Eds.), *The uncommon child. The genesis of behavior* (Vol. 3, pp. 151–172). New York: Plenum.

Rice, M. L. (1983). Contemporary accounts of the cognition/language relationship: Implications for speech-language clinicians. *Journal of Speech and Hearing Disorders, 48*, 347–359.

Richards, R. G. (1985). Wasting teacher time. *Academic Therapy, 20*, 411–418.

Richardson, G. (1984). Word recognition under spatial transformation in retarded and normal readers. *Journal of Experimental Child Psychology, 38*, 220–240.

Richardson, S. A., Koller, H., & Katz, M. (1985a). Appearance and mental retardation: Some first steps in the development and application of a measure. *American Journal of Mental Deficiency, 89*, 475–484.

Richardson, S. A., Koller, H., & Katz, M. (1985b). Relationship of upbringing to later behavior disturbance of mildly mentally retarded young people. *American Journal of Mental Deficiency, 90*, 1–8.

Richardson, S. A., Koller, H., & Katz, M. (1988). Job histories in open employment of a population of young adults with mental retardation. *American Journal on Mental Retardation, 92*, 483–491.

Richardson, S. A., Koller, H., Katz, M., & McClaren, J. (1984). Career paths through mental retardation services: An epidemiological perspective. *Applied Research in Mental Retardation, 5*, 53–67.

Riese, M. L. (1988). Temperament in full-term and preterm infants: Stability over ages 6 to 24 months. *Journal of Developmental and Behavioral Pediatrics, 9*, 6–11.

Rieser, J. J., Guth, D. A., & Weatherford, D. L. (1987). Mentally retarded and nonretarded adults' sensitivity to spatial structure. *American Journal of Mental Deficiency, 91*, 379–391.

Rincover, A. (1986). Behavioral research in self-injury and self-stimulation. *Psychiatric Clinics of North America, 9*, 755–766.

Rincover, A., & Ducharme, J. M. (1987). Variables influencing stimulus overselectivity and "tunnel vision" in developmentally delayed children. *American Journal of Mental Deficiency, 91*, 422–430.

Ripich, D. N., & Griffith, P. L. (1988). Narrative abilities of children with learning disabilities and non disabled children: Story structure, cohesion, and propositions. *Journal of Learning Disabilities, 21*, 165–173.

Roberton, M. A. (1986). Developmental changes in the relative timing of locomotion. In H. T. A. Whiting & M. G. Wade (Eds.), *Themes in motor development* (pp. 279–296). Dordrecht: Nijhoff.

Roberts, M. A., Ray, R. S., & Roberts, R. J. (1984). A playroom observational procedure for assessing hyperactive boys. *Journal of Pediatric Psychology, 9*, 177–191.

Robins, L. N., & Helzer, J. E. (1986). Diagnosis and clinical assessment: The current state of psychiatric diagnosis. *Annual Review of Psychology, 37*, 409–432.

Rock, P. J. (1988). Independence: What it means to six disabled people living in the community. *Disability, Handicap and Society, 3*, 27–35.

Rodger, S. (1986). Parents as therapists: A responsible alternative or abrogation of responsibility. *Exceptional Child, 33*, 17–27.

Rodgers, C. (1987). Maternal support of the Down's syndrome stereotype: The effect of direct experience of the condition. *Journal of Mental Deficiency Research, 31*, 271–278.

Rodick, J. D., Henggeler, S. W., & Hanson, C. L. (1986). An evaluation of the Family Adaptability and Cohesion Evaluation Scales and the Circumplex Model. *Journal of Abnormal Child Psychology, 14*, 77–87.

Roessler, R. T., & Johnson, V. A. (1987). Developing job maintenance skills in learning disabled youth. *Journal of Learning Disabilities, 20*, 428–432.

Rogan, L. L., & Hartman, L. D. (1990). Adult outcome of learning disabled students ten years after initial follow-up. *Learning Disabilities Focus, 5*, 91–102.

Rom, A. (1985). Verb usage by educable mentally retarded children. *Journal of Mental Deficiency Research, 29*, 165–172.

Romski, M. A., Sevcik, R. A., & Joyner, S. E. (1984). Nonspeech communication systems: Implications for language intervention with mentally retarded children. *Topics in Language Disorders, 5*, 66–81.

Romski, M. A., Sevcik, R. A., & Pate, J. L. (1988). Establishment of symbolic communication in persons with severe retardation. *Journal of Speech and Hearing Disorders, 53*, 94–107.

Romski, M. A., Sevcik, R. A., & Rumbaugh, D. M. (1985). Retention of symbolic communication skills by severely mentally retarded persons. *American Journal of Mental Deficiency, 89*, 441–444.

Rondal, J. A. (1988). Language development in Down's syndrome: A life-span perspective. *International Journal of Behavioral Development, 11*, 21–36.

Ronnberg, J., & Nilsson, L. (1987). The modality effect, sensory handicap, and compensatory functions. *Acta Psychologica, 65*, 263–283.

Rose, S. A., & Wallace, I. F. (1985). Visual recognition memory: A predictor of later cognitive functioning in preterms. *Child Development, 56*, 843–852.

Rose, S. A., Feldman, J. F., McCarton, C. M., & Wolfson, J. (1988). Information processing in 7-month-old infants as a function of risk status. *Child Development, 59*, 589–603.

Rosenbaum, P. L., Armstrong, R. W., & King, S. M. (1986). Improving attitudes toward the disabled: A randomized controlled trial of direct contact versus Kids-on-the-Block. *Journal of Developmental and Behavioral Pediatrics, 7,* 302–307.

Rosenberg, L. A., Harris, J. C., & Reifler, J. P. (1988). Similarities and differences between parents' and teachers' observations of the behavior of children with learning problems. *Journal of Learning Disabilities, 21,* 189–190.

Rosenberg, R. P., & Beck, S. (1986). Preferred assessment methods and treatment modalities for hyperactive children among clinical child and school psychologists. *Journal of Clinical Child Psychology, 15,* 142–147.

Ross, G. (1987). Temperament of preterm infants: Its relationship to perinatal factors and 1-year outcome. *Journal of Developmental and Behavioral Pediatrics, 8,* 106–110.

Ross, L. E. (1966). Classical conditioning and discrimination learning research with the mentally retarded. In N. R. Ellis (Ed.), *International review of research in mental retardation* (pp. 21–54). New York: Academic Press.

Ross, R. T., Begab, M. J., Dondis, E. H., Giampiccolo, Jr., J. S., Meyers, C. E. (1985). *Lives of the mentally retarded: A 40 year followup study.* Stanford, CA: Stanford University Press.

Roth, F. P., & Clark, D. M. (1987). Symbolic play and social participation abilities of language-impaired and normally developing children. *Journal of Speech and Hearing Disorders, 52,* 17–29.

Roth, K., Eisenberg, N., & Sell, E. R. (1984). The relation of preterm and full-term infants' temperament to test-taking behaviors and developmental status. *Infant Behavior and Development, 7,* 495–505.

Rovet, J. F., Ehrlich, R. M., & Hoppe, M. (1988). Specific intellectual deficits in children with early onset diabetes mellitus. *Child Development, 59,* 226–234.

Rowe, D. C., & Plomin, R. (1981). The importance of nonshared (E1) Environmental influences in behavioral development. *Developmental Psychology, 17,* 517–531.

Rowitz, L. (1987). The American mental retardation service system. *Journal of Mental Deficiency Research, 31,* 337–347.

Rowlandson, P. H., & Stephens, J. A. (1985). Cutaneous reflex responses recorded in children with various neurological disorders. *Developmental Medicine and Child Neurology, 27,* 434–447.

Rowley, P. T. (1984). Genetic screening: Marvel or menace? *Science, 225,* 138–144.

Royal, G. P., & Roberts, M. C. (1987). Students' perceptions of and attitudes toward disabilities: A comparison of twenty conditions. *Journal of Clinical Child Psychology, 16,* 122–132.

Rubin, K. H., & Howe, N. (1985). Toys and play behaviors: An overview. *Topics in Early Childhood Special Education, 5,* 1–9.

Rudel, R. G., & Helfgott, E. (1984). Effect of Piracetam on verbal memory of dyslexic boys. *Journal of the American Academy of Child Psychiatry, 23,* 695–699.

Rudie, F., & Riedl, G. (1984). Attitudes of parents/guardians of mentally retarded former state hospital residents toward current community placement. *American Journal of Mental Deficiency, 89,* 295–297.

Ruff, H. A., McCarton, C., Kurtzberg, D., & Vaughan, Jr., H. G. (1984). Preterm infants' manipulative exploration of objects. *Child Development, 55,* 1166–1173.

Ruhl, K. L., & Hughes, C. A. (1985). The nature and extent of aggression in special education settings serving behaviorally disordered students. *Behavioral Disorders, 10,* 95–104.

Rumsey, J. M., Berman, K. F., Denckla, M. B., Hamburger, S. D., Kruesi, M. J., & Weinberger, D. R. (1987). Regional cerebral blood flow in severe developmental dyslexia. *Archives of Neurology, 44,* 1144–1150.

Rumsey, J. M., Grimes, A. M., Pikus, A. M., Duara, R., & Ismond, D. R. (1984). Auditory brainstem responses in pervasive developmental disorders. *Biological Psychiatry, 19,* 1403–1418.

Runco, M. A., & Schreibman, L. (1987). Brief report: Socially validating behavioral objectives in the treatment of autistic children. *Journal of Autism and Developmental Disorders, 17,* 141–147.

Russell, T. (1984). Respite care: A means of rest and recuperation for parents of retarded individuals. *The Pointer, 28,* 4–7.

Rutter, M. (1983). Cognitive deficits in the pathogenesis of autism. *Journal of Child Psychology and Psychiatry, 24,* 513–531.

Rutter, M. (1985a). Family and school influences on behavioural development. *Journal of Child Psychology and Psychiatry, 26,* 349–368.

Rutter, M. (1985b) The treatment of autistic children. *Journal of Child Psychology and Psychiatry, 26,* 193–214.

Rutter, M., Cox, A., Tupling, C., Berger, M., & Yule, W. (1975). Attainment and adjustment in two geographical areas: 1. the prevalence of psychiatric disorder. *British Journal of Psychiatry, 126,* 493–509.

Rutter, M., & Garmezy, N. (1983). Developmental psychopathology. In E. M. Hetherington (Ed.), *Handbook of child psychology* (Vol. 4, pp. 775–911). New York: Wiley.

Rutter, M., & Quinton, D. (1984). Long-term follow-up of women institutionalized in childhood: Factors promoting good functioning in adult life. *British Journal of Developmental Psychology, 2,* 191–204.

Rutter, M., & Schopler, E. (1987). Autism and pervasive developmental disorders: Concepts and diagnostic issues. *Journal of Autism and Developmental Disorders, 17,* 159–186.

Rutter, M., Tizard, J., & Whitmore, K. (1970). The epidemiology of handicap: Summary of findings. In *Education, health and behavior* (pp. 347–357). London: Longman.

Ryan, C., Longstreet, C. L., & Morrow, L. (1985). The effects of diabetes mellitus on the school attendance and school achievement of adolescents. *Child: Care, Health and Development, 11,* 229–240.

Ryckman, D. B., & Nolen, P. A. (1985). Bisensory integration: An encoding replication. *Journal of Learning Disabilities, 18,* 35–41.

Sabatino, D. A. (1982). Research on achievement motivation with learning disabled populations. *Advances in Learning and Behavioral Disabilities, 1,* 75–116.

Sabornie, E. J. (1987). Bi-directional social status of behaviorally disordered and nonhandicapped elementary school pupils. *Behavioral Disorders, 13,* 45–57.

Sabornie, E. J., & Kauffman, J. M. (1985). Regular classroom sociometric status of behaviorally disordered adolescents. *Behavioral Disorders, 10,* 268–274.

Sabornie, E. J., & Kauffman, J. M. (1987). Assigned, received, and reciprocal social status of adolescents with and without mild mental retardation. *Education and Training in Mental Retardation, 22,* 139–149.

Sack, W. H., Mason, R., & Collins, R. (1987). A long-term follow-up study of a children's psychiatric day treatment center. *Child Psychiatry and Human Development, 18,* 58–68.

Sack, W. H., Mason, R., & Higgins, J. E. (1985). The single-parent family and abusive child punishment. *American Journal of Orthopsychiatry, 55,* 252–259.

Saco-Pollitt, C., Pollitt, E., & Greenfield, D. (1985). The cumulative deficit hypothesis in the light of cross-cultural evidence. *International Journal of Behavioral Development, 8,* 75–97.

Safer, D. J., & Allen, R. P. (1989). Absence of tolerance to the behavioral effects of methylphenidate in hyperactive and inattentive children. *Journal of Pediatrics, 115,* 1003–1008.

Safran, J. S., & Safran, S. P. (1985). A developmental view of children's behavioral tolerance. *Behavioral Disorders, 10,* 87–94.

Salend, S. J., & Giek, K. A. (1988). Independent living arrangements for individuals with mental retardation: The landlords' perspective. *Mental Retardation, 26,* 89–92.

Salomon, G., & Parving, A. (1985). Hearing disability and communication handicap for compensation purposes based on self-assessment and audiometric testing. *Audiology, 24,* 135–145.

Saloner, M. R., & Gettinger, M. (1985). Social inference skills in learning disabled and nondisabled children. *Psychology in the Schools, 22,* 201–207.

Salt, P., Galler, J. R., & Ramsey, F. C. (1988). The influence of early malnutrition on subsequent behavioral development: 2. The effects of maternal depressive symptoms. *Journal of Developmental and Behavioral Pediatrics, 9,* 1–5.

Salzberg, C. L., Agran, M., & Lignugaris/Kraft, B. (1986). Behaviors that contribute to entry-level employment: A profile of five jobs. *Applied Research in Mental Retardation, 7,* 299–314.

Sameroff, A. J. (1982). Development and the dialectic: The need for a systems approach. In W. A. Collins (Ed.), *The concept of development* (pp. 83–103). Hillsdale, NJ: Lawrence Erlbaum Associates.

Sameroff, A. J., & Chandler, M. J. (1975). Reproductive risk and the continuum of caretaking casualty. *Review of child development research* (Vol. 4, pp. 187–244). Chicago: University of Chicago Press.

Samuels, S. J. (1987). Why it is difficult to characterize the underlying cognitive deficits in special education populations. *Exceptional Children, 54,* 60–62.

Samuels, S. J., & Miller, N. L. (1985). Failure to find attention differences between learning disabled and normal children on classroom and laboratory tasks. *Exceptional Children, 51,* 358–375.

Sandler, A. G., & McLain, S. C. (1987). Sensory reinforcement: Effects of response-contingent vestibular stimulation on multiply handicapped children. *American Journal of Mental Deficiency, 91,* 373–378.

Sandman, C. A., Barron, J. L., & Colman, H. (1990). An orally administered opiate blocker, Naltrexone, attenuates self-injurious behavior. *American Journal on Mental Retardation, 95,* 93–102.

Sansone, J., & Zigmond, N. (1986). Evaluating mainstreaming through an analysis of students' schedules. *Exceptional Children, 52,* 452–458.

Sasso, G. M., Simpson, R. L., & Novak, C. G. (1985). Procedures for facilitating integration of autistic children in public school settings. *Analysis and Intervention in Developmental Disabilities, 5,* 233–246.

Satz, P., & Fletcher, J. M. (1987). Left-handedness and dyslexia: An old myth revisited. *Journal of Pediatric Psychology, 12,* 291–298.

Saunders, R. R., Saunders, K. J., Kirby, K. C., & Spradlin, J. E. (1988). The merger and development of equivalence classes by unreinforced conditional selection of comparison stimuli. *Journal of the Experimental Analysis of Behavior, 50,* 145–162.

Saunders, R. R., Saunders, K. J., & Spradlin, J. E. (1990). Long-term stability of equivalence relations in the absence of training or practice. *American Journal on Mental Retardation, 95,* 297–303.

Scafidi, F. A., Field, T. M., Schanberg, S. M., Bauer, C. R., Vega-Lahr, N., Garcia, R., Poirier, J., Nystrom, G., & Kuhn, C. M. (1986). Effects of tactile/kinesthetic stimulation on the clinical course and sleep/wake behavior of preterm neonates. *Infant Behavior and Development, 9,* 91–104.

Scarborough, H. S. (1984). Continuity between childhood dyslexia and adult reading. *British Journal of Psychology, 75,* 329–348.

Schachar, R., Logan, G., Wachsmuth, R., & Chajczyk, D. (1988). Attaining and maintaining preparation: A comparison of attention in hyperactive, normal, and disturbed control children. *Journal of Abnormal Child Psychology, 16,* 361–378.

Schachter, F. F., & Stone, R. K. (1985). Pediatricians' and psychologists' implicit personality theory: Significance of sibling differences. *Journal of Developmental and Behavioral Pediatrics, 6,* 295–297.

Schaie, K. W. (1984). Midlife influences upon intellectual functioning in old age. *International Journal of Behavioral Development, 7,* 463–478.

Schalock, R. L., Foley, J. W., Toulouse, A., & Stark, J. A. (1985). Medication and programming in controlling the behavior of mentally retarded individuals in community settings. *American Journal of Mental Deficiency, 89,* 503–509.

Schalock, R. L., & Jensen, C. M. (1986). Assessing the goodness-of-fit between persons and their environments. *Journal of the Association for Persons with Severe Handicaps, 11,* 103–109.

Schalock, R. L., & Lilley, M. A. (1986). Placement from community-based mental retardation programs: How well do clients do after 8 to 10 years? *American Journal on Mental Deficiency, 90,* 669–676.

Schaughency, E., Frame, C. L., & Strauss, C. C. (1987). Self-concept and aggression in elementary school students. *Journal of Clinical Child Psychology, 16,* 116–121.

Scheerenberger, R. C. (1983). *A history of mental retardation.* Baltimore: Paul H. Brookes.

Scheiner, A. P., Sexton, M. E., Rockwood, J., Sullivan, D., & Davis, H. (1985). The vulnerable child syndrome: Fact and theory. *Journal of Developmental and Behavioral Pediatrics, 6,* 298–301.

Schery, T. K. (1985). Correlates of language development in language-disordered children. *Journal of Speech and Hearing Disorders, 50,* 73–83.

Schirmer, B. R. (1985). An analysis of the language of young hearing-impaired children in terms of syntax, semantics, and use. *American Annals of the Deaf, 130,* 15–19.

Schloss, P. J., Espin, C. A., Smith, M. A., & Suffolk, D. R. (1987). Developing assertiveness during employment interviews with young adults who stutter. *Journal of Speech and Hearing Disorders, 52,* 30–36.

Schmidt, K., Solant, M. V., & Bridger, W. H. (1985). Electrodermal activity of under-socialized aggressive children: A pilot study. *Journal of Child Psychology and Psychiatry, 26,* 653–660.

Schneider, B. H., & Byrne, B. M. (1987). Individualizing social skills training for behavior-disordered children. *Journal of Consulting and Clinical Psychology, 55,* 444–445.

Schneider, B. H., Ledingham, J. E., Byrne, B. M., Oliver, J., & Poirier, C. A. (1985). Social consequences of hyperactivity in a children's treatment center. *Journal of Pediatric Psychology, 10,* 429–438.

Schneider, S. G., & Asarnow, R. F. (1987). A comparison of cognitive/ neuropsychological impairments of nonretarded autistic and schizophrenic children. *Journal of Abnormal Child Psychology, 15,* 29–46.

Schnittjer, C. J., & Hirshoren, A. (1984). Consistency of the Behavior Problem Checklist across deaf, blind, and non-handicapped children. *International Journal of Behavioral Development, 7,* 243–252.

Schultz, A. H. (1956). The occurrence and frequency of pathological and teratological conditions and of twinning among non-human primates. *Primatologia, 1,* 965–1014.

Schumacher, K., Qvammen, B., & Wisland, M. (1986). A critical examination of intra-agency relocation effects. *Applied Research in Mental Retardation, 7,* 329–336.

Schumaker, J. B., & Hazel, J. S. (1984). Social skills assessment and training for the learning disabled: Who's on first and what's on second?: 1. *Journal of Learning Disabilities, 17,* 422–431.

Schunk, D. H., & Cox, P. D. (1986). Strategy training and attributional feedback with learning disabled students. *Journal of Educational Psychology, 78,* 201–209.

Schunk, D. H., Hanson, A. R., & Cox, P. D. (1987). Peer-model attributes and children's achievement behaviors. *Journal of Educational Psychology, 79,* 54–61.

Schuster, J. W. (1990). Sheltered workshops: Financial and philosophical liabilities. *Mental Retardation, 28,* 233–239.

Schwartz, H. (1956). *Samuel Gridley Howe.* Cambridge, MA: Harvard University Press.

Schwethelm, B., & Mahoney, G. (1986). Task persistence among organically impaired mentally retarded children. *American Journal of Mental Deficiency, 90,* 432–439.

Sciarillo, W. G., Brown, M. M., Robinson, N. M., Bennett, F. C., & Sells, C. J. (1986). Effectiveness of the Denver Developmental Screening Test with biologically vulnerable infants. *Journal of Developmental and Behavioral Pediatrics, 7,* 77–83.

Scott, M. S., Greenfield, D. B., & Partridge, M. F. (1989). Classification of normally achieving and mildly mentally retarded students on the basis of their oddity transfer performance. *American Journal on Mental Retardation, 93,* 527–534.

Scruggs, T. E., & Mastropieri, M. A. (1983). Intelligence and learning of learning disabled adolescents under three conditions. *Psychological Reports, 53,* 1117–1118.

Scruggs, T. E., Mastropieri, M. A., Tolfa, D., & Jenkins, V. (1985). Attitudes of behaviorally disordered students toward tests. *Perceptual and Motor Skills, 60,* 467–470.

Seagull, E. A. W., & Scheurer, S. L. (1986). Neglected and abused children of mentally retarded parents. *Child Abuse and Neglect, 10,* 493–500.

Searleman, A., Cunningham, T. F., & Goodwin, W. (1988). Association between familial sinistrality and pathological left-handedness: A comparison of mentally retarded and nonretarded subjects. *Journal of Clinical and Experimental Neuropsychology, 10,* 132–138.

Seguin, E. (1907). *Idiocy and its treatment by the physiological method.* New York: Teachers College.

Seibert, J. M., Hogan, A. E., & Mundy, P. C. (1986). On the specifically cognitive nature of early object and social skill domain associations. *Merrill-Palmer Quarterly, 32,* 21–36.

Seidenberg, M. S., Bruck, M., Fornarolo, G., & Backman, J. (1985). Word recognition processes of poor and disabled readers: Do they necessarily differ? *Applied Psycholinguistics, 6,* 161–179.

Seltzer, G. B., Finaly, E., & Howell, M. (1988). Functional characteristics of elderly persons with mental retardation in community settings and nursing homes. *Mental Retardation, 26,* 213–217.

Seltzer, M. M. (1985). Informal supports for aging mentally retarded persons. *American Journal on Mental Deficiency, 90,* 259–265.

Seltzer, M. M. (1988). Structure and patterns of service utilization by elderly persons with mental retardation. *Mental Retardation, 26,* 181–185.

Seltzer, M. M., & Krauss, M. W. (1984). Family, community residence, and institutional placements of a sample of mentally retarded children. *American Journal on Mental Deficiency, 89,* 257–266.

Semrud-Clikeman, M., & Hynd, G. W. (1990). Right hemisphere dysfunction in nonverbal learning disabilities: Social, academic, and adaptive functioning in adults and children. *Psychological Bulletin, 107,* 196–209.

Sergeant, J. A., & Scholten, C. A. (1985a). On data limitations in hyperactivity. *Journal of Child Psychology and Psychiatry, 26,* 111–124.

Sergeant, J. A., & Scholten, C. A. (1985b). On resource strategy limitations in hyperactivity: Cognitive impulsivity reconsidered. *Journal of Child Psychology and Psychiatry, 26,* 97–109.

Seymour, P. H., & MacGregor, C. J. (1984). Developmental dyslexia: A cognitive experimental analysis of phonological, morphemic, and visual impairments. *Cognitive Neuropsychology, 1,* 43–82.

Seys, D., & Duker, P. (1988). Effects of staff management on the quality of residential care for mentally retarded individuals. *American Journal of Mental Retardation, 93,* 290–299.

Shafer, M. S., Hill, J., Seyfarth, J., & Wehman, P. (1987). Competitive employment and workers with mental retardation: Analysis of employers' perceptions and experiences. *American Journal on Mental Retardation, 92,* 304–311.

Shafer, M. S., Kregel, J., Banks, P. D., & Hill, M. L. (1988). An analysis of employer evaluations of workers with mental retardation. *Research in Developmental Disabilities, 9,* 377–391.

Shaffer, J., Friedrich, W. N., Shurtleff, D. B., & Wolf, L. (1985). Cognitive and achievement status of children with myelomeningocele. *Journal of Pediatric Psychology, 10,* 325–336.

Shah, A., & Holmes, N. (1985). Brief report: The use of the Leiter International Performance Scale with autistic children. *Journal of Autism and Developmental Disorders, 15,* 195–203.

Shalev, R. S., Weirtman, R., & Amir, N. (1988). Developmental dyscalculia. *Cortex, 24*, 555–561.

Shapiro, T., Sherman, M., Calamari, G., & Koch, D. (1987). Attachment in autism and other developmental disorders. *Journal of the American Academy of Child and Adolescent Psychiatry, 26*, 480–484.

Share, D. L., Moffitt, T. E., & Silva, P. A. (1988). Factors associated with arithmetic-and-reading disability and specific arithmetic disability. *Journal of Learning Disabilities, 21*, 313–320.

Shaywitz, B. A., & Waxman, S. G. (1987). Dyslexia. *New England Journal of Medicine, 316*, 1268–1270.

Shen, Y., Wang, Y., & Yang, X. (1985). An epidemiological investigation of Minimal Brain Dysfunction in six elementary schools in Beijing. *Journal of Child Psychology and Psychiatry, 26*, 777–787.

Shepherd, M. J., Gelzheiser, L. M., & Solar, R. A. (1985). How good is the evidence for a production deficiency among learning disabled students? *Journal of Educational Psychology, 77*, 553–561.

Sheppard, L. C., Ballinger, B. R., & Fenton, G. W. (1987). Anticonvulsant medication in a mental handicap hospital: 1972–1982. *British Journal of Psychiatry, 150*, 513–517.

Sherman, B. R. (1988). Predictors of the decision to place developmentally disabled family members in residential care. *American Journal on Mental Retardation, 92*, 344–351.

Sherman, M., Nass, R., & Shapiro, T. (1984). Brief report: Regional cerebral blood flow in autism. *Journal of Autism and Developmental Disorders, 14*, 439–446.

Sherman, S. R., Frenkel, E. R., & Newman, E. S. (1984). Foster family care for older persons who are mentally retarded. *Mental Retardation, 22*, 302–308.

Sherrod, K. B., O'Connor, S., Vietze, P. M., & Altemeier, III, W. A. (1984). Child health and maltreatment. *Child Development, 55*, 1174–1183.

Shibagaki, M., & Kiyono, S. (1985). Skin potential responses of mentally retarded children during nocturnal sleep. *American Journal of Mental Deficiency, 90*, 206–211.

Shibagaki, M., Kiyono, S., & Matsuno, Y. (1985). Nocturnal sleep of severely mentally retarded children and adolescents: Ontogeny of sleep patterns. *American Journal of Mental Deficiency, 90*, 212–216.

Shinn-Strieker, T. (1986). Patterns of cognitive style in normal and handicapped children. *Journal of Learning Disabilities, 19*, 572–576.

Shisler, L., Osguthorpe, R. T., & Eiserman, W. D. (1987). The effects of reverse-role tutoring on the social acceptance of students with behavioral disorders. *Behavioral Disorders, 13*, 35–44.

Shonkoff, J. P., Hauser-Cram, P., Krauss, M. W., & Upshur, C. C. (1988). Early intervention efficacy research: What have we learned and where do we go from here? *Topics in Early Childhood Special Education, 8*, 81–93.

Shriberg, L. D., & Kwiatkowski, J. (1988). A follow-up study of children with phonologic disorders of unknown origin. *Journal of Speech and Hearing Disorders, 53*, 144–155.

Shucard, D. W., Cummins, K. R., & McGee, M. G. (1984). Event-related brain potentials differentiate normal and disabled readers. *Brain and Language, 21*, 318–334.

Sidman, M., Kirk, B., & Willson-Morris, M. (1985). Six-member stimulus classes generated by conditional-discrimination procedures. *Journal of the Experimental Analysis of Behavior, 43,* 21–42.

Siegel, B., Anders, T. F., Ciaranello, R. D., Bienenstock, B., & Kraemer, H. C. (1986). Empirically derived subclassification of the autistic syndrome. *Journal of Autism and Developmental Disorders, 16,* 275–293.

Siegel, G. M., Pick, Jr., H. L., & Garber, S. R. (1984). Auditory feedback and speech development. *Advances in Child Development and Behavior, 18,* 49–79.

Siegel, G. M., & Spradlin, J. E. (1985). Therapy and research. *Journal of Speech and Hearing Disorders, 50,* 226–230.

Siegel, L., & Ryan, E. B. (1988). Development of grammatical sensitivity, phonological, and short-term memory skills in normally achieving and learning disabled children. *Developmental Psychology, 24,* 28–37.

Siegel, L. I. (1987). Confrontation and support in group therapy in the residential treatment of severely disturbed adolescents. *Adolescence, 22,* 681–690.

Siegel, L. S., Cunningham, C. E., & Van der Spuy, H. I. J. (1985). Interactions of language-delayed and normal preschool boys with their peers. *Journal of Child Psychology and Psychiatry, 26,* 77–83.

Siegel, L. S., Saigal, S., Rosenbaum, P., Morton, R. A., Young, A., Berenbaum, S., & Stoskopf, B. (1982). Predictors of development in preterm and fullterm infants: A model for detecting the at risk child. *Journal of Pediatric Psychology, 7,* 135–148.

Siegler, R. S. (1983). Five generalizations about cognitive development. *American Psychologist, 38,* 263–277.

Sigelman, C. K., & Begley, N. L. (1987). The early development of reactions to peers with controllable and uncontrollable problems. *Journal of Pediatric Psychology, 12,* 99–115.

Sigelman, C. K., & Shorokey, J. J. (1986). Effects of treatments and their outcomes on peer perceptions of a hyperactive child. *Journal of Abnormal Child Psychology, 14,* 397–410.

Sigman, M., Cohen, S. E., Beckwith, L., & Parmelee, A. H. (1986). Infant attention in relation to intellectual abilities in childhood. *Developmental Psychology, 22,* 788–792.

Sigman, M., & Mundy, P. (1989). Social attachments in autistic children. *Journal of the American Academy of Child and Adolescent Psychiatry, 28,* 74–81.

Sigman, M., Mundy, P., Sherman, T., & Ungerer, J. (1986). Social interactions of autistic, mentally retarded and normal children and their caregivers. *Journal of Child Psychology and Psychiatry, 27,* 647–656.

Sigman, M., & Ungerer, J. A. (1984). Attachment behaviors in autistic children. *Journal of Autism and Developmental Disorders, 14,* 231–244.

Silva, P. A., Hughes, P., Williams, S., & Faed, J. M. (1988). Blood lead, intelligence, reading attainment, and behaviour in eleven year old children in Dunedin, New Zealand. *Journal of Child Psychology and Psychiatry, 29,* 43–52.

Silva, P. A., McGee, R., & Williams, S. M. (1983). Developmental language delay from 3 to 7 years and its significance for low intelligence and reading difficulties at age 7. *Developmental Medicine and Child Neurology, 25,* 783–793.

Silva, P. A., McGee, R., & Williams, S. M. (1985). Some general characteristics of

9-year-old boys with general reading backwardness or specific reading retardation. *Journal of Child Psychology and Psychiatry, 26,* 407–421.

Silver, E. J., Lubin, R. A., & Silverman, W. P. (1984). Serving profoundly mentally retarded persons: Staff attitudes and job satisfaction. *American Journal of Mental Deficiency, 89,* 297–301.

Silver, L. B. (1987). The "Magic Cure": A review of the current controversial approaches for treating learning disabilities. *Journal of Learning Disabilities, 20,* 498–512.

Silverman, F. H., & Klees, J. (1989). Adolescents' attitudes toward peers who wear visible hearing aids. *Journal of Communication Disorders, 22,* 147–150.

Silverman, W. P., Silver, E. J., Sersen, E. A., Lubin, R. A., & Schwartz, A. A. (1986). Factors related to adaptive behavior changes among profoundly mentally retarded, physically disabled persons. *American Journal on Mental Deficiency, 90,* 651–658.

Silverstein, B. J., Olvera, D. R., & Schalock, R. (1987). Allocating direct-care resources for treatment of maladaptive behavior: The staff intensity scale. *Mental Retardation, 25,* 91–100.

Simons, C. J. R., Ritchie, S. K., Mullett, M. D., & Liechty, E. A. (1986). Parental recall of infant medical complications and its relationship to delivery method and education level. *Journal of Developmental and Behavioral Pediatrics, 7,* 355–360.

Sinclair, E., & Alexson, J. (1985). Creating diagnostic related groups: A manageable way to deal with DSM-III. *American Journal of Orthopsychiatry, 55,* 426–433.

Sinclair, E., Guthrie, D., & Forness, S. R. (1984). Establishing a connection between severity of learning disabilities and classroom attention problems. *Journal of Educational Research, 78,* 18–21.

Singer, G. S., & Irvin, L. K. (1987). Human rights review of intrusive behavioral treatments for students with severe handicaps. *Exceptional Children, 54,* 46–52.

Singer, L. M., Brodzinsky, D. M., Ramsey, D., Steir, M., & Waters, E. (1985). Mother-infant attachment in adoptive families. *Child Development, 56,* 1543–1551.

Singer, L. T., & Fagan, III, J. F. (1984). Cognitive development in the failure-to-thrive infant: A 3-year longitudinal study. *Journal of Pediatric Psychology, 9,* 363–383.

Singer, L. T., Wood, R., & Lambert, S. (1985). Developmental follow-up of long-term infant tracheostomy: A preliminary report. *Journal of Developmental and Behavioral Pediatrics, 6,* 132–136.

Singh, N. N., Watson, J. E., & Winton, A. S. (1987). Parents' acceptability ratings of alternative treatments for use with mentally retarded children. *Behavior Modification, 11,* 17–26.

Siperstein, G. N., & Bak, J. J. (1989). Social relationships of adolescents with moderate mental retardation. *Mental Retardation, 27,* 5–10.

Siperstein, G. N., Bak, J. J., & O'Keefe, P. (1988). Relationship between children's attitudes toward and their social acceptance of mentally retarded peers. *American Journal on Mental Retardation, 93,* 24–27.

Siperstein, G. N., & Goding, M. J. (1985). Teachers' behavior toward LD and non-LD children: A strategy for change. *Journal of Learning Disabilities, 18,* 139–144.

Skiba, R., & Casey, A. (1985). Interventions for behaviorally disordered students: A quantitative review and methodological critique. *Behavioral Disorders, 10,* 239–252.

Slaghuis, W. L., & Lovegrove, W. J. (1986). The effect of physical flicker on visible persistence in normal and specifically disabled readers. *Australian Journal of Psychology, 38*, 1–11.

Slate, J. R., & Saudargas, R. A. (1987). Classroom behaviors of LD, seriously emotionally disturbed and average children: A sequential analysis. *Learning Disability Quarterly, 10*, 125–134.

Slife, B. D., Weiss, J., & Bell, T. (1985). Separability of metacognition and cognition: Problem solving in learning-disabled and regular students. *Journal of Educational Psychology, 77*, 437–445.

Smeets, P. M., Hoogeveen, F. R., Striefel, S., & Lancioni, G. E. (1985). Stimulus overselectivity in TMR children: establishing functional control of simultaneous multiple stimuli. *Analysis and Intervention in Developmental Disabilities, 5*, 247–267.

Smit, A. B., & Bernthal, J. E. (1983). Performance of articulation-disordered children on language and perception measures. *Journal of Speech and Hearing Research, 26*, 124–136.

Smith, C., Algozzine, B., Schmid, R., & Hennly, T. (1990). Prison adjustment of youthful inmates with mental retardation. *Mental Retardation, 28*, 177–181.

Smith, D. E., Miller, S. D., Stewart, M., Walter, T. L., & McConnell, J. V. (1988). Conductive hearing loss in autistic, learning-disabled, and normal children. *Journal of Autism and Developmental Disorders, 18*, 53–65.

Smith, K., & Griffiths, P. (1987). Defective lateralized attention for non-verbal sounds in developmental dyslexia. *Neuropsychologia, 25*, 259–268.

Smith, L., & Hagen, V. (1984). Relationship between the home environment and sensorimotor development of Down syndrome and nonretarded infants. *American Journal of Mental Deficiency, 89*, 124–132.

Smith, L., & Von Tetzchner, S. (1986). Communicative, sensorimotor, and language skills of young children with Down syndrome. *American Journal of Mental Deficiency, 91*, 57–66.

Smith, M. D., & Coleman, D. (1986). Managing the behavior of adults with autism in the job setting. *Journal of Autism and Developmental Disorders, 16*, 145–154.

Smith, M. O., Shaywitz, S. E., Shaywitz, B. A., Gertner, J. M., Raskin, L. A., & Gelwan, E. M. (1985). Exogenous growth hormone levels predict attentional performance: A preliminary report. *Journal of Developmental and Behavioral Pediatrics, 6*, 273–278.

Smith, R. W., Osborne, L. T., Crim, D., & Rhu, A. H. (1986). Labeling theory as applied to learning disabilities: Survey findings and policy suggestions. *Journal of Learning Disabilities, 19*, 195–202.

Smith, W. P., & Rossman, B. B. R. (1986). Developmental changes in trait and situational denial under stress during childhood. *Journal of Child Psychology and Psychiatry, 27*, 227–235.

Snider, V. E. (1987). Use of self-monitoring of attention with LD students: Research and application. *Learning Disability Quarterly, 10*, 139–151.

Snow, J. H., Barnett, L., Cunningham, K., & Ernst, M. (1988). Cross-modal development with normal and learning disabled children. *International Journal of Clinical Neuropsychology, 10*, 74–80.

Snowling, M., & Frith, U. (1986). Comprehension in "Hyperlexic" readers. *Journal of Experimental Child Psychology, 42*, 392–415.

Snowling, M., Goulandris, N., Bowlby, M., & Howell, P. (1986). Segmentation and speech perception in relation to reading skill: A developmental analysis. *Journal of Experimental Child Psychology, 41,* 489–507.

Solecki, R. S. (1971). Neanderthal is not an epithet but a worthy ancestor. *Smithsonian, 1,* 20–27.

Sollee, N. D., & Kindlon, D. J. (1987). Lateralized brain injury and behavior problems in children. *Journal of Abnormal Child Psychology, 15,* 479–490.

Soodak, L. C. (1990). Social behavior and knowledge of social 'scripts' among mentally retarded adults. *American Journal on Mental Retardation, 94,* 515–521.

Soper, H. V., Satz, P., Orsini, D. L., Van Grop, W. G., & Green, M. F. (1987). Handedness distribution in a residential population with severe or profound mental retardation. *American Journal of Mental Deficiency, 92,* 94–102.

Soraci, Jr., S. A., Deckner, C. W., Baumeister, A. A., & Carlin, M. T. (1990). Attentional functioning and relational learning. *American Journal on Mental Retardation, 95,* 304–315.

Soyster, H. D., & Ehly, S. W. (1986). Parent-rated adaptive behavior and in-school ratings of students referred for EMR evaluation. *American Journal of Mental Deficiency, 90,* 460–463.

Soyster, H. D., & Ehly, S. W. (1987). Relation between parent-rated adaptive behavior and school ratings of students referred for evaluation as educable mentally retarded. *Psychological Reports, 60,* 271–277.

Spangler, P. F., & Gilman, B. (1985). The frequency of serious behavioral and medical incidents occurring in community-based living arrangements. *Mental Retardation, 23,* 246–248.

Sparks, G. G. (1986). Developmental differences in children's reports of fear induced by the mass media. *Child Study Journal, 16,* 55–66.

Spaulding, B. R., & Morgan, S. B. (1986). Spina bifida children and their parents: A population prone to family dysfunction? *Journal of Pediatric Psychology, 11,* 359–374.

Spaulding, J., & Balch, P. (1983). A brief history of primary prevention in the twentieth century: 1908–1980. *American Journal of Community Psychology, 11,* 59–80.

Spearman, C. (1927). *The nature of intelligence and the principles of cognition.* London: MacMillan.

Speece, D. L., McKinney, J. D., & Appelbaum, M. I. (1985). Classification and validation of behavioral subtypes of learning disabled children. *Journal of Educational Psychology, 77,* 67–77.

Spence, S. H. (1986). Behavioural treatments of childhood obesity. *Journal of Child Psychology and Psychiatry, 27,* 447–453.

Spiker, D., & Ricks, M. (1984). Visual self-recognition in autistic children: Developmental relationships. *Child Development, 55,* 214–225.

Spitz, H. H. (1986). Disparities in mentally retarded persons' IQs derived from different intelligence tests. *American Journal of Mental Deficiency, 90,* 588–591.

Spitz, H. H., Minsky, S. K., & Bessellieu, C. L. (1985). Influence of planning time and first-move strategy on Tower of Hanoi problem-solving performance of mentally retarded young adults and nonretarded children. *American Journal of Mental Deficiency, 90,* 46–56.

Spooner, F. (1984). Comparisons of backward chaining and total task presentation in training severely handicapped persons. *Education and Training of the Mentally Retarded, 19,* 15–22.

Sprafkin, J., & Gadow, K. (1987). An observational study of emotionally disturbed and learning disabled children in school settings. *Journal of Abnormal Child Psychology, 15,* 393–408.

Sprafkin, J., & Gadow, K. (1987). An observational study of emotionally disturbed and learning disabledd children in school settings. *Journal of Abnormal Child Psychology, 15,* 393–408.

Sprafkin, J., Gadow, K. D., & Grayson, P. (1988). Effects of cartoons on emotionally disturbed children's social behavior in school settings. *Journal of Child Psychology and Psychiatry, 29,* 91–99.

Spreat, S., Telles, J. L., Conroy, J. W., Feinstein, C., & Colombatto, J. J. (1987). Attitudes toward deinstitutionalization: National survey of families of institutionalized persons with mental retardation. *Mental Retardation, 25,* 267–274.

Spreen, O. (1988). Prognosis of learning disability. *Journal of Consulting and Clinical Psychology, 56,* 836–842.

Spreen, O. (1989). The relationship between learning disability, emotional disorders, and neuropsychology; some results and observations. *Journal of Clinical and Experimental Neuropsychology, 11,* 117–140.

Spreen, O., & Haaf, R. G. (1986). Empirically derived learning disability subtypes: A replication attempt and longitudinal patterns over 15 years. *Journal of Learning Disabilities, 19,* 170–180.

Springer, N. S. (1987). From institution to foster care: Impact on nutritional status. *American Journal of Mental Deficiency, 91,* 321–327.

Spruill, J., & May, J. (1988). The mentally retarded offender: Prevalence rates based on individual versus group intelligence tests. *Criminal Justice and Behavior, 15,* 484–491.

Spungen, L. B., & Farran, A. C. (1986). Effect of intensive care unit exposure on temperament in low birth weight preterm infants. *Journal of Behavioral and Developmental Pediatrics, 7,* 288–292.

Spungen, L. B., Kurtzberg, D., & Vaughan, Jr., H. G. (1985). Patterns of looking behavior in full-term and low birth weight infants at 40 weeks post-conceptional age. *Journal of Developmental and Behavioral Pediatrics, 6,* 287–294.

Srikameswaran, S., & Martin, G. L. (1984). A component analysis of a self-management program for improving work rates of mentally handicapped persons. *Mental Retardation and Learning Disability Bulletin, 12,* 39–52.

St. Louis, K. O., Hinzman, A. R., & Hull, F. M. (1985). Studies of cluttering: Disfluency and language measures in young possible clutterers and stutterers. *Journal of Fluency Disorders, 10,* 151–172.

Stahlecker, J. E., & Cohen, M. C. (1985). Application of the strange situation attachment paradigm to a neurologically impaired population. *Child Development, 56,* 502–507.

Stan, E. A., & Mosley, J. L. (1988). Semantic encoding by mildly retarded and non-retarded individuals. *Journal of Mental Deficiency Research, 32,* 371–382.

Stanley, M. A., & Comer, R. J. (1988). Reacting to mentally retarded persons: The impact of labels and observed behaviors. *Journal of Social and Clinical Psychology, 6,* 279–292.

Stanovich, K. E. (1985). Explaining the variance in reading ability in terms of psychological processes: What have we learned? *Annals of Dyslexia, 35,* 67–96.

Stark, J., & Goldsbury, T. (1988). Analysis of labor and economics: Needs for the next decade. *Mental Retardation, 26,* 363–368.

Stark, K. D., Reynolds, W. M., & Kaslow, N. J. (1987). A comparison of the relative efficacy of self-control therapy and a behavioral problem-solving therapy for depression in children. *Journal of Abnormal Child Psychology, 15,* 91–113.

Stark, R. E., Bernstein, L. E., Condino, R., Bender, M., Tallal, P., & Catts, III, H. (1984). Four-year follow-up study of language impaired children. *Annals of Dyslexia, 34,* 49–68.

Stehouwer, R. S., Bultsma, C. A., & Blackford, I. T. (1985). Developmental differences in depression: Cognitive-perceptual distortion in adolescent versus adult female depressives. *Adolescence, 20,* 291–299.

Stein, M. A., & O'Donnell, J. P. (1985). Classification of children's behavior problems: Clinical and quantitative approaches. *Journal of Abnormal Child Psychology, 13,* 269–279.

Stein, N. L. (1987). Lost in the learning maze. *Journal of Learning Disabilities, 20,* 409–410.

Stein, Z., & Susser, M. (1985). Effects of early nutrition on neurological and mental competence in human beings. *Psychological Medicine, 15,* 717–726.

Stein, Z., Susser, M., Saenger, G., & Marolla, F. (1972). Nutrition and mental performance. *Science, 178,* 708–713.

Stelmack, R. M., Saxe, B. J., Noldy-Cullum, N., Campbell, K. B., & Armitage, R. (1988). Recognition memory for words and event-related potentials: A comparison of normal and disabled readers. *Journal of Clinical and Experimental Neuropsychology, 10,* 185–200.

Stemberger, J. P. (1984). Structural errors in normal and agrammatic speech. *Cognitive Neuropsychology, 1,* 281–313.

Stern, M., & Hildebrandt, K. A. (1986). Prematurity stereotyping: Effects on mother–infant interaction. *Child Development, 57,* 308–315.

Stern, M., & Karraker, K. H. (1988). Prematurity stereotyping by mothers of premature infants. *Journal of Pediatric Psychology, 13,* 255–263.

Stevens, Jr., J. H., & Bakeman, R. (1985). A factor analytic study of the HOME scale for infants. *Developmental Psychology, 21,* 1196–1203.

Stevens, S., & Gruzelier, J. (1984). Electrodermal activity to auditory stimuli in autistic, retarded, and normal children. *Journal of Autism and Developmental Disorders, 14,* 245–260.

Stevenson, D. T., & Romney, D. M. (1984). Depression in learning disabled children. *Journal of Learning Disabilities, 17,* 579–582.

Stevenson, J., & Graham, P. (1988). Behavioral deviance in 13-year-old twins: An item analysis. *Child and Adolescent Psychiatry, 27,* 791–797.

Stevenson, J., Graham, P., Fredman, G., & McLoughlin, V. (1987). A twin study of genetic influences on reading and spelling ability and disability. *Journal of Child Psychology and Psychiatry, 28,* 229–247.

Stewart, T. D. (1958). Report of committee on research: Anthropology. *Yearbook of the American Philosophical Society,* 274–278.

Stiefel, G. S., Plunkett, J. W., & Meisels, S. J. (1987). Affective expression among *preterm infants of varying levels of biological risk. Infant Behavior and Development, 10,* 151–164.

Stipek, D. J., & Sanborn, M. E. (1985). Teachers' task-related interactions with handicapped and nonhandicapped preschool children. *Merrill-Palmer Quarterly, 31,* 285–300.

Stone, C. A. (1985). Vygotsky's developmental model and the concept of proleptic instruction: Some implications for theory and research in the field of learning disabilities. *Research Communications in Psychology, Psychiatry, and Behavior, 10,* 129–152.

Stone, R. K., Alvarez, W. F., & May, J. E. (1988). Dyskinesia, antipsychotic-drug exposure and risk factors in a developmentally-disabled population. *Pharmacology, Biochemistry and Behavior, 29,* 45–51.

Stone, R. K., May, J. E., Alvarez, W. F., & Ellman, G. (1989). Prevalence of dyskinesia and related movement disorders in a developmentally disabled population. *Journal of Mental Deficiency Research, 33,* 41–53.

Stoneman, Z. (1989). Comparison groups in research on families with mentally retarded members: A methodological and conceptual review. *American Journal of Mental Retardation, 94,* 195–215.

Stoneman, Z., Brody, G. H., Davis, C. H., & Crapps, J. M. (1987). Mentally retarded children and their older same-sex siblings: Naturalistic in-home observations. *American Journal on Mental Retardation, 92,* 290–298.

Stoneman, Z., Brody, G. H., Davis, C. H., & Crapps, J. M. (1988). Childcare responsibilities, peer relations, and sibling conflict: Older siblings of mentally retarded children. *American Journal on Mental Retardation, 93,* 174–183.

Stoneman, Z., & Crapps, J. M. (1988). Correlates of stress, perceived competence, and depression among family care providers. *American Journal on Mental Retardation, 93,* 166–173.

Stoner, S. B., & Glynn, M. A. (1987). Cognitive styles of school-age children showing attention deficit disorders with hyperactivity. *Psychological Reports, 61,* 119–125.

Stouthamer-Loeber, M., & Loeber, R. (1986). Boys who lie. *Journal of Abnormal Child Psychology, 14,* 551–564.

Strain, P. (1985). Social and nonsocial determinants of acceptability in handicapped preschool children. *Topics in Early Childhood Special Education, 4,* 47–58.

Strain, P. S., Odom, S. L., & McConnell, S. (1984). Prompting social reciprocity of exceptional children: Identification, target behavior selection, and intervention. *Remedial and Special Education, 5,* 21–28.

Strain, P. S., Sainto, D. M., & Maheady, L. (1984). Toward a functional assessment of severely handicapped learners. *Educational Psychologist, 19,* 180–187.

Strand, S. C., & Morris, R. C. (1986). Programmed training of visual discriminations: A comparison of techniques. *Applied Research in Mental Retardation, 7,* 165–182.

Strand, S. C., & Morris, R. C. (1988). Criterion-related versus non-criterion-related prompt training with severely mentally handicapped children. *Journal of Mental Deficiency Research, 32,* 137–151.

Straus, W. L., Jr., & Cave, A. J. E. (1957). Pathology and the posture of Neanderthal man. *Quarterly Review of Biology, 32,* 348–363.

Strauss, A. A., & Lehtinen, L. E. (1947). *Psychopathology of the brain-injured child* (Vol. 1). New York: Grune & Stratton.

Strauss, C. C., Forehand, R. L., Frame, C., & Smith, K. (1984). Characteristics of children with extreme scores on the children's depression inventory. *Journal of Clinical Child Psychology, 13,* 227–231.

Strauss, C. C., Last, C. G., Hersen, M., & Kazdin, A. E. (1988). Association between anxiety and depression in adolescents with anxiety disorders. *Journal of Abnormal Child Psychology, 16,* 57–68.

Strawser, S., & Weller, C. (1985). Use of adaptive behavior and discrepancy criteria to determine learning disabilities severity subtypes. *Journal of Learning Disabilities, 18,* 205–212.

Streissguth, A. P., Landesman-Dwyer, S., Martin, J., & Smith, D. W. (1980). Teratogenic effects of alcohol in humans and laboratory animals. *Science, 209,* 353–361.

Strom, R., Daniels, S., Wurster, S., Rees, R., & Goldman, R. (1984). A comparison of childrearing attitudes of parents of handicapped and non-handicapped children. *Journal of Instructional Psychology, 11,* 89–103.

Strupp, H. H. (1986). The nonspecific hypothesis of therapeutic effectiveness: A current assessment. *American Journal of Orthopsychiatry, 56,* 513–520.

Sugden, D. A. (1986). The development of proprioceptive control. In H. T. A. Whiting, & M. G. Wade (Eds.), *Themes in motor development* (pp. 21–40). Dordrecht: Nijhoff.

Summers, E. G. (1986). The information flood in learning disabilities: A bibliometric analysis of the journal literature. *Remedial and Special Education, 7,* 49–60.

Sumner, E. G. (1940). *Folkways.* Boston: Ginn & Company. (Original work published 1904)

Sumpton, R. C., Raynes, N. V., & Thorp, D. (1987). The residential careers of a group of mentally handicapped people: The influence of early residential experience. *British Journal of Mental Subnormality, 33,* 3–9.

Susman, E. J., & Hollenbeck, A. R. (1984). Sequential variations in the interactions of caregivers and hospitalized seriously ill children and adolescents. *International Journal of Behavioral Development, 7,* 395–421.

Sutton, J. P., Whitton, J. L., Topa, M., & Moldofsky, H. (1986). Evoked potential maps in learning disabled children. *Electroencephalography and Clinical Neurophysiology, 65,* 399–404.

Swanson, H. L. (1985). Assessing learning disabled children's intellectual performance: An information processing perspective. *Advances in Learning and Behavioral Disabilities, 4,* 225–272.

Swanson, H. L. (1986). Do semantic memory deficiencies underlie learning disabled readers' encoding processes? *Journal of Experimental Child Psychology, 41,* 461–488.

Swanson, H. L. (1987). Developmental changes in LD readers' encoding preferences. *Learning Disability Quarterly, 10,* 164–174.

Swanson, H. L. (1988a). Learning disabled children's problem solving: Identifying mental processes underlying intelligent performance. *Intelligence, 12,* 261–278.

Swanson, H. L. (1988b). Memory subtypes in learning disabled readers. *Learning Disabilities Quarterly, 11,* 342–357.

Swanson, H. L. (1989). Strategy instruction: Overview of principles and procedures for effective use. *Learning Disability Quarterly, 12,* 3–14.

Swanson, H. L., & Rathgeber, A. J. (1986). The effects of organizational dimension on memory for words in learning-disabled and nondisabled readers. *Journal of Educational Research, 79,* 155–162.

Swanson, H. L., & Rhine, B. (1985). Strategy transformations in learning disabled children's math performance: Clues to the development of expertise. *Journal of Learning Disabilities, 18,* 596–603.

Swicegood, P. R., & Crump, W. D. (1984). Piagetian cognitive development of learning disabled and nonhandicapped students. *Journal of Human Behavior and Learning, 1,* 13–21.

Swift, C., & Lewis, R. B. (1985). Leisure preferences of elementary-aged learning disabled boys. *Remedial and Special Education, 6,* 37–42.

Szatmari, P., Offord, D. R., & Boyle, M. H. (1989). Ontario Child Health Study: Prevalence of attention deficit disorder with hyperactivity. *Journal of Child Psychology and Psychiatry, 30,* 219–230.

Szeszulski, P. A., & Manis, F. R. (1987). A comparison of word recognition processes in dyslexic and normal readers at two reading-age levels. *Journal of Experimental Child Psychology, 44,* 364–376.

Szymanski, L., Kedesdy, J., Sulkes, S., Cutler, A., & Stevens-Our, P. (1987). Naltrexone in treatment of self-injurious behavior: A clinical study. *Research in Developmental Disabilities, 8,* 179–190.

Tager-Flusberg, H. (1985). Basic level and superordinate level categorization by autistic, mentally retarded, and normal children. *Journal of Experimental Child Psychology, 40,* 450–469.

Tager-Flusberg, H., Calkins, S., Nolin, T., Baumberger, T., Anderson, M., & Chadwick-Dias, A. (1990). A longitudinal study of language acquisition in autistic and Down syndrome children. *Journal of Autism and Developmental Disorders, 20,* 1–21.

Tait, C. A., Roush, J., & Johns, J. (1983). Normal ABR's in children classified as learning disabled. *Journal of Auditory Research, 23,* 56–62.

Tallal, P. (1984). Temporal or phonetic processing deficit in dyslexia? That is the question. *Applied Psycholinguistics, 5,* 167–169.

Tamaroff, M. H., Nir, Y., & Straker, N. (1986). Children reared in a reverse isolation environment: Effects on cognitive and emotional development. *Journal of Autism and Developmental Disorders, 16,* 415–424.

Tannock, R. (1988). Mothers' directiveness in their interactions with their children with and without Down syndrome. *American Journal on Mental Retardation, 93,* 154–165.

Tanoue, Y., Oda, S., Asano, F., & Kawashima, K. (1988). Epidemiology of infantile autism in southern Ibaraki, Japan: Differences in prevalence in birth cohorts. *Journal of Autism and Developmental Disorders, 18,* 155–166.

Tarnowski, K. J., Rasnake, L. K., Mulick, J. A., & Kelly, P. A. (1989). Acceptability of behavioral interventions for self-injurious behavior. *American Journal on Mental Retardation, 93,* 575–580.

Tarver-Behring, S., Barkley, R. A., & Karlsson, J. (1985). The mother–child interactions of hyperactive boys and their normal siblings. *American Journal of Orthopsychiatry, 55,* 202–209.

Taylor, A. R., Asher, S. R., & Williams, G. A. (1987). The social adaptation of mainstreamed mildly retarded children. *Child Development, 58,* 1321–1334.

Taylor, C. R., & Chamove, A. S. (1986). Vibratory or visual stimulation reduces self-injury. *Australia and New Zealand Journal of Developmental Disabilities, 12,* 243–248.

Taylor, E., & Sandberg, S. (1984). Hyperactive behavior in English schoolchildren: A questionnaire survey. *Journal of Abnormal Child Psychology, 12*, 143–155.

Taylor, H. G., & Fletcher, J. M. (1983). Biological foundations of specific developmental disorders': Methods, findings and future directions. *Journal of Child Clinical Psychology, 12*, 46–65.

Terwogt, M. M., Schene, J., & Harris, P. L. (1986). Self-control of emotional reactions by young children. *Journal of Child Psychology and Psychiatry, 27*, 357–366.

Tew, B., & Laurence, K. M. (1985). Possible personality problems among 10-year-old spina bifida children. *Child: Care, Health and Development, 11*, 375–390.

Thase, M. E., Tigner, R., Smeltzer, D. J., & Liss, L. (1984). Age-related neuropsychological deficits in Down's syndrome. *Biological Psychiatry, 19*, 571–585.

Thomas, A. P., Bax, M. C. O., & Smyth, D. P. (1988). The social skill difficulties of young adults with physical disabilities. *Child: Care, Health and Development, 14*, 255–264.

Thomas, M., Felce, D., De Kock, U., Saxby, H., & Repp, A. (1986). The activity of staff and of severely and profoundly mentally handicapped adults in residential settings of different sizes. *British Journal of Mental Subnormality, 32*, 82–92.

Thompson, R. A., Cicchetti, D., Lamb, M. E., & Malkin, C. (1985). Emotional responses of Down syndrome and normal infants in the strange situation: The organization of affective behavior in infants. *Developmental Psychology, 21*, 828–841.

Thompson, R. J. (1985). Delineation of children's behavior problems: A basis for assessment and intervention. *Journal of Developmental and Behavioral Pediatrics, 6*, 37–50.

Thompson, T., Robinson, J., Graff, M., & Ingenmey, R. (1990). Home-like architectural features of residential environments. *American Journal on Mental Retardation, 95*, 328–341.

Thorley, G. (1983). Childhood hyperactivity and food additives. *Developmental Medicine and Child Neurology, 25*, 527–539.

Till, J. A., Reich, A., Dickey, S., & Seiber, J. (1983). Phonatory and manual reaction times of stuttering and nonstuttering children. *Journal of Speech and Hearing Research, 26*, 171–180.

Tisdelle, D. A., & St. Lawrence, J. S. (1988). Adolescent interpersonal problem-solving skill training: Social validation and generalization. *Behavior Therapy, 19*, 171–182.

Tittemore, J. A., Lawson, J. S., & Inglis, J. (1985). Validation of a Learning Disability Index (LDI) derived from a principal components analysis of the WISC-R. *Journal of Learning Disabilities, 18*, 449–454.

Todman, J. B., & File, P. E. (1985). Output organization in the free recall of mildly retarded children. *Acta Psychologica, 58*, 287–291.

Todman, J. B., & Gibb, C. M. (1985). High speed memory scanning in retarded and non-retarded adolescents. *British Journal of Psychology, 76*, 49–57.

Togonu-Bickersteth, F., & Odebiyi, A. I. (1985). Influence of Yoruba beliefs about abnormality on the socialization of deaf children: A research note. *Journal of Child Psychology and Psychiatry, 26*, 639–652.

Tollison, P., Palmer, D. J., & Stowe, M. L. (1987). Mothers' expectations, interactions, and achievement attributions for their learning disabled or normally achieving sons. *Journal of Special Education, 21*, 83–93.

Tomporowski, P. D., & Allison, P. (1988). Sustained attention of adults with mental retardation. *American Journal on Mental Retardation, 92*, 525–530.

Tomporowski, P. D., & Ellis, N. R. (1984). Effects of exercise on the physical fitness, intelligence, and adaptive behavior of institutionalized mentally retarded adults. *Applied Research in Mental Retardation, 5,* 329–337.

Tomporowski, P. D., Hayden, A. M., & Applegate, B. (1990). Effects of background event rate on sustained attention of mentally retarded and nonretarded adults. *American Journal on Mental Retardation, 94,* 499–508.

Tonge, B. J., Lipton, G. L., & Crawford, G. (1984). Psychological and educational correlates of strabismus in school children. *Australia and New Zealand Journal of Psychiatry, 18,* 71–77.

Torello, M. W., & Duffy, F. H. (1985). Using brain electrical activity mapping to diagnose learning disabilities. *Theory into Practice, 24,* 95–99.

Torgesen, J. K. (1985). Memory processes in reading disabled children. *Journal of Learning Disabilities, 18,* 350–357.

Torgesen, J. K. (1986). Learning disabilities theory: Its current state and future prospects. *Journal of Learning Disabilities, 19,* 399–407.

Torgesen, J. K. (1988). Studies of children with learning disabilities who perform poorly on memory span tasks. *Journal of Learning Disabilities, 21,* 605–612.

Torgesen, J. K., Rashotte, C. A., & Greenstein, J. (1988). Language comprehension in learning disabled children who perform poorly on memory span tests. *Journal of Educational Psychology, 80,* 480–487.

Torneus, M. (1984). Phonological awareness and reading: A chicken and egg problem? *Journal of Educational Psychology, 76,* 1346–1358.

Towle, P. O., & Schwarz, J. C. (1987). The Child Behavior Checklist as applied to archival data: Factor structure and external correlates. *Journal of Clinical Child Psychology, 16,* 69–79.

Trach, J. S., & Rusch, F. R. (1989). Supported employment program evaluation: Evaluating degree of implementation and selected outcomes. *American Journal on Mental Deficiency, 94,* 134–140.

Tramontana, M. G., Hooper, S. R., & Selzer, S. C. (1988). Research on the preschool prediction of later academic achievement: A review. *Developmental Review, 8,* 89–146.

Travis, L. W., Thomas, A. R., & Fuller, G. B. (1985). Handicapped students in the least restrictive environment: A longitudinal study. *School Psychology Review, 14,* 521–530.

Treffert, D. A. (1988). The Idiot Savant: A review of the syndrome. *American Journal of Psychiatry, 145,* 563–572.

Treiber, F. A., & Mabe, P. A. (1987). Child and parent perceptions of children's psychopathology in psychiatric outpatient children. *Journal of Abnormal Child Psychology, 15,* 115–124.

Trickett, P. K., & Susman, E. J. (1988). Parental perceptions of child-rearing practices in physically abusive and nonabusive families. *Developmental Psychology, 24,* 270–276.

Tsai, L. Y. (1984). Brief report: The development of hand laterality in infantile autism. *Journal of Autism and Developmental Disorders, 14,* 447–450.

Tsukahara, R., Aoki, H., Mita, K., & Yabe, K. (1985). Postural adjustments for jumping reaction movement in mentally retarded children: Findings from EMG patterns. *Journal of Mental Deficiency Research, 29,* 359–372.

Turner, L. A., & Bray, N. W. (1985). Spontaneous rehearsal by mildly mentally retarded children and adolescents. *American Journal of Mental Deficiency, 90,* 57–63.

Turnure, J. E. (1987). Social influences on cognitive strategies and cognitive development: The role of communication and instruction. *Intelligence, 11,* 77–89.

Tymchuk, A. J., Andron, L., & Rahbar, B. (1988). Effective decision-making/problem-solving training with mothers who have mental retardation. *American Journal on Mental Retardation, 92,* 510–516.

Tymitz-Wolf, B. (1984). An analysis of EMR children's worries about mainstreaming. *Education and Training of the Mentally Retarded, 19,* 157–168.

Tzuriel, D., & Golinsky, H. (1985). Teachers' social orientation and classroom achievements. *British Journal of Mental Subnormality, 31,* 9–18.

Tzuriel, D., & Klein, P. S. (1985). The assessment of analogical thinking modifiability among regular, special education, disadvantaged, and mentally retarded children. *Journal of Abnormal Child Psychology, 13,* 539–552.

Udwin, O., & Yule, W. (1983). Imaginative play in language disordered children. *British Journal of Disorders of Communication, 18,* 197–205.

Ulvund, S. E. (1984). Predictive validity of assessments of early cognitive competence in light of some current issues in developmental psychology. *Human Development, 27,* 76–83.

Umetani, T., Kitao, S., & Katada, A. (1985). Discrimination shift learning and response inhibition of moderately and severely mentally retarded and non-retarded children. *Journal of Mental Deficiency Research, 29,* 219–224.

Ungerer, J. A., & Sigman, M. (1987). Categorization skills and receptive language development in autistic children. *Journal of Autism and Developmental Disorders, 17,* 3–16.

Unruh, D., Cronin, M., & Gilliam, J. E. (1987). Locus of control in normal and emotionally disturbed/behavior disordered children. *Child Study Journal, 17,* 15–20.

Unruh, D., & Gilliam, J. E. (1986). Selective attention in emotionally disturbed/behavior-disordered children. *Psychological Reports, 59,* 1035–1039.

Van Bourgondien, M. E. (1987). Children's responses to retarded peers as a function of social behaviors, labeling, and age. *Exceptional Children, 53,* 432–439.

Van Engeland, H. (1984). The electrodermal orienting response to auditive stimuli in autistic children, normal children, mentally retarded children, and child psychiatric patient. *Journal of Autism Developmental Disorders, 14,* 261–279.

Van Engeland, H., Bodnar, F. A., & Bolhuis, G. (1985). Some qualitative aspects of the social behaviour of autistic children: An ethological approach. *Journal of Child Psychology and Psychiatry, 26,* 879–893.

Van Hasselt, V. B., Kazdin, A. E., & Hersen, M. (1986). Assessment of problem behavior in visually handicapped adolescents. *Journal of Clinical Child Psychology, 15,* 134–141.

Van Ijzendoorn, M. H., & Van Vliet-Visser, S. (1988). The relationship between quality of attachment in infancy and IQ in kindergarten. *Journal of Genetic Psychology, 149,* 23–28.

Van den Bos, K. P. (1984). Letter processing in dyslexic subgroups. *Annals of Dyslexia, 34,* 179–193.

Van der Meere, J., & Sergeant, J. (1988a). Acquisition of attention skill in pervasively hyperactive children. *Journal of Child Psychology and Psychiatry, 29,* 301–310.

Van der Meere, J., & Sergeant, J. (1988b). Controlled processing and vigilance in hyperactivity: Time will tell. *Journal of Abnormal Child Psychology, 16,* 641–655.

Van der Meere, J., & Sergeant, J. (1988c). Focused attention in pervasively hyperactive children. *Journal of Abnormal Child Psychology, 16,* 627–639.

Van der Wissel, A. (1987). IQ profiles of learning disabled and mildly mentally retarded children: A psychometric selection effect. *British Journal of Developmental Psychology, 5,* 45–51.

Vandenberg, B. (1981). The role of play in the development of insightful tool-using strategies. *Merrill-Palmer Quarterly, 27,* 97–109.

Vandenberg, B. R. (1985). The effects of retardation on exploration. *Merrill-Palmer Quarterly, 31,* 397–409.

Varnhagen, C. K., Das, J. P., & Varnhagen, S. (1987). Auditory and visual memory span: Cognitive processing by TMR individuals with Down syndrome or other etiologies. *American Journal of Mental Deficiency, 91,* 398–405.

Varni, J. W., & Banis, H. T. (1985). Behavior therapy techniques applied to eating, exercise, and diet modification in childhood obesity. *Journal of Developmental & Behavioral Pediatrics, 6,* 367–372.

Vaughn, S., Bos, C. S., Harrell, J. E., & Lasky, B. A. (1988). Parent participation in the initial placement/IEP Conference 10 years after mandated involvement. *Journal of Learning Disabilities, 21,* 82–89.

Vellutino, F. R., & Scanlon, D. M. (1986). Experimental evidence for the effects of instructional bias on word identification. *Exceptional Children, 53,* 145–155.

Verglas, G. du, Banks, S. R., & Guyer, K. E. (1988). Clinical effects of fenfluramine on children with autism: A review of the research. *Journal of Autism and Developmental Disorders, 18,* 297–308.

Vig, S., Kaminer, R. K., & Jedrysek, E. (1987). A later look at borderline and mildly retarded preschoolers. *Journal of Developmental and Behavioral Pediatrics, 8,* 12–17.

Vikan, A. (1985). Psychiatric epidemiology in a sample of 1510 10-year-old children: 1. Prevalence. *Journal of Child Psychology and Psychiatry, 26,* 55–75.

Vitiello, B., Spreat, S., & Behar, D. (1989). Obsessive-compulsive disorder in mentally retarded patients. *Journal of Nervous and Mental Disease, 177,* 232–236.

Volkmar, F. R., Cohen, D. J., Bregman, J. D., Hooks, M. Y., & Stevenson, J. M. (1989). An examination of social typologies in autism. *Journal of the American Academy of Child and Adolescent Psychiatry, 28,* 82–86.

Volkmar, F. R., Cohen, D. J., Hoshino, Y., Rende, R. D., & Paul, R. (1988). Phenomenology and classification of the childhood psychoses. *Psychological Medicine, 18,* 191–201.

Volpe, J. J. (1981). The neurological examination-normal and abnormal features. *Neurology of the newborn.* Philadelphia: W. B. Saunders.

Vyse, S. A., & Rapport, M. D. (1989). The effects of methylphenidate on learning in children with ADDH: The stimulus equivalence paradigm. *Journal of Consulting and Clinical Psychology, 57,* 425–435.

Waas, G. A. (1988). Social attributional biases of peer-rejected and aggressive children. *Child Development, 59,* 969–975.

Wacker, D. P., Wiggins, B., Fowler, M., & Berg, W. K. (1988). Training students with profound or multiple handicaps to make requests via microswitches. *Journal of Applied Behavior Analysis, 21,* 331–343.

Wade, M. G., Hoover, J. H., & Newell, K. M. (1984). Training reaction and movement times of moderately and severely mentally retarded persons in aiming movements. *American Journal of Mental Deficiency, 89,* 174–179.

Wagner, W. G., & Geffken, G. (1986). Enuretic children: How they view their wetting behavior. *Child Study Journal, 16,* 13–18.

Walbran, B. B., & Hile, M. G. (1988). Observing staff-resident interactions: Methological considerations. *Mental Retardation, 26,* 161–165.

Waldron, M. B., Diebold, T. J., & Rose, S. (1985). Hearing impaired students in regular classrooms: A cognitive model for educational services. *Exceptional Children, 52,* 39–43.

Walker, H. M., & Lamon, W. E. (1987). Social behavior standards and expectations of Australian and U.S. teacher groups. *Journal of Special Education, 21,* 56–82.

Wallander, J. L. (1988). The relationship between attention problems in childhood and antisocial behavior eight years later. *Journal of Child Psychology and Psychiatry, 29,* 53–61.

Wallander, J. L., Schroeder, S. R., Michelli, J. A., & Gualtieri, C. T. (1987). Classroom social interactions of attention deficit disorder with hyperactivity children as a function of stimulant medication. *Journal of Pediatric Psychology, 12,* 61–76.

Wann, J. P. (1986). Handwriting disturbances: Developmental trends. In H. T. A. Whiting & M. G. Wade (Eds.), *Themes in motor development* (pp. 207–226). Dordrecht: Nijhoff.

Ward, J., & Center, Y. (1987). Attitudes to the integration of disabled children into regular classes: A factor analysis of functional characteristics. *British Journal of Educational Psychology, 57,* 221–224.

Warren, C. A., & Karrer, R. (1984). Movement-related potentials during development: A replication and extension of relationships to age, motor control, mental status and IQ. *International Journal of Neuroscience, 24,* 81–96.

Wasik, B. H. (1987). Sociometric measures and peer descriptors of kindergarten children: A study of reliability and validity. *Journal of Clinical Child Psychology, 16,* 218–224.

Wasserman, G. A., & Allen, R. (1985). Maternal withdrawal from handicapped toddlers. *Journal of Child Psychology and Psychiatry, 26,* 381–387.

Wasserman, G. A., Allen, R., & Linares, L. O. (1988). Maternal interaction and language development in children with and without speech-related anomalies. *Journal of Communication Disorders, 21,* 319–331.

Waterhouse, L., & Fein, D. (1984). Developmental trends in cognitive skills for children diagnosed as autistic and schizophrenic. *Child Development, 55,* 236–248.

Watson, B., & Goldgar, D. E. (1988). Evaluation of a typology of reading disability. *Journal of Clinical and Experimental Neuropsychology, 10,* 432–450.

Watt, J. (1987). Temperament in small-for-dates and pre-term infants: A preliminary study. *Child Psychiatry and Human Development, 17,* 177–188.

Webster, R. E., & Johnson, M. M. (1987). Teacher–student verbal communication patterns in regular and special classrooms. *Psychology in the Schools, 24,* 174–179.

Webster-Stratton, C. (1985a). Comparison of abusive and nonabusive families with conduct-disordered children. *American Journal of Orthopsychiatry, 55,* 59–69.

Webster-Stratton, C. (1985b). Comparisons of behavior transactions between conduct-disordered children and their mothers in the clinic and at home. *Journal of Abnormal Child Psychology, 13,* 169–194.

Webster-Stratton, C. (1985c). The effects of father involvement in parent training for conduct problem children. *Journal of Child Psychology and Psychiatry, 26,* 801–810.

Webster-Stratton, C. (1988). Mothers' and fathers' perceptions of child deviance: Roles of parent and child behaviors and parent adjustment. *Journal of Consulting and Clinical Psychology, 56,* 909–915.

Wehman, P. (1988). Supported employment: Toward equal employment opportunity for persons with severe disabilities. *Mental Retardation, 26,* 357–361.

Wehman, P., Hill, J. W., Wood, W., & Parent, W. (1987). A report on competitive employment histories of persons labeled severely mentally retarded. *Journal of Association for Persons with Severe Handicaps, 12,* 11–17.

Wehmer, F., & Porter, R. (1970). Environmental inheritance: The "grandmother effect." *Aging and Human Development, 1,* 251–260.

Wehr, S. H., & Kaufman, M. E. (1987). The effects of assertive training on performance in highly anxious adolescents. *Adolescence, 22,* 195–205.

Weiss, B., Weisz, J. R., & Bromfield, R. (1986). Performance of retarded and nonretarded persons on information-processing tasks: Further tests of the similar structure hypothesis. *Psychological Bulletin, 100,* 157–175.

Weiss, E. (1984). Learning disabled children's understanding of social interactions of peers. *Journal of Learning Disabilities, 17,* 612–615.

Weiss, G., & Hechtman, L. (1980). The hyperactive child syndrome. *Annual Progress in Child Psychiatry and Child Development,* 319–335.

Welch, J., Nietupski, J., & Hamre-Nietupski, S. (1985). Teaching public transportation problem solving skills to young adults with moderate handicaps. *Education and Training of the Mentally Retarded, 20,* 287–295.

Weller, C., & Strawser, S. (1987). Adaptive behavior of subtypes of learning disabled individuals. *Journal of Special Education, 21,* 101–115.

Weller, C., Strawser, S., & Buchanan, M. (1985). Adaptive behavior: Designator of a continuum of severity of learning disabled individuals. *Journal of Learning Disabilities, 18,* 200–204.

Wenar, C., Ruttenberg, B. A., Kalish-Weiss, B., & Wolf, E. G. (1986). The development of normal and autistic children: A comparative study. *Journal of Autism and Developmental Disorders, 16,* 317–333.

Wender, E. H. (1986). The food additive-free diet in the treatment of behavior disorders: A review. *Journal of Developmental and Behavioral Pediatrics, 7,* 35–42.

Werry, J. S. (1985). ICD 9 & DSM III classification for the clinician. *Journal of Child Psychology and Psychiatry, 26,* 1–6.

Werry, J. S. (1988). Drugs, Learning and cognitive function in children—An update. *Journal of Child Psychology and Psychiatry, 29,* 129–141.

Wertlieb, D., Hauser, S. T., & Jacobson, A. M. (1986). Adaptation to diabetes: Behavior symptoms and family context. *Journal of Pediatric Psychology, 11,* 463–479.

Wertlieb, D., Weigel, C., Springer, T., & Feldstein, M. (1987). Temperament as a moderator of children's stressful experiences. *American Journal of Orthopsychiatry, 57,* 234–245.

West, M. O., & Prinz, R. J. (1987). Parental alcoholism and childhood psychopathology. *Psychological Bulletin, 102,* 204–218.

Westling, D. L. (1985). Similarities and differences in instructional tactics used by teachers of TMR and PMR students. *Education and Training of the Mentally Retarded, 20,* 253–259.

Wetherby, A. M. (1986). Ontogeny of communicative functions in autism. *Journal of Autism and Developmental Disorders, 16,* 295–316.

Whalen, C. K., Henker, B., Castro, J., & Granger, D. (1987). Peer perceptions of hyperactivity and medication effects. *Child Development, 58,* 816–828.

Whalen, C. K., Henker, B., Swanson, J. M., Granger, D., Kliewer, W., Spencer, J. (1987). Natural social behaviors in hyperactive children: Dose effects of methylphenidate. *Journal of Consulting and Clinical Psychology, 55,* 187–193.

Wharry, R. E., & Kirkpatrick, S. W. (1986). Vision and academic performance of learning disabled children. *Perceptual and Motor Skills, 62,* 323–336.

Wheldall, K., & Lam, Y. Y. (1987). Rows versus Tables: 2. The effects of two classroom seating arrangements on classroom disruption rate, on-task behaviour and teacher behaviour in three special school classes. *Educational Psychology, 7,* 303–312.

White, K. R. (1982). The relation between socioeconomic status and academic achievement. *Psychological Bulletin, 91,* 461–481.

White, R., Benedict, M. I., Wulff, L., & Kelley, M. (1987). Physical disabilities as risk factors for child maltreatment: A selected review. *American Journal of Orthopsychiatry, 57,* 93–101.

White, S., Halpin, B. M., Strom, G. A., & Santilli, G. (1988). Behavioral comparisons of young, sexually abused, neglected, and nonreferred children. *Journal of Clinical Child Psychology, 17,* 53–61.

Whitehouse, D., & Harris, J. C. (1984). Hyperlexia in infantile autism. *Journal of Autism and Developmental Disorders, 14,* 281–289.

Whiteley, J. H., & Krenn, M. J. (1986). Uses of the Bayley mental scale with nonambulatory profoundly mentally retarded children. *American Journal of Mental Deficiency, 90,* 425–431.

Whitman, B. Y., Graves, B., & Accardo, P. (1987). Mentally retarded parents in the community: Identification method and needs assessment survey. *American Journal of Mental Deficiency, 91,* 636–638.

Whitman, T. L. (1987). Self-instruction, individual differences, and mental retardation. *American Journal of Mental Deficiency, 92,* 213–223.

Whyte, J., Curry, C., & Hale, D. (1985). Inspection time and intelligence in dyslexic children. *Journal of Child Psychology and Psychiatry, 26,* 423–428.

Widen, J. E., Folsom, R. C., Thompson, G., & Wilson, W. R. (1987). Auditory brainstem responses in young adults with Down syndrome. *American Journal of Mental Deficiency, 91,* 472–479.

Widom, C. S. (1988). Sampling biases and implications for child abuse research. *American Journal of Orthopsychiatry, 58,* 260–270.

Widom, C. S. (1989). Does violence beget violence? A critical examination of the literature. *Psychological Bulletin, 106,* 3–28.

Wieseler, N. A., Hanson, R. H., Chamberlain, T. P., & Thompson, T. (1988). Stereotypic behavior of mentally retarded adults adjunctive to a positive reinforcement schedule. *Research in Developmental Disabilities, 9,* 393–403.

Wikler, L. M. (1986). Periodic stresses of families of older mentally retarded children: An exploratory study. *American Journal of Mental Deficiency, 90,* 703–706.

Williams, H., McClenaghan, B., Ward, D., Carter, W., Brown, C., Byde, R., Johnson, D. Lasalle, D. (1986). Sensory-motor control and balance: A behavioural perspective. In H.T.A. Whiting, & M. G. Wade, (Eds.), *Themes in motor development* (pp. 247–264) Dordrecht: Nijhoff.

Williams, J. P. (1986). Teaching children to identify the main idea of expository texts. *Exceptional Children, 53,* 163–168.

Willich, Y., Prior, M., Cumming, G., & Spanos, T. (1988). Are disabled readers delayed or different? An approach using an objective miscue analysis. *British Journal of Educational Psychology, 58,* 315–329.

Wilson, B. J., Cantor, J., Gordon, L., & Zillman, D. (1986). Affective response of nonretarded and retarded children to the emotions of a protagonist. *Child Study Journal, 16,* 77–93.

Wilson, L., Cone, T., Bradley, C., & Reese, J. (1986). The characteristics of learning disabled and other handicapped students referred for evaluation in the state of Iowa. *Journal of Learning Disabilities, 19,* 553–557.

Wilson, L. R. (1985). Large-scale learning disability identification: The reprieve of a concept. *Exceptional Children, 52,* 44–51.

Wilson, R. S. (1985). Risk and resilience in early development. *Developmental Psychology, 21,* 795–805.

Windle, M. (1988). Psychometric strategies of measures of temperament: A methodological critique. *International Journal of Behavioral Development, 11,* 171–201.

Wing, L. (1981). Language, social, and cognitive impairments in autism and severe mental retardation. *Journal of Autism and Developmental Disorders, 11,* 31–44.

Wingate, M. E. (1983). Speaking unassisted: Comments on a paper by Andrews et al. *Journal of Speech and Hearing Disorders, 48,* 255–263.

Winnega, M., & Berkson, G. (1986). Analyzing the stimulus properties of objects used in stereotyped behavior. *American Journal of Mental Deficiency, 91,* 277–285.

Winters, Jr., J. J., & Hoats, D. L. (1985). Comparison of verbal typicality judgments of mentally retarded and nonretarded persons. *American Journal of Mental Deficiency, 90,* 335–341.

Winters, Jr., J. J., & Semchuk, M. T. (1986). Retrieval from long-term store as a function of mental age and intelligence. *American Journal of Mental Deficiency, 90,* 440–448.

Wolf, L., & Goldberg, B. (1986). Autistic children grow up: An eight to twenty-four year followup study. *Canadian Journal of Psychiatry, 31,* 550–556.

Wolf, T. (1973). *Alfred Binet.* Chicago: University of Chicago.

Wolfe, D. A. (1985). Child-abusive parents: An empirical review and analysis. *Psychological Bulletin, 97,* 462–482.

Wolfe, D. A., Zak, L., Wilson, S., & Jaffe, P. (1986). Child witnesses to violence between parents: Critical issues in behavioral and social adjustment. *Journal of Abnormal Child Psychology, 14,* 95–104.

Wolff, D. E., Desberg, P., & Marsh, G. (1985). Analogy strategies for improving word recognition in competent and learning disabled readers. *The Reading Teacher, 38,* 412–416.

Wolff, P. H., Cohen, C., & Drake, C. (1984). Impaired motor timing control in specific reading retardation. *Neuropsychologia, 22,* 587–600.

Wolk, S. (1985). Biasing influences on test level assignment for hearing impaired students. *Exceptional Children, 52,* 161–169.

Wolraich, M. L., & Siperstein, G. N. (1986). Physicians' and other professionals' expectations and prognoses for mentally retarded individuals. *American Journal of Mental Deficiency, 91,* 244–249.

Wood, K. M., Richman, L. C., & Eliason, M. J. (1989). Immediate memory functions in reading disability subtypes. *Brain and Language, 36,* 181–192.

Woodley-Zanthos, P., & Ellis, N. R. (1989). Memory for frequency of occurrence: Intelligence level and retrieval cues. *Intelligence, 13,* 53–61.

Woolfson, R. C. (1984). Historical perspective on mental retardation. *American Journal on Mental Deficiency, 89,* 231–235.

Woollacott, M. H. (1986). Postural control and development. In H. T. A. Whiting & M. G. Wade (Eds.), *Themes in motor development* (pp. 3–20). Dordrecht: Nijhoff.

Woollacott, M. H., & Shumway-Cook, A. (1986). The development of the postural and voluntary motor control systems in Down's syndrome children. In M. G. Wade (Ed.), *Motor skill acquisition of the mentally handicapped* (pp. 45–72). Amsterdam: Elsevier.

Worrell, B. (1987). Walking the fine line: The people first advisor. *Entourage, 2,* 30–35.

Wright, L. S. (1985). Suicidal thoughts and their relationship to family stress and personal problems among high school seniors and college undergraduates. *Adolescence, 20,* 575–580.

Wright, L. S., & Stimmel, T. (1984). Perceptions of parents and self among college students reporting learning disabilities. *The Exceptional Child, 31,* 203–208.

Wulff, S. B. (1985). The symbolic and object play of children with autism: A review. *Journal of Autism and Developmental Disorders, 15,* 139–148.

Wurtele, S. K., & Miller, C. L. (1987). Children's conceptions of sexual abuse. *Journal of Clinical Child Psychology, 16,* 184–191.

Wynne, M. E., & Rogers, J. J. (1985). Variables discriminating residential placement of severely handicapped children. *American Journal of Mental Deficiency, 89,* 515–523.

Yao, K., Solanto, M. V., & Wender, E. H. (1988). Prevalence of hyperactivity among newly immigrated Chinese-American children. *Journal of Developmental and Behavioral Pediatrics, 9,* 367–373.

Yawkey, T. D., & Toro-Lopez, J. A. (1985). Examining descriptive and empirically based typologies of toys for handicapped and nonhandicapped children. *Topics in Early Childhood Special Education, 5,* 47–57.

Yeates, K. O., & Weisz, J. R. (1985). On being called "mentally retarded": Do developmental and professional perspectives limit labeling effects? *American Journal of Mental Deficiency, 90,* 349–352.

Yoder, P. J. (1987). Relationship between degree of infant handicap and clarity of infant cues. *American Journal of Mental Deficiency, 91,* 639–641.

Yoder, P. J., & Feagans, L. (1988). Mothers' attributions of communication to prelinguistic behavior of developmentally delayed and mentally retarded infants. *American Journal on Mental Retardation, 93*, 36–43.

Yoder, P. J., & Layton, T. L. (1988). Speech following sign language training in autistic children with minimal verbal language. *Journal of Autism and Developmental Disorders, 18*, 217–229.

Younger, A. J., & Boyko, K. A. (1987). Aggression and withdrawal as social schemas underlying children's peer perceptions. *Child Development, 58*, 1094–1100.

Ysseldyke, J. E., Christenson, S. L., Thurlow, M. L., & Bakewell, D. (1989). Are different kinds of instructional tasks used by different categories of students in different settings? *School Psychology Review, 18*, 98–111.

Ysseldyke, J. E., Thurlow, M. L., Christenson, S. L., & McVicar, R. (1988). Instructional grouping arrangements used with mentally retarded, learning disabled, emotionally disturbed, and nonhandicapped elementary students. *Journal of Educational Research, 81*, 305–311.

Ysseldyke, J. E., Thurlow, M. L., Christenson, S. L., & Weiss, J. (1987). Time allocated to instruction of mentally retarded, learning disabled, emotionally disturbed, and nonhadicapped elementary students. *Journal of Special Education, 21*, 43–55.

Zametkin, A. J., & Rapoport, J. L. (1987). Neurobiology of attentional deficit disorder with hyperactivity: Where have we come in 50 years? *Journal of the American Academy of Child and Adolescent Psychiatry, 26*, 676–686.

Zarling, C. L., Hirsch, B. J., & Landry, S. (1988). Maternal social networks and mother–infant interactions in full-term and very low birthweight, preterm infants. *Child Development, 59*, 178–185.

Zeaman, D., & House, B. J. (1963). The role of attention in retardate discrimination learning. In N. R. Ellis (Ed.), *Handbook of mental deficiency* (pp. 159–223). New York: McGraw-Hill.

Zeanah, C. H., Keener, M. A., Anders, T. F., & Levine, R. (1986). Measuring difficult temperament in infancy. *Journal of Developmental and Behavioral Pediatrics, 7*, 114–119.

Zentall, S. S. (1984). Context effects in the behavioral ratings of hyperactivity. *Journal of Abnormal Child Psychology, 12*, 345–352.

Zentall, S. S. (1985). Stimulus-control factors in search performance of hyperactive children. *Journal of Learning Disabilities, 18*, 480–485.

Zentall, S. S., & Kruczek, T. (1988). The attraction of color for active attention-problem children. *Exceptional Children, 54*, 357–362.

Zetlin, A., & Murtaugh, M. (1990). Whatever happened to those with borderline IQs? *American Journal on Mental Retardation, 94*, 463–469.

Zetlin, A. G. (1986). Mentally retarded adults and their siblings. *American Journal of Mental Deficiency, 91*, 217–225.

Zetlin, A. G., & Turner, J. L. (1988). Salient domains in the self-conception of adults with mental retardation. *Mental Retardation, 26*, 219–222.

Zigler, E. (1967). Familial mental retardation: A continuing dilemma. *Science, 155*, 292–298.

Zigler, E., Balla, D., & Hodapp, R. (1984). On the definition and classification of mental retardation. *American Journal on Mental Deficiency, 89*, 215–230.

Zigler, E., Balla, D., & Kossan, N. (1986). Effects of types of institutionalization on responsiveness to social reinforcement, wariness, and outerdirectedness among low M. A. residents. *American Journal on Mental Deficiency, 91*, 10–17.

Zigmond, N., Kerr, M. M., & Schaeffer, A. (1988). Behavior patterns of learning disabled and non-learning disabled adolescents in high school academic classes. *Remedial and Special Education, 9,* 6–11.

Zigmond, N., Levin, E., & Laurie, T. E. (1985). Managing the mainstream: An analysis of teacher attitudes and student performance in mainstream high school programs. *Journal of Learning Disabilities, 18,* 535–541.

Zirpoli, T. J., Snell, M. E., & Loyd, B. H. (1987). Characteristics of persons with mental retardation who have been abused by caregivers. *Journal of Special Education, 21,* 31–41.

Zubrick, S. R., Macartney, H., & Stanley, F. (1988). Hidden handicap in school-age children who received neonatal intensive care. *Developmental Medicine and Child Neurology, 30,* 145–152.

Zuravin, S. J. (1988). Child maltreatment and teenage first births: A relationship mediated by chronic sociodemographic stress? *American Journal of Orthopsychiatry, 58,* 91–103.

Zwiebel, A., & Mertens, D. M. (1985). A comparison of intellectual structure in deaf and hearing children. *American Annals of the Deaf, 130,* 27–31.

Author Index

Subject Index